Lecture Notes in Computer Science 1883

Edited by G. Goos, J. Hartmanis and J. van Leeuwen

Springer
Berlin
Heidelberg
New York
Barcelona
Hong Kong
London
Milan
Paris
Singapore
Tokyo

Bill Triggs   Andrew Zisserman
Richard Szeliski (Eds.)

Vision Algorithms: Theory and Practice

International Workshop on Vision Algorithms
Corfu, Greece, September 21-22, 1999
Proceedings

Springer

Series Editors

Gerhard Goos, Karlsruhe University, Germany
Juris Hartmanis, Cornell University, NY, USA
Jan van Leeuwen, Utrecht University, The Netherlands

Volume Editors

Bill Triggs
INRIA Rhône-Alpes
655 avenue de l'Europe, Montbonnot 38330, France
E-mail: Bill.Triggs@inrialpes.fr

Andrew Zisserman
Oxford University, Department of Engineering Science
19 Parks Road, OX1 3PJ, UK
E-mail: az@robots.ox.ac.uk

Richard Szeliski
Microsoft Research
Redmond, WA 98052-6399, USA
E-mail: szeliski@microsoft.com

Cataloging-in-Publication Data applied for

Die Deutsche Bibliothek - CIP-Einheitsaufnahme

Vision algorithms : theory and practice ; proceedings / International
Workshop on Vision Algorithms, Corfu, Greece, September 21 - 22, 1999.
Bill Triggs ... (ed.). - Berlin ; Heidelberg ; New York ; Barcelona ;
Hong Kong ; London ; Milan ; Paris ; Singapore ; Tokyo : Springer, 2000
  (Lecture notes in computer science ; Vol. 1883)
  ISBN 3-540-67973-1

CR Subject Classification (1998): I.4, I.3, I.5, F.2

ISSN 0302-9743
ISBN 3-540-67973-1 Springer-Verlag Berlin Heidelberg New York

Springer-Verlag Berlin Heidelberg New York
a member of BertelsmannSpringer Science+Business Media GmbH
© Springer-Verlag Berlin Heidelberg 2000
Printed in Germany

Typesetting: Camera-ready by author, data conversion by Steingräber Satztechnik GmbH, Heidelberg
Printed on acid-free paper   SPIN: 10722442   06/3142   5 4 3 2 1 0

Preface

This volume contains the final versions of papers originally given at the workshop *Vision Algorithms: Theory and Practice*, which was held on 21–22 September 1999 during the *Seventh International Conference on Computer Vision* at the Corfu Holiday Palace Hotel in Kanoni, Corfu, Greece.

The subject of the workshop was algorithmic issues in computer vision, and especially in vision geometry: correspondence, tracking, structure and motion, and image synthesis. Both theoretical and practical aspects were considered. A particular goal was to take stock of the 'new wave' of geometric and statistical techniques that have been developed over the last few years, and to ask which of these are proving useful in real applications. To encourage discussion, we asked the presenters to stand back from their work and reflect on its context and longer term prospects, and we encouraged the audience to actively contribute questions and comments. The current volume retains some of the flavour of this, as each paper is followed by a brief edited transcript of the discussion that followed its presentation.

The theme was certainly topical, as we had 65 submitted papers for only 15 places (an acceptance rate of only 23%), and around 100 registered participants in all (nearly 1/3 of the ICCV registration). With so many submissions, there were some difficult decisions to make, and our reviewers deserve many thanks for their thoroughness and sound judgment in paper evaluation. As several authors commented, the overall quality of the reviews was exceptionally high. The accepted papers span the full range of algorithms for geometric vision, and we think that their quality will speak for itself.

To complement the submitted papers, we commissioned two invited talks "from the shop floor", two "expert reviews" on topical technical issues, and a panel session.

The invited talks were by two industry leaders with a great deal of experience in building successful commercial vision systems:

- Keith Hanna of the Sarnoff Corporation described Sarnoff's real time video alignment and annotation systems, which are used routinely in applications ranging from military reconnaissance to inserting advertisements and annotations on the Super Bowl field. This work is presented in the paper *Annotation of Video by Alignment to Reference Imagery* on page 253).
- Luc Robert of REALViZ S.A. described REALViZ's MatchMover and ReTimer post-production systems for movie special effects, which are used in a number of large post-production houses. Unfortunately there is no paper for this presentation, but the discussion that followed it is summarized on page 265.

Both presenters tried to give us some of the fruits of their experience in the difficult art of "making it work", illustrated by examples from their own systems.

The two "expert reviews" were something of an experiment. Each was a focused technical summary prepared jointly by a small team of people that we consider to be domain experts. In each case, the aim was to provide a concise technical update and state of the art, and then to discuss the advantages of the various implementation choices in a little more depth.

The motivation for these review sessions was as follows. As active members of the vision community and referees of many papers, we continually find that certain basic topics are poorly understood. This applies particularly to areas where a cultural split has occurred, with two or more camps following more or less separate lines of development. There are several such splits in the vision community, and we feel that every effort must be made to heal them. For one thing, it is fruitless for one group to reduplicate the successes and failures of another, or to continue with a line of research that others know to be unprofitable. More positively, intercommunication breeds innovation, and it is often at the boundaries between fields that the most rapid progress is made. The workshop as a whole was intended to take stock of the rapid progress made in vision geometry over the past decade, and hopefully to narrow the gap between "the geometers" and "the rest". Within this scope, we singled out the following two areas for special treatment: (*i*) the choice between direct and feature-based correspondence methods; and (*ii*) bundle adjustment.

Direct versus feature-based correspondence methods: One of the significant splits that has emerged in the vision community over the past 15–20 years is in the analysis of image sequences and multi-view image sets. Two classes of techniques are used:

- **"Feature-based" approaches:** Here, the problem is broken down into three stages: (*i*) local geometric features are extracted from each image (*e.g.* "points of interest", linear edges . . .); (*ii*) these features are used to compute multi-view relations, such as the epipolar geometry, and simultaneously are put into correspondence with one another using a robust search method; (*iii*) the estimated multi-view relations and correspondences are used for further computations such as refined correspondences, 3D structure recovery, plane recovery and alignment, moving object detection, *etc*.
- **"Direct" approaches:** Here, rather than extracting isolated features, dense spatio-temporal variations of image brightness (or color, texture, or some other dense descriptor) are used directly. Instead of a combinatorial search over feature correspondences, there is a search over the continuous parameters of an image motion model (translation, 2D affine, homographic), that in principle establishes dense correspondences as well as motion parameters. Often, a multi-scale search is used.

The experts in this session were P. Anandan & Michal Irani, who present the direct approach in the paper *About Direct Methods* on page 267, and Phil Torr & Andrew Zisserman, who present the feature-based approach in the paper *Feature Based Methods for Structure and Motion Estimation* on page 278. In each case, the authors try: (*i*) to give a brief, clear description of the two classes of methods; (*ii*) to identify the applications in which each has been most successful; and (*iii*) to discuss the limitations of each approach. The discussion that followed the session is summarized on page 295.

Bundle adjustment for visual reconstruction: Bundle adjustment is the refinement of visual reconstructions by simultaneous optimization over both structure and camera parameters. It was initially developed in the late 1950's and 1960's in the aerial photogrammetry community, where already by 1970 extremely accurate reconstruction of networks of thousands of images was feasible. The computer vision community is only now starting to consider problems of this size, and is still largely ignorant of the theory and methods of bundle adjustment. In part this is because cultural differences make the photogrammetry literature relatively inaccessible to most vision researchers, so one aim of this session was to present the basic photogrammetric techniques from a computer vision perspective. The issues raised in the session are reported in the survey paper *Bundle Adjustment — A Modern Synthesis* on page 298. This paper is rather long, but we publish it in the hope that it will be useful to the community to have the main elements of the theory collected in one place.

The workshop ended with an open panel session, with Richard Hartley, P. Anandan, Jitendra Malik, Joe Mundy and Olivier Faugeras as panelists. Each panelist selected a topic related to the workshop theme that he felt was important, and gave a short position statement on it followed by questions and discussion. The panel finished with more general discussion. A brief summary of the discussion and the issues raised by the panel is given on page 376.

Finally, we would like to thank the many people who helped to organize the workshop, and without whom it would not have been possible. The scientific helpers are listed on the following pages, but thanks must also go to: John Tsotsos, the chairman of ICCV'99, for his help with the logistics and above all for hosting a great main conference; to Mary-Kate Rada and Maggie Johnson of the IEEE Computer Society, and to Danièle Herzog of INRIA for their efficient organizational support; to the staff of the Corfu Holiday Palace for some memorable catering; and to INRIA Rhône-Alpes and the IEEE Computer Society for agreeing to act as sponsors.

June 2000   Bill Triggs, Andrew Zisserman and Richard Szeliski

Workshop Organizers

Bill Triggs   INRIA Rhône-Alpes, Grenoble, France
Andrew Zisserman   Dept. of Engineering Science, Oxford University
Richard Szeliski   Microsoft Research, Redmond, WA

Sponsors

INRIA Rhône-Alpes
IEEE Computer Society

Program Committee

Michael Black	Michal Irani	Harpreet Sawhney
Stefan Carlsson	Philip McLauchlan	Amnon Shashua
Olivier Faugeras	Steve Maybank	Chris Taylor
Andrew Fitzgibbon	John Oliensis	Phil Torr
Wolfgang Förstner	Shmuel Peleg	Luc Van Gool
Pascal Fua	Jean Ponce	Thierry Viéville
Greg Hager	Long Quan	Zhengyou Zhang
Richard Hartley	Ian Reid	Kalle Åström

Invited Speakers

Keith Hanna   Sarnoff Corporation, Princeton, NJ
Luc Robert   REALViZ S.A., Sophia Antipolis, France

Panelists

P. Anandan	Richard Hartley	Joe Mundy
Olivier Faugeras	Jitendra Malik	

Additional Reviewers

Peter Belhumeur	John Illingworth	Cordelia Schmid
Ingemar Cox	Michael Isard	Steve Seitz
Patrick Gros	Bart Lamiroy	Harry Shum
Radu Horaud	Jitendra Malik	Ramin Zabih
	Peter Meer	

Review Helpers

Yaron Caspi	Yanlin Guo	Garbis Salgian
Athos Georghiades	Steve Hsu	Peter Sturm
Jacob Goldberger	Robert Mandelbaum	Hai Tao
	Bogdan Matei	

Student Helpers and Session Transcripts

Eric Hayman	Antonio Criminisi	Geoff Cross	Joss Knight

Table of Contents

Invited Talks

Special Sessions

An Experimental Comparison
of Stereo Algorithms

Richard Szeliski[1] and Ramin Zabih[2]

[1] Microsoft Research, Redmond, WA 98052-6399, szeliski@microsoft.com
[2] Cornell University, Ithaca, NY 14853-7501, rdz@cs.cornell.edu

Abstract. While many algorithms for computing stereo correspondence
have been proposed, there has been very little work on experimentally
evaluating algorithm performance, especially using real (rather than synthetic) imagery. In this paper we propose an experimental comparison of several different stereo algorithms. We use real imagery, and explore two different methodologies, with different strengths and weaknesses. Our first methodology is based upon manual computation of
dense ground truth. Here we make use of a two stereo pairs: one of
these, from the University of Tsukuba, contains mostly fronto-parallel
surfaces; while the other, which we built, is a simple scene with a slanted
surface. Our second methodology uses the notion of prediction error,
which is the ability of a disparity map to predict an (unseen) third
image, taken from a known camera position with respect to the input pair. We present results for both correlation-style stereo algorithms
and techniques based on global methods such as energy minimization.
Our experiments suggest that the two methodologies give qualitatively
consistent results. Source images and additional materials, such as the
implementations of various algorithms, are available on the web from
http://www.research.microsoft.com/~szeliski/stereo.

1 Introduction

The accurate computation of stereo depth is an important problem in early
vision, and is vital for many visual tasks. A large number of algorithms have
been proposed in the literature (see [8, 10] for literature surveys). However, the
state of the art in evaluating stereo methods is quite poor. Most papers do not
provide quantitative comparisons of their methods with previous approaches.
When such comparisons are done, they are almost inevitably restricted to synthetic imagery. (However, see [13] for a case where real imagery was used to
compare a hierarchical area-based method with a hierarchical scanline matching
algorithm.)

The goal of this paper is to rectify this situation, by providing a quantitative
experimental methodology and comparison among a variety of different methods
using real imagery. There are a number of reasons why such a comparison is valuable. Obviously, it allows us to measure progress in our field and motivates us to
develop better algorithms. It allows us to carefully analyze algorithm characteristics and to improve overall performance by focusing on sub-components. It allows

B. Triggs, A. Zisserman, R. Szeliski (Eds.): Vision Algorithms'99, LNCS 1883, pp. 1–19, 2000.

us to ensure that algorithm performance is not unduly sensitive to the setting of "magic parameters". Furthermore, it enables us to design or tailor algorithms for specific applications, by tuning these algorithms to problem-dependent cost or fidelity metrics and to sample data sets.

We are particularly interested in using these experiments to obtain a deeper understanding of the behavior of various algorithms. To that end, we focus on image phenomena that are well-known to cause difficulty for stereo algorithms, such as depth discontinuities and low-texture regions.

Our work can be viewed as an attempt to do for stereo what Barron *et al.*'s comparative analysis of motion algorithms [3] accomplished for motion. The motion community benefited significantly from that paper; many subsequent papers have made use of these sequences. However, Barron *et al.* rely exclusively on synthetic data for their numerical comparisons; even the well-known "Yosemite" sequence is computer-generated. As a consequence, it is unclear how well their results apply to real imagery.

This paper is organized as follows. We begin by describing our two evaluation methodologies and the imagery we used. In section 3 we describe the stereo algorithms that we compare and give some implementation details. Section 4 gives experimental results from our investigations. We close with a discussion of some extensions that we are currently investigating.

2   Evaluation Methodologies

We are currently studying and comparing two different evaluation methodologies: comparison with ground truth depth maps, and the measurement of novel view prediction errors.

2.1   Data Sets

The primary data set that we used is a multi-image stereo set from the University of Tsukuba, where every pixel in the central *reference* image has been labeled by hand with its correct disparity. The image we use for stereo matching and the ground truth depth map are shown in figure 1. Note that the scene is fairly fronto-planar, and that the ground truth contains a small number of integer-valued disparities.

The most important limitation of the Tsukuba imagery is the lack of slanted surfaces. We therefore created a simple scene containing a slanted surface. The scene, together with the ground truth, are shown in figure 2. The objects in the scene are covered with paper that has fairly high-texture pictures on it. In addition, the scene geometry is quite simple. Additional details about this imagery can be found at the web site for this paper,
http://www.research.microsoft.com/~szeliski/stereo.

2.2   Comparison with Ground Truth

The ground truth images are smaller than the input images; we handle this by ignoring the borders (i.e., we only compute error statistics at pixels which are

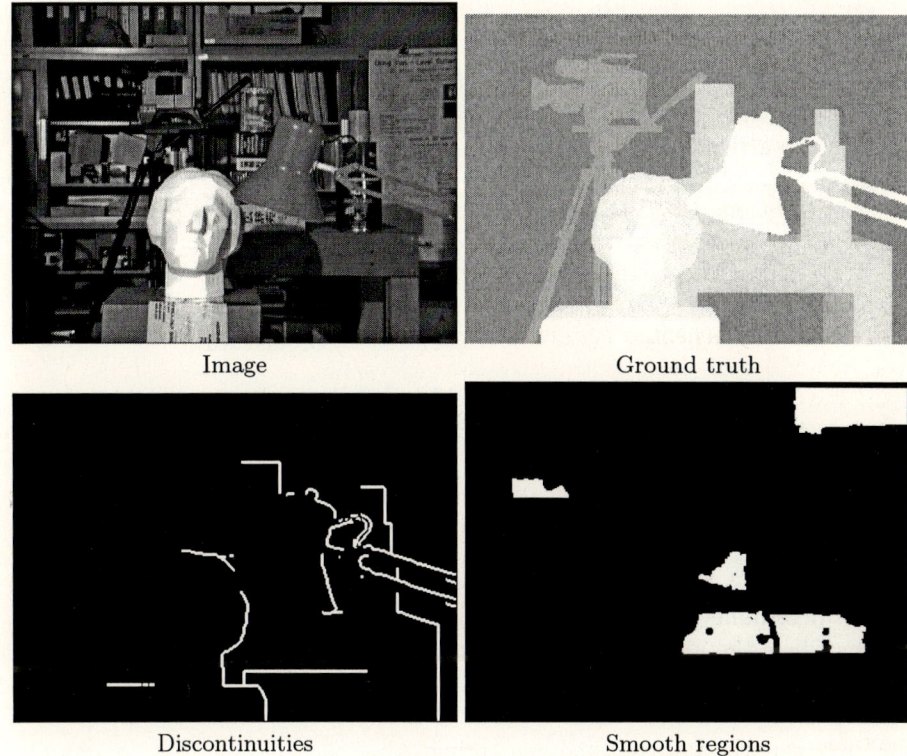

Image	Ground truth
Discontinuities	Smooth regions

Fig. 1. Imagery from the University of Tsukuba

given a label in the ground truth). Discarding borders is particularly helpful for correlation-based methods, since their output near the border is not well-defined.

The interesting regions in the Tsukuba imagery include:

- Specular surfaces, including the gray shelves in the upper left of the image, the orange lamp, and the white statue of a face. Specularities cause difficulty in computing depth, due to the reflected motion of the light source.
- Textureless regions, including the wall at the top right corner and the deeply shadowed area beneath the table. Textureless regions are locally ambiguous, which is a challenge for stereo algorithms.
- Depth discontinuities, at the borders of all the objects. It is difficult to compute depth at discontinuities, for a variety of reasons. It is especially difficult for thin objects, such as the orange lamp handle.
- Occluded pixels, near some of the object borders. Ideally, a stereo algorithm should detect and report occlusions; in practice, many algorithms do not do this, and in fact tend to give incorrect answers at unoccluded pixels near the occlusions.

Our goal is to analyze the effectiveness of different methods in these different regions. We have used the ground truth to determine the depth discontinuities and the occluded pixels. A pixel is a depth discontinuity if any of its

Image   Ground truth

Fig. 2. Imagery from Microsoft Research.

(4-connected) neighbors has a disparity that differs by more than 1 from its disparity.[1] A pixel is occluded if according to the ground truth it is not visible in both images.

While the Tsukuba imagery contains textureless regions, there is no natural way to determine these from the ground truth. Instead, we looked for large regions where the image gradient was small. We found five such regions, which are shown in figure 1. These regions correspond to major features in the scene; for example, one is the lamp shade, while two come from shadowed regions under the table.

We have computed error statistics for the depth discontinuities and for the textureless regions separately from our statistics for the other pixels. Since the methods we wish to compare include algorithms that do not detect occlusions, we have ignored the occluded pixels for the purpose of our statistics. Our statistics count the number of pixels whose disparity differs from the ground truth by more than ± 1. This makes sense because the true disparities are usually fractional. Therefore, having an estimate which differs from the true value by a tiny amount could be counted as an error if we required exact matches. In fact, we also computed exact matches, and obtained quite similar overall results.

2.3   Comparison Using Prediction Error

An alternative approach to measuring the quality of a stereo algorithm is to test how well it predicts novel views.[2] This is a particularly appropriate test when the stereo results are to be used for image-based rendering, but it is also useful for other tasks such as motion-compensated prediction in video coding and frame rate conversion. This approach parallels methodologies that are prevalent

---

[1] Neighboring pixels that are part of a sloped surface can easily differ by 1 pixel, but should not be counted as discontinuities.

[2] A third possibility is to run the stereo algorithm on several different pairs within a multi-image data set, and to compute the *self-consistency* between different disparity estimates [16]. We will discuss this option in more detail in section 5.

in many other research areas, such as speech recognition, machine learning, and information retrieval. In these disciplines, it is traditional to partition data into *training* data that is used to tune up the system, and *test* data that is used to evaluate it. In statistics, it is common to leave some data out during model fitting to prevent over-fitting (*cross-validation*).

To apply this methodology to stereo matching, we compute the depth map using a pair of images selected from a larger, multi-image stereo dataset, and then measure how well the original *reference* image plus depth map predicts the remaining views. The University of Tsukuba data set is an example of such a multi-image data set: the two images in figure 1 are part of a 5×5 grid of views of this scene. Many other examples of multi-image data sets exist, including the *Yosemite* fly-by, the *SRI Trees* set, the *NASA (Coke can)* set, the MPEG-4 *flower garden* data set, and many of the data sets in the CMU Image Database (`http://www.ius.cs.cmu.edu/idb`). Most of these data sets do not have an associated ground truth depth map, and yet all of them can be used to evaluate stereo algorithms if prediction error is used as a metric.

When developing a prediction error metric, we must specify two different components: an algorithm for predicting novel views, and a metric for determining how well the actual and predicted images match. A more detailed description of these issues can be found in our framework paper, which lays the foundations for prediction error as a quality metric [20].

In terms of view prediction, we have a choice of two basic algorithms. We can generate novel views from a color/depth image using *forward warping* [22], which involves moving the source pixels to the destination image and potentially filling in gaps. Alternatively, we can use *inverse warping* to pull pixels from the new (unseen) views back into the coordinate frame of the original reference image. This is easier to implement, since no decision has to be made as to which gaps need to be filled.

Unfortunately, inverse warping will produce erroneous results at pixels which are occluded (invisible) in the novel views, unless a separate occlusion (or visibility) map is computed for each novel view. Without this occlusion masking, certain stereo algorithms actually outperform the ground truth in terms of prediction error, since they try to match occluded pixels to *some* other pixel of the same color. In our experiments, therefore, we do not include occluded pixels in the computation of prediction error.

The simplest error metric that can be used in an L_2 (root mean square) distance between the pixel values. It is also possible to use a robust measure, which downweights large error, and to count the number of outliers [17]. Another possibility is to compute the per-pixel *residual motion* between the predicted and real image, and to compensate one of the two images by this motion to obtain a *compensated* RMS or robust error measure [20]. For simplicity, we use the raw (uncompensated and un-robustified) RMS error.

3   Algorithms

Loosely speaking, methods for computing dense stereo depth can be divided into two classes.[3] The first class of methods allow every pixel to independently select its disparity, typically by analyzing the intensities in a fixed rectangular window. These methods use statistical methods to compare the two windows, and are usually based on correlation. The second class of methods relies on global methods, and typically find the depth map that minimizes some function, called the energy or the objective function. These methods generally use an iterative optimization technique, such as simulated annealing.

3.1   Local Methods Based on Correlation

We implemented a number of standard correlation-based methods that use fixed-size square windows. We define the *radius* of a square whose side length is $2r+1$ to be r. The methods we chose were:

- Correlation using the L_2 and L_1 distance. The L_2 distance is the simplest correlation-based method, while the L_1 distance is more robust.
- Robust correlation using M-estimation with a truncated quadratic [5].
- Robust correlation using Least Median Squares [17].

3.2   Global Methods

Most global methods are based on energy minimization, so the major variable is the choice of energy function. Some stereo methods minimize a 1-dimensional energy function independently along each scanline [1, 4, 15]. This minimization can be done efficiently via dynamic programming [14]. More recent work has enforced some consistency between adjacent scanlines. We have found that one of these methods, MLMHV [9], performs quite well in practice, so we have included it in our study.

The most natural energy functions for stereo are two-dimensional, and contain a data term and a smoothness term. The data term is typically of the form $\sum_p [I(p) - I'(p + d(p))]^2$, where d is the depth map, p ranges over pixels, and I and I' are the input images. For our initial experiments, we have chosen a simple smoothness term which behaves well for largely front-planar imagery (such as that shown in figure 1). This energy function is the *Potts energy*, and is simply the number of adjacent pixels with different disparities.

In the energy minimization framework, it is difficult to determine whether an algorithm fails due to the choice of energy function or due to the optimization method. This is especially true because minimizing the energy functions that arise in early vision is almost inevitably NP-hard [21]. By selecting a single energy function for our initial experiments, we can control for this variable.

---

[3] There are a number of stereo methods that compute a sparse depth map. We do not consider these methods for two reasons. First, a dense output is required for a number of interesting applications, such as view synthesis. Second, a sparse depth map makes it difficult to identify statistically significant differences between algorithms.

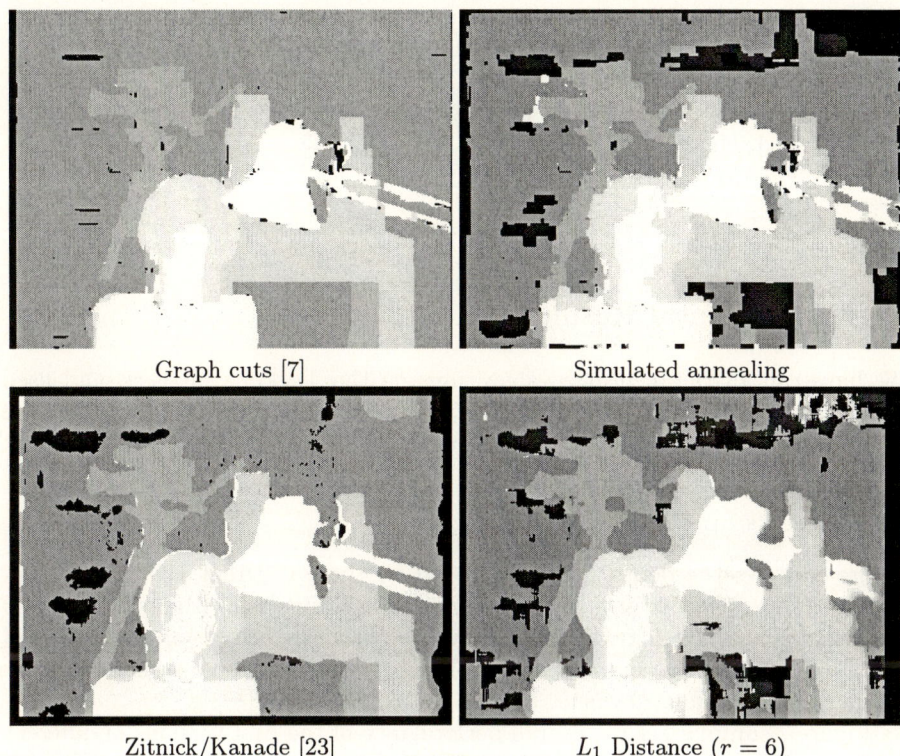

Graph cuts [7]   Simulated annealing

Zitnick/Kanade [23] L_1 Distance ($r = 6$)

Fig. 3. Results for several algorithms, on the imagery of figure 1

We used three methods to minimize the energy:

- Simulated annealing [12, 2] is the most common energy minimization technique. Following [6], we experimented with several different annealing schedules; our data is from the one that performed best.
- Graph cuts are a combinatorial optimization technique that can be used to minimize a number of different energy functions [7]. Other algorithms based on graph cuts are given in [18, 15].
- Mean field methods replace the stochastic update rules of simulated annealing with deterministic rules based either on the behavior of the *mean* or *mode* disparity at each pixel [11], or the local *distribution* of probabilities across disparity [19]. We present results for the latter algorithm.

The final method we experimented with is a global method that is not based on energy minimization. This algorithm, due to Zitnick and Kanade [23], is a cooperative method in the style of the Marr-Poggio algorithm. A particularly interesting feature of the algorithm is that it enforces various physical constraints, such as uniqueness. The uniqueness constraint states that a non-occluded pixel in one image should map to a unique pixel in the other image.

# errors (> ±1)	Total pixels	Discontinuities	Low-texture areas
Image	84,863	1,926	6,037
L_1 distance	10,457	1,025	967
Annealing	4,244	720	765
Zitnick/Kanade [23]	2,191	749	60
Graph cuts [7]	1,591	572	0

Fig. 4. Errors on ground truth data, from the results shown in figure 3.

4   Experimental Results

We have run all the mentioned algorithms on the Tsukuba imagery, and used both ground truth and prediction error to analyze the results. In addition, we have run the correlation-based algorithms on the Microsoft Research imagery.

4.1   Results on the Tsukuba Imagery

Figure 3 shows the depth maps computed by three different algorithms. Figures 5–7 show the performance of various algorithms using the ground truth performance methodology. Figure 5 shows the performance of correlation-based methods as a function of window size. Figure 6 shows the performance of two global optimization methods.

Figure 7 summarizes the overall performance of the best versions of different methods. The graph cuts algorithm has the best performance, and makes no errors in the low-textured areas shown in figure 1. Simulated annealing, mean-field estimation, M-estimation, and MLMHV [9] seem to have comparable performance. Note that the differences in overall performance between methods cannot be explained simply by their performance at discontinuities or in low-textured areas. For example, consider the data for annealing and for graph cuts, shown in figure 4. There is a substantial difference in performance at discontinuities and in textureless regions, but most errors occur in other portions of the image.

4.2   Analysis of Ground-Truth Data

Our data contains some unexpected results. First of all, it is interesting that the different correlation-based methods are so similar in terms of their performance. In addition, there was surprisingly little variation as a function of window size, once the windows were sufficiently large. Finally, the overall performance of the correlation-based methods was disappointing, especially near discontinuities. Note that an algorithm that assigned every pixel a random disparity would be within ±1 of the approximately 20% of the time, and thus correct under our definition.

It is commonly believed that it is important for matching algorithms to gracefully handle outliers. In terms of statistical robustness, the L_2 distance is the worst, followed by the L_1 distance. M-estimation is better still, and least median squares is best of all. There is some support for this argument in our

Total accuracy

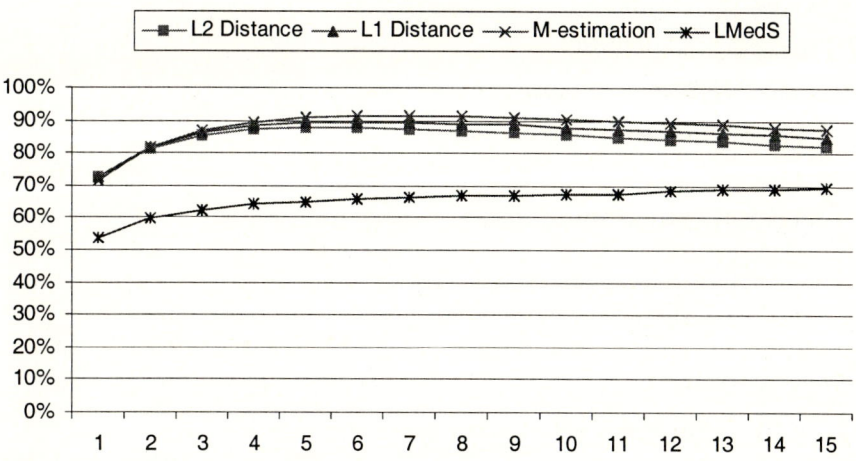

Discontinuity accuracy

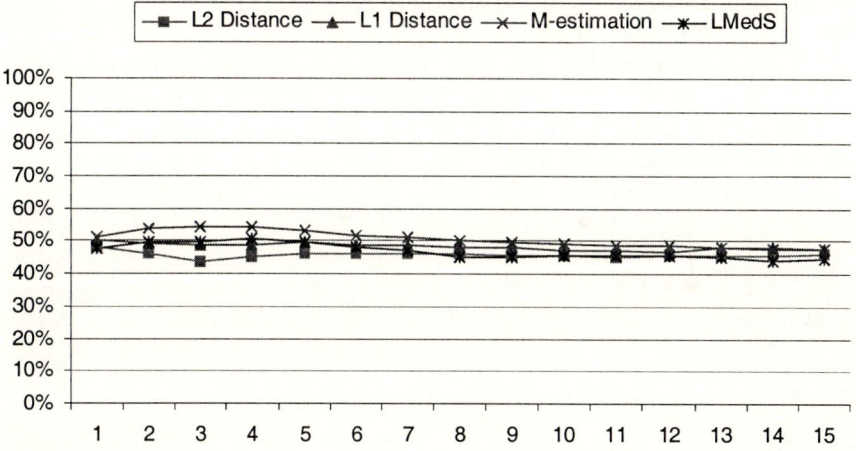

Fig. 5. Performance of standard correlation-based methods as a function of window radius, using the ground truth of figure 1. The graph at top shows errors for all pixels (discarding those that are occlusions according to the ground truth). The graph at bottom only considers pixels that are discontinuities according to the ground truth.

data, but it is not clear cut. The L_1 distance has a small advantage over the L_2 distance, and M-estimation has a slightly larger advantage over the L_1 distance. Least median squares does quite badly (although to the naked eye it looks fairly good, especially with small windows). The regions where it makes the most

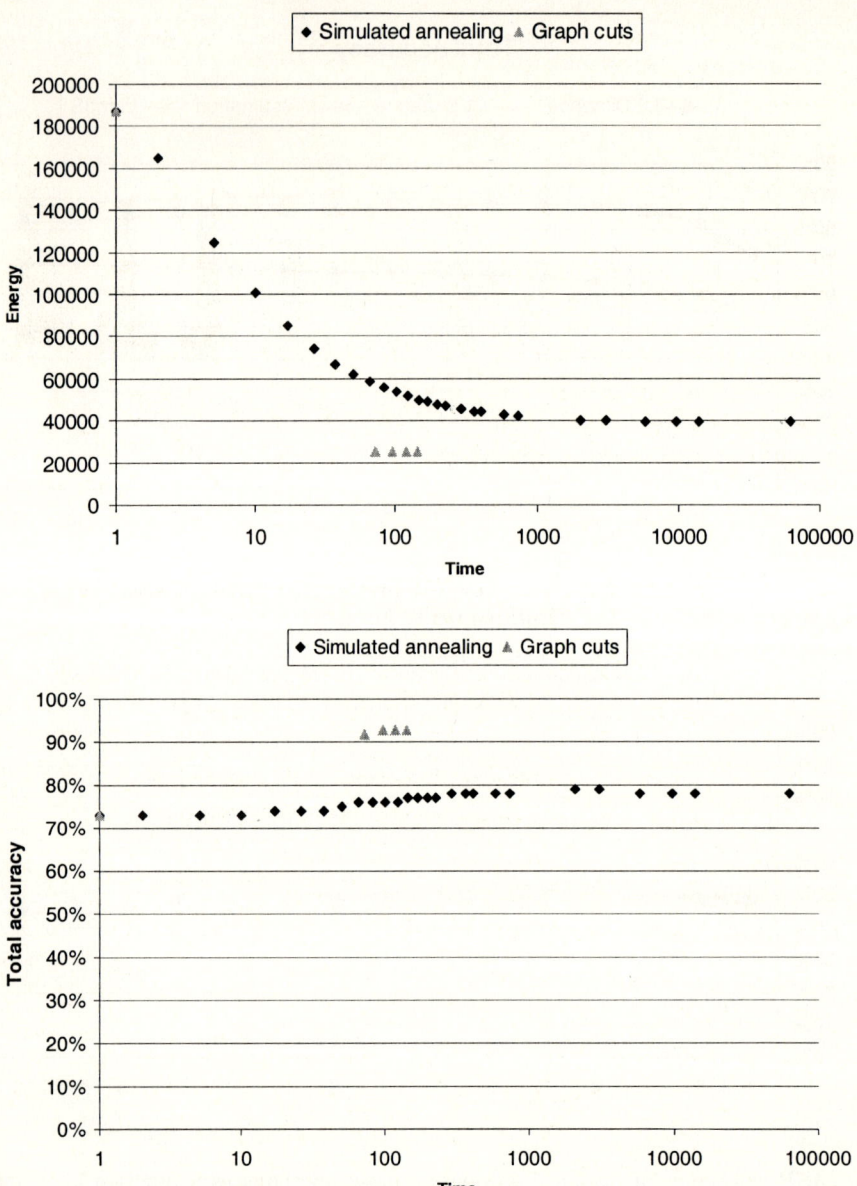

Fig. 6. Performance of global optimization methods as a function of running time, using the Potts model energy on the imagery of figure 1.

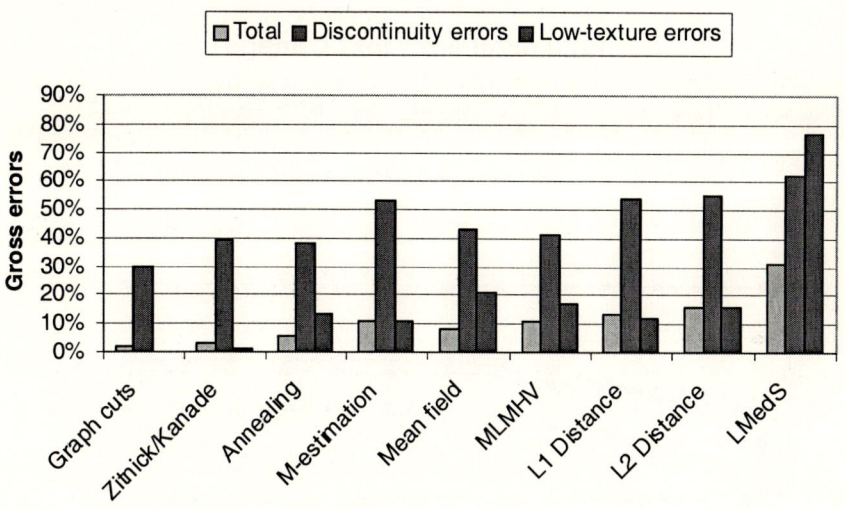

Fig. 7. Performance comparison, using the best results for each algorithm, on the imagery of figure 1.

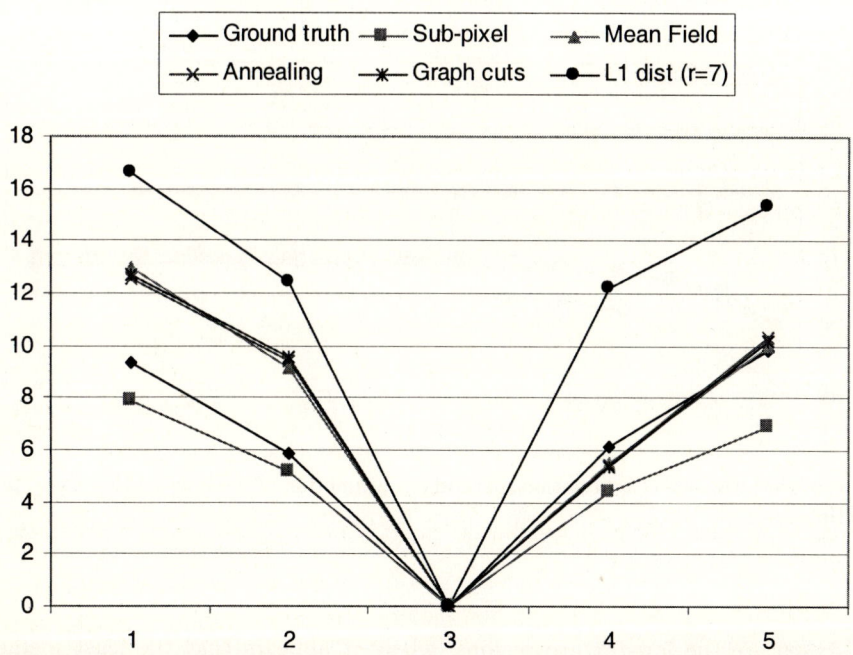

Fig. 8. RMS prediction error (in gray levels) as a function of frame number using the imagery of figure 1.

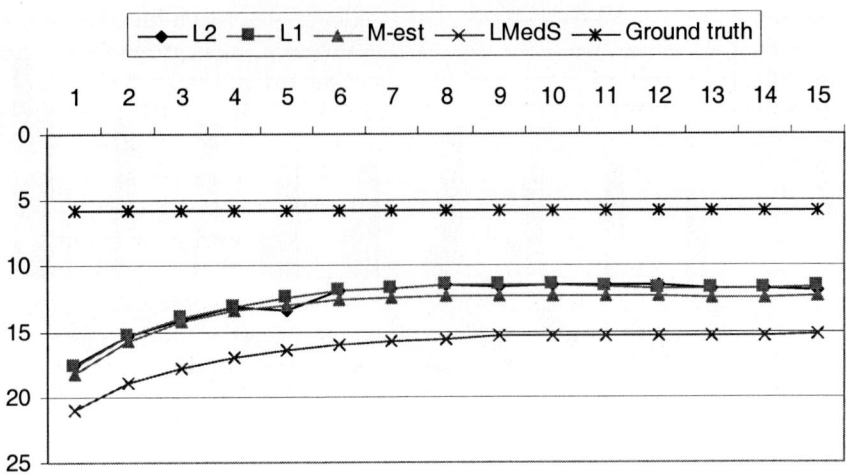

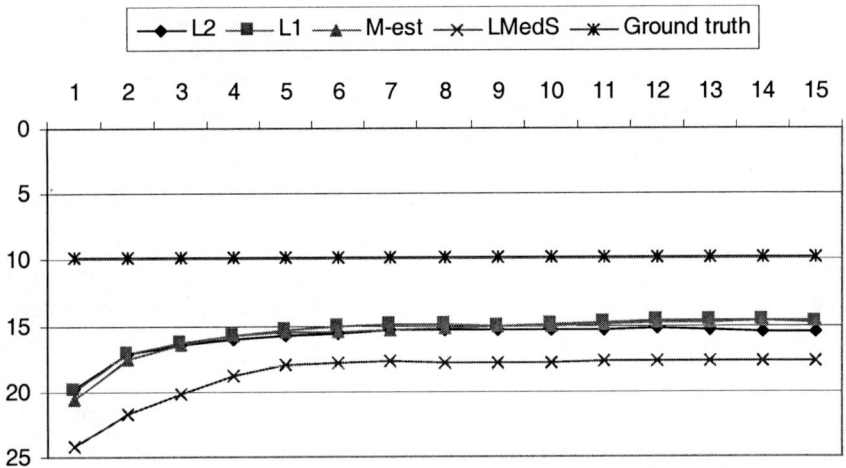

Fig. 9. Performance of correlation methods as a function of window radius, using prediction error.

mistakes are the low-texture regions, where it appears that the least median squares algorithm treats useful textured pixels (e.g., the bolts on the front of the workbench) as outliers.

4.3   Analysis of Prediction Error Data

The prediction error metrics for various algorithms are shown in figures 8 and 9. Figure 8 shows the RMS (uncorrected) prediction error as a function of frame number for four different algorithms and two versions of the ground truth data. The frames being tested are the ones in the middle row of the 5×5 University of Tsukuba data set (we will call these images LLL, LL, L, R, and RR in subsequent discussions). The ground truth data was modified to give sub-pixel estimates using a sub-pixel accurate correlation-based technique whose search range was constrained to stay within a $\frac{1}{2}$ pixel disparity of the original ground truth. As we can see in figure 8, this reduces the RMS prediction error by about 2 gray levels.

We can also see from this figure that error increases monotonically away from the reference frame 3 (the left image), and that prediction errors are worse when moving leftward. This is because errors in the depth map due to occlusions in the right image are more visible when moving leftward (these areas are being exposed, rather than occluded). It is also interesting that the graph cut, mean field, and annealing approaches have very similar prediction errors, even though their ground truth errors differ. Our current conjecture is that this is because graph cuts do a better job of estimating disparity in textureless regions, which is not as important for the prediction task.

Figure 9 shows the prediction error as a function of window size for the four correlation-based algorithms we studied. These figures also suggest that a window size of 7 is sufficient if prediction error is being used as a metric. The shape of these curves is very similar to the ground truth error (figure 5), which suggests that the two metrics are producing consistent results.

4.4   Results on the Microsoft Research Imagery

The results from running different variants of correlation on the imagery of figure 2 are shown in figure 11. Selected output images are given in figure 10. The overall curves are quite consistent with the results from the Tsukuba imagery. Here, the least median squares algorithm does slightly bettern than the other techniques. This is probably because there are no low-texture regions in this dataset.

5   Discussion

In this paper, we have compared two methodologies for evaluating stereo matching algorithms, and also compared the performance of several widely used stereo algorithms. The two methodologies produce different, but somewhat consistent results, while emphasizing (or de-emphasizing) certain kinds of errors.

The ground truth methodology gives the best possible evaluation of a stereo matcher's quality, since it supposedly knows what the perfect result ("gold standard") should be. However, it is possible for the ground truth to be inaccurate, and it typically is so near discontinuities where pixels are mixtures of values

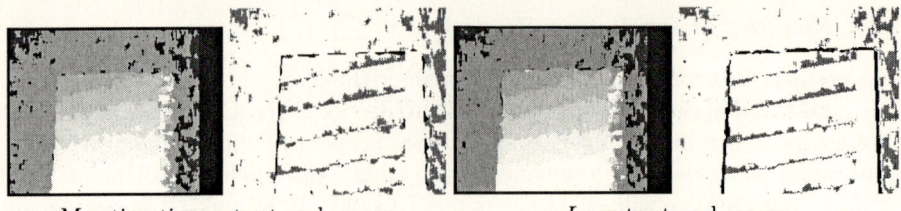

M-estimation output and errors L_2 output and errors

Fig. 10. Results for correlation algorithms ($r = 4$), on the imagery of figure 2. Errors $> \pm 1$ are shown in black, while errors of ± 1 are shown in gray.

from different surfaces. Quantization to the nearest integer disparity is a further source of error, which we compensate for by only counting errors $> \pm 1$ disparity. Ground truth also weights regions such as textureless or occluded regions (where it is very difficult, if not impossible, to get a reliable result) equally with regions where all algorithms should perform well. In our experiments, we have deliberately excluded occluded regions from our analysis. It may be desirable to treat these regions on the same footing as other potential problem areas (textureless regions and discontinuities). Breaking down the error statistics by their location in the image, is a step towards trying to rationalize this situation.

Intensity prediction error is a different metric, which de-emphasizes errors in low-texture areas, but emphasizes small (one pixel or sub-pixel) errors in highly textured areas. The former is a reasonable idea if the stereo maps are going to be used in an image-based rendering application. Those regions where the depth estimates are unreliable due to low texture are also regions where the errors are less visible. The problem with sub-pixel errors should be fixable by modifying or extending the algorithms being evaluated to return sub-pixel accurate disparity estimates.

A third methodology, which we have not yet evaluated, is the self-consistency metric of Leclerc *et al.* [16]. In this methodology, the consistency in 3D location (or re-projected pixel coordinates) of reconstructed 3D points from different pairs of images is calculated. This shares some characteristics with the intensity prediction metric error used in this paper, in that more than two images are used to perform the evaluation. However, this metric is more stringent than intensity prediction. In low texture areas where the results tend to be error-prone, it is unlikely that the self-consistency will be good (whereas intensity prediction may be good). There is a possibility that independently run stereo matchers may accidentally produce consistent results, but this seems unlikely in practice. In the future, we hope to collaborate with the authors of [16] to apply our different methodologies to the same sets of data.

5.1 Extensions

In work to date, we have already obtained interesting results about the relative performance of various algorithms and their sensitivity to certain parameters

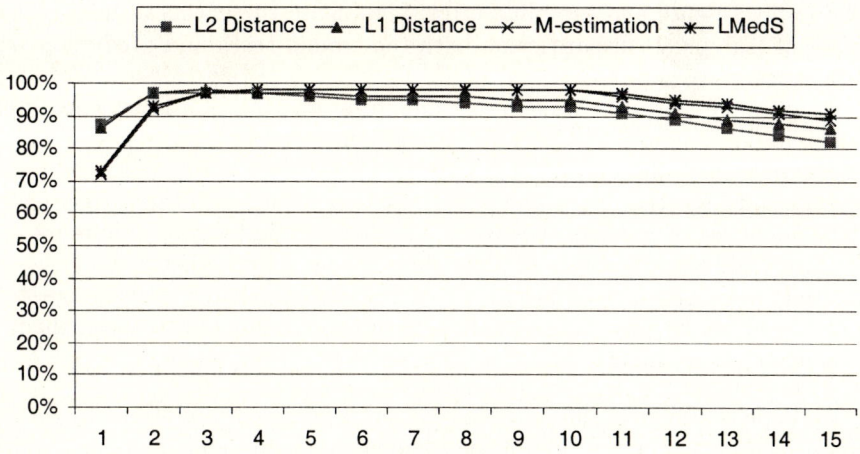

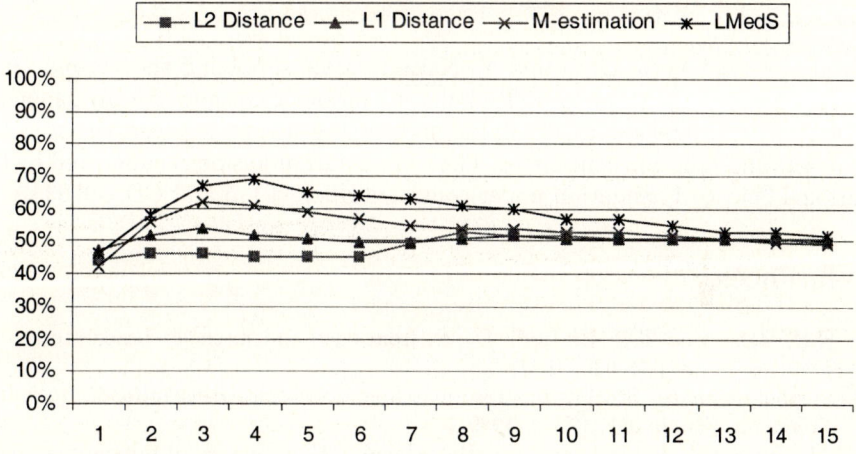

Fig. 11. Performance of standard correlation-based methods as a function of window radius, using the ground truth of figure 2. The graph at top shows errors for all pixels (discarding those that are occlusions according to the ground truth). The graph at bottom only considers pixels that are discontinuities according to the ground truth.

(such as window size). However, there are many additional issues and questions that we are planning to examine in ongoing work. These issues include:

- Sub-pixel issues and sampling error: investigate the effects of using a finer set of (sub-pixel) disparities on both the ground truth and prediction error metrics.
- Study more algorithms, including minimization with non-Potts energy and the use of weighted windows for correlation.
- Evaluate more data sets.
- Determine whether it is more important to come up with the correct energy to minimize, or whether it is more important to find a good minimum.
- Investigate the sensitivity of algorithms to various parameter values.
- Study whether cross-validation (using prediction error in a multi-image stereo dataset) can be used to fine-tune algorithm parameters or to adapt them locally across an image.

We hope that our results on stereo matching will motivate others to perform careful quantitative evaluation of their stereo algorithm, and that our inquiries will lead to a deeper understanding of the behavior (and failure modes) of stereo correspondence algorithms.

Acknowledgements

We are grateful to Y. Ohta and Y. Nakamura for supplying the ground truth imagery from the University of Tsukuba, to various colleagues for furnishing us with their algorithms and/or results, and for the helpful suggestions from the reviewers and program committee. The second author has been supported by the National Science Foundation under contracts IIS-9900115 and CDA-9703470.

References

1. H.H. Baker and T.O. Binford. Depth from edge and intensity based stereo. In *IJCAI81*, pages 631–636, 1981.
2. Stephen Barnard. Stochastic stereo matching over scale. *International Journal of Computer Vision*, 3(1):17–32, 1989.
3. J.L. Barron, D.J. Fleet, and S.S. Beauchemin. Performance of optical flow techniques. *International Journal of Computer Vision*, 12(1):43–77, February 1994.
4. P. N. Belhumeur and D. Mumford. A Bayesian treatment of the stereo correspondence problem using half-occluded regions. In *Computer Vision and Pattern Recognition*, pages 506–512, Champaign-Urbana, Illinois, 1992.
5. Michael Black and P. Anandan. A framework for the robust estimation of optical flow. In *4th International Conference on Computer Vision*, pages 231–236, 1993.
6. Andrew Blake. Comparison of the efficiency of deterministic and stochastic algorithms for visual reconstruction. *IEEE Transactions on Pattern Analysis and Machine Intelligence*, 11(1):2–12, January 1989.
7. Yuri Boykov, Olga Veksler, and Ramin Zabih. Fast approximate energy minimization via graph cuts. In *Seventh International Conference on Computer Vision (ICCV'99)*, pages 377–384, Kerkyra, Greece, September 1999.

8. Lisa Brown. A survey of image registration techniques. *ACM Computing Surveys*, 24(4):325–376, December 1992.
9. I. Cox, S. Hingorani, S. Rao, and B. Maggs. A maximum likelihood stereo algorithm. *Computer Vision, Graphics and Image Processing*, 63(3):542–567, 1996.
10. U. Dhond and J. Aggarwal. Structure from stereo — a review. *IEEE Transactions on Systems, Man and Cybernetics*, 19(6), 1989.
11. Davi Geiger and Federico Girosi. Parallel and deterministic algorithms from MRF's: Surface reconstruction. *IEEE Transactions on Pattern Analysis and Machine Intelligence*, 13(5):401–412, May 1991.
12. S. Geman and D. Geman. Stochastic relaxation, Gibbs distributions, and the Bayesian restoration of images. *IEEE Transactions on Pattern Analysis and Machine Intelligence*, 6:721–741, 1984.
13. Y. C. Hsieh, D. McKeown, and F. P. Perlant. Performance evaluation of scene registration and stereo matching for cartographic feature extraction. *IEEE Transactions on Pattern Analysis and Machine Intelligence*, 14(2):214–238, February 1992.
14. S. S. Intille and A. F. Bobick. Disparity-space images and large occlusion stereo. In *Proc. Third European Conference on Computer Vision (ECCV'94)*, volume 1, Stockholm, Sweden, May 1994. Springer-Verlag.
15. H. Ishikawa and D. Geiger. Occlusions, discontinuities, and epipolar lines in stereo. In *Fifth European Conference on Computer Vision (ECCV'98)*, pages 332–248, Freiburg, Germany, June 1998. Springer-Verlag.
16. Y. G. Leclerc, Q.-T. Luong, and P. Fua. Self-consistency: A novel approach to characterizing the accuracy and reliability of point correspondence algorithms. In *DARPA Image Understanding Workshop*, Monterey, California, November 1998.
17. Peter Rousseeuw and Annick Leroy. *Robust Regression and Outlier Detection*. New York: Wiley, 1987.
18. S. Roy and I. J. Cox. A maximum-flow formulation of the n-camera stereo correspondence problem. In *Sixth International Conference on Computer Vision (ICCV'98)*, pages 492–499, Bombay, January 1998.
19. D. Scharstein and R. Szeliski. Stereo matching with nonlinear diffusion. *International Journal of Computer Vision*, 28(2):155–174, July 1998.
20. R. Szeliski. Prediction error as a quality metric for motion and stereo. In *Seventh International Conference on Computer Vision (ICCV'99)*, pages 781–788, Kerkyra, Greece, September 1999.
21. Olga Veksler. *Efficient Graph-based Energy Minimization Methods in Computer Vision*. PhD thesis, Cornell University, July 1999.
22. G. Wolberg and T. Pavlidis. Restoration of binary images using stochastic relaxation with annealing. *Pattern Recognition Letters*, 3:375–388, 1985.
23. Charles Zitnick and Takeo Kanade. A cooperative algorithm for stereo matching and occlusion detection. Technical Report CMU-RI-TR-99-35, Robotics Institute, Carnegie Mellon University, Pittsburgh, PA, October 1999.

Discussion

Jean Ponce: You only showed one data set, how much can you say from one data set?

Ramin Zabih: Yes, that's clearly the major weakness so far — there's only one data set. The two different methodologies point in the same direction. It might still be that there's something strange about the way the ground truth was presented, but I think that the agreement is encouraging. So far the state of the art has been just to show off different pictures. We're trying to move beyond that, but getting ground truth for the ground-truth methodology is very difficult. At the least the prediction error stuff allows you to work on lots of different data sets, which we're in the process of doing.

Jean Ponce: Yes, but prediction error is so application dependent. It works very well for image-based rendering, but if you want to do navigation or whatever, then it's not really appropriate.

Ramin Zabih: Yes, I agree.

Yvan Leclerc: Yesterday I talked about our self-consistency methodology for comparing stereo algorithms. I was wondering if you could comment on the relationship between your approach and ours.

Rick Szeliski: For those who missed Yvan's talk, his technique is similar in that you start with a multi-image data set. But instead of what we call prediction error, where you take a depth map computed with one image pair and predict the appearance in all the other images, Yvan's methodology computes depth maps between all possible pairs, and then sees whether they're consistently predicting the same 3D point. I think that it's a very valid methodology. What we hope to do is to test a wider range of data sets with more algorithms, and eventually publish a survey paper, along the lines of the kind of comparative work that we see already in motion estimation. I think it will be essential to include Yvan's methodology as well. Hopefully we'll be able to work out some sort of a joint evaluation. The two metrics won't necessarily give the same results — appearance prediction is oriented towards image-based rendering and is tolerant of errors in low texture regions, whereas Yvan's method is oriented towards structure and might heavily penalize those. Jean's comment is very well taken — this is application-dependent. But you know, in computer vision we've worked on robotics, robotics, robotics. Even when we stopped working on that we still kept the same mind set. But if you look for example at what happens with stereo algorithms when you try to do z-keying — you try to extract the foreground person from a textured background and put something synthetic behind him — the result is horrible, it's just not acceptable, you get these spiky halos full of the wrong pixels. As Luc Robert commented yesterday, we can't use computer vision yet in Hollywood. The reason is basically that we're not focusing on the right problems. That's why I like prediction error — it penalizes you heavily for those visible little single pixels errors.

Yvan Leclerc: Combining our methodologies would be a great idea. Let's do it.

Ramin Zabih: One comment about Jean's point is that in many situations there do seem to be consistent differences between the algorithms. We don't have enough ground truth to do convincing statistics yet, but it looks like the optimization-based approaches are doing better, certainly at discontinuities, and often in low texture areas as well.

Rick Szeliski: One final comment. We have made these data sets available on `http://www.research.microsoft.com/~szeliski/stereo/`, so that people can run their stereo algorithms on them. We are interested in hearing about the results, as we intend to publish a comparative survey of the performance of the different methods we have access to.

A General Method for Feature Matching and Model Extraction

Clark F. Olson

Jet Propulsion Laboratory, California Institute of Technology
4800 Oak Grove Drive, Mail Stop 125-209, Pasadena, CA 91109-8099
http://robotics.jpl.nasa.gov/people/olson/homepage.html

Abstract. Popular algorithms for feature matching and model extraction fall into two broad categories, generate-and-test and Hough transform variations. However, both methods suffer from problems in practical implementations. Generate-and-test methods are sensitive to noise in the data. They often fail when the generated model fit is poor due to error in the selected features. Hough transform variations are somewhat less sensitive the noise, but implementations for complex problems suffer from large time and space requirements and the detection of false positives. This paper describes a general method for solving problems where a model is extracted from or fit to data that draws benefits from both generate-and-test methods and those based on the Hough transform, yielding a method superior to both. An important component of the method is the subdivision of the problem into many subproblems. This allows efficient generate-and-test techniques to be used, including the use of randomization to limit the number of subproblems that must be examined. However, the subproblems are solved using pose space analysis techniques similar to the Hough transform, which lowers the sensitivity of the method to noise. This strategy is easy to implement and results in practical algorithms that are efficient and robust. We apply this method to object recognition, geometric primitive extraction, robust regression, and motion segmentation.

1 Introduction

The generate-and-test paradigm is a popular strategy for solving model matching problems such as recognition, detection, and fitting. The basic idea of this method is to generate (or predict) many hypothetical model positions using the minimal amount of information necessary to identify unique solutions. A sequence of such positions is tested, and the positions that meet some criterion are retained. Examples of this technique include RANSAC [6] and the alignment method [10].

The primary drawback to generate-and-test paradigm is sensitivity to noise. Let us call the features that are used in predicting the model position for some test the *distinguished features*, since they play a more important role in whether the test is successful. The other features are *undistinguished features*. Error in

B. Triggs, A. Zisserman, R. Szeliski (Eds.): Vision Algorithms'99, LNCS 1883, pp. 20–36, 2000.

the distinguished features causes the predicted position to be in error. As the error grows, the testing step becomes more likely to fail.

To deal with this problem, methods have been developed to propagate errors in the locations of the distinguished features [1, 8]. Under the assumption of a bounded error region for each of the distinguished image features, these methods can place bounds on the locations to which the undistinguished model features can be located in an image. When we count the number of undistinguished model features that can be aligned with image features (with the constraint that the distinguished features must always be in alignment up to the error bounds) these techniques can guarantee that we never undercount the number of alignable features. The techniques will thus never report that the model is not present according to some counting criterion when, in fact, the model does meet the criterion.

On the other hand, this method is likely to overcount the number of alignable features, even if the bounds on the location of each individual feature are tight. The reason for this is that, while this method checks whether there is a model position that brings each of the undistinguished model features into alignment with image features (along with all of the distinguished features) up to the error bounds, it does not check whether there is a position that brings all of the counted undistinguished features into alignment up to the error bounds.

A competing technique for feature matching and model extraction is based on the Hough transform. This method also generates hypothetical model positions solutions using minimal information, but rather than testing each solution separately, the testing is performed by analyzing the locations of the solutions in the space of possible model positions (or *poses*). This is often, but not always, accomplished through a histogramming or clustering procedure. The large clusters in the pose space indicate good model fits. We call techniques that examine the pose space for sets of consistent matches among all hypothetical matches *Hough-based methods*, since they derive from the Hough transform [11, 15]. While these techniques are less sensitive to noise in the features, they are prone to large computational and memory requirements, as well as the detection of false positive instances [7], if the pose space analysis is not careful.

In this paper, we describe a technique that combines the generate-and-test and Hough-based methods in a way that draws ideas and advantages from each, yielding a method that improves upon both. Like the generate-and-test method, (partial) solutions based on distinguished features are generated for further examination. However, each such solution is under-constrained and Hough-based methods are used to determine and evaluate the remainder of the solution. This allows both randomization to be used to reduce the computational complexity of the method and error propagation techniques to be used in order to better extract the relevant models. We call this technique RUDR (pronounced "rudder"), for Recognition Using Decomposition and Randomization.

First, it is shown that the problem can be treated as many subproblems, each of which is much simpler than the original problem. We next discuss various methods by which the subproblems can be solved. The application of randomization to reduce the number of subproblems that must be examined is then described. These techniques yield efficiency gains over conventional generate-and-test and Hough-based methods. In addition, the subdivision of the problem allows us to examine a much smaller parameter space in each of the subproblems than in the original problem and this allows the error inherent in localization procedures to be propagated accurately and efficiently in the matching process.

This method has a large number of applications. It can be applied to essentially any problem where a model is fit to cluttered data (i.e. with outliers or multiple models present). We discuss the application of this method to object recognition, curve detection, robust regression, and motion segmentation.

The work described here is a generalization of previous work on feature matching and model extraction [19, 20, 22]. Similar ideas have been used by other researchers. A simple variation of this method has been applied to curve detection by Murakami et al. [18] and Leavers [14]. In both of these cases, the problem decomposition was achieved through the use of a single distinguished feature in the image for each of the subproblems. We argue that the optimal performance is achieved when the number of distinguished features is one less than the number necessary to fully define the model position in the errorless case. This has two beneficial effects. First, it reduces the amount of the pose space that must be considered in each problem (and the combinatorial explosion in the sets of undistinguished features that are examined). Second, it allows a more effective use of randomization in reducing the computational complexity of the method. A closely related decomposition and randomization method has been described by Cass [4] in the context of pose equivalence analysis. He uses a *base match* to develop an approximation algorithm for feature matching under uncertainty.

2   General Problem Formalization

The class of problems that we attack using RUDR are those that require a model to be fit to a set of observed data features, where a significant portion of the observed data may be outliers or there may be multiple models present in the data. These problems can, in general, be formalized as follows.

Given:
• $\mathcal{M}$: The model to be fit. This model may be a set of distinct features as is typical in object recognition, or it may be a parameterized manifold such as a curve or surface, as in geometric primitive extraction and robust regression.
• $\mathcal{D}$: The data to match. This data consists of a set of features or measurements, $\{\delta_1, ..., \delta_d\}$, that have been extracted, for example, from an image.
• $\mathcal{T}$: The possible positions or transformations of the model. We use τ to denote individual transformations in this space.
• $A(\mathcal{M}, \mathcal{D}, \mathcal{T}, \tau, D)$: A binary-valued acceptance criterion that specifies whether a transformation, τ, satisfactorily brings the model into agreement with a set of data features, $D \in \mathcal{D}$. We allow this criterion to be a function of the full set of data features and the set of transformations to allow the criterion to select the

single best subset of data features according to some criterion or to take into account global matching information.

Determine and report:
• All maximal sets of data features, $D \in \mathcal{D}$, for which there is a transformation, $\tau \in \mathcal{T}$, such that the acceptance criterion, $A(\mathcal{M}, \mathcal{D}, \mathcal{T}, \tau, D)$, is satisfied.

This formalization is very general. Many problems can be formalized in this manner, including object recognition, geometric primitive extraction, motion segmentation, and robust regression.

A useful acceptance criterion is based on bounding the fitting error between the model and the data. Let $C(\mathcal{M}, \delta, \tau)$ be a function that determines whether the specified position of the model fits the data feature δ (e.g. up to a bounded error). We let $C(\mathcal{M}, \delta, \tau) = 1$, if the criterion is satisfied, and $C(\mathcal{M}, \delta, \tau) = 0$, otherwise. The model is said to be brought into alignment with a set of data features, $D = \{\delta_1, ..., \delta_x\}$ up to the error criterion, if all of the individual features are brought into alignment:

$$\prod_{i=1}^{x} C(\mathcal{M}, \delta_i, \tau) = 1 \qquad (1)$$

The bounded-error acceptance criterion specifies that a set of data features, $D = \{\delta_1, ..., \delta_x\}$, should be reported, if the cardinality of the set meets some threshold ($x \geq c$), there is a position of the model that satisfies (1), and the set is not a subset of some larger set that is reported.

While this criterion cannot incorporate global information, such as mean-square-error or least-median-of-squares, RUDR is not restricted to using this bounded-error criterion. This method has been applied to least-median-of-squares regression with excellent results [19].

Example As a running example, we will consider the detection of circles in two-dimensional image data. For this case, our model, $\mathcal{M}$, is simply the parameterization of a circle, $(x - x_c)^2 + (y - y_c)^2 = r^2$, and our data, $\mathcal{D}$, is a set of image points. The space of possible transformations is the space of circles, $\mathcal{T} = [x_c, \ y_c, \ r]^T$. We use a bounded-error acceptance criterion such that a point is considered to be on the circle if $\left| \sqrt{(x - x_c)^2 + (y - y_c)^2} - r \right| < \epsilon$. We will report the circles that have $\sum_{i=1}^{d} C_\epsilon(\mathcal{M}, \delta_i, \tau) > \pi r$. In other words, we search for the circles that have half of their perimeter present in the image.

3 Approach

Let us call the hypothetical correspondence between a set of data features and the model a *matching*. The generate-and-test paradigm and many Hough-based strategies solve for hypothetical model positions using matchings of the minimum cardinality to constrain the model position up to a finite ambiguity (assuming errorless features). We call the matchings that contain this minimal amount of information the *minimal matchings* and we denote their cardinality k. We consider two types of models. One type of model consists of a set of discrete features similar to the data features. The other is a parameterized model such as a curve or surface. When the model is a set of discrete features, the minimal matchings specify the model features that match each of the data features in the minimal matching and we call these *explicit matchings*. Otherwise, the data features are matched implicitly to the parameterized model and we thus call these *implicit matchings*.

In the generate-and-test paradigm, the model positions generated using the minimal matchings are tested by determining how well the undistinguished features are fit according to the predicted model position. In Hough-based methods, it is typical to determine the positions of the model that align each of the minimal matchings and detect clusters of these positions in the parameter space that describes the set of possible model positions, but other pose space analysis techniques can be used (e.g. [3, 4]).

The approach that we take draws upon both generate-and-test techniques and Hough-based techniques. The underlying matching method may be any one of several pose space analysis techniques in the Hough-based method (see Section 4), but unlike previous Hough-based methods, the problem is subdivided into many smaller problems, in which only a subset of the minimal matchings is examined. When randomization is applied to selecting which subproblems to solve, a low computational complexity can be achieved with a low probability of failure.

The key to this method is to subdivide the problem into many small subproblems, in which a *distinguished matching* of some cardinality $g < k$ between data features and the model is considered. Only those minimal matchings that contain the distinguished matching are examined in each subproblem and this constrains the portion of the pose space that the subproblem considers. We could consider each possible distinguished matching of the appropriate cardinality as a subproblem, but we shall see that this is not necessary in practice.

Let's consider the effect of this decomposition of the problem on the matchings that are detected by a system using a bounded-error criterion, $C(\mathcal{M}, d, t)$, as described above. For now, we assume that we have some method of determining precisely those sets of data features that should be reported according to the bounded-error acceptance criterion. The implications of performing matching only approximately and the use of an acceptance criterion other than the bounded-error criterion are discussed subsequently.

Proposition 1. *For any transformation, $\tau \in \mathcal{T}$, the following statements are equivalent:*
1. Transformation τ brings at least x data features into alignment with the model up to the error criterion.
2. Transformation τ brings at least $\binom{x}{k}$ sets of data features with cardinality k into alignment with the model up to the error criterion.

3. For any distinguished matching of cardinality g that is brought into alignment with the model up to the error criterion by τ, there are $\binom{x-g}{k-g}$ minimal matchings that contain the distinguished matching that are brought into alignment up to the error criterion by τ.

The proof of this proposition, which follows directly from combinatorics, is sketched in [20]. This result indicates that as long as we examine one distinguished matching that belongs to each of the matchings that should be reported, the strategy of subdividing the problem into subproblems yields equivalent results to examining the original problem as long as the threshold on the number of matches is set appropriately.

This decomposition of the problem allows our method to be viewed as a class of generate-and-test methods, where distinguished matchings (rather than minimal matchings) are generated and the testing step is performed using a pose space analysis method (such as clustering or pose space equivalence analysis) rather than comparing a particular model position against the data.

While distinguished matchings of any cardinality could be considered, we must balance the complexity of the subproblems with the number of subproblems that are examined. Increasing the cardinality of the distinguished matching is beneficial up to a point. As the size of the distinguished matching is increased, the number of minimal matchings that is examined in each subproblem is decreased and we have more constraint on the position of the model. The subproblems are thus simpler to solve. By itself, this does not improve matters, since there are more subproblems to examine. However, since we use randomization to limit the number of subproblems that are examined, we can achieve a lower computational complexity by having more simple subproblems than fewer difficult ones. On the other hand, when we reach $g = k$, the method becomes equivalent to a generate-and-test technique and we lose both the benefits gained through the Hough-based analysis of the pose space and the property that the subproblems become simpler with larger distinguished matchings. We thus use distinguished matchings with cardinality $g = k - 1$.

Now, for practical reasons, we may not wish to use an algorithm that reports exactly those matchings that satisfy the error criterion, since such algorithms are often time consuming. In this case, we cannot guarantee that examining a distinguished matching that belongs to a solution that should be reported will result in detecting that solution. However, empirical evidence suggests that the examination of these subproblems yields superior results when an approximation algorithm is used [20], owing to failures that occur in the examination of full problem.

We can also use these techniques with acceptance criteria other than the bounded-error criterion. With other criteria, the proposition is no longer always true, but if an approximation algorithm is used to detect good matchings, examination of the subproblems often yields good results. For example, an application of these ideas to least-median-of-squares regression has yielded an approximation algorithm that is provably accurate with high probability, while previous approximation algorithms do not have this property [19].

Example For our circle detection example, $k = 3$, since three points are sufficient to define a circle in the noiseless case. The above analysis implies that, rather than examining individual image features, or all triples of features, we should examine trials (or subproblems) where only the triples that share some distinguished pair of features in common. Multiple trials are examined to guard against missing a circle.

4   Solving the Subproblems

Now, we must use some method to solve each of the subproblems that are examined. We can use any method that determines the number of matchings of a given cardinality can be brought approximately into alignment with the model at a particular position. The simplest method is one that uses a multi-dimensional histogramming step in order to locate large clusters in the pose space. This method can be implemented efficiently in both time and space [20]. However, errors in the data cause the clusters to spread in a manner that can be difficult to handle using this technique. For complex problems, it can become problematic to detect the clusters without also detecting a significant number of false positives [7]. Alternatively, recently developed pose equivalence analysis techniques developed by Breuel [3] and Cass [4] can be applied that allow localization error to be propagated accurately. Breuel's experiments indicate that his techniques can operate in linear expected time in the number of matchings, so we can, in general, perform this step efficiently.

In our method, only a small portion of the parameter space is examined in each subproblem. If it is assumed that there is no error in the data features in the distinguished matching, then each subproblem considers only a sub-manifold of the parameter space. In general, if there are p transformation parameters and each feature match yields b constraints on the transformation, then a subproblem where the distinguished matchings have cardinality g considers only a $(p - gb)$-dimensional manifold of the transformation space in the errorless case. This allows us to parameterize the sub-manifold (using $p - gb$ parameters) and perform analysis in this lower dimensional space. A particularly useful case is when the resulting manifold has only one dimension (i.e. it is a curve). In this case, the subproblem can be solved very simply by parameterizing the curve and finding positions on the curve that are consistent with many minimal matchings.

When localization error in the data features is considered, the subproblems must (at least implicitly) consider a larger space than the manifold described above. The subproblems are still much easier to solve. A technique that is useful in this case is to project the set of transformations that are consistent with a minimal matching up to the error criterion onto the manifold that results in the errorless case and then perform clustering only in the parameterization of this manifold as discussed above [22].

Example For circle detection, the circle positions that share a pair of points lie on a curve in the pose space. (The center of the circle is always on the perpendicular bisector of the two distinguished points.) We parameterize the positions using the signed distance d from the center of the circle to the midpoint between the distinguished points (positive if above, negative if below). This yields a unique descriptor for every circle containing the distinguished points. For each triple that is considered, we can project the pose space consistent with the triple onto the parameterization by considering which centers are possible given some error bounds on the point locations [22]. We determine if a circle is present in each trial by finely discretizing d and performing a simple Hough transform variation, where the counter for each bin is incremented for each triple that is consistent with the span represented by the counter. Peaks in the accumulator are accepted if they surpass some predetermined threshold.

5 Randomization and Complexity

A deterministic implementation of these ideas examines each possible distinguished matching with the appropriate cardinality. This requires $O(n^k)$ time, where n is the number of possible matches between a data feature and the model. When explicit matchings are considered, $n = md$, where m is the number of model features and d is the number of data features. When implicit matchings are considered, $n = d$. Such a deterministic implementation performs much redundant work. There are many distinguished matchings that are part of each of the large consistent matchings that we are seeking. We thus find each matching that meets the acceptance criterion many times (once for each distinguished matching that is contained in the maximal matching). We can take advantage of this redundancy through the use of a common randomization technique to limit the number of subproblems that we must consider while maintaining a low probability of failure.

Assume that some minimum number of the image features belong to the model. Denote this number by b. Since our usual acceptance criterion is based on counting the number of image features that belong to the model, we can allow the procedure to fail when too few image features belong to the model. Otherwise, the probability that some set of image features with cardinality $g = k - 1$ completely belongs to the model is approximately bounded by $\left(\frac{b}{d}\right)^{k-1}$. If we take t trials that select sets of $k - 1$ image features randomly, then the probability that none of them will completely belong to the model is:

$$p_t \approx \left(1 - \left(\frac{b}{d}\right)^{k-1}\right)^t. \tag{2}$$

Setting this probability below some arbitrarily small threshold ($p_t < \gamma$) yields:

$$t \approx \frac{\ln \gamma}{\ln(1 - (\frac{b}{d})^{k-1})} \approx \left(\frac{d}{b}\right)^{k-1} \ln \frac{1}{\gamma}. \tag{3}$$

Now, for explicit matches, we assume that some minimum fraction f_e of the model features appear in the image. In this case, the number of trials necessary is approximately $\left(\frac{d}{f_e m}\right)^{k-1}\ln\frac{1}{\gamma}$. For each trial, we must consider matching the set of image features against each possibly matching set of model features, so the total number of distinguished matchings that are considered is approximately $\left(\frac{d}{f_e}\right)^{k-1}(k-1)!\ln\frac{1}{\gamma}$. Each explicit distinguished matching requires $O(md)$ time to process, so the overall time required is $O(md^k)$.

For implicit matches, we may assume that each significant model in the image comprises some minimum fraction f_i of the image features. The number of trials necessary to achieve a probability of failure below γ is approximately $f_i^{1-k}\ln\frac{1}{\gamma}$, which is a constant independent of the number of model or image features. Since each trial can be solved in $O(d)$ time, the overall time required is $O(d)$.

Note that the complexity can be reduced further by performing subsampling among the matchings considered in each trial. Indeed, $O(1)$ complexity is possible with some assumptions about the number of features present and the rate of errors allowable [2]. We have not found this further complexity reduction to be necessary in our experiments. However, it may be useful when the number of image features is very large.

Example Our circle detection case uses implicit matchings. If we assume that each circle that we wish to detect comprises at least $f_i = 5\%$ of the image data and require that the probability of failure is below $\gamma = 0.1\%$, then the number of trials necessary is 2764. Each trial considers the remaining $d-2$ image features. Note that techniques considering all triples will surpass the number of triples considered here when $d > 53$.

6   Comparison with Other Techniques

This section gives a comparison of the RUDR approach with previous generate-and-test and Hough-based techniques.

Deterministic generate-and-test techniques require $O(n^{k+1})$ time to perform model extraction in general, since there are $O(n^k)$ minimal matchings and the testing stage can be implemented $O(n)$ time. This can often be reduced slightly through the use of efficient geometric searching techniques during the testing stage (e. g. [16]). RUDR yields a superior computational complexity requirement for this case. When randomization is applied to generate-and-test techniques, the computation complexity becomes $O(md^{k+1})$ (or slightly better using efficient geometric search) for explicit matches and $O(d)$ for implicit matches. RUDR yields a superior computational complexity for the case of explicit matches and, while the generate-and-test approach matches the complexity for the case of implicit matches, RUDR examines less subproblems by a constant factor (approximately $\frac{1}{f_i}$) and is thus faster in practice.

In addition, previous generate-and-test techniques are inherently less precise in the propagation of localization error. The basic generate-and-test algorithm introduces false positives unless care is taken to propagate the errors correctly [1, 8], since error in the data features leads to error in the hypothetical model pose and this error causes some of the models to be missed as a result of a poor fit. A more serious problem is that, while the generate-and-test techniques that propagate errors correctly ensure that each of the undistinguished features can be separately brought into alignment (along with the distinguished set) up to some error bounds by a single model position, this position may be different for each such feature match. It does not guarantee that *all* of the features can be brought into alignment up to the error bounds by a single position and thus causes false positives to be found.

Hough-based methods are capable of propagating localization error such that neither false positives nor false negatives occur (in the sense that only matchings meeting the acceptance criterion are reported) [3, 4]. However, previous Hough-based methods have had large time and space requirements. Deterministic Hough-based techniques that examine minimal matchings require $O(n^k)$ time and considerable memory [20].

Randomization has been previously applied to Hough transform techniques [2, 13, 14, 24]. However, in previous methods, randomization has been used in a different manner than it is used here. While RUDR examines all of the data in each of the subproblems, previous uses of randomization in Hough-based methods subsample the overall data examined, causing both false positives and false negatives to occur as a result. While false negatives can occur due to the use of randomization in the RUDR approach, the probability of such an occurrence can be set arbitrarily low.

Our method draws the ability to propagate localization error accurately from Hough-based methods and combines it with the ability to subdivide the problem into many smaller subproblems and thus reap the full benefit of randomization techniques. The result is a model extraction algorithm with superior computational complexity to previous methods that is also robust with respect to false positives and false negatives.

All of the techniques considered so far have been model-based methods. The primary drawback to such techniques is a combinatorial complexity that is polynomial in the number of features, but exponential in the complexity of the pose space (as measured by k). This can be subverted in some cases by assuming that some fraction of the data features arises from the model (this shifts the base of the exponent to the required fraction). An alternative that can be useful in reducing this problem is the use of grouping or perceptual organization methods that use data-driven techniques to determine features that are likely to belong to the same model (for example, [12, 17]). In cases where models can be identified by purely data-driven methods, such techniques are likely to be faster than the techniques described here. However, work has shown the even imperfect feature grouping methods can improve both the complexity and the rate of false positives in the RUDR method [21].

There are some situations where RUDR can not be applied effectively. If a single data feature is sufficient to constrain the position of the model, the RUDR problem decomposition will not be useful. In addition, the techniques we describe will be of less value is when there is a small number of features in the image. In this case, the randomization may not yield an improvement in the speed of the algorithm. However, the error propagation benefits will still apply.

7   Applications of RUDR

RUDR has been applied to several problems. We review the important aspects of these applications here and discuss additional areas where RUDR can be applied.

7.1   Extraction of Geometric Primitives

The Hough transform is a well known technique for geometric primitive extraction [11, 15]. The application of RUDR to this method improves the efficiency of the technique, allows the localization error to be propagated accurately, and reduces the amount of memory that is required [22].

Consider the case of detecting curves from feature points in two-dimensional image data. If we wish to detect curves with p parameters, then we use distinguished matchings consisting of $p-1$ feature points, since, in general, p points are required to solve for the curve parameters. Each distinguished matching maps to a one-dimensional manifold (a curve) in the parameter space, if the points are errorless and in general position. Methods have been developed to map minimal matchings with bounded errors into segments of this curve for the case of lines and circles [22]. $O(d)$ time and space is required for curve detection with these techniques, where d is the number of data points extracted from the image.

Figure 1 shows the results of using RUDR to detect circles in a binary image of an engineering drawing. The results are very good, with the exception of circles found with a low threshold that are not perceptually salient. However, these circles meet the acceptance criterion specified, so this is not a failure of the algorithm.

The image in Figure 1 contains 9299 edge pixels. In order to detect circles comprising 4% of the image, RUDR examines 4318 trials and considers 4.01×10^7 triples. Contrast this to the 8.04×10^{11} possible triples. A generate-and-test technique using the same type of randomization examines 1.08×10^5 trials (1.00×10^9 triples) to achieve the same the same probability of examining a trial where the distinguished features belong to some circle, but will still miss circles due to the error in the features.

7.2   Robust Regression

RUDR can be applied to the problem of finding the least-median-of-squares (LMS) regression line. The most commonly considered problem is to fit a line to points in the plane. We apply RUDR to this problem by considering a series of distinguished points in the data. A single distinguished point is examined in each trial (since only two are required to define a line). For each trial, we determine the line that is optimal with respect to the median residual, but with the constraint that the line must pass through the distinguished point.

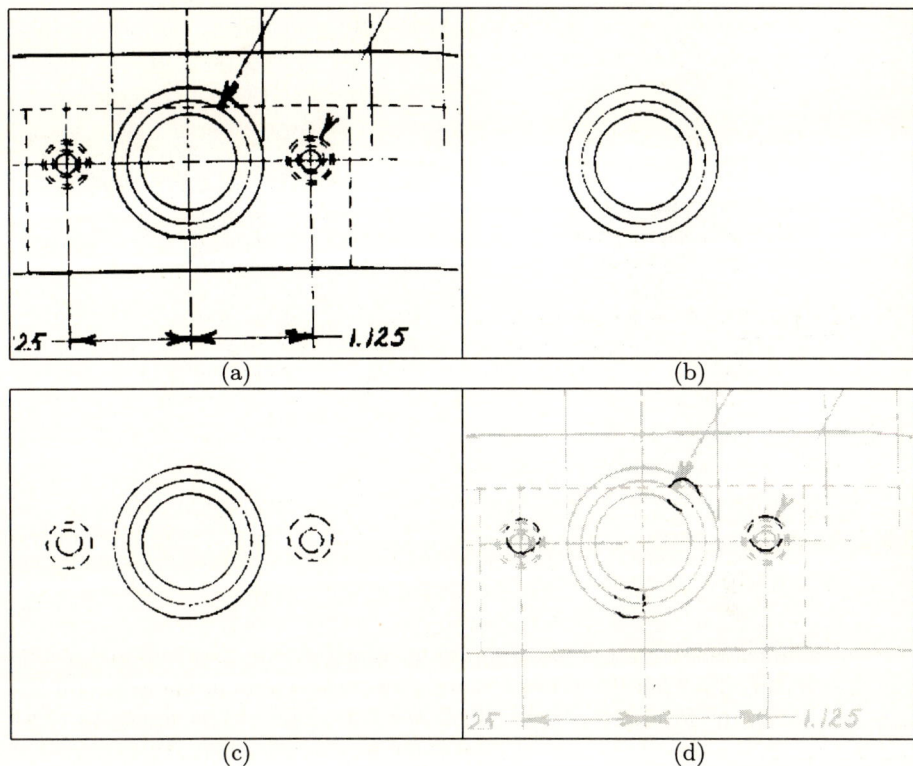

Fig. 1. Circle detection. (a) Engineering drawing. (b) Circles found comprising 4% of the image. (c) Perceptually salient circles found comprising 0.8% of the image. (d) Insalient circles found comprising 0.8% of the image.

It can be shown that the solution to this constrained problem has a median residual that is no more than the sum of the optimal median residual and the distance of the distinguished point from the optimal LMS regression line [19]. Now, at least half of the data points must lie no farther from the optimal regression line than the optimal median residual (by definition). Each trial thus has a probability of at least 0.5 of obtaining a solution with a residual no worse than twice the optimal median residual. The use of randomization implies that we need to perform only a constant number of trials to achieve a good solution with high probability (approximately $-\log_2 \delta$ trials are necessary to achieve an error rate of δ).

Each subproblem (corresponding to a distinguished point) can be solved using a specialized method based on parametric search techniques [19]. This allows each subproblem to be solved exactly in $O(n \log^2 n)$ time or in $O(n \log n)$ time for a fixed precision solution using numerical techniques. These techniques have also been extended to problems in higher dimensional spaces.

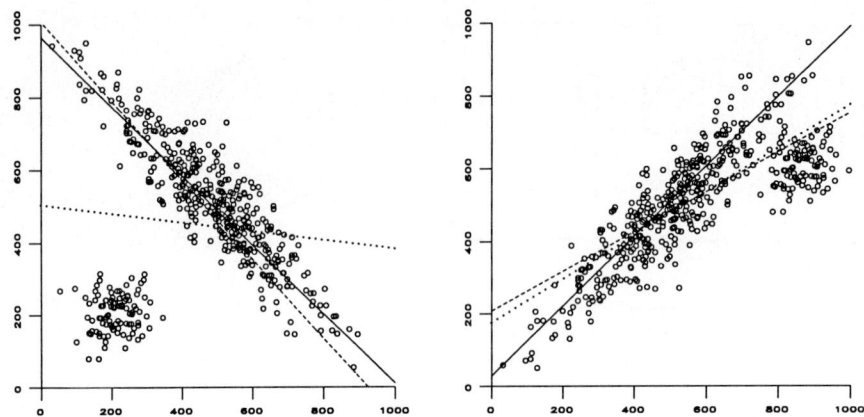

Fig. 2. Robust regression examples. The solid lines are the RUDR LMS estimate. The dashed lines are the PROGRESS LMS estimate. The dotted lines are the least-squares fit.

The complexity of our method is superior to the best known exact algorithms for this problem [5]. The PROGRESS algorithm [23] is a commonly used approximation algorithm for LMS regression that is based on the generate-and-test paradigm. It requires $O(n)$ time. However, unlike our algorithm, this algorithm yields no lower bounds (with high probability) on the quality of the solution detected.

Figure 2 shows two examples where RUDR, PROGRESS, and least-squares estimation were used to perform regression. In these examples, there were 400 inliers and 100 outliers, both from two-dimensional normal distributions. For these experiments, 10 trials of the RUDR algorithm were considered, and 50 trials of the PROGRESS algorithm. For both cases, RUDR produces the best fit to the inliers. The least-squares fit is known to be non-robust, so it is not surprising that it fairs poorly. The PROGRESS algorithm has difficulty, since, even in 50 trials, it does not generate a solution very close to the optimal solution.

7.3   Object Recognition

The application of RUDR to object recognition yields an algorithm with $O(md^k)$ computational complexity, where m is the number of model features, d is the number of data features, and k is the minimal number of feature matches necessary to constrain the position of the model up to a finite ambiguity in the case of errorless features in general position.

For recognizing three-dimensional objects using two-dimensional image data, $k = 3$. In each subproblem, we compute the pose for each minimal matching containing the distinguished matching using the method of Huttenlocher and Ullman [10]. We then use a multi-dimensional histogramming technique that

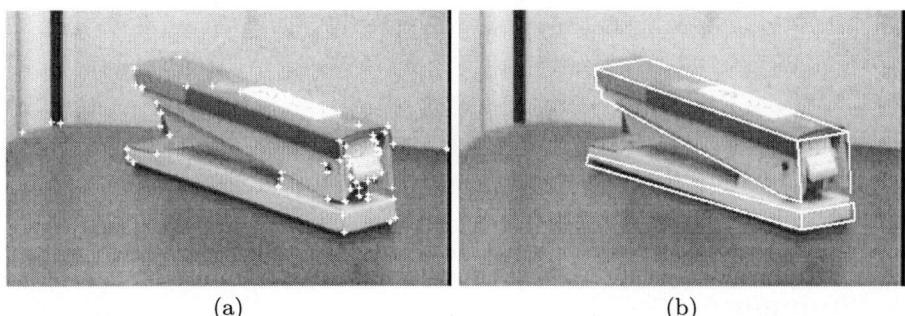

(a)   (b)

Fig. 3. Three-dimensional object recognition. (a) Corners detected in the image. (b) Best hypothesis found.

examines each axis of the pose space separately. After finding the clusters along some axis in the pose space, the clusters of sufficient size are then analyzed recursively in the remainder of the pose space [20]. The poses for all sets of points sharing a distinguished matching of cardinality $k - 1$ lie in a two-dimensional subspace for this case. Despite this, we perform the histogramming in the full six-dimensional space, since this requires little extra time and space with this histogramming method. Feature error has been treated in an ad hoc manner in this implementation through the examination of overlapping bins in the pose space. Complex images may require a more thorough analysis of the errors.

We can also apply these techniques to images in which imperfect grouping techniques have determined sets of points that are likely to derive from the same object [21]. This allows a reduction in both the computational complexity and the rate of false positives. Figure 3 shows an example where this approach has been applied to the recognition of a three-dimensional object.

7.4   Motion Segmentation

RUDR can be used to perform motion segmentation with any technique for determining structure and motion from corresponding data features in multiple images. In this problem, we are given sets of data features in multiple images. We assume that we know the feature correspondences between images (e.g. from a tracking mechanism), but not which sets of features belong to coherent objects.

Say that we have an algorithm to determine structure and motion using k feature correspondences in i images and that there are d features for which we know the correspondences between the images (see [9] for a review of such techniques). We examine distinguished matchings of $k - 1$ sets of feature correspondences between the images. Each subproblem is solved by determining the hypothetical structure and motion of each minimal matching (k sets of feature correspondences) containing the distinguished matching and then determining how many of the minimal matchings yield consistent structures for the distinguished matching and motions that are consistent with them belonging to a single object. This is repeated for enough distinguished matchings to find all of the rigidly moving objects consisting of some minimum fraction of all image features.

Our analysis for implicit matchings implies that we must examine approximately $\epsilon^{1-k} \ln \frac{1}{\gamma}$ trials to find objects whose fraction of the total number of data features is at least ϵ with a probability of failure for a particular object no larger than γ.

8   Summary

This paper has described a technique that we have named RUDR for solving model extraction and fitting problems such as recognition and regression. This approach is very general and can be applied to a wide variety problems where a model is fit to a set of data features and it is tolerant to noisy data features, occlusion, and outliers.

The RUDR method draws advantages from both the generate-and-test paradigm and from parameter space methods based on the Hough transform. The key ideas are: (1) Break down the problem into many small subproblems in which only the model positions consistent with some distinguished matching of features are examined. (2) Use randomization techniques to limit the number of subproblems that need to be examined to guarantee a low probability of failure. (3) Use clustering or parameter space analysis techniques to determine the matchings that satisfy the criteria.

The use of this technique yields two primary advantages over previous methods. First, RUDR is computationally efficient and has a low memory requirement. Second, we can use methods by which the localization error in the data features is propagated precisely, so that false positives and false negatives do not occur.

Acknowledgments

The research described in this paper was carried out in part by the Jet Propulsion Laboratory, California Institute of Technology, and was sponsored in part by the Air Force Research Laboratory at Tyndall Air Force Base, Panama City, Florida, through an agreement with the National Aeronautics and Space Administration. Portions of this research were carried out while the author was with Cornell University and the University of California at Berkeley.

References

1. T. D. Alter and D. W. Jacobs. Uncertainty propagation in model-based recognition. *International Journal of Computer Vision*, 27(2):127–159, 1998.
2. J. R. Bergen and H. Shvaytser. A probabilistic algorithm for computing Hough transforms. *Journal of Algorithms*, 12:639–656, 1991.

3. T. M. Breuel. Fast recognition using adaptive subdivisions of transformation space. In *Proceedings of the IEEE Conference on Computer Vision and Pattern Recognition*, pages 445–451, 1992.

4. T. A. Cass. Polynomial-time geometric matching for object recognition. *International Journal of Computer Vision*, 21(1/2):37–61, January 1997.

5. H. Edelsbrunner and D. L. Souvaine. Computing least median of squares regression lines and guided topological sweep. *Journal of the American Statistical Association*, 85(409):115–119, March 1990.

6. M. A. Fischler and R. C. Bolles. Random sample consensus: A paradigm for model fitting with applications to image analysis and automated cartography. *Communications of the ACM*, 24:381–396, June 1981.

7. W. E. L. Grimson and D. P. Huttenlocher. On the sensitivity of the Hough transform for object recognition. *IEEE Transactions on Pattern Analysis and Machine Intelligence*, 12(3):255–274, March 1990.

8. W. E. L. Grimson, D. P. Huttenlocher, and D. W. Jacobs. A study of affine matching with bounded sensor error. *International Journal of Computer Vision*, 13(1):7–32, 1994.

9. T. S. Huang and A. N. Netravali. Motion and structure from feature correspondences: A review. *Proceedings of the IEEE*, 82(2):252–268, February 1994.

10. D. P. Huttenlocher and S. Ullman. Recognizing solid objects by alignment with an image. *International Journal of Computer Vision*, 5(2):195–212, 1990.

11. J. Illingworth and J. Kittler. A survey of the Hough transform. *Computer Vision, Graphics, and Image Processing*, 44:87–116, 1988.

12. D. W. Jacobs. Robust and efficient detection of salient convex groups. *IEEE Transactions on Pattern Analysis and Machine Intelligence*, 18(1):23–37, 1996.

13. N. Kiryati, Y. Eldar, and A. M. Bruckstein. A probabilistic Hough transform. *Pattern Recognition*, 24(4):303–316, 1991.

14. V. F. Leavers. The dynamic generalized Hough transform: Its relationship to the probabilistic Hough transforms and an application to the concurrent detection of circles and ellipses. *CVGIP: Image Understanding*, 56(3):381–398, November 1992.

15. V. F. Leavers. Which Hough transform? *CVGIP: Image Understanding*, 58(2):250–264, September 1993.

16. R. J. Lipton and R. E. Tarjan. Applications of a planar separator theorem. *SIAM Journal on Computing*, 9(3):615–627, 1980.

17. D. G. Lowe. *Perceptual Organization and Visual Recognition*. Kluwer, 1985.

18. K. Murakami, H. Koshimizu, and K. Hasegawa. On the new Hough algorithms without two-dimensional array for parameter space to detect a set of straight lines. In *Proceedings of the IAPR International Conference on Pattern Recognition*, pages 831–833, 1986.

19. C. F. Olson. An approximation algorithm for least median of squares regression. *Information Processing Letters*, 63(5):237–241, September 1997.

20. C. F. Olson. Efficient pose clustering using a randomized algorithm. *International Journal of Computer Vision*, 23(2):131–147, June 1997.

21. C. F. Olson. Improving the generalized Hough transform through imperfect grouping. *Image and Vision Computing*, 16(9-10):627–634, July 1998.

22. C. F. Olson. Constrained Hough transforms for curve detection. *Computer Vision and Image Understanding*, 73(3):329–345, March 1999.

23. P. J. Rousseeuw and A. M. Leroy. *Robust Regression and Outlier Detection*. John Wiley and Sons, 1987.

24. L. Xu, E. Oja, and P. Kultanen. A new curve detection method: Randomized Hough transform (RHT). *Pattern Recognition Letters*, 11:331–338, May 1990.

Discussion

Tom Drummond: It seems to me that there's an asymmetry between the noise-fitting of the points you choose for your $(k-1)$-D model and the noise distribution in pose space. Can you comment on how you cope with this?

Clark Olson: The features of the distinguished matching (the $(k-1)$-D model) do play a more important role in each trial than the remaining features. The error in each feature is treated the same way in each minimal matching that is examined, but the features in the distinguished matching are seen in *every* minimal matching for a particular trial. The use of a distinguished matching constrains the pose to a sub-manifold of the pose space. Within this sub-manifold, the poses of the minimal matchings will be clustered in a smaller area, and the center will be shifted from the center of the set of all correct minimal matchings. However, with a precise method to process each trial, proposition 1 implies that the use of distinguished matchings has no effect on the overall result of the algorithm so long as we include at least one distinguished matching belonging to each model that should be reported.

Andrew Fitzgibbon: Just an observation. As well as reducing the dimensionality of the loci in the Hough space, in the circle case you also make them simpler — they're cones with raw Hough, but just lines with your case. That makes them easier to cluster, *etc.*

Clark Olson: Yes, that's correct.

Characterizing the Performance of Multiple-Image Point-Correspondence Algorithms Using Self-Consistency

Yvan G. Leclerc[1], Q.-Tuan Luong[1], and P. Fua[2,] [*]

[1] Artificial Intelligence Center, SRI International, Menlo Park, CA
leclerc,luong@ai.sri.com
[2] LIG, EPFL, Lausanne, Switzerland, fua@lig.di.epfl.ch fua@lig.di.epfl.ch

Abstract. A new approach to characterizing the performance of point-correspondence algorithms is presented. Instead of relying on any "ground truth', it uses the self-consistency of the outputs of an algorithm independently applied to different sets of views of a static scene. It allows one to evaluate algorithms for a given class of scenes, as well as to estimate the accuracy of every element of the output of the algorithm for a given set of views. Experiments to demonstrate the usefulness of the methodology are presented.

1   Introduction and Motivation

One way of characterizing the performance of a stereo algorith is to compare its matches against "ground truth." If sufficient quantities of accurate ground truth were available, estimating the distribution of errors over many image pairs of many scenes (within a class of scenes) would be relatively straightforward. This distribution could then be used to predict the accuracy of matches in new images. Unfortunately, acquiring ground truth for any scene is an expensive and problematic proposition at best.

Instead, we propose to estimate a related distribution, which can be derived automatically from the matches of many image pairs of many scenes, assuming only that the projection matrices for the image pairs (and their covariances) have been correctly estimated, up to an unknown projective transformation.

The related *self-consistency* distribution, as we call it, is the distribution of the normalized difference between triangulations of matches obtained when one image is fixed and the projection matrix of the second image is changed, averaged over all matches, many images, and many scenes.

---

[*] This work was sponsored in part by the Defense Advanced Research Projects Agency under contract F33615-97-C-1023 monitored by Wright Laboratory. The views and conclusions contained in this document are those of the authors and should not be interpreted as representing the official policies, either expressed or implied, of the Defense Advanced Research Projects Agency, the United States Government, or SRI International.

B. Triggs, A. Zisserman, R. Szeliski (Eds.): Vision Algorithms'99, LNCS 1883, pp. 37–52, 2000.

Intuitively, a perfect stereo algorithm is one for which the triangulations are invariant to changes in the second image, that is, one for which the mean and variance of the self-consistency distribution are zero. The extent to which the distribution deviates from this is a measure of the accuracy of the algorithm. Of course, a stereo algorithm that is perfectly self-consistent in this sense can still have systematic biases. We will discuss such biases in a more complete version of this paper.

Although the self-consistency distribution is an important global characterization of a stereo algorithm, it would be better if we could refine the predicted accuracy of individual matches given just a pair of images. We propose to do this by estimating the self-consistency distribution as a function of some type of "score" (such as sum of squared difference) that can be computed for each match using only the image pair. Conditionalizing the self-consistency distribution like this not only allows us to better predict the accuracy of individual matches, it also allows us to compare different scoring functions to see which one best correlates with the self-consistency of matches.

The self-consistency distribution is a very simple idea that has powerful consequences. It can be used to compare algorithms, compare scoring functions, evaluate the performance of an algorithm across different classes of scenes, tune algorithm parameters, reliably detect changes in a scene, and so forth. All of this can be done for little manual cost beyond the precise estimation of the camera parameters and perhaps manual inspection of the output of the algorithm on a few images to identify systematic biases.

In the remainder of this paper we will describe the algorithm we use for estimating the self-consistency distribution of general n-point correspondence algorithms given prior collections of images. This includes the development of a method to normalize the triangulation (or reprojection) differences due to the inherent errors arising from the nominal accuracy of the matches, the projection matrices, and their covariances. Monte Carlo experiments are presented to justify the normalization method. We will then show how the self-consistency distribution can be used to to compare stereo algorithms and scoring functions.

2   Previous Work in Estimating Uncertainty

Existing work on estimating uncertainty without ground truth falls into two categories: analytical approaches and statistical approaches.

The analytical approaches are based on the idea of error propagation [17]. When the output is obtained by optimizing a certain criterion (like a correlation measure), the shape of the optimization curve [5, 12, 8] or surface [1] provides estimates of the covariance through the second-order derivatives. These approaches make it possible to compare the uncertainty of different outputs given by the same algorithm. However, it is problematic to use them to compare different algorithms.

Statistical approaches make it possible to compute the covariance given only one data sample and a black-box version of an algorithm, by repeated runs of the algorithm, and application of the law of large numbers [4].

Both of the above approaches characterize the performance of a given output only in terms of its expected variation with respect to additive white noise. In [15], the accuracy was characterized as a function of image resolution. The bootstrap methodology [3] goes further, since it makes it possible to characterize the accuracy of a given output with respect to IID noise of unknown distribution. Even if such an approach could be applied to the multiple image correspondence problem, it would characterize the performance with respect to IID sensor noise. Although this is useful for some applications, for other applications it is necessary to estimate the expected accuracy and reliability of the algorithms as viewpoint, scene domain, or other imaging conditions are varied. This is the problem we seek to address with the self-consistency methodology.

3   The Self-Consistency Distribution

To understand the self-consistency distribution, consider the following thought experiment. Consider a match (m_A, m_B) derived from two images, A and B. Now, fix image A and m_A, vary the projection matrix of the second image to produce image B', and apply the stereo algorithm to images A and B' producing the match $(m_A, m_{B'})$. Because the coordinates of the matches are identical in image A, the two matches should triangulate to the same point in space, within the expected error induced by the nominal precision of the matches, the projection matrices, and their covariances.

The distribution of the difference between the triangulations of the two matches, after suitable normalization, averaged over all matches derived from many image pairs of many scenes, is what we call the self-consistency distribution for that algorithm. We will discuss in detail the normalization later in the paper.

When the triangulations are equal to within the expected error, the matches are said to be consistent. When an an algorithm produces matches that are always consistent in this sense, we say that the algorithm is self-consistent.

Note that the self-consistency distribution is directly applicable to change detection by using the $x\%$ confidence interval for a match. The $x\%$ confidence interval is the largest normalized distance that two matches (with the same coordinate in one image) can have $x\%$ of the time. Thus, two matches derived from images of a scene taken at different times can then be compared against this confidence interval to see if the scene has changed over time at that point (see [9]).

3.1   A Methodology for Estimating the Self-Consistency Distribution

Ideally, the self-consistency distribution should be computed using all possible variations of viewpoint and camera parameters (within some class of variations) over all possible scenes (within some class of scenes). However, we can compute an estimate of the distribution using some small number of images of a scene, and average this distribution over many scenes.

In the thought experiment above, we first found a match, fixed the coordinate of the match in one image, varied the camera parameter of the second image to get a second match, and then computed the normalized distance between their triangulations.

Here we start with some fixed collection of images assumed to have been taken at exactly the same time (or, equivalently, a collection of images of a static scene taken over time). Each image has a unique index and associated projection matrix and (optionally) projection covariances. We then apply a stereo algorithm independently to all pairs of images in this collection.[1]. The image indices, match coordinates, and score, are reported in *match* files for each image pair.

We now search the match files for pairs of matches that have the same coordinate in one image. For example, if a match is derived from images 1 and 2, another match is derived from images 1 and 3, and these two matches have the same coordinate in image 1, then these two matches correspond to one instance of the thought experiment. Such a pair of matches, which we call a *common-point match set*, should be self-consistent because they should correspond to the same point in the world. This extends the principle of the trinocular stereo constraint [16, 2] to arbitrary camera configurations and multiple images.

Given two matches in a common-point match set, we can now compute the distance between their triangulations, after normalizing for the camera configurations. The histogram of these normalized differences, computed over all common-point matches, is our estimate of the self-consistency distribution.

Another distribution that one could compute using the same data files would involve using all the matches in a common-point match set, rather than just pairs of matches. For example, one might use the deviation of the triangulations from the mean of all triangulations within a set. This is problematic for several reasons.

First, there are often outliers within a set, making the mean triangulation less than useful. One might mitigate this by using a robust estimation of the mean. But this depends on various (more or less) arbitrary parameters of the robust estimator that could change the overall distribution.

Second, and perhaps more importantly, we see no way to extend the normalization used to eliminate the dependence on camera configurations, described in Sect. 4, to the case of multiple matches.

Third, we see no way of using the above variants of the self-consistency distribution for change detection.

---

[1] Note that the "stereo" algorithm can find matches in $n > 2$ images. In this case, the algorithm would be applied to all subsets of size n. We use $n = 2$ to simplify the presentation here.

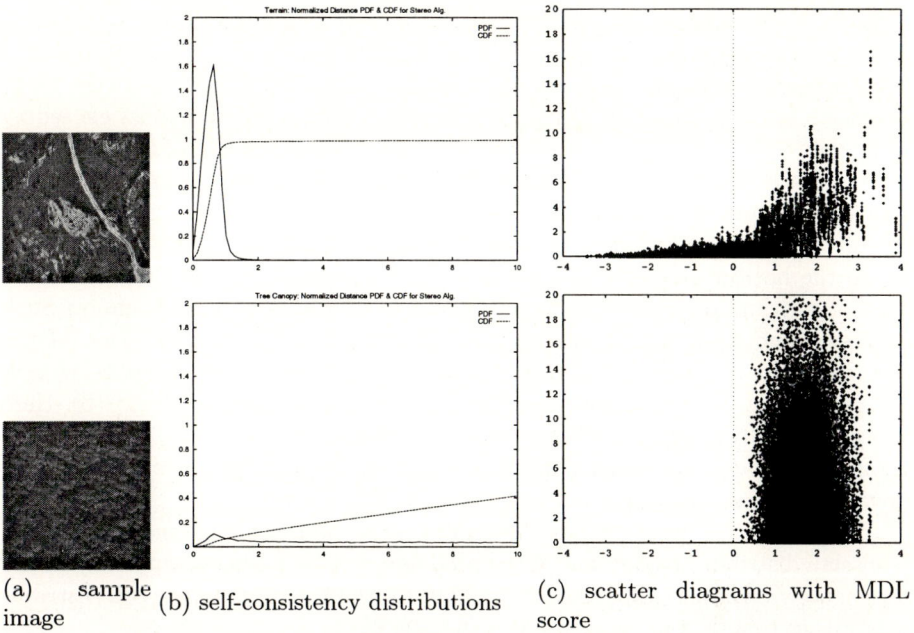

(a) sample image (b) self-consistency distributions (c) scatter diagrams with MDL score

Fig. 1. Results on two different types of images: terrain (top) vs. tree canopy (bottom).

3.2 An Example of the Self-Consistency Distribution

To illustrate the self-consistency distribution, we first apply the above methodology to the output of a simple stereo algorithm [6]. The algorithm first rectifies the input pair of images and then searches for 7×7 windows along scan lines that maximize a normalized cross-correlation metric. Sub-pixel accuracy is achieved by fitting a quadratic to the metric evaluated at the pixel and its two adjacent neighbours. The algorithm first computes the match by comparing the left image against the right and then comparing the right image against the left. Matches that are not consistent between the two searches are eliminated.

The stereo algorithm was applied to all pairs of five aerial images of bare terrain, one of which is illustrated in the top row of Fig. 1(a). These images are actually small windows from much larger images (about 9000 pixels on a side) for which precise ground control and bundle adjustment were applied to get accurate camera parameters.

Because the scene consists of bare, relatively smooth, terrain with little vegetation, we would expect the stereo algorithm described above to perform well. This expectation is confirmed anecdotally by visually inspecting the matches.

However, we can get a quantitative estimate for the accuracy of the algorithm for this scene by computing the self-consistency distribution of the output of the algorithm applied to the ten images pairs in this collection. Figure 1(b) shows two versions of the distribution. The solid curve is the probability density (the probability that the normalized distance equals x). It is useful for seeing the mode and the general shape of the distribution. The dashed curve is the cumulative probability distribution (the probability that the normalized distance is less than x). It is useful for seeing the median of the distribution (the point where the curve reaches 0.5) or the fraction of match pairs with normalized distances exceeding some value.

In this example, the self-consistency distribution shows that the mode is about 0.5, about 95% of the normalized distances are below 1, and that about 2% of the match pairs have normalized distances above 10.

In the bottom row of Fig. 1 we see the self-consistency distribution for the same algorithm applied to all pairs of five aerial images of a tree canopy. Such scenes are notoriously difficult for stereo algorithms. Visual inspection of the output of the stereo algorithm confirms that most matches are quite wrong. This can be quantified using the self-consistency distribution in Fig. 1(b). Here we see that, although the mode of the distribution is still about 0.5, only 10% of the matches have a normalized distance less than 1, and only 42% of the matches have a normalized distance less than 10.

Note that the distributions illustrated above are not well modelled using Gaussian distributions because of the predominance of outliers (especially in the tree canopy example). This is why we have chosen to compute the full distribution rather than use its variance as a summary.

3.3   Conditionalization

As mentioned in the introduction, the global self-consistency distribution, while useful, is only a weak estimate of the accuracy of the algorithm. This is clear from the above examples, in which the unconditional self-consistency distribution varied considerably from one scene to the next.

However, we can compute the self-consistency distribution for matches having a given "score" (such as the MDL-base score described in detail below). This is illustrated in Fig. 1(c) using a scatter diagram. The scatter diagram shows a point for every pair of matches, the x coordinate of the point being the larger of the scores of the two matches, and the y coordinate being the normalized distance between the matches.

There are several points to note about the scatter diagrams. First, the terrain example (top row) shows that most points with scores below 0 have normalized distances less than about 1. Second, most of the points in the tree canopy example (bottom row) are not self-consistent. Third, none of the points in the tree canopy example have scores below 0. Thus, it would seem that this score is able to segregate self-consistent matches from non-self-consistent matches, even when the scenes are radically different (see Sect. 5.3).

4   Projection Normalization

To apply the self-consistency method to a set of images, all we need is the set of projection matrices in a common projective coordinate system. This can be obtained from point correspondences using projective bundle adjustment [13, 14] and does not require camera calibration. The Euclidean distance is not invariant to the choice of projective coordinates, but this dependance can often be reduced by using the normalization described below. Another way to do so, which actually cancels the dependance on the choice of projective coordinates, is to compute the difference between the reprojections instead of the triangulations, as described in more detail in [11]. This, however, does not cancel the dependance on the relative geometry of the cameras.

4.1   The Mahalanobis Distance

Assuming that the contribution of each individual match to the statistics is the same ignores many imaging factors like the geometric configuration of the cameras and their resolution, or the distance of the 3D point from the cameras. There is a simple way to take into account all of these factors, applying a normalization which make the statistics invariant to these imaging factors. In addition, this mechanism makes it possible to take into account the uncertainty in camera parameters, by including them into the observation parameters.

We assume that the observation error (due to image noise and digitalization effects) is Gaussian. This makes it possible to compute the covariance of the reconstruction given the covariance of the observations. Let us consider two reconstructed estimates of a 3-D point, M_1 and M_2 to be compared, and their computed covariance matrices Λ_1 and Λ_2. We weight the squared Euclidean distance between M_1 and M_2 by the sum of their covariances. This yields the squared *Mahalanobis distance*: $(\mathbf{M}_1 - \mathbf{M}_2)^T (\Lambda_1 + \Lambda_2)^{-1} (\mathbf{M}_1 - \mathbf{M}_2)$.

4.2   Determining the Reconstruction and Reprojection Covariances

If the measurements are modeled by the random vector $\mathbf{x}$, of mean $\mathbf{x}_0$ and of covariance $\Lambda_{\mathbf{x}}$, then the vector $\mathbf{y} = f(\mathbf{x})$ is a random vector of mean is $f(\mathbf{x}_0)$ and, up to the first order, covariance $\mathbf{J}_f(\mathbf{x}_0)\Lambda_{\mathbf{x}}\mathbf{J}_f(\mathbf{x}_0)^T$, where $\mathbf{J}_f(\mathbf{x}_0)$ is the Jacobian matrix of f, at the point $\mathbf{x}_0$.

In order to determine the 3-D distribution error in reconstruction, the vector $\mathbf{x}$ is defined by concatenating the 2-D coordinates of each point of the match, ie $[x_1, y_1, x_2, y_2, \ldots x_n, y_n]$ and the result of the function is the 3-D coordinates X, Y, Z of the point M reconstructed from the match, in the least-squares sense. The key is that M is expressed by a closed-form formula of the form $\mathbf{M} = (\mathbf{L}^T\mathbf{L})^{-1}\mathbf{L}^T\mathbf{b}$, where $\mathbf{L}$ and $\mathbf{b}$ are a matrix and vector which depend on the projection matrices and coordinates of the points in the match. This makes it possible to obtain the derivatives of M with respect to the $2n$ measurements $w_i, i = 1 \ldots n, w = x, y$. We also assume that the errors at each pixel are independent, uniform, and isotropic. The covariance matrix $\Lambda_{\mathbf{x}}$ is then diagonal, therefore each element of Λ_M can be computed as a sum of independent terms for each image.

The above calculations are exact when the mapping between the vector of coordinates of m_i and M (resp. m'_j and M') is linear, since it is only in that case that the distribution of M and M' is Gaussian. The reconstruction operation is exactly linear only when the projection matrices are affine. However, the linear approximation is expected to remain reasonable under normal viewing conditions, and to break down only when the projection matrices are in configurations with strong perspective.

5   Experiments

5.1   Synthetic Data

In order to gain insight into the nature of the normalized self-consistency distributions, we investigate the case when the noise in point localization is Gaussian.

We first derive the analytical model for the self-consistency distribution in that case. We then show, using monte-carlo experiments that, provided that the geometrical normalization described in Sec.4 is used, the experimental self-consistency distributions fit this model quite well when perspective effects are not strong. A consequence of this result is that under the hypothesis that the error localization of the features in the images is Gaussian, the difference self-consistency distribution could be used to recover exactly the accuracy distribution.

Modeling the Gaussian Self-Consistency Distributions The squared Mahalanobis distance in 3D follows a chi-square distribution with three degrees of freedom:

$$\chi_3^2 = \frac{1}{\sqrt{2\pi}} \sqrt{x} e^{-x/2} \ .$$

In our model, the Mahalanobis distance is computed between M, M', reconstructions in 3D, which are obtained from matches m_i, m'_j of which coordinates are assumed to be Gaussian, zero-mean and with standard deviation σ. If M, M' are obtained from the coordinates m_i, m'_j with a linear transformation A, A', then the covariances are $\sigma^2 A A^T$, $\sigma^2 A' A'^T$. The Mahalanobis distance follows the distribution:

$$d_3 = x^2/\sigma^3 \sqrt{2/\pi} e^{-x^2/2\sigma^2} \ . \tag{1}$$

Using the Mahalanobis distance, the self-consistency distributions should be *statistically* independent of the 3D points and projection matrices. Of course, if we were just using the Euclidean distance, there would be no reason to expect such an independence.

Comparison of the Normalized and Unnormalized Distributions. To explore the domain of validity of the first-order approximation to the covariance, we have considered three methods to generate random projection matrices:

1. General projection matrices are picked randomly.
2. Projection matrices are obtained by perturbing a fixed, realistic matrix (which is close to affine). Entries of this matrix are each varied randomly within 500% of the initial value.

3. Affine projection matrices are picked randomly.

Each experiment in a set consisted of picking random 3D points, random projection matrices according to the configuration previously described, projecting them, adding random Gaussian noise to the matches, and computing the self-consistency distributions by labelling the matches so that they are perfect.

To illustrate the invariance of the distribution that we can obtain using the normalization, we performed experiments where we computed both the normalized version and the unnormalized version of the self-consistency. As can be seen in Fig. 2, using the normalization reduced dramatically the spread of the self-consistency curves found within each experiment in a set. In particular, in the two last configurations, the resulting spread was very small, which indicates that the geometrical normalization was successful at achieving invariance with respect to 3D points and projection matrices.

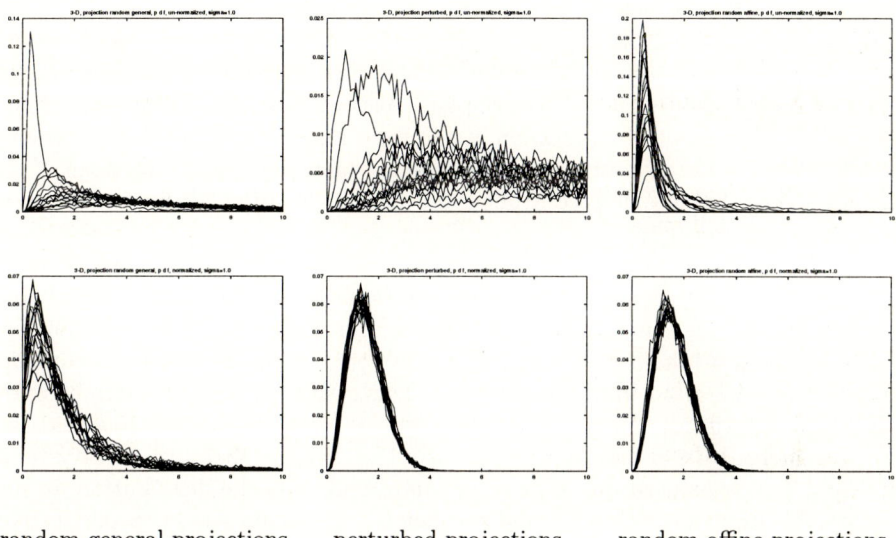

random general projections   perturbed projections   random affine projections

Fig. 2. Un-normalized (top) vs normalized (bottom) self-consistency distributions.

Comparison of the Experimental and Theoretical Distributions. Using the Mahalanobis distance, we then averaged the density curves within each set of experiments, and tried to fit the model described in Eq. 1 to the resulting curves, for six different values of the standard deviation, $\sigma = 0.5, 1, 1.5, 2, 2.5, 3$. As illustrated in Fig. 3, the model describes the average self-consistency curves very well when the projection matrices are affine (as expected from the theory), but also when they are obtained by perturbation of a fixed matrix. When the projection matrices are picked totally at random, the model does not describe the curves very well, but the different self-consistency curves corresponding to each noise level are still distinguishable.

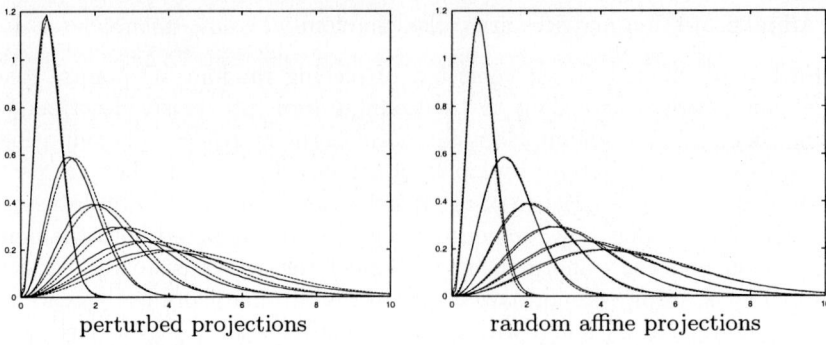

perturbed projections   random affine projections

Fig. 3. Averaged theoretical (solid) and experimental (dashed) curves.

5.2   Comparing Two Algorithms

The experiments described here and in the following section are based on the application of stereo algorithms to seventeen scenes, each comprising five images, for a total of 85 images and 170 image pairs. At the highest resolution, each image is a window of about 900 pixels on a side from images of about 9000 pixels on a side. Some of the experiments were done on gaussian-reduced versions of the images. These images were controlled and bundle-adjusted to provide accurate camera parameters.

A single self-consistency distribution for each algorithm was created by merging the scatter data for that algorithm across all seventeen scenes. In previous papers, [11, 10], we compared two algorithms, but using data from only four images. By merging the scatter data as we do here, we are now able to compare algorithms using data from many scenes. This results in a much more comprehensive comparison.

The merged distributions are shown in Fig. 4 as probability density functions for the two algorithms. The solid curve represents the distribution for our deformable mesh algorithm [7], and the dashed curve represents the distribution for the stereo algorithm described above.

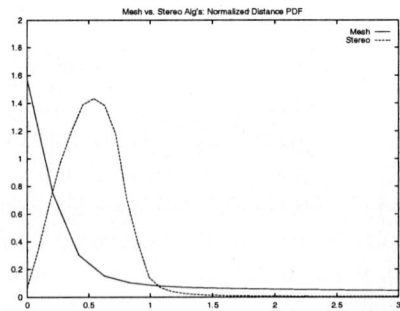

Fig. 4. Comparing two stereo algorithms (Mesh vs Stereo) using the self-consistency distributions.

Comparing these two graphs shows some interesting differences between the two algorithms. The deformable mesh algorithm clearly has more outliers (matches with normalized distances above 1), but has a much greater proportion of matches with distances below 0.25. This is not unexpected since the strength of the deformable meshes is its ability to do very precise matching between images. However, the algorithm can get stuck in local minima. Self-consistency now allows us to quantify how often this happens.

But this comparison also illustrates that one must be very careful when comparing algorithms or assessing the accuracy of a given algorithm. The distributions we get are very much dependent on the scenes being used (as would also be the case if we were comparing the algorithms against ground truth—the "gold standard" for assessing the accuracy of a stereo algorithm). In general, the distributions will be most useful if they are derived from a well-defined class of scenes. It might also be necessary to restrict the imaging conditions (such as resolution or lighting) as well, depending on the algorithm. Only then can the distribution be used to predict the accuracy of the algorithm when applied to images of similar scenes.

5.3   Comparing Three Scoring Functions

To eliminate the dependency on scene content, we propose to use a score associated with each match. We saw scatter diagrams in Fig. 1(c) that illustrated how a scoring function might be used to segregate matches according to their expected self-consistency.

In this section we will compare three scoring functions, one based on Minimum Description Length Theory (the MDL score, Appendix A), the traditional sum–of–squared–differences (SSD) score, and the SSD score normalized by the localization covariance (SSD/GRAD score) [5]. All scores were computed using the same matches computed by our deformable mesh algorithm applied to all image pairs of the seventeen scenes mentioned above. The scatter diagrams for all of the areas were then merged together to produce the scatter diagrams show in Fig. 5.

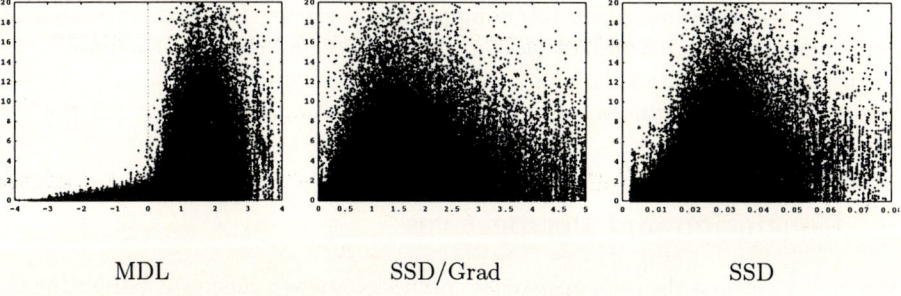

MDL   SSD/Grad   SSD

Fig. 5. Scatter diagrams for three different scores.

The MDL score has the very nice property that the confidence interval (as defined earlier) rises monotonically with the score, at least until there is a paucity of data, when then score is greater than 2. It also has a broad range of scores (those below zero) for which the normalized distances are below 1, with fewer outliers than the other scores.

The SSD/GRAD score also increases monotonically (with perhaps a shallow dip for small values of the score), but only over a small range.

The traditional SSD score, on the other hand, is distinctly not monotonic. It is fairly non-self-consistent for small scores, then becomes more self-consistent, and then rises again.

Another way that we can compare the scores is with a measure we call the *efficiency* of the scoring function. This is the number of match pairs for which the confidence interval is below some value d divided by the total number of match pairs having normalized distances less than d. Intuitively, the efficiency represents how well the scoring function can predict that match pairs will have normalized differences below some value given just the score. An ideal score would have an efficiency of 1 for all values of d.

The 99% efficiency of all three scores is illustrated in Fig. 6. Note that, overall, the MDL score is somewhat more efficient than the SSD/GRAD score, both of which are significantly more efficient than the SSD score.

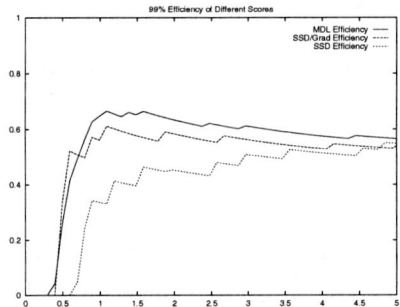

Fig. 6. Comparing three scoring schemes (MDL vs. SSD/GRAD vs. SSD) using the efficiency measure.

Our previous publication [11] compared two scoring function by comparing their cumulative distributions in two different scenes. Here we compare scores using the merged data from many scenes using confidence-interval and efficiency graphs, again providing a more comprehensive comparison than was possible before.

6   Conclusion and Perspectives

We have proposed the self-consistency methodology as a means of estimating the accuracy and reliability of point-correspondence algorithms algorithms, comparing different algorithms, and comparing different scoring functions. We have presented a detailed prescription for applying this methodology to multiple-image point-correspondence algorithms, without any need for ground truth or camera calibration, and have demonstrated it's utility in two experiments.

The self-consistency distribution is a very simple idea that has powerful consequences. It can be used to compare algorithms, compare scoring functions, evaluate the performance of an algorithm across different classes of scenes, tune algorithm parameters, reliably detect changes in a scene, and so forth. All of this can be done for little manual cost beyond the precise estimation of the camera parameters and perhaps manual inspection of the output of the algorithm on a few images to identify systematic biases.

Readers of this paper are invited to visit the self-consistency web site to download an executable version of the code, documentation, and examples at http://www.ai.sri.com/sct/ described in this paper.

Finally, we believe that the core idea of our methodology, which examines the *self-consistency* of an algorithm across independent experimental trials, can be used to assess the accuracy and reliability of algorithms dealing with a range of computer vision problems. This could lead to algorithms that can learn to be self-consistent over a wide range of scenes over a wide range of scenes without the need for external training data or "ground truth."

A   The MDL Score

Given N images, let M be the number of pixels in the correlation window and let g_i^j be the image gray level of the ith pixel observed in image j. For image j, the number of bits required to describe these gray levels as IID white noise can be approximated by:

$$C_j = M(\log \sigma_j + c) \ , \qquad (2)$$

where σ_j is the measured variance of the $g_i^j{}_{1 \leq i \leq N}$ and $c = (1/2)\log(2\pi e)$.

Alternatively, these gray levels can be expressed in terms of the mean gray level $\overline{g_i}$ across images and the deviations $g_i^j - \overline{g_i}$ from this average in each individual image. The cost of describing the means, can be approximated by

$$\overline{C} = M(\log \overline{\sigma} + c) \ , \qquad (3)$$

where $\overline{\sigma}$ is the measured variance of the mean gray levels. Similarly the coding length of describing deviations from the mean is given by

$$C_j^d = M(\log \sigma_j^d + c) \qquad (4)$$

where σ_j^d is the measured variance of those deviations in image j. Note that, because we describe the mean across the images, we need only describe $N - 1$ of the C_j^d. The description of the Nth one is implicit.

The MDL score is the difference between these two coding lengths, normalized by the number of samples, that is

$$Loss = \overline{C} + \sum_{1 \leq j \leq N-1} C_j^d - \sum_{1 \leq j \leq N} C_j \ . \qquad (5)$$

When there is a good match between images, the $g_i^j{}_{1 \leq j \leq N}$ have a small variance. Consequently the C_j^d should be small, $\overline{C}$ should be approximately equal to any of the C_j and *Loss* should be negative. However, C_j can only be strongly negative if these costs are large enough, that is, if there is enough texture for a reliable match. See [9] for more details.

References

1. P. Anandan. A computational framework and an algorithm for the measurement of visual motion. *IJCV*, 2:283–310, 1989.
2. N. Ayache and F. Lustman. Fast and reliable passive trinocular stereovision. In *ICCV*, pages 422–427, 1987.
3. K. Cho, P. Meer, and J. Cabrera. Performance assessment through bootstrap. *PAMI*, 19(11):1185–1198, November 1997.
4. G. Csurka, C. Zeller, Z. Zhang, and O. Faugeras. Characterizing the uncertainty of the fundamental matrix. *CVGIP-IU*, 1996.
5. W. Forstner. On the geometric precision of digital correlation. In *International archives of photogrammetry and remote sensing*, volume 24-III, pages 176–189, Helsinki, 1982.
6. P. Fua. Combining Stereo and Monocular Information to Compute Dense Depth Maps that Preserve Depth Discontinuities. In *Int. Joint Conf. on AI*, pages 1292–1298, Sydney, Australia, August 1991.
7. P. Fua and Y. G. Leclerc. Object-Centered Surface Reconstruction: Combining Multi-Image Stereo and Shading. *IJCV*, 16:35–56, 1995.
8. T. Kanade and M. Okutomi. A stereo matching algorithm with an adaptive window: Theory and experiment. *PAMI*, 16(9):920–932, 1994.
9. Y. Leclerc, Q.-T. Luong, and P. Fua. A framework for detecting changes in terrain. In *Proc. Image Understanding Workshop*, pages 621–630, Monterey, CA, 1998.
10. Y. Leclerc, Q.-T. Luong, and P. Fua. Self-consistency: a novel approach to characterizing the accuracy and reliability of point correspondence algorithms. In *Proc. Image Understanding Workshop*, pages 793–807, Monterey, CA, 1998.
11. Y. Leclerc, Q.-T. Luong, and P. Fua. Self-consistency: a novel approach to characterizing the accuracy and reliability of point correspondence algorithms. In *Proceedings of the One-day Workshop on Performance Characterisation and Benchmarking of Vision Systems*, Las Palmas de Gran Canaria, Canary Islands, Spain, 1999.
12. L. Matthies. Stereo vision for planetary rovers: Stochastic modeling to near real-time implementation. *IJCV*, 8(1):71–91, July 1992.
13. R. Mohr, F. Veillon, and L. Quan. Relative 3d reconstruction using multiple uncalibrated images. In *CVPR*, pages 543–548, NYC, 1993.
14. R. Szeliski and S.B. Kang. Recovering 3d shape and motion from image streams using nonlinear least squares. *JVCIR*, pages 10–28, 1994.
15. P.H.S. Torr and A. Zissermann. Performance characterization of fundamental matrix estimation under image degradation. *mva*, 9:321–333, 1997.
16. M. Yachida, Y. Kitamura, and M. Kimachi. Trinocular vision: New approach for correspondence problem. In *ICPR*, pages 1041–1044, 1986.
17. S. Yi, R.M. Haralick, and L.G. Shapiro. Error propagation in machine vision. *MVA*, 7:93–114, 1994.

Discussion

Andrew Fitzgibbon: The metric you propose sounds a little like a quantification of Jacobs work on the generic view assumption, where solutions to shape from shading algorithms are consistent if, when you move the camera a little bit, they don't change much. Are you aware of that, and have you looked at it?

Yvan Leclerc: I'm well aware of the work. What they do is ask as a thought experiment, if I was to change my viewpoint a little bit, how would the output of the algorithm change. That's the generic viewpoint constraint. Here what I do is look at how the real algorithm behaves under real changes in viewpoint provided by real new imagery. Also, as I understand the generic viewpoint thing, you look at local perturbations in viewpoint or viewing conditions, see how that affects the output, and pick the output that is most generic — that gives you the smallest change. The philosophy is a little different from what we are trying to do here. There's a relationship between them, but I'm not sure that I can go further than that right now.

Joe Mundy: The stereo case and the 3D model you reconstruct is pretty well defined and constrained. What if there was a large space of possible solutions, all of which could explain the data? How would you approach that?

Yvan Leclerc: Well, I'm not sure exactly what you mean by that, but the methodology as I've described it should still let you pick out the sets of hypotheses that are consistent. I certainly agree that for any single image or image pair there may be many hypotheses that can explain them. But as you get more and more observations, more and more views, the set of hypotheses that are consistent with the data should shrink until you get down to a core set that are consistent with all the images. That would be my expectation.

Rick Szeliski: Perhaps this is a follow-on from Joe's question. In stereo matching when you have textureless regions there are a lot of equivalent hypotheses, each as good as the others. So depth predictions from independent groups of measurements are unlikely to agree with each other. Is there a mechanism where the algorithms could say, this is my estimate but I have very low confidence in it, or perhaps even have a confidence interval.

Yvan Leclerc: Exactly, that's what the score is for. For each pair of matches, the algorithm supplies a score. Here I used the MDL score, for which scores near zero usually correspond to textureless regions. So you can tell which matches are in textureless regions, and which have large outliers. If you want, you can just keep the matches with good scores. So you have a fairly general algorithm that is able to separate good matches from bad ones. What is nice here is that you can guess "Oh yes, the MDL score ought to do that" and then actually verify that it does with the methodology.

Bill Triggs: Given your experience with testing stereo on these difficult scenes with dirt ground and tree cover and things like that, which correlation or pixel correspondence method works the best?

Yvan Leclerc: So far I've only compared the two examples that I gave, a simple stereo algorithm and the deformable patches. As I showed, the deformable patches tend to give a much more accurate solution in some circumstances where the score is negative. When the surface is somewhat smooth and it isn't like a tree canopy, they are much better than traditional stereo. What I'd like to do is to have people try their stereo algorithms on sets of images and use self-consistency to characterize the results. Then we'd have a nice quantitative measure to compare different algorithms under different conditions, for various classes of images. That's why I'm providing the software, so that people can download it and try it for themselves. (Provisional site: `http://www.ai.sri.com/sct/`).

A Sampling Algorithm for Tracking Multiple Objects

Hai Tao, Harpreet S. Sawhney, and Rakesh Kumar

Sarnoff Corporation
201 Washington Rd., Princeton NJ 08543
{htao,hsawhney,rkumar}@sarnoff.com

Abstract. The recently proposed CONDENSATION algorithm and its variants enable the estimation of arbitrary multi-modal posterior distributions that potentially represent multiple tracked objects. However, the specific state representation adopted in the earlier work does not explicitly supports counting, addition, deletion and occlusion of objects. Furthermore, the representation may increasingly bias the posterior density estimates towards objects with dominant likelihood as the estimation progresses over many frames. In this paper, a novel formulation and an associated CONDENSATION-like sampling algorithm that explicitly support counting, addition and deletion of objects are proposed. We represent all objects in an image as an object configuration. The *a posteriori* distribution of all possible configurations are explored and maintained using sampling techniques. The dynamics of configurations allow addition and deletion of objects and handle occlusion. An efficient hierarchical algorithm is also proposed to approximate the sampling process in high dimensional space. Promising comparative results on both synthetic and real data are demonstrated.

1 Introduction

Tracking multiple objects in videos is a key problem in many applications such as video surveillance, human computer interaction, and video conferencing. It is also a challenging research topic in computer vision. Some difficult issues involved are cluttered background, unknown number of objects, and complicated interaction between objects. Many tracking algorithms can be interpreted in a probabilistic framework called hidden Markov model (HMM) [1], explicitly or implicitly.

As shown in Fig.1, the states of an object $x_t \in X$ at different time instances $t = 1,2,\ldots n$ form a Markov chain. State x_t contains object deformation parameters such as positions and scale factors. At each time instance t, conditioned on x_t, observation z_t is independent of other previous object states or observations. This model is summarized as

$$P(x_1, x_2, \ldots x_n; z_1, z_2, \ldots z_n) =$$

$$P(x_1)P(z_1 \mid x_1)\prod_{i=2}^{n}[P(x_t \mid x_{t-1})P(z_t \mid x_t)] \tag{1}$$

B. Triggs, A. Zisserman, R. Szeliski (Eds.): Vision Algorithms'99, LNCS 1883, pp. 53-68, 2000.

The tracking problem can be posed as the computation of the *a posteriori* distribution $P(x_t | \mathbf{Z}_t)$ for given observations $\mathbf{Z}_t = \{z_1, z_2, ..., z_t\}$. When a single object is tracked, the maximum *a posteriori* (MAP) solution is desired. If both the object dynamics $P(x_t | x_{t-1})$ and the observation likelihood $P(z_t | x_t)$ are Gaussian distributions, $P(x_t | \mathbf{Z}_t)$ is also a Gaussian distribution. The MAP solution is $E(x_t | \mathbf{Z}_t)$.

In order to compute $P(x_t | \mathbf{Z}_t)$, a forward algorithm [1] is applied. It computes $P(x_t | \mathbf{Z}_t)$ based on $P(x_{t-1} | \mathbf{Z}_{t-1})$ inductively and is formulated as

$$P(x_t | \mathbf{Z}_t) \propto P(z_t | x_t) P(x_t | \mathbf{Z}_{t-1})$$
$$= P(z_t | x_t) \int P(x_t | x_{t-1}) P(x_{t-1} | \mathbf{Z}_{t-1}) dx_{t-1}$$

(2)

Using this formula, the well-known Kalman filter that computes $E(x_t | \mathbf{Z}_t)$ for a Gaussian process can be derived [2]. When multiple objects present, if the number of objects is fixed and the posterior of each object is Gaussian, similar solution in analytic form is obtained. If the number of objects may change over time, data association method such as multiple-hypothesis tracking (MHT) [3] has to be used. The complexity of MHT algorithm is exponential with respect to the time and pruning techniques are necessary for real applications [4].

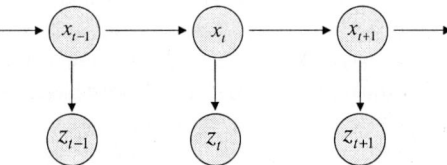

Fig. 1. The hidden Markov model.

When the analytic form of either $P(x_t | x_{t-1})$ or $P(z_t | x_t)$ is not available, sampling techniques such as the CONDENSATION algorithm [5] are preferred. The idea is to represent $P(x_t | \mathbf{Z}_t)$ with samples and to propagate the posterior distribution over time by computing the likelihood function $P(z_t | x_t)$ and simulating the dynamics $P(x_t | x_{t-1})$. In [6], a variance reduction method called importance sampling algorithm is used to reduce the number of samples and to handle data associate problems. A more recent paper [8] deal with fixed number of object using a sampling scheme.

The original CONDENSATION algorithm and its variants use a single object state as the basic state representation. Presence of multiple objects is *implicitly* contained in the multiple peaks of the posterior distribution. When the CONDENSATION algorithm is applied to such a representation, it is very likely that a peak corresponding to the dominant likelihood value will increasingly dominate over all other peaks when the estimation progresses over time. In other words, a *dominant peak* is established if some objects obtain larger likelihood values more frequently. If the posterior is propagated with fixed number of samples, eventually, all samples will be around the dominant peak. Dominant peak may occur in many model based tracking algorithms. For example, a head-shoulder contour deformable model may fit one person better than another in most frames of a video sequence. This phenomenon is further illustrated here with a synthetic example.

Fig. 6 shows two frames of the synthetic sequence. More details of the sequence can be found in Section 6. In Fig. 9, the tracking results using the original CONDENSATION algorithm are illustrated. Since the likelihood function is biased to certain objects, the differences between these objects and the other objects in the posterior distribution increase exponentially with respect to the number of frames observed. In frame 15 (Fig. 9b), three peaks can be identified. In frame 25 (Fig. 9c), one object looses most of its samples because of its constantly relatively smaller likelihood. . In frame 65 (Fig. 9d), another object vanishes due to its smaller likelihood. This phenomenon can also be observed in Fig. 9e and Fig. 9f.

Besides the dominant peak problem, the above example also illustrates that the events such as addition, deletion, and occlusion can not be naturally handled. In Fig. 9d, a new object appears but no samples are allocated to it. In Fig. 9h, an object disappears, but the samples are not redistributed to the other object.

Importance sampling [6] is a data-driven mechanism that may alleviate some of the above problems. However, in order to maintain and update the count and state of multiple objects explicitly, a new representation is required.

It should be noticed that the limitation described here is not of the CONDENSATION process but of the state representation that is used by the tracker. In this paper we present a new representation and apply a CONDENSATION-like sampling algorithm for the estimation of the joint distribution of multiple objects under the presence of clutter, varying object counts and appearance/disappearance of objects.

2   Tracking Multiple Objects

Our goal is to (i) track multiple instances of an object template, (ii) maintain an expected value of the number of objects at any time instant, and (iii) be resilient to clutter, occlusion/deocclusion and appearance/disappearance of objects. In order to be able to represent multiple objects, we enhance the basic representation by representing all objects in the image as an *object configuration* (the term configuration is used in the rest of this paper for conciseness). A configuration is represented by a set of object deformation parameters $s_t = \{x_{t,1}, x_{t,2}, \ldots, x_{t,m}\} \in X^m$, where m is the number of objects. If K is the maximum possible number of objects in an image, the configuration space is $\bigcup_{m=0}^{K} X^m$. Given the enhanced representation, the goal is to compute the *a posteriori* probability of the configuration parameters $P(s_t | \mathbf{Z}_t)$ instead of the *a posteriori* probability of object parameters $P(x_t | \mathbf{Z}_t)$. The posterior for a configuration is given by

$$P(s_t | \mathbf{Z}_t) \propto P(z_t | s_t) P(s_t | \mathbf{Z}_{t-1})$$
$$= P(z_t | s_t) \int P(s_t | s_{t-1}) P(s_{t-1} | \mathbf{Z}_{t-1}) ds_{t-1} \tag{3}$$

To estimate this distribution, the configuration dynamics $P(s_t | s_{t-1})$ and the configuration likelihood $P(z_t | s_t)$ need to be modeled. Then a CONDENSATION-like sampling algorithm can be applied. Distribution $P(s_t | s_{t-1})$ describes the temporal behavior of a configuration in terms of how each of the individual objects changes, how a new object is introduced, how an existing object is deleted, and how to handle occlusion. The likelihood $P(z_t | s_t)$ measures how well the configuration fits the current observation.

2.1   Dynamics of a Configuration - $P(s_t | s_{t-1})$

$P(s_t | s_{t-1})$ is decomposed into object-level and configuration-level dynamics. Suppose s_{t-1} contains m objects, or $s_{t-1} = \{x_{t-1,1}, x_{t-1,2}, \ldots, x_{t-1,m}\}$. Object-level dynamics $P(\bar{x}_{t,i} | x_{t-1,i})$ is first applied to predict the behavior of each object. The resulted configuration is $\bar{s}_t = \{\bar{x}_{t-1,1}, \bar{x}_{t-1,2}, \ldots, \bar{x}_{t-1,m}\}$. Then, the configuration-level dynamics $P(s_t | \bar{s}_t)$ will perform the object deletion and addition.

2.1.1 Object-Level Dynamics $P(\bar{x}_{t,i} | x_{t-1,i})$
A commonly used model is:

$$\bar{x}_{t,i} = \mathbf{A} x_{t-1,i} + w \tag{4}$$

where $w: N(0, \Sigma)$ is a Gaussian noise and $\mathbf{A}$ is the state transition matrix. According to this model, $P(\bar{x}_{t,i} | x_{t-1,i})$ has Gaussian distribution $N(\mathbf{A} x_{t-1,i}, \Sigma)$.

2.1.2 Configuration-Level Dynamics - $P(s_t | \bar{s}_t)$
The configuration-level dynamics should allow deletion and addition of objects in $\bar{s}_t$. Domain-dependent information should be brought in to model these events. For instance, knowledge about deletion and addition can be described as spatial birth and death processes [9].

Deletion probability $\beta(x, y)$ is defined as a function of the image coordinates (x, y). For example, $\beta(x, y)$ may have higher values around the scene boundaries because objects usually disappear at those locations. For an object at (x, y), its chance of survival in the current frame is $1 - \beta(x, y)$. When occlusion happen in an area with low deletion probability, the occluded object is unlikely to be deleted.

By the same token, addition probability is defined as $\alpha(x, y)$. Since new objects always cause image changes, motion blobs are used to construct $\alpha(x, y)$. For video with static background, motion blobs are detected by image differencing method. $\alpha(x, y)$ is non-zero only in the regions of the motion blobs. For the case of a pan/tilt or moving camera, the blob detection may be accomplished using background alignment techniques and change detection algorithms [10].

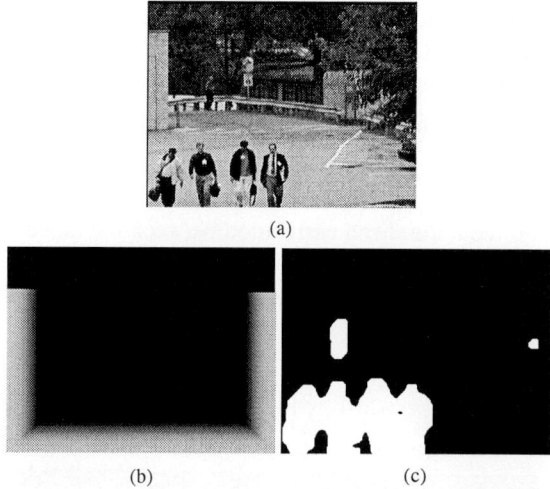

Fig. 2. Configuration-level dynamics: (a) a video frame with static background (b) deletion probability $\beta(x, y)$ (c) motion blobs.

In Fig. 2a, a frame from a test video clip is shown. Fig. 2b shows the deletion probability $\beta(x, y)$. The highest value in the image is around the border. The motion corresponding blobs are shown in Fig. 2c. The addition probability $\alpha(x, y)$ is 0.01 in these blobs.

2.2   Likelihood of a Configuration $\pi_t = P(z_t \mid s_t)$

$P(z_t \mid s_t)$ is a very complicated distribution. One possible type of approximation is observation decomposition [7]. The image is spatially decomposed into small regions and the likelihood is formulated as the product of local likelihood. Since the configuration is not decomposed, it will lead to algorithms manipulating in a high-dimensional configuration space. In this paper, we propose an approximation using configuration decomposition. The likelihood is replaced by an energy function and decomposed into object-level and configuration-level terms. The energy function is designed to gives the more desired configurations higher values. Intuitively, three factors should be considered. The first factor is, in average, how well individual objects in a configuration fit the observation. This is noted as the object-level likelihood. For example, a contour matcher may be applied to calculate the likelihood of each object in a configuration, and their geometric average is computed as the object-level likelihood for that configuration. The average is taken to make it independent of the number of objects. The second factor is how much of the observation has been explained by the configuration. This is noted as the configuration coverage. The third factor is the compactness. It is always desirable to explain the observation using minimum number of objects. All these three factors are indispensable. In Fig. 3, the likelihood of some configurations is illustrated.

2.2.1 Object-Level Likelihood

For a given object, the likelihood $L(z_t, x_{t,i})$ measures how well the image data supports the presence of this object. The likelihood can be defined as any reasonable match measures, e.g. the normalized correlation between the object and the image, or the Chamfer matching score for a contour representation of an object. For a configuration with m objects, the object-level likelihood is computed as the geometric average of $L(z_t, x_{t,i})$. More precisely,

$$\lambda = \left(\prod_{i=1}^{m} L(z_t, x_{t,i}) \right)^{\frac{1}{m}}. \tag{5}$$

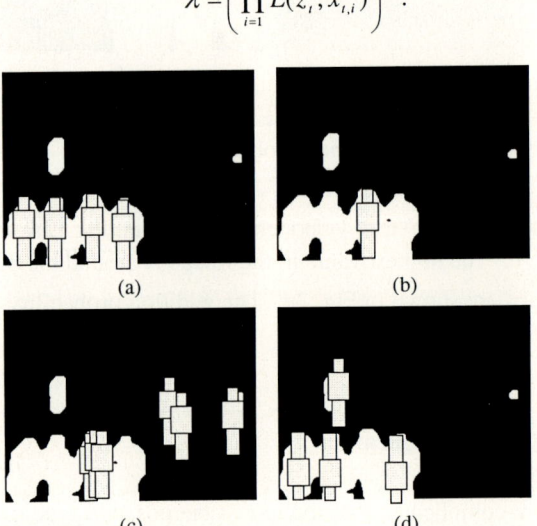

(a)   (b)

(c)   (d)

Fig. 3. Likelihood of a configuration (a) highest (b) low: interested region is not covered (c) low: too many object are used to explain the data (d) low: likelihood of individual objects are low.

2.2.2 Configuration Coverage

In general, it is difficult to compute configuration coverage. However, for moving object tracking, motion blobs are good cues. If we assume all the motion blobs in a frame are caused by the objects to be tracked, the configuration coverage can be computed as the percentage of the motion blob areas being covered by objects. It is formulated as

$$\gamma = \frac{|A \cap (\bigcup_{i=1}^{m} B_i) + b|}{|A| + b} \tag{6}$$

where A is the union of motion blobs. B_i is the area covered by object i in a configuration. b is a small positive constant used to avoid zero division. If $|A| = 0$, $\gamma = 1$.

2.2.3 Configuration Compactness

The compactness is defined as the ratio between data that has been explained and the amount of cost. In terms of motion blobs, it can be computed as

$$\xi = \frac{|A \cap (\bigcup_{i=1}^{m} B_i) + c|}{(|\bigcup_{i=1}^{m} B_i| + a)} \tag{7}$$

where a is a small positive constant like b. If too many objects are used to explain a small area, ξ will be small. c is a positive number so that when $|A| = 0$, the configurations with smaller number of objects have higher score.

Finally, the overall likelihood of configuration s_t is approximated by

$$\pi_t = \lambda \cdot (\gamma \xi)^\beta \tag{8}$$

where β, a positive constant that controls the relative importance of the last two terms. It should be mentioned that, depending on the application, different cues may be used to compute the configuration coverage and compactness. For instance, color blobs with skin colors can be applied for face tracking.

3   A Sampling Algorithm

Given the above formulation of configuration dynamics and likelihood, we now present a CONDENSATION-like algorithm to estimate the *a posteriori* configuration densities. Subsequently, we show how the standard CONDENSATION algorithm can be approximated using a fast hierarchical algorithm.

Suppose $\pi_t^j = P(z_t | s_t^j)$, $j = 1, 2, \ldots R_s$ is the likelihood of the j th configuration s_t^j, where R_s is the total number of configuration samples. R_s is a constant in the algorithm.

For j from 1 to R_s, perform the following three steps.

Step 1. At time instance $t > 1$, randomly select the jth configuration sample $s_{t-1}^{\prime j}$ from all R_s samples s_{t-1}^i, $i = 1, 2, \ldots R_s$ in the previous frame according to their corresponding likelihood π_{t-1}^i, $i = 1, 2, \ldots R_s$.

Step 2. Apply the dynamics to predict the current configuration s_t^j from $s_{t-1}^{\prime j}$ using $P(s_t^j | s_{t-1}^{\prime j})$

Step 3: Compute the new likelihood $\pi_t^j = P(z_t | s_t^j)$

To initialize this process, s_1^j is sampled randomly in the configuration space $\bigcup_{m=0}^{K} X^m$. For example, if the maximum possible number of objects in a configuration is $K = 9$ and 1000 configuration samples are initiated ($R_s = 1000$), then for the 10 categories of configurations that contain 0 to 9 objects, 100 samples are assigned to each category. For a configuration sample with m objects, the parameters of each object are randomly chosen in the parameter space. The configuration likelihood is then computed. If the likelihood of a configuration is high, according to Step 1, in the next iteration, this configuration is likely to be selected. The expected number of objects in a frame can also be computed as $\sum_{j=1}^{R_s} |s_t^j| \pi_t^j$, where $|s_t^j|$ is the number of objects in s_t^j.

The above algorithm samples the *a posteriori* distribution of the configurations in a high dimensional space $\bigcup_{m=0}^{K} X^m$. If there are m objects in the scene, the posterior has to be sampled in the space X^m. To maintain the same sample density, the number of samples needs to be exponential with respect to m, which makes the algorithm impractical. Importance sampling techniques [6] alleviate the problem to some extent by reducing the volume of the parameter space X, however, the dimensionality of the sampling space is not reduces. A possible solution to this problem is to sample from configurations with high likelihood. More specifically, in the first step, $s_{t-1}'^j$ is only drawn from s_{t-1}^i with relatively large π_{t-1}^i. This strategy makes the sampling process focus on the posterior distribution around the MAP solution, which is desirable because the goal of the tracking process is to actually obtain the MAP configuration. A problem of this method is that the tracker is easily trapped by local maximum solutions.

4   An Efficient Hierarchical Sampling Algorithm

In this section, we describe an efficient hierarchical algorithm that decouples the sampling process into two stages: local configuration sampling stage and global configuration sampling stage. The local sampling stage track the motion of individual objects, while the configuration sampling process handles object addition, deletion. Strictly speaking, it does not propagate the configuration posterior distribution. It reinforces the likelihood portion to some extent so that the tracker is less likely to be trapped by local optimal solutions. To explain the algorithm more clearly, examples will be provided for each step of the algorithm.

The first step is selecting new configuration samples based on the previous samples and their corresponding likelihood (see Section 3). For example, in Fig. 4a, four configurations are selected. They contain two, three, four, and four objects respectively. There are total of thirteen objects in these four configurations. Different shapes are used in the figure to distinguish objects in different configurations.

The second step is local sampling of the object-level *a posteriori* distribution conditioned on given configurations. More specifically, the image is first partitioned into non-overlapping regions and configurations are broken into *sub-configurations* according to the partition. For example, in Fig. 4b, the configuration marked by "△" is decomposed into three sub-configurations in region 2, 3, and 4. The sub-configuration in region 4 contains two objects. In region 4, there are three other sub-configurations containing 1, 1, and 2 objects respectively. After the partitioning, in each region, object-level dynamics is applied to every object and likelihood is computed for each sub-configuration (Fig. 4c). Note that the configuration-level dynamics such as object deletion and object addition is not performed in this step.

Next, in each image region, all sub-configurations with the same number of objects are grouped together. According to their likelihood, they are sampled to produce the same number of new sub-configurations. These samples are then assigned back to the global configurations randomly (because there is no identity left after sampling). For example, in region 4, based on the two resulted two-object sub-configurations in Fig. 4c and their corresponding likelihood, sampling process is applied to obtain two "new" sub-configurations (Fig. 4d). Actually, these two sub-configurations are identical because the sub-configuration with higher likelihood has been selected twice. The resulted configurations are assigned arbitrarily back to the global configuration.

In the third step, configuration-level dynamics computation (see Section 2.1.2) is applied and likelihood is computed for each configuration (see Section 2.2). Fig. 4e shows the result after configuration-level dynamics being applied. A new "△" object is added and a "○" object is deleted.

The hierarchical tracking algorithm is summarized as follows:

Step 1. Select configurations: At time $t > 1$, select R_s configuration samples. The jth configuration sample $s_{t-1}^{'j}$ is select randomly from all R_s samples s_{t-1}^i, $i = 1,2,...R_s$ in the previous frame according to their likelihood π_{t-1}^i, $i = 1,2,...R_s$.

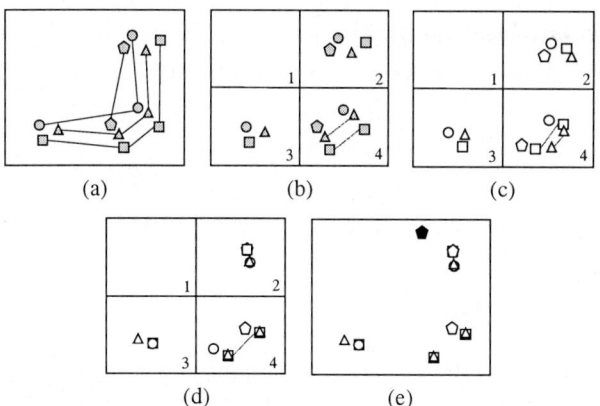

(a)   (b)   (c)

(d)   (e)

Fig. 4. The hierarchical sampling algorithm for tracking multiple objects. (a) select configurations (b) partition configurations into sub-configurations (c) local object-level sampling (d) recover configurations from new sub-configurations (e) global configuration-level dynamics and likelihood computation.

Step 2. Local object-level sampling: Partition the 2D image into regions and break configurations into sub-configurations. In each region, apply object-level dynamics. For sub-configurations containing the same number of objects, do sampling according to their local configuration-level likelihood. Assign them randomly back to the global configurations.

Step 3: Global configuration-level sampling: The configuration-level samples are recovered. The likelihood $\pi_t^j = P(z_t \mid s_t^j)$ is computed. Go to the next frame.

5   Implementation

The proposed hierarchical algorithm has been implemented on a Pentium II 400 MHz PC. It runs at 1 frame/s when 300 configuration samples are used on 320x240 video frames.

5.1   Video Preprocessing

Detecting motion blobs is an important step for computing configuration-level likelihood. Several methods such as background subtraction, two-image or three-image differencing algorithms are available. Three-image differencing method is used in our implementation [10].

5.2   Object Representation

As shown in Fig. 5, a contour-plus-region representation is designed. To track multiple people, the head-shoulder contour in Fig. 5a is compared with the edge images in order to obtain object likelihood $L(z_t, x_{t,i})$. The contour template is divided into several line segments. $L(z_t, x_{t,i})$ is computed as the weighted average of the matching score for individual template contour segments. The regions of the template are represented by rectangles and are used to compute γ and ξ using Equation (6) and (7). The parameter β, which controls the relative importance of the object-level likelihood and the configuration-level likelihood, equals 1.5.

5.3   The Hierarchical Algorithm

A fixed number of configuration samples are used in the algorithm. These samples are evenly distributed to configurations with different number of objects at the initialization stage. For the first frame, several iterations of the algorithm are executed to obtain the initial prior (with different dynamics). The size of each local image region in our implementation is 10×10 pixels.

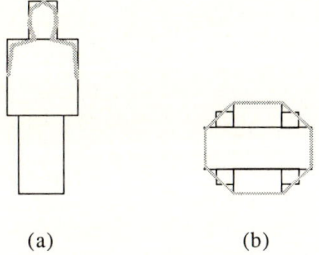

(a)   (b)

Fig. 5. (a) A simple contour-region representation of people, (b) a coarse 2D contour-region representation of spherical objects.

6   Experimental Results

6.1   The Synthetic Sequence

Both a synthetic image sequence and natural video data are tested. The synthetic sequence contains four moving objects of similar shapes (Fig. 6). They approximate a circle with six, seven, eight, and thirty laterals. These objects undergo only translations in this test sequence. A translation invariant object-level likelihood function is computed based on a generic contour model and a contour matching algorithm. The likelihood values of these four objects remain consistent over time and have small differences due to their different shapes. This setup resembles many model based trackers in the way that a generic model (built either by learning or designing) is used to track an entire class of objects. These objects enter and leave the scene at the image boundaries. There is one instance of object occlusion in this sequence.

The background image is formed by Gaussian noise. To simulate some random irrelevant moving objects, white noise is added to the background at two locations that gives rise to some spurious motions blobs. Finally, noise is added to the appearance of the moving objects. Quantitative analysis is conducted based on the tracking results and the actual number and positions of objects in each frame.

For the synthetic sequence, we compared the results of the CONDENSATION algorithm and the hierarchical algorithm. In the CONDENSATION algorithm, 600 object samples are used. In the latter one, 300 configuration samples are initialized. These 300 samples are evenly distributed in terms of number of objects in a configuration and object parameter values.

In Fig. 9, the tracking results of the original CONDENSATION algorithm with a single object state representation are shown. Importance sampling is used in the first frame to obtain a better prior. Object samples are represented by white dots. In Fig. 9i, marginal sample distributions on vertical image axis for every five frames are shown. As explained in Section 1, dominant peaks and inappropriate handling of object addition and deletion are observed.

In Fig. 10, the corresponding results of the hierarchical tracking algorithm with the multiple object representation are demonstrated. Four distinct trajectories are observed in Fig. 10i. Events such as addition, deletion, and occlusion can be easily distinguished.

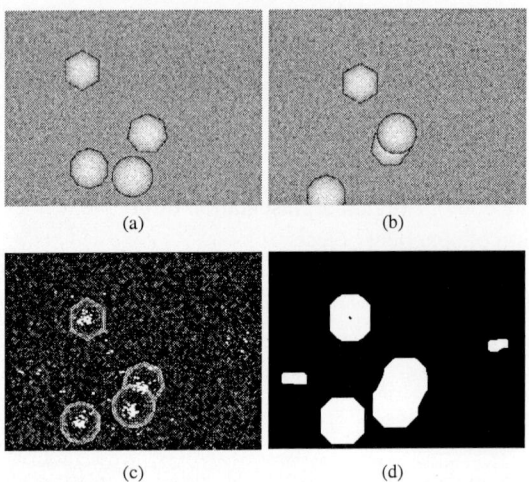

Fig. 6. (a)(b) Two frames in the synthetic sequence (c) the edge map and the tracking result (white dots are object samples) (d) motion blobs.

As mentioned in Section 3, by applying the new representation, expected number of objects in each frame is computed from configuration samples. In Fig. 7, the expected number of objects in each frame using the hierarchical algorithm is shown. In the same figure, the actual number of objects is also drawn. (The first 20 iterations are used the algorithm initialization and are not significant in the comparison). The number of objects in most of frames is correctly estimated, even during the occlusion period.

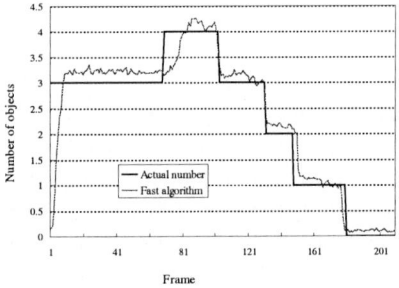

Fig. 7. Object counts in the synthetic sequence.

6.2   Tracking Multiple People

Both algorithms have been tested on real video sequences. For tracking multiple people, a simple contour-plus-region template is designed (Fig. 5a). Only translation is modeled in the transformation. A frame is shown in Fig. 2a. Its corresponding motion blobs are shown in Fig. 2c. For this particular sequence, deletion is only allowed in the gray regions drawn in Fig. 2b. Fig. 8 demonstrates the tracking results in some frames. Four persons are simultaneously tracked. The number of persons in the scene is automatically estimated in the hierarchical algorithm.

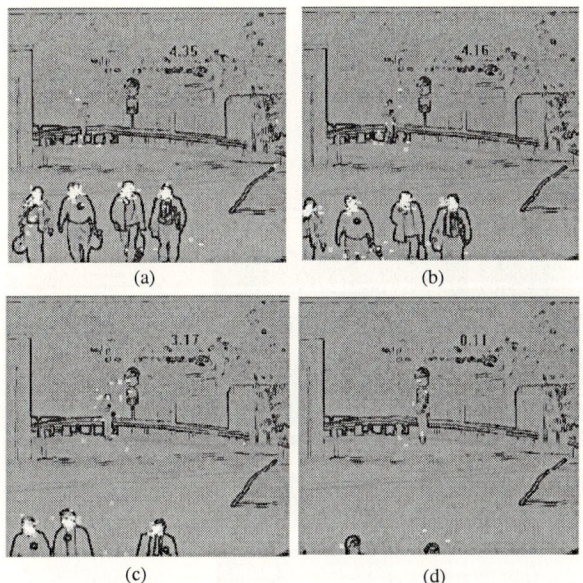

(a)   (b)

(c)   (d)

Fig. 8. The results of tracking multiple people.

7   Conclusions

The new representation proposed in this paper explicitly models multiple objects in a video frame as an object configuration. The events such as object addition, deletion, and occlusion are modeled in configuration-level dynamics. With this formulation, CONDENSATION-like tracking algorithms can be designed to propagate the configuration posterior. A hierarchical sampling algorithm is also proposed in this paper. Promising comparative experimental results of the CONDENSATION algorithm and the new algorithm on both synthetic and real data are demonstrated. Compared to the multiple-hypothesis tracking method, which is an approximation of the Viterbi algorithm based on local maximums of likelihood function, the proposed algorithm explores the likelihood function in the whole parameter space. However, the concept of configuration tracks needs to be introduced to fully model the data association over time.

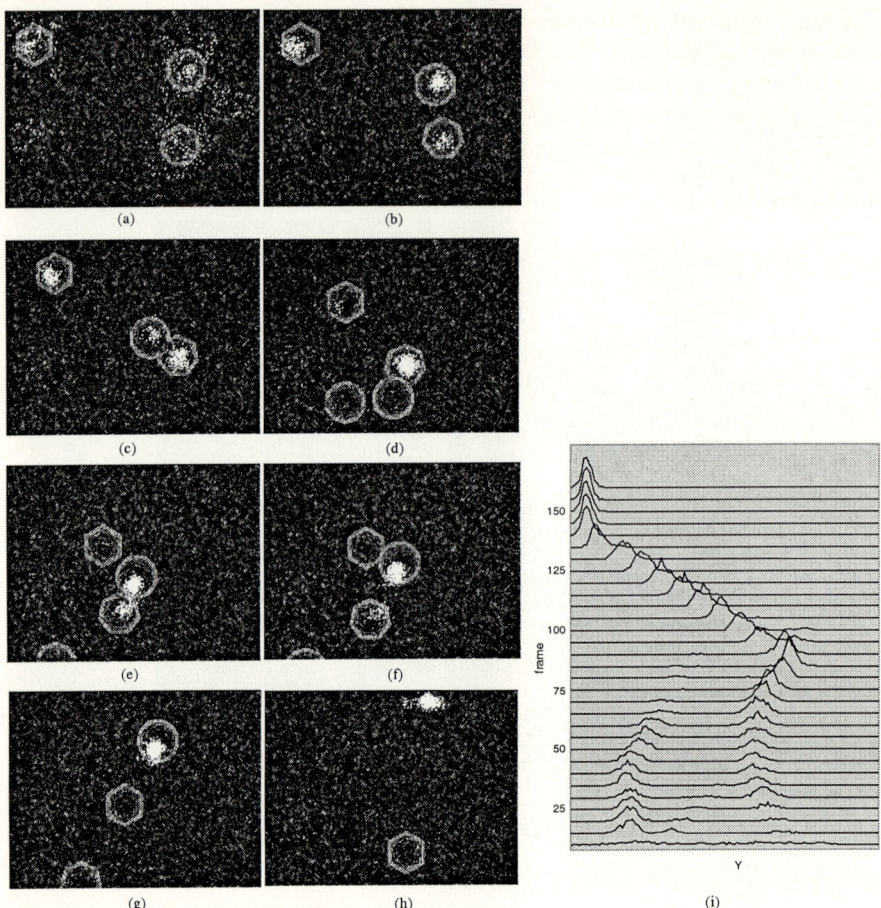

Fig. 9. Results of the CONDENSATION algorithm in frame (a) 1 (b) 10 (c) 25 (d) 65 (e) 85 (f) 90 (g) 110 (h) 140 and (i) the marginal sample distribution along the vertical image axis. Left side is the top of the images.

References

[1] L. R. Rabiner, "A tutorial on hidden Markov models and selected applications in speech recognition," *Proceedings of the IEEE*, vol. 77, pp. 257-286, Feb. 1989.

[2] Z. Ghahramani and G. E. Hinton, "Parameter estimation for linear dynamical systems," Technical Report CRG-TR-96-2, Univ. of Toronto, 1996.

[3] D. B. Reid, "An algorithm for tracking multiple targets," *IEEE Trans. Automatic Control*, vol. 24, no. 6, pp. 843-854, Dec. 1979.

[4] I. J. Cox, S. L.Hingorani, "An efficient implementation of Reid's multiple hypothesis tracking algorithm and tts evaluation for the purpose of visual tracking," *IEEE Trans. Pattern Anal. Machine Intell.*, vol. 18, no. 2, pp. 138-150, Feb. 1996.

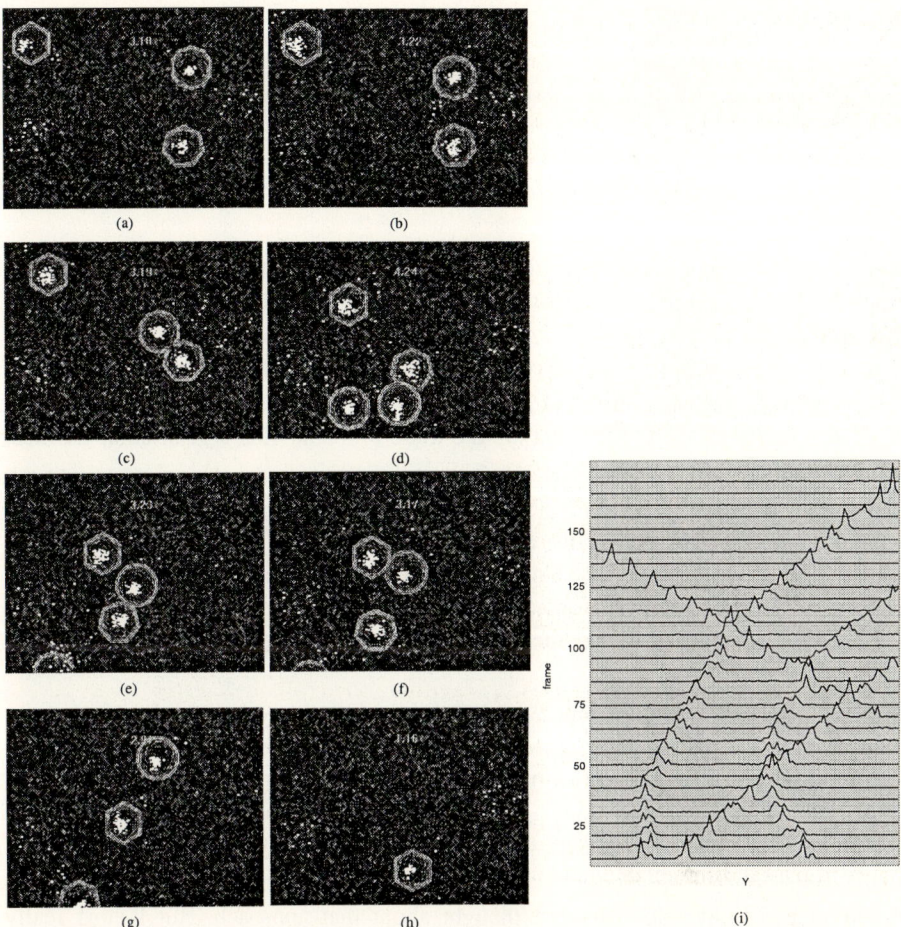

Fig. 10. Results of the hierarchical algorithm in frame (a) 1 (b) 10 (c) 25 (d) 65 (e) 85 (f) 90 (g) 110 (h) 140 (i) and the marginal sample distribution along the vertical image axis. Left side is the top of the images.

[5] M. Isard and A. Blake, "Contour tracking by stochastic propagation of conditional density," in *Proc. European Conf. on Computer Vision*, pp. 343-356, Cambridge UK, 1996.

[6] M. Isard and A. Blake, "ICONDENSATION: unified low-level and high-level tracking in a stochastic framework," in *Proc. European Conf. on Computer Vision*, pp. 893-908, 1998.

[7] J. Sullivan, A. Blake, M. Isard, and J. MacCormick, "Object localization by Bayesian correlation," *Proc. Int. Conf. Computer Vision*, 1999.

[8] J. MacCormick and A. Blake, "A probabilistic exclusion principle for tracking multiple objects," *Proc. Int. Conf. Computer Vision*, 1999.

[9] N. A. C. Cressie, *Statistics for Spatial Data*, John Wiley & Sons Inc., 1991.

[10] A. Selinger and L. Wixson, "Classifying moving objects as rigid or non-rigid without correspondences," *Proc. DARPA Image Understanding Workshop*, pp. 341-347, Monterey, CA, Nov. 1998.

Discussion

Tom Drummond: It's clear that insertion is harder than deletion because you have to generate a whole new set of parameters to describe the new object. Judging by your results, you allocated maybe 10-15% of the samples to insertion. Did you find that you needed to artificially amplify the probability of a new object to provide dense enough samples for insertion?

Harpreet Sawhney: We selected the addition and deletion probabilities empirically, but there wasn't a lot of tuning as there are very few free parameters.

Bill Triggs: You suggested combining multiple hypothesis tracking and CONDENSATION. With classical MH tracking there's a combinatorial search over the joint hypotheses, to enforce the exclusion principle / unicity. How would you put that together with CONDENSATION, what are the trade-offs and what sort of computational complexities would you expect?

Harpreet Sawhney: I haven't done any real experiments to explore this, but the trade-offs you mention are certainly the questions to ask for multiple hypothesis tracking. Something like CONDENSATION, but with more explicit data associations, might allow us to maintain the identity of object configurations over time without doing all the combinatorics that multiple hypotheses imply. But this is just a vague idea that we are beginning to explore.

Olivier Faugeras: I think that the Bayesian formalisms that you and others have been using recently are just not the right way to do tracking, because you are really pushing reality into being Bayesian and using Bayes Rule. I don't think these probabilities are really attainable in practice. Have you considered an alternative approach based on variational calculus, using the very efficient and well developed and practically useful theory of partial differential equations?

Harpreet Sawhney: No, I haven't thought about that approach. But I don't really agree that the probabilistic models are not the right ones. For one thing, in tracking the specific object models can be very complex and difficult to capture in a complete state description. You could have an ideal model, but real objects will vary from that both statistically and systematically. Secondly, when you need to discover new objects in the data, it seems to me that probabilistic representations offer an efficient method of capturing what is going on. I don't see how you would use a variational representation for doing something like tracking, but I am happy to talk to you about that.

Real-Time Tracking of Complex Structures for Visual Servoing

Tom Drummond and Roberto Cipolla

Department of Engineering, University of Cambridge,
Trumpington Street, Cambridge, UK, CB2 1PZ
twd20@eng.cam.ac.uk
http://www-svr.eng.cam.ac.uk/~twd20/

Abstract. This paper presents a visual servoing system which incorporates a novel three-dimensional model-based tracking system. This tracking system extends constrained active contour tracking techniques into three dimensions, placing them within a Lie algebraic framework. This is combined with modern graphical rendering technology to create a system which can track complex three dimensional structures in real time at video frame rate (25 Hz) on a standard workstation without special hardware. The system is based on an internal CAD model of the object to be tracked which is rendered using binary space partition trees to perform hidden line removal. The visible features are identified on-line at each frame and are tracked in the video feed. Analytical and statistical edge saliency are then used as a means of increasing the robustness of the tracking system.

1   Introduction

The tracking of complex three-dimensional objects is useful for numerous applications, including motion analysis, surveillance and robotic control tasks.

This paper tackles two problems. Firstly, the accurate tracking of a known three-dimensional object in the field of view of a camera with known internal parameters. The output of this tracker is a continuously updated estimate of the pose of the object being viewed. Secondly, the use of this information to close the loop in a robot control system to guide a robotic arm to a previously taught target location relative to a workpiece. This work is motivated by problems such as compensation for placement errors in robotic manufacturing. The example presented in this paper concerns the welding of ship parts.

1.1   Model-Based Tracking

Because a video feed contains a very large amount of data, it is important to extract only a small amount of salient information, if real-time frame (or field) rate performance is to be achieved [11]. This observation leads to the notion of *feature based* tracking [9] in which processing is restricted to locating strong image features such as contours [19, 3].

B. Triggs, A. Zisserman, R. Szeliski (Eds.): Vision Algorithms'99, LNCS 1883, pp. 69–84, 2000.

A number of successful systems have been based on tracking the image contours of a known model. Lowe [15] used the Marr-Hildreth edge detector to extract edges from the image which were then chained together to form lines. These lines were matched and fitted to those in the model. A similar approach using the Hough transform has also been used [21]. The use of two-dimensional image processing incurs a significant computational cost and both of these systems make use of special purpose hardware in order to achieve frame rate processing.

An alternative approach is to render the model first and then use sparse one-dimensional search to find and measure the distance to matching (nearby) edges in the image. This approach has been used in RAPID [10], CONDENSATION [14] and other systems [4, 20, 17]. The efficiency yielded by this approach allows all these systems to run in real-time on standard workstations. The approach is also used here and discussed in more detail in Section 2.1.

Using either of these approaches, most systems (except CONDENSATION) then compute the pose parameters by linearising with respect to image motion. This process is reformulated here in terms of the Lie group $SE(3)$ and its Lie algebra. This formulation is a natural one to use since the group $SE(3)$ exactly represents the space of poses that form the output of the system. The Lie algebra of a group is the tangent space to the group at the identity and is therefore the natural space in which to represent differential quantities such as velocities and small motions in the group. Thus the representation provides a canonical method for linearising the relationship between image motion and pose parameters. Further, this approach can be generalised to other transformation groups and has been successfully applied to deformations of a planar contour using the groups $GA(2)$ and $P(2)$ [5].

Outliers are a key problem that must be addressed by systems which measure and fit edges. They frequently occur in the measurement process since additional edges may be present in the scene in close proximity to the model edges. These may be caused by shadows, for example, or strong background scene elements. Such outliers are a particular problem for the traditional least-squares fitting method used by many of the algorithms. Methods of improving robustness to these sorts of outliers include the use of RANSAC [1], factored sampling [14] or regularisation, for example the Levenberg-Marquadt scheme used in [15]. The approach used here employs iterative re-weighted least squares (a robust M-estimator) which is then extended to incorporate a number of additional saliency measures. This is discussed in more detail in Section 4.

There is a trade-off to be made between robustness and precision. The CONDENSATION system, for example, obtains a high degree of robustness by taking a large number of sample hypotheses of the position of the tracked structure with a comparatively small number of edge measurements per sample. By contrast, the system presented here uses a large number of measurements for a single position hypothesis and is thus able to obtain very high precision in its positional estimates. This is particularly relevant in tasks such as visual servoing since the dynamics and environmental conditions can be controlled so as to constrain the robustness problems, while high precision is needed in real-time in order for the system to be useful.

Occlusion is also a significant cause of instabilities and may occur when the object occludes parts of itself (self occlusion) or where another object lies between the camera and the target (external occlusion). RAPID handles the first of these problems by use of a pre-computed table of visible features indexed by what is essentially a view-sphere. By contrast, the system presented here uses graphical rendering techniques to dynamically determine the visible features and is thus able to handle more complex situations (such as objects with holes) than can be tabulated on a view-sphere.

External occlusion can be treated by using outlier rejection, for example in [1] which discards primitives for which insufficient support is found, or by modifying statistical descriptions of the observation model (as in [16]). If a model is available for the intervening object, then it is possible to use this to re-estimate the visible features [8, 21]. Both of these methods are used within the system presented here.

1.2   Visual Servoing

The use of visual feedback output by such tracking systems for robotic control is increasingly becoming an attractive proposition. A distinction is often made [13] between *image-based* [7] and *position-based* [2] visual servoing. The approach presented here is position-based but closes the control loop by projecting the action of three-dimensional camera motion into the image where it is fitted to image measurements. Since the eye-in-hand approach is used, this generates a motion-to-image Jacobian (also known as the interaction screw [7]) which can be used to generate robot control commands to minimise the image error.

2   Theoretical Framework

The approach proposed here for tracking a known 3-dimensional structure is based upon maintaining an estimate of the camera projection matrix, P, in the co-ordinate system of the structure. This projection matrix is represented as the product of a matrix of internal camera parameters:

$$K = \begin{bmatrix} f_u & s & u_0 \\ 0 & f_v & v_0 \\ 0 & 0 & 1 \end{bmatrix} \tag{1}$$

and a Euclidean projection matrix representing the position and orientation of the camera relative to the target structure:

$$E = \begin{bmatrix} R & t \end{bmatrix} \qquad \text{with } RR^T = I \text{ and } |R| = 1 \tag{2}$$

The projective co-ordinates of an image feature are then given by

$$\begin{pmatrix} u \\ v \\ w \end{pmatrix} = P \begin{pmatrix} x \\ y \\ z \\ 1 \end{pmatrix} \tag{3}$$

with the actual image co-ordinates given by

$$\begin{pmatrix} \tilde{u} \\ \tilde{v} \end{pmatrix} = \begin{pmatrix} u/w \\ v/w \end{pmatrix} \tag{4}$$

Rigid motions of the camera relative to the target structure between consecutive video frames can then be represented by right multiplication of the projection matrix by a Euclidean transformation of the form:

$$M = \begin{bmatrix} R & t \\ 0\,0\,0 & 1 \end{bmatrix} \tag{5}$$

These M, form a 4×4 matrix representation of the group SE(3) of rigid body motions in 3-dimensional space, which is a 6-dimensional Lie Group. The generators of this group are typically taken to be translations in the x, y and z directions and rotations about the x, y and z axes, represented by the following matrices:

$$G_1 = \begin{bmatrix} 0\,0\,0\,1 \\ 0\,0\,0\,0 \\ 0\,0\,0\,0 \\ 0\,0\,0\,0 \end{bmatrix}, G_2 = \begin{bmatrix} 0\,0\,0\,0 \\ 0\,0\,0\,1 \\ 0\,0\,0\,0 \\ 0\,0\,0\,0 \end{bmatrix}, G_3 = \begin{bmatrix} 0\,0\,0\,0 \\ 0\,0\,0\,0 \\ 0\,0\,0\,1 \\ 0\,0\,0\,0 \end{bmatrix}, \tag{6}$$

$$G_4 = \begin{bmatrix} 0\,0\,0\,0 \\ 0\,0\,1\,0 \\ 0\,-1\,0\,0 \\ 0\,0\,0\,0 \end{bmatrix}, G_5 = \begin{bmatrix} 0\,0\,-1\,0 \\ 0\,0\,0\,0 \\ 1\,0\,0\,0 \\ 0\,0\,0\,0 \end{bmatrix}, G_6 = \begin{bmatrix} 0\,1\,0\,0 \\ -1\,0\,0\,0 \\ 0\,0\,0\,0 \\ 0\,0\,0\,0 \end{bmatrix}$$

These generators form a basis for the vector space (the Lie algebra) of derivatives of SE(3) at the identity. Consequently, the partial derivative of projective image co-ordinates under the ith generating motion can be computed as:

$$\begin{pmatrix} u' \\ v' \\ w' \end{pmatrix} = PG_i \begin{pmatrix} x \\ y \\ z \\ 1 \end{pmatrix} \tag{7}$$

with

$$L_i = \begin{pmatrix} \tilde{u}' \\ \tilde{v}' \end{pmatrix} = \begin{pmatrix} \frac{u'}{w} + \frac{uw'}{w^2} \\ \frac{v'}{w} + \frac{vw'}{w^2} \end{pmatrix} \tag{8}$$

giving the motion in true image co-ordinates. A least squares approach can then be used to fit the observed motion of image features between adjacent frames. This process is detailed in Section 3.3.

This method can be extended to include the motion of image features due to the change in internal camera parameters [6] or internal model parameters by incorporating the vector fields they generate into the least squares process.

2.1   Tracking Edges

An important aspect of the approach presented here is the decision to track the edges of the model (which appear as intensity discontinuities in the video feed). Edges are strong features that can be reliably found in the image because they have a significant spatial extent. Furthermore, this means that a number of

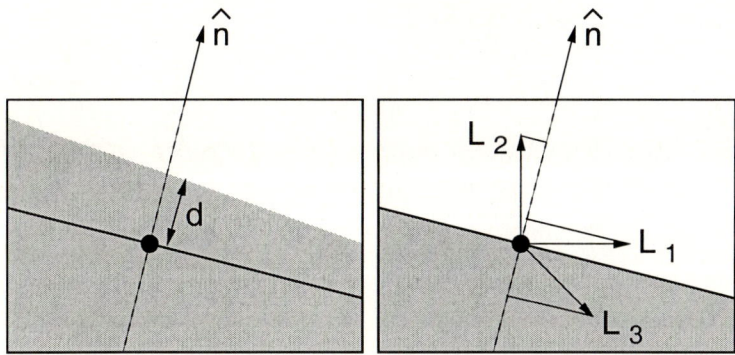

Fig. 1. Computing the normal component of the motion

measurements can be made along each edge, and thus they may be accurately localised within an image.

This approach also takes advantage of the aperture problem (that the component of motion of an edge, tangent to itself, is not observable locally). This problem actually yields a substantial benefit since the search for intensity discontinuities in the video image can be limited to a one dimensional path that lies along the edge normal, $\hat{n}$ (see Figure 1) and thus has linear complexity in the search range, rather than quadratic as for a two-dimensional feature search. This benefit is what makes it possible to track complex structures in real time on a standard workstation without additional hardware. The normal component of the motion fields, L_i are then also computed (as $L_i \cdot \hat{n}$).

3   Tracking System

The three-dimensional tracking system makes use of constrained snake technology [3] to the follow edges of the workpiece that are visible in the video image. One novel aspect of this work is the use of a real-time hidden-line-removal rendering system (using binary space partition trees [18]) to dynamically determine the visible features of the model in real-time. This technique allows accurate frame rate tracking of complex structures such as the ship part shown in Figure 2.

Figure 3 shows system operation. At each cycle, the system renders the expected view of the object (a) using its current estimate of the projection matrix, P. The visible edges are identified and tracking nodes are assigned at regular intervals in image co-ordinates along these edges (b). The edge normal is then searched in the video feed for a nearby edge (c). Typically $m \approx 400$ nodes are assigned and measurements made in this way. The system then projects this m-dimensional measurement vector onto the 6-dimensional subspace corresponding to Euclidean transformations (d) using the least squares approach described in Section 3.3 to give the motion, M. The Euclidean part of the projection matrix,

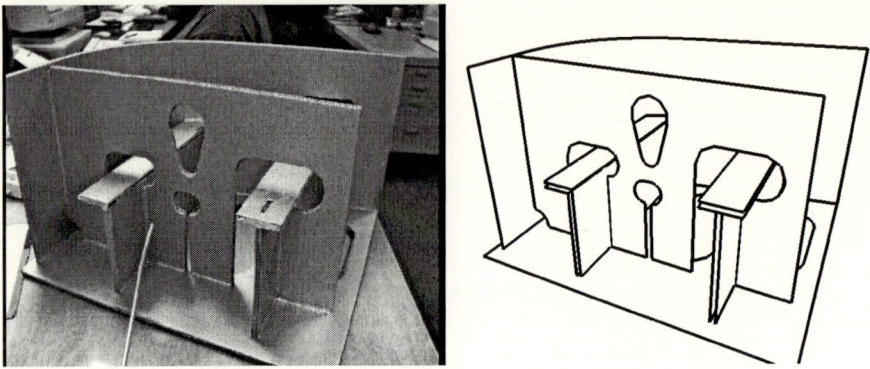

Fig. 2. Image and CAD model of ship part

E is then updated by right multiplication with this transformation (e). Finally, the new projection matrix P is obtained by multiplying the camera parameters K with the updated Euclidean matrix to give a new current estimate of the local position (f). The system then loops back to step (a).

3.1   Rendering the Model

In order to accurately render a CAD model of a complex structure such as the one shown in Figure 2 at frame rate, an advanced rendering technique such as the use of binary space partition trees is needed [18]. This approach represents the object as a tree, in which each node contains the equation of a plane in the model, together with a list of edges and convex polygons in that plane. Each plane partitions 3-dimensional space into the plane and the two open regions either side of the plane. The two branches of the tree represent those parts of the model that fall into these two volumes. Thus the tree recursively partitions space into small regions which, in the limit, contain no remaining model features. The rendering takes place by performing an *in-order* scan of the tree, where at

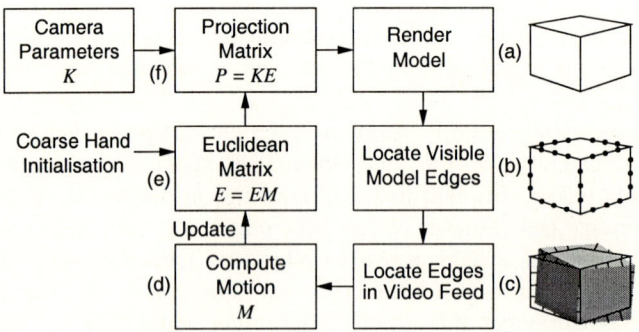

Fig. 3. Tracking system operation

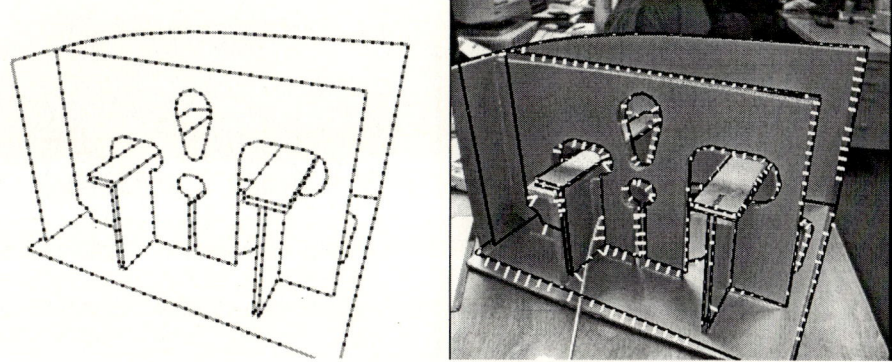

Fig. 4. Tracking nodes assigned and distances measured

each node, the viewpoint is tested to see if it lies in front, or behind the plane. When this is determined, those features lying closer to the camera are rendered first, then the plane itself, and finally, the more distant features. The use of a stencil buffer prevents over-writing of nearer features by more distant ones and also provides a layer map when the rendering is complete. The ship part contains 12 planes, but since 8 of these (corresponding to the T and L beams) are split into two parts by a vertical plane partition, there are 20 nodes in the tree.

3.2 Locating Edges

Once rendering is complete, the layer map is used to locate the visible parts of each edge by comparing the assigned layer of the plane for each edge in the model with the layer in the stencil buffer at a series of points along that edge. Where the depths agree, trackers are assigned to search for the nearest edge in the video feed along the edge normal (see Figure 4).

The result of this process is a set of trackers with known position in the model co-ordinate system, with computed edge normals and the distance along those normals to the nearest image edge. Grouping these distances together provides an m-dimensional measurement vector.

3.3 Computing the Motion

Step (d) in the process involves the projection of the measurement vector onto the subspace defined by the Euclidean transformation group. The action of each of the generators of SE(3) on the tracking nodes in image co-ordinates can be found by computing PG_i and applying this to the homogeneous co-ordinates of the node in 3-space. This can be projected to give a vector, L_i^ξ describing the image motion of the ξth node for the ith generator of Euclidean motion of the object. $L_i^\xi \cdot \hat{n}^\xi$ then describes the magnitude of the edge normal motion that would be observed in the image at each node for each group generator. These can be considered as a set of m-dimensional vectors which describe the

Fig. 5. Frames from tracking sequence

motion in the image for each mode of Euclidean transformation. The system then projects the m-vector corresponding to the measured distances to the observed edges onto the subspace spanned by the transformation vectors. This provides a solution to finding the geometric transformation of the part which best fits the observed edge positions, minimising the square error between the transformed edge position and the actual edge position (in pixels). This process is performed as follows:

$$O_i = \sum_\xi d^\xi (L_i^\xi \cdot \hat{n}^\xi) \tag{9}$$

$$C_{ij} = \sum_\xi (L_i^\xi \cdot \hat{n}^\xi)(L_j^\xi \cdot \hat{n}^\xi) \tag{10}$$

$$\alpha_i = C_{ij}^{-1} O_j \tag{11}$$

(with Einstein summation convention over Latin indices). The α_i are then the coefficients of the vector in the Lie algebra representing the quantity of each mode of Euclidean motion that has been observed. The final step is to compute the actual motion of the model and apply it to the matrix E in (2). This is done by using the exponential map relating α_i to SE(3).

$$E_{t+1} = E_t \exp(\sum_i \alpha_i G_i) \tag{12}$$

This section has described the basic version of the tracking system. This system performs well over a wide range of configurations (see Figure 5). However, in order to improve robustness to occlusion and critical configurations which cause instability, saliency characteristics are introduced.

4   Extended Iterative Re-weighted Least Squares

The naïve least squares algorithm presented in Section 3.3 is vulnerable to instabilities caused by the presence of outliers. This is because the sum-of-squares objective function can be significantly affected by a few measurements with large errors. Equivalently, the corresponding Gaussian distribution dies off far too quickly to admit many sample measurements at a large number of standard deviations.

A standard technique for handling this problem is the substitution of a robust M-estimator for least squares estimator by replacing the objective function with one that applies less weighting to outlying measurements [12]. This can be achieved by modifying the least squares algorithm and replacing(9) and (10) with:

$$O_i = \sum_\xi s(d^\xi) d^\xi (L_i^\xi \cdot \hat{n}^\xi) \tag{13}$$

$$C_{ij} = \sum_\xi s(d^\xi)(L_i^\xi \cdot \hat{n}^\xi)(L_j^\xi \cdot \hat{n}^\xi) \tag{14}$$

A common choice for the weighting function, s is:

$$s(d^\xi) = \frac{1}{c + d^\xi} \tag{15}$$

which corresponds to replacing the Gaussian error distribution with one that lies between Gaussian and Laplacian. The parameter c is chosen here to be approximately one standard deviation of the inlying data. This approach is known as iterative re-weighted least squares (IRLS) since s depends on d, which changes with each iteration. In the current implementation, only a single iteration is performed for each frame of the video sequence and convergence occurs rapidly over sequential frames. Incorporating IRLS into the system improves its robustness to occlusion (see Figure 6). The function s controls the confidence with which each measurement is fitted in the least squares procedure and thus can be viewed as representing the saliency of the measurement.

This can be further exploited by extending IRLS by incorporating a number of additional criteria into the saliency estimate. These are chosen to improve

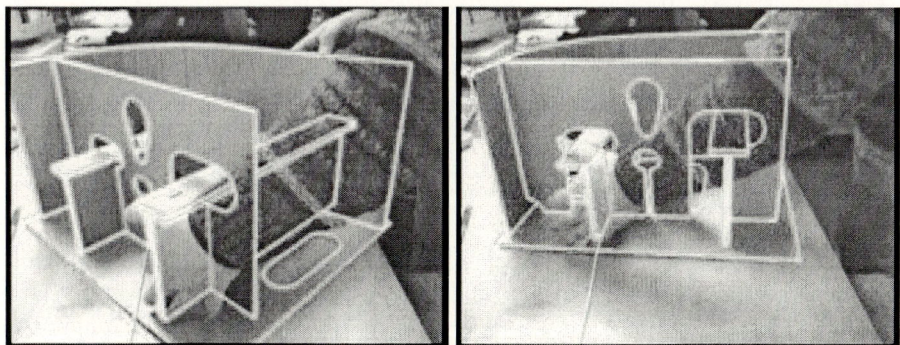

Fig. 6. Frames from tracking sequence with occlusion

the robustness of the system when it is exposed to critical configurations which have been identified as causing instabilities. The saliency or re-weighting of each measurement is modified to include four additional terms. The first three of these terms address statistical saliency (can a feature be detected reliably?) while the fourth is concerned with analytical saliency (does the feature constrain the motion?).

Multiple edges: When the tracker sees multiple edges within its search range, it is possible for the wrong one to be chosen. Typically many trackers on the same edge will do this, compounding the problem. To reduce this problem, the saliency is inversely proportional to the number of edge strength maxima visible within the search path.

Many trackers disappear simultaneously: If a major edge is aligned along an image axis then it is possible for the entire edge to leave the field of view between two frames. This entails a sudden change in the set of trackers used and may cause a sudden apparent motion of the model. This sudden change in the behaviour of the tracker can be removed by constructing a border at the edge of the image. The saliency of nodes within this border is weakened linearly to zero as the pixel approaches the edge. A border of 40 pixels has been found to be sufficiently large for this purpose.

Poor visibility: Generally the best measurements come from the strongest edges in the image, since weak edges may be difficult to locate precisely. This is taken into account by examining the edge strengths found in the search path. If the edge strength along a search path is below a threshold, no measurement is made for that node. Between this threshold and a higher threshold (equal to double the lower one), the saliency of the node is varied linearly. Above the higher threshold, the visibility does not affect the saliency.

Weak conditioning: If the majority of the trackers belong to a single plane of the model (for example the feature rich front plane of the ship part) which is front on to the camera then the least squares matrix generated by these nodes becomes more weakly conditioned than in the general configuration. This can be improved by increasing the saliency of measurements that help to condition the least squares matrix. If the vector comprising the six image motions at node i lies in the subspace spanned by the eigen vectors of C_{ij} corresponding to the smallest eigen values, then that node is particularly important in constraining the estimated motion. This is implemented by the simple expedient of doubling the saliency when $(L_i^\xi \cdot \hat{n}^\xi)(L_j^\xi \cdot \hat{n}^\xi)C_{ij}^{-1}$ is greater than the geometric mean of that quantity, computed over the visible features in the image.

These measures have been found to provide increased robustness and while they represent a heuristic method of dealing with critical configurations, the general approach of modifying the re-weighting function, s, provides a powerful method of incorporating domain knowledge within the least squares framework in a conceptually intuitive manner.

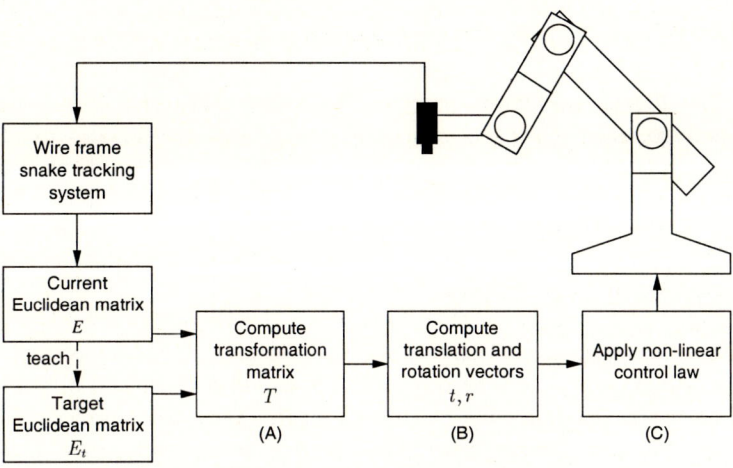

Fig. 7. Visual servoing system operation

5   Visual Servoing System

The visual servoing system (shown in Figure 7) takes the Euclidean matrix, E as output from the tracking system and uses this within a non-linear control law to provide feedback to servo the robot to a stored target position. These are learned by acquiring the Euclidean matrix with the robot placed in the target position by the supervisor. The inverse of this target matrix, E_t^{-1}, is easily computed and the product of this with the current position matrix yields the transformation from the target position to the current position (A).

$$T = EE_t^{-1} \tag{16}$$

The translation and rotation vectors that must be applied to the robot are then easily extracted from this representation (B). (here $i, j, k = 1,2,3$):

$$t_i = T_{i4} \tag{17}$$

$$r_i' = \tfrac{1}{2} \sum_{jk} \epsilon_{ijk} T_{jk}$$

$$r_i = \frac{r_i' \sin^{-1}(|r'|)}{|r'|} \tag{18}$$

The vectors t and r are then multiplied by a gain factor and sent to the robot as end effector translation and rotation velocities (C). The gain is dependent on the magnitudes of t and r so that small velocities are damped to obtain higher precision, while large errors in position may be responded to quickly. A maximum velocity clamp is also applied for safety reasons and to prevent possible instabilities due to latency. Figures 8 and 9 show the visual servoing system in action tracing a path between recorded waypoints and performing closed loop control tracking a moving part.

6   Results

The tracking system and visual servoing system have been tested in a number of experiments to assess their performance both quantitatively and qualitatively. These experiments were conducted with an SGI O2 workstation (225 MHz) controlling a Mitsubishi RV-E2 robot.

6.1   Stability of the Tracker

The stability of the tracker with a stationary structure was measured to assess the effect of image noise on the tracker. The standard deviation of position and rotation as measured from the Euclidean matrix were measured over a run of 100 frames. From a viewing distance of 30cm, the apparent rms translational motion was found to be 0.03mm with the rms rotation being 0.015 degrees.

6.2   Accuracy of Positioning

The accuracy of positioning the robot was measured with two experiments. Firstly, the ship part was held fixed and the robot asked to home to a given position from a number of different starting points. When the robot had ceased to move, the program was terminated and the robots position queried. The standard deviation of these positions was computed and the r.m.s. translational motion was 0.08mm with the r.m.s. rotation being 0.06 degrees.

The second accuracy experiment was performed by positioning the ship part on an accurate turntable. The part was turned through fifteen degrees, one degree at a time and the robot asked to return to the target position each time. Again, the position of the robot was queried and a circle was fitted to the data. The residual error was computed and found to give an r.m.s. positional error of 0.12mm per measurement (allowing for the three degrees of freedom absorbed into fitting the circle).

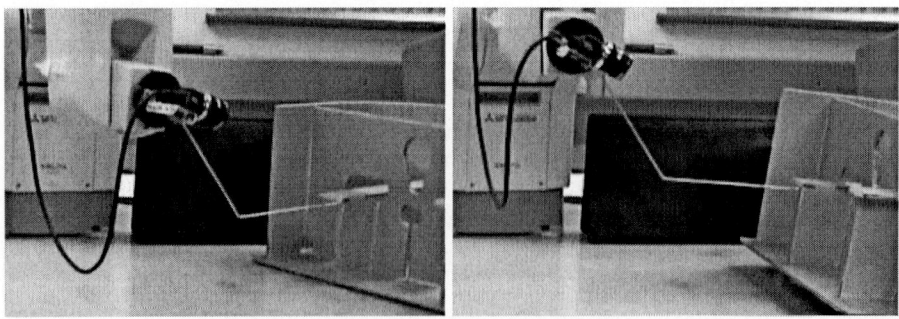

Fig. 8. Closed-loop visual servoing. The task is to maintain a fixed spatial position relative to the workpiece.

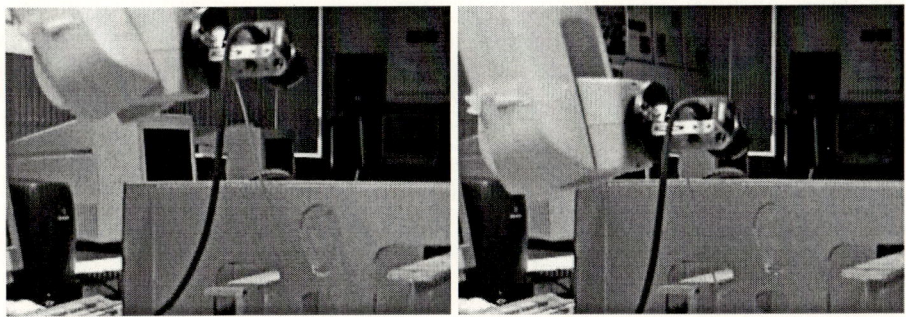

Fig. 9. Visual servoing. The task is to trace out a trajectory relative to the workpiece.

6.3   Closed Loop Tracking

The qualitative performance of the tracking and servoing systems were assessed in a closed loop tracking experiment. The robot was asked to maintain a fixed position relative to the part whilst it was moved through a series of perturbations. This experiment is shown in Figure 8.

6.4   Saliency Enhancements

The modifications to the least squares fitting procedure were tested by running two versions (with and without the modifications) of the tracking system concurrently. A series of ten experiments were conducted in which the model was moved through a configuration known to cause difficulties. Because two processes were running concurrently, the average frame rate attained by both was only 12 frames per second. Of the ten experiments, the unmodified version lost track of the model on five occasions. The modified version successfully tracked on all ten experiments, although on two of these the tracking suffered a significant temporary deviation.

6.5   Path Following

The servoing system made to perform path following by recording the Euclidean matrices at a series of waypoints along the path. The system was then made to home to each of these in succession, moving on to the next node as soon as the current one had been reached. This experiment is shown in Figure 9.

7   Conclusion

This paper has introduced a real-time three-dimensional tracking system based on an active wire frame model which is rendered with hidden line removal. A formulation which uses the Lie algebra of the group of rigid body transformations

(SE(3)) to linearise the tracking problem has been presented and saliency measurements have been described which enhance the robustness of the tracker. A visual servoing system which uses the tracker has been implemented and results from a number of experiments presented.

Acknowledgements

This work was supported by an EC (ESPRIT) grant no. LTR26247 (VIGOR) and by an EPSRC grant no. K84202.

References

1. M. Armstrong and A. Zisserman. Robust object tracking. In *Proceedings of Second Asian Conference on Computer Vision*, pages 58–62, 1995.
2. R. Basri, E. Rivlin, and I. Shimshoni. Visual homing: Surfing on the epipoles. In *Proceedings of International Conference on Computer Vision (ICCV '98)*, pages 863–869, 1998.
3. R. Cipolla and A. Blake. Image divergence and deformation from closed curves. *International Journal of Robotics Research*, 16(1):77–96, 1997.
4. N. Daucher, M. Dhome, J. T. Lapresté, and G. Rives. Modelled object pose estimation abd tracking by monocular vision. In *Proceedings of the British Machine Vision Conference*, pages 249–258, 1993.
5. T. Drummond and R. Cipolla. Visual tracking and control using Lie algebras. In *Proceedings of IEEE Conference on Computer Vision and Pattern Recognition (CVPR'99)*, volume 2, pages 652–657, 1999.
6. T. Drummond and R. Cipolla. Real-time tracking of complex structures with on-line camera calibration. In *Proceedings of the 10th British Machine Vision Conference (BMVC'99)*, 1999. to appear.
7. B. Espiau, F. Chaumette, and P. Rives. A new approach to visual servoing in robotics. *IEEE T-Robotics and Automation*, 8(3), 1992.
8. M. Haag and H-H. Nagel. Tracking of complex driving manoeuvres in traffic image sequences. *Image and Vision Computing*, 16:517–527, 1998.
9. G. Hager, G. Grunwald, and K. Toyama. Feature-based visual servoing and its application to telerobotics. In V. Graefe, editor, *Intelligent Robotic Systems*. Elsevier, 1995.
10. C. Harris. Tracking with rigid models. In A. Blake, editor, *Active Vision*, chapter 4, pages 59–73. MIT Press, 1992.
11. C. Harris. Geometry from visual motion. In A. Blake, editor, *Active Vision*, chapter 16, pages 263–284. MIT Press, 1992.
12. P. J. Huber. *Robust Statistics*. Wiley series in probability and mathematical statistics. Wiley, 1981.
13. S. Hutchinson, G.D. Hager, and P.I. Corke. A tutorial on visual servo control. *IEEE T-Robotics and Automation*, 12(5):651–670, 1996.
14. M. Isard and A. Blake. CONDENSATION - conditional density propagation for visual tracking. *International Journal of Computer Vision*, 29(1):5–28, 1998.
15. D. G. Lowe. Robust model-based motion tracking through the integration of search and estimation. *International Journal of Computer Vision*, 8(2):113–122, 1992.

16. J. MacCormick and A. Blake. Spatial dependence in the observation of visual contours. In *Proceedings of the Fifth European Conference on Computer vision (ECCV'98)*, pages 765–781, 1998.

17. E. Marchand, P. Bouthemy, F. Chaumette, and V. Moreau. Robust real-time visual tracking using a 2d-3d model-based approach. In *Proceedings of IEEE International Conference on Computer Vision (ICCV'99)*, 1999. to appear.

18. M. Paterson and F. Yao. Efficient binary space partitions for hidden surface removal and solid modeling. *Discrete and Computational Geometry*, 5(5):485–503, 1990.

19. D. Terzopoulos and R. Szeliski. Tracking with Kalman snakes. In A. Blake, editor, *Active Vision*, chapter 1, pages 3–20. MIT Press, 1992.

20. A. D. Worrall, G. D. Sullivan, and K. D. Baker. Pose refinement of active models using forces in 3d. In J. Eklundh, editor, *Proceedings of the Third European Conference on Computer vision (ECCV'94)*, volume 2, pages 341–352, May 1994.

21. P. Wunsch and G. Hirzinger. Real-time visual tracking of 3-d objects with dynamic handling of occlusion. In *Proceedings of the 1997 International Conference on Robotics and Automation*, pages 2868–2873, 1997.

Discussion

Kenichi Kanatani: I've seen this kind of model tracking problem many times and each uses different techniques. You project the model edge and look at gray levels along the perpendicular to find discontinuities. Many other authors use edge images and look for edge pixels. What are the advantages of gray levels over edge pixels?

Tom Drummond: Edges are a very popular approach, but there's an enormous cost in processing the entire image to find edges first. All of the systems I know that do this rely on special image processing hardware like the DataCube. With gray levels, we only have to process at tiny fraction of the image pixels — say 400 tracks of 40 pixels each — and we can do this with a standard Silicon Graphics workstation.

Yongduek Seo: How precisely can you control the robot?

Tom Drummond: There are two issues: global precision and repeatability. When we control the robot we teach it the position by putting the camera at the target viewpoint. It learns the view, and this gives us a very high repeatability. At a distance of about 25 cm we get about 0.1mm repeatability, because the camera just has to move to make the image identical to the training one. But that's much higher than the global precision — from a different relative viewpoint the relative mesh of the tracker and real structure are slightly different and the precision is less.

Direct Recovery of Planar-Parallax
from Multiple Frames

Michal Irani[1], P. Anandan[2], and Meir Cohen[1]

[1] Dept. of Computer Science and Applied Math, The Weizmann Inst. of Science,
Rehovot, Israel,
`irani@wisdom.weizmann.ac.il`
[2] Microsoft Research, One Microsoft Way, Redmond, WA 98052, USA,
`anandan@microsoft.com`

Abstract. In this paper we present an algorithm that estimates dense planar-parallax motion from *multiple uncalibrated* views of a 3D scene. This generalizes the "plane + parallax" recovery methods to more than two frames. The parallax motion of pixels across multiple frames (relative to a planar surface) is related to the 3D scene structure and the camera epipoles. The parallax field, the epipoles, and the 3D scene structure are estimated directly from image brightness variations across multiple frames, without pre-computing correspondences.

1 Introduction

The recovery of the 3D structure of a scene and the camera epipolar-geometries (or camera motion) from multiple views has been a topic of considerable research. The large majority of the work on structure-from-motion (SFM) has assumed that correspondences between image features (typically a sparse set of image points) is given, and focused on the problem of recovering SFM based on this input. Another class of methods has focused on recovering dense 3D structure from a set of dense correspondences or an optical flow field. While these have the advantage of recovering *dense* 3D structure, they require that the correspondences are known. However, correspondence (or flow) estimation is a notoriously difficult problem.

A small set of techniques have attempted to combine the correspondence estimation step together with SFM recovery. These methods obtain dense correspondences while *simultaneously* estimating the 3D structure and the camera geometries (or motion) [3, 11, 13, 16, 15]. By inter-weaving the two processes, the local correspondence estimation process is constrained by the current estimate of (global) epipolar geometry (or camera motion), and vice-versa. These techniques minimize the violation of the brightness gradient constraint with respect to the unknown structure and motion parameters. Typically this leads to a significant improvement in the estimated correspondences (and the attendant 3D structure) and some improvement in the recovered camera geometries (or motion). These methods are sometimes referred to as "direct methods" [3], since they directly

B. Triggs, A. Zisserman, R. Szeliski (Eds.): Vision Algorithms'99, LNCS 1883, pp. 85–99, 2000.

use image brightness information to recover 3D structure and motion, without explicitly computing correspondences as an intermediate step.

While [3, 16, 15] recover 3D information relative to a *camera-centered* coordinate system, an alternative approach has been proposed for recovering 3D structure in a *scene-centered* coordinate system. In particular, the "Plane+Parallax" approach [14, 11, 13, 7, 9, 8], which analyzes the parallax displacements of points relative to a (real or virtual) physical planar surface in the scene (the "reference plane"). The underlying concept is that after the alignment of the reference plane, the residual image motion is due only to the *translational* motion of the camera and to the *deviations* of the scene structure from the planar surface. All effects of camera rotation or changes in camera calibration are eliminated by the plane stabilization. Hence, the residual image motion (the planar-parallax displacements) form a *radial flow field* centered at the epipole.

The "Plane+Parallax" representation has several benefits over the traditional camera-centered representation, which make it an attractive framework for correspondence estimation and for 3D shape recovery:

1. *Reduced search space:*   By parametrically aligning a visible image structure (which usually corresponds to a planar surface in the scene), the search space of unknowns is significantly reduced. Globally, all effects of unknown rotation and calibration parameters are folded into the homographies used for patch alignment. The only remaining unknown global camera parameters which need to be estimated are the epipoles (i.e., 3 global unknowns per frame; gauge ambiguity is reduced to a single global scale factor for all epipoles across all frames). Locally, because after plane alignment the unknown displacements are constrained to lie along radial lines emerging from the epipoles, local correspondence estimation reduces from a 2-D search problem into a simpler 1-D search problem at each pixel. The 1-D search problem has the additional benefit that it can uniquely resolve correspondences, even for pixels which suffer from the aperture problem (i.e., pixels which lie on line structures).

2. *Provides shape relative to a plane in the scene:*   In many applications, distances from the camera are not as useful information as fluctuations with respect to a plane in the scene. For example, in robot navigation, heights of scene points from the ground plane can be immediately translated into obstacles or holes, and can be used for obstacle avoidance, as opposed to distances from the camera.

3. *A compact representation:*   By removing the mutual global component (the plane homography), the residual parallax displacements are usually very small, and hence require significantly fewer bits to encode the shape fluctuations relative to the number of bits required to encode distances from the camera. This is therefore a compact representation, which also supports progressive encoding and a high resolution display of the data.

4. *A stratified 2D-3D representation:*   Work on motion analysis can be roughly classified into two classes of techniques: 2D algorithms which handle cases with no 3D parallax (e.g., estimating homographies, 2D affine transforma-

tions, etc), and 3D algorithms which handle cases with dense 3D parallax (e.g., estimating fundamental matrices, trifocal tensors, 3D shape, etc). Prior *model selection* [17] is usually required to decide which set of algorithms to apply, depending on the underlying scenario. The Plane+Parallax representation provides a *unified* approach to 2D and 3D scene analysis, with a strategy to gracefully bridge the gap between those two extremes [10]. Within the Plane+Parallax framework, the analysis always starts with 2D estimation (i.e., the homography estimation). When that is all the information available in the image sequence, that is where the analysis stops. The 3D analysis then gradually builds *on top* of the 2D analysis, with the gradual increase in 3D information (in the form of planar-parallax displacements and shape-fluctuations w.r.t. the planar surface).

[11, 13] used the Plane+Parallax framework to recover dense structure relative to the reference plane from *two* uncalibrated views. While their algorithm linearly solves for the structure directly from brightness measurements in two frames, it does not naturally extend to multiple frames. In this paper we show how dense planar-parallax displacements and relative structure can be recovered directly from brightness measurements in *multiple* frames. Furthermore, we show that many of the ambiguities existing in the two-frame case of [11, 13] are resolved by extending the analysis to multiple frames. Our algorithm assumes as input a sequence of images in which a planar surface has been previously aligned with respect to a reference image (e.g., via one of the 2D parametric estimation techniques, such as [1, 6]). We do *not* assume that the camera calibration information is known. The output of the algorithm is: (i) the epipoles for all the images with respect to the reference image, (ii) dense 3D structure of the scene relative to a planar surface, and (iii) the correspondences of all the pixels across all the frames, which must be consistent with (i) and (ii). The estimation process uses the *exact* equations (as opposed to *instantaneous* equations, such as in [4, 15]) relating the residual parallax motion of pixels across *multiple* frames to the relative 3D structure and the camera epipoles. The 3D scene structure and the camera epipoles are computed directly from image measurements by minimizing the variation of image brightness across the views without pre-computing a correspondence map.

The current implementation of our technique relies on the prior alignment of the video frames with respect to a planar surface (similar to other plane+parallax methods). This requires that a real physical plane exists in the scene and is visible in all the video frames. However, this approach can be extended to arbitrary scenes by folding in the plane homography computation also into the simultaneous estimation of camera motion, scene structure, and image displacements (as was done by [11] for the case of *two* frames).

The remainder of the paper describes the algorithm and shows its performance on real and synthetic data. Section 2 shows how the 3D structure relates to the 2D image displacement under the plane+parallax decomposition. Section 3 outlines the major steps of our algorithm. The benefits of applying the algorithm to multiple frames (as opposed to two frames) are discussed in Section 4. Section 5 shows some results of applying the algorithm to real data. Section 6 concludes the paper.

2   The Plane+Parallax Decomposition

The induced 2D image motion of a 3D scene point between two images can be decomposed into two components [9, 7, 10, 11, 13, 14, 8, 2]: (i) the image motion of a reference planar surface Π (i.e., a homography), and (ii) the residual image motion, known as "planar parallax". This decomposition is described below.

To set the stage for the algorithm described in this paper, we begin with the derivation of the plane+parallax motion equations shown in [10]. Let $p = (x, y, 1)$ denote the image location (in homogeneous coordinates) of a point in one view (called the "reference view"), and let $p' = (x', y', 1)$ be its coordinates in another view. Let $\mathbf{B}$ denote the homography of the plane Π between the two views. Let $\mathbf{B}^{-1}$ denote its inverse homography, and $\mathbf{B}^{-1}{}_3$ be the third row of B^{-1}. Let $p_w = (x_w, y_w, 1) = \frac{\mathbf{B}^{-1}p'}{\mathbf{B}^{-1}{}_3p'}$, namely, when the second image is warped towards the first image using the inverse homography B^{-1}, the point p' will move to the point p_w in the *warped image*. For 3D points on the plane Π, $p_w = p$, while for 3D points which are not on the plane, $p_w \neq p$. It was shown in [10] that[1]:

$$p' - p = (p' - p_w) + (p_w - p)$$

and

$$p_w - p = -\gamma(t_3 p_w - t) \tag{1}$$

where $\gamma = H/Z$ represents the 3D structure of the point p, where H is the perpendicular distance (or "height") of the point from the reference plane Π, and Z is its depth with respect to the reference camera. All *unknown* calibration parameters are folded into the terms in the parenthesis, where t denotes the epipole in projective coordinates and t_3 denotes its third component: $t = (t_1, t_2, t_3)$.

In its current form, the above expression cannot be directly used for estimating the unknown correspondence p_w for a given pixel p in the reference image, since p_w appears on both sides of the expression. However, p_w can be eliminated from the right hand side of the expression, to obtain the following expression:

$$p_w - p = -\frac{\gamma}{1 + \gamma t_3}(t_3 p - t). \tag{2}$$

This last expression will be used in our direct estimation algorithm.

3   Multi-frame Parallax Estimation

Let $\{\Phi_j\}_{j=0}^l$ be $l+1$ images of a rigid scene, taken using cameras with unknown calibration parameters. Without loss of generality, we choose Φ_0 as a reference

---

[1] The notation we use here is slightly different than the one used in [10]. The change to projective notation is used to unify the two separate expressions provided in [10], one for the case of a finite epipole, and the other for the case of an infinite epipole.

frame. (In practice, this is usually the middle frame of the sequence). Let Π be a plane in the scene that is visible in all l images (the "reference plane"). Using a technique similar to [1, 6], we estimate the image motion (homography) of Π between the reference frame Φ_0 and each of the other frames Φ_j $(j = 1, \ldots, l$). Warping the images by those homographies $\{\mathbf{B}_j\}_{j=1}^{l}$ yields a new sequence of l images, $\{I_j\}_{j=1}^{l}$, where the image of Π is aligned across all frames. Also, for the sake of notational simplicity, let us rename the reference image to be I, i.e., $I = \Phi_0$. The only residual image motion between reference frame I and the warped images, $\{I_j\}_{j=1}^{l}$, is the residual planar-parallax displacement $\boldsymbol{p}_w^j - \boldsymbol{p}$ $(j = 1..l)$ due to 3D scene points that are *not* located on the reference plane Π. This residual planar parallax motion is what remains to be estimated.

Let $\boldsymbol{u}^j = (u^j, v^j)$ denote the first two coordinates of $\boldsymbol{p}_w^j - \boldsymbol{p}$ (the third coordinate is 0). From Eq. (2) we know that the residual parallax is:

$$\boldsymbol{u}^j = \begin{bmatrix} u^j \\ v^j \end{bmatrix} = -\frac{\gamma}{1 + \gamma t_3^j} \begin{bmatrix} t_3^j x - t_1^j \\ t_3^j y - t_2^j \end{bmatrix}, \tag{3}$$

where the superscripts j denote the parameters associated with the jth frame.

In the *two*-frame case, one can define $\alpha = \frac{\gamma}{1+\gamma t_3}$, and then the problem posed in Eq. (3) becomes a bilinear problem in α and in $\boldsymbol{t} = (t_1, t_2, t_3)$. This can be solved using a standard iterative method. Once α and $\boldsymbol{t}$ are known, γ can be recovered. A similar approach was used in [11] for shape recovery from two-frames. However, this approach does not extend to multiple (> 2) frames, because α is *not* a shape invariant (as it depends on t_3), and hence varies from frame to frame. In contrast, γ *is* a shape invariant, which is shared by all image frames. Our multi-frame process directly recovers γ from *multi-frame* brightness quantities.

The basic idea behind our direct estimation algorithm is that rather than estimating l separate $\boldsymbol{u}^j$ vectors (corresponding to each frame) for each pixel, we can simply estimate a single γ (the shape parameter), which for a particular pixel, is common over all the frames, and a single $\boldsymbol{t}^j = (t_1, t_2, t_3)$ which for each frame I_j is common to all image pixels. There are two advantages in doing this:

1. For n pixels over l frames we reduce the number of unknowns from $2nl$ to $n + 3l$.
2. More importantly, the recovered flow vector is constrained to satisfy the epipolar structure implicitly captured in Eq. (2). This can be expected to significantly improve the quality of the recovered parallax flow vectors.

Our direct estimation algorithm follows the same computational framework outlined in [1] for the *quasi-parametric* class of models. The basic components of this framework are: (i) pyramid construction, (ii) iterative estimation of global (motion) and local (structure) parameters, and (iii) coarse-to-fine refinement. The overall control loop of our algorithm is therefore as follows:

1. Construct pyramids from each of the images I_j and the reference frame I.
2. Initialize the structure parameter γ for each pixel, and motion parameter t^j for each frame (usually we start with $\gamma = 0$ for all pixels, and $t^j = (0, 0, 1)^T$ for all frames).
3. Starting with the coarsest pyramid level, at each level, refine the structure and motion using the method outlined in Section 3.1.
4. Repeat this step several times (usually about 4 or 5 times per level).
5. Project the final value of the structure parameter to the next finer pyramid level. Propagate the motion parameters also to the next level. Use these as initial estimates for processing the next level.
6. The final output is the structure and the motion parameters at the finest pyramid level (which corresponds to the resolution of the input images) and the residual parallax flow field synthesized from these.

Of the various steps outline above, the pyramid construction and the projection of parameters are common to many techniques for motion estimation (e.g., see [1]), hence we omit the description of these steps. On the other hand, the refinement step is specific to our current problem. This is described next.

3.1   The Estimation Process

The inner loop of the estimation process involves refining the current values of the structure parameters γ (one per pixel) and the motion parameters t^j (3 parameters per frame). Let us denote the "true" (but unknown) values of these parameters by $\gamma(x, y)$ (at location (x, y) in the reference frame) and t^j. Let $u^j(x, y) = (u^j, v^j)$ denote the corresponding unknown true parallax flow vector. Let γ_c, t_c^j, u_c^j denote the *current estimates* of these quantities. Let $\delta\gamma = \gamma - \gamma_c$, $\delta t^j = (\delta t_1^j, \delta t_2^j, \delta t_3^j) = t^j - t_c^j$, and $\delta u^j = (\delta u^j, \delta v^j) = u^j - u_c^j$. These δ quantities are the refinements that are estimated during each iteration.

Assuming brightness constancy (namely, that corresponding image points across all frames have a similar brightness value)[2], we have:

$$I(x, y) \approx I_j(x^j, y^j) = I_j(x + u^j, y + v^j) = I_j(x + u_c^j + \delta u^j, y + v_c^j + \delta v^j)$$

For small δu^j we make a further approximation:

$$I(x - \delta u^j, y - \delta v^j) \approx I_j(x + u_c^j, y + v_c^j).$$

Expanding I to its first order Taylor series around (x, y) :

$$I(x - \delta u^j, y - \delta v^j) \approx I(x, y) - I_x \delta u^j - I_y \delta v^j$$

---

[2] Note that over multiple frames the brightness will change somewhat, at least due to global illumination variation. We can handle this by using the Laplacian pyramid (as opposed to the Gaussian pyramid), or otherwise pre-filtering the images (e.g., normalize to remove global mean and contrast changes), and applying the brightness constraint to the filtered images.

where I_x, I_y denote the image intensity derivatives for the reference image (at pixel location (x, y)). From here we get the brightness constraint equation:

$$I_j(x + u_c^j, y + v_c^j) \approx I(x, y) - I_x \delta u^j - I_y \delta v^j$$

Or:

$$I_j(x + u_c^j, y + v_c^j) - I(x, y) + I_x \delta u^j + I_y \delta v^j \approx 0$$

Substituting $\delta u^j = u^j - u_c^j$ yields:

$$I_j(x + u_c^j, y + v_c^j) - I(x, y) + I_x(u^j - u_c^j) + I_y(v^j - v_c^j) \approx 0$$

Or, more compactly:

$$I_j^\tau(x, y) + I_x u^j + I_y v^j \approx 0 \tag{4}$$

where

$$I_j^\tau(x, y) \stackrel{\text{def}}{=} I_j(x + u_c^j, y + v_c^j) - I(x, y) - I_x u_c^j - I_y v_c^j$$

If we now substitute the expression for the local parallax flow vector u^j given in Eq. (3), we obtain the following equation that relates the structure and motion parameters directly to image brightness information:

$$I_j^\tau(x, y) + \frac{\gamma(x,y)}{1+\gamma(x,y)t_3^j}\left(I_x(t_3^j x - t_1^j) + I_y(t_3^j y - t_2^j)\right) \approx 0 \tag{5}$$

We refer to the above equation as the "epipolar brightness constraint".

Each pixel and each frame contributes one such equation, where the unknowns are: the relative scene structure $\gamma = \gamma(x, y)$ for each pixel (x, y), and the epipoles t^j for each frame $(j = 1, 2, \ldots, l)$. Those unknowns are computed in two phases. In the first phase, the "Local Phase", the relative scene structure, γ, is estimated separately for each pixel via least squares minimization over multiple frames simultaneously. This is followed by the "Global Phase", where all the epipoles t^j are estimated between the reference frame and each of the other frames, using least squares minimization over all pixels. These two phases are described in more detail below.

Local Phase In the local phase we assume all the epipoles are given (e.g., from the previous iteration), and we estimate the unknown scene structure γ from all the images. γ is a local quantity, but is common to all the images at a point. When the epipoles are known (e.g., from the previous iteration), each frame I_j provides one constraint of Eq. (5) on γ. Therefore, theoretically, there is sufficient geometric information for solving for γ. However, for increased numerical stability, we locally assume each γ is constant over a small window around each pixel in the reference frame. In our experiments we used a 5×5 window. For each pixel (x, y), we use the error function:

$$Err(\gamma) \stackrel{\text{def}}{=} \sum_j \sum_{(\tilde{x},\tilde{y}) \in \text{Win}(x,y)} \left(\tilde{I}_j^\tau(1 + \gamma t_3^j) + \gamma\left(\tilde{I}_x(t_3^j \tilde{x} - t_1^j) + \tilde{I}_y(t_3^j \tilde{y} - t_2^j)\right)\right)^2 \tag{6}$$

where $\gamma = \gamma(x, y)$, $\tilde{I}_j^{\tau} = I_j^{\tau}(\tilde{x}, \tilde{y})$, $\tilde{I}_x = I_x(\tilde{x}, \tilde{y})$, $\tilde{I}_y = I_y(\tilde{x}, \tilde{y})$, and $\text{Win}(x, y)$ is a 5×5 window around (x, y). Differentiating $Err(\gamma)$ with respect to γ and equating it to zero yields a single linear equation that can be solved to estimate $\gamma(x, y)$. The error term $Err(\gamma)$ was obtained by multiplying Eq. (5) by the denominator $(1 + \gamma t_3^j)$ to yield a <u>linear</u> expression in γ. Note that without multiplying by the denominator, the local estimation process (after differentiation) would require solving a polynomial equation in γ whose order increases with l (the number of frames). Minimizing $Err(\gamma)$ is in practice equivalent to applying *weighted* least squares minimization on the collection of original Eqs. (5), with weights equal to the denominators. We could apply *normalization* weights $\frac{1}{1 + \gamma_c t_3^j}$ (where γ_c is the estimate of the shape at pixel (x, y) from the previous iteration) to the linearized expression, in order to assure minimization of meaningful quantities (as is done in [18]), but in practice, for the examples we used, we found it was not necessary to do so during the local phase. However, such a normalization weight was important during the global phase (see below).

Global Phase In the global phase we assume the structure γ is given (e.g., from previous iteration), and we estimate for each image I_j the position of its epipole t^j with respect to the reference frame. We estimate the set of epipoles $\{t^j\}$ by minimizing the following error with respect each of the epipoles:

$$Err(t^j) \stackrel{\text{def}}{=} \sum_{(x,y)} \left(W_j(x, y) \left[I_j^{\tau}(1 + \gamma t_3^j) + \gamma \left(I_x(t_3^j x - t_1^j) + I_y(t_3^j y - t_2^j) \right) \right] \right)^2$$

(7)

where $I_x = I_x(x, y), I_y = I_y(x, y), I_j^{\tau} = I_j^{\tau}(x, y), \gamma = \gamma(x, y)$. Note that, when $\gamma(x, y)$ are fixed, this minimization problem decouples into a set of separate individual minimization problems, each a function of one epipole t^j for the jth frame. The inside portion of this error term is similar to the one we used above for the local phase, with the addition of a scalar weight $W_j(x, y)$. The scalar weight is used to serve two purposes. First, if Eq. (7) did not contain the weights $W_j(x, y)$, it would be equivalent to a *weighted* least squares minimization of Eq. (5), with weights equal to the denominators $(1 + \gamma(x, y)t_3^j)$. While this provides a convenient linear expression in the unknown t^j, these weights are not physically meaningful, and tend to skew the estimate of the recovered epipole. Therefore, in a fashion similar to [18], we choose the weights $W_j(x, y)$ to be $(1 + \gamma(x, y)t_{3,c}^j)^{-1}$, where the γ is the updated estimate from the local phase, whereas the $t_{3,c}^j$ is based on the current estimate of t^j (from the previous iteration).

The scalar weight also provides us an easy way to introduce additional robustness to the estimation process in order to reduce the contribution of pixels that are potentially outliers. For example, we can use weights based on residual misalignment of the kind used in [6].

4   Multi-frame vs. Two-Frame Estimation

The algorithm described in Section 3 extends the plane+parallax estimation
to multiple frames. The most obvious benefit of multi-frame processing is the
improved signal-to-noise performance that is obtained due to having a larger
set of independent samples. However, there are two additional benefits to multi-
frame estimation: (i) overcoming the *aperture problem*, from which the two-frame
estimation often suffers, and (ii) resolving the singularity of shape recovery in
the vicinity of the epipole (we refer to this as the *epipole singularity*).

4.1   Eliminating the Aperture Problem

When only two images are used as in [11, 13], there exists only one epipole. The
residual parallax lies along epipolar lines (centered at the epipole, see Eq. (3)).
The epipolar field provides one line constraint on each parallax displacement,
and the Brightness Constancy constraint forms another line constraint (Eq. (4)).
When those lines are not parallel, their intersection uniquely defines the parallax
displacement. However, if the image gradient at an image point is parallel to the
epipolar line passing through that point, then its parallax displacement (and
hence its structure) can not be uniquely determined. However, when multiple
images with multiple epipoles are used, then this ambiguity is resolved, because
the image gradient at a point can be parallel to at most one of the epipolar lines
associated with it. This observation was also made by [4, 15].

To demonstrate this, we used a sequence composed of 9 images (105×105
pixels) of 4 squares (30×30 pixels) moving over a stationary textured background
(which plays the role of the aligned reference plane). The 4 squares have the same
motion: first they were all shifted to the right (one pixel per frame) to generate
the first 5 images, and then they were all shifted down (one pixel per frame) to
generate the next 4 images. The width of the stripes on the squares is 5 pixels.
A sample frame is shown in Fig. 1.a (the fifth frame).

The epipoles that correspond to this motion are at infinity, the horizontal
motion has an epipole at $(\infty, 52.5]$, and the vertical motion has an epipole at
$[52.5, \infty)$. The texture on the squares was selected so that the spatial gradients of
one square are parallel to the direction of the horizontal motion, another square
has spatial gradients parallel to the direction of the vertical motion, and the two
other squares have spatial gradients in multiple directions. We have tested the
algorithm on three cases: (i) pure vertical motion, (ii) pure horizontal motion,
and (iii) mixed motions.

Fig. 1.b is a typical depth map that results from applying the algorithm to
sequences with purely vertical motion. (Dark grey corresponds to the reference
plane, and light grey corresponds to elevated scene parts, i.e., the squares). The
structure for the square with vertical bars is not estimated well as expected,
because the epipolar constraints are parallel to those bars. This is true even
when the algorithm is applied to multiple frames with the same epipole.

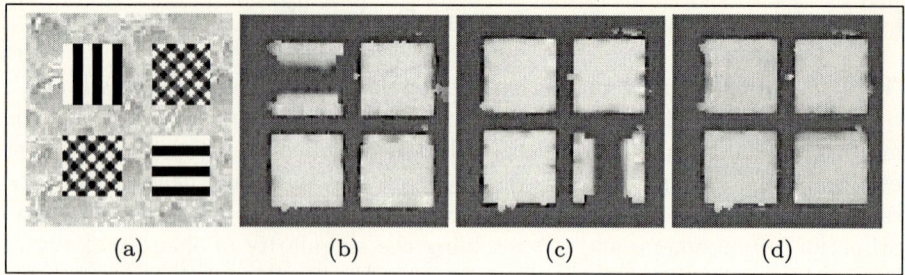

Fig. 1. Resolving aperture problem: (a) A sample image, (b) Shape recovery for pure vertical motion. Ambiguity along vertical bars, (c) Shape recovery for pure horizontal motion. Ambiguity along horizontal bars, (d) Shape recovery for a sequence with mixed motions. No ambiguity.

Fig. 1.c is a typical depth map that results from applying the algorithm to sequences with purely horizontal motion. Note that the structure for the square with horizontal bars is not estimated well.

Fig. 1.d is a typical depth map that results from applying the algorithm to multiple images with mixed motions (i.e., more than one distinct epipole). Note that now the shape recovery does not suffer from the aperture problem.

4.2   Epipole Singularity

From the planar parallax Eq. (3), it is clear that the structure γ cannot be determined at the epipole, because at the epipole: $t_3^j x - t_1^j = 0$ and $t_3^j y - t_2^j = 0$. For the same reason, the recovered structure at the *vicinity* of the epipole is highly sensitive to noise and unreliable. However, when there are multiple epipoles, this ambiguity disappears. The singularity at one epipole is resolved by information from another epipole.

To test this behavior, we compared the results for the case with only one epipole (i.e., two-frames) to cases with multiple epipoles at different locations. Results are shown in Fig. 2. The sequence that we used was composed of images of a square that is elevated from a reference plane and the simulated motion (after plane alignment) was a looming motion (i.e., forward motion). Fig. 2.a,b,c show three sample images from the sequence. Fig. 2.d shows singularity around the epipole in the two-frame case. Figs. 2.e,h,i,j show that the singularity at the epipoles is *eliminated* when there is more than one epipole. Using more images also increases the signal to noise ratio and further improves the shape reconstruction.

5   Real World Examples

This section provides experimental results of applying our algorithm to real world sequences. Fig. 3 shows an example of shape recovery from an indoor sequence

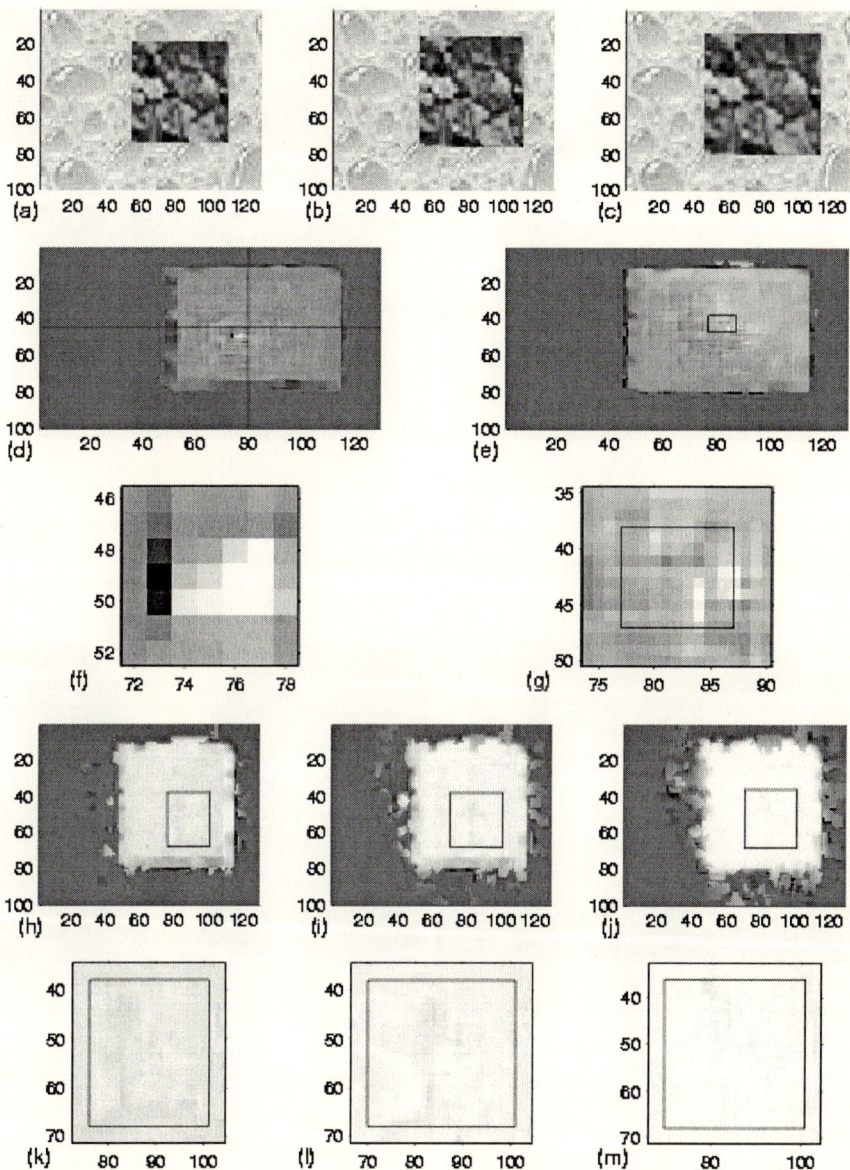

Fig. 2. Resolving epipole singularity in case of multiple epipoles. (a-c) sample images
from a 9-frame sequence with multiple epipoles, (d,f) shape recovery using 2 images
(epipole singularity exist in this case), (e,g) using 3 images with 2 different epipoles,
(h,k) using 5 images with multiple epipoles, (i,l) using 7 images with multiple epipoles,
(j,m) using 9 images with multiple epipoles. Note that epipole singularity disappears
once multiple epipoles exist. (f,g,k,l,m) show an enlarge view of the depth image at the
vicinity of the epipoles. The box shows the region where the epipoles are. For visibility
purposes, different images are shown at different scales. For reference, coordinate rulers
are attached to each image.

Fig. 3. Blocks sequence. (a) one frame from the sequence. (b) The recovered shape (relative to the carpet). Brighter values correspond to taller points.

Fig. 4. Flower-garden sequence. (a) one frame from the sequence. (b) The recovered shape (relative to the facade of the house). Brighter values correspond to points farther from the house.

(the "block" sequence from [11]). The reference plane is the carpet. Fig. 3.a shows one frame from the sequence. Fig. 3.b shows the recovered structure. Brighter grey levels correspond to taller points relative to the carpet. Note the fine structure of the toys on the carpet.

Fig. 4 shows an example of shape recovery for a sequence of five frames (part of the flower garden sequence). The reference plane is the house. Fig. 4.a shows the reference frame from the sequence. Fig. 4.b shows the recovered structure. Note the gradual change of depth in the field.

Fig. 5. Stairs sequence. (a) one frame from the sequence. (b) The recovered shape (relative to the ground surface just in front of the building). Brighter values correspond to points above the ground surface, while darker values correspond to points below the ground surface.

Fig. 5 shows an example of shape recovery for a sequence of 5 frames. The reference plane is the flat region in front of the building. Fig. 5.a show one frame from the sequence. Fig. 5.b shows the recovered structure. The brightness reflects the magnitude of the structure parameter γ (brighter values correspond to scene points above the reference plane and darker values correspond to scene points below the reference plane). Note the fine structure of the stairs and the lamp-pole. The shape of the building wall is not fully recovered because of lack of texture in that region.

6   Conclusion

We presented an algorithm for estimating dense planar-parallax displacements from multiple uncalibrated views. The image displacements, the 3D structure, and the camera epipoles, are estimated *directly* from image brightness variations across multiple frames. This algorithm extends the two-frames plane+parallax estimation algorithm of [11, 13] to multiple frames. The current algorithm relies on prior plane alignment. A natural extension of this algorithm would be to fold the homography estimation into the simultaneous estimation of image displacements, scene structure, and camera motion (as was done by [11] for *two* frames).

References

1. Bergen J. R., Anandan P., Hanna K. J., Hingorani R., *Hierarchical Model-Based Motion Estimation*, In European Conference on Computer Vision, pages 237-252, Santa Margarita Ligure, May 1992.
2. Criminisi C., Reid I., Zisserman Z., *Duality, Rigidity, and Planar Parallax*, In European Conference on Computer Vision, vol.II, 1998.
3. Hanna K. J., *Direct Multi-Resolution Estimation of Ego-Motion and Structure From Motion*, Workshop on Visual Motion, pp. 156-162, Princeton, NJ, Oct. 1991.
4. Hanna K. J. and Okamoto N. E., *Combining Stereo and Motion for Direct Estimation of Scene Structure*, International Conference on Computer Vision, 357-365, 1993.
5. Hartley R. I., *In Defense of the Eight-Point Algorithm*, In IEEE Trans. on Pattern Analysis and Machine Intelligence, 19(6):580-593, June 1997.
6. Irani M., Rousso B., and Peleg S., *Computing Occluding and Transparent Motions*, In International Journal of Computer Vision 12(1):5-16, Jan. 1994. (also in ECCV-92).
7. Irani M. and Anandan P., *Parallax Geometry of Pairs of Points for 3D Scene Analysis*, In European Conference on Computer Vision, A, pages 17-30, Cambridge, UK, April 1996.
8. Irani M., Rousso B. and peleg P., *Recovery of Ego-Motion Using Region Alignment*, In IEEE Trans. on Pattern Analysis and Machine Intelligence, 19(3), pp.268-272, March 1997. (also in CVPR-94).
9. Irani M., Anandan P., Weinshall D., *From Reference Frames to Reference Planes: Multi-View Parallax Geometry and Applications*, In European Conference on Computer Vision, vol.II, pp.829-845, 1998.
10. Irani M. and P. Anandan, *A Unified Approach to Moving Object Detection in 2D and 3D Scenes*, In IEEE Trans. on Pattern Analysis and Machine Intelligence, 20(6), pp. 577-589, June 1998.
11. Kumar R., Anandan P. and Hanna K., *Direct Recovery of shape From Multiple Views: a Parallax Based Approach*, International Conference on Pattern Recognition pp. 685-688, Oct. 1994.
12. Longuet-Higgins H.C., and Prazdny K., *The Interpretation of a Moving Retinal Image*, Proceedings of the Royal Society of London B, 208:385–397, 1980.
13. Sawhney H. S., *3D Geometry From Planar Parallax*, In IEEE Conference on Computer Vision and Pattern Recognition, pages 929-934, June 1994.
14. Shashua A. and Navab N., *Relative affine Structure: Theory and Application to 3D Reconstruction From Perspective Views*, In IEEE Conference on Computer Vision and Pattern Recognition, pages 483-489, 1994.
15. Stein G. P. and Shashua A., *Model-based Brightness constraints: On Direct Estimation of Structure and Motion*, In IEEE Conference on Computer Vision and Pattern Recognition, pages 400-406, 1997.
16. Szeliski R. and Kang S.B., *Direct Methods for Visual Scene Reconstruction*, In Workshop on Representations of Visual Scenes, 1995.
17. Torr P.H.S., *Geometric motion segmentation and model selection*, Proceedings of The Royal Society of London A, 356:1321–1340, 1998.
18. Zhang Z., *Determining the Epipolar Geometry and its Uncertainty: A Review*, IJCV, 27(2):161-195, 1997.

Discussion

Rick Szeliski: How do you initialize? – You have a sort of back and forth, two phase method for solving a bilinear problem. But when you have your first plane stabilized in a set of images, how do you guess the initial epipole or depth-map?

Michal Irani: We start with a zero depth map, and for the epipoles we try five different positions, one in the centre and one in each of the four quadrants. This does provide a good enough initialization — even in the case where the epipoles are at infinity we converge to the correct solution.

Bill Triggs: Just a comment on a comment you made about linearized methods being stabler than fully nonlinear ones. Assuming that the nonlinear method optimizes the statistically correct error model, its stability is by definition the true stability of the problem. If a linear method appears stabler it must be because it's either estimating a simplified model, or biased. So linear methods are not intrinsically stabler, they're just more often allowed to give wrong results.

Michal Irani: Well, linear algorithms are much simpler, and when their approximations are valid, they *don't* give the wrong results. So that's exactly the question — when *are* they valid, because when they are you would like to use them. The case I was talking about — the intermediate approximation where the global component of the homography is exact and only the local component is approximated — turns out to be valid in many, many cases. That's what we're checking right now. It has the potential to produce very simple algorithms without making any severe assumptions, whereas the original Longuet-Higgins approximation was very restrictive.

P. Anandan: I want to make a comment on Bill's comment. I think you see a similar thing about nonlinear methods being unstable in the work on encoding epipolar geometry. I recall Adiv's work, where at each iteration you normalize by the current depth to make the flow look more like the exact equation. So in some sense, by using weights based on the current estimate, you reduce the error introduced by the linear approximation during the iterative process. I'm not sure whether linear methods with varying weights should count as linear or nonlinear for stability. The same issues come up in correspondence based methods for structure-from-motion as well.

Michal Irani: I'm not sure whether this is what you meant Anandan, but generally when you solve a nonlinear iteration step you make some approximations that may not be correct. It's better to start with valid approximations than to start with bad ones. So, when you're assuming linear models, at least you know which approximations you're making.

Generalized Voxel Coloring

W. Bruce Culbertson[1], Thomas Malzbender[1], and Greg Slabaugh[2]

[1] Hewlett-Packard Laboratories
1501 Page Mill Road, Palo Alto, CA 94306 USA
{bruce_culbertson, tom_malzbender}@hp.com

[2] Georgia Institute of Technology
slabaugh@ece.gatech.edu

Abstract. Image-based reconstruction from randomly scattered views is a challenging problem. We present a new algorithm that extends Seitz and Dyer's Voxel Coloring algorithm. Unlike their algorithm, ours can use images from arbitrary camera locations. The key problem in this class of algorithms is that of identifying the images from which a voxel is visible. Unlike Kutulakos and Seitz's Space Carving technique, our algorithm solves this problem exactly and the resulting reconstructions yield better results in our application, which is synthesizing new views. One variation of our algorithm minimizes color consistency comparisons; another uses less memory and can be accelerated with graphics hardware. We present efficiency measurements and, for comparison, we present images synthesized using our algorithm and Space Carving.

1 Introduction

We present a new algorithm for volumetric scene reconstruction. Specifically, given a handful of images of a scene taken from arbitrary but known locations, the algorithm builds a 3D model of the scene that is consistent with the input images. We call the algorithm Generalized Voxel Coloring or GVC. Like two earlier solutions to the same problem, Voxel Coloring [1] and Space Carving [2], our algorithm uses voxels to model the scene and exploits the fact that surface points in a scene, and voxels that represent them, project to consistent colors in the input images. Although Voxel Coloring and Space Carving are particularly successful solutions to the scene reconstruction problem, our algorithm has advantages over each of them. Unlike Voxel Coloring, GVC allows input cameras to be placed at arbitrary locations in and around the scene. This is why we call it *Generalized* Voxel Coloring. When checking the color consistency of a voxel, GVC uses the entire set of images from which the voxel is visible. Space Carving usually uses only a subset of those images. Using full visibility during reconstruction yields better results in our application, which is synthesizing new views.

New-view synthesis, a problem in image-based rendering, aims to produce new views of a scene, given a handful of existing images. Conventional computer graphics typically creates new views by projecting a manually generated 3D model of the scene. Image-based rendering has attracted considerable interest recently because images are so much easier to acquire than 3D models. We solve the new-view

B. Triggs, A. Zisserman, R. Szeliski (Eds.): Vision Algorithms'99, LNCS 1883, pp. 100-115, 2000.

synthesis problem by first using GVC to create a model of the scene and then projecting the model to the desired viewpoint.

We first describe earlier solutions to the new-view synthesis and volumetric reconstruction problems. We compare the merits of those solutions to our own. Next, we discuss GVC in detail. We have implemented two versions of GVC. One uses *layered depth images* (LDIs) to eliminate unnecessary color consistency comparisons. The other version makes more efficient use of memory. Next, we present our experimental results. We compare our two implementations with Space Carving in terms of computational efficiency and quality of synthesized images. Finally, we describe our future work.

2   Related Work

View Morphing [3] and Light Fields [4] are solutions to the new-view synthesis problem that do not create a 3D model as an intermediate step. View Morphing is one of the simplest solutions to the problem. Given two images of a scene, it uses interpolation to create a new image intermediate in viewpoint between the input images. Because View Morphing uses no 3D information about the scene, it cannot in general render images that are strictly correct, although the results often look convincing. Most obviously, the algorithm has limited means to correctly render objects in the scene that occlude one another.

Lumigraph [5] and Light Field techniques use a sampling of the light radiated in every direction from every point on the surface of a volume. In theory, such a collection of data can produce nearly perfect new views. In practice, however, the amount of input data required to synthesize high quality images is far greater than what we use with GVC and is impractical to capture and store. Concentric Mosaics [6] is a similar technique that makes the sampling and storage requirements more practical by restricting the range over which new views may be synthesized. These methods have an advantage over nearly all competing approaches: they treat view-dependent effects, like refraction and specular reflections, correctly.

Stereo techniques [7, 8] find points in two or more input images that correspond to the same point in the scene. They then use knowledge of the camera locations and triangulation to determine the depth of the scene point. Unfortunately, stereo is difficult to apply to images taken from arbitrary viewpoints. If the input viewpoints are far apart, then corresponding image points are hard to find automatically. On the other hand, if the viewpoints are close together, then small measurement errors result in large errors in the calculated depths. Furthermore, stereo naturally produces a 2D depth map and integrating many such maps into a true 3D model is a challenging problem [9].

Roy and Cox [10] and Szeliski and Golland [11] have developed variations of stereo that, in one respect, resemble voxel coloring: they project discrete 3D grid points into an arbitrary number of images to collect correlation or color variance statistics. Roy and Cox impose a smoothness constraint both along and across epipolar lines, which produces better reconstructions compared with conventional stereo. A major shortcoming of their algorithm is that it does not model occlusion.

Szeliski and Golland's algorithm models occlusion but not as generally as GVC. Specifically, their scheme for finding an initial set of occluding gridpoints is unlikely to work when the cameras surround the scene. However, the authors are ambitious in recovering fractional opacity and correct color for voxels whose projections in the images span occlusion boundaries—a goal we have not attempted.

Faugeras and Keriven [12] have produced impressive reconstructions by applying variational methods within a level set formulation. Surfaces, initially larger than the scenes, are refined using PDEs to successively better approximations of the scenes. Like GVC, their method can employ arbitrary numbers of images, account for occlusion correctly, and deduce arbirary topologies. It is not clear under what conditions their method converges or whether it can be easily extended to use color images. Neither Szeliski and Golland nor Faugeras and Keriven have provided runtime and memory statistics so it is not clear if their methods are practical for reconstructing large scenes.

Voxel Coloring, Space Carving, and GVC all exploit the fact that points on Lambertian surfaces are *color-consistent*—they project onto similar colors in all the images from which they are visible. These methods start with an arbitrary number of calibrated[1] images of the scene and a set of voxels that is a superset of the scene. Each voxel is projected into the images from which it is visible. If the voxel projects onto inconsistent colors in several images, it must not be on a surface and, so, it is *carved*—that is, declared to be transparent. Otherwise, the voxel is *colored, i.e.,* declared to be opaque and assigned the color of its projections. These algorithms stop when all the opaque voxels project into consistent colors in the images. Because the final set of opaque voxels is color-consistent, it is a good model of the scene.

Voxel Coloring, Space Carving and GVC all differ in the way they determine *visibility*, the knowledge of which voxels are visible from which pixels in the images. A voxel fails to be visible from an image if it projects outside the image or it is blocked by other voxels that are currently considered to be opaque. When the opacity of a voxel changes, the visibility of other voxels potentially changes, so an efficient means is needed to update the visibility.

Voxel Coloring puts constraints on the camera locations to simplify the visibility computation. It requires the cameras be placed in such a way that the voxels can be visited, on a single scan, in front-to-back order relative to every camera. Typically, this condition is met by placing all the cameras on one side of the scene and scanning voxels in planes that are successively further from the cameras. Thus, the transparency of all voxels that might occlude a given voxel is determined before the given voxel is checked for color consistency. Although it simplifies the visibility computation, the restriction on camera locations is a significant limitation. For example, the cameras cannot surround the scene, so some surfaces will not be visible in any image and hence cannot be reconstructed.

Space Carving and GVC remove Voxel Coloring's restriction on camera locations. These are among the few reconstruction algorithms for which arbitrarily and widely dispersed image viewpoints are not a hindrance. With the cameras placed arbitrarily, no single scan of the voxels, regardless of its order, will enable each voxel's visibility in the final model (and hence its color consistency) to be computed correctly.

---

[1] We define an image to be *calibrated* if, given any point in the 3D scene, we know where it projects in the image. However, Saito and Kanade [13] have shown a weaker form of calibration can also be used.

Several key insights of Kutulakos and Seitz enable algorithms to be designed that evaluate the consistency of voxels multiple times during carving, using changing and incomplete visibility information, and yet yield a color-consistent reconstruction at the end. Space Carving and GVC initially consider all voxels to be opaque, *i.e.* uncarved, and only change opaque voxels to transparent, never the reverse. Consequently, as some voxels are carved, the remaining uncarved voxels can only become more visible from the images. In particular, if S is the set of pixels that have an unoccluded view of an uncarved voxel at one point in time and if S^* is the set of such pixels at a later point in time, then $S \subseteq S^*$. Kutulakos and Seitz assume a color consistency function will be used that is *monotonic*, meaning for any two sets of pixels S and S^* with $S \subseteq S^*$, if S is inconsistent, then S^* is inconsistent also. This seems intuitively reasonable since a set of pixels with dissimilar color will continue to be dissimilar if more pixels are added to the set. Given that the visibility of a voxel only increases as the algorithm runs and the consistency function is monotonic, it follows that carving is *conservative*—no voxel will ever be carved if it would be color-consistent in the final model.

Space Carving scans voxels for color consistency similarly to Voxel Coloring, evaluating a plane of voxels at a time. It forces the scans to be front-to-back, relative to the cameras, by using only images whose cameras are currently behind the moving plane. Thus, when a voxel is evaluated, the transparency is already known of other voxels that might occlude it from the cameras currently being used. Unlike Voxel Coloring, Space Carving uses multiple scans, typically along the positive and negative directions of each of the three axes. Because carving is conservative, the set of uncarved voxels is a shrinking superset of the desired color-consistent model as the algorithm runs.

While Space Carving never carves voxels it shouldn't, it is likely to produce a model that includes some color-*in*consistent voxels. During scanning, cameras that are ahead of the moving plane are not used for consistency checking, even when the voxels being checked are visible from those cameras. Hence, the color consistency of a voxel is, in general, never checked over the entire set of images from which it is visible. In contrast, every voxel in the final model constructed by GVC is guaranteed to be color consistent over the entire set of images from which it is visible. We find the models that GVC produces, using full visibility, project to better new views.

3 Generalized Voxel Coloring

We have developed two variants of our Generalized Voxel Coloring algorithm. GVC-LDI is an enhancement of GVC, the basic algorithm. The carving of one voxel potentially changes the visibility of other voxels. When an uncarved voxel's visibility changes, its color consistency should be reevaluated and it, too, should be carved if it is then found to be inconsistent. GVC-LDI uses *layered depth images* (LDIs) [14, 15] to determine exactly which voxels have their visibility changed when another voxel is carved and thus can reevaluate exactly the right voxels. In the same situation, GVC does not know which voxels need to be reevaluated and so reevaluates all voxels in the current model. Therefore, GVC-LDI performs significantly fewer color-

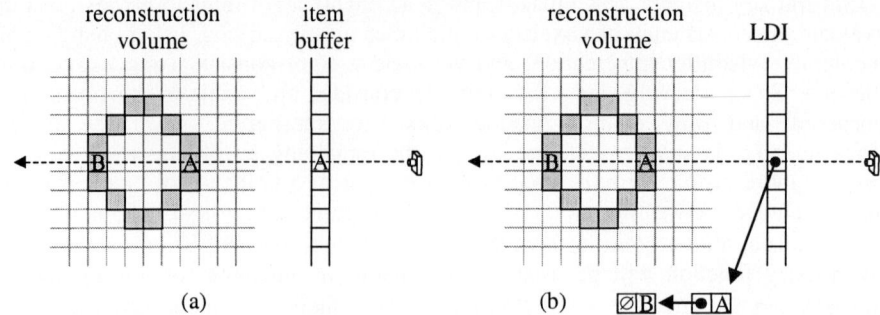

Fig. 1. The data structures used compute visibility. An item buffer *(a)* is used by GVC and records the ID of the surface voxel visible from each pixel in an image. A layered depth image (LDI) *(b)* is used by GVC-LDI and records all surface voxels that project onto each pixel.

consistency evaluations than GVC during a reconstruction. However, GVC uses considerably less memory than GVC-LDI.

Like Space Carving, both GVC and GVC-LDI initially assume all voxels are opaque, *i.e.* uncarved. They carve inconsistent voxels until all those that remain project into consistent colors in the images from which they are visible.

3.1   The Basic GVC Algorithm

GVC determines visibility as follows. First, every voxel is assigned a unique ID. Then, an *item buffer* [16] is constructed for each image. An item buffer, shown in figure 1a, contains a voxel ID for every pixel in the corresponding image. While the item buffer is being computed, a distance is also stored for every pixel. A voxel V is *rendered* to the item buffer as follows. Scan conversion is used to find all the pixels that V projects onto. If the distance from the camera to V is less than the distance stored for the pixel, then the pixel's stored distance and voxel ID are over-written with those of V. Thus, after a set of voxels have been rendered, each pixel will contain the ID of the closest voxel that projects onto it. This is exactly the visibility information we need.

Once valid item buffers have been computed for the images, it is then possible to compute the set vis(V) of all pixels from which the voxel V is visible. Vis(V) is computed as follows. V is projected into each image. For every pixel P in the projection of V, if P's item buffer value equals V's ID, then P is added to vis(V). To check the color consistency of a voxel V, we apply a consistency function consist() to vis(V) or, in other words, we compute consist(vis(V)).

Since carving a voxel changes the visibility of the remaining uncarved voxels, and since we use item buffers to maintain visibility information, the item buffers need to be updated periodically. GVC does this by recomputing the item buffers from scratch. Since this is time consuming, we allow GVC to carve many voxels between updates. As a result, the item buffers are out-of-date much of the time and the computed set *vis(V)* is only guaranteed to be a subset of all the pixels from which a voxel V is visible. However, since carving is conservative, no voxels will be carved that shouldn't be. During the final iteration of GVC, no carving occurs so the visibility

```
initialize SVL
for every voxel V
   carved(V) = false
loop {
   visibilityChanged = false
   compute item buffers by rendering voxels on SVL
   for every voxel V ∈ SVL {
      compute vis(V)
      if (consist(vis(V)) = false) {
         visibilityChanged = true
         carved(V) = true
         remove V from SVL
         for all voxels N that are adjacent to V
            if (carved(N) = false and N ∉ SVL)
               add N to SVL
      }
   }
   if (visibilityChanged = false) {
      save voxel space
      quit
   }
}
```

Fig. 2. Pseudo-code for the GVC algorithm. See text for details.

information stays up-to-date. Every voxel is checked for color consistency on the final iteration so it follows that the final model is color-consistent.

As carving progresses, each voxel is in one of three categories:

- it has been found to be inconsistent and has been carved;
- it is on the surface of the set of uncarved voxels and has been found to be consistent whenever it has been evaluated; or
- it is surrounded by uncarved voxels, so it is visible from no images and its consistency is undefined.

We use an array of bits, one per voxel, to record which voxels have been carved. This data structure is called *carved* in the pseudo-code and is initially set to false for every voxel. We maintain a data structure called the *surface voxel list* (SVL) to identify the second category of voxels. The SVL is initialized to the set of voxels that are not surrounded by other voxels. The item buffers are computed by rendering all the voxels on the SVL into them. We call voxels in the third category *interior* voxels. Though interior voxels are uncarved, they do not need to be rendered into the item buffers because they are not visible from any images. When a voxel is carved, adjacent interior voxels become surface voxels and are added to the SVL. To avoid adding a voxel to the SVL more than once, we need a rapid means of determining if the voxel is already on the SVL; we maintain a hash table for this purpose.

When GVC has finished, the final set of uncarved voxels may be recorded by saving the function carved() or the SVL. Pseudo-code for GVC appears in figure 2.

3.2   The GVC-LDI Algorithm

Basic GVC computes visibility in a relatively simple manner that also makes efficient use of memory. However, the visibility information is time-consuming to update. Hence, GVC updates it infrequently and it is out-of-date much of the time. This does not lead to incorrect results but it does result in inefficiency because a voxel that would be evaluated as *in*consistent using all the visibility information might be evaluated as *consistent* using a subset of the information. Ultimately, all the information is collected but, in the meantime, voxels can remain uncarved longer than necessary and can therefore require more than an ideal number of consistency evaluations. Furthermore, GVC reevaluates the consistency of voxels on the SVL even when their visibility (and hence their consistency) has not changed since their last evaluation. By using layered depth images instead of item buffers, GVC-LDI can efficiently and immediately update the visibility information when a voxel is carved and also can precisely determine the voxels whose visibility has changed.

Unlike the item buffers used by the basic GVC method, which record at each pixel P just the closest voxel that projects onto P, the LDIs store at each pixel a list of *all* the surface voxels that project onto P. See figure 1b. These lists, which in the pseudo-code are called LDI(P), are sorted according to the distance of the voxel to the image's camera. The head of LDI(P) stores the voxel closest to P, which is the same voxel an item buffer would store. Since the information stored in an item buffer is also available in an LDI, vis(V) can be computed in the same way as before. The LDIs are initialized by rendering the SVL voxels into them.

The uncarved voxels whose visibility changes when another voxel is carved come from two sources:

- They are interior voxels adjacent to the carved voxel and become surface voxels when the carved voxel becomes transparent. See figure 3a.
- They are already surface voxels (hence they are in the SVL and LDIs) and are often distant from the carved voxel. See figure 3b.

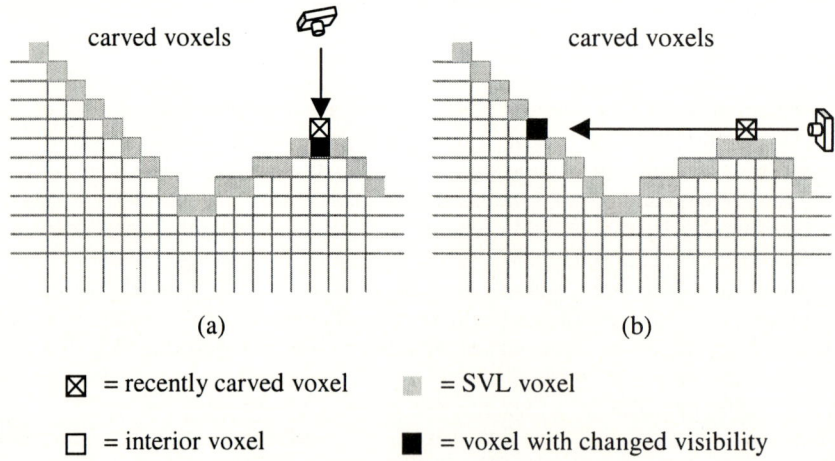

(a)   (b)

⊠ = recently carved voxel   ▨ = SVL voxel

☐ = interior voxel   ■ = voxel with changed visibility

Fig. 3. When a voxel is carved, there are two categories of other voxels whose visibility changes: *(a)* interior voxels that are adjacent to the carved voxel and *(b)* voxels that are already on the SVL and are often distant from the carved voxel.

Voxels in the first category are trivial to identify since they are next to the carved voxel. Voxels in the second category are impossible to identify efficiently in the basic GVC method; hence, that method must repeatedly evaluate the entire SVL for color consistency. In GVC-LDI, voxels in the second category can be found easily with the aid of the LDIs; they will be the second voxel on LDI(P) for some pixel P in the projection of the carved voxel. GVC-LDI keeps a list of the SVL voxels whose visibility has changed, called the *changed visibility SVL* (*CVSVL* in the pseudo-code). These are the only voxels whose consistency must be checked. Carving is finished when the CVSVL is empty.

When a voxel is carved, the LDIs (and hence the visibility information) can be updated immediately and efficiently. The carved voxel can be easily deleted from LDI(P) for every pixel P in its projection. The same process automatically updates the visibility information for the second category of uncarved voxels whose visibility has changed; these voxels move to the head of LDI lists from which the carved voxel has been removed and they are also added to the CVSVL. Interior voxels adjacent to the carved voxel are pushed onto the LDI lists for pixels they project onto. As a byproduct of this process, we learn if the voxel is visible; if it is, we put it on the CVSVL. Pseudo-code for GVC-LDI appears in figure 4.

```
initialize SVL
render SVL to LDIs
for every voxel V
   carved(V) = false
copy SVL to CVSVL
while (CVSVL is not empty) {
   delete V from CVSVL
   compute vis(V)
   if (consist(vis(V)) = false) {
      carved(V) = true
      remove V from SVL
      for every pixel P in projection of V into all images {
         if (V is head of LDI(P))
            add next voxel on LDI(P) (if any) to CVSVL
         delete V from LDI(P)
      }
      for every voxel N adjacent to V with N ∉ SVL {
         N_is_visible = false
         for every pixel P in projection of N to all images {
            add N to LDI(P)
            if (N is head of LDI(P))
               N_is_visible = true
         }
         add N to SVL
         if (N_is_visible)
            add N to CVSVL
      }
   }
}
save voxel space
```

Fig. 3. Pseudo-code for the GVC-LDI algorithm. See text for details.

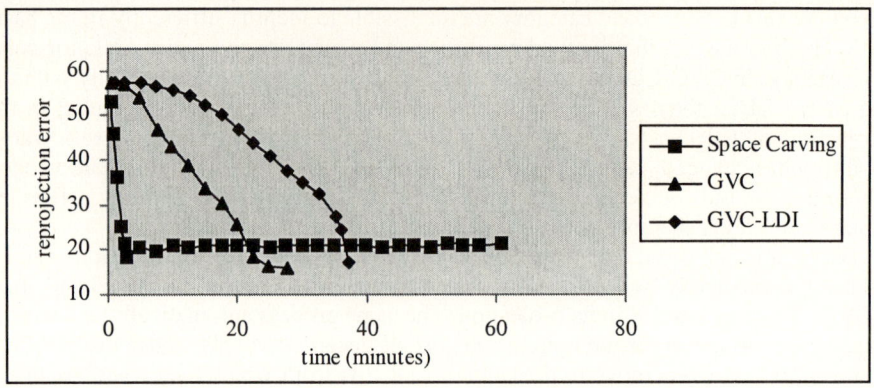

Fig. 4. Convergence of the algorithms while reconstructing the "toycar" scene.

4   Results

We present the results of running Space Carving, GVC, and GVC-LDI on two image sets that we call "toycar" and "bench". In particular, we present runtime statistics and provide, for side-by-side comparison, images synthesized with Space Carving and our algorithms. The experiments were run on a 440 MHz HP J5000 computer.

The toycar and bench image sets represent opposite extremes in terms of how difficult they are to reconstruct. The toycar scene is ideal for reconstruction. The seventeen 800×600-pixel images are computer-rendered and perfectly calibrated. The colors and textures make the various surfaces in the scene easy to distinguish from each other. The bench images are photographs of a natural, real-world scene. In contrast to the toycar scene, the bench scene is challenging to reconstruct for a number of reasons: the images are somewhat noisy, the calibration is not as good, and the scene has large areas with relatively little texture and color variation.

We reconstructed the toycar scene in a 167×121×101-voxel volume. Four of the input images are shown in figure 7. New views synthesized from Space Carving and GVC-LDI reconstructions are shown in figure 8. There are some holes visible along one edge of the blue-striped cube in the Space Carving reconstruction. The coloring in the Space Carving image has a noisier appearance than the GVC-LDI image.

We used fifteen 765×509-pixel images of the bench scene and reconstructed a 75×71×33-voxel volume. We calibrated the images with a product called PhotoModeler Pro [17]. The points used to calibrate the images are well dispersed throughout the scene and their estimated 3D coordinates project within a maximum of 1.2 pixels of their measured locations in the images. Four of the input images are shown in figure 9. New views synthesized from Space Carving and GVC reconstructions are shown in figure 10. The Space Carving image is considerably noisier and more distorted than the GVC image.

Figures 5 and 6 show the total time Space Carving, GVC, and GVC-LDI ran on the toycar and bench scenes until carving completely stopped. They also illustrate the

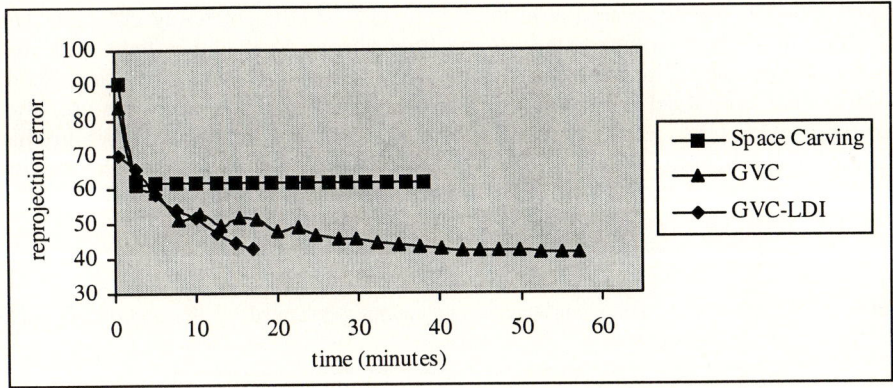

Fig. 5. Convergence of the algorithms while reconstructing the "bench" scene.

rates at which the algorithms converged to good visual representations of the scene. We used *reprojection error* to estimate visual quality. Specifically, we projected models to the same viewpoint as an extra image of the actual scene, and computed the errors by comparing corresponding pixels in the projected and actual images.

Due to the widely varied color and texture in the toycar scene, the color consistency of most voxels can be correctly determined using a small fraction of the input image pixels that will ultimately be able to view the voxel in the final model. Thus, many voxels that must be carved can, in fact, be carved the first time their consistency is checked. Space Carving, with its lean data structures, checks the consistency of voxels faster (albeit, less completely) than the other algorithms and hence, as shown in figure 5, was the first to converge to a good representation of the scene. After producing a good model, Space Carving spent a long time carving a few additional voxels and was the last to completely stop carving. However, this additional carving is not productive visually. Unlike the other two algorithms, GVC-LDI spends extra time to find *all* the pixels that can view a voxel when checking a voxel's consistency. In the toycar scene, this precision was not helpful and caused GVC-LDI to converge the slowest to a good visual model. Ultimately, GVC and GVC-LDI reconstructed models with somewhat lower reprojection error than Space Carving.

The convergence characteristics of the algorithms were different for the bench scene, as shown in figure 6. The color and texture of this scene make reconstruction difficult but are probably typical of the real-world scenes that we are most interested in reconstructing. In contrast to the toycar scene, many voxels in the bench scene are very close to the color-consistency threshold. Hence, many voxels that must be carved cannot be shown to be inconsistent until they become visible from a large number of pixels. Initially, all three algorithms converge at roughly the same rate. Then Space Carving stops improving in reprojection error but continues slow carving. GVC and GVC-LDI produce models of similar quality, both with considerably less error than Space Carving. After an initial period of relatively rapid carving, GVC then slows to a carving rate of several hundred voxels per iteration. Because, on each of these iterations, GVC recalculates all its item buffers and checks the consistency of thousands of voxels, it takes GVC a long time to converge to a color-consistent model. For the bench scene, the efficiency of GVC-LDI's relatively complex data structures more than compensates for the time needed to maintain them. Because GVC-LDI finds all the pixels from which a voxel is visible, it can carve many voxels sooner, when the model is less refined, than the other algorithms. Furthermore, after carving a voxel, GVC-LDI only reevaluates the few other voxels whose visibility has changed. Consequently, GVC-LDI is faster than GVC by a large margin. On both the toycar and the bench scene, GVC-LDI used the fewer color consistency checks than the other algorithms, as shown in table 1.

Table 1. The number of color consistency evaluations performed by the algorithms while reconstructing the "toycar" and "bench" scenes.

	toycar	bench
Space Carving	12.70 M	4.24M
GVC	3.15 M	2.54M
GVC-LDI	2.14 M	526M

All three algorithms keep copies of the input images in memory. The images dominate the memory usage for Space Carving. GVC uses an equal amount of memory for the images and the item buffers and, consequently, uses about twice as much memory as Space Carving, as shown in table 2. The LDIs dominate the memory usage in GVC-LDI and consume an amount of memory roughly proportional to the number of image pixels times the depth complexity of the scene. The table shows that GVC-LDI uses considerably more memory than the other two algorithms. Memory consumed by the carve and SVL data structures is relatively insignificant and, therefore, the voxel resolution has little bearing on the memory requirements for GVC and GVC-LDI.

Table 2. The memory used by the algorithms while reconstructing the "toycar" and "bench" scenes.

	toycar	bench
Space Carving	43.2 MB	26.1 MB
GVC	85.7 MB	53.9 MB
GVC-LDI	462.0 MB	385.0 MB

Kutulakos and Seitz have shown that for a given image set and monotonic consistency function, there is a unique maximal color-consistent set of voxels, which they call V^*. Since GVC and GVC-LDI do not stop carving until the remaining uncarved voxels are all color-consistent and since they never carve consistent voxels, we expect them to produce identical results, namely V^*, when used with a monotonic consistency function. However, monotonic consistency functions can be hard to construct. An obvious choice for consist(S) would take the maximum difference between the colors of any two pixels in S. However, using distance in the RGB cube as a difference measure, this function is $O(n^2)$ on the size of S and has poor immunity to noise and high-frequency color variation. We actually use standard deviation for the consistency function and it is not monotonic. Consequently, GVC and GVC-LDI generally produce models that are different but similar in quality.

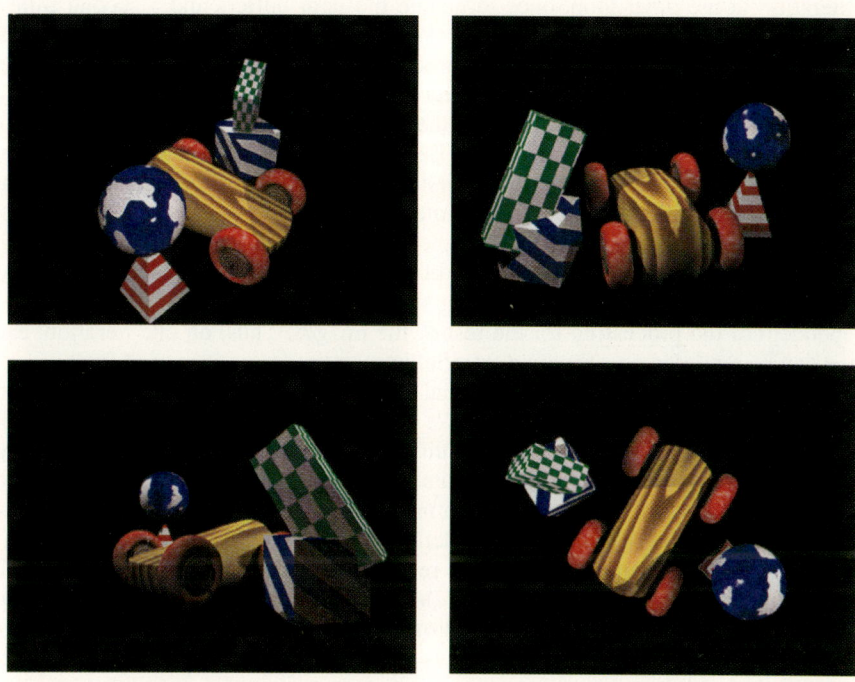

Fig. 7. Four of the seventeen images of the toycar scene.

Fig. 8. New views projected from reconstructions of the toycar scene. The image on the left was created with Space Carving, the image on the right with GVC-LDI. There are some holes visible along one edge of the blue-striped cube in the Space Coloring reconstruction. The coloring in the Space Carving image has a noisier appearance than the GVC-LDI image.

5   Future Work

We have devised a reformulation of the GVC algorithm that we hope to implement in the near future. Our current implementation renders each voxel into each image twice per iteration in the outer loop, once to update the item buffers and a second time to gather color statistics for consistency checking. We treat voxels as cubes and render them by scan-converting their faces, a process that is time-consuming. In our new implementation, we will eliminate the second rendering. Instead, after updating an item buffer, we will scan its pixels, using the voxel IDs to accumulate the pixel colors into the statistics for the correct voxels. Besides reducing the amount of rendering, this approach has three other benefits. First, we will not need the item buffer again after processing an image. Thus, the same memory can be used for all the item buffers, reducing the memory requirement relative to our current implementation. Second, the rendering that is still required can be easily accelerated with a hardware graphics processor. Third, the processing that must be performed on one image is independent of the processing for the rest of the images. Thus, on one iteration, each image can be rendered on a separate, parallel processor.

We believe LDIs have great potential for use in voxel-based reconstruction algorithms. A hybrid algorithm could make the memory requirements for LDIs more practical. In such an approach, an algorithm like GVC would be used to find a rough model. GVC runs most efficiently during its earliest iterations, when many voxels can be carved on each iteration. Once a rough model has been obtained, GVC-LDI could be used to refine local regions of the model. The rough model should be sufficient to find the subset of images from which the region is visible. The subset is likely to be considerably smaller than the original set, so the memory requirements for the LDIs should be much smaller. GVC-LDI would run until the model of the region converges to color-consistency. If the convergence is slow, GVC-LDI should be much faster than GVC.

The algorithms described in this paper find a set of voxels whose color inconsistency falls below a threshold. It would be preferable to have an algorithm that would attempt to minimize color inconsistency—to find the model that is most consistent with the input images. We have already mentioned that LDIs can efficiently maintain visibility information when voxels are removed from the model, *i.e.* carved, but, in fact, they can also be used to efficiently maintain visibility information when voxels are moved or added to the model. Thus, LDIs could be a key element in an algorithm that would add, delete, and move voxels in a model to minimize its reprojection error.

6   Conclusion

We have described a new algorithm, Generalized Voxel Coloring, for constructing a model of a scene from images. We use GVC for image-based modeling and rendering—specifically, for synthesizing new views of the scene. Unlike most earlier solutions to the new-view synthesis problem, GVC accommodates arbitrary numbers of images taken from arbitrary viewpoints. Like Voxel Coloring and Space Carving, GVC colors voxels using color consistency, but it generalizes these algorithms by

Fig. 9. Four of the fifteen input images of the bench scene.

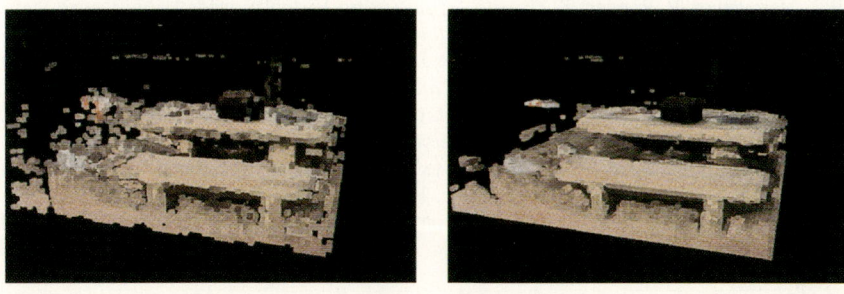

Fig. 10. New views projected from reconstructions of the bench scene. The image on the left was created with Space Carving. The image on the right was created with GVC. The Space Carving image is considerably noisier and more distorted than the GVC image.

allowing arbitrary viewpoints and using all possible images for consistency checking. Furthermore, GVC-LDI uses layered depth images to significantly reduce the number of color consistency checks needed to build a model. We have presented experimental data and new images, synthesized using our algorithms and Space Carving, that demonstrate the benefit of using full visibility when checking color consistency.

Acknowledgements

We would like to thank Steve Seitz for numerous discussions. We are indebted to Mark Livingston, who performed the difficult task of calibrating the bench image set. We are grateful for the support of our management, especially Fred Kitson.

References

1. S. Seitz, Charles R. Dyer, "Photorealistic Scene Reconstruction by Voxel Coloring", *Proceedings of Computer Vision and Pattern Recognition Conference*, 1997, pp. 1067-1073.
2. K. N. Kutulakos and S. M. Seitz, "What Do N Photographs Tell Us about 3D Shape?" *TR680*, Computer Science Dept. U. Rochester, January 1998.
3. S. Seitz, Charles R. Dyer, "View Morphing", *Proceedings of SIGGRAPH 1996*, pp. 21-30.
4. M. Levoy and P. Hanrahan, "Light Field Rendering", *Proceedings of SIGGRAPH 1996*, pp. 31-42.
5. S. Gortler, R. Grzeszczuk, R. Szeliski, M. Cohen, "The Lumigraph", *Proceedings of SIGGRAPH 1996*, pp. 43-54.
6. H. Shum, H. Li-Wei, "Rendering with Concentric Mosaics", *Proceedings of SIGGRAPH 99*, pp. 299-306.
7. W. E. L. Grimson, "Computational experiments with a feature based stereo algorithm", *IEEE Transactions on Pattern Analysis and Machine Intelligence*, vol. 7, no. 1, January 1985, pp. 17-34.
8. M. Okutomi, T. Kanade, "A Multi-baseline Stereo", *IEEE Transactions on Pattern Analysis and Machine Intelligence*, vol. 15, No. 4, April 1993, pp. 353-363.
9. P. J. Narayanan, P. Rander, T. Kanade, "Constucting Virtual Worlds Using Dense Stereo", *IEEE International Conference on Computer Vision*, 1998, pp. 3-10.
10. S. Roy, I. Cox, "A Maximum-Flow Formulation of the N-camera Stereo Correspondence Problem", *IEEE International Conference on Computer Vision*, 1998, pp. 492-499.
11. R. Szeliski, P. Golland, "Stereo Matching with Transparency and Matting", *IEEE International Conference on Computer Vision*, 1998, pp. 517-524.
12. O. Faugeras, R. Keriven, "Complete Dense Stereovision using Level Set Methods", *Fifth European Conference on Computer Vision*, 1998.
13. H. Saito, T. Kanade, "Shape Reconstruction in Projective Grid Space from Large Number of Images", *Proceedings of Computer Vision and Pattern Recognition Conference*, 1999, volume 2, pp. 49-54.
14. N. Max, "Hierarchical Rendering of Trees from Precomputed Multi-Layer Z-Buffers", *Eurographics Rendering Workshop 1996*, pp 165-174.
15. J. Shade, S. Gortler, L. He, R. Szeliski, "Layered Depth Images", *Proceedings of SIGGRAPH 98*, pp. 231-242.
16. H. Weghorst, G. Hooper, D. P. Greenberg, "Improving Computational Methods for Ray Tracing", *ACM Transactions on Graphics*, 3(1), January 1984, pp. 52-69.
17. Eos Systems Inc., 205-2034 West 12th Ave., Vancouver B.C. V6J 2G2, Canada.

Discussion

Yvan Leclerc: Do GVC and GVCLDI give you exactly the same answers?

Bruce Culbertson: That's a very good question. They would if we used a strictly monotonic consistency function, but for various reasons we haven't. We found that it was hard to design a strictly monotonic consistency function that was relatively immune to image noise. We need to do some averaging, and that upsets the monotonicity. So we don't get voxel-for-voxel identical models with the two algorithms. But we found that they usually \emph{look} identical and have nearly identical reprojection errors.

Rick Szeliski: What can you say about sampling issues? - A voxel projects into several pixels with partial fill. What do you do about that?

Bruce Culbertson: In general we've used voxels that project into many pixels. We really haven't explored what happens when we use very small voxels, so I can't say too much about that. I will say that by using voxels that are large relative to the image resolution, we get very good noise immunity. It also extends the runtime, but it's worth exploring.

Bill Triggs: Two questions. One: in all of these voxel-based

approaches there's an n^3 scaling rule - the voxel resolution cubed - whereas a surface-based approach would be only n^2. That seems to suggest that if you have a very high resolution or very large scenes, maybe a voxel-based approach would be inefficient compared to a surface-based one.

Bruce Culbertson: Well, there's one detail that I had to leave out to make my talk short enough. Although our model consists of all the opaque voxels, the vast majority of these are on the interior of the model and can't be seen from any of the images. That makes them really uninteresting, so we've minimized the amount of memory and time devoted to dealing with them. So our in-memory representation is actually just the surface.

Bill Triggs: The second question follows on from that. If you somehow get a pixel wrong and carve it accidentally when you shouldn't have, it makes a hole in the model. Do the holes tend to remain relatively shallow, or can they become deep or even punch right through the model, so that the cameras on the other side start carving away material too and you eventually end up with empty space?

Bruce Culbertson: Our color-consistency functions usually have some threshold for deciding what we mean by consistency, and if we set that too low we do get holes in the model. That makes the algorithm think that the cameras can see right through those holes onto the other side of the object's surface, so errors can sometimes propagate very badly. When that happens it's often difficult to get intuition about what went wrong and figure out which camera saw through what hole to make the model so poor.

Bill Triggs: So do you have any any "repair heuristics" for this ?

Bruce Culbertson: It would be great to have something like that, but we haven't tried it.

Projective Reconstruction from N Views Having One View in Common *

M. Urban, T. Pajdla, and V. Hlaváč

Center for Machine Perception
Czech Technical University, Prague
Karlovo nám. 13, 121 35 Prague, Czech Republic,
urbanm@cmp.felk.cvut.cz
http://cmp.felk.cvut.cz

Abstract. Projective reconstruction recovers projective coordinates of 3D scene points from their several projections in 2D images. We introduce a method for the projective reconstruction based on concatenation of trifocal constraints around a reference view. This configuration simplifies computations significantly. The method uses only linear estimates which stay "close" to image data. The method requires correspondences only across triplets of views. However, it is not symmetrical with respect to views. The reference view plays a special role. The method can be viewed as a generalization of Hartley's algorithm [11], or as a particular application of Triggs' [21] closure relations.

1 Introduction

Finding a projective reconstruction of the scene from its images is a problem which was addressed in many works [7, 22, 12, 13, 9]. It is a difficult problem mainly because of two reasons. Firstly, if more images of a scene are available, it is difficult to see all scene points in all images as some of the points become often occluded by the scene itself. Secondly, image data are affected by noise so that there is usually no 3D reconstruction that is consistent with raw image data. In order to find an approximate solution which would be optimal with respect to errors in image data, a nonlinear bundle adjustment has to be performed or an approximate methods have to be used.

In past, the research addressed both problems. Methods for finding a projective reconstruction of the scene from many images assuming that all correspondences are available were proposed [20, 21, 18]. On the other hand, if only two, three, or four images were used, methods for obtaining a projective reconstruction by a linear Least Squares method were presented [11, 9].

We concentrate on the situation when there are more than four views and not all correspondences are available. We show that a linear Least Squares method

---

* This research is supported by the Grant Agency of the Czech Republic under the grants 102/97/0480, 102/97/0855, and 201/97/0437, and by the Czech Ministry of Education under the grant VS 96049.

B. Triggs, A. Zisserman, R. Szeliski (Eds.): Vision Algorithms'99, LNCS 1883, pp. 116–131, 2000.
© Springer-Verlag Berlin Heidelberg 2000

can be used if there is a common reference view so that the correspondences between the reference view and other views exist.

The proposed approach extends the Hartley's method for computing camera projection matrices [11, 9] for more views than four. His method computes the matrices in two steps. Firstly, the epipoles are computed by a Least Squares method. Secondly, using the epipoles and image data, the rest of camera projection matrices – infinite homographies – are estimated, again, by a Least Squares method.

We assume to have views arranged so that all have some correspondences with a same reference view. Therefore we can compute all the epipoles between the reference view and the other views. Let the correspondences be, for instance, available among triplets of views. Then, trifocal tensors can be estimated independently in each triplet and the epipoles can be computed from the tensors. Having the epipoles, one large linear Least Squares problem for computing the homographies can be constructed.

The paper is organized as follows. In section 1.1, the definition of the projective reconstruction is given. Section 1.2 reviews multifocal constraints. Brief overview of existing methods for projective reconstruction is given in section 1.3. The method for projective reconstruction from many views sharing a reference view is introduced in section 2. Experiments showing the feasibility of the proposed method are given in section 3. The work is summarized in section 4.

1.1 Projective Reconstruction

Let a camera be modeled by a projection from a projective space P^3 to P^2. The homogeneous coordinates of points in the i-th image are denoted by $\tilde{\mathbf{u}}^{(i)} \in P^2$ and homogeneous coordinates of points in P^3 are denoted by $\tilde{\mathbf{x}}$.

Then, the projections of a set of m points by n cameras can be expressed as

$$s_j^{(i)} \tilde{\mathbf{u}}_j^{(i)} = \tilde{\mathbf{P}}^{(i)} \tilde{\mathbf{x}}_j, \ i = 1, \ldots, n, \ j = 1, \ldots, m, \tag{1}$$

where 3×4 real matrix $\tilde{\mathbf{P}}^{(i)} \in M^{3,4}$ is a camera projection matrix, $s_j^{(i)} \in R \backslash \{0\}$ are scale factors.

The goal of a projective reconstruction is to find camera matrices $\tilde{\mathbf{P}}^{(i)}$ and homogeneous coordinates $\tilde{\mathbf{x}}_j$ so that the equation (1) is satisfied for all image points $\tilde{\mathbf{u}}_j^{(i)}$, $i = 1, \ldots, n$, $j = 1, \ldots, m$.

Since both $\tilde{\mathbf{P}}^{(i)}$ and $\tilde{\mathbf{x}}_j$ are unknown, it is obvious that they can be recovered up to a choice of a coordinate system in P^3, i.e. up to a homography. Once having camera matrices $\tilde{\mathbf{P}}^{(i)}$, the consequent recovery of points $\tilde{\mathbf{x}}_j$ is trivial (and vice versa). Therefore, the following definition of projective reconstruction is introduced:

Definition 1 (Projective reconstruction). *The recovery of the equivalence class P*

$$P = \Big\{ \ \left(\mathbf{P}^{(1)}, \ldots, \mathbf{P}^{(n)}\right) \ | \ \left(\mathbf{P}^{(1)}, \ldots, \mathbf{P}^{(n)}\right) = \left(\tilde{\mathbf{P}}^{(1)} \mathbf{H}, \ldots, \tilde{\mathbf{P}}^{(n)} \mathbf{H}\right),$$

$$\mathbf{H} \in M^{4,4}, \ \det(\mathbf{H}) \neq 0 \ \Big\}$$

from a set of points $\tilde{\mathbf{u}}_j^{(i)}$ $i = 1, \ldots, n$, $j = 1, \ldots, m$, *such that there exists a corresponding set of points* $\tilde{\mathbf{x}}_j \in \mathrm{P}^3$ *and* $s_j^{(i)} \in \mathrm{R} \backslash \{0\}$ *so that* $s_j^{(i)} \tilde{\mathbf{u}}_j^{(i)} = \tilde{\mathbf{P}}^{(i)} \tilde{\mathbf{x}}_j$, *is called the* **projective reconstruction**.

1.2   Multifocal Constraints

The algorithms for a projective reconstruction are usually based on so-called multifocal constraints. The multifocal constraints are derived from (1) by eliminating $s_j^{(i)}$ and $\tilde{\mathbf{x}}_j$. Introducing matrix

$$\mathbf{L}_j^{(i)} = \begin{bmatrix} 0 & -\tilde{u}_j^{(i)3} & \tilde{u}_j^{(i)2} \\ \tilde{u}_j^{(i)3} & 0 & -\tilde{u}_j^{(i)1} \\ -\tilde{u}_j^{(i)2} & \tilde{u}_j^{(i)1} & 0 \end{bmatrix}, \tag{2}$$

the equations (1) can be transformed into the equivalent system

$$\begin{bmatrix} \mathbf{L}_j^{(1)} \tilde{\mathbf{P}}^{(1)} \\ \vdots \\ \mathbf{L}_j^{(n)} \tilde{\mathbf{P}}^{(n)} \end{bmatrix} \tilde{\mathbf{x}}_j = \mathbf{M}_j \tilde{\mathbf{x}}_j = \mathbf{0}, \ j = 1, \ldots, m \ .$$

Then, the multifocal constraints between $\tilde{\mathbf{P}}^{(i)}$ and $\tilde{\mathbf{u}}_j^{(i)}$, assuring the existence of $\tilde{\mathbf{x}}_j \in \mathrm{P}^3$, $\tilde{\mathbf{x}}_j \neq 0$, can be written as

$$\det \mathbf{M}_j^{\iota \kappa \lambda \mu} = 0 \ , \quad \forall \, \mathbf{M}_j^{\iota \kappa \lambda \mu}, \ j = 1 \ldots, m \tag{3}$$

where $\mathbf{M}_j^{\iota \kappa \lambda \mu}$ is the sub-matrix of $\mathbf{M}_j$ consisting of rows $\iota, \kappa, \lambda, \mu$. It is seen from the size of $\mathbf{M}_j$ that $m \binom{3n}{4}$ such constraints can be constructed. Since rank $\mathbf{L}^{(i)} = 2$, it follows that at most $\binom{2n}{4}$ of them are linearly independent. Depending on the chosen rows, $\mathbf{M}_j^{\iota \kappa \lambda \mu}$ can comprise coordinates of points from two, three, or four images and therefore we speak about bifocal, trifocal, or quadrifocal constraints respectively. The terms formed by $\tilde{\mathbf{P}}^{(i)}$ are just the components of the well-known multi-view (matching) tensors: epipoles, fundamental matrices, trifocal and quadrifocal tensors.

Hence the solution of a projective reconstruction from m points projected to n views can be described by a system of $m \binom{3n}{4}$ polynomial equations (3) of degree four. To solve such a system appears to be a difficult problem [14][1]. In addition, the measured data $\tilde{\mathbf{u}}_j^{(i)}$ involve errors in real situations and thus this over-constrained system (3) need not have any non-trivial solution. Therefore, only an approximate solution can be obtained.

---

[1] In this context, we shall mention the paper from Bondyfalat, Mourrain, Pan [3]. They present a method for resolving of over-constraint polynomial systems.

1.3   Brief Overview of Existing Methods

The "ideal" optimization technique for projective reconstruction is based on a bundle adjustment, i.e. on minimizing the distances between the original and the reprojected image points. Due to the non-linearity and the complexity of the problem, this can be solved only by a numerical search (e.g. by a gradient descent), which assumes an initial estimate of multi-view geometry, see [6, 12]. Let us review the main principles used to obtain an initial estimate of multi-view geometry which appeared in the literature and compare them with our approach.

Method based on a six point projective invariant. The principle of the method was firstly introduced by Quan in [16]. He showed that the solution of a projective reconstruction from three views can be expressed in a closed form using six point correspondences. It was found that the main disadvantage of the method in a practical situations is that even a small error in one of the six selected correspondences can completely corrupt the result. Therefore, if the reconstruction should be correct even in presence of errors in the correspondences, some additional optimization has to be employed. An algorithm based on random sampling of the input set of correspondences applied by Torr's [2] is an example.

Methods based on linearization of matching constraints. The linearization means that a non-linear task is decomposed into several subtasks, which can be solved by a least-squares estimate of a linear system. The approaches based on linearization are not optimal with respect to noise in image data. They minimize imaginary algebraic distances instead of the image discrepancies. Therefore the estimates should be formulated in a way, so that noise in input data does not skew the solution too much. The results provided by a linearization can be used as an initial estimate for the numerical search in a gradient optimization technique.

The linearization of matching constraints makes use of the two facts: (i) the matching constraints (3) are linear in multi-view tensors, (ii) the multi-view tensors or their special combinations can be linearly decomposed into projection matrices $\tilde{\mathbf{P}}^{(i)}$. Thus, the nonlinear problem of projective reconstruction can be approximated in two linear[2] steps:

1. Estimate multi-focal tensor(s) from image data.
2. Decompose multiple view tensor(s) to projection matrices $\tilde{\mathbf{P}}^{(i)}$, $i = 1, \ldots, n$.

Firstly, the methods based only on one matching tensor (bifocal, trifocal, or quadrifocal) were developed, i.e. the methods only for projective reconstruction from 2, 3, or 4 views. For detailed description see [6, 5, 9, 11, 10, 12, 19, 17, 25].

Considering more than four views, the task becomes more complicated. Triggs described in [21] the method how to concatenate more matching tensors such

---

[2] "Linear problem" is meant in the sense that the problem is equivalent to a Least Square solution of a system of linear equations.

that they cover n views and that the relations[3] between the tensors and the projection matrices are linear. However, the tensors have to be scaled consistently at first. A general way of concatenating the trifocal tensors was presented also by Avidan and Shahsua in [18]. A different approach [1] is based on threading of fundamental matrices using trifocal tensors. The estimation is performed only by triplets of views in a sequence and not from all n views at once. Therefore, errors of consecutive estimations may cumulate during the process. A reconstruction from many views under additional constraints was presented e.g. by Fitzgibbon et al. [8].

The decomposition of the non-linear problem to two consecutive steps brings the following controversy: since the image data are affected by noise, only approximations of matching tensors are received by the first estimate. These approximations does not have to fulfill all the tensor constraints and the successive decomposition to projection matrices becomes unstable.

Hartley [11, 9] has introduced the following improvement: estimate only the epipoles from the given tensor and then estimate the projective matrices directly from image data. This finesse stabilizes the process significantly. So far, this important improvement was known only for the projective reconstruction based on one matching tensor, i.e. only for projective reconstruction from 2, 3, or 4 views. The improvement is impossible in general for the chains of tensors derived by Triggs.

Sturm and Triggs [20] improved the method for n views in a different way. They proposed to recover only 'projective' depths of image points from closure relations. Then, so-called *joint image matrix* can be constructed from the scaled image points. This matrix can be directly factorized into projection matrices (using SVD). The disadvantage of this technique is that the joint image matrix can contain only the points which are observed in all n views. The points seen only in some of n views cannot be involved in computations.

In section 2, we present an algorithm for projective reconstruction from $n \geq 4$ views. The algorithm is based on a linearization of the trifocal constraints concatenated around a reference view. This configuration is a special application of Trigg's $\mathbf{e}-\mathbf{G}-\mathbf{e}$ closure relation and the common reference view simplifies the computations significantly.

It allows to estimate projection matrices (using the epipoles) directly from image data analogically to Hartley's improvement [11, 9]. Furthermore, the problem of the consistent tensor scaling disappears in this case. The used image points have not to be observed in all n views. It is sufficient if they are observed in a triplet of views, where one of the views is the reference view.

---

[3] They are called *joint image closure relations* in [21]

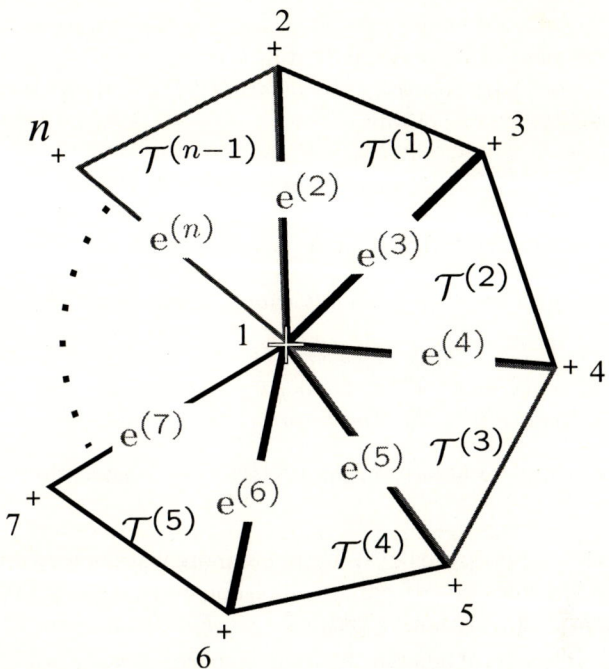

Fig. 1. Cake configuration of $n-1$ triplets of views.

2   Projective Reconstruction from Trifocal Constraints with a Common Reference View

Let us consider that n views are covered by trifocal constraints so that they have the common reference view. (The example of such a configuration is for instance the "Cake" configuration, see Figure 1.) Then, the following two facts hold.

Theorem 1. *The trifocal tensor $\mathcal{T}^{(a)}$ is related to image data by the linear constraint*

$$u^{(1)i} l_j^{(b)\lambda} l_k^{(c)\mu} \, \mathcal{T}_i^{(a)jk} = 0 \;, \quad \lambda, \mu = 1, 2, 3 \;, \tag{4}$$

where $a = 1, \ldots, n-1$ indexes the triplets of views, $b = a+1$ and $c = (a+2) \bmod n$ indexes the views and $l_j^{(b)\lambda}$ denotes λ-th row of $\mathbf{L}_j^{(b)}$ from (2).

Proof. See [17, 11].   □

Theorem 2. *The tensors $\mathcal{T}^{(a)}$ can be expressed as linear forms of the projection matrices $\tilde{\mathbf{P}}^{(b)}$ and the epipoles $\mathbf{e}^{(b)}$.*

Proof. The general relation between the trifocal tensor $\mathcal{T}^{(a)}$, epipoles $\mathbf{e}^{(b)}, \mathbf{e}^{(c)}$, and $\tilde{\mathbf{P}}^{(1)}, \tilde{\mathbf{P}}^{(b)}, \tilde{\mathbf{P}}^{(c)}$ is

$$\mathcal{T}_\bullet^{(a)\bullet k} \tilde{\mathbf{P}}^{(1)} = e^{(c)k} \tilde{\mathbf{P}}^{(b)} - \mathbf{e}^{(b)} \tilde{\mathbf{p}}^{(c)k} \;, \quad k = 1, 2, 3 \;, \tag{5}$$

where $\mathcal{T}_\bullet^{(a)\bullet k}$ is 3×3 matrix ($\bullet$ denotes the free indexes), $e^{(c)k}$ denotes the k-th component of $\mathbf{e}^{(c)}$, and $\tilde{\mathbf{p}}^{(c)k}$ the k-th row of $\tilde{\mathbf{P}}^{(c)}$, see [21, 23] (Triggs calls it $\mathbf{e}-\mathbf{G}-\mathbf{e}$ closure relation). Considering $\tilde{\mathbf{P}}^{(1)} = [\mathbf{I}, \mathbf{0}]$, $\tilde{\mathbf{P}}^{(b)} = [\mathbf{A}^{(b)}, \mathbf{e}^{(b)}]$, and $\tilde{\mathbf{P}}^{(c)} = [\mathbf{A}^{(c)}, \mathbf{e}^{(c)}]$, we obtain

$$\mathcal{T}_\bullet^{(a)\bullet k} = e^{(c)k}\mathbf{A}^{(b)} - \mathbf{e}^{(b)}\mathbf{a}^{(c)k} , \quad k = 1, 2, 3 , \tag{6}$$

where $\mathbf{a}^{(c)k}$ denotes the k-th row of $\tilde{\mathbf{A}}^{(c)}$. $\qquad\qquad\square$

When combining (4) with (6), the following consequence is evident.

Consequence 1 *Let n views be covered by trifocal tensors so that they all have a common reference view. Then, having the epipoles $\mathbf{e}^{(b)}$, the camera matrices $\tilde{\mathbf{P}}^{(b)}$ can be estimated directly (and linearly) from image data.*

Thus, the complete algorithm for projective reconstruction can be outlined as follows:

1. **Estimation of epipoles $\mathbf{e}^{(c)}$.** There are more ways how to estimate epipoles $\mathbf{e}^{(c)}$, e.g. via bifocal, trifocal or quadrifocal constraints. We consider the estimation from neighboring tensors $\mathcal{T}^{(a)}, \mathcal{T}^{(a+1)}$ as the most "natural" (i.e. as the common perpendicular to six null spaces of matrices $\mathcal{T}_\bullet^{(a)\bullet k}, \mathcal{T}_\bullet^{(a+1)\bullet k}$, $k = 1, 2, 3$). where $a = 1, \ldots, n-1$, $c = (a + 2) \bmod n$.

2. **Estimation of $\mathbf{A}^{(b)}$ from image data using $\mathbf{e}^{(b)}$, $b = 2, \ldots, n$.**
   The detail description of the estimation for the "Cake" configuration is given in Appendix A.

3   Experiments

In all experiments, the "Cake" configuration of the trifocal constraints is used, i.e. the trifocal constraints arise from the view triplets $\langle 1, 2, 3 \rangle$, $\langle 1, 3, 4 \rangle$, $\ldots$, $\langle 1, n, 2 \rangle$, see Figure 1.

3.1   Experiment on Synthetic Data

In the first experiment, we have tested the accuracy and the stability of the algorithm with respect to noise for 3 and 5 views. An artificial scene consisted of a set of 40 points distributed randomly (uniform distribution) in a cube of size 1 meter. A camera with viewing angle $63°$ was used. Image size was 1000×1000 units[4]. Image data were corrupted by Gaussian noise with standard deviation increasing gradually from 0.5 to 25 image units. The reprojection error of the reconstruction provided by the above proposed algorithm was evaluated for 200

---

[4] The image units get a physical meaning with respect to the focal length f. One image unit is $\frac{1}{500}\sin(\frac{1}{2}\alpha)f$ in this experiment, where α is the viewing angle.

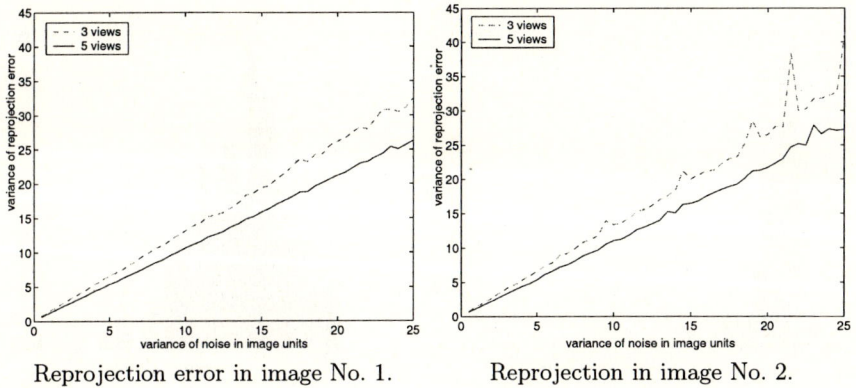

Reprojection error in image No. 1.   Reprojection in image No. 2.

Fig. 2. Variance of the reprojection error *vs.* variance of noise in image data.

measurements for a given value of noise. The camera positions were selected randomly in the distance between 2 and 2.5 meters from the scene center.

The results of the experiment are illustrated on Figures 2, and 3. Since the tested algorithm is symmetric with respect to images 2, 3, 4, and 5, we present the errors only for image 1 and 2. It is seen from Figures 2 and 3, that the reprojection error increases linearly in the tested range of noise. Furthermore, it is seen, that the accuracy of the results increases with the number of images.

3.2   Experiments on Real Data

The behavior of the proposed algorithm was tested on two sets of real images. The first set captures the house from Kampa, the second sets captures a cardboard model of a toy house. The experimental software CORRGUI [4, 24] was used to select the correspondences manually, to define polygonal faces of the reconstruction, and to map texture from images onto the reconstruction.

House at Kampa.   We have taken 7 images of a house using an uncalibrated photographic camera, see Figure 4. Then, the photographs were digitized in the resolution 2393×3521 pixels.

Point correspondences in image triplets were assigned manually. The following numbers of correspondences were selected:

Image triplet	$(1,2,3)$	$(1,3,4)$	$(1,4,5)$	$(1,5,6)$	$(1,6,7)$	$(1,7,2)$
Number of correspondences	67	62	46	51	82	82

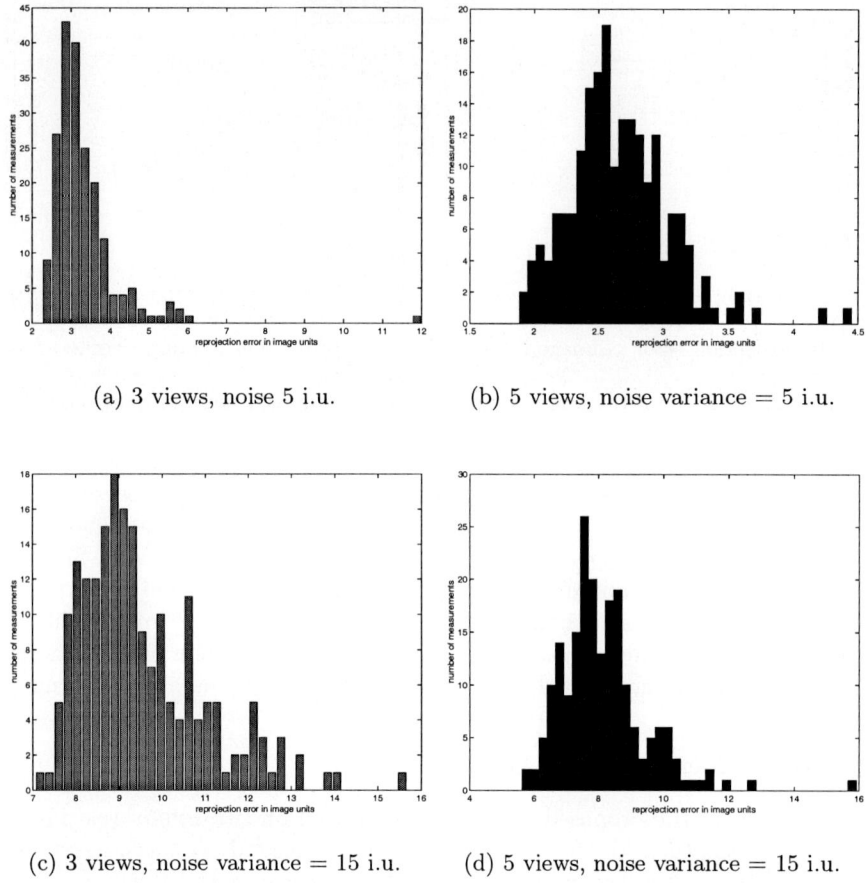

(a) 3 views, noise 5 i.u. (b) 5 views, noise variance = 5 i.u.

(c) 3 views, noise variance = 15 i.u. (d) 5 views, noise variance = 15 i.u.

Fig. 3. Histograms of 200 measurements of the reprojection error in image No. 2 for noise level 5 and 15 image units.

The projective reconstruction from all 7 images was performed. The following table shows the maximal and the average distances between input and reprojected image points:

image No.	1	2	3	4	5	6	7
Maximal error [pxl]	13.4	27.2	12.2	8.6	14.1	8.8	8.9
Mean error [pxl]	1.3	2.3	2.6	1.9	6.7	1.4	3.1
Median [pxl]	1.0	1.7	1.9	1.6	6.2	1.1	3.4

The recovered class P of the projective reconstruction was used as the input for Pollefeys' algorithm [15] computing a similarity reconstruction of the house, see Figure 5.

Fig. 4. Seven input images of the house at Kampa.

Fig. 5. Two views on the recovered 3D model of the house at Kampa with image texture mapped onto the reconstruction.

"Toy" House. In this experiment, 10 images of a "toy" house model were taken, see Figure 6, by an uncalibrated photographic camera and then digitized in the resolution 2003×2952 pixels. Point correspondences were assigned manually across image triplets.

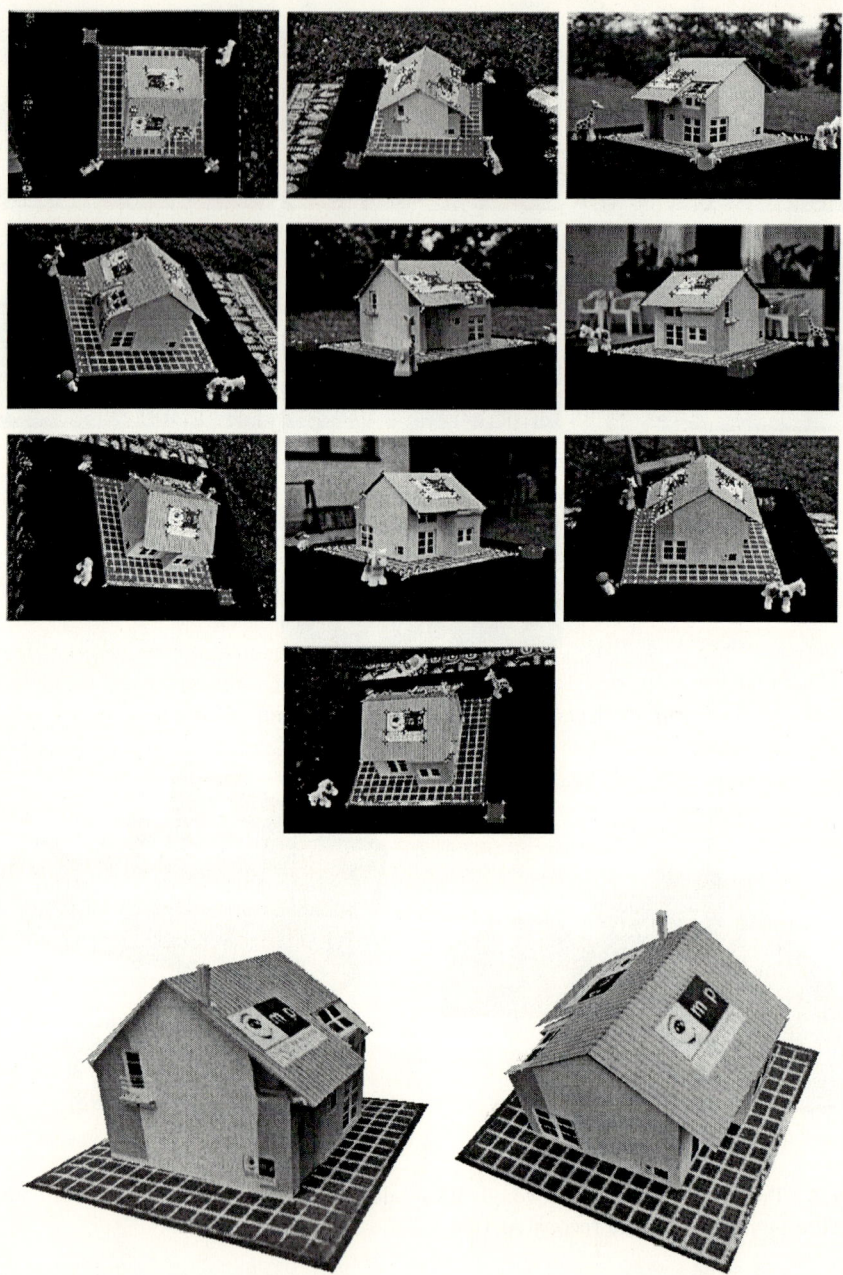

Fig. 6. Ten input images of the "toy" house and two views of the recovered 3D Euclidean model.

The following numbers of correspondences were selected:

Image triplets	$(1,2,3)$	$(1,3,4)$	$(1,4,5)$	$(1,5,6)$	$(1,6,7)$
Number of correspondences	48	60	54	20	41

Image triplets	$(1,7,8)$	$(1,8,9)$	$(1,9,10)$	$(1,10,2)$	
Number of correspondences	56	41	59	71	

The projective reconstruction from all 10 images was done. The following table shows the maximal and the average distances between the input and the reprojected image points:

Image No.	1	2	3	4	5	6	7	8	9	10
Maximal error [pxl]	4.9	10.1	8.2	5.7	9.9	7.9	6.4	5.9	8.9	8.0
Mean error [pxl]	1.4	3.7	2.9	2.0	3.1	2.7	1.7	2.1	1.66	2.0
Median [pxl]	1.1	3.4	2.7	1.7	2.7	2.2	1.5	1.7	1.4	1.8

The Euclidean model (Figure 6) was recovered from the projective one by assigning 3D Euclidean coordinates to 5 points.

4 Conclusions

We have presented a new approach for projective reconstruction from a set of n views if $n > 4$. The views are grouped by triplets having a reference view in common. There are two important advantages of the proposed approach. Firstly, the existence of a common reference view allows to construct one large over-determined linear system for all homographies in the projection matrices. Secondly, correspondences are needed only among the triplets of views containing the reference view. Thus, in this special arrangement with one reference view, a simultaneous estimate of all the homographies can be obtained even though not all correspondences are available. On the other hand, since there is a reference view in a special position, the method is not symmetrical with respect to all images.

A   Complete Algorithm

1. **Estimate the epipoles $\mathbf{e}^{(b)}$, $b = 2, \ldots, n$,**
   e.g. through the trifocal tensors.

2. **Estimate $\mathbf{A}^{(b)}$, $b = 2, \ldots, n$.**
   The matrices $\mathbf{A}^{(b)}$ are constrained by $\mathcal{T}^{(a)}$, and $\mathbf{e}^{(b)}$ up to three free parameters (see Appendix B)

$$\begin{bmatrix} \mathbf{a}_i^{(2)} \\ \vdots \\ \mathbf{a}_i^{(n)} \end{bmatrix} \in \kappa_i , \quad \kappa_i = \left\{ \begin{bmatrix} \mathbf{y}_i^{(2)} \\ \vdots \\ \mathbf{y}_i^{(n)} \end{bmatrix} + \omega_i \begin{bmatrix} \mathbf{e}^{(2)} \\ \vdots \\ \mathbf{e}^{(n)} \end{bmatrix} , \quad \omega_i \in \mathrm{R} \right\} , \quad i = 1, 2, 3.$$

a) Let us select the element of κ_i orthogonal (for instance) to $\mathbf{f} =$
$\begin{bmatrix} \mathbf{e}^{(2)} \\ \vdots \\ \mathbf{e}^{(n)} \end{bmatrix}$. Let $\mathbf{V}^0$, $\mathbf{V}^0 \in \mathrm{M}^{3(n-1),3(n-1)-1}$, is a matrix which columns form a basis of the space orthogonal to vector $\mathbf{f}$ and let $\mathbf{z}_i \in \mathrm{R}^{3(n-1)-1}$, then the selected solution can be expressed as

$$\begin{bmatrix} \mathbf{a}_i^{(2)} \\ \vdots \\ \mathbf{a}_i^{(n)} \end{bmatrix} = \mathbf{V}^0 \mathbf{z}_i , \quad i = 1, 2, 3 . \tag{7}$$

b) Substituting (8) and (6) to (4) we can formulate the linear estimate directly for $\mathbf{z}_i$, $i = 1, 2, 3$,

$$\text{minimize} \left\| \mathbf{D} \begin{bmatrix} \mathbf{GV}^0 & \mathbf{0} & \mathbf{0} \\ \mathbf{0} & \mathbf{GV}^0 & \mathbf{0} \\ \mathbf{0} & \mathbf{0} & \mathbf{GV}^0 \end{bmatrix} \begin{bmatrix} \mathbf{z}_1 \\ \mathbf{z}_2 \\ \mathbf{z}_3 \end{bmatrix} \right\| \quad \text{subject to} \quad \left\| \begin{bmatrix} \mathbf{z}_1 \\ \mathbf{z}_2 \\ \mathbf{z}_3 \end{bmatrix} \right\| = 1 ,$$

where the matrix $\mathbf{D}$ is composed from image data $u^{(1)i} l_j^{(b)\lambda} l_k^{(c)\mu}$.

c) The columns $\mathbf{a}_i^{(2)}, \ldots, \mathbf{a}_i^{(n)}$, $i = 1, 2, 3$, can be easily obtained by the back projection (7).

B   From $\mathcal{T}^{(a)}$ and $\mathbf{e}^{(b)}$ to $\mathbf{A}^{(b)}$

Consider $n-1$ tensors $\mathcal{T}^{(1)}, \ldots, \mathcal{T}^{(n-1)}$ of the triplets $\langle 1, 2, 3 \rangle, \ldots, \langle 1, n, 2 \rangle$. Assume that we have already performed the estimations of $\mathbf{e}^{(j)}$, $j = 2, \ldots, n$.

Equations (6) can be rewritten to the matrix form

$$\begin{bmatrix} \text{vector}_9(\mathcal{T}_i^{(1)\bullet\bullet}) \\ \vdots \\ \text{vector}_9(\mathcal{T}_i^{(n-1)\bullet\bullet}) \end{bmatrix} = \mathbf{G} \begin{bmatrix} \mathbf{a}_i^{(2)} \\ \vdots \\ \mathbf{a}_i^{(n)} \end{bmatrix} , \quad i = 1, 2, 3 \tag{8}$$

where $\mathbf{G}$ is $9(n-1) \times 3(n-1)$ matrix

$$\mathbf{G} = \begin{bmatrix} \begin{bmatrix} e^{(3)1}\mathbf{I} \\ e^{(3)2}\mathbf{I} \\ e^{(3)3}\mathbf{I} \end{bmatrix} & \begin{bmatrix} -e^{(2)} & 0 & 0 \\ 0 & -e^{(2)} & 0 \\ 0 & 0 & -e^{(2)} \end{bmatrix} & \begin{bmatrix} 0\,0\,0 \\ 0\,0\,0 \\ 0\,0\,0 \end{bmatrix} & \cdots \\ \begin{bmatrix} 0\,0\,0 \\ 0\,0\,0 \\ 0\,0\,0 \end{bmatrix} & \begin{bmatrix} e^{(4)1}\mathbf{I} \\ e^{(4)2}\mathbf{I} \\ e^{(4)3}\mathbf{I} \end{bmatrix} & \begin{bmatrix} -e^{(3)} & 0 & 0 \\ 0 & -e^{(3)} & 0 \\ 0 & 0 & -e^{(3)} \end{bmatrix} & \cdots \\ \vdots & \vdots & & \ddots \\ \begin{bmatrix} -e^{(n)} & 0 & 0 \\ 0 & -e^{(n)} & 0 \\ 0 & 0 & -e^{(n)} \end{bmatrix} & \begin{bmatrix} 0\,0\,0 \\ 0\,0\,0 \\ 0\,0\,0 \end{bmatrix} & \cdots & \begin{bmatrix} e^{(2)1}\mathbf{I} \\ e^{(2)2}\mathbf{I} \\ e^{(2)3}\mathbf{I} \end{bmatrix} \end{bmatrix}$$

Since the kernel of $\mathbf{G}$ is generated by the vector[5]

$$\begin{bmatrix} \mathbf{e}^{(2)} \\ \vdots \\ \mathbf{e}^{(n)} \end{bmatrix},$$

for given $\mathcal{T}^{(a)}$ and $\mathbf{e}^{(b)}$ there exists a one dimensional set satisfying (8)

$$\begin{bmatrix} \mathbf{a}_i^{(2)} \\ \vdots \\ \mathbf{a}_i^{(n)} \end{bmatrix} \in \kappa_i, \quad \kappa_i = \left\{ \begin{bmatrix} \mathbf{y}_i^{(2)} \\ \vdots \\ \mathbf{y}_i^{(n)} \end{bmatrix} + \omega_i \begin{bmatrix} \mathbf{e}^{(2)} \\ \vdots \\ \mathbf{e}^{(n)} \end{bmatrix}, \quad \omega_i \in \mathrm{R} \right\}. \tag{9}$$

The vector $\begin{bmatrix} \mathbf{y}_i^{(2)} \\ \vdots \\ \mathbf{y}_i^{(n)} \end{bmatrix}$ denotes a particular solution of (8) different from $\begin{bmatrix} \mathbf{e}^{(2)} \\ \vdots \\ \mathbf{e}^{(n)} \end{bmatrix}$.

References

1. S. Avidan and A. Shashua. Threading fundamental matrices. In *ECCV-98*, Frieburg, Germany, June 1998. Springer - Verlag.
2. P. Beardsley, P. Torr, and A. Zisserman. 3D model acquisition from extended image sequences. In Bernard Buxton and Roberto Cippola, editors, *ECCV-96*. Springer-Verlag, 1996.
3. D. Bondyfalat, B. Mourrain, and V.Y. Pan. Controlled iterative methods for solving polynomials systems. ISSAC'98. ACM Press, 1998.
4. J. Buriánek. Korespondence pro virtualní kameru. Master's thesis, Czech Technical University, FEL ČVUT, Karlovo náměstí 13, Praha, Czech Republic, 1998. In Czech.
5. O. Faugeras. *Three-Dimensional Computer Vision: A Geometric Viewpoint*. The MIT Press, 1993.
6. O. Faugeras and T. Papadopoulo. Grassmann-Cayley algebra for modeling systems of cameras and the algebraic equations of the manifold of trifocal tensors. Technical Report 3225, INRIA, Jully 1997.
7. O. Faugeras and B. Mourrain. The geometry and algebra of the point and line correspondences between n images. Technical Report RR-2665, INRIA - Sophia Antipolis, Octobre 1995.
8. Fitzgibbon, A.W. and Cross, G. and Zisserman, A. Automatic 3D Model Construction for Turn-Table Sequences. SMILE98, Freiburg, Germany, Springer-Verlag LNCS 1506, June 1998.
9. R. I. Hartley. Computation of the quadrifocal tensor. In *ECCV-98*, volume I, pages 20–35. Springer Verlag, 1998.
10. R. I. Hartley. Projective reconstruction from line correspondences. Technical report, GE–Corporate Research and Development, P.O. Box 8, Schenectady, NY, 12301., 1995.

---

[5] for $\mathbf{e}^{(i)} \neq \mathbf{0}$

11. R.I. Hartley. Lines and points in three views and the trifocal tensor. *International Journal of Computer Vision*, 22(2):125–140, March 1997.
12. A. Heyden. A common framework for multiple view tensors. In *ECCV-98*, volume I, pages 3–19. Springer Verlag, 1998.
13. A. Heyden. Reduced multilinear constraints - theory and experiments. *International Journal of Computer Vision*, 30:5–26, 1998.
14. R.H. Lewis and P.F. Stiller. Solving the recognition problem for six lines using the Dixon resultant. *Preprint submitted to Elsevier Preprint*, 1999.
15. M. Pollefeys, R. Koch, and L. VanGool. Self-calibration and metric reconstruction in spite of varying and unknown internal camera parameters. In *ICCV98*, page Session 1.4, 1998.
16. L. Quan. Invariants of 6 points and projective reconstruction from 3 uncalibrated images. *PAMI*, 17(1):34–46, January 1995.
17. A. Shashua. Trilinear tensor: The fundamental construct of multiple-view geometry and its applications. In *International Workshop on Algebraic Frames For The Perception Action Cycle (AFPAC97)*, Kiel Germany, September 1997.
18. A. Shashua and S. Avidan. The rank 4 constraint in multiple (≥ 3) view geometry. In Bernard Buxton and Roberto Cipolla, editors, *ECCV-96*, pages 196–206. Springer Verlag, April 1996.
19. A. Shashua and M. Werman. Fundamental tensor: On the geometry of three perspective views. Technical report, Hebrew University of Jerusalem, Institut of Computer Science, 91904 Jerusalem, Israel, 1995.
20. P. Sturm and B. Triggs. A factorization based algorithm for multi-image projective structure and motion. In *ECCV-96*. Springer - Verlag, 1996.
21. B. Triggs. Linear projective reconstruction from matching tensors. Technical report, Edinburgh, 1996. *British Machine Vision Conference*.
22. B. Triggs. The geometry of projective reconstruction I: Matching constraints and the joint image. Technical report, 1995. unpublished report.
23. M. Urban, T. Pajdla, and V. Hlaváč. Projective reconstruction from multiple views. Technical Report CTU-CMP-1999-5, CMP, FEL ČVUT, Karlovo náměstí 13, Praha, Czech Republic, December 1999.
24. T. Werner, T. Pajdla, and M. Urban. Rec3d: Toolbox for 3d reconstruction from uncalibrated 2d views. Technical Report CTU-CMP-1999-4, Czech Technical University, FEL ČVUT, Karlovo náměstí 13, Praha, Czech Republic, December 1999.
25. Zhengyou Zhang. Determining the epipolar geometry and its uncertainty: A review. *IJCV*, 1997.

Discussion

Richard Hartley: In my algorithm I compute the epipoles, then there's an optional phase in which you iterate over the positions of the epipoles to get a global minimum of algebraic error. Could you do the same sort of thing here?

Tomáš Pajdla: Yes, our method can be seen as the first step where we get some kind of initial estimate. We could follow this with iterations or proceed with bundle adjustment to optimize the real reprojection error in the images. We haven't done this here, but if the initialization is good the bundle adjustment will converge.

Richard Hartley: Just iterating over the position of the epipoles would be a lot simpler and faster than bundle adjustment, if you have a lot of matched points.

Tomáš Pajdla: Yes.

Kalle Åström: In your house sequence there seemed to be something wrong with the texture mapping.

Tomáš Pajdla: Yes, you're right. The texture mapping is provided by the VRML viewer, which can only map textures that were taken frontoparallelly. It splits the polygons into triangles, then maps each triangle independently using an affine transformation. For non-frontoparallel textures, this introduces discontinuities across the edges, which are visible for big polygons. It's a problem with the VRML standard and the VRML consortium ought to fix it.

Note: The texture mapping was fixed in the final version of the paper, by recursively subdividing the triangles until the error of the affine texture mapping was less than one pixel.

Marc Pollefeys: In some cases it may be very hard to have a global common view, but you might have a lot of views from all around an object. Could you use this technique to reconstruct small patches around several central views, and then somehow stitch all these patches together? I mean something like the Kanade dome, where you could choose some of the cameras as central ones, surrounded by others. Could you patch the whole cage structure together? Or would you work with trifocal tensors in this case?

Tomáš Pajdla: We only developed the work for a single central view. One advantage is that we can estimate the homographies from all the image data. But it would probably be possible to generalize it by gluing things together, maybe using the trifocal tensor as in other works. I don't know whether it would be any better than just using the trifocal tensor — you'd have to try it.

Point- and Line-Based Parameterized Image Varieties for Image-Based Rendering

Yakup Genc [*] and Jean Ponce

Department of Computer Science and Beckman Institute
University of Illinois, Urbana, IL 61801, USA
{y-genc,ponce}@cs.uiuc.edu

Abstract. This paper generalizes the parameterized image variety approach to image-based rendering proposed in [5] so it can handle both points and lines in a unified setting. We show that the set of all images of a rigid set of m points and n lines observed by a weak perspective camera forms a six-dimensional variety embedded in $\mathbb{R}^{2(m+n)}$. A parameterization of this variety by the image positions of three reference points is constructed via least squares techniques from point and line correspondences established across a sequence of images. It is used to synthesize new pictures without any explicit 3D model. Experiments with real image sequences are presented.

1 Introduction

The set of all images of m points and n lines can be embedded in a $2(m+n)$-dimensional vector space E, but it forms in fact a low-dimensional subspace V of E: as will be shown in the next section, V is a variety (i.e., a subspace defined by polynomial equations) of dimension eight for affine cameras, and an eleven-dimensional variety for projective cameras. But V is only a *six-dimensional* variety of E for weak perspective and full perspective cameras. We propose to construct an explicit representation of V, the *Parameterized Image Variety* (or PIV) from a set of point and line correspondences established across a sequence of weak perspective or paraperspective images. The PIV associated with a rigid scene is parameterized by the position of three image points, and it can be used to synthesize new pictures of this scene from arbitrary viewpoints, with applications in virtual reality.

Like other recent approaches to image synthesis without explicit 3D models [12, 13, 18], our method completely by-passes the estimation of the motion and structure parameters, and works fully in image space. Previous techniques exploit the affine or projective structure of images [4, 10, 11] but ignore the Euclidean constraints associated with real cameras; consequently, as noted in [13], the synthesized pictures may be subjected to affine or projective deformations. Our

---

[*] Present Address: Siemens Corporate Research, 755 College Road East, Princeton, NJ, 08540, USA. E-mail: ygenc@scr.siemens.com

B. Triggs, A. Zisserman, R. Szeliski (Eds.): Vision Algorithms'99, LNCS 1883, pp. 132–148, 2000.
© Springer-Verlag Berlin Heidelberg 2000

method takes Euclidean constraints into account explicitly and outputs correct images.

Parameterized image varieties were first introduced in [5] as a technique for parameterizing the set of images of a fixed set of points. Here we recall the original method and present a completely new extension to the problem of parameterizing the set of images of a fixed set of lines (a potential advantage of lines over points is that they can be localized very accurately in edge maps). We show how both the point and line PIVs can be integrated in a general framework for image synthesis without explicit 3D models, and present preliminary experiments with real images.

1.1   Background

Recent work in computer graphics [3, 8, 14] and computer vision [1, 12, 13, 18] has demonstrated the possibility of displaying 3D scenes without explicit 3D models (*image-based rendering*). The *light field* techniques developed by Chen [3], Gortler, Grzeszczuk, Szeliski and Cohen [8], and Levoy and Hanrahan [14] are based on the idea that the set of all visual rays is four-dimensional, and can thus be characterized from a two-dimensional sample of images of a rigid scene.

In contrast, the methods proposed by Laveau and Faugeras [13], Seitz and Dyer [18], Kutulakos and Vallino [12], and Avidan and Shashua [1] only use a discrete (and possibly small) set of views among which point correspondences have been established by feature tracking or conventional stereo matching. These approaches are related to the classical problem of *transfer* in photogrammetry: given the image positions of *tie points* in a set of reference images and in a new image, and given the image positions of a ground point in the reference images, predict the position of that point in the new image [2].

In the projective case, Laveau and Faugeras [13] have proposed to first estimate the pair-wise epipolar geometry between the set of reference views, then reproject the scene points into a new image by specifying the position of the new optical center in two reference images and the position of four reference points in the new image. Once the feature points have been reprojected, realistic rendering is achieved using classical computer graphics techniques such as ray tracing and texture mapping. Since then, related methods have been proposed by several authors in both the affine and projective cases [1, 12, 18]. The main drawback of these techniques is that the synthesized images are in general separated from the "correct" pictures by arbitrary planar affine or projective transformations (this is not true for the method proposed by Avidan and Shashua [1], which synthesizes correct Euclidean images, but assumes calibrated cameras and actually estimates the (small) rotation between the cameras used at modeling time).

The approach presented in the rest of this paper generates correct images by explicitly taking into account the Euclidean constraints associated with real cameras. In addition, it integrates both point- and line-based image synthesis in a common framework. We are not aware of any other line-based approach to image-based rendering, although structure-from-line-motion methods have of course been proposed in the past (see, for example, [9, 17, 21] for recent approaches), and image-based rendering is close in spirit to methods for transfer based on the trifocal tensor [19], that are in principle applicable to lines [9].

1.2   The Set of Images of a Rigid Scene

Let us first consider an *affine* camera observing some 3D scene, i.e., let us assume that the scene is first submitted to a 3D affine transformation and then ortho-graphically projected onto the image plane of the camera. We denote the coordi-nate vector of a scene point P in the world coordinate system by $\boldsymbol{P} = (x, y, z)^T$. Let $\boldsymbol{p} = (u, v)^T$ denote the coordinate vector of the projection p of P onto the image plane, the affine camera model can be written as

$$\boldsymbol{p} = \mathcal{M}\boldsymbol{P} + \boldsymbol{p}_0 \tag{1}$$

with

$$\mathcal{M} = \begin{pmatrix} \boldsymbol{a}^T \\ \boldsymbol{b}^T \end{pmatrix} \quad \text{and} \quad \boldsymbol{p}_0 = \begin{pmatrix} u_0 \\ v_0 \end{pmatrix}.$$

Note that $\boldsymbol{p}_0$ is the image of the origin of the world coordinate system.

Suppose we observe a fixed set of points P_i $(i = 1, .., m)$ with coordinate vectors $\boldsymbol{P}_i$, and let $\boldsymbol{p}_i$ denote the coordinate vectors of the corresponding image points. Writing (1) for all the scene points yields

$$\begin{pmatrix} \boldsymbol{u} \\ \boldsymbol{v} \end{pmatrix} = \begin{pmatrix} \boldsymbol{x} \; \boldsymbol{y} \; \boldsymbol{z} \; \boldsymbol{0} \; \boldsymbol{0} \; \boldsymbol{0} \; \boldsymbol{1} \; \boldsymbol{0} \\ \boldsymbol{0} \; \boldsymbol{0} \; \boldsymbol{0} \; \boldsymbol{x} \; \boldsymbol{y} \; \boldsymbol{z} \; \boldsymbol{0} \; \boldsymbol{1} \end{pmatrix} \begin{pmatrix} \boldsymbol{a} \\ \boldsymbol{b} \\ \boldsymbol{p}_0 \end{pmatrix},$$

where

$$\begin{cases} \boldsymbol{u} = (u_1, \dots, u_m)^T, \\ \boldsymbol{v} = (v_1, \dots, v_m)^T, \\ \boldsymbol{1} = (1, \dots, 1)^T, \\ \boldsymbol{0} = (0, \dots, 0)^T, \end{cases} \quad \begin{cases} \boldsymbol{x} = (x_1, \dots, x_m)^T, \\ \boldsymbol{y} = (y_1, \dots, y_m)^T, \\ \boldsymbol{z} = (z_1, \dots, z_m)^T, \end{cases}$$

and it follows that the set of images of m points is an eight-dimensional vector space V_p embedded in $\mathbb{R}^{2m}$.

Let us now consider a line Δ parameterized by its direction $\boldsymbol{\Omega}$ and the vector $\boldsymbol{D}$ joining the origin of the world coordinate system to its projection onto Δ. We can parameterize the projection δ of Δ onto the image plane by the image vector $\boldsymbol{d}$ that joins the origin of the image coordinate system to its orthogonal projection onto δ. This vector is defined by the two constraints

$$\begin{cases} \boldsymbol{d} \cdot (\mathcal{M}\boldsymbol{\Omega}) = 0, \\ \boldsymbol{d} \cdot (\mathcal{M}\boldsymbol{D} + \boldsymbol{p}_0) = |\boldsymbol{d}|^2. \end{cases} \tag{2}$$

It follows that the set of all affine images of n lines is an eight-dimensional variety V_l embedded in $\mathbb{R}^{2n}$ and defined by the $2n$ equations in $2n+8$ unknowns (namely, the coordinates of the vectors d_i ($i = 1, .., n$) associated with the n lines and the coordinates of the vectors a, b and p_0) obtained by writing (2) for n lines. More generally, the set of all affine images of m points and n lines is an eight-dimensional variety V embedded in $\mathbb{R}^{2(m+n)}$.

Let us now suppose that the camera observing the scene has been calibrated so that image points are represented by their normalized coordinate vectors. Under orthographic projection, a^T and b^T are the first two rows of a rotation matrix, and it follows that an orthographic camera is an affine camera with the additional constraints

$$|a|^2 = |b|^2 = 1 \quad \text{and} \quad a \cdot b = 0. \tag{3}$$

Likewise, a weak perspective camera is an affine camera with the constraints

$$|a|^2 = |b|^2 \quad \text{and} \quad a \cdot b = 0. \tag{4}$$

Finally, a paraperspective camera is an affine camera with the constraints

$$a \cdot b = \frac{u_r v_r}{2(1 + u_r^2)}|a|^2 + \frac{u_r v_r}{2(1 + v_r^2)}|b|^2$$

and

$$(1 + v_r^2)|a|^2 = (1 + u_r^2)|b|^2,$$

where (u_r, v_r) denote the coordinates of the image of the reference point associated with the scene (see [16] for the use of similar constraints in Euclidean shape and motion recovery).

As shown earlier, the set of affine images of a fixed scene is an eight-dimensional variety. If we restrict our attention to weak perspective cameras, the set of images becomes the six-dimensional sub-variety defined by the additional constraints (4). Similar constraints apply to paraperspective and true perspective projection, and they also define six-dimensional varieties. We only detail the weak perspective case in the next three sections; the extension to the paraperspective case is straightforward [7]. Extending the proposed approach to the full perspective case would require eliminating three motion parameters among five quadratic Euclidean constraints, a formidable task in elimination theory [15].

2   Parameterized Image Varieties

We propose a parameterization of the six-dimensional variety formed by the weak perspective images of m points and n lines in terms of the image positions of three points in the scene. This parameterization defines the *parameterized image variety* (or *PIV*) associated with the scene. Let us suppose that we observe three points A_0, A_1, A_2 whose images are not collinear (see Fig. 1). We can choose (without loss of generality) a Euclidean coordinate system such that the coordinate vectors of the three points in this system are $A_0 = (0,0,0)^T$, $A_1 = (1,0,0)^T$, $A_2 = (p,q,0)^T$ (the values of p and q are nonzero but unknown). These points will be used to parameterize the PIV in the next two sections.

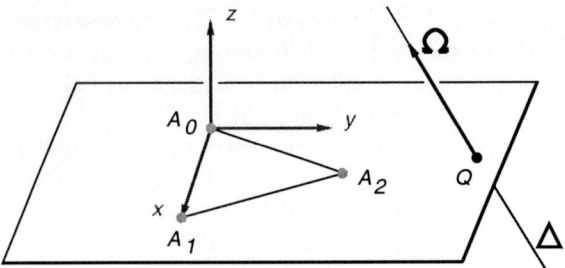

Fig. 1. Geometric setup used in the rest of the paper.

2.1   The Point PIV

This section briefly summarizes the presentation of [5]. Let us consider a point P and its projection p in the image plane, and denote by $\boldsymbol{P} = (x, y, z)^T$ and $\boldsymbol{p} = (u, v)^T$ their coordinate vectors. The values of (x, y, z) are of course unknown. We will also assume that $u_0 = v_0 = 0$ since we can go back to the general case via an image translation. Applying (1) to A_1, A_2 and P yields

$$\boldsymbol{u} \stackrel{\text{def}}{=} \begin{pmatrix} u_1 \\ u_2 \\ u \end{pmatrix} = \mathcal{A}\boldsymbol{a} \quad \text{and} \quad \boldsymbol{v} \stackrel{\text{def}}{=} \begin{pmatrix} v_1 \\ v_2 \\ v \end{pmatrix} = \mathcal{A}\boldsymbol{b}, \tag{5}$$

where

$$\mathcal{A} \stackrel{\text{def}}{=} \begin{pmatrix} \boldsymbol{A}_1^T \\ \boldsymbol{A}_2^T \\ \boldsymbol{P}^T \end{pmatrix} = \begin{pmatrix} 1 & 0 & 0 \\ p & q & 0 \\ x & y & z \end{pmatrix}.$$

In turn, we have $\boldsymbol{a} = \mathcal{B}\boldsymbol{u}$ and $\boldsymbol{b} = \mathcal{B}\boldsymbol{v}$, where

$$\mathcal{B} \stackrel{\text{def}}{=} \mathcal{A}^{-1} = \begin{pmatrix} 1 & 0 & 0 \\ \lambda & \mu & 0 \\ \alpha/z & \beta/z & 1/z \end{pmatrix} \quad \text{and} \quad \begin{cases} \lambda = -p/q, \\ \mu = 1/q, \\ \alpha = -(x + \lambda y), \\ \beta = -\mu y. \end{cases}$$

Letting $\mathcal{C} \stackrel{\text{def}}{=} z^2 \mathcal{B}^T \mathcal{B}$, the weak perspective constraints (4) can now be rewritten as

$$\begin{cases} \boldsymbol{u}^T \mathcal{C} \boldsymbol{u} - \boldsymbol{v}^T \mathcal{C} \boldsymbol{v} = 0, \\ \boldsymbol{u}^T \mathcal{C} \boldsymbol{v} = 0, \end{cases}$$

with

$$\mathcal{C} = \begin{pmatrix} \xi_1 & \xi_2 & \alpha \\ \xi_2 & \xi_3 & \beta \\ \alpha & \beta & 1 \end{pmatrix} \quad \text{and} \quad \begin{cases} \xi_1 = (1 + \lambda^2)z^2 + \alpha^2, \\ \xi_2 = \lambda\mu z^2 + \alpha\beta, \\ \xi_3 = \mu^2 z^2 + \beta^2. \end{cases}$$

This equation defines a pair of linear constraints on the coefficients ξ_i ($i = 1, 2, 3$), α and β; they can be rewritten as

$$\begin{pmatrix} \boldsymbol{d}_1^T - \boldsymbol{d}_2^T \\ \boldsymbol{d}^T \end{pmatrix} \boldsymbol{\xi} = 0, \tag{6}$$

where

$$\begin{cases} \boldsymbol{d}_1 \overset{\text{def}}{=} (u_1^2, 2u_1u_2, u_2^2, 2u_1u, 2u_2u, u^2)^T, \\ \boldsymbol{d}_2 \overset{\text{def}}{=} (v_1^2, 2v_1v_2, v_2^2, 2v_1v, 2v_2v, v^2)^T, \\ \boldsymbol{d} \overset{\text{def}}{=} (u_1v_1, u_1v_2 + u_2v_1, u_2v_2, u_1v + uv_1, u_2v + uv_2, uv)^T, \\ \boldsymbol{\xi} \overset{\text{def}}{=} (\xi_1, \xi_2, \xi_3, \alpha, \beta, 1)^T. \end{cases}$$

When the four points A_0, A_1, A_2, and P are rigidly attached to each other, the five structure coefficients ξ_1, ξ_2, ξ_3, α and β are fixed. For a rigid scene formed by m points, choosing three of the points as a reference triangle and writing (6) for the remaining ones yields a set of $2m - 6$ quadratic equations in $2m$ unknowns that define a parameterization of the set of all weak perspective images of the scenes. This is the PIV. Note that the weak perspective constraints (6) are linear in the five structure coefficients. Thus, given a collection of images and point correspondences, we can compute these coefficients through linear least-squares (see [6] for an alternative solution).

Once the vector $\boldsymbol{\xi}$ has been estimated, we can specify arbitrary image positions for our three reference points and use (6) to compute u and v. A more convenient form for this equation is obtained by introducing

$$\mathcal{E} \overset{\text{def}}{=} \begin{pmatrix} \xi_1 - \alpha^2 & \xi_2 - \alpha\beta \\ \xi_2 - \alpha\beta & \xi_3 - \beta^2 \end{pmatrix} = \begin{pmatrix} (1 + \lambda^2)z^2 & \lambda\mu z^2 \\ \lambda\mu z^2 & \mu^2 z^2 \end{pmatrix},$$

and defining $\boldsymbol{u}_2 = (u_1, u_2)^T$ and $\boldsymbol{v}_2 = (v_1, v_2)^T$. This allows us to rewrite (4) as

$$\begin{cases} X^2 - Y^2 + e_1 - e_2 = 0, \\ 2XY + e = 0, \end{cases} \tag{7}$$

where

$$\begin{cases} e_1 = \boldsymbol{u}_2^T \mathcal{E} \boldsymbol{u}_2, \\ e_2 = \boldsymbol{v}_2^T \mathcal{E} \boldsymbol{v}_2, \quad \text{and} \quad \begin{cases} X = u + \alpha u_1 + \beta u_2, \\ Y = v + \alpha v_1 + \beta v_2. \end{cases} \\ e = 2\boldsymbol{u}_2^T \mathcal{E} \boldsymbol{v}_2, \end{cases}$$

It is easy to show [5] that only two of the (X, Y) pairs of solutions of (7) are physically correct, and that they can be computed in closed form. The values of u and v are then trivially obtained.

2.2   The Line PIV

Line position. Let us now consider a line Δ and assume that its intersection with the reference plane spanned by the points A_0, A_1 and A_2 is transversal (see

Fig. 1). Without loss of generality, we can parameterize this line by the affine coordinates (χ_1, χ_2) of the point Q in the basis (A_0, A_1, A_2), i.e.,

$$Q = A_0 + \chi_1 A_1 + \chi_2 A_2,$$

and by the coordinate vector $\boldsymbol{\Omega} = (x, y, 1)^T$ of its direction in the Euclidean world coordinate system.

Let δ denote the projection of Δ. We can parameterize this line by the position of the image q of the point Q and the unit coordinate vector $\boldsymbol{\omega} = (\cos\theta, \sin\theta)^T$ of its direction (see Fig. 2). If we take as before a_0 as the origin of the image plane, and denote by d the distance between a_0 and δ, the equation of δ is

$$-u\sin\theta + v\cos\theta - d = 0, \tag{8}$$

where (u, v) denote image coordinates. Since the point Q lies in the reference plane, the affine coordinates of q in the coordinate system a_0, a_1, a_2 are also χ_1 and χ_2 and substituting in (8) yields

$$(u_1\sin\theta - v_1\cos\theta)\chi_1 + (u_2\sin\theta - v_2\cos\theta)\chi_2 + d = 0,$$

which is a linear equation in χ_1 and χ_2. Given several images of the line Δ, we can thus estimate χ_1 and χ_2 via linear least-squares. These affine coordinates can then be used to predict the position of q in any new image once a_0, a_1 and a_2 have been specified.

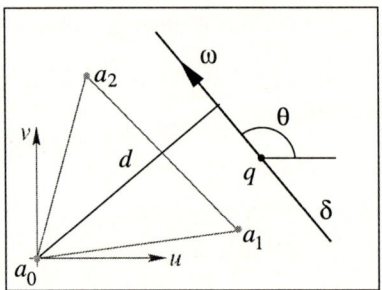

Fig. 2. Parameterization of δ.

Line orientation. Let us now turn to the prediction of the orientation θ of the image line. The equations derived in Section 2.1 still apply when we take $\boldsymbol{P} = \boldsymbol{\Omega}$ and $\boldsymbol{p} = \rho\boldsymbol{\omega}$, where ρ is an image-dependent scale factor. Note that since the overall value of ρ is irrelevant, we can take $z = 1$ without loss of generality.

There are two differences with the point case: (a) the parameters ξ_i ($1 = 1, 2, 3$), α and β are no longer independent since there is no z parameter to take into account, and (b) the equations in (7) contain terms in ρ, that depend on the image considered since this time

$$X = \rho\cos\theta + \alpha u_1 + \beta u_2 \quad \text{and} \quad Y = \rho\sin\theta + \alpha v_1 + \beta v_2.$$

Substituting these values in (7) and eliminating ρ yields, after some algebraic manipulation

$$f_{12} - g_{12}\cos 2\theta - g\sin 2\theta = \sqrt{(e_1 - e_2)^2 + e^2}, \qquad (9)$$

with

$$\begin{cases} f_{12} \stackrel{\text{def}}{=} u_2^T \mathcal{F} u_2 + v_2^T \mathcal{F} v_2, \\ g \stackrel{\text{def}}{=} 2u_2 \mathcal{G} v_2, \\ g_{12} \stackrel{\text{def}}{=} u_2 \mathcal{G} u_2 - v_2 \mathcal{G} v_2, \end{cases} \quad \text{and} \quad \begin{cases} \mathcal{F} \stackrel{\text{def}}{=} \begin{pmatrix} \alpha^2 & \alpha\beta \\ \alpha\beta & \beta^2 \end{pmatrix}, \\ \mathcal{G} \stackrel{\text{def}}{=} \begin{pmatrix} \xi_1 & \xi_2 \\ \xi_2 & \xi_3 \end{pmatrix}. \end{cases}$$

This allows us to construct a minimal set of four structure parameters ε_1, ε_2, ε_3 and Θ by introducing $\gamma = \sqrt{\alpha^2 + \beta^2}$ and defining

$$\begin{cases} \varepsilon_1 = (1 + \lambda^2)/\gamma^2, \\ \varepsilon_2 = \lambda\mu/\gamma^2, \\ \varepsilon_3 = \mu^2/\gamma^2, \end{cases} \quad \text{and} \quad \Theta = \text{Arg}(\alpha, \beta).$$

With this notation, (9) becomes

$$(i_1 + i_2) - (h_1 - h_2 + i_1 - i_2)\cos 2\theta - (h + i)\sin 2\theta = \sqrt{(h_1 - h_2)^2 + h^2}, \quad (10)$$

where

$$\begin{cases} h \stackrel{\text{def}}{=} 2u_2 \mathcal{H} v_2, \\ h_1 \stackrel{\text{def}}{=} u_2^T \mathcal{H} u_2, \\ h_2 \stackrel{\text{def}}{=} v_2^T \mathcal{H} v_2, \\ i \stackrel{\text{def}}{=} u_2 \mathcal{I} v_2, \\ i_1 \stackrel{\text{def}}{=} \frac{1}{2} u_2^T \mathcal{I} u_2, \\ i_2 \stackrel{\text{def}}{=} \frac{1}{2} v_2^T \mathcal{I} v_2, \end{cases} \quad \text{and} \quad \begin{cases} \mathcal{H} \stackrel{\text{def}}{=} \begin{pmatrix} \varepsilon_1 & \varepsilon_2 \\ \varepsilon_2 & \varepsilon_3 \end{pmatrix}, \\ \mathcal{I} \stackrel{\text{def}}{=} \begin{pmatrix} \frac{1}{2}(1 + \cos 2\Theta) & \sin 2\Theta \\ \sin 2\Theta & \frac{1}{2}(1 - \cos 2\Theta) \end{pmatrix}. \end{cases}$$

Given a set of line correspondences, the four structure parameters ε_1, ε_2, ε_3 and Θ can be estimated via non-linear least-squares. At synthesis time, (10) becomes a trigonometric equation in 2θ, with two solutions that are easily computed in closed form. Each of this solution only determines θ up to a π ambiguity, which is immaterial in our case.

Note that directly minimizing the error corresponding to (10) is a biased process. A better method is to minimize $\sum_{i=1}^{p}(\theta_i - \hat{\theta}_i)^2$, where $\hat{\theta}_i$ is the line orientation empirically measured in image number i, and θ_i is the orientation predicted from (10). This is a constrained minimization problem, and the derivatives of θ_i with respect to the structure parameters are easily computed from the partial derivatives of (10) with respect to θ and these parameters.

From lines to line segments. Infinite lines are inappropriate for realistic graphical display. Thus we must associate with each of them a finite line segment that can be passed to a rendering module. On the other hand, while lines can be localized very accurately in the input images, the position of their end-points cannot in general be estimated reliably since most edge finders behave poorly near edge junctions. Additional line breaks can also be introduced by the program that segments edges into straight lines. Here we present a method for computing an estimate of the endpoints of a line from its PIV.

Let R denote one of the endpoints of the segment associated with the line Δ, and let r denote its image. We have $r - q = l\omega$, and $R - Q = L\Omega$, and we can once again write $\rho\omega = \mathcal{M}\Omega$, where this time $\rho = l/L$. The (signed) distance l is known at training time and unknown at synthesis time, while the (signed) distance L is unknown at training time and known at synthesis time. It is easily shown that

$$X^2 + Y^2 = \gamma^2 \sqrt{(h_1 - h_2)^2 + h^2},$$

and expanding this expression yields a quadratic equation in ρ

$$\rho^2 - 2c\rho + d = 0, \tag{11}$$

where

$$\begin{cases} c \stackrel{\text{def}}{=} \gamma((u_1 \cos \Theta + u_2 \sin \Theta) \cos \theta + (v_1 \cos \Theta + v_2 \sin \Theta) \sin \theta), \\ d \stackrel{\text{def}}{=} \gamma^2(i_{12} - \sqrt{h_{12}^2 + h^2}). \end{cases}$$

Note that we can compute γ from the vector $(\varepsilon_1, \varepsilon_2, \varepsilon_3)^T$ as

$$\gamma = \sqrt{\varepsilon_3/(\varepsilon_1 \varepsilon_3 - \varepsilon_2^2)}.$$

During training, (11) can be used to estimate $|L|$ from a single image or from several ones (via non-linear least squares). During image synthesis, we estimate $|l|$ as $|\rho L|$, and give a sign to l using tracking from a real image.

3   Image Synthesis

Once the PIV parameters have been estimated, the scene can be rendered from a new viewpoint by specifying interactively the image positions of the three reference points, and computing the corresponding image positions of all other points and lines. To create a shaded picture, we can construct a constrained Delaunay triangulation of these lines and points [20], whose vertices and edges will be a subset of the input points and line segments. Texture mapping is then easily achieved by using the triangulation of one of the input images. This section details the main stages of the rendering process.

3.1   Integration of Point and Line PIVs

Once the structure parameters associated with all the points and lines have been computed, these can be used to construct a refined estimate of the parameters $1 + \lambda^2$, $\lambda\mu$ and μ^2 that are common across all features. Indeed, the vectors $(\xi_1 - \alpha^2, \xi_2 - \alpha\beta, \xi_3 - \beta^2)^T$ and $(\varepsilon_1, \varepsilon_2, \varepsilon_3)^T$ associated with the various lines and points all belong to the one-dimensional vector space spanned by $(1 + \lambda^2, \lambda\mu, \mu^2)^T$. A representative unit vector $(\eta_1, \eta_2, \eta_3)^T$ can be found via singular value decomposition, and we obtain

$$\begin{cases} 1 + \lambda^2 = \eta_1\eta_3/(\eta_1\eta_3 - \eta_2^2), \\ \lambda\mu = \eta_2\eta_3/(\eta_1\eta_3 - \eta_2^2), \\ \mu^2 = \eta_3\eta_3/(\eta_1\eta_3 - \eta_2^2). \end{cases}$$

Once these common structure parameters have been estimated, a better estimate of the point PIV can be constructed via linear least squares [5]. In the case of lines, (10) becomes an equation in γ^2 and 2Θ only, and better estimates of these parameters can be computed once again via non-linear least squares.

With the line segments associated to each line and the refined structure parameters in hand, we are now in a position to construct a shaded picture. As noted before, we can construct a constrained Delaunay triangulation of the line segments and points (using, for example Shewuck's Triangle public-domain software [20]) whose vertices and edges form a superset of the input points and line segments. Texture mapping is then easily achieved by using the triangulation of one of the input images.

3.2   Hidden-Surface Removal

Here we show how traditional z-buffer techniques can be used to perform hidden-surface elimination even though no explicit 3D reconstruction is performed. The technique is the same as in [5] and it is summarized here for completeness. Let Π denote the image plane of one of our input images, and Π' the image plane of our synthetic image. To render correctly two points P and Q that project onto the same point r' in the synthetic image, we must compare their depths.

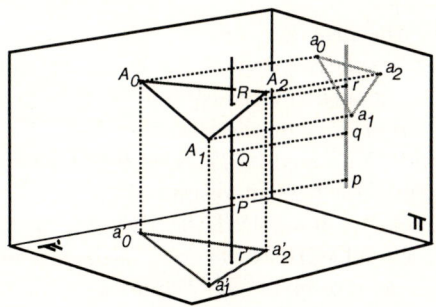

Fig. 3. Using a z-buffer without actual depth values.

Let R denote the intersection of the viewing ray joining P to Q with the plane spanned by the reference points A_0, A_1 and A_2, and let p, q, r denote the projections of P, Q and R into the reference image. Suppose for the time being that P and Q are two of the points tracked in the input image; it follows that the positions of p and q are known. The position of r is easily computed by remarking that its coordinates in the affine basis of Π formed by the projections a_0, a_1, a_2 of the reference points are the same as the coordinates of R in the affine basis formed by the points A_0, A_1, A_2 in their own plane, and thus are also the same as the coordinates of r' in the affine basis of Π' formed by the projections a_0', a_1', a_2' of the reference points.

The ratio of the depths of P and Q relative to the plane Π is simply the ratio $\overline{pr}/\overline{qr}$. Not that deciding which point is actually visible requires orienting the line supporting the points p, q, r, which is simply the epipolar line associated with the point r'. A coherent orientation should be chosen for all epipolar lines and all frames. This is easily done, up to a two-fold ambiguity, using the technique described in [5].

3.3   Rendering

Given an input triangulation, the entire scene can now be rendered as follows: (1) pick the correct orientation for the epipolar lines (using one of the point correspondences and the previous orientation); (2) compute, for each of the data points P, the position of r in the reference image and the "depth" $\overline{pr}$ and store it as its "z" coordinate; (3) render the triangles forming the scenes using a z-buffer algorithm with orthographic projection along the z-axis. Texture mapping is easily incorporated in the process. It should be noted that this process can generate two families of images corresponding to the initial choice of epipolar line orientation. The choice can be made by the user during interactive image synthesis.

4   Implementation and Results

We have implemented the proposed approach and tested it on real data sets. The LQBOX data set is kindly provided by Dr. Long Quan from CNRS, the TOWER and XL1BOX data sets were acquired by the authors in the Computer Vision and Robotics Laboratory at the Beckman Institute, using a Canon XL1 Digital Camcorder kindly provided by Dr. David Kriegman.

For completeness, we first present results of point PIV experiments. Along with the above data sets we have used the HOUSE data set kindly provided by Dr. Carlo Tomasi, the KITCHEN data set kindly provided by the Modeling by Videotaping Research Group at the Department of Computer Science of Carnegie Mellon University and the FLOWER and FACE data sets acquired by the authors. Note that for both point and line features, we have four variants of the PIV algorithm, namely, the first and second passes of the weak perspective and paraperspective algorithms (or W1, P1, W2 and P2 in short). Fig. 4 shows some quantitative results where we have estimated the PIVs for each data set using different numbers of images in training. In particular we have used the

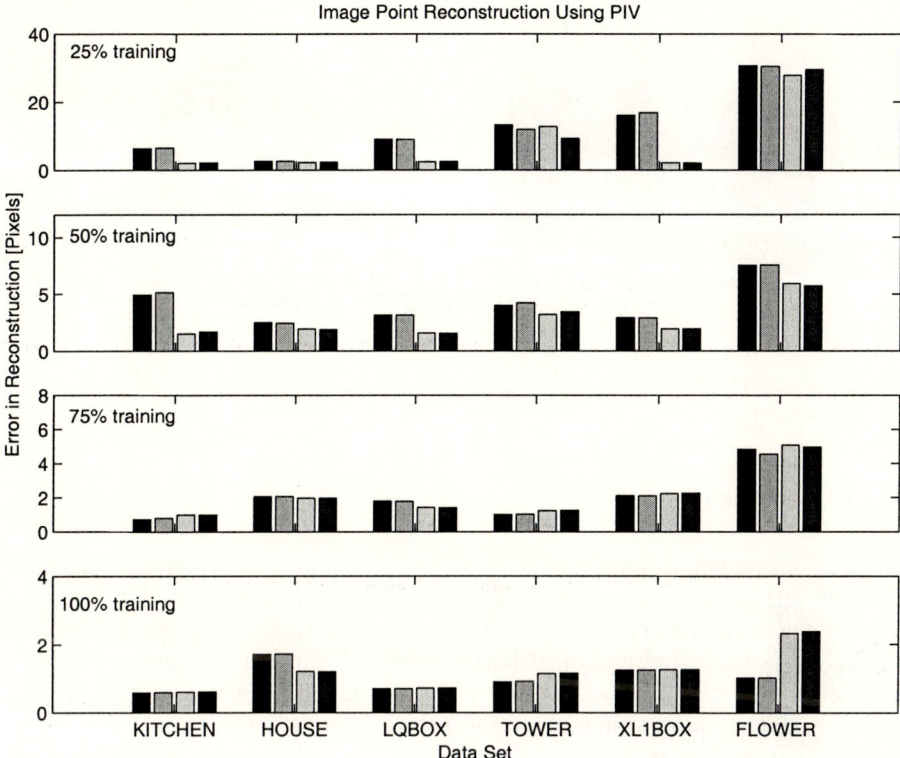

Fig. 4. Average error in image point reconstruction on real data sets: for each data the bars from left to right represents the W1, P1, W2 and P2 methods. In training, from top to bottom, the first 25%, 50%, 75% and 100% of the images are used.

first 25%, 50%, 75%, or 100% of the data in training and used the rest of the data as test images to compute the reprojection errors (except in the last case where all the data is used in training and testing). Figure 5 shows synthesized images for novel views using point PIVs.

Fig. 6 shows the mean errors for the reconstruction of images of line features for four different methods as it is done for point features above. Note that the line position is computed using affine notions only. We have recorded the error in reconstruction of the line position in pixels and the line direction in degrees.

Fig. 7 shows the line features with their extents reconstructed for the last frame in the TOWER data, with the first half of the images used for training. The original lines plotted as dotted lines.

Finally, Fig. 8 shows view-synthesis results where we have used the line and point PIVs together. More view synthesis results in the form of movies can found in http://www-cvr.ai.uiuc.edu/~ygenc/thesis/index.html.

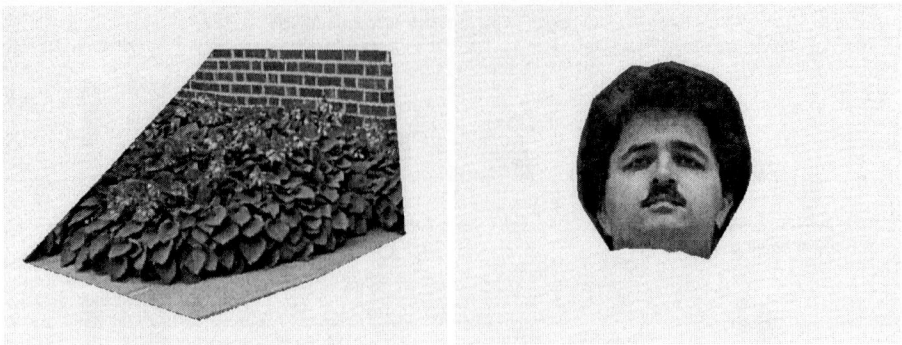

Fig. 5. Image synthesis for novel views using point features for the FLOWER and FACE data sets.

5   Discussion

We have presented an integrated method for image-based rendering from point and line correspondences established across image sequences, and demonstrated an implementation using real images. A very interesting problem that we plan to explore is the construction of better meshes from image sequences. This is a difficult issue for any image-based rendering technique that does not attempt to estimate the camera motion or the actual scene structure, and it is also a very important one in practice since rendering a scene from truely arbitrary viewpoints requires constructing a mesh covering its whole surface.

Acknowledgments

This work was partially supported by the National Science Foundation under grant IRI-9634312, by the National Aeronautics and Space Administration under grant NAG 1-613, and by the Beckman Institute at the University of Illinois at Urbana-Champaign. We wish to thank Andrew Fitzgibbon, David Kriegman, Conrad J. Poelman, Long Quan, Carlo Tomasi, Andrew Zisserman, and the Modeling by Videotaping Research Group at Carnegie Mellon University for providing us with the data used in our experiments.

References

1. S. Avidan and A. Shashua. Novel view synthesis in tensor space. In *Proc. CVPR*, pp. 1034–1040, 1997.
2. E.B. Barrett, M.H. Brill, N.N. Haag, and P.M. Payton. Invariant linear models in photogrammetry and model-matching. In J. Mundy and A. Zisserman, eds., *Geometric Invariance in Computer Vision*, pp. 277–292. MIT Press, 1992.
3. S.E. Chen. Quicktime VR: An image-based approach to virtual environment navigation. In *SIGGRAPH*, pp. 29–38, 1995.

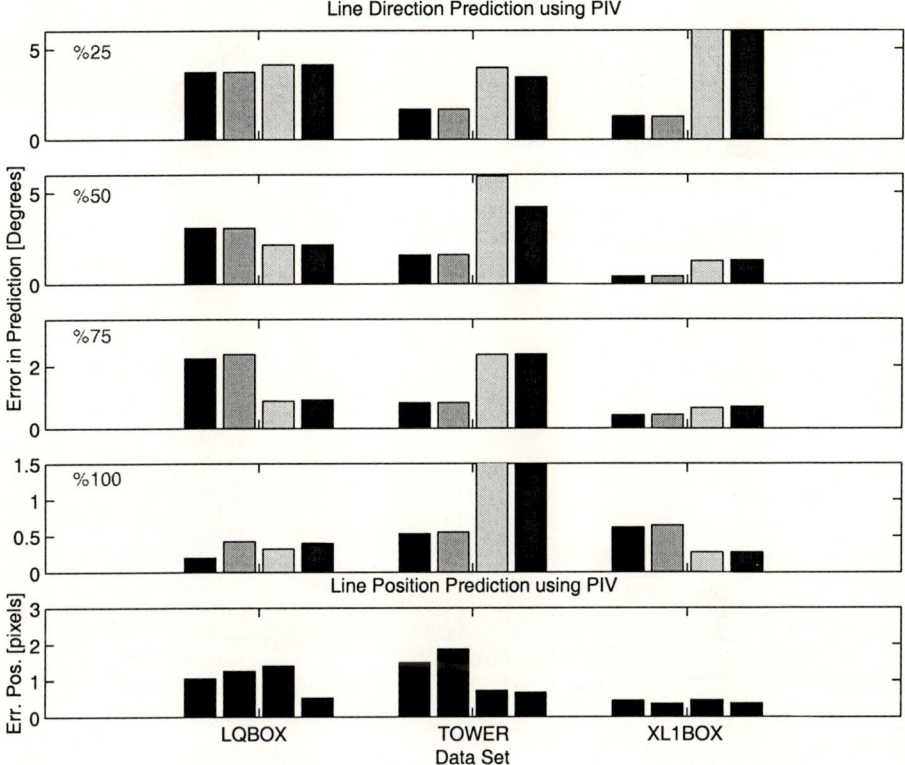

Fig. 6. Image line reconstruction on real data sets. The upper four graphs show the error in line directions where the bars from left to right represents the W1, P1, W2 and P2 methods. From top to bottom, the first 25%, 50%, 75% and 100% of the images are used in training. The last graph shows the error in line position from left to right the first 25%, 50%, 75% and 100% of the images were used in training.

4. O.D. Faugeras. What can be seen in three dimensions with an uncalibrated stereo rig? In *Proc. ECCV*, pp. 563–578, 1992.

5. Y. Genc and J. Ponce. Parameterized image varieties: A novel approach to the analysis and synthesis of image sequences. In *Proc. ICCV*, pp. 11–16, 1998.

6. Y. Genc, J. Ponce, Y. Leedan, and P. Meer. Parameterized image varieties and estimation with bilinear constraints. In *Proc. CVPR*, 1999.

7. Yakup Genc. *Weak Calibration and Image-Based Rendering Algorithms*. PhD thesis, University of Illinois at Urbana-Champaign, September 1999.

8. S.J. Gortler, R. Grzeszczuk, R. Szeliski, and M. Cohen. The lumigraph. In *SIGGRAPH*, pp. 43–54, 1996.

9. R.I. Hartley. A linear method for reconstruction from lines and points. In *Proc. ICCV*, pp. 882–887, 1995.

10. R.I. Hartley, R. Gupta, and T. Chang. Stereo from uncalibrated cameras. In *Proc. CVPR*, pp. 761–764, 1992.

W1

P1

W2

P2

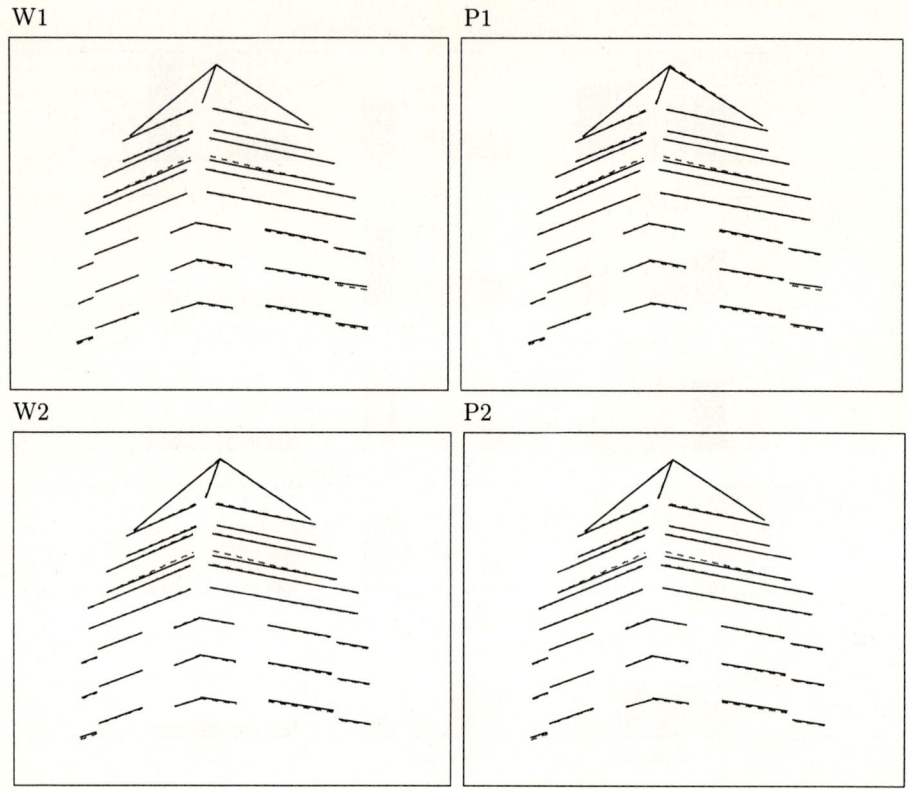

Fig. 7. Reconstructed lines (solid) together with the original lines (dotted) for the last image in the TOWER data set.

11. J.J. Koenderink and A.J. Van Doorn. Affine structure from motion. *J. Opt. Soc. Am. A*, 8:377–385, 1990.
12. K.N. Kutulakos and J. Vallino. Calibration-free augmented reality. *IEEE Trans. Vis. Comp. Gr.*, 4(1):1–20, 1998.
13. S. Laveau and O.D. Faugeras. 3D scene representation as a collection of images and fundamental matrices. Tech. Rep. 2205, INRIA, 1994.
14. M. Levoy and P. Hanrahan. Light field rendering. In *SIGGRAPH*, pp. 31–42, 1996.
15. F.S. Macaulay. *The Algebraic Theory of Modular Systems.* Cambridge Univ. Press, 1916.
16. C.J. Poelman and T. Kanade. A paraperspective factorization method for shape and motion recovery. *PAMI*, 19(3):206–218, 1997.
17. L. Quan and T. Kanade. Affine structure from line correspondences with uncalibrated affine cameras. *PAMI*, 19(8):834–845, 1997.
18. S.M. Seitz and C.R. Dyer. Physically-valid view synthesis by image interpolation. In *Work. on Representation of Visual Scenes*, 1995.
19. A. Shashua. Trilinearity in visual recognition by alignment. In *Proc. ECCV*, pp. 479–484, 1994.

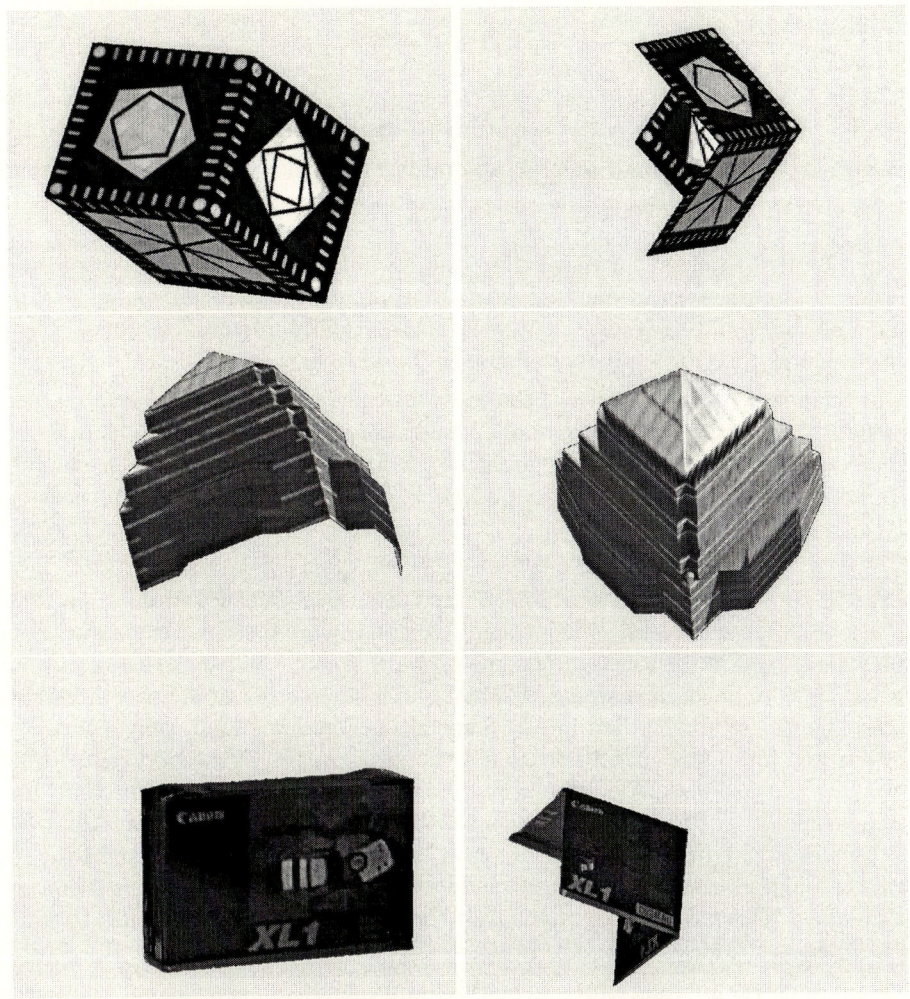

Fig. 8. Image synthesis for novel views using both line and point features.

20. J.R. Shewchuk. Triangle: Engineering a 2D quality mesh generator and Delaunay triangulator. In *ACM Work. Applied Computational Geometry*, pp. 124–133, 1996.
21. C.J. Taylor and D.J. Kriegman. Structure and motion from line segments in multiple images. *PAMI*, 17(10):1021–1032, 1995.

Discussion

Yongduek Seo: In the tower movie I see that there are shadows. Would it be possible to change the shadow according to the motion?

Jean Ponce: That would be nice, but I don't know how to do it. David Kriegman did something like that for fixed illumination and Lambertian objects. In principal you could take this funny linear illumination model and put it in, but if you wanted to use it for real I think there would be a lot of engineering work to do. It's not clear how much the graphics companies want these things. Yakup tells me that building geometric models is not very interesting for them — they can just buy a set of scanners and do the job like that.

Bill Triggs: Following on from the previous talk, your six-dimensional variety obviously supports some sort of embedding of Euclidean structure, including the Euclidean group motions. So it might be possible to use Lie algebra techniques to move yourself around with your joystick. Secondly, you talk about varieties but it isn't clear to me that the global structure is of any use to you — really you are looking at just one point on the variety.

Jean Ponce: I agree on both points. Let me answer the second question first. The points are completely independent except when we estimate the structure coefficients and put it together. There two ways it could be better. First, instead of the three point basis it would be nice to do it some other way. Second, ideally, you should take all the data into account at once and we don't know how yet.

For the first question on how to use the joystick, yes we could do something like that. For example Avidan and Shashua use the trifocal tensor for that, but they explicitly put in a representation of the rotation. In our case we didn't try it because we didn't want either motion or 3D structure. We wanted to work only in the image and see what we could do there. Even then, there is still a lot of implicit 3D stuff. But yes, if you wanted you could probably go back to some Euclidean embedding and make it work.

Yvan Leclerc: In your experiments, did you manually segment out the tower or was it automatic?

Jean Ponce: We built a simple tracker/segmenter and after that cleaned the results by hand.

Recovery of Circular Motion from Profiles of Surfaces

Paulo R. S. Mendonça, Kwan-Yee K. Wong, and Roberto Cipolla

Department of Engineering, University of Cambridge,
Trumpington Street, Cambridge, CB2 1PZ, UK
{prdsm2, kykw2, cipolla}@eng.cam.ac.uk

Abstract. This paper addresses the problem of motion recovery from image profiles, in the important case of turntable sequences. No correspondences between points or lines are used. Symmetry properties of surfaces of revolution are exploited to obtain, in a robust and simple way, the image of the rotation axis of the sequence and the homography relating epipolar lines. These, together with geometric constraints for images of rotating objects, are used to obtain epipoles and, consequently, the full epipolar geometry of the camera system. This sequential approach (image of rotation axis — homography — epipoles) avoids many of the problems usually found in other algorithms for motion recovery from profiles. In particular, the search for the epipoles, by far the most critical step for the estimation of the epipolar geometry, is carried out as a one-dimensional optimization problem, with a smooth unimodal cost function. The initialization of the parameters is trivial in all three stages of the algorithm. After the estimation of the epipolar geometry, the motion is recovered using the fixed intrinsic parameters of the camera, obtained either from a calibration grid or from self-calibration techniques. Results from real data are presented, demonstrating the efficiency and practicality of the algorithm.

1 Introduction

Points and lines have long been used for the recovery of structure and motion from images of 3D objects. Nevertheless, for a smooth surface the predominant feature in the image is its *profile* or *apparent contour*, defined as the projection of a *contour generator* of the surface. A contour generator corresponds to the set of points on a surface where the normal vector to the surface is orthogonal to the rays joining the points in the set and the camera center (for details, see [3, 4]). If the surface does not have noticeable texture, the profile may actually be the only source of information available for estimating the structure of the surface and the motion of the camera.

The problem of motion recovery from image profiles has been tackled in several works. The concept of *frontier point*, defined as a point on a surface tangent to any plane of the pencil of epipolar planes related to a pair of images, was introduced in [15]. The idea was further developed in [14], where the frontier point was recognized as a fixed point on a surface, created by the intersection of two contour generators. A frontier point projects on its associated images as an *epipolar tangency*. The use of frontier points and epipolar tangencies for motion recovery was first shown in [2]. A parallax based technique, using a reference planar contour was shown in [1], where the images are registered using the reference contour and common tangents are used

B. Triggs, A. Zisserman, R. Szeliski (Eds.): Vision Algorithms'99, LNCS 1883, pp. 149–165, 2000.
© Springer-Verlag Berlin Heidelberg 2000

to determine the projections of the frontier point. The techniques described above face two main difficulties: the likely non-uniqueness of the solution, due to the presence of local minima, and the unrealistic requirement of having at least 7 corresponding epipolar tangencies available on each image pair. Better results can be achieved when an affine approximation is used, as shown in [11]. In this case the problem can be solved when as few as 4 epipolar tangencies are available, but the application of the method is constrained to situations where the affine approximation is valid.

In the case of circular motion, the envelope of the profiles exhibits symmetry properties that greatly simplify this estimation problem. This is an idea well developed for orthographic projection. In [15] it is shown that, when the image plane is parallel to the axis of rotation, the image of the axis of rotation will be perpendicular to common tangents to the images of the profile. The use of bilateral symmetry to obtain the axis of rotation was first introduced in [13]. The condition of parallelism between the image plane and the axis of rotation was relaxed in [8], but orthographic projection was still used.

In this paper we introduce a novel technique for the estimation of the motion parameters of turntable sequences. It based on symmetry properties of the set of apparent contours generated by the object that undergoes the rotation. In Section 2, a method for obtaining the images of the axis of rotation and a special vanishing point is presented. The algorithm is simple, efficient and robust, and it does not make direct use of the profiles. Therefore, its use can be extended to non-smooth objects, and the quality of the results obtained justifies doing so. Section 3 makes use of the previous results to introduce a parameterization of the fundamental matrix based on the *harmonic homology*. This parameterization allows for the estimation of the epipoles to be carried out as independent one-dimensional searches, avoiding local minima points and greatly decreasing the computational complexity of the estimation. These results are used in Section 4, which presents the algorithm for motion estimation. Experimental results are shown in Section 5, and conclusions and future work are described in Section 6.

2   Theoretical Background

An object rotating about a fixed axis sweeps out a surface of revolution [8]. Symmetry properties [18, 19] of the image of this surface of revolution can be exploited to estimate the parameters of the motion of the object in a simple and elegant way, as will be shown next.

2.1   Symmetry Properties of Images of Surfaces of Revolution

In the definitions that follow, points and lines will be referred to by their representation as vectors in homogeneous coordinates.

A 2D homography that keeps the pencil of lines through a point u and the set of points on a line l fixed is called a *perspective collineation* with center u and axis l. An *homology* is a perspective collineation whose center and axis are not incident (otherwise the perspective homology is called an *elation*). Let a be a point mapped by an homology onto a point a'. It is easy to show that the center of the homology u, a and a' are collinear.

Let $\mathbf{q}_a$ be the line passing through these points, and $\mathbf{v}_a$ the intersection of $\mathbf{q}_a$ and the axis $\mathbf{l}$. If $\mathbf{a}$ and $\mathbf{a}'$ are harmonic conjugates with respect to $\mathbf{u}$ and $\mathbf{v}_a$, i.e., their cross-ratio is one, the homology is said to be a *harmonic homology* (see details in [16, 5]). The matrix $\mathbf{W}$ representing a harmonic homology with center $\mathbf{u}$ and axis $\mathbf{l}$ in homogeneous coordinates is given by

$$\mathbf{W} = \mathbb{I} - 2\frac{\mathbf{u}\mathbf{l}^{\mathrm{T}}}{\mathbf{u}^{\mathrm{T}}\mathbf{l}}. \tag{1}$$

Henceforth a matrix representing a projective transformation in homogeneous coordinates will be used in reference to the transformation itself whenever an ambiguity does not arise.

An important property of profiles of surfaces of revolution is stated in the next theorem:

Theorem 1. *The profile of a surface of revolution S viewed by a pinhole camera is invariant to the harmonic homology with axis given by the image of the axis of rotation of the surface of revolution and center given by the image of the point at infinity in a direction orthogonal to a plane that contains the axis of rotation and the camera center.*

The following lemma will be used in the proof of Theorem 1.

Lemma 1. *Let $\mathbf{T} : \Gamma \mapsto \Gamma$ be a harmonic homology with axis $\mathbf{l}$ and center $\mathbf{u}$ on the plane Γ, and let $\mathbf{H} : \Gamma \mapsto \Gamma'$ be a bijective 2D homography. Then, the transformation $\mathbf{W} = \mathbf{H}\mathbf{T}\mathbf{H}^{-1} : \Gamma' \mapsto \Gamma'$ is a harmonic homology with axis $\mathbf{l}' = \mathbf{H}^{-\mathrm{T}}\mathbf{l}$ and center $\mathbf{u}' = \mathbf{H}\mathbf{u}$.*

Proof. Since $\mathbf{H}$ is bijective, $\mathbf{H}^{-1}$ exists. Then

$$\mathbf{W} = \mathbf{H}\left(\mathbb{I} - 2\frac{\mathbf{u}\mathbf{l}^{\mathrm{T}}}{\mathbf{u}^{\mathrm{T}}\mathbf{l}}\right)\mathbf{H}^{-1}$$

$$= \mathbb{I} - 2\frac{\mathbf{u}'\mathbf{l}'^{\mathrm{T}}}{\mathbf{u}'^{\mathrm{T}}\mathbf{l}'}, \tag{2}$$

since $\mathbf{u}^{\mathrm{T}}\mathbf{l} = \mathbf{u}'^{\mathrm{T}}\mathbf{l}'$. $\qquad\square$

The following corollary is a trivial consequence of Lemma 1:

Corollary 1. *Let $\mathbf{T}$, $\mathbf{H}$ and $\mathbf{W}$ be defined as in Lemma 1. The transformation $\mathbf{H}$ is a isomorphism between the structures $(\mathbf{T}, \Gamma)$ and $(\mathbf{W}, \Gamma')$, i.e, $\forall \gamma \in \Gamma, \mathbf{H}\mathbf{T}\gamma = \mathbf{W}\mathbf{H}\gamma$.*

An important consequence of Lemma 1 and Corollary 1 is that if a set of points s, e.g., the profile of a surface of revolution, is invariant to a harmonic homology $\mathbf{T}$, the set $\hat{s}$ obtained by transforming s by a 2D projective transformation $\mathbf{H}$ is invariant to the harmonic homology $\mathbf{W} = \mathbf{H}\mathbf{T}\mathbf{H}^{-1}$.

Without loss of generality assume that the axis of rotation of the surface of revolution S is coincident with the y-axis of an right-handed orthogonal coordinate system. Considering a particular case of Theorem 1 where the pinhole camera $\mathbf{P}$ is given by $\mathbf{P} = [\mathbb{I}\,|\,\mathbf{t}]$, where $\mathbf{t} = [0\ 0\ \alpha]^T$, for any $\alpha > 0$, symmetry considerations show that the profile s of S will be bilaterally symmetric with respect to the image of y (a proof is presented in the Appendix 1), which corresponds to the line $\mathbf{q_s} = [1\ 0\ 0]^T$ in (homogeneous) image coordinates.

Proof of Theorem 1 (particular case). Since s is bilaterally symmetrical about $\mathbf{q_s}$, there is a transformation $\mathbf{T}$ that maps each point of s on its symmetrical counterpart, given by

$$\mathbf{T} = \begin{bmatrix} -1 & 0 & 0 \\ 0 & 1 & 0 \\ 0 & 0 & 1 \end{bmatrix}. \tag{3}$$

However, as any bilateral symmetry transformation, $\mathbf{T}$ is also a harmonic homology, with axis $\mathbf{q_s}$ and center $\mathbf{v}_x = [1\ 0\ 0]^T$, since

$$\mathbf{T} = \mathbb{I} - 2\frac{\mathbf{v}_x\mathbf{q_s}^T}{\mathbf{v}_x^T\mathbf{q_s}}. \tag{4}$$

The transformation $\mathbf{T}$ maps the set s onto itself (although the points of s are not mapped onto themselves by $\mathbf{T}$, but on their symmetrical counterparts), and thus s is invariant to the harmonic homology $\mathbf{T}$. Since the camera center lies on the z-axis of the coordinate system, the plane that contains the camera center and the axis of rotation is in fact the yz-plane, and the point at infinity orthogonal to the yz-plane is $\mathbf{U}_x = [1\ 0\ 0\ 0]^T$, whose image is $\mathbf{v}_x$. □

Let $\hat{\mathbf{P}}$ be an arbitrary pinhole camera. The camera $\hat{\mathbf{P}}$ can be obtained by rotating $\mathbf{P}$ about its optical center by a rotation $\mathbf{R}$ and transforming the image coordinate system of $\mathbf{P}$ by introducing the intrinsic parameters represented by the matrix $\mathbf{K}$. Let $\mathbf{KR} = \mathbf{H}$. Thus, $\hat{\mathbf{P}} = \mathbf{H}[\mathbf{I}\,|\,\mathbf{t}]$, and the point $\mathbf{U}_x$ in space with the image $\mathbf{v}_x$ in $\mathbf{P}$ will project as a point $\mathbf{u}_x = \mathbf{H}\mathbf{v}_x$ in $\hat{\mathbf{P}}$. Analogously, the line $\mathbf{q_s}$ in $\mathbf{P}$ will correspond to a line $\mathbf{l_s} = \mathbf{H}^{-T}\mathbf{q_s}$ in $\hat{\mathbf{P}}$. It is now possible to derive the proof of Theorem 1 in the general case.

Proof of Theorem 1 (general case). Let $\hat{s}$ be the profile of the surface of revolution S obtained from the camera $\hat{\mathbf{P}}$. Thus, the counter-domain of the bijection $\mathbf{H}$ acting on the profile s is $\hat{s}$ (or $\mathbf{H}s = \hat{s}$), and, using Lemma 1, the transformation $\mathbf{W} = \mathbf{H}\mathbf{T}\mathbf{H}^{-1}$ is a harmonic homology with center $\mathbf{u}_x = \mathbf{H}\mathbf{v}_x$ and axis $\mathbf{l_s} = \mathbf{H}^{-T}\mathbf{q_s}$. Moreover, from Corollary 1, $\mathbf{W}\mathbf{H}s = \mathbf{H}\mathbf{T}s$, or $\mathbf{W}\hat{s} = \mathbf{H}\mathbf{T}s$. From the particular case of the Theorem 1 it is known that the profile s will be invariant to the harmonic homology $\mathbf{T}$, so $\mathbf{W}\hat{s} = \mathbf{H}s = \hat{s}$. □

The images of a rotating object are the same as the images of a fixed object taken by a camera rotating around the same axis, or by multiple cameras along that circular trajectory. Consider any two of such cameras, denoted by $\mathbf{P}$ and $\mathbf{P}'$. If $\mathbf{P}$ and $\mathbf{P}'$ point towards the axis of rotation, their epipoles $\mathbf{e}$ and $\mathbf{e}'$ will be symmetrical with respect to the image of the rotation axis, or $\mathbf{e}' = \mathbf{T}\mathbf{e}$, according to Figure 2. In a general situation, the epipoles will simply be related by the transformation $\mathbf{e}' = \mathbf{W}\mathbf{e}$. It is then straightforward to show that the corresponding epipolar lines $\mathbf{l}$ and $\mathbf{l}'$ are related by $\mathbf{l}' = \mathbf{W}^{-T}\mathbf{l}$. This means that the pair of epipoles can be represented with only two parameters once $\mathbf{W}$ is

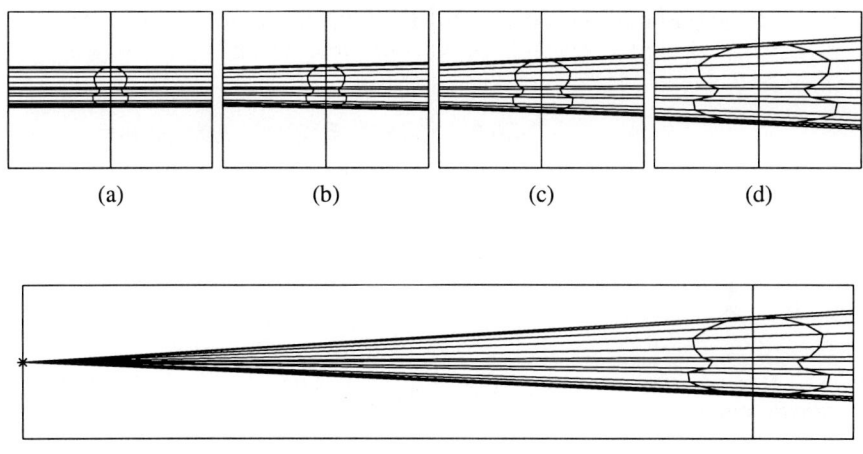

Fig. 1. Lines joining symmetric points with respect to the image of rotation axis $\mathbf{l}_s$ (images are scaled and translated independently for better observation). (a) The optical axis points directly towards the rotation axis. (b) The camera is rotated about its optical center by an angle ρ of $20°$ in a plane orthogonal to the rotation axis. (c) $\rho = 40°$. (d) $\rho = 60°$. (e) Same as (d), but the vanishing point $\mathbf{v}_x$ is also shown.

known. From (2) it can be seen that $\mathbf{W}$ has only four degrees of freedom (dof). Therefore, the fundamental matrix relating views of an object under circular motion must have only 6 dof, in agreement with [17].

3   Parameterization of the Fundamental Matrix

3.1   Epipolar Geometry under Circular Motion

The fundamental matrix corresponding to a pair of cameras related by a rotation around a fixed axis has a very special parameterization, as shown in [17, 7]. A simpler derivation of this result will be shown here.

Consider the pair of camera matrices $\mathbf{P}_1$ and $\mathbf{P}_2$, given by

$$\mathbf{P}_1 = [\mathbb{I}\,|\,\mathbf{t}\,] \tag{5}$$
$$\mathbf{P}_2 = [\mathbf{R}_y(\theta)\,|\,\mathbf{t}\,]\,,$$

where

$$\mathbf{t} = \begin{bmatrix} 0 \ 0 \ 1 \end{bmatrix}^{\mathrm{T}} \text{ and} \tag{6}$$

$$\mathbf{R}_y(\theta) = \begin{bmatrix} \cos\theta & 0 & \sin\theta \\ 0 & 1 & 0 \\ -\sin\theta & 0 & \cos\theta \end{bmatrix}.$$

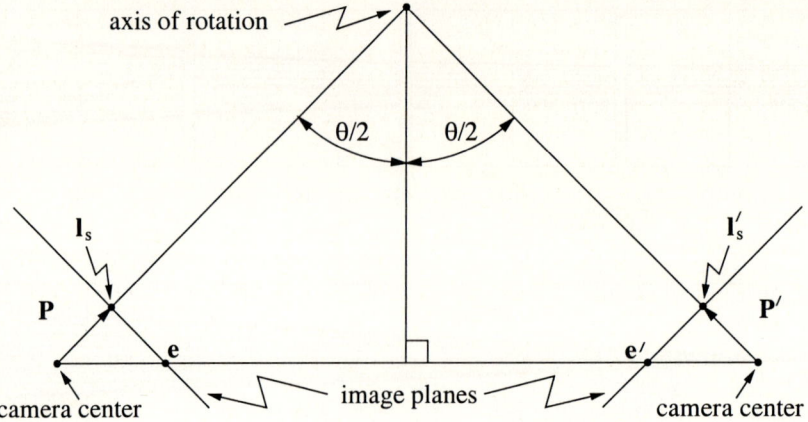

Fig. 2. If the cameras are pointing towards the axis of rotation, the epipoles **e** and **e′** are symmetric with respect to the image of the axis of rotation.

Let $\mathbf{F}$ be the fundamental matrix relating $\mathbf{P}_1$ and $\mathbf{P}_2$. From (5) and (6), it is easy to see that

$$\mathbf{F} = \begin{bmatrix} 0 & \cos\theta - 1 & 0 \\ \cos\theta - 1 & 0 & \sin\theta \\ 0 & -\sin\theta & 0 \end{bmatrix} \tag{7}$$

$$= -\sin\theta \begin{bmatrix} 1 \\ 0 \\ 0 \end{bmatrix}_\times + (\cos\theta - 1)\left(\begin{bmatrix} 1 \\ 0 \\ 0 \end{bmatrix} [0\ 1\ 0] + \begin{bmatrix} 0 \\ 1 \\ 0 \end{bmatrix} [1\ 0\ 0] \right). \tag{8}$$

Let now $\mathbf{U}_X$, $\mathbf{U}_Y$ and $\mathbf{U}_Z$ be the points at infinity in the x, y and z direction, respectively, in world coordinates. Projecting these points using the camera $\mathbf{P}_1$, we obtain $\mathbf{u}_x$, $\mathbf{u}_y$ and $\mathbf{u}_z$ given by

$$\mathbf{u}_x = \begin{bmatrix} 1 \\ 0 \\ 0 \end{bmatrix}, \mathbf{u}_y = \begin{bmatrix} 0 \\ 1 \\ 0 \end{bmatrix} \text{ and } \mathbf{u}_z = \begin{bmatrix} 0 \\ 0 \\ 1 \end{bmatrix}. \tag{9}$$

The image of the horizon is the line $\mathbf{q}_h$, and the image of the screw axis is the line $\mathbf{q}_s$, where

$$\mathbf{q}_s = \begin{bmatrix} 1 \\ 0 \\ 0 \end{bmatrix} \text{ and } \mathbf{q}_h = \begin{bmatrix} 0 \\ 1 \\ 0 \end{bmatrix}. \tag{10}$$

Substituting (9) and (10) in (8), the desired parameterization is obtained:

$$\mathbf{F} = -\sin\theta \left[[\mathbf{u}_x]_\times + \tan\frac{\theta}{2}(\mathbf{q}_s\mathbf{q}_h^T + \mathbf{q}_h\mathbf{q}_s^T) \right]. \tag{11}$$

The factor "$-\sin\theta$" can be eliminated since the fundamental matrix is defined only up to an arbitrary scale. Assume now that the cameras $\mathbf{P}_1$ and $\mathbf{P}_2$ are transformed by a rotation $\mathbf{R}$ about their optical centers and the introduction of a set of intrinsic parameters represented by the matrix $\mathbf{K}$. The new pair of cameras, $\hat{\mathbf{P}}_1$ and $\hat{\mathbf{P}}_2$, is related to $\mathbf{P}_1$ and $\mathbf{P}_2$ by

$$\hat{\mathbf{P}}_1 = \mathbf{HP}_1 \text{ and}$$
$$\hat{\mathbf{P}}_2 = \mathbf{HP}_2, \tag{12}$$

where $\mathbf{H} = \mathbf{KR}$. The fundamental matrix $\hat{\mathbf{F}}$ of the new pair of cameras $\hat{\mathbf{P}}_1$ and $\hat{\mathbf{P}}_2$ is given by

$$\hat{\mathbf{F}} = \mathbf{H}^{-\mathrm{T}}\mathbf{F}\mathbf{H}^{-1}$$
$$= \det(\mathbf{H})[\mathbf{v}_x]_\times + \tan\frac{\theta}{2}(\mathbf{l}_s\mathbf{l}_h^{\mathrm{T}} + \mathbf{l}_h\mathbf{l}_s^{\mathrm{T}}), \tag{13}$$

where $\mathbf{v}_x = \mathbf{H}\mathbf{u}_x$, $\mathbf{l}_h = \mathbf{H}^{-\mathrm{T}}\mathbf{q}_h$ and $\mathbf{l}_s = \mathbf{H}^{-\mathrm{T}}\mathbf{q}_s$.

3.2 Parameterization via Planar Harmonic Homology

The epipole $\mathbf{e}'$ in the image obtained from the camera $\mathbf{P}_2$ in (5) is given by

$$\mathbf{e}' = \mathbf{u}_x - \tan\frac{\theta}{2}\mathbf{u}_z, \tag{14}$$

which can be obtained from (5). The planar harmonic homography $\mathbf{T}$ relating the symmetric elements in the stereo camera system $\mathbf{P}_1$ and $\mathbf{P}_2$ (e.g. epipoles and pencils of epipolar lines) can be parameterized as

$$\mathbf{T} = \mathbb{I} - 2\frac{\mathbf{u}_x\mathbf{q}_s^{\mathrm{T}}}{\mathbf{u}_x^{\mathrm{T}}\mathbf{q}_s}. \tag{15}$$

Direct substitution of (14) and (15) in (11) shows that the fundamental matrix can be parameterized by $\mathbf{e}'$ and $\mathbf{T}$ as:

$$\mathbf{F} = [\mathbf{e}']_\times\mathbf{T}. \tag{16}$$

Again, it is easy to show that the result does not depend on the transformation $\mathbf{H}$, and the general result becomes

$$\hat{\mathbf{F}} = [\hat{\mathbf{e}}']_\times\mathbf{W}, \text{ with } \hat{\mathbf{e}}' = \mathbf{v}_x - \tan\frac{\theta}{2}\mathbf{v}_z. \tag{17}$$

Thus, we have proved that the transformation $\mathbf{W}$ corresponds to a plane induced homography (see [9]). This means that the registration of the images can be done by using $\mathbf{W}$ instead of a planar contour as proposed in [1, 6]. It is known that different choices of the plane that induces the homography in a *plane plus parallax* parameterization of the fundamental matrix will result in different homographies, although they will all generate the same fundamental matrix, since

$$\hat{\mathbf{F}} = [\hat{\mathbf{e}}']_\times\mathbf{W} = [\hat{\mathbf{e}}']_\times[\mathbf{W} + \hat{\mathbf{e}}'\mathbf{a}^{\mathrm{T}}] \; \forall\mathbf{a} \in \mathbb{R}^3. \tag{18}$$

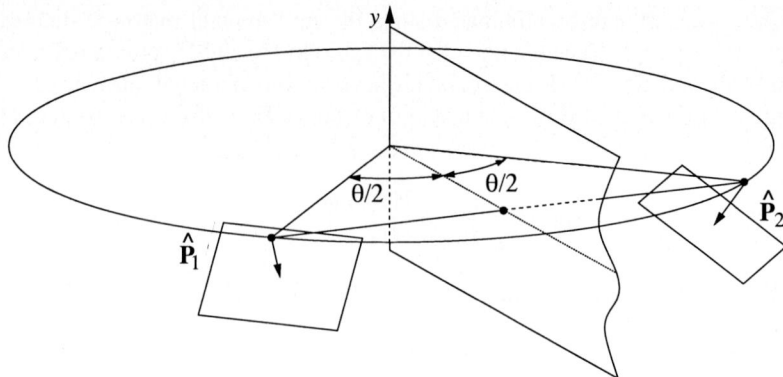

Fig. 3. The harmonic homology is a homography induced by the plane that contains the axis of rotation and bisects the segment joining the camera centers.

The three parameter family of homographies $[\mathbf{W}+\hat{\mathbf{e}}'\mathbf{a}^{\mathrm{T}}]$ has a one to one correspondence with the set of planes in $\mathbb{R}^3$. In particular, the homology $\mathbf{W}$ relating the cameras $\hat{\mathbf{P}}_1$ and $\hat{\mathbf{P}}_2$ is induced by a plane $\varXi$ that contains the axis of rotation y and bisects the segment joining the optical centers of the cameras, as shown in Figure 3.

4 Algorithms for Motion Recovery

4.1 Estimation of the Harmonic Homology

Consider an object that undergoes a full rotation around a fixed axis. The envelope ϵ of the profiles is found by overlapping the image sequence and applying a Canny edge detector to the resultant image (Figure 4(b)). The homography $\mathbf{W}$ is then found by sampling N points $\mathbf{x}_i$ along ϵ and optimizing the cost function

$$f_{\mathbf{W}}(\mathbf{v}_x, \mathbf{l}_s) = \sum_{i=1}^{N} \mathrm{dist}(\epsilon, \mathbf{W}(\mathbf{v}_x, \mathbf{l}_s)\mathbf{x}_i)^2, \tag{19}$$

where $\mathrm{dist}(\epsilon, \mathbf{W}(\mathbf{v}_x, \mathbf{l}_s)\mathbf{x}_i)$ is the distance between the curve ϵ and the transformed sample point $\mathbf{W}(\mathbf{v}_x, \mathbf{l}_s)\mathbf{x}_i$.

The initialization of the line $\mathbf{l}_s$ is trivial, and can be made simply by picking a coarse approximation for the axis of symmetry of ϵ. This can be done via user intervention or by automatically locating one or more pairs of corresponding bitangents. In all practical situations, the camera should be roughly pointing towards the rotation axis, which means that the point $\mathbf{v}_x$ is far (or even at infinity) and at a direction orthogonal to $\mathbf{l}_s$. The estimation of $\mathbf{W}$ is summarized in Algorithm 1.

4.2 Estimation of the Epipoles

After obtaining a good estimation of $\mathbf{W}$, one can then search for *epipolar tangencies* between pairs of images in the sequence. Epipolar tangencies are important for motion

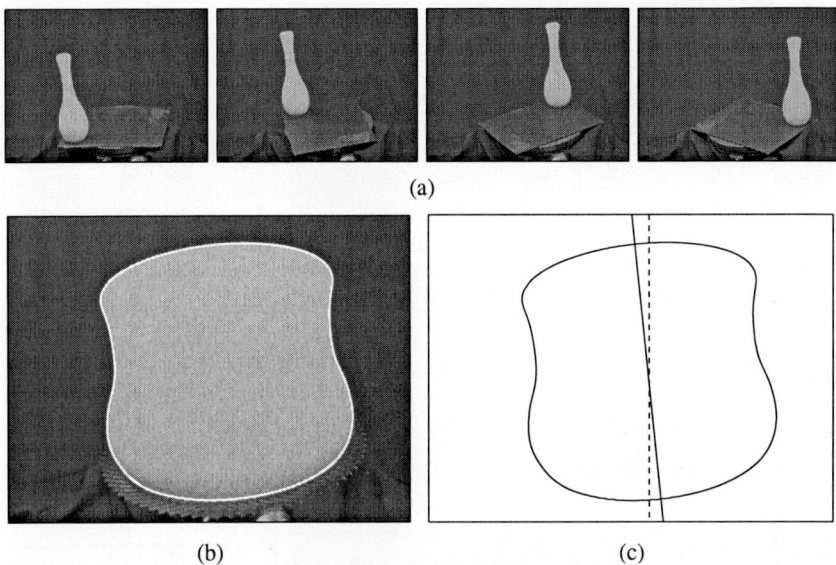

Fig. 4. (a) Image 1, 8, 15 and 22 in the sequence of 36 images of a rotating vase. (b) Envelope of apparent contours produced by overlapping all images in the sequence. (c) Initial guess (dashed line) and final estimation (solid line) of the image of the rotation axis.

Algorithm 1 Estimation of the harmonic homology $\mathbf{W}$.

---

  overlap the images in sequence;
  extract the envelope ϵ of the profiles using Canny edge detector;
  sample N points $\mathbf{x}_i$ along ϵ;
  initialize the axis of symmetry $\mathbf{l}_s$ and the vanishing point $\mathbf{v}_x$;
  while not converged **do**
    transfer the points $\mathbf{x}_i$ using $\mathbf{W}$;
    compute the distances between ϵ and the transferred points;
    update $\mathbf{l}_s$ and $\mathbf{v}_x$ to minimize the function in (19);
  end while

---

estimation from profiles since they are the only correspondences that can be established between image pairs [2]. To obtain a pair of corresponding epipolar tangencies in two images, it is necessary to find a line tangent to one profile which is transferred by $\mathbf{W}^{-T}$ to a line tangent to the profile in the other image (see Figure 6). The search for corresponding tangent lines may be carried out as a one-dimensional optimization problem. The single parameter is the angle α that defines the orientation of the epipolar line $\mathbf{l}$ in the first image, and the cost function is given by

$$f_\alpha = \text{dist}(\mathbf{W}^{-T}\mathbf{l}(\alpha), \mathbf{l}'_{\parallel}(\alpha)), \tag{20}$$

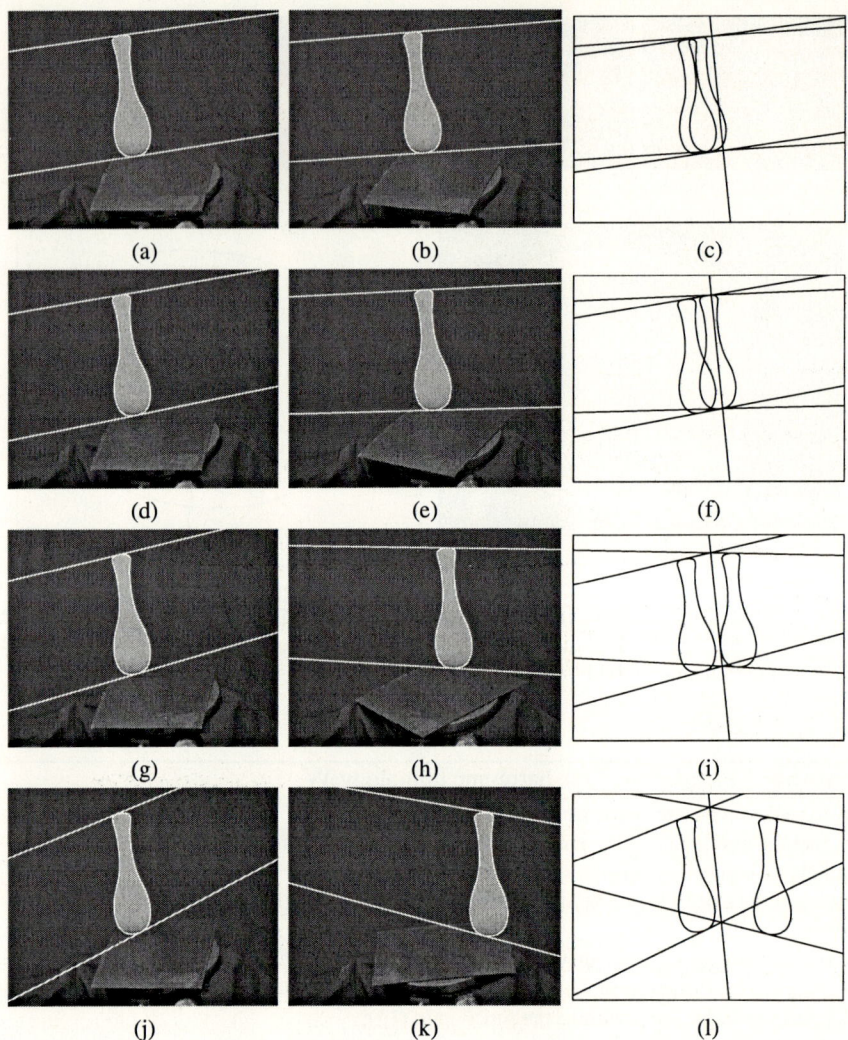

Fig. 5. Five images from a single camera and circular motion after a rotation of $10°$, $20°$, $40°$ and $80°$ are shown in (b), (e), (h) and (k), and the base image at $0°$ can be seen in (a), (d), (g), (g). The epipolar geometry between image pairs is shown. The overlapping of corresponding pairs can be seen in (c), (f), (i) and (l). Corresponding epipolar lines intersect at the image of the rotation axis, and all epipoles lie on a common horizon.

where $\mathrm{dist}(\mathbf{W}^{-T}\mathbf{l}(\alpha), \mathbf{l}'_{\parallel}(\alpha))$ is the distance between the transferred line $\mathbf{l}' = \mathbf{W}^{-T}\mathbf{l}$ and a parallel line $\mathbf{l}'_{\parallel}$ tangent to the profile in the second image. Typical values of α lie between -0.5 rad and 0.5 rad, or $-30°$ and $30°$.

Given a pair of epipolar lines near the top and the bottom of a profile, the epipole can be computed as the intersection point of the two epipolar lines, and the fundamental

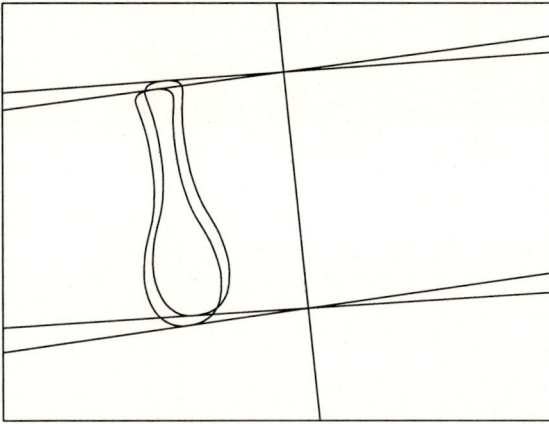

Fig. 6. Corresponding pairs of epipolar tangencies near the top and bottom of two images.

Algorithm 2 Estimation of the orientation of the epipolar lines.

---

extract the profiles of two adjacent images using Canny edge detector;
fit b-splines to the top and the bottom of the profiles;
initialize α;
while not converge **do**
    find l, l' and l'$_{\parallel}$;
    compute the distance between l' and l'$_{\parallel}$;
    update α to minimize the function in (20);
end while

---

matrix relating the two cameras follows from (17). Using the camera calibration matrix obtained either from a calibration grid or from self-calibration techniques, the essential matrix can be found. The decomposition of the essential matrix gives the relative motion between two cameras.

4.3   Critical Configurations

There is a configuration where the algorithm described in Algorithm 2 fails. Let $\mathcal{N}_t$ and $\mathcal{N}'_t$ be subsets of two adjacent apparent contours, with $\mathcal{N}_t$ and $\mathcal{N}'_t$ related by the homography $\mathbf{W}$ found in Algorithm 1. Any value of α in Algorithm 2 such that the resulting epipolar tangencies are in $\mathcal{N}_t$ and $\mathcal{N}'_t$ will minimize the cost function in (19). The proof follows from observing that if α is the orientation of a putative epipolar line with corresponding epipolar tangency in $\mathcal{N}_t$ in the first contour, the mapping of the epipolar line tangency via $\mathbf{W}$, as required by Algorithm 2, will result in a line tangent to the second contour, as shown in Figure 7. To overcome this problem it is enough then to choose another contour as the first one of the pair where the problem appeared, and proceed with the algorithm.

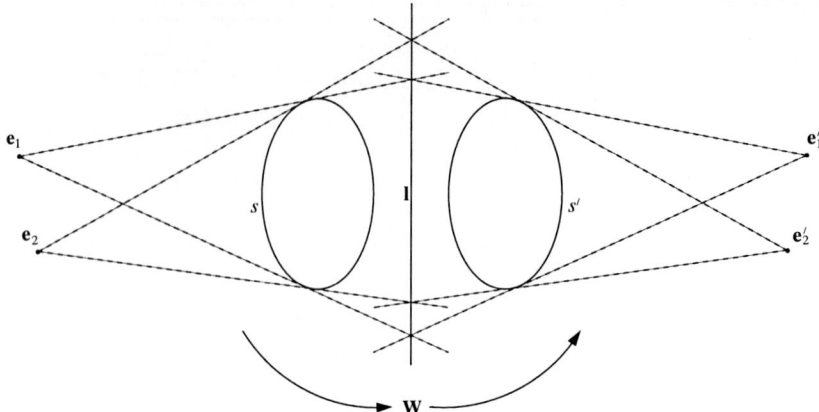

Fig. 7. If the apparent contours are related by the homography $\mathbf{W}$, there will be multiple solutions for the positions of the epipoles. Both pairs $(\mathbf{e}_1, \mathbf{e}_1{}')$ and $(\mathbf{e}_2, \mathbf{e}_2{}')$ are valid epipoles, consistent with the transformation $\mathbf{W}$ (and thus with l) and the contours s and s'.

The ultimate degenerate configuration occurs when the surface being viewed is a surface of revolution (if not completely, at least in the neighbourhood of the frontier points), and the axis of rotation of the turntable is coincident with the axis of rotation of the surface (or the axis of rotation of the rotationally symmetric neighbourhoods). In this case, all the contours are the same, since the contour generator is a fixed curve in space, and the substitution of one contour for another will not make any difference.

5   Implementation and Experimental Results

The algorithms described in the previous session were tested using a set of 36 images of a vase placed on a turntable (see Figure 4(a)) rotated by an angle of $10°$ between successive snapshots. To obtain $\mathbf{W}$, the Algorithm 1 was implemented with 40 evenly spaced sample points along the envelope ($N = 40$). An approximation for the image of the rotation axis was manually picked by observing the symmetry of the envelope. This provided an initial guess for $\mathbf{l}_s$. The vanishing point $\mathbf{v}_x$ was initialized at infinity, at a direction orthogonal to $\mathbf{l}_s$. The cost function (19) was minimized using the BFGS algorithm [10]. The initial and final configurations can be seen in Figure 4(c).

For the estimation of the motion, the Algorithm 2 was applied for pairs of images to obtain the essential matrix $\mathbf{E}$. The camera calibration matrix was obtained using a calibration grid. The cost function in (20) was minimized using the Golden Section method. This optimization problem is rather simple since the cost function is smooth and unimodal (see Figure 8).

The direction of the axis of rotation was initialized as that obtained from the first pair of images. The quality of each subsequent estimation was checked by comparing the direction of the rotation axis computed from the current pair with the average direction found for all the previous pairs. If the deviation was greater than $10°$, the motion was

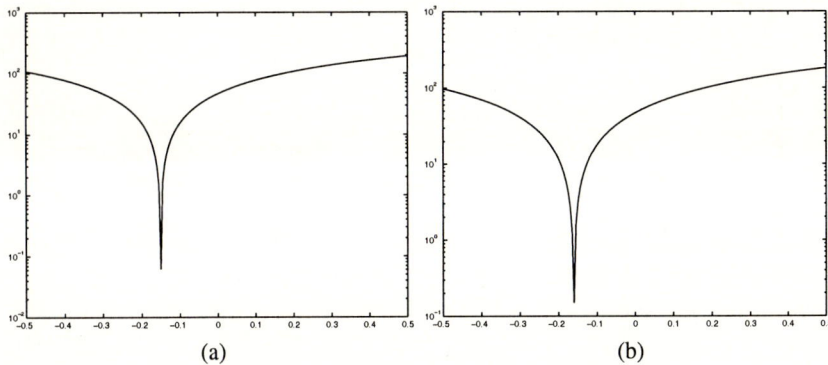

(a)   (b)

Fig. 8. Plot of the cost function (20) for a pair of images in the sequence. (a)/(b) Cost function for a pair of corresponding epipolar tangencies near the top/bottom of the profile.

Algorithm 3 Motion estimation.

estimate motion between IMAGE(1) and IMAGE(2);
update the direction of the axis of rotation;
for i = 3 TO END **do**
  j = i - 1;
  while motion is bad **do**
    estimate motion between IMAGE(j) and IMAGE(i);
    j = j - 1;
  end while
  update the direction of the axis of rotation;
end for

---

estimated by using a different combination of images (see Algorithm 3). Such process of quality control is completely automatic.

The remaining problem was to fix the ratio of the norm of the relative translations. Since the camera is performing circular motion, it is easy to show that the relative translations are proportional to $\sin \theta/2$, where θ is the angle of the relative rotation between the two cameras. The resulting camera configurations are presented in Figure 9(a-c). The estimated relative angles between adjacent cameras are accurate, as shown in fig 9(d) and the camera centers are virtually on the same plane and the motion closely follows a circular path.

6   Conclusions and Future Work

This paper introduces a new method of motion estimation by using profiles of a rotating object. No affine approximation has been used and only minimal information (two epipolar tangencies) is required, as long as the object performs a complete rotation. This means that the algorithm can be applied in any practical situation involving circular motion. If more information is available, the estimation problem will be more constrained,

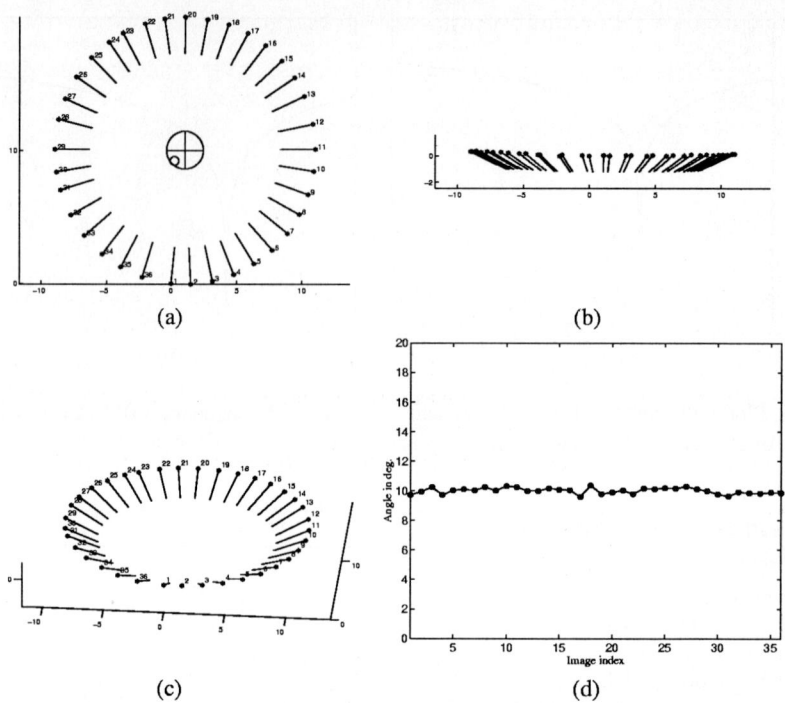

Fig. 9. (a-c) Final configuration of the estimated motion of the cameras. (d) Estimated angles of rotation.

and numerical results can be further improved. By proceeding in a divide-and-conquer approach, the difficulties due to initialization and presence of local minima are overcome. The search space in the main loop of the algorithm is one-dimensional, making the technique highly efficient.

Some ideas can be explored to further improve the results presented in this work. A promising approach is to make simultaneous use of the parameterizations shown in (11) and (17). After estimating the position of the epipoles using Algorithm 2, the horizon line can be found by fitting a line l_h to the epipoles, such that $l_h^T v_x = 0$. This should be done by using a robust method, such as Hough transform or RANSAC. Then, Algorithm 2 can be run again, now with the constraint that all the epipoles must lie on the horizon line. This procedure constrains the cameras to exactly follow a circular path, and integrates information from all images in the estimation of the horizon. This approach has already been proved to produce more accurate results, allowing for high quality reconstructions [12].

Appendix A: Bilateral Symmetry of Images of Surfaces of Revolution

Let S be the surface of revolution parameterized as

$$S = \{\mathbf{S}(\tau, \phi) = [f(\tau)\sin\phi \quad g(\tau) \quad -f(\tau)\cos\phi]^{\mathrm{T}}, (\tau, \phi) \in I_\tau \times I_\phi\}, \qquad (21)$$

where $f : \mathbb{R} \supset I_\tau \mapsto \mathbb{R}$ is a differentiable map for which $\exists a > 0$ such that $0 < f(\tau) < a$ $\forall \tau \in I_\tau$, and $g : \mathbb{R} \supset I_\tau \mapsto \mathbb{R}$ is a differentiable map for which $\exists b, c$ such that $b < g(\tau) < c \ \forall \tau \in I_\tau$. Also, $\dot{f}^2 + \dot{g}^2 > 0$, where $\dot{f}$ and $\dot{g}$ are the derivatives of the maps f and g. The normal vector at the point $\mathbf{S}(\tau, \phi)$ is given by $\mathbf{n} = \mathbf{S}_\phi \times \mathbf{S}_\tau = f(\tau)[-\dot{g}\sin\phi \quad \dot{f} \quad \dot{g}\cos\phi]^{\mathrm{T}}$, where $\mathbf{S}_\chi$ is the partial derivative of $\mathbf{S}$ with respect to the variable χ. Let $\mathbf{P} = [\mathbb{I}\,|\,\mathbf{t}]$ be the matrix of a pinhole camera, with $\mathbf{t} = [0\ 0\ \alpha]^{\mathrm{T}}$ and $\alpha > a$.

The profile s of S obtained from $\mathbf{P}$ is the projection of the set of points of S where $(\mathbf{S}(\tau, \phi) + \mathbf{t}) \cdot \mathbf{n} = 0$. This constraint can be expressed as $g(\tau)\dot{f} - \dot{g}f(\tau) + \alpha\dot{g}\cos\phi = 0$, and for $\tau \in I_\tau$ such that $\dot{g}(\tau) \neq 0$ the resulting expression for $\mathbf{s} \in s$ after removing the dependence on ϕ is given by

$$\mathbf{s}(\tau) = \begin{bmatrix} \pm\dfrac{f\sqrt{(\alpha\dot{g})^2 - (\dot{g}f - g\dot{f})^2}}{\alpha^2\dot{g} - f(\dot{g}f - g\dot{f})} \\[2ex] \dfrac{g}{\alpha^2\dot{g} - f(\dot{g}f - g\dot{f})} \end{bmatrix} \qquad (22)$$

$\forall \tau$ such that $|(\dot{g}f - g\dot{f})/(\alpha\dot{g})| < 1$. Observe that this condition implies that $\alpha^2\dot{g} - f(\dot{g}f - g\dot{f}) \neq 0$, otherwise one would have $|(\dot{g}f - g\dot{f})/(\alpha\dot{g})| = |\alpha/f| > 1$. From (22), one can see that the profile s is bilaterally symmetric about the line $\mathbf{q}_s = [1\ 0\ 0]^{\mathrm{T}}$ (observe the sign "$\pm$").

Acknowledgements

Paulo R. S. Mendonça gratefully acknowledges the financial support of CAPES, Brazilian Ministry of Education, grant BEX1165/96-8. Roberto Cipolla acknowledges the support of the EPSRC and EC project Vigor.

References

1. K. Åström, R. Cipolla, and P. J. Giblin. Generalised epipolar constraints. In B. F. Buxton and R. Cipolla, editors, *Proc. 4th European Conf. on Computer Vision*, volume II, pages 97–108. Springer–Verlag, 1996.

2. R. Cipolla, K. Åström, and P. J. Giblin. Motion from the frontier of curved surfaces. In *Proc. 5th Int. Conf. on Computer Vision*, pages 269–275, 1995.

3. R. Cipolla and A. Blake. Surface shape from the deformation of apparent contours. *Int. Journal of Computer Vision*, 9(2):83–112, 1992.

4. R. Cipolla and P. J. Giblin. *Visual Motion of Curves and Surfaces*. Cambridge University Press, Cambridge, 1999.

5. H. S. M. Coxeter. *Introduction to Geometry*. John Wiley and Sons, New York, second edition, 1969.

6. G. Cross, A. Fitzgibbon, and A. Zisserman. Parallax geometry of smooth surfaces in multiple views. In *Proc. 7th Int. Conf. on Computer Vision*, volume I, pages 323–329, 1999.

7. A. W. Fitzgibbon, G. Cross, and A. Zisserman. Automatic 3D model construction for turntable sequences. In *3D Structure from Multiple Images of Large-Scale Environments, European Workshop SMILE'98*, Lecture Notes in Computer Science 1506, pages 155–170, 1998.

8. P. J. Giblin, F. E. Pollick, and J. E. Rycroft. Recovery of an unknown axis or rotation from the profiles of a rotating surface. *J. Opt. Soc. America A*, 11:1976–1984, 1994.

9. R. Hartley. Projective reconstruction and invariants from multiple images. *IEEE Trans. Pattern Analysis and Machine Intell.*, 16(10):1036–1041, 1994.

10. D. G. Luenberger. *Linear and Nonlinear Programming*. Addison-Wesley, USA, second edition, 1984.

11. P. R. S. Mendonça and R. Cipolla. Estimation of epipolar geometry from apparent contours: Affine and circular motion cases. In *Proc. Conf. Computer Vision and Pattern Recognition*, volume I, pages 9–14, 1999.

12. P. R. S. Mendonça, K-Y. K. Wong, and R. Cipolla. Camera pose estimation and reconstruction from image profiles under circular motion. In *Proc. 6th European Conf. on Computer Vision*, Dublin, Ireland, 2000. Springer–Verlag.

13. V. S. Nalwa. Line-drawing interpretation: Bilateral symmetry. *IEEE Trans. Pattern Analysis and Machine Intell.*, 11(10):1117–1120, 1989.

14. J. Porrill and S. B. Pollard. Curve matching and stereo calibration. *Image and Vision Computing*, 9(1):45–50, 1991.

15. J. H. Rieger. Three dimensional motion from fixed points of a deforming profile curve. *Optics Letters*, 11:123–125, 1986.

16. J. G. Semple and G. T. Kneebone. *Algebraic Projective Geometry*. Oxford University Press, 1952.

17. T. Vieville and D. Lingrand. Using singular displacements for uncalibrated monocular visual systems. In *Proc. 4th European Conf. on Computer Vision*, volume II, pages 207–216, 1996.

18. A. Zisserman, D. Forsyth, J. Mundy, and C. A. Rothwell. Recognizing general curved objects efficiently. In J.L Mundy and A. Zisserman, editors, *Geometric Invariance in Computer Vision*, chapter 11, pages 228–251. MIT Press, Cambridge, Mass., 1992.

19. A. Zisserman, J. L. Mundy, D. A. Forsyth, J. Liu, N. Pillow, C. Rothwell, and S. Utcke. Class-based grouping in perspective images. In *Proc. 5th Int. Conf. on Computer Vision*, pages 183–188, 1995.

Discussion

Jean Ponce: This is all very interesting, but given that the motion is circular and the aim is to model an object, why not calibrate the camera, at least internally, and maybe the turntable too. After all the camera just sits there on its tripod, and you have the turntable there.

Paulo Mendonça: For the internal parameters I agree, we can calibrate off line and we don't even need the turntable to do it. In fact, in the particular experiment I showed, we used an off-line internal calibration, not the one extracted from the harmonic homology. But for the external parameters and the motion I'd rather not do that because I like the flexibility of not having to rely on a calibration grid.

Andrew Fitzgibbon: To continue that answer, there were several calibrated turntable systems at SIGGRAPH, and every one was knocked at least ten times during the day and had to be recalibrated. It was impossible to precalibrate a system there.

My question is: for your object, do the epipolar tangencies have to be far from the rotation axis to get a good estimate of the epipole?

Paulo Mendonça: No, not really. The thing I have to avoid is contours that are related to one other by the harmonic homology. That doesn't mean that the epipolar tangencies have to be far from the rotation axis. With an irregular object that doesn't have symmetries with itself that are close to the symmetry given by the surface of revolution, there's no problem.

Andrew Fitzgibbon: OK. Also, in your results it appeared that your camera centres were not coplanar.

Paulo Mendonça: Yes, as I said the results are preliminary. I haven't implemented all the theory I talked about, such as the bit where the epipoles are constrained to lie on the same horizon. What I used is the cloud of points I showed in one of the slides.

Andrew Fitzgibbon: So you would expect your results to improve.

Paulo Mendonça: Oh yes, I've improved on that result already. What I haven't done yet is use the full sequence of images to escape from the algorithm's critical configurations. There should be a way of doing that, so that if I can't use a particular pair of images to get the angle associated with a camera, I can just jump to another pair.

Yvan Leclerc: I was wondering if the harmonic homology for this kind of skew symmetry you are talking about, would hold even for objects for which the outline is partially self-occluding from a certain viewpoint? If you think of a dumb bell you get an occluding edge for example.

Paulo Mendonça: Yes, we still get the symmetry and it is actually better for the initialization of the rotation axis. Self-occlusions give non-smooth points in the profile of the surface of revolution. These are good for initialization because they are symmetry points that are both accurate and trustworthy.

Kalle Åström: Is there a connection between the rotation angles and the epipoles?

Paulo Mendonça: Yes. The angle is directly related to the position of the epipole along the horizon line.

Optimization Criteria, Sensitivity and Robustness of Motion and Structure Estimation

Jana Košecká[1], Yi Ma[2], and Shankar Sastry[2]

[1] Computer Science Department, George Mason University, Fairfax, VA 22030
[2] EECS Department, University of California at Berkeley, Berkeley, CA 94720-1772
kosecka@cs.gmu.edu, {mayi, sastry}@eecs.berkeley.edu

Abstract. The prevailing efforts to study the standard formulation of motion and structure recovery have been recently focused on issues of sensitivity and robustness of existing techniques. While many cogent observations have been made and verified experimentally, many statements do not hold in general settings and make a comparison of existing techniques difficult. With an ultimate goal of clarifying these issues we study the main aspects of the problem: the choice of objective functions, optimization techniques and the sensitivity and robustness issues in the presence of noise.

We clearly reveal the relationship among different objective functions, such as "(normalized) epipolar constraints", "reprojection error" or "triangulation", which can all be be unified in a new " optimal triangulation" procedure formulated as a constrained optimization problem. Regardless of various choices of the objective function, the optimization problems all inherit the same unknown parameter space, the so called "essential manifold", making the new optimization techniques on Riemanian manifolds directly applicable.

Using these analytical results we provide a clear account of sensitivity and robustness of the proposed linear and nonlinear optimization techniques and study the analytical and practical equivalence of different objective functions. The geometric characterization of critical points of a function defined on essential manifold and the simulation results clarify the difference between the effect of bas relief ambiguity and other types of local minima leading to a consistent interpretations of simulation results over large range of signal-to-noise ratio and variety of configurations. [1]

1 Introduction

While the geometric relationships governing the motion and structure recovery problem have been long understood, the robust solutions in the presence of noise are still sought. New studies of sensitivity of different algorithms, search for intrinsic local minima and new algorithms are still subject of great interest.

The seminal work of Longuet-Higgins [9] on the characterization of the so called *epipolar constraint*, enabled the decoupling of the structure and motion

---

[1] This work is supported by ARO under the MURI grant DAAH04-96-1-0341

B. Triggs, A. Zisserman, R. Szeliski (Eds.): Vision Algorithms'99, LNCS 1883, pp. 166–182, 2000.

problems and led to the development of numerous linear and nonlinear algorithms for motion estimation (see [14, 7, 21] for overviews). The appeal of linear algorithms which use the epipolar constraint (in the discrete case [21, 7, 9, 14] and in the differential case [6, 13]) is the closed form solution to the problem which, in the absence of noise, provides true estimate of the motion. However, a further analysis of linear techniques revealed an inherent bias in the translation estimates [6, 7]. The sensitivity studies of the motion estimation problem have been done both in an analytical [1, 18] and experimental setting [19] and revealed the superiority of the nonlinear optimization schemes over the linear ones. Numerous nonlinear optimization schemes differed in the choice of objective functions [23], different parameterizations of the unknown parameter space [22, 23, 5] and means of initialization of the iterative schemes (e.g. monte-carlo simulations [21, 17], or linear techniques [6]). In most cases, the underlying search space has been parameterized for computational convenience instead of being loyal to its intrinsic geometric structure. Algebraic manipulation of intrinsic geometric relationships typically gave rise to different objective functions, making the comparison of the performance of different techniques inappropriate and often obstructing the key issues of the problem. The goal of this paper is to evaluate intrinsic difficulties of the structure and motion recovery problem in the presence of *large* levels of noise, in terms of intrinsic local minima, bias, sensitivity and robustness. This evaluation is done with respect to the choice of objective function and optimization technique, in the simplified two-view, point-feature scenario. The main contributions presented in this paper are summarized briefly below:

1. We present a new optimal triangulation procedure and show that it can be formulated as an iterative two step constrained optimization: Motion estimation is formulated as optimization on the essential manifold and is followed by additional well conditioned minimization of two Raleigh quotients for estimating the structure. The procedure clearly reveals the relationship between existing objective functions used previously and exhibits superior (provable) convergence properties. This is possible thanks to the intrinsic nonlinear search schemes on the essential manifold, utilizing Riemanian structure of the unknown parameter space.

2. We demonstrate analytically and by extensive simulations how the choice of the objective functions and configurations affects the sensitivity and robustness of the estimates, making a clear distinction between the two. We both observe and geometrically characterize how the patterns of critical points of the objective function change with increasing levels of noise for general configurations. We show the role of linear techniques for initialization and detection of these incorrect local minima. Further more we utilize the second order information to characterize the nature of the bas relief ambiguity and rotation and translation confounding for special class of "sensitive" motions/configurations.

Based on analytical and experimental results, we will give a clear profile of the performance of different algorithms over a large range of signal-to-noise ratio, and under various motion and structure configurations.

2   Optimization on the Essential Manifold

Suppose the camera motion is given by $(R, S) \in SE(3)$ (the special Euclidean group) where R is a rotation matrix in $SO(3)$ (the special orthogonal group) and $S \in \mathbb{R}^3$ is the translation vector. The intrinsic geometric relationship between two corresponding projections of a single 3D point in two images p and q (in homogeneous coordinates) then gives the so called *epipolar constraint* [9]:

$$p^T R \widehat{S} q = \qquad\qquad (1)$$

where $\widehat{S} \in \mathbb{R}^{3 \times 3}$ is defined such that $\widehat{S} v = S \times v$ for all $v \in \mathbb{R}^3$. Epipolar constraint decouples the problem of motion recovery from that of structure recovery. The first part of this paper will be devoted to recovering motion from directly using this constraint or its variations. In Section 3, we will see how this constraint has to be adjusted when we consider recovering motion and structure simultaneously.

The entity of our interest is the matrix $R\widehat{S}$ in the epipolar constraint; the so called *essential matrix*. The *essential manifold* is defined to be the space of all such matrices, denoted by $\mathcal{E} = \{R\widehat{S} \mid R \in SO(3), \widehat{S} \in so(3)\}$, where $SO(3)$ is a Lie group of 3×3 rotation matrices, and $so(3)$ is the Lie algebra of $SO(3)$, *i.e.*, the tangent plane of $SO(3)$ at the identity. $so(3)$ then consists of all 3×3 skew-symmetric matrices. The problem of motion recovery is equivalent to optimizing functions defined on the so called *normalized essential manifold*:

$$\mathcal{E}_1 = \{R\widehat{S} \mid R \in SO(3), \widehat{S} \in so(3), \frac{1}{2}tr(\widehat{S}^T \widehat{S}) = 1\}.$$

Note that $\frac{1}{2}tr(\widehat{S}^T \widehat{S}) = S^T S$. In order to formulate properly the optimization problem, it is crucial to understand the Riemannian structure of the normalized essential manifold. In our previous work we showed [11] that the space of essential matrices can be identified with the unit tangent bundle of the Lie group $SO(3)$, *i.e.*, $T_1(SO(3))^2$. Further more its Riemannian metric g induced from the bi-invariant metric on $SO(3)$ is the same as that induced from the Euclidean metric with $T_1(SO(3))$ naturally embedded in $\mathbb{R}^{3 \times 4}$. $(T_1(SO(3)), g)$ is the product Riemannian manifold of $(SO(3), g_1)$ and $(\mathbb{S}^2, g_2)$ with g_1 and g_2 canonical metrics for $SO(3)$ and $\mathbb{S}^2$ as Stiefel manifolds. Given this Riemannian structure of our unknown parameter space, we showed [13] that one can generalize Edelman *et al*'s methods [3] to the product Riemannian manifolds and obtain intrinsic geometric Newton's or conjugate gradient algorithms for solving such an optimization problem. Given the epipolar constraint, the problem of motion recovery R, S from a given set of image correspondences $p_i, q_i \in \mathbb{R}^3, i = 1, \dots, N$, in the presence of noise can be naturally formulated as a minimization of the

---

[2] However, the unit tangent bundle $T_1(SO(3))$ is not exactly the normalized essential manifold $\mathcal{E}_1$. It is a double covering of the normalized essential space $\mathcal{E}_1$, *i.e.*, $\mathcal{E}_1 = T_1(SO(3))/\mathbb{Z}^2$ (for details see [11]).

following objective function:

$$F(R,S) = \sum_{i=1}^{N} (p_i^T R \widehat{S} q_i)^2 \tag{2}$$

for $p_i, q_i \in \mathbb{R}^3$, where $F(R,S)$ is a function defined on $T_1(SO(3)) \cong SO(3) \times \mathbb{S}^2$ with $R \in SO(3)$ represented by a 3×3 rotation matrix and $S \in \mathbb{S}^2$ a vector of unit length in $\mathbb{R}^3$. Due to the lack of space below we present only a summary of the Newton's algorithm for optimization of the above objective function on the essential manifold. Please refer for more details to [13] for this particular objective function and to [3] for the details of the Newton's or other conjugate gradient algorithms for general Stiefel or Grassmann manifolds.

Riemannian Newton's algorithm for minimizing $F(R,S)$:

1. *At the point (R, S),*
   - *Compute the gradient $G = (F_R - RF_R^T R, F_S - SF_S^T S)$,*
   - *Compute $\Delta = - Hess^{-1}G$.*
2. *Move (R, S) in the direction Δ along the geodesic to $(\exp(R, \Delta_1), \exp(S, \Delta_2))$.*
3. *Repeat if $\|G\| \geq \epsilon$ for pre-determined $\epsilon > 0$.*

$F_R(F_S)$ is a derivative of the objective function $F(R,S)$ with respect to its parameters.

The basic ingredients of the algorithm is the computation of the gradient and Hessian whose explicit formulas can be found in [13]. These formulas can be alternatively obtained by directly using the explicit expression of geodesics on this manifold. On $SO(3)$, the formula for the geodesic at R in the direction $\Delta_1 \in T_R(SO(3)) = R_*(so(3))$ is $R(t) = \exp(R, \Delta_1 t) = R \exp \widehat{\omega} t = R(I + \widehat{\omega} \sin t + \widehat{\omega}^2(1 - \cos t))$, where $t \in \mathbb{R}, \widehat{\omega} = R^T \Delta_1 \in so(3)$. The last equation is called the *Rodrigues' formula* (see [16]). $\mathbb{S}^2$ (as a Stiefel manifold) also has very simple expression of geodesics. At the point S along the direction $\Delta_2 \in T_S(\mathbb{S}^2)$ the geodesic is given by $S(t) = \exp(S, \Delta_2 t) = S \cos \sigma t + U \sin \sigma t$, where $\sigma = \|\Delta_2\|$ and $U = \Delta_2/\sigma$, then $S^T U = 0$ since $S^T \Delta_2 = 0$. Using these formulae for geodesics, we can calculate the first and second derivatives of $F(R,S)$ in the direction $\Delta = (\Delta_1, \Delta_2) \in T_R(SO(3)) \times T_S(\mathbb{S}^2)$. The explicit formula for the Hessian obtained in this manner plays an important role for sensitivity analysis of the motion estimation [1] as we will point out in the second part of the paper. Furthermore, using this formula, we have shown [13] that the conditions when the Hessian is guaranteed non-degenerate are the same as the conditions for the linear 8-point algorithm having a unique solution; whence the Newton's algorithm has quadratic rate of convergence.

2.1 Minimizing Normalized Epipolar Constraints

Although the epipolar constraint (1) gives the only necessary (depth independent) condition that image pairs have to satisfy, motion estimates obtained from minimizing the objective function (2) are not necessarily statistically or geometrically optimal for the commonly used noise model of image correspondences. In general, in order to get less biased estimates, we need to *normalize* (or weight) the epipolar constraints properly, which has been initially observed in [22]. In this section, we will give a brief account of these normalized versions of epipolar constraints. In the perspective projection case[3], coordinates of image points p and q are of the form $p = (p^1, p^2, 1)^T \in \mathbb{R}^3$ and $q = (q^1, q^2, 1)^T \in \mathbb{R}^3$. Suppose that the actual measured image coordinates of N pairs of image points are: $p_i = \tilde{p}_i + x_i$, $q_i = \tilde{q}_i + y_i$ for $i = 1, \ldots, N$, where $\tilde{p}_i$ and $\tilde{q}_i$ are ideal (noise free) image coordinates, $x_i = (x_i^1, x_i^2, 0)^T \in \mathbb{R}^3$, $y_i = (y_i^1, y_i^2, 0)^T \in \mathbb{R}^3$ and $x_i^1, x_i^2, y_i^1, y_i^2$ are independent Gaussian random variables of identical distribution $N(0, \sigma^2)$. Substituting p_i and q_i into the epipolar constraint (1), we obtain:

$$p_i^T R \widehat{S} q_i = x_i^T R \widehat{S} \tilde{q}_i + \tilde{p}_i^T R \widehat{S} y_i + x_i^T R \widehat{S} y_i.$$

Since the image coordinates p_i and q_i usually are magnitude larger than x_i and y_i, one can omit the last term in the equation above. Then $p_i^T R \widehat{S} q_i$ are independent random variables *approximately* of Gaussian distribution $N(0, \sigma^2(\|\widehat{e}_3 R \widehat{S} q_i\|^2 + \|p_i^T R \widehat{S} \widehat{e}_3\|^2))$, where $e_3 = (0, 0, 1)^T \in \mathbb{R}^3$. If we assume the *a prior* distribution of the motion (R, S) is uniform, the maximum *a posterior* (MAP) estimates of (R, S) is then the global minimum of the objective function:

$$F_s(R, S) = \sum_{i=1}^{N} \frac{(p_i^T R \widehat{S} q_i)^2}{\|\widehat{e}_3 R \widehat{S} q_i\|^2 + \|p_i^T R \widehat{S} \widehat{e}_3\|^2} \tag{3}$$

for $p_i, q_i \in \mathbb{R}^3, (R, S) \in SO(3) \times \mathbb{S}^2$. We here use F_s to denote the *statistically normalized* objective function associated with the epipolar constraint. This objective function is also referred in the literature under the name *gradient criteria* or *epipolar improvement*. Therefore, we have $(R, S)_{MAP} \approx \arg\min F_s(R, S)$. Note that in the noise free case, F_s achieves zero, just like the unnormalized objective function F of equation (2). Asymptotically, MAP estimates approach the unbiased minimum mean square estimates (MMSE). So, in general, the MAP estimates give less biased estimates than the unnormalized objective function F. Note that F_s is still a function defined on the manifold $SO(3) \times \mathbb{S}^2$. Another commonly used criteria to recover motion is to minimize the geometric distances between image points and corresponding epipolar lines. This objective function is given as:

$$F_g(R, S) = \sum_{i=1}^{N} \frac{(p_i^T R \widehat{S} q_i)^2}{\|\widehat{e}_3 R \widehat{S} q_i\|^2} + \frac{(p_i^T R \widehat{S} q_i)^2}{\|p_i^T R \widehat{S} \widehat{e}_3^T\|^2} \tag{4}$$

for $p_i, q_i \in \mathbb{R}^3, (R, S) \in SO(3) \times \mathbb{S}^2$. We here use F_g to denote this *geometrically normalized* objective function. Notice that, similar to F and F_s, F_g is also a function defined on the essential manifold and can be minimized using the given Newton's algorithm. As we know from the differential case [12], the normalization has no effect when the translational motion is in the image plane, *i.e.*, the

---

[3] The spherical projection case is similar and is omitted for simplicity.

unnormalized and normalized objective functions are in fact equivalent. For the discrete case, we have similar claim [8]. Therefore in such case the normalization will have very little effect on motion estimation as will be verified by simulation.

3   Optimal Triangulation

Note that, in the presence of noise, for the motion (R, S) recovered from minimizing the unnormalized or normalized objective functions F, F_s or F_g, the value of the objective functions is not necessarily zero. Consequently, if one directly uses p_i and q_i to recover the 3D location of the point to which the two images p_i and q_i correspond, the two rays corresponding to p_i and q_i may not be coplanar, hence may not intersect at one 3D point. Also, when we derived the normalized epipolar constraint F_s, we ignored the second order terms. Therefore, rigorously speaking, it does not give the exact MAP estimates. Under the assumption of Gaussian noise model, in order to obtain the optimal (MAP) estimates of camera motion and a consistent 3D structure reconstruction, in principle we need to solve the following optimal triangulation problem: Seek camera motion (R, S) and points $\tilde{p}_i, \tilde{q}_i \in \mathbb{R}^3$ on the image plane such that they minimize the distance from p_i and q_i:

$$F_t(R, S, \tilde{p}_i, \tilde{q}_i) = \sum_{i=1}^{N} \|\tilde{p}_i - p_i\|^2 + \|\tilde{q}_i - q_i\|^2 \tag{5}$$

subject to the conditions: $\tilde{p}_i^T R \widehat{S} \tilde{q}_i = 0$, $\tilde{p}_i^T e_3 = 1$, $\tilde{q}_i^T e_3 = 1$ for $i = 1, \ldots, N$. We here use F_t to denote the objective function for triangulation. This objective function is also referred in literature as the reprojection error. Unlike [4], we do not assume a known essential matrix $R\widehat{S}$. Instead we seek $\tilde{p}_i, \tilde{q}_i$ and (R, S) which minimize the objective function F_t given by (5). The objective function F_t then implicitly depends on the variables (R, S) through the constraints. Clearly, the optimal solution to this problem is exactly equivalent to the optimal MAP estimates of both motion *and* structure. Using Lagrangian multipliers, we can convert the minimization problem to an unconstrained one:

$$\min_{R, S, \tilde{p}_i, \tilde{q}_i} \sum_{i=1}^{N} \|\tilde{p}_i - p_i\|^2 + \|\tilde{q}_i - q_i\|^2 + \lambda_i \tilde{p}_i^T R \widehat{S} \tilde{q}_i + \beta_i (\tilde{p}_i^T e_3 - 1) + \gamma_i (\tilde{q}_i^T e_3 - 1).$$

The necessary conditions for minima of this objective function are:

$$2(\tilde{p}_i - p_i) + \lambda_i R \widehat{S} \tilde{q}_i + \beta_i e_3 = 0 \tag{6}$$

$$2(\tilde{q}_i - q_i) + \lambda_i \widehat{S}^T R^T \tilde{p}_i + \gamma_i e_3 = \tag{7}$$

From necessary conditions we get $\tilde{p}_i, \tilde{q}_i$. Substituting these and λ_i obtained from (6) back to into F_t we get:

$$F_t(R, S, \tilde{p}_i, \tilde{q}_i) = \sum_{i=1}^{N} \frac{(p_i^T R \widehat{S} \tilde{q}_i + \tilde{p}_i^T R \widehat{S} q_i)^2}{\|\widehat{e}_3 R \widehat{S} \tilde{q}_i\|^2 + \|\tilde{p}_i^T R \widehat{S} \widehat{e}_3^T\|^2} \tag{8}$$

and alternatively using (7) for λ_i instead, we get:

$$F_t(R, S, \tilde{p}_i, \tilde{q}_i) = \sum_{i=1}^{N} \frac{(p_i^T R \widehat{S} \tilde{q}_i)^2}{\|\widehat{e}_3 R S \tilde{q}_i\|^2} + \frac{(\tilde{p}_i^T R \widehat{S} q_i)^2}{\|\tilde{p}_i^T R S \widehat{e}_3^T\|^2}. \tag{9}$$

Geometrically, both expressions of F_t are the distances from the image points p_i and q_i to the epipolar lines specified by $\tilde{p}_i, \tilde{q}_i$ and (R, S). Equations (8) and (9) give explicit formulae of the residue of $\|\tilde{p}_i - p_i\|^2 + \|\tilde{q}_i - q_i\|^2$ as p_i, q_i being triangulated by $\tilde{p}_i, \tilde{q}_i$. Note that the terms in F_t are normalized *crossed epipolar constraints* between p_i and $\tilde{q}_i$ or between $\tilde{p}_i$ and q_i. These expressions of F_t can be further used to solve for (R, S) which minimizes F_t. This leads to the following iterative scheme for obtaining optimal estimates of both motion and structure, without explicitly introducing scale factors (or depths) of the 3D points.

Optimal Triangulation Algorithm Outline: *The procedure for minimizing F_t can be outlined as follows:*

1. *Initialize $\tilde{p}_i^*(R, S), \tilde{q}_i^*(R, S)$ as p_i, q_i.*
2. **Motion:** *Update (R, S) by minimizing $F_t^*(R, S) = F_t(R, S, \tilde{p}_i^*(R, S), \tilde{q}_i^*(R, S))$ given by (8) or (9) as a function defined on the manifold $SO(3) \times \mathbb{S}^2$.*
3. **Structure (Triangulation):** *Solve for $\tilde{p}_i^*(R, S)$ and $\tilde{q}_i^*(R, S)$ which minimize the objective function F_t (5) with respect to (R, S) computed in the previous step.*
4. *Back to step 2 until updates are small enough.*

At step 3, for a fixed (R, S), $\tilde{p}_i^*(R, S)$ and $\tilde{q}_i^*(R, S)$ can be computed by minimizing the distance $\|\tilde{p}_i - p_i\|^2 + \|\tilde{q}_i - q_i\|^2$ for each pair of image points. Let $t_i \in \mathbb{R}^3$ be the normal vector (of unit length) to the (epipolar) plane spanned by $(\tilde{q}_i, S)$. Given such a t_i, $\tilde{p}_i$ and $\tilde{q}_i$ are determined by:

$$\tilde{p}_i(t_i) = \frac{\widehat{e}_3 t_i' t_i'^T \widehat{e}_3^T p_i + \widehat{t'}_i^T \widehat{t'}_i e_3}{e_3^T \widehat{t'}_i^T \widehat{t'}_i e_3}, \quad \tilde{q}_i(t_i) = \frac{\widehat{e}_3 t_i t_i^T \widehat{e}_3^T q_i + \widehat{t}_i^T \widehat{t}_i e_3}{e_3^T \widehat{t}_i^T \widehat{t}_i e_3} \tag{10}$$

where $t_i' = R t_i$. Then the distance can be explicitly expressed as:

$$\|\tilde{q}_i - q_i\|^2 + \|\tilde{p}_i - p_i\|^2 = \|q_i\|^2 + \frac{t_i^T A_i t_i}{t_i^T B_i t_i} + \|p_i\|^2 + \frac{t_i'^T C_i t_i'}{t_i'^T D_i t_i'},$$

where

$$\begin{aligned} A_i &= I - (\widehat{e}_3 q_i q_i^T \widehat{e}_3^T + \widehat{q}_i \widehat{e}_3 + \widehat{e}_3 \widehat{q}_i), & B_i &= \widehat{e}_3^T \widehat{e}_3 \\ C_i &= I - (\widehat{e}_3 p_i p_i^T \widehat{e}_3^T + \widehat{p}_i \widehat{e}_3 + \widehat{e}_3 \widehat{p}_i), & D_i &= \widehat{e}_3^T \widehat{e}_3 \end{aligned} \tag{11}$$

Then the problem of finding $\tilde{p}_i^*(R, S)$ and $\tilde{q}_i^*(R, S)$ becomes one of finding t_i^* which minimizes the function of a sum of two *singular Rayleigh quotients*:

$$\min_{t_i^T S = 0, t_i^T t_i = 1} V(t_i) = \frac{t_i^T A_i t_i}{t_i^T B_i t_i} + \frac{t_i^T R^T C_i R t_i}{t_i^T R^T D_i R t_i}. \tag{12}$$

This is an optimization problem on a unit circle $\mathbb{S}^1$ in the plane orthogonal to the vector S. If $n_1, n_2 \in \mathbb{R}^3$ are vectors such that S, n_1, n_2 form an orthonormal basis of $\mathbb{R}^3$, then $t_i = \cos(\theta)n_1 + \sin(\theta)n_2$ with $\theta \in \mathbb{R}$. We only need to find θ^* which minimizes the function $V(t_i(\theta))$. From the geometric interpretation of the optimal solution, we also know that the global minimum θ^* should lie between two values: θ_1 and θ_2 such that $t_i(\theta_1)$ and $t_i(\theta_2)$ correspond to normal vectors of the two planes spanned by (q_i, S) and $(R^T p_i, S)$ respectively (if p_i, q_i are already triangulated, these two planes coincide). Therefore, in our approach the local minima is no longer an issue for triangulation, as oppose to the method proposed in [4]. The problem now becomes a simple bounded minimization problem for a scalar function and can be efficiently solved using standard optimization routines (such as "fmin" in Matlab or the Newton's algorithm). If one properly parameterizes $t_i(\theta)$, t_i^* can also be obtained by solving a 6-degree polynomial equation, as shown in [4] (and an approximate version results in solving a 4-degree polynomial equation [21]). However, the method given in [4] involves coordinate transformation for each image pair and the given parameterization is by no means canonical. For example, if one chooses instead the commonly used parameterization of a circle $\mathbb{S}^1$: $\sin(2\theta) = \frac{2\lambda}{1+\lambda^2}$, $\cos(2\theta) = \frac{1-\lambda^2}{1+\lambda^2}$, $\lambda \in \mathbb{R}$, then it is straightforward to show from the Rayleigh quotient sum (12) that the necessary condition for minima of $V(t_i)$ is equivalent to a 6-degree polynomial equation in λ.[4] The triangulated pairs $(\tilde{p}_i, \tilde{q}_i)$ and the camera motion (R, S) obtained from the minimization automatically give a consistent (optimal) 3D structure reconstruction by two-frame stereo.

In the expressions of F_t given by (18) or (19), if we simply approximate $\tilde{p}_i, \tilde{q}_i$ by p_i, q_i respectively, we may obtain the normalized versions of epipolar constraints for recovering camera motion. Although subtle difference between F_s, F_g and F_t has previously been pointed out in [23], our approach discovers that all these three objective functions can be unified in the same optimization procedure – they are just slightly different approximations of the same objective function F_t^*. Practically speaking, using either normalized objective function F_s or F_g, one can already get camera motion estimates which are very close to the optimal ones. This will be demonstrated by extensive simulations in the next section.

4   Critical Values and Ambiguous Solutions

We devote the remainder of this paper to study of the robustness and sensitivity of motion and structure estimation problem in the presence of large levels of noise. We emphasize here the role of the linear techniques for initialization and utilize the characterization of the space of essential matrices and the intrinsic optimization techniques on the essential manifold. The focus of our robustness

---

[4] Since there is no closed form solution to 6-degree polynomial equations, directly minimizing the Rayleigh quotient sum (12) avoids unnecessary transformations hence can be much more efficient.

study deals with the appearance of new local minima. Like any nonlinear system, when increasing the noise level, new critical points of the objective function can be introduced through bifurcation. Although in general an objective function could have numerous critical points, numbers of different types of critical points have to satisfy the so called *Morse inequalities*, which are associated to topological invariants of the underlying manifold (see [15]). Key to this study is the computation of the *Euler characteristic* $\chi(M)$ of the underlying manifold $SO(3) \times \mathbb{RP}^2$ which is in this case 0; $\chi(SO(3) \times \mathbb{RP}^2) = 0$. Euler characteristic is equal to $\sum_{\lambda=0}^n (-1)^\lambda D_\lambda$, where D_λ is the dimension of the λth homology group $H_\lambda(M, \mathbb{K})$ of M over any field $\mathbb{K}$, the so called λ^{th} *Betti number*. In our case $D_\lambda = 1, 2, 3, 3, 2, 1$ for $\lambda = 0, 1, 2, 3, 4, 5$ types of critical points respectively. For details of this computation see [13]. Among all the critical points, those belonging to type 0 are called (local) *minima*, type n are (local) *maxima*, and types 1 to $n - 1$ are *saddles*. From the above computation any Morse function defined on $SO(3) \times \mathbb{RP}^2$ must have all three kinds of critical values. The nonlinear search algorithms proposed in the above are trying to find the global minimum of given objective functions. We study the effect of initialization by linear techniques and apperance of new critical points on different slices of the nonlinear objective function which we can be easily visualized. The choice of the section is determined by the estimate of rotation where the nonlinear algorithm converged by initialization of the linear algorithm.

Rewriting the epipolar constraint as $p_i^T E q_i = 0, i = 1, \ldots, N$, minimizing the objective function F is (approximately) equivalent to the following least square problem $\min \|Ae\|^2$, where A is a $N \times 9$ matrix function of entries of p_i and q_i, and $e \in \mathbb{R}^9$ is a vector of the nine entries of E. Then e is the (usually one dimensional) null space of the 9×9 symmetric matrix $A^T A$. In the presence of noise, e is simply chosen to be the eigenvector corresponding to the least eigenvalue of $A^T A$. At a low noise level, this eigenvector in general gives a good initial estimate of the essential matrix. However, at a certain high noise level, the smallest two eigenvalues may switch roles, as do the two corresponding eigenvectors – topologically, a bifurcation as shown in Figure 2 occurs. This phenomena is very common in the motion estimation problem: at a high noise level, the translation estimate may suddenly change direction by roughly 90°, especially in the case when translation is parallel to the image plane. We will refer to such estimates as the *second eigenmotion*. A similar situation for the differential case and small field of view has previously been reported in [2].

Figure 1 and 2 demonstrate such a sudden appearance of the second eigenmotion. They are the simulation results of the proposed nonlinear algorithm of minimizing the function F_s for a cloud of 40 randomly generated pairs of image correspondences (in a field of view 90°, depth varying from 100 to 400 units of focal length.). Gaussian noise of standard deviation of 6.4 or 6.5 pixels is added on each image point (image size 512×512 pixels). To make the results comparable, we used the same random seeds for both runs. The actual rotation is 10° about the Y-axis and the actual translation is along the X-axis.[5] The ratio between translation and rotation is 2.[6] In the figures, "+" marks the actual translation, "*" marks the translation estimate from linear algorithm (see [14] for detail) and "∘" marks the estimate from nonlinear optimization. Up to the noise level of 6.4 pixels, both rotation and translation estimates are very close to the actual motion. Increasing the noise level further by 0.1 pixel, the translation estimate suddenly switches to one which is roughly $90°$ away from the actual translation. Geometrically, this estimate corresponds to the second smallest eigenvector of the matrix $A^T A$ as we discussed before. Topologically, this estimate corresponds to the local minimum introduced by a bifurcation as shown by Figure 2. Clearly, in Figure 1, there is 1 maximum, 1 saddle and 1 minimum on $\mathbb{RP}^2$; in Figure 2, there is 1 maximum, 2 saddles and 2 minima. Both patterns give the Euler characteristic of $\mathbb{RP}^2$ as 1. Rotation is fixed at the estimate from nonlinear algorithm. The errors are expressed in terms of canonical metric on $SO(3)$ for rotation and in terms of angle for translation.

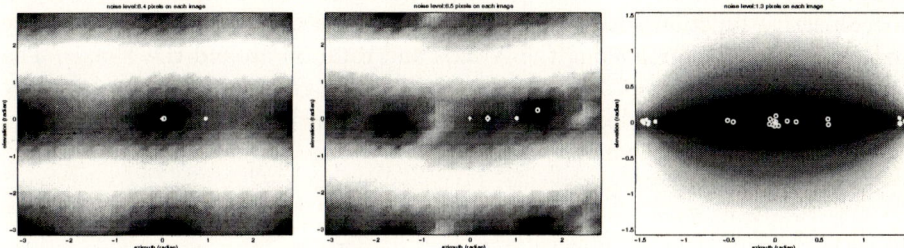

Fig. 1. Value of objective function F_s for all S at noise level 6.4 pixels. Estimation errors: 0.014 in rotation estimate and $2.39°$ in translation estimate.

Fig. 2. Value of objective function F_s for all S at noise level 6.5 pixels. Estimation errors: 0.227 in rotation estimate and $84.66°$ in translation estimate.

Fig. 3. Bas relief ambiguity. FOV is $20°$, points depths vary from 100 to 150 units of focal length, rotation magnitude is $2°$, T/R ratio is 2. 20 runs with noise level 1.3 pixels.

From the Figure 2, we can see that the the second eigenmotion ambiguity is even more likely to occur (at certain high noise level) than the other local minimum marked by "⋄" in the figure which is a legitimate estimate of the actual one. These two estimates always occur in pair and exist for general configuration even when both the FOV and depth variation are sufficiently large. We propose a way for resolving the second eigenmotion ambiguity by linear algorithm which is used for initialization. An indicator of the configuration being close to critical

---

[5] We here use the convention that Y-axis is the vertical direction of the image and X-axis is the horizontal direction and the Z-axis coincides with the optical axis of the camera.

[6] Rotation and translation magnitudes are compared with respect to the center of the cloud of 3D points generated.

is the ratio of the two smallest eigenvalues of $A^T A$ σ_9 and σ_8 . By using both eigenvectors v_9 and v_8 for computing the linear motion estimates, the one which satisfies the positive depth constraint by larger margin (i.e. larger number of points satisfies the positive depth constraint) leads to the motion estimates closer to the true one (see [8] for details).

This second eigenmotion effect has a quite different interpretation as the one which was previously attributed to the bas relief ambiguity. The bas relief effect is only evident when FOV and depth variation is small, but the second eigen-motion ambiguity may show up for general configurations. Bas relief estimates are statistically meaningful since they characterize a sensitive direction in which translation and rotation are the most likely to be confound. The second eigen-motion, however, is not statistically meaningful: it is an effect of initialization which with increasing noise level causes a perturbation to a different slice of the objective function with a different topology of the residual. This effect occurs only at a high noise level and this critical noise level gives a measure of the *robustness* of linear initialization of the given algorithm. For comparison, Figure 3 demonstrates the effect of the bas relief ambiguity: the long narrow valley of the objective function corresponds to the direction that is the most sensitive to noise.[7] Translation is along the X-axis and rotation around the Y-axis. The (translation) estimates of 20 runs, marked as "o", give a distribution roughly resembling the shape of this valley – the actual translation is marked as "+"in the center of the valley which is covered by circles.

5   Experiments and Sensitivity Analysis

In this section, we clearly demonstrate by experiments the relationship among the linear algorithm (as in [14]), nonlinear algorithm (minimizing F), normalized nonlinear algorithm (minimizing F_s) and optimal triangulation (minimizing F_t). Due to the nature of the second eigenmotion ambiguity (when not corrected), it gives statistically meaningless estimates. Such estimates should be treated as "outliers" if one wants to properly evaluate a given algorithm and compare simulation results. We will demonstrate that seemingly conflicting statements in the literature about the performance of existing algorithms can in fact be given a *unified* explanation if we systematically compare the simulation results with respect to a *large range* of noise levels (as long as the results are statistically meaningful).

The following simulations were carried out with the points in general config-uration and camera parameters described in Section 4. All nonlinear algorithms are initialized by the estimates from the standard 8-point linear algorithm (see [14]), instead of from the ground truth. The criteria for all nonlinear algorithms to stop are: (a) The norm of gradient is less than a given error tolerance, which

---

[7] This direction is given by the eigenvector of the Hessian associated with the smallest eigenvalue.

usually we pick as 10^{-8} unless otherwise stated;[8] and (b) The smallest eigenvalue of the Hessian matrix is positive.[9]

Axis Dependency Profile It has been well known that the sensitivity of the motion estimation depends on the camera motion. However, in order to give a clear account of such a dependency, one has to be careful about two things: 1. The signal-to-noise ratio and 2. Whether the simulation results are still statistically meaningful while varying the noise level. Figure 4, 5, 6 and 7 give simulation results of 100 trials for each combination of translation and rotation ("T-R") axes, for example, "X-Y" means translation is along the X-axis and the rotation axis is the Y-axis. Rotation is always $10°$ about the axis and the T/R ratio is 2. In the figures, "linear" stands for the standard 8-point linear algorithm; "nonlin" is the Riemannian Newton's algorithm minimizing the epipolar constraints F, "normal" is the Riemannian Newton's algorithm minimizing the normalized epipolar constraints F_s.

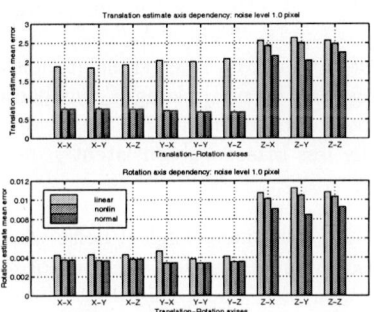

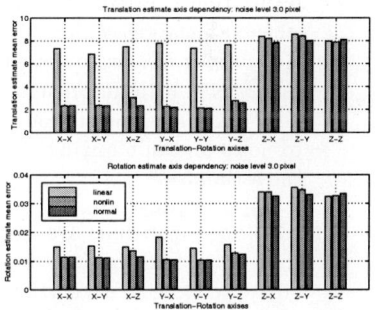

Fig. 4. Axis dependency: estimation errors in rotation and translation at noise level 1.0 pixel. T/R ratio $= 2$ and rotation $= 10°$.

Fig. 5. Axis dependency: estimation errors in rotation and translation at noise level 3.0 pixels. T/R ratio $= 2$ and rotation $= 10°$.

By carefully comparing the simulation results in Figure 4, 5, 6 and 7, we can draw the following conclusions:

1. **Optimization Techniques (linear vs. nonlinear)**
   (a) Minimizing F in general gives better estimates than the linear algorithm at low noise levels (Figure 4 and 5). At higher noise levels, this is no longer true (Figure 6 and 7), due to the more global nature of the linear technique.
   (b) Minimizing the normalized F_s in general gives better estimates than the linear algorithm at moderate noise levels (all figures).

---

[8] Our current implementation of the algorithms in Matlab has a numerical accuracy at 10^{-8}.

[9] Since we have the explicit formulae for Hessian, this condition would keep the algorithms from stopping at saddle points.

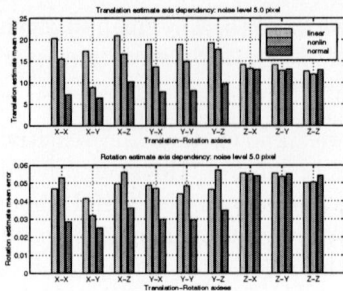

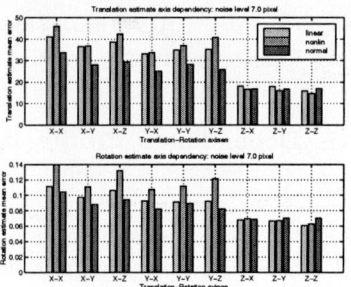

Fig. 6. Axis dependency: estimation errors in rotation and translation at noise level 5.0 pixel. T/R ratio = 2 and rotation = 10°.

Fig. 7. Axis dependency: estimation errors in rotation and translation at noise level 7.0 pixels. T/R ratio = 2 and rotation = 10°.

2. **Optimization Criteria (F vs. F_s)**
   (a) At relatively low noise levels (Figure 4), normalization has little effect when translation is parallel to the image plane; and estimates are indeed improved when translation is along the Z-axis.
   (b) However, at moderate noise levels (Figure 5, 6 and 7), when translation is along the Z-axis, little improvement can be gained by minimizing F_s instead of F; however, when translation is parallel to the image plane, F is more sensitive to noise and minimizing the statistically less biased F_s consistently improves the estimates.
3. **Axis Dependency**
   (a) All three algorithms are the most robust to the increasing of noise when the translation is along Z. At moderate noise levels (all figures), their performances are quite close to each other.
   (b) Although, at relatively low noise levels (Figure 4, 5 and 6), estimation errors seem to be larger when the translation is along the Z-axis, estimates are in fact much less sensitive to noise and more robust to increasing of noise in this case. The larger estimation error in case of translation along Z-axis is because the displacements of image points are smaller than those when translation is parallel to the image plane, thus the signal-to-noise ratio is in fact smaller.
   (c) At a noise level of 7 pixels (Figure 7), estimation errors seem to become smaller when the translation is along Z-axis. This is due to the fact that, at a noise level of 7 pixels, the second eigenmotion ambiguity already occurs in some of the trials when the translation is parallel to the image plane.

The second statement about the axis dependency supplements the observation given in [20]. In fact, the motion estimates are both robust and less sensitive to increasing of noise when translation is along the Z-axis. For a fixed base line, high noise level results resemble those for a smaller base line at a moderate noise level. Figure 7 is therefore a generic picture of the axis dependency profile for the differential or small base-line case (for more details see [12]).

Non-iterative vs. Iterative In general, the motion estimates obtained from directly minimizing the normalized epipolar constraints F_s or F_g are already very close to the solution of the optimal triangulation obtained by minimizing F_t iteratively between motion and structure. It is already known that, at low noise levels, the estimates from the non-iterative and iterative schemes usually differ by less than a couple of percent [23].

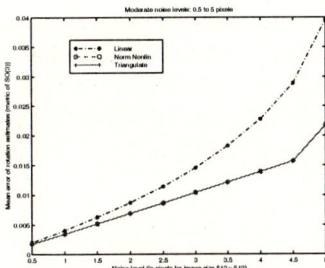

Fig. 8. Estimation errors of rotation (in canonical metric on $SO(3)$). 50 trials, rotation 10 degree around Y-axis and translation along X-axis, T/R ratio is 2. Noises range from 0.5 to 5 pixels.

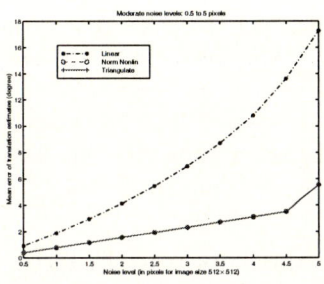

Fig. 9. Estimation errors of translation (in degree). 50 trials, rotation 10 degree around Y-axis and translation along X-axis, T/R ratio is 2. Noises range from 0.5 to 5 pixels.

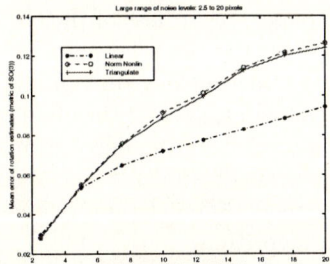

Fig. 10. Estimation errors of rotation (in canonical metric on $SO(3)$). 40 points, 50 trials, rotation 10 degree around Y-axis and translation along Z-axis, T/R ratio is 2. Noises range from 2.5 to 20 pixels.

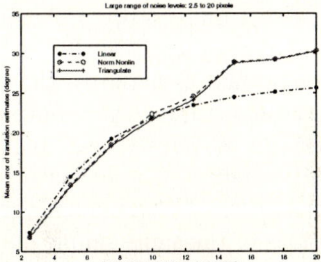

Fig. 11. Estimation errors of translation (in degree). 40 points, 50 trials, rotation 10 degree around Y-axis and translation along Z-axis, T/R ratio is 2. Noises range from 2.5 to 20 pixels.

By comparing the simulation results in Figures 8, 9, 10 and 11 we can draw the following conclusions:

1. Although the iterative optimal triangulation algorithm usually gives better estimates (as it should), the non-iterative minimization of the normalized epipolar constraints F_s or F_g gives motion estimates with only a few percent larger errors for all range of noise levels. The higher the noise level, the more evident the improvement of the iterative scheme is.

2. Within moderate noise levels, normalized nonlinear algorithms consistently give significantly better estimates than the standard linear algorithm, especially when the translation is parallel to the image plane. At very high noise levels, the performance of the standard linear algorithm, out performs nonlinear algorithms. This is due to the more global nature of the linear algorithm. However, such high noise levels are barely realistic in real applications.

For low level Gaussian noises, the iterative optimal triangulation algorithm gives the MAP estimates of the camera motion and scene structure, the estimation error can be shown close to the theoretical error bounds, such as the Cramer-Rao bound. This has been shown experimentally in [21]. Consequently, minimizing the normalized epipolar constraints F_s or F_g gives motion estimates close to the error bound as well.

6   Discussions and Future Work

Although previously proposed algorithms already have good performance in practice, the geometric concepts behind them have not yet been completely revealed. The non-degeneracy conditions and convergence speed of those algorithms are usually not explicitly addressed. Due to the recent development of optimization methods on Riemannian manifolds, we now can have a better mathematical understanding of these algorithms, and propose new geometric algorithms or filters, which exploit the intrinsic geometric structure of the motion and structure recovery problem. As shown in this paper, regardless of the choice of different objectives, the problem of optimization on the essential manifold is common and essential to the optimal motion and structure recovery problem. Furthermore, from a pure optimization theoretic viewpoint, most of the objective functions previously used in the literature can be unified in a single optimization procedure. Consequently, "minimizing (normalized) epipolar constraints", "triangulation", "minimizing reprojection errors" are all different (approximate) versions of the same simple optimal triangulation algorithm.

In this paper, we have studied in detail the problem of recovering a discrete motion (displacement) from image correspondences. Similar ideas certainly apply to the differential case where the rotation and translation are replaced by angular and linear velocities respectively [13]. One can show that they all in fact minimize certain normalized versions of the differential epipolar constraint. We hope the Riemannian optimization theoretic viewpoint proposed in this paper will provide a different perspective to revisit these schemes. Although the study of the proposed algorithms is carried out in a calibrated camera framework, due to a clear geometric connection between the calibrated and uncalibrated case [10], the same approach and optimization schemes can be generalized with little effort to the uncalibrated case as well. Details will be presented in future work.

References

1. K. Danilidis. *Visual Navigation*, chapter "Understanding Noise Sensitivity in Structure from Motion". Lawrence Erlbaum Associates, 1997.

2. K. Danilidis and H.-H. Nagel. Analytical results on error sensitivity of motion estimation from two views. *Image and Vision Computing*, 8:297–303, 1990.
3. A. Edelman, T. Arias, and S. T. Smith. The geometry of algorithms with orthogonality constraints. *SIAM J. Matrix Analysis Applications*, to appear.
4. R. Hartley and P. Sturm. Triangulation. *Computer Vision and Image Understanding*, 68(2):146–57, 1997.
5. B. Horn. Relative orientation. *International Journal of Computer Vision*, 4:59–78, 1990.
6. A. D. Jepson and D. J. Heeger. Linear subspace methods for recovering translation direction. *Spatial Vision in Humans and Robots, Cambridge Univ. Press*, pages 39–62, 1993.
7. K. Kanatani. *Geometric Computation for Machine Vision*. Oxford Science Publications, 1993.
8. J. Košecká, Y. Ma, and S. Sastry. Optimization criteria, sensitivity and robustness of motion and structure estimation. In *Vision Algorithms Workshop, ICCV*, pages 9–16, 1999.
9. H. C. Longuet-Higgins. A computer algorithm for reconstructing a scene from two projections. *Nature*, 293:133–135, 1981.
10. Y. Ma, J. Košecká, and S. Sastry. A mathematical theory of camera self-calibration. *Electronic Research Laboratory Memorandum, UC Berkeley*, UCB/ERL M98/64, October 1998.
11. Y. Ma, J. Košecká, and S. Sastry. Motion recovery from image sequences: Discrete viewpoint vs. differential viewpoint. In *Proceeding of European Conference on Computer Vision, Volume II, (also Electronic Research Laboratory Memorandum M98/11, UC Berkeley)*, pages 337–53, 1998.
12. Y. Ma, J. Košecká, and S. Sastry. Linear differential algorithm for motion recovery: A geometric approach. *Submitted to IJCV*, 1999.
13. Y. Ma, J. Košecká, and S. Sastry. Optimization criteria and geometric algorithms for motion and structure estimation. *submitted to IJCV*, 1999.
14. S. Maybank. *Theory of Reconstruction from Image Motion*. Springer-Verlag, 1993.
15. J. Milnor. *Morse Theory*. Annals of Mathematics Studies no. 51. Princeton University Press, 1969.
16. R. M. Murray, Z. Li, and S. S. Sastry. *A Mathematical Introduction to Robotic Manipulation*. CRC press Inc., 1994.
17. S. Soatto and R. Brockett. Optimal and suboptimal structure from motion. *Proceedings of International Conference on Computer Vision*, to appear.
18. M. Spetsakis. Models of statistical visual motion estimation. *CVIPG: Image Understanding*, 60(3):300–312, November 1994.
19. T. Y. Tian, C. Tomasi, and D. Heeger. Comparison of approaches to egomotion computation. In *CVPR*, 1996.
20. J. Weng, T.S. Huang, and N. Ahuja. Motion and structure from two perspective views: Algorithms, error analysis, and error estimation. *IEEE Transactions on Pattern Analysis and Machine Intelligence*, 11(5):451–475, 1989.
21. J. Weng, T.S. Huang, and N. Ahuja. *Motion and Structure from Image Sequences*. Springer Verlag, 1993.
22. J. Weng, T.S. Huang, and N. Ahuja. Optimal motion and structure estimation. *IEEE Transactions on Pattern Analysis and Machine Intelligence*, 15(9):864–84, 1993.
23. Z. Zhang. Understanding the relationship between the optimization criteria in two-view motion analysis. In *Proceeding of International Conference on Computer Vision*, pages 772–77, Bombay, India, 1998.

Discussion

Kenichi Kanatani: You compare your method with other techniques, but in my view what you should really do is compare it with the theoretical accuracy bound, the lower bound beyond which accuracy can't be improved. For the problems you have described so far it is very easy to derive this bound.

Jana Košecká: Theoretical accuracy is usually expressed in terms of the Cramér-Rao bound, but there's an alternative way to look at it. If one bases the optimization on the epipolar constraint, it turns out that no matter what you do, half of the variance always gets absorbed by the structure. You can not do better than that — the error along the epipolar line gets absorbed by the structure, so you can only improve the error perpendicular to the epipolar line. One can even consider this as an alternative means of putting some lower bound on the estimates using these kind of techniques. Also, Weng, Huang and Ahuja [21] already did the comparision with the theoretical bound. Rather than repeating this analysis, we preferred to give a complementary viewpoint.

Gauge Independence
in Optimization Algorithms for 3D Vision

Philip F. McLauchlan

School of Electrical Engineering, Information Technology and Mathematics,
University of Surrey,
Guildford GU2 5XH.
`P.McLauchlan@ee.surrey.ac.uk`

Abstract. We attack the problem of coordinate frame dependence and
gauge freedoms in structure-from-motion. We are able to formulate a
bundle adjustment algorithm whose results are independent of both the
coordinate frame chosen to represent the scene and the ordering of the
images. This method is more efficient that existing approaches to the
problem in photogrammetry.
We demonstrate that to achieve coordinate frame independent results,
(i) Rotations should be represented by quaternions or local rotation parameters, not angles, and (ii) the translation vector describing the cam-
era/scene motion should be represented in scene 3D coordinates, not
camera 3D coordinates, two representations which are normally treated
as interchangeable. The algorithm allows 3D point and line features to be
reconstructed. Implementation is via the efficient recursive partitioning
algorithm common in photogrammetry. Results are presented demonstrating the advantages of the new method in terms of the stability of
the bundle adjustment iterations.

1 Introduction

Parameter estimation is usually posed as the minimization of the geometric
error in the image measurements, and solved by a suitable non-linear optimization algorithm. Convergence and stability are two recurrent important issues in
implementing such algorithms. There are usually several factors at work here,
from the obvious ones, such as design of the algorithm, and its ability to sup-
press noise, to less obvious ones such as correlations in the measurements. Given
many candidates for culprits when experiencing problems, it is often difficult to
determine which factor(s) are at fault. We shall attack one of these, with the aim
of eliminating it. This effect is the **coordinate frame** ambiguity, which arises
from the fact that simply selecting different coordinate frames for the space of
parameters may affect the results of algorithms using that representation.

Coordinate frame ambiguities (or *gauge freedoms*) arise in problems where the
natural representations *over-parametrize* the problem. The "extra" parameters
are those that specify a coordinate frame. Problems of interpreting geometric
aspects of a scene (e.g. its 3D shape) by combining multiple observations of it,

B. Triggs, A. Zisserman, R. Szeliski (Eds.): Vision Algorithms'99, LNCS 1883, pp. 183–199, 2000.

using a sensor lacking an absolute frame of reference, *always* have this property. This is because to compute geometrical quantities, one must define a frame of reference, and because no absolute frame of reference is provided by the sensor, there is no natural frame and the choice of coordinate frame is arbitrary. One can obtain different, equivalent answers using different frames of reference. However designing algorithms the necessary independence property to make the choice truly arbitrary, in the sense that the algorithm behaves in equivalent ways given different choices, is not trivial.

Achieving coordinate frame independence may seem like a small advance, especially when good results have been achieved in 3D reconstruction without much care given to this issue. However we argue that if reconstruction algorithms are to be integrated into larger vision systems, it is vital that they have predictable performance. Elimination of the effect of arbitrary choices inside algorithms is an important step in this direction. Moreover we have found in the case of projective 3D reconstruction that our methods deliver improvements in the convergence compared with alternative methods [9].

One of the surprising results of our work is that even where strong non-linearity is present in the projection equations, such as in the projective and perspective models, the effective choice of coordinate frame can be reduced to an orthogonal transformation without affecting our desideratum of independence to image ordering. This is achieved by a combination of appropriate choice of scene motion and structure representation, suitable rank-deficient linear system solution methods, and a *normalisation* step which eliminates the non-orthogonal part of the coordinate frame ambiguity. In [9] we presented the algorithm for projective reconstruction. Here we discuss the principles of gauge independence in general while restricting detailed discussion to the case of Euclidean reconstruction.

1.1   Examples of Gauge Freedoms in Vision

There are many examples of optimisation algorithms in vision where the natural representation of the parameters to be estimated contains gauge freedoms:–

- The fundamental matrix is a 3×3 matrix defining the epipolar geometry of two uncalibrated views of a scene. It has two redundant degrees of freedom, one being a scale gauge freedom, the other being the constraint that the matrix is singular.
- The problem of registering multiple range images is typically attacked by selecting a single "reference" range map, and registering the others to the coordinate frame of the reference map [3]. Clearly the results will depend on the choice of reference range map.
- Any optimisation involving quantities whose natural representation is in homogeneous coordinates, and so has a scale freedom. This turns up in projective reconstruction, such as estimating the fundamental matrix as above, and also applies when computing structure and motion. There is always a choice whether to fix one of the elements of the vector/matrix to unity or to keep the full representation and use constrained optimisation.

– Structure-from-motion and photogrammetry share the coordinate frame problem (known as the ZOD or zero-order design problem by photogrammetrists [1]). This is the main subject of the current work.

1.2 Three-Stranded Approach

To achieve gauge independent algorithms, our design has three separate but interrelated strands, which we introduce here. Because of the ubiquity of the phrase "gauge independence" in the paper, we shall abbreviate it to "GI". The meaning of gauge independence in this context is that if two reconstructions are related by a coordinate frame transformation, which can be thought of as two separate "runs" of the algorithm, then the optimisation algorithm should maintain the same coordinate frame transformation throughout, so that at the end of the algorithm the two reconstructions are still equivalent.

Representation. There are often choices of representation available which are difficult to distinguish on first appearance. Some examples relevant to the discussion here:–

1. 3D rotations can be represented in a variety of angle systems, such as Euler or Cardan angles, quaternions, or local rotation parameters.
2. In projective reconstruction, projective points and projection matrices can be represented in homogeneous coordinates, or in non-homogeneous coordinates formed by fixing a chosen coordinate at unity.
3. In Euclidean reconstruction, the translation vector can be represented in either camera coordinates or scene coordinates.

One of the major contributions of this work is to show that for many optimisation problems the choice of representation may at least partly be decided by gauge dependence criteria. We shall see that indeed all the three choices of representation above can be decided by GI (gauge independence) criteria, in favour of (1) Local rotation parameters or quaternions, (2) homogeneous coordinates normalised to unit norm, and (3) translation vector in scene coordinate frame. It may be somewhat surprising that the last case can be decided in this way, so we demonstrate the problems with the camera coordinate representation of translation in section 4.6.

Rank-deficient linear system methods. We will be considering here the solution of optimisation problems with coordinate frame ambiguities, using Gauss-Newton iterative methods. This gives rise to a rank-deficient linear system to be solved at each iteration. We shall show how this can be done, maintaining GI. Matrix pseudo-inverse has been suggested as a solution to this problem both in photogrammetry [1] and recently in computer vision [10]. We propose a more flexible approach involving the introduction of artificial extra constraints applies to the updated solution. With suitable choice of constraints, the two methods can be made equivalent.

Coordinate frame normalisation. To facilitate the application of the rank-deficient linear system methods, it turns out to be necessary in some cases, and advantageous in others, to adjust the coordinate system among the space of possible frames and thus impose some pre-specified constraints, which will typically be the same as the artificial constraints used to solve the rank-deficient system; in other words the same constraints are employed before each iteration (normalisation) and also to the updated solution (when eliminating rank deficiencies). However the linear system methods are only able to impose the constraints to first order, which in a non-linear system implies that the normalisation must be applied between iterations to re-impose the constraints. The normalisation reduces the *effective* space of possible coordinate frames, but of course it must itself be applied in a GI manner, as defined in section 3.3

We propose that these three techniques constitute a good general framework for applying GI to optimisation problems involving gauge freedoms. In the following sections we shall fill out these ideas in more detail. Section 2 introduces the concepts mathematically and defines the notation used in the remainder of the paper. Section 3 defines the Gauss-Newton method, and derives the general GI criteria in detail, to be applied in later sections to our models. The perspective projection model for point features is then discussed in detail in section 4. We demonstrate that our chosen model obeys the GI criteria. The complete algorithm for gauge-independent Euclidean reconstruction is summarised in section 5. Some preliminary results are presented in section 6.

2   Definitions and Notation

Let us consider a general iterative algorithm that estimates a set of parameters $\mathbf{x}$ from an observation

$$\mathbf{z} = \mathbf{h}(\mathbf{x}) + \mathbf{w}$$

where $\mathbf{h}(.)$ is the observation function and $\mathbf{w}$ a noise vector with covariance R. With a realistic scenario with multiple observations in multiple images, one may consider at this point that all the observations are "stacked" into this single vector $\mathbf{z}$, and like wise all the unknowns (e.g. the structure and motion parameters for the structure-from-motion problem) are stacked into a single vector $\mathbf{x}$. At each iteration, the algorithm takes as input the previous estimate $\mathbf{x}^-$, and computes a new estimate $\mathbf{x}^+$, which is based solely on the old value $\mathbf{x}^-$ and the measurement $\mathbf{z}$. We shall assume that an *additive* rule is being employed, as is the case for the Gauss-Newton variants used almost exclusively in optimization algorithms for 3D vision and photogrammetry. Then the update rule may be written in general as

$$\mathbf{x}^+ = \mathbf{x}^- + \mathbf{f}(\mathbf{h}, \mathbf{x}^-, \mathbf{z}). \tag{1}$$

The algorithm is thus defined by the observation function $\mathbf{h}(.)$, the latest state estimate $\mathbf{x}^-$ and the measurement vector $\mathbf{z}$. As more iterations are made, and with a good wind, the estimates $\mathbf{x}^+$ converge towards the true parameter vector, as closely as possible given the inevitable errors in the measurements. Now let us consider redefining the space of parameters in a different way, using parameters $\mathbf{y}$, which may be assumed to be related by an invertible mapping $\mathbf{g}(.)$ to the original parameter vector $\mathbf{x}$:

$$\mathbf{y} = \mathbf{g}(\mathbf{x}), \quad \mathbf{x} = \mathbf{g}^{-1}(\mathbf{y}).$$

In the case of $\mathbf{g}(.)$ representing a genuine gauge freedom, the transformation has no effect on the measurements:

$$\mathbf{h}(\mathbf{y}) = \mathbf{h}(\mathbf{g}(\mathbf{x})) = \mathbf{h}(\mathbf{x}). \tag{2}$$

In other words different choices of $\mathbf{g}(.)$ represent purely internal choices of coordinate frame in which to represent $\mathbf{x}$. The iterative update rule in this transformed space is then

$$\mathbf{y}^+ = \mathbf{y}^- + \mathbf{f}(\mathbf{h}, \mathbf{y}^-, \mathbf{z}). \tag{3}$$

We can now define our algorithm as independent of the choice of coordinates if when applying the algorithm from different starting points $\mathbf{x}_0^-$ and $\mathbf{y}_0^-$, related by the coordinate transformation $\mathbf{g}(.)$, remain related by the same $\mathbf{g}(.)$ at each corresponding iteration. Thus combining equations (1) and (3) with this criterion, we need to show that for a particular problem that, given the latest state estimates $\mathbf{x}^-$, $\mathbf{y}^-$ in the two algorithm instances, and the coordinate transformation $\mathbf{g}(.)$ between them, that

$$\begin{aligned}\mathbf{g}(\mathbf{x}^- + \mathbf{f}(\mathbf{h}, \mathbf{x}^-, \mathbf{z})) &= \mathbf{y}^- + \mathbf{f}(\mathbf{h}, \mathbf{y}^-, \mathbf{z}) \\ &= \mathbf{g}(\mathbf{x}^-) + \mathbf{f}(\mathbf{h}, \mathbf{g}(\mathbf{x}^-), \mathbf{z})\end{aligned} \tag{4}$$

This is the *gauge independence (GI) criterion*. If we can prove it for a particular problem, we have eliminated the effect of coordinate frame choice.

Throughout the paper we will take the vector norm $\|\mathbf{x}\|$ of a vector $\mathbf{x}$ to indicate the 2-norm $(\mathbf{x}^\top \mathbf{x})^{\frac{1}{2}}$.

3   The Gauss-Newton Method

We now specialize further to the Gauss-Newton method, a least-squares method commonly used to obtain maximum likelihood or maximum *a posteori* estimates of parameters. An adjusted version of the Gauss-Newton scheme that deals with conditioning problems is known as the Levenberg-Marquardt algorithm, but we first consider the simpler form. We first define an error function to be minimized, based on discrepancies in observations, and extrapolate second-order approximations to the error function from the current parameter estimate, which then yields the new estimate as the minimum of the second-order hypersurface, which may be easily computed.

Following the usual theory of maximum likelihood parameter estimation [4], we assume that we have made several noisy observations $\mathbf{z}(j)$, $j = 1, \ldots, k$, (which can where appropriate be bundled into a single vector $\mathbf{z}$ as above), related to the parameter vector $\mathbf{x}$ through measurement functions $\mathbf{h}(j)$:

$$\mathbf{z}(j) = \mathbf{h}(j; \mathbf{x}) + \mathbf{w}(j), \quad j = 1, \ldots, k \tag{5}$$

Here $\mathbf{w}(j)$ is random independently distributed noise with covariance $R(j)$, and is assumed to have zero mean, i.e. it is unbiased.

We construct the error function J from as the sum-of-squares of discrepancies between the actual observations and those predicted by a modelling parameter estimate $\mathbf{x}$:

$$J(\mathbf{x}) = \sum_{j=1}^{k} (\mathbf{z}(j) - \mathbf{h}(j; \mathbf{x}))^{\top} R(j)^{-1} (\mathbf{z}(j) - \mathbf{h}(j; \mathbf{x})). \tag{6}$$

We form a second-order (quadratic) approximation to $J(.)$ around the latest estimate $\mathbf{x}^-$, and locate the minimum of the quadratic extrapolation of $J(.)$ to obtain a new estimate $\mathbf{x}^+$. Omitting details of this standard procedure, we obtain

$$A(\mathbf{x}^+ - \mathbf{x}^-) = \sum_{j=1}^{k} H(j)^{\top} R(j)^{-1} \boldsymbol{\nu}(j) = \mathbf{a}, \tag{7}$$

where:–

- The matrix $A = \sum_{j=1}^{k} H(j)^{\top} R(j)^{-1} H(j)$ may be identified as the state information (inverse covariance) matrix;
- The *innovation vectors* $\boldsymbol{\nu}(j)$ are $\boldsymbol{\nu}(j) = \mathbf{z}(j) - \mathbf{h}(j; \mathbf{x}^-)$;
- The Jacobian matrices $H(j)$ are $H(j) = \frac{\partial \mathbf{h}(j)}{\partial \mathbf{x}}$, evaluated at $\mathbf{x}^-$.

Equation (7) represents one Gauss-Newton update iteration.

3.1   G-N Iterations with Gauge Freedoms

Summarising the above discussion, our Gauss-Newton update consists of solving the symmetric matrix equation

$$A\,\Delta\mathbf{x} = \mathbf{a} \tag{8}$$

for state change vector $\Delta\mathbf{x} = \mathbf{x}^+ - \mathbf{x}^-$, given matrix A and vector $\mathbf{a}$ computed from the measurement vectors $\mathbf{z}(j)$, measurement functions $\mathbf{h}(j)$ and Jacobians $H(j) = \partial \mathbf{h}(j)/\partial \mathbf{x}$, evaluated at the latest solution $\mathbf{x}^-$. A is rank-deficient, because of gauge freedoms, and so extra constraints must be introduced in order to provide a unique solution to the matrix equation. These are the choices we shall consider for the form of these constraints:–

1. **Gauge Fixing** methods enforce *gauge conditions*

$$\mathbf{c}(\mathbf{x}) = \mathbf{0}$$

   to force a chosen gauge on the solution. We shall assume that the gauge conditions apply exactly to the previous solution, i.e. $\mathbf{c}(\mathbf{x}^-) = \mathbf{0}$. There are two ways to impose gauge $\mathbf{c}(\mathbf{x}^+) = \mathbf{0}$ on the new solution $\mathbf{x}^+$:
   (a) **Weighting** methods incorporate the gauge conditions $\mathbf{c}(\mathbf{x}^+)$ as extra "virtual" observations to be integrated with the actual measurements.

(b) **Projection** project the state space into a smaller space in which the gauge conditions are approximately satisfied; solve for the update in the reduced state space; finally project the solution back into the original space.

For brevity we shall consider the latter technique only.

2. **Pseudo-Inverse** methods attack the matrix equation (8) directly using a form of pseudo-inverse applied to A to solve for $\Delta\mathbf{x}$. This method has been suggested by Morris & Kanatani [10], and possesses the same GI properties as our proposed gauge fixing method. However it is somewhat slower and less flexible.

3. **Elimination** methods eliminate the necessary number of state parameters by setting them to special values. The remaining parameters can then be solved for directly. Such a procedure is also referred to as selecting a canonical frame [8, 12, 2], or a normal form [14]. This method can be used to eliminate the effect of coordinate frame ambiguity, simply by fixing the same number of parameters as there are gauge freedoms, but in the context of 3D reconstruction from multiple images this procedure introduces a new dependence on the order of the images.

3.2   Gauge Fixing

Enforcing a chosen gauge $\mathbf{c}(.)$ by linearising $\mathbf{c}(.)$ about the latest solution $\mathbf{x}^-$ gives us the system of equations

$$A\,\Delta\mathbf{x} = \mathbf{a}, \quad C\,\Delta\mathbf{x} = \mathbf{0}, \quad \text{where } C = \left.\frac{\partial\mathbf{c}}{\partial\mathbf{x}}\right|_{\mathbf{x}^-}. \tag{9}$$

The equation $C\Delta\mathbf{x} = \mathbf{0}$ ensures that the gauge conditions will be enforced to first order on the solution vector $\mathbf{x}^+$. In order for the constraint to entirely remove the gauge freedoms, it is clear that the rows of C must span the null-space of A, although the two linear spaces do not have to be equal. Equation (9) is a standard linear system with equality constraints, and [6] suggest the following method of solution:

To apply the alternative "projection" method of gauge fixing we first write the Singular Value Decomposition (SVD) of the constraint Jacobian matrix $C = \partial\mathbf{c}/\partial\mathbf{x}$ as

$$C = UWV^\mathsf{T} = U \begin{pmatrix} W_1 & 0 \\ 0 & 0 \end{pmatrix} \begin{pmatrix} V_1^\mathsf{T} \\ V_2^\mathsf{T} \end{pmatrix}.$$

If there are r gauge conditions, the size of W_1 is $r \times r$. Now define a transformed state vector

$$\begin{pmatrix} \mathbf{y}' \\ \mathbf{y} \end{pmatrix} = \begin{pmatrix} V_1^\mathsf{T} \\ V_2^\mathsf{T} \end{pmatrix} \Delta\mathbf{x} \tag{10}$$

If we convert the equations (9) into the transformed state space $\mathbf{y}$, $\mathbf{y}'$, we obtain

$$A(V_1\ V_2) \begin{pmatrix} \mathbf{y}' \\ \mathbf{y} \end{pmatrix} = \mathbf{a}, \quad C(V_1\ V_2) \begin{pmatrix} \mathbf{y}' \\ \mathbf{y} \end{pmatrix} = \mathbf{0}.$$

The latter equation simplifies to

$$U \begin{pmatrix} W_1 & 0 \\ 0 & 0 \end{pmatrix} \begin{pmatrix} \mathbf{y}' \\ \mathbf{y} \end{pmatrix} = \mathbf{0} \quad \text{or} \quad \mathbf{y}' = \mathbf{0},$$

enforcing the gauge conditions $C\,\Delta\mathbf{x} = \mathbf{0}$. The main equation now becomes

$$AV_2\mathbf{y}' = \mathbf{a}$$

from which we can obtain the solutions for $\mathbf{y}$ and $\mathbf{x}^+$:

$$\mathbf{y} = (V_2^\top AV_2)^{-1}V_2^\top \mathbf{a}, \quad \mathbf{x}^+ = \mathbf{x}^- + V_2\mathbf{y} \tag{11}$$

Thus this method of solution involves projecting $\mathbf{x}$ into the smaller state space $\mathbf{y}$, in which the gauge conditions are enforced to first order, solving the unconstrained linear system in that space and projecting back into $\mathbf{x}$ space to obtain the final solution (11).

Gauge independence of projection method. If we hypothesise that coordinate frame changes are always linear orthogonal,

$$\mathbf{y} = \phi\mathbf{x} \tag{12}$$

for orthogonal matrix ϕ, and also that the constraint function $\mathbf{c}(.)$ transforms similarly as

$$\mathbf{c}(\mathbf{y}) = \theta\mathbf{c}(\mathbf{x}) \tag{13}$$

for orthogonal matrix θ, then we can demonstrate gauge independence. Firstly we write the SVD of the constraint Jacobian C' in the transformed frame as

$$C' = U'W'V'^\top = \theta C\phi^{-1} = \theta UWV^\top\phi^{-1} = (\theta U)W(\phi V)^\top$$

and so we have $V_2' = \phi V_2$. Also the innovation vectors are

$$\boldsymbol{\nu}'(j) = \mathbf{z}(j) - \mathbf{h}(j;\mathbf{y}^-) = \boldsymbol{\nu}(j),$$

because of the pure gauge freedom assumption (2). The measurement Jacobians $H'(j)$ in the transformed space are related to $H(j)$ as

$$H'(j) = \frac{\partial\mathbf{h}(j)}{\partial\mathbf{y}} = \frac{\partial\mathbf{h}(j)}{\partial\mathbf{x}}\frac{\partial\mathbf{x}}{\partial\mathbf{y}} = H(j)\phi^{-1}$$

Thus the information matrix A and RHS vector $\mathbf{a}$ transform to

$$A' = \phi A\phi^{-1}, \quad \mathbf{a}' = \phi\mathbf{a}. \tag{14}$$

This leads to the update rule is the transformed frame:–

$$\begin{aligned}\mathbf{y}^+ &= \mathbf{y}^- + V_2'(V_2'^\top A'V_2')^{-1}V_2'^\top \mathbf{a}' = \mathbf{y}^- + \phi V_2(V_2^\top AV_2)^{-1}V_2^\top \mathbf{a} \\ &= \mathbf{y}^- + \phi(\mathbf{x}^+ - \mathbf{x}^-)\end{aligned}$$

which is gauge-independent in the sense of preserving the same ϕ between the solutions before and after the iteration, given that $\mathbf{y}^- = \phi\mathbf{x}^-$, thus satisfying the main GI criterion (4).

The criteria (12) and (13) can be applied to specific models in order to select the state representation and constraint functions in specific scenarios, which is what we do in later sections for the structure-from-motion problem.

3.3   Coordinate Frame Normalisation

The third strand of our method of dealing with gauge freedoms is to normalise the coordinate frame of our estimated parameters before applying Gauss-Newton iterations. We select a coordinate frame among the space of frames that agrees with pre-specified *normalisation conditions*. There is a strong link with the gauge fixing conditions discussed, since the most natural choice of gauge fixing conditions is then to re-impose the same conditions as were used to select the initial coordinate frame.

The intended effect of coordinate frame normalisation is illustrated in figure 1 As before we consider a general change of coordinates $\mathbf{y} = \mathbf{g}(\mathbf{x})$ relating two

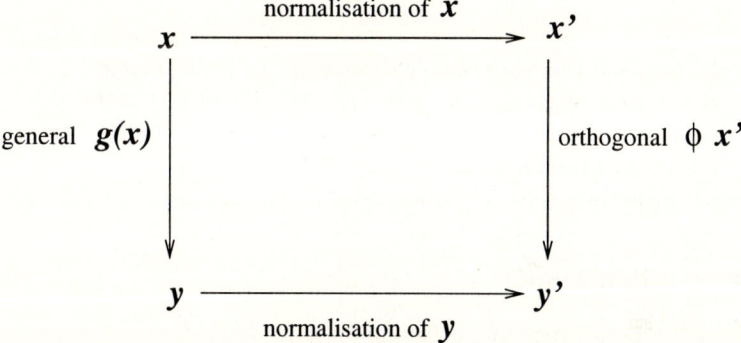

Fig. 1. Illustration of coordinate frame normalisation. Applying normalisation to two different parameter vectors $\mathbf{x}$ related by a general coordinate frame transformation $\mathbf{y} = \mathbf{g}(\mathbf{x})$ reduces the space of transformations after normalisation of both to the space of orthogonal transformations $\mathbf{y}' = \phi\mathbf{x}'$ for orthogonal matrix ϕ.

equivalent parameter vector estimates. The idea of normalisation is to reduce the effective space of coordinate frames, ideally to the space of (possibly scaled) linear orthogonal transformations. If this can be achieved, we can proceed to use the GI Gauss-Newton methods described above. We assume in figure 1 that no scale factor β remains after normalisation, because in the problems we have looked at we have been able to remove any scale factors, including, perhaps surprisingly, projective 3D reconstruction.

In the following sections we shall treating each different type of gauge freedom separately in demonstrating satisfaction of the GI criteria. This is a valid approach because when considered in combination we obtain a product of the orthogonal transformations corresponding to all the gauge freedoms together, which is another orthogonal transformation. Hence if we prove that the GI criteria are satisfied for all sub-parts of our representation, we automatically have GI for the whole system.

4   Perspective Projection Model

The projection model corresponding to Euclidean SFM is the perspective model [11]. It is the most detailed model and applies when the camera calibration is known. We can write perspective projection for 3D points $\mathbf{X} = (X\ Y\ Z)^\top$ as

$$\mathbf{p} = \lambda K (R\ |\ -R\mathbf{T}) \begin{pmatrix} \mathbf{X} \\ 1 \end{pmatrix} \tag{15}$$

$$= \lambda \begin{pmatrix} f_x & \alpha & x_0 \\ 0 & f_y & y_0 \\ 0 & 0 & 1 \end{pmatrix} R(I_{3\times3}\ |\ -\mathbf{T}) \begin{pmatrix} X \\ Y \\ Z \\ 1 \end{pmatrix}$$

where

- $\mathbf{p}$ is the projected image point in homogeneous coordinates;
- K is the matrix of calibration parameters, defined by the focal lengths f_x, f_y, the image centre coordinates x_0, y_0 and skew parameter α;
- R is a 3×3 rotation matrix;
- $\mathbf{T}$ is a translation vector in scene coordinates, the camera position.

4.1   Observation Model

To construct a measurement vector for use in Gauss-Newton iterations, $\mathbf{p}$ is converted to non-homogeneous form by dividing through by z. Then the measurement vector $\mathbf{z}_{i(j)}$ is the image feature position for scene feature i in image j, for instance a corner feature.

4.2   Representing Rotations

Representing a 3D rotation is problematic in the context of gauge invariance. Angle representations do not have the GI properties, because they clearly do not transform according to the GI criterion (12). There is also the problem that angle representations, and indeed any non-redundant representations of rotation, have singularities near which small changes in rotations have uncontrollably large changes in the rotation parameters. There are however two good choices, one redundant and one non-redundant. *Quaternions* are a good choice, and can provide the solutions to many problems in vision, such can computing the camera rotation between images [16] or camera pose estimation [7]. However they have the problem that quaternions are a redundant representation, having a scale freedom. This is easy to handle using the gauge methods employed in this paper, but we prefer the *local rotation* approach, employed in 3D reconstruction by Taylor & Kriegman [15]. A local rotation representation has also been developed independently by Pennec & Thirion [13]. The idea is that if an estimate R_0 of the rotation is available, one can factorise a rotation R as

$$R = R_s R_0 \tag{16}$$

where R_s is a small rotation. Because R_s is small, we can use a representation that is specialised to small rotations. The exponential representation is ideal for this purpose. This represents a rotation using a 3-vector $\mathbf{r}$ by the Rodriguez formula

$$
\begin{aligned}
R_s &= e^{[\mathbf{r}]_\times} \\
&= I_{3\times 3} + \frac{\sin\theta}{\theta}[\mathbf{r}]_\times + \frac{(1 - \cos\theta)}{\theta^2}(\mathbf{r}\mathbf{r}^\top - \|\mathbf{r}\|^2 I_{3\times 3})
\end{aligned} \tag{17}
$$

where $\theta = \|\mathbf{r}\|$ is the rotation angle, and $[\mathbf{r}]_\times$ is the "cross-product" matrix for $\mathbf{r}$. In an iterative algorithm, the small rotation change R_s is compounded with the previous value R_0 to form the new rotation estimate $R_s R_0$ to be fed in as the new R_0 at the next iteration.

4.3   Euclidean Ambiguities and Constraints

The global coordinate frame ambiguity for the Euclidean case is a 3D similarity transformation, as we can see by rewriting (15) as

$$
\begin{aligned}
\mathbf{p} &= \lambda(R \mid -R\mathbf{T}) \begin{pmatrix} \mathbf{X} \\ 1 \end{pmatrix} \\
&= \lambda K(R \mid -R\mathbf{T}) K \begin{pmatrix} R_H\mathbf{T}_H \\ \mathbf{0}^\top & h \end{pmatrix}^{-1} \begin{pmatrix} R_H\mathbf{T}_H \\ \mathbf{0}^\top & h \end{pmatrix} \begin{pmatrix} \mathbf{X} \\ 1 \end{pmatrix} \\
&= \lambda(R' \mid -R'\mathbf{T}') \begin{pmatrix} \mathbf{X}' \\ 1 \end{pmatrix}
\end{aligned}
$$

where R_H is a 3×3 rotation matrix, $\mathbf{T}_H$ a translation vector, h a scale factor, and $R' = RR_H^{-1}$, $\mathbf{T}' = h^{-1}(R_H\mathbf{T} + \mathbf{T}_H)$ and $\mathbf{X}' = h^{-1}(R_H\mathbf{X} + \mathbf{T}_H)$. The Euclidean coordinate frame ambiguity is represented by R_H, $\mathbf{T}_H$ and h. This provides 7 degrees of freedom in setting up the global coordinate frame.

4.4   Euclidean Normalisation

We first normalise the coordinate frame using constraints on the translation vectors (three constraints) and overall scale (one). No normalisation needs to be applied to the rotations. Then we introduce a constraint function $\mathbf{c}(.)$ such that the rows of its Jacobian C are linear combinations of the null-space vectors of A, thus guaranteeing elimination of all seven gauge freedoms.

The coordinate frame normalisation subtracts the centroid of the camera translation vectors from each translation vector, and then scales the translation vectors so that their average squared length is unity. Given that the original centroid of the translations is $\bar{\mathbf{T}}$, and writing

$$s = \sqrt{\frac{\sum_{j=1}^{k} \|\mathbf{T}_{(j)} - \bar{\mathbf{T}}\|^2}{k}},$$

averaging over the k images, we need to make the following modifications to all the parameters:

$$\mathbf{T}_{(j)} \leftarrow \frac{1}{s}(\mathbf{T}_{(j)} - \bar{\mathbf{T}})$$

$$\mathbf{X} \leftarrow \frac{1}{s}(\mathbf{X} - \bar{\mathbf{X}}) \text{ for all 3D points,}$$

The modifications being made together ensures that the modified reconstruction is equivalent to the original. After the normalisation, the centroid of the translations is fixed at zero and the scale set to unity. The normalisation leaves only rotation unchanged. Now under a rotation R_H of initial coordinate frame as above, normalising both coordinate frames as in figure 1, the rotations and translations in the two frames are related after normalisation as

$$R'_{(j)} = R_{(j)}R_H^{-1}, \quad \mathbf{T}'_{(j)} = R_H \mathbf{T}.$$

Since the reference rotations will be reset to the normalised rotations in both cases, both sets of local rotation parameters will be set to zero. This means that the motion parameters after normalisation will have the relationship

$$\begin{pmatrix} \mathbf{r}'_{(j)} \\ \mathbf{T}'_{(j)} \end{pmatrix} = \begin{pmatrix} I & 0 \\ 0 & R_H \end{pmatrix} \begin{pmatrix} \mathbf{r}_{(j)} \\ \mathbf{T}_{(j)} \end{pmatrix}, \tag{18}$$

an orthogonal change of coordinates, agreeing with the GI criterion (12). Similarly the point 3D features are normalised in the two coordinate frames to $\mathbf{X}'$ which will be related as $\mathbf{X}' = R_H \mathbf{X}$, again agreeing with (12). So our normalisation procedure has successfully achieved its aim of reducing the coordinate frame freedom to a combination of orthogonal transformations.

4.5   Euclidean Gauge Conditions

Having normalised the coordinate frame, we separate the seven gauge conditions into three rotation conditions $\mathbf{c_r}(.)$, three translation $\mathbf{c_T}(.)$ and one scale $c_s(.)$, as follows:

$$\mathbf{c} = \begin{pmatrix} \mathbf{c_r} \\ \mathbf{c_T} \\ c_s \end{pmatrix} = \begin{pmatrix} \sum_j (\mathbf{r}_{(j)} + [\hat{\mathbf{T}}_{(j)}] \times \mathbf{T}_{(j)}) \\ \sum_j \mathbf{T}_{(j)} \\ \frac{1}{2}\|\mathbf{T}_{(j)}\|^2 \end{pmatrix}$$

We include the vectors $\hat{\mathbf{T}}_{(j)}$ with the convention that they are represented as *constant* vectors in $\mathbf{c}(.)$, equal to $\mathbf{T}_{(j)}$ but not considered as variables. Thus the Jacobian of $\mathbf{c}(.)$ i

$$C = \begin{pmatrix} \frac{\partial \mathbf{c_r}}{\partial \mathbf{r}(1)} & \frac{\partial \mathbf{c_r}}{\partial \mathbf{T}(1)} & \cdots\cdots & \frac{\partial \mathbf{c_r}}{\partial \mathbf{r}(k)} & \frac{\partial \mathbf{c_r}}{\partial \mathbf{T}(k)} \\ \frac{\partial \mathbf{c_T}}{\partial \mathbf{r}(1)} & \frac{\partial \mathbf{c_T}}{\partial \mathbf{T}(1)} & \cdots\cdots & \frac{\partial \mathbf{c_T}}{\partial \mathbf{r}(k)} & \frac{\partial \mathbf{c_T}}{\partial \mathbf{T}(k)} \\ \frac{\partial \mathbf{c_s}}{\partial \mathbf{r}(1)} & \frac{\partial \mathbf{c_s}}{\partial \mathbf{T}(1)} & \cdots\cdots & \frac{\partial \mathbf{c_s}}{\partial \mathbf{r}(k)} & \frac{\partial \mathbf{c_s}}{\partial \mathbf{T}(k)} \end{pmatrix}$$

$$= \begin{pmatrix} R_{(1)}{}^\top - [\mathbf{T}_{(1)}]_\times & \ldots\ldots & R_{(k)}{}^\top - [\mathbf{T}_{(k)}]_\times \\ 0 & I & \ldots\ldots & 0 & I \\ \mathbf{0}^\top & \mathbf{T}_{(1)}{}^\top & \ldots\ldots & \mathbf{0}^\top & \mathbf{T}_{(k)}{}^\top \end{pmatrix}$$

To demonstrate agreement with the GI criterion (13), we use the relation (18), obtaining under the transformed normalised coordinate frame,

$$\mathbf{c}'_{\mathbf{r}} = \sum_j (\mathbf{r}'_{(j)} + [\hat{\mathbf{T}}'_{(j)}]_\times \mathbf{T}'_{(j)})$$

$$= \sum_j (\mathbf{r}_{(j)} + [R_H \hat{\mathbf{T}}_{(j)}]_\times R_H \mathbf{T}_{(j)})$$

$$= R_H \mathbf{c}_{\mathbf{r}}$$

Trivially we also have $\mathbf{c}'_{\mathbf{T}} = R_H \mathbf{c}_{\mathbf{T}}$ and finally $c'_s = c_s$.

4.6   Translation Represented in Camera Frame

We now discuss an alternative model whereby we represent the translation vector in camera coordinates. In other words the projection model (15) converts to $\mathbf{p} = \lambda K(R\mathbf{X} + \mathbf{T})$. We can follow through the previous model, and we find that the results do *not* agree with the GI criteria (details omitted).

5   Algorithm Description

1. Start with a prior estimate $\mathbf{x}^-$ for the state parameters $\mathbf{x}$. Some of them may be provided in advance, for instance camera calibration parameters where applicable. Others may be given initial estimates directly from the observations. In 3D reconstruction, the multi-view tensorial approach is the latest way to generate motion and structure parameters directly from images [5]. The first step is to normalise the coordinate frame as specified by any normalisation conditions (section 3.3). Then if there are gauge fixing constraints to be enforced, these must be enforced prior to starting the iterations. They are then re-enforced between each iteration, as described below.

2. Build the linear system (8) by linearising the measurement equations for each observation around the latest state parameters $\mathbf{x}^-$. For the 3D reconstruction problem, these are the non-homogeneous versions of the point projection equation (15). If gauge constraints are to be enforced to first order by the

weighting or projection methods, the linear system is adjusted to (11). When the state vector $\mathbf{x}$ is partitioned into blocks, constraints can be applied separately to single blocks or combinations of blocks, and arbitrary mixtures of different constraint types are allowed for each constraint.

3. Perform a Gauss-Newton iteration (7), to produce a new estimate $\mathbf{x}^+$ for the state parameters. We actually use Levenberg-Marquardt iterations, which are basic Gauss-Newton iterations with added damping.

4. Re-impose any normalisation and gauge fixing conditions by manipulation of the state vector $\mathbf{x}^+$. Because this only corrects internal gauge freedoms, the error function $J(\mathbf{x}^+)$ is not affected.

5. Other internal degrees of freedom that are not gauge freedoms may be reset. For instance, in the case of Euclidean reconstruction, the reference rotations $R_0(j)$ are adjusted to $R_s(j)R_0(j)$, where $R_s(j)$ is the small rotation formed from the updated rotation parameters $\mathbf{r}(j)$. This allows $\mathbf{r}(j)$ to be reset to zero. All such changes are fed back to the state vector $\mathbf{x}^+$.

6. If the error function $J(\mathbf{x}^+)$ in (6) is has decreased from $J(\mathbf{x}^-)$, replace $\mathbf{x}^-$ with the updated and adjusted state vector $\mathbf{x}^+$, and decrease the Levenberg-Marquardt damping factor. Otherwise increase the damping factor and make no change to $\mathbf{x}^-$.

7. If a termination criterion has been reached (e.g. limit on number of iterations or on the size of a decrease in J), exit. Otherwise loop back to step 2 and perform another iteration.

6   Results

In figure 2 we show some preliminary results on a test-set of seven simulated images of fifteen 3D points. To make the reconstruction difficult, the points were placed so that they almost aligned in a single plane, a critical surface for 3D reconstruction. This allows the advantages of imposing gauge conditions to be made apparent. The convergence of the algorithm on this test set is quicker than the other algorithms here on test, which are:–

- **Camera**-centred translation (Camera T-1 and Camera T-2). These results for the camera-centred translation vector representation were obtained for different initial coordinate frames, and show that the convergence rate in this case is affected by coordinate frame choice. The total time taken by this version was 1.60s on a 233MHz PC.
- **Free Gauge** is the method advocated in [5], whereby Levenberg-Marquardt damping is used to deal with the gauge freedoms. In well-conditioned situations this method is comparable in performance with imposing explicit gauge conditions, but as we see here when the conditioning is quite bad, having gauge conditions helps because Levenberg-Marquardt is left to deal with the conditioning of the system, which in the free gauge algorithm are "masked" by the gauge freedoms. Total time: 1.63s.
- **Pseudo-inverse** is the of taking the pseudo-inverse of the information matrix used by photogrammetrists [1] and suggested by Morris & Kanatani [10],

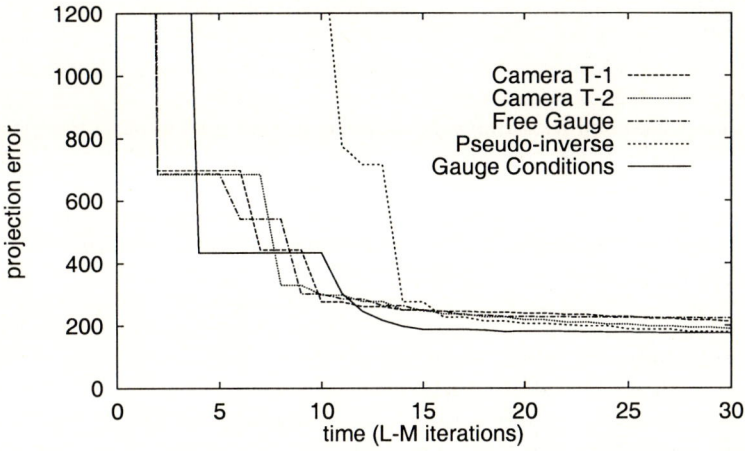

Fig. 2. Results showing convergence rate for a test set of simulated data, testing various types of bundle adjustment (see text).

although adjusted to firstly eliminate the structure parameters from the system to improve the performance. Total time: 11.91s.
- **Gauge Conditions** is the gauge condition method. Total time: 10.95s.

In other experiments, not shown here because of lack of space, we have shown that the convergence rates for a well-conditioned 3D Euclidean reconstruction problem are comparable for all these methods, and others we have tried. It is only when the conditioning is bad that the gauge condition method is likely to show great advantages, and it is considerable slower than the free-gauge algorithm, because of the extra expense of factorizing the gauge condition matrix. Nevertheless where reliability is important, the explicit gauge condition method should be considered, and in any case our discussions of representation and coordinate frame normalisation still apply. The speed difference will reduce if the ratio of features to images is increased.

7   Conclusions

We have developed the theory of gauge independence in some detail for the problem of 3D scene reconstruction. The methods are applicable to many optimisation problems having internal gauge freedoms, especially those resulting in a sparse information matrix structure. We have omitted the generalisation of the method to reconstructions of lines and other projection models; they will appear in a longer treatment.

References

1. K.B. Atkinson. *Close Range Photogrammetry and Machine Vision.* Whittles Publishing, Caithness, Scotland, 1996.
2. A. Azarbayejani and Alex P. Pentland. Recursive estimation of motion, structure, and focal length. *IEEE Transactions on Pattern Analysis and Machine Intelligence,* 17(6):562–575, 1995.
3. R. Bergevin, M. Soucy, H. Gagnon, and D. Laurendeau. Towards a general multiview registration technique. *IEEE Transactions on Pattern Analysis and Machine Intelligence,* 18(5):540–547, May 1996.
4. A. Gelb (ed). *Applied Optimal Estimation.* MIT press, 1974.
5. A.W. Fitzgibbon and A. Zisserman. Automatic camera recovery for closed or open image sequences. In *Proc. 5th European Conf. on Computer Vision, Freiburg,* volume 1, pages 311–326. Springer-Verlag, June 1998.
6. G. H. Golub and C. F. van Loan. *Matrix Computations, 3rd edition.* The John Hopkins University Press, Baltimore, MD, 1996.
7. J. Heuring and D. W. Murray. Visual head tracking and slaving for visual telepresence. In *Proc. IEEE Int'l Conf. on Robotics and Automation,* 1996.
8. Q.-T. Luong and T. Viéville. Canonic representations for the geometries of multiple projective views. In *Proc. 3rd European Conf. on Computer Vision, Stockholm,* pages 589–599, May 1994.
9. P. F. McLauchlan. Gauge invariance in projective 3d reconstruction. In *IEEE Workshop on Multi-View Modeling and Analysis of Visual Scenes, Fort Collins, CO, June 1999,* 1999.
10. D. Morris and K. Kanatani. Uncertainty modeling for optimal structure from motion. In *Proc. ICCV'99 Vision Algorithms Workshop,* 1999.
11. J. L. Mundy and A. P. Zisserman, editors. *Geometric Invariance in Computer Vision.* MIT Press, Cambridge, MA, 1992.
12. P.A.Beardsley, A.Zisserman, and D.W.Murray. Sequential updating of projective and affine structure from motion. *International Journal of Computer Vision,* 23(3), 1997.
13. X. Pennec and J.P. Thirion. A framework for uncertainty and validation of 3-d registration methods based on points and frames. *International Journal of Computer Vision,* 25(3):203–229, December 1997.
14. L. Quan and T. Kanade. Affine structure from line correspondences with uncalibrated affine cameras. *IEEE Transactions on Pattern Analysis and Machine Intelligence,* 19(8):834–845, 1997.
15. C.J. Taylor and D.J. Kriegman. Structure and motion from line segments in multiple images. *IEEE Transactions on Pattern Analysis and Machine Intelligence,* 17(11):1021–1032, November 1995.
16. J. Weng, T. S. Huang, and N. Ahuja. Motion and structure from two perspective views: algorithms, error analysis and error estimation. *IEEE Transactions on Pattern Analysis and Machine Intelligence,* 11(5):451–476, 1989.

Discussion

Kenichi Kanatani: As you mentioned, gauge freedom is something that occurs in our description of the problem. It is nothing to do with the real world, the observations, or the noise. Changing the gauge doesn't affect these, the final results should be the same or at least geometrically equivalent.

Philip McLauchlan: Yes, that's correct.

Kenichi Kanatani: But you showed some convergence graphs where the final results seem to be different for different gauge fixing methods. Apart from computational efficiency, do the results depend on the gauge or not?

Philip McLauchlan: They are all converging to the same answer — if you leave them to run long enough they do converge to the same global minimum. But the speed at which they do it, and whether they do it at different rates for completely arbitrary reasons like changing the coordinate frame, depends a lot on the gauge fixing method.

Kenichi Kanatani: So there are two issues for the choice, speed of convergence and computational efficiency, like fill-in problems.

Philip McLauchlan: Yes, that's right.

Rick Szeliski: This is a clarification question. In addition to renormalizing at each step to keep the centroid at zero and the scale at unity, do you also impose this as a gauge condition so that the delta, the change in movement has zero centroid and there is no change in scale?

Philip McLauchlan: That is correct.

Rick Szeliski: You also made a comment that by eliminating either the structure or the motion you can get more efficient. Does that just depend on the problem, whether there are more frames or more points?

Philip McLauchlan: That's right. Usually these problem have a large number of features and a relatively small number of images, so it makes sense to eliminate the structure parameters first because that is fast, and then to solve for the motion and then back-substitute to obtain the structure, whereas the photogrammetrists' main solution involves doing it the other way round. They argue that they can do this in an approximate way which doesn't give them a big performance problem, but it seems like the whole reason for doing this is flawed, and it makes more sense to me that we should aim for the more efficient solution which has no disadvantages.

Joss Knight: Does the gauge conditioning help at all with problems of local minima in the minimization?

Philip McLauchlan: No, not really. The different versions all assume that the initial solution is close enough to the global minimum to avoid the local minima.

Uncertainty Modeling
for Optimal Structure from Motion

Daniel D. Morris[1], Kenichi Kanatani[2], and Takeo Kanade[1]

[1] Robotics Institute, Carnegie Mellon University,
Pittsburgh, PA 15213, USA
{ddmorris, tk}@ri.cmu.edu
[2] Department of Computer Science, Gunma University,
Kiryu, Gunma 376-8515, Japan
kanatani@cs.gunma-u.ac.jp

Abstract. The parameters estimated by Structure from Motion (SFM) contain inherent indeterminacies which we call gauge freedoms. Under a perspective camera, shape and motion parameters are only recovered up to an unknown similarity transformation. In this paper we investigate how covariance-based uncertainty can be represented under these gauge freedoms. Past work on uncertainty modeling has implicitly imposed gauge constraints on the solution before considering covariance estimation. Here we examine the effect of selecting a particular gauge on the uncertainty of parameters. We show potentially dramatic effects of gauge choice on parameter uncertainties. However the inherent geometric uncertainty remains the same irrespective of gauge choice. We derive a Geometric Equivalence Relationship with which covariances under different parametrizations and gauges can be compared, based on their true geometric uncertainty. We show that the uncertainty of gauge invariants exactly captures the geometric uncertainty of the solution, and hence provides useful measures for evaluating the uncertainty of the solution. Finally we propose a fast method for covariance estimation and show its correctness using the Geometric Equivalence Relationship.

1 Introduction

It is well known that, for accurate 3D reconstruction from image sequences, statistically optimal results are obtained by bundle adjustment [2, 3, 5, 6, 13, 16]. This is just Maximum Likelihood estimation for independent, isotropic Gaussian noise, and is also used by photogrammetrists. Current research generally focuses on two areas: (1) simplicity of solution, which includes finding a closed form approximate solutions such as the Factorization method [4, 8–12], and (2) efficiency, which includes finding fast or robust numerical schemes [1, 2].

An important third area to address is the quantitative assessment of the reliability of the solution. While some work has incorporated uncertainty analyzes of the results [9, 14–16], none has investigated the effect of parameter indeterminacies on the uncertainty modeling. These indeterminacies are inherent to SFM

B. Triggs, A. Zisserman, R. Szeliski (Eds.): Vision Algorithms'99, LNCS 1883, pp. 200–217, 2000.

and have a significant effect on parameter uncertainties. Our goal is to create a framework for describing the uncertainties and indeterminacies of parameters used in Structure from Motion (SFM). We can then determine how both these uncertainties and indeterminacies affect the real geometric measurements recovered by SFM.

The standard measure for uncertainty is the covariance matrix. However in SFM there is a uniqueness problem for the solution and its variance due to inherent indeterminacies: the estimated object feature positions and motions are only determined up to a overall translation, rotation and scaling. Constraining these global quantities we call choosing a *gauge*. Typically a covariance matrix describes the second order moments of a perturbation around a unique solution. In past work [9, 15, 16] indeterminacies are removed by choosing an arbitrary gauge, and then the optimization is performed under these gauge constraints and the recovered shape and motion parameters along with their variances are expressed in this gauge.

In this paper we provide an analysis of the effects of indeterminacies and gauges on covariance-based uncertainty models. While the choice of gauge can dramatically affect the magnitude and values in a covariance matrix, we show that these effects are superficial and the underlying geometric uncertainty is unaffected. To show this we derive a Geometric Equivalence Relationship between the covariance matrices of the parameters that depends only on the essential geometric component in the covariances. Hence we are able to propose a covariance-based description of parameter uncertainties that does not require gauge constraints. Furthermore we show how this parametric uncertainty model can be then used to obtain an uncertainty model for actual geometric properties of the shape and motion which are gauge-invariant. Optimization is achieved in an efficient free-gauge manner and we propose a fast method for obtaining covariance estimates when there are indeterminacies.

2   Geometric Modeling

2.1   Camera Equations

Here we describe an object and camera system in a camera–centered coordinate system. Analogous equations could be derived in other coordinate systems. Suppose we track N rigidly moving feature points $\mathbf{p}_\alpha$, $\alpha = 1, \ldots, N$, in M images. Let $\mathbf{p}_{\kappa\alpha}$ be the 2–element image coordinates of $\mathbf{p}_\alpha$ in the κth image. We identify the camera coordinate system with the XYZ world coordinate system, and choose an object coordinate system in the object. Let $\mathbf{t}_\kappa$ be the origin of the object coordinate system in the κ'th image, $\mathbf{R}_\kappa$ be a 3×3 rotation matrix which specifies its orientation and $\mathbf{s}_\alpha$ be the coordinates of the feature point, $\mathbf{p}_\alpha$, in the object coordinate system. Thus the position of feature point $\mathbf{p}_\alpha$ with respect to the camera coordinate system in the κth image is $\mathbf{R}_\kappa \mathbf{s}_\alpha + \mathbf{t}_\kappa$.

Assume we have a projection operator $\Pi : \mathcal{R}^3 \to \mathcal{R}^2$ which projects a point in 3D to the 2D image plane. We can then express the image coordinates, of feature $\mathbf{p}_\alpha$ as:

$$\mathbf{p}_{\kappa\alpha} = \Pi[\mathbf{K}_\kappa(\mathbf{R}_\kappa\mathbf{s}_\alpha + \mathbf{t}_\kappa)] \tag{1}$$

where $\mathbf{K}_\kappa$ is a 3×3 internal camera parameter matrix [2] containing quantities such as focal length for each image. While these parameters can be estimated along with shape and motion parameters, for simplicity we ignore them in the rest of the paper and assume $\mathbf{K}_\kappa$ is just the identity matrix for orthography and $diag([f, f, 1])$ for perspective projection with focal length f. Various camera models can be defined by specifying the action of this projection operator on a vector $(X, Y, Z)^\top$. For example we define the projection operators for orthography and perspective projection respectively in the following way:

$$\Pi_o\left[\begin{pmatrix} X \\ Y \\ Z \end{pmatrix}\right] = \begin{pmatrix} X \\ Y \end{pmatrix}, \quad \Pi_p\left[\begin{pmatrix} X \\ Y \\ Z \end{pmatrix}\right] = \begin{pmatrix} X/Z \\ Y/Z \end{pmatrix}, \tag{2}$$

Equation (1) can be applied to all features in all images, and then combined in the form:

$$\mathbf{p} = \mathbf{\Pi}(\boldsymbol{\theta}) \tag{3}$$

where $\mathbf{p} = (\mathbf{p}_{11}^\top, \mathbf{p}_{12}^\top, \mathbf{p}_{13}^\top, \ldots, \mathbf{p}_{MN}^\top)^\top$ is a vector containing all the image feature coordinates in all images, and $\boldsymbol{\theta}$ is a vector containing the shape and motion parameters, $\mathbf{R}_\kappa$, $\mathbf{s}_\alpha$, $\mathbf{t}_\kappa$, and possibly unknown internal camera parameters, for all object features and images, and $\mathbf{\Pi}$ is the appropriate combination of the projection matrices. More details can be found in [7].

2.2   Parameter Constraints

Not all of the parameters in $\boldsymbol{\theta}$ are independent and some need to be constrained. In particular the columns of each rotation matrix, $\mathbf{R}_\kappa$, must remain unit orthogonal vectors. Small perturbations of rotations are parametrized by a 3-vector: $\Delta\boldsymbol{\Omega}_\kappa$ which to first order maintain the rotation properties [3]. Let $\mathcal{T}$ be the manifold of valid vectors $\boldsymbol{\theta}$ such that all solutions for $\boldsymbol{\theta}$ lie in $\mathcal{T}$. $\mathcal{T}$ will be a manifold of dimension n, where n is the number of parameters needed to locally specify the shape and motion, 3 for each rotation, 3 for each translation, and 3 for each 3D feature point, plus any internal camera parameters that must be estimated. So in general for just motion and shape, the number of unknown parameters is: $n = 3N + 6M$.

2.3   Indeterminacies

The camera equations (1) and (3) contain a number of indeterminacies. There are two reasons for these indeterminacies: first the object coordinate system can be selected arbitrarily, and second the projection model maps many 3D points to a single 2D point. These are specified as follows:

Coordinate System Indeterminacies

If we rotate and then translate the coordinate system by $\mathbf{R}$ and $\mathbf{t}$ respectively, we obtain the following transformed shape and motion parameters:

$$\mathbf{s}'_\alpha = \mathbf{R}^\top(\mathbf{s}_\alpha - \mathbf{t}), \quad \mathbf{R}'_\kappa = \mathbf{R}_\kappa\mathbf{R}, \quad \mathbf{t}'_\kappa = \mathbf{R}_\kappa\mathbf{t} + \mathbf{t}_\kappa. \tag{4}$$

We note that $\mathbf{R}'_\kappa\mathbf{s}'_\alpha + \mathbf{t}'_\kappa = \mathbf{R}_\kappa\mathbf{s}_\alpha + \mathbf{t}_\kappa$, and hence irrespective of the projection model, equations (1) and (3) must be ambiguous to changes in coordinates.

Projection Indeterminacies

Many different geometric solutions project onto the same points in the image. In orthography the depth or Z component does not affect the image, and hence the projection is invariant to the transformation:

$$\mathbf{t}'_\kappa = \mathbf{t}_\kappa + d_\kappa\mathbf{k} \tag{5}$$

for any value d_κ. Orthography has a discrete reflection ambiguity, but since it is not differential we do not consider it. Perspective projection has a scale ambiguity such that if we transform the shape and translation by a scale s:

$$\mathbf{s}'_\alpha = s\mathbf{s}_\alpha, \quad \text{and} \quad \mathbf{t}'_\kappa = s\mathbf{t}_\kappa, \tag{6}$$

we find that $\Pi_p[\mathbf{K}_\kappa(\mathbf{R}_\kappa\mathbf{s}'_\alpha + \mathbf{t}'_\kappa)] = \Pi_p[\mathbf{K}_\kappa(\mathbf{R}_\kappa\mathbf{s}_\alpha + \mathbf{t}_\kappa)]$.

2.4   Solution Manifold

Since the camera equations contain these indeterminacies, then given the measurement data, $\mathbf{p}$, there is not a unique shape and motion parameter set, $\boldsymbol{\theta}$, that maps to this. Rather equation (3) is satisfied by a manifold, $\mathcal{M}$, of valid solutions within $\mathcal{T}$ which are all mapped to the same $\mathbf{p}$. This manifold has dimension, r, given by the number of infinitesimal degrees of freedom at a given point. From the ambiguity equations (4-6) we obtain $r = 7$ for perspective projection and $r = M + 6$ under orthography. Figure 1 illustrates a solution $\boldsymbol{\theta} \in \mathcal{M}$.

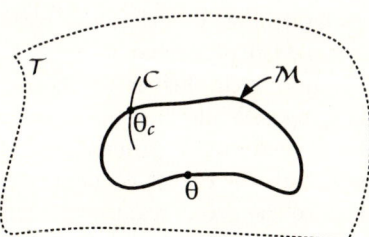

Fig. 1. An illustration of a curve representing a manifold $\mathcal{M}$ of solution vectors $\boldsymbol{\theta}$, all lying in the parameter space $\mathcal{T}$. Choosing a gauge $\mathcal{C}$, which intersects the manifold at one point, defines a unique solution $\boldsymbol{\theta}_\mathcal{C}$.

2.5   Gauge Constraints

In order to remove the ambiguity of the solution we can define a gauge or manifold of points: $\mathcal{C}$. Let $\mathcal{C}$ contain all those points in $\mathcal{T}$ that satisfy a set of r constraint equations:

$$c_i(\boldsymbol{\theta}) = 0 \ \text{ for } \ 1 \le i \le r. \tag{7}$$

The gauge $\mathcal{C}$ will thus have dimension $n - r$. We require that $\mathcal{C}$ intersect $\mathcal{M}$ transversally and at most at one point per connected component of $\mathcal{M}$. The intersection of $\mathcal{C}$ and $\mathcal{M}$ thus provides unique solution within a connected component of $\mathcal{M}$, as illustrated in Figure 1. However there may be ambiguities between components of $\mathcal{M}$, such as the reflection ambiguity in orthography.

For example, we could define an arbitrary gauge with the following constraints:

$$\sum_{\alpha=1}^{N} \mathbf{s}_\alpha = \mathbf{0}, \ \ \mathbf{R}_1 = \mathbf{I}, \ \ \sum_{\alpha=1}^{N} \mathbf{s}_\alpha^\top \mathbf{s}_\alpha = 1. \tag{8}$$

This fixes the origin of the object coordinate system in its centroid, aligns the object coordinate system with the first image, and fixes the scale. In orthography the scale constraint is omitted, but we add the constraint set: $t_{z_\kappa} = 0$ on the Z component of translation.

We note that this, or any other choice of gauge is arbitrary, and does not affect the geometry. It does affect our parameter estimates and their uncertainties, but in ways that do not affect the geometric meaning of the results.

3   Uncertainty in Data Fitting

When there is noise in the measured data, there will be a resulting uncertainty in the recovered parameters, which we would like to represent by a covariance matrix. However, when indeterminacies exist, the solution will be a manifold rather than a point, and standard perturbation analysis cannot be performed. The usual approach, in dealing with this, is to choose a gauge and constrain the solution to lie in this gauge. While this approach is a valid, it introduces additional constraints into the estimation process, and the resulting uncertainty values are strongly dependent on the choice of gauge. In this section we ask the question: How can we estimate the geometric uncertainty without depending on an arbitrary selection of a gauge? To answer this we introduce gauge invariants whose uncertainty does not depend on gauge choice. We also derive a Geometric Equivalence Relationship that considers only this "true" geometric uncertainty. Along the way we derive the *normal form* for the covariance which gives us a convenient way to calculate uncertainty without having to explicitly specify a gauge.

3.1   Perturbation Analysis

First we derive an uncertainty measure in an arbitrary gauge. We assume that the noise is small, and thus that the first order terms dominate. When the noise is Gaussian the first order terms exactly describe the noise. The measured data, $\mathbf{p}$ is a result of the true feature positions, $\bar{\mathbf{p}}$, corrupted by noise, $\Delta\mathbf{p}$:

$$\mathbf{p} = \bar{\mathbf{p}} + \Delta\mathbf{p}. \tag{9}$$

The noise $\Delta\mathbf{p}$ is a random variable of the most general type, not necessarily independent for different points, but it is assumed to have zero mean and known variance[1]:

$$V_p[\mathbf{p}] = E\{\Delta\mathbf{p}\Delta\mathbf{p}^\top\}. \tag{10}$$

We note that in the special case when feature points are independent, $V[\mathbf{p}]$ will be block diagonal with the 2×2 block diagonal elements giving the independent feature covariances.

Given this uncertainty in the measured data, let $\hat{\boldsymbol{\theta}}$ be our estimator of the shape and motion parameters. There is no unique true solution unless we restrict our estimation to a particular gauge. If we choose gauge $\mathcal{C}$ our estimator can be written as: $\hat{\boldsymbol{\theta}}_\mathcal{C} = \bar{\boldsymbol{\theta}}_\mathcal{C} + \Delta\boldsymbol{\theta}_\mathcal{C}$, for true solution $\bar{\boldsymbol{\theta}}_\mathcal{C}$ and perturbation $\Delta\boldsymbol{\theta}_\mathcal{C}$. The perturbation $\Delta\boldsymbol{\theta}_\mathcal{C}$ and its variance, $V[\Delta\boldsymbol{\theta}_\mathcal{C}]$, both lie in the tangent plane to the gauge manifold, $T_{\bar{\boldsymbol{\theta}}_\mathcal{C}}[\mathcal{C}]$.

We expand equation (3) around $\bar{\boldsymbol{\theta}}_\mathcal{C}$ and get to first order:

$$\nabla_{\boldsymbol{\theta}}^{\mathcal{T}}\boldsymbol{\Pi}(\bar{\boldsymbol{\theta}}_\mathcal{C})\Delta\boldsymbol{\theta}_\mathcal{C} = \Delta\mathbf{p} \tag{11}$$

where $\nabla_{\boldsymbol{\theta}}^{\mathcal{T}}$ is the gradient with respect to $\boldsymbol{\theta}$ in the manifold $\mathcal{T}$. We then split the perturbations, $\Delta\boldsymbol{\theta}_\mathcal{C}$ into two components, those in $T_{\boldsymbol{\theta}_\mathcal{C}}[\mathcal{M}]$ and those in $T_{\boldsymbol{\theta}_\mathcal{C}}[\mathcal{M}]^\perp$ as shown in Figure 2:

$$\Delta\boldsymbol{\theta}_\mathcal{C} = \Delta\boldsymbol{\theta}_\mathcal{C}{}^{\|\mathcal{M}} + \Delta\boldsymbol{\theta}_\mathcal{C}{}^{\perp\mathcal{M}}. \tag{12}$$

The gradient $\nabla_{\boldsymbol{\theta}}^{\mathcal{T}}\boldsymbol{\Pi}(\bar{\boldsymbol{\theta}})$ is orthogonal to the tangent plane of $\mathcal{M}$ and has rank $n - r$. We can thus solve for the orthogonal perturbations:

$$\Delta\boldsymbol{\theta}_\mathcal{C}{}^{\perp\mathcal{M}} = (\nabla_{\boldsymbol{\theta}}^{\mathcal{T}}\boldsymbol{\Pi}(\bar{\boldsymbol{\theta}}_\mathcal{C}))_{n-r}^{-}\Delta\mathbf{p}, \tag{13}$$

where "$-$" denotes the Moore-Penrose generalized inverse[2] constrained to have rank $n - r$. We call the covariance of this orthogonal component the *normal covariance*:

$$V_{\perp\mathcal{M}}[\boldsymbol{\theta}] = (\nabla_{\boldsymbol{\theta}}^{\mathcal{T}}\boldsymbol{\Pi}(\bar{\boldsymbol{\theta}}))_{n-r}^{-}V_p(\nabla_{\boldsymbol{\theta}}^{\mathcal{T}}\boldsymbol{\Pi}(\bar{\boldsymbol{\theta}}))_{n-r}^{-\top}. \tag{14}$$

The normal covariance is expressed at a particular solution, $\boldsymbol{\theta}$, and depends on our choice of parametrization and implicitly assumes a metric over parameter

---

[1] We can extend this to the case when variance is known only up to a scale factor
[2] The Moore-Penrose generalized inverse is defined such that if $A = U\Lambda V^\top$ by SVD, then $A_N^- = V\Lambda_N^- U^\top$, where Λ_N^- has the first N singular values inverted on the diagonal, and the rest zeroed.

space. But it does not require explicit gauge constraints, (rather implicitly assumes a gauge normal to the manifold), and as we shall see, it incorporates all of the essential geometric uncertainty in the solution.

When the indeterminacies are removed by adding constraints the normal covariance must be obliquely projected onto the appropriate constraint surface. The uncertainty in the gauge will be in its tangent plane: $\Delta\boldsymbol{\theta}_C \in T[\mathcal{C}]$. We already know the perturbation, $\Delta\boldsymbol{\theta}_C{}^{\perp\mathcal{M}}$, orthogonal to $T[\mathcal{M}]$, and so it only remains to derive the component parallel to $T[\mathcal{M}]$ as illustrated in Figure 2.

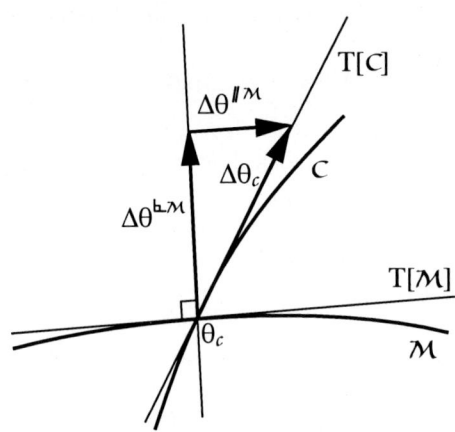

Fig. 2. An illustration of the oblique projection of perturbations along the solution tangent space, $T[\mathcal{M}]$, and onto the gauge manifold tangent space $T[\mathcal{C}]$: $\Delta\boldsymbol{\theta}_C = \Delta\boldsymbol{\theta}_C{}^{\perp\mathcal{M}} + \Delta\boldsymbol{\theta}_C{}^{\|\mathcal{M}}$. This projection transforms the normal covariance matrix into the local gauge covariance.

Let U be a matrix with r columns spanning $T[\mathcal{M}]$ at $\boldsymbol{\theta}_C$, and let V be a matrix with r columns spanning the space orthogonal to $T[\mathcal{C}]$ at $\boldsymbol{\theta}_C$. Then we can express equation (12) as:

$$\Delta\boldsymbol{\theta}_C = \Delta\boldsymbol{\theta}_C{}^{\perp\mathcal{M}} + U\mathbf{x}. \tag{15}$$

for some unknown coefficients $\mathbf{x}$. The fact that this perturbation is in the constraint tangent plane, implies that $V^{\top}\Delta\boldsymbol{\theta}_C = 0$. Applying this to (15) and eliminating $\mathbf{x}$ we obtain:

$$\Delta\boldsymbol{\theta}_C = Q^{\mathcal{C}}\Delta\boldsymbol{\theta}_C{}^{\perp\mathcal{M}} \tag{16}$$

where $Q^{\mathcal{C}} = \mathbf{I} - U(V^{\top}U)^{-1}V^{\top}$ is our oblique projection operator along $T[\mathcal{M}]$. The covariance of $\boldsymbol{\theta}$ in this gauge is then given by:

$$V_{\mathcal{C}}[\boldsymbol{\theta}_C] = Q^{\mathcal{C}}V_{\perp\mathcal{M}}[\boldsymbol{\theta}_C]Q^{\mathcal{C}^{\top}}. \tag{17}$$

3.2   Inherent Geometric Uncertainty

The camera equations provide geometric constraints on the measurements. Parameters containing indeterminacies correspond to entities not fully constrained by the camera equations, whereas parameters which have a unique value over the solution manifold are fully constrained. These fully constrained parameters describe the "true" geometric entities. They can be uniquely recovered, (up to possibly a discrete ambiguity), from the camera equations. Having a unique value on the solution manifold means that the parameter is invariant to gauge transformations on the solution. We call these gauge invariants.

Not only are the values of gauge invariants unique, but given the covariance of the measured data, the covariance of the invariant is uniquely obtainable. However, the covariance of parameters containing indeterminacies will not be uniquely specified and many possible "geometrically equivalent" covariances can be obtained that correspond to the same measurement covariance. In this section we derive a Geometric Equivalence Relationship for parameters that contain indeterminacies. This permits us to test whether covariances of these parameters under different gauges correspond to the same underlying measurement covariance or not. Finally we propose a fast method for covariance estimation and show its correctness using the Geometric Equivalence Relationship.

Let us assume that we are measuring an invariant property, $I(\boldsymbol{\theta})$, of the solution. Consider the estimators in two gauges: $\boldsymbol{\theta}_C$ and $\boldsymbol{\theta}_{C'}$ with uncertainties: $\Delta\boldsymbol{\theta}_C$ and $\Delta\boldsymbol{\theta}_{C'}$ in their corresponding tangent planes. Let $\frac{\partial\boldsymbol{\theta}_C}{\partial\boldsymbol{\theta}_{C'}}$ be the Jacobian matrix that maps perturbations in the tangent plane of C' to perturbations in the tangent plane of C:

$$\Delta\boldsymbol{\theta}_C = \frac{\partial\boldsymbol{\theta}_C}{\partial\boldsymbol{\theta}_{C'}}\Delta\boldsymbol{\theta}_{C'}. \tag{18}$$

The invariant property will have the same value for both solutions: $I(\boldsymbol{\theta}_C) = I(\boldsymbol{\theta}_{C'})$. Moreover, since I is invariant to all points in $\mathcal{M}$, it must also be invariant to infinitesimal perturbations in $\mathcal{M}$, and hence its gradient must be orthogonal to the tangent plane of $\mathcal{M}$:

$$\nabla_{\boldsymbol{\theta}}^T I \in T[\mathcal{M}]^{\perp}. \tag{19}$$

A perturbation of the invariant at $\boldsymbol{\theta}_C$ can be written:

$$\Delta I(\boldsymbol{\theta}_C) = \nabla_{\boldsymbol{\theta}}^T I \Delta\boldsymbol{\theta}_C = \nabla_{\boldsymbol{\theta}}^T I \frac{\partial\boldsymbol{\theta}_C}{\partial\boldsymbol{\theta}_{C'}}\Delta\boldsymbol{\theta}_{C'}. \tag{20}$$

The variance of the invariant can be calculated using both components of this equation:

$$V[I] = \nabla_{\boldsymbol{\theta}}^T I V[\boldsymbol{\theta}_C]\nabla_{\boldsymbol{\theta}}^T I^T = \nabla_{\boldsymbol{\theta}}^T I \frac{\partial\boldsymbol{\theta}_C}{\partial\boldsymbol{\theta}_{C'}} V[\boldsymbol{\theta}_{C'}]\frac{\partial\boldsymbol{\theta}_C}{\partial\boldsymbol{\theta}_{C'}}^T \nabla_{\boldsymbol{\theta}}^T I^T. \tag{21}$$

The covariances of parameters with indeterminacies may have "non-geometric" components along the tangent plane of the solution manifold. This equation transforms these covariances into the uniquely defined covariance of a gauge invariant.

We then apply the orthogonal constraint from equation (19) to both expressions for $V[I]$ and obtain the following result:

$$\mathbf{u}^T(V[\boldsymbol{\theta}_C] - \frac{\partial\boldsymbol{\theta}_C}{\partial\boldsymbol{\theta}_{C'}} V[\boldsymbol{\theta}_{C'}]\frac{\partial\boldsymbol{\theta}_C}{\partial\boldsymbol{\theta}_{C'}}^T)\mathbf{u} = 0, \quad \forall\mathbf{u} \in T_{\boldsymbol{\theta}_c}[\mathcal{M}]^{\perp}. \tag{22}$$

This means that the difference between the covariance and the transformed co-variance: $V[\boldsymbol{\theta}_C] - \frac{\partial \boldsymbol{\theta}_c}{\partial \boldsymbol{\theta}_{c'}} V[\boldsymbol{\theta}_{C'}] \frac{\partial \boldsymbol{\theta}_c}{\partial \boldsymbol{\theta}_{c'}}^{\mathsf{T}}$ must lie in the the tangent space $T_{\boldsymbol{\theta}_c}[\mathcal{M}]$. Or equivalently we can say that these two variances have the same orthogonal component to $T[\mathcal{M}]$ at $\boldsymbol{\theta}_C$. We denote this relationship as: $V[\boldsymbol{\theta}_C] \equiv V[\boldsymbol{\theta}_{C'}] \bmod \mathcal{M}$. Thus we have:

Geometric Equivalence Relationship *The covariance matrices $V[\boldsymbol{\theta}_C]$ and $V[\boldsymbol{\theta}_{C'}]$ are geometrically equivalent if and only if*

$$V[\boldsymbol{\theta}_C] \equiv V[\boldsymbol{\theta}_{C'}] \bmod \mathcal{M}. \tag{23}$$

In essence this says that at a point $\boldsymbol{\theta} \in \mathcal{M}$, it is only the component of the covariance that is not in the tangent plane that contributes to the geometric uncertainty. Any matrix satisfying this equivalence relationship captures the geometric uncertainty of the parameters. The normal form of the covariance calculated from equation (14) is a natural choice that captures this uncertainty for a given parametrization, and does not require constraints to be specified. From this relationship we see that the covariance in any gauge is equivalent to the normal covariance, i.e.: $V_C[\boldsymbol{\theta}_C] \equiv V_{\perp\mathcal{M}}[\boldsymbol{\theta}] \bmod \mathcal{M}$. Thus the covariance of an invariant can be calculated directly from either of these covariances by transforming them with the invariant gradient, $\nabla_{\boldsymbol{\theta}}^{\mathsf{T}} I$, as in equation (21).

4   Maximum Likelihood Estimation

It is known that *Maximum Likelihood* (ML) estimation is unbiased and obtains the optimal shape and motion parameters. The ML solution is obtained by minimizing the cost:

$$J = (\mathbf{p} - \boldsymbol{\Pi}(\boldsymbol{\theta}))^{\mathsf{T}} V_p^{-1} (\mathbf{p} - \boldsymbol{\Pi}(\boldsymbol{\theta}))). \tag{24}$$

where $\boldsymbol{\theta} \in \mathcal{T}$. The minimum value of this will have the same camera indeterminacies described in section 2.3, and hence determine a manifold, $\mathcal{M}$, of geometrically equivalent solutions. A unique solution can be obtained by choosing an arbitrary gauge $\mathcal{C}$.

4.1   Free-Gauge Solution

Instead of constraining our minimization process with our chosen gauge $\mathcal{C}$, at each step we would like to choose a gauge orthogonal to the solution manifold $\mathcal{M}$, and proceed in that direction. We expect this to give better convergence to the manifold $\mathcal{M}$ especially when our desired gauge $\mathcal{C}$ has a large oblique angle to $\mathcal{M}$. Once any point on $\mathcal{M}$ is achieved, it is easy to transform this solution into any desired gauge.

Levenberg-Marquardt (LM) minimization is a combination of Gauss-Newton and gradient descent. The gradient of J is obtained as

$$\nabla_{\boldsymbol{\theta}} J = -2\nabla_{\boldsymbol{\theta}}^{\mathsf{T}} \boldsymbol{\Pi}(\boldsymbol{\theta}) V_p^{-1} (\mathbf{p} - \boldsymbol{\Pi}(\boldsymbol{\theta})), \tag{25}$$

and the Gauss-Newton approximation for the Hessian:

$$\nabla_{\boldsymbol{\theta}}^2 J \approx \frac{1}{2} E\{\nabla_{\boldsymbol{\theta}} J \nabla_{\boldsymbol{\theta}} J^\top\} = 2\nabla_{\boldsymbol{\theta}}^{\mathcal{T}} \boldsymbol{\Pi}(\boldsymbol{\theta}) V_p^{-1} \nabla_{\boldsymbol{\theta}}^{\mathcal{T}} \boldsymbol{\Pi}(\boldsymbol{\theta})^\top. \tag{26}$$

Gauss-Newton proceeds iteratively by solving the linear equation:

$$\nabla_{\boldsymbol{\theta}}^2 J \Delta\boldsymbol{\theta} = -\nabla_{\boldsymbol{\theta}} J. \tag{27}$$

However, in our case the Hessian, $\nabla_{\boldsymbol{\theta}}^2 J$, is singular due to the ambiguity directions with rank $n - r$. Hence we take steps in the direction:

$$\Delta\boldsymbol{\theta} = -(\nabla_{\boldsymbol{\theta}}^2 J)_{n-r}^{-} \nabla J, \tag{28}$$

which proceeds orthogonally towards the manifold $\mathcal{M}$. This is called free-gauge minimization. To implement LM we add a gradient term.

At the solution, $\boldsymbol{\theta} \in \mathcal{M}$, the covariance of the ML estimation of shape and motion parameters is obtained as:

$$V[\boldsymbol{\theta}] = E\{\Delta\boldsymbol{\theta}\Delta\boldsymbol{\theta}^\top\} = 2(\nabla_{\boldsymbol{\theta}}^2 J)_{n-r}^{-} \tag{29}$$

$$= \frac{1}{2}(\nabla_{\boldsymbol{\theta}}^{\mathcal{T}} \boldsymbol{\Pi}(\boldsymbol{\theta}) V_p^{-1} \nabla_{\boldsymbol{\theta}}^{\mathcal{T}} \boldsymbol{\Pi}(\boldsymbol{\theta})^\top)_{n-r}^{-} \tag{30}$$

It can be shown that this is identical to the normal covariance expression in equation (14), $V[\boldsymbol{\theta}] \equiv V_{\perp\mathcal{M}}[\boldsymbol{\theta}]$, and not just up to a geometric equivalence, and so we use this as an alternate expression to for the normal covariance.

4.2   Efficient Covariance Estimation

The calculation of the generalized inverse in equations (28) and (30) involves use of SVD which takes $O(n^3)$ operations, and so for many feature points or images is slow. The Hessian often has sparse structure and when it is multiplied by the gradient, as in LM, the generalized inverse can be avoided and efficient minimization methods for J have been proposed [1, 2]. Here, however, we not only want a fast LM method, but also an efficient method to estimate the full covariance. We propose an efficient method in this section.

Let us assume that our parameter vector is divided into a shape and a motion part, $\boldsymbol{\theta}_s$ and $\boldsymbol{\theta}_m$ respectively, such that $\boldsymbol{\theta} = (\boldsymbol{\theta}_s^\top, \boldsymbol{\theta}_m^\top)^\top$. The Hessian is then split into its shape and motion components:

$$\nabla_{\boldsymbol{\theta}}^2 J = \begin{pmatrix} \nabla_{\boldsymbol{\theta}_s}^2 J & \nabla_{\boldsymbol{\theta}_{sm}} J \\ \nabla_{\boldsymbol{\theta}_{ms}} J & \nabla_{\boldsymbol{\theta}_m}^2 J \end{pmatrix} = \begin{pmatrix} U & W \\ W^\top & V \end{pmatrix}. \tag{31}$$

When noise in the feature points specified by V_p are independent of each other, U and V are full rank[3] and sparse with $O(N)$ and $O(M)$ non-zero elements respectively, where N is the number of features and M is the number of images [2].

---

[3] U is full rank for affine and perspective projection, but not when homogeneous coordinates are used as the general projective case, but then we do not obtain Euclidean shape.

The cross-term matrix W is not sparse however, and so applying a standard sparse techniques will not reduce the complexity of determining the generalized inverse.

First we define the full rank matrix T as follows:

$$T = \begin{pmatrix} I & 0 \\ -W^\top U^{-1} & I \end{pmatrix} \tag{32}$$

and obtain the block diagonal matrix:

$$T \nabla_\theta^2 J T^\top = \begin{pmatrix} U & 0 \\ 0 & V - W^\top U^{-1} W \end{pmatrix}. \tag{33}$$

Then we define the covariance $V_T[\theta]$ by:

$$V_T[\theta] = T^\top (T \nabla_\theta^2 J T^\top)^-_{n-r} T \tag{34}$$

$$= T^\top \begin{pmatrix} U^{-1} & 0 \\ 0 & (V - W^\top U^{-1} W)^-_{m-r} \end{pmatrix} T,$$

where $m = 6M$ is the number of motion parameters. This can be obtained in $O(N^2 M + M^3)$ operations which, when when the number of images is small (i.e. $M \ll N$), is much faster than the original SVD which is $O(N^3 + M^3)$.

In order for $V_T[\theta]$ to be a valid description of the uncertainty, we must show that it is geometrically equivalent to $V_{\perp \mathcal{M}}[\theta]$. Let $A = \frac{1}{2} \nabla_\theta^2 J$ be half the Hessian, and consider the equation:

$$A\mathbf{x} = \mathbf{u} \tag{35}$$

where $\mathbf{u}$ is in the column space of A. The general solution is a combination of a unique particular solution, $\mathbf{x}_p = A^- \mathbf{u}$, in the column space of A, and a homogeneous solution, $\mathbf{x}_h$, which is any vector in the nullspace of A, i.e. $A\mathbf{x}_h = 0$. We left multiply equation (35) by T and rearrange to obtain:

$$(TAT^\top)T^{-\top}\mathbf{x} = T\mathbf{u}. \tag{36}$$

Then changing variables: $\mathbf{y} = T^{-\top}\mathbf{x}$, and solving for $\mathbf{y}$ we obtain: $\mathbf{y} = (TAT^\top)^- T\mathbf{u} + \mathbf{y}_h$ where $(TAT^\top)\mathbf{y}_h = 0$. Now transforming back to $\mathbf{x}$ we can decompose the solution into the particular and homogeneous parts:

$$\mathbf{x} = T^\top (TAT^\top)^- T\mathbf{u} + T^\top \mathbf{y}_h = \mathbf{x}_p + \mathbf{x}_h, \tag{37}$$

where $\mathbf{x}_p = A^- \mathbf{u}$ is the particular solution obtained in equation (35). It is easy to see that $T^\top \mathbf{y}_h$ is in the nullspace of A, and hence $T^\top (TAT^\top)^- T\mathbf{u} = \mathbf{x}_p + \mathbf{x}'_h$ for some vector $\mathbf{x}'_h$ in the nullspace of A.

We now apply the geometric equivalence test to $V_{\perp \mathcal{M}}[\theta] = A^-$ and $V_T[\theta] = T^\top (TAT^\top)^- T$. The change of constraint Jacobian is the identity: $\frac{\partial \theta_c}{\partial \theta_{c'}} = I$, and the orthogonal component to the tangent space of $\mathcal{M}$, $T_\theta[\mathcal{M}]^\perp$, is spanned by the columns of A and so $\mathbf{u}$ is any vector in the column space of A. Applying the equivalence relationship we obtain:

$$\mathbf{u}^\top (A^- - T^\top (TAT^\top)^- T)\mathbf{u} = \mathbf{u}^\top (\mathbf{x}_p - \mathbf{x}_p - \mathbf{x}'_h) = \mathbf{u}^\top (-\mathbf{x}'_h) = 0, \tag{38}$$

for all $\mathbf{u}$ in the column and row space of A, since $\mathbf{x}'_h$ is in the nullspace. We thus conclude that $V_T[\boldsymbol{\theta}]$ can be efficiently estimated and is geometrically equivalent to the normal covariance $V_{\perp\mathcal{M}}[\boldsymbol{\theta}]$.

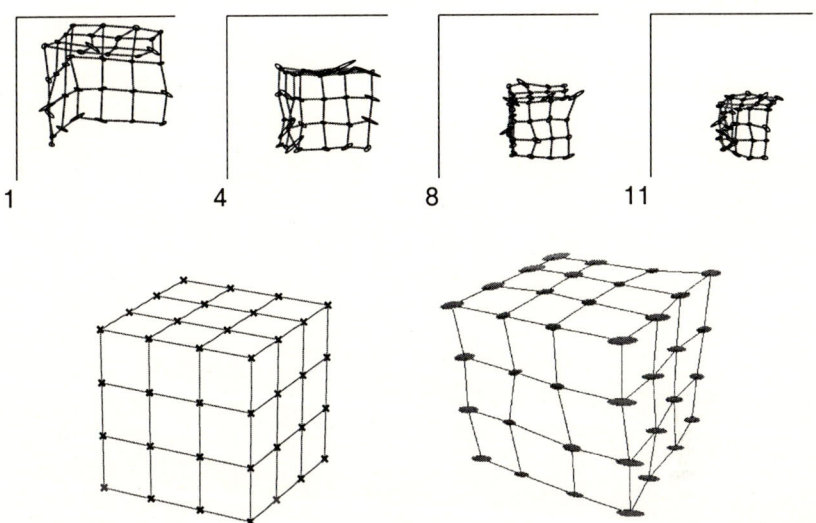

Fig. 3. Four images of an eleven image sequence with significant noise added and the scaled standard deviation of each point illustrated with an ellipse. (The lines connecting points are only present for viewing). The synthetic object is shown bottom left. The optimal reconstruction, given the noise estimates, is shown on the right with uncertainty ellipsoids. These ellipsoids, corresponding to the 3×3 block diagonal elements of a full shape covariance, are significantly correlated as shown in the full covariance matrix in Figure 5.

5   Results

We give some sample synthetic and real results illustrating our uncertainty modeling. A set of features in an image sequence with known correspondences is shown in Figure 3. The synthetic object is also shown along with a sample optimal reconstruction and ellipsoids illustrating feature-based uncertainty. The individual feature uncertainties are strongly correlated as illustrated in the subsequent Figures.

The normal covariance for this shape and motion recovery is shown in Figure 4. This contains a full description of the uncertainty in the features, but to experimentally confirm it using Monte Carlo simulation requires that we select a gauge such as that in equation (8). In Figure 5 we show the predicted covariance obtained by projecting the normal covariance into this gauge using equation (17). Even though the normal covariance and the predicted covariance have significantly different values and correlations, they contain the same geometric uncertainty (as they are equivalent under the Geometric Equivalence Relationship) and will give the same predictions for uncertainties of gauge invariants. Figure 5 also contains the Monte Carlo covariance estimate in this gauge, involving 400 SFM reconstruction runs. It is very similar to the predicted covariance confirming that our uncertainty model is correct. An easier way to visually compare the covariances is to plot the square root of their diagonal elements. This gives the net standard deviation in each parameter in this gauge as illustrated in Figure 6.

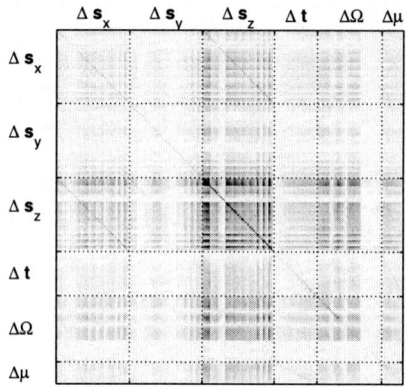

Fig. 4. The predicted normal covariance matrix giving us the geometric uncertainty of the reconstructed synthetic object. The scaled absolute value is shown by the darkness of the shading. Here weak perspective was used and μ is the recovered scale for each image. We note that it can be altered by adding components in the tangent plane to $\mathcal{M}$ without changing the underlying uncertainty, as we see in Figure 5.

The problem with the shape and motion covariance plots is their dependence on choice of gauge. Gauge invariants, however, will give us unambiguous measures for the uncertainty of the results. We chose two invariants on our synthetic object: an angle between two lines and the ratio of two lengths. Their statistics are shown in Table 1, confirming very good matching between predicted uncertainty and actual uncertainty.

Table 1. Predicted and measured values, along with their uncertainties in standard deviations, of two gauge independent properties of the synthetic object in Figure 3: (left) the angle between two lines, and (right) the ratio of two lengths.

Angle	*Mean*	*Uncertainty*	**Ratio**	*Mean*	*Uncertainty*
Predicted:	90.11°	±2.10°	Predicted:	0.9990	±0.0332
Recovered:	90.02°	±2.10°	Recovered:	1.0005	±0.0345

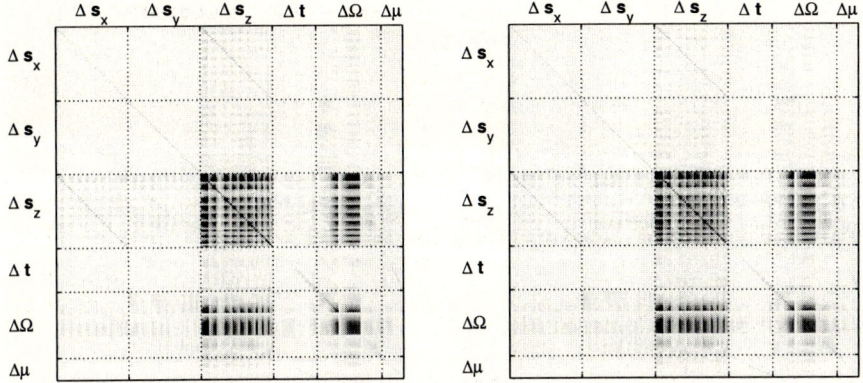

Fig. 5. (Left diagram) The predicted covariance in an arbitrary gauge, see equation (8). We note that the values and correlations are significantly different from the normal covariance in Figure 4, and yet it still contains the same geometric uncertainty. The Monte Carlo estimation of covariance in this gauge is shown on the right. It shows close similarity to the predicted covariance in this gauge as can also be seen in Figure 6.

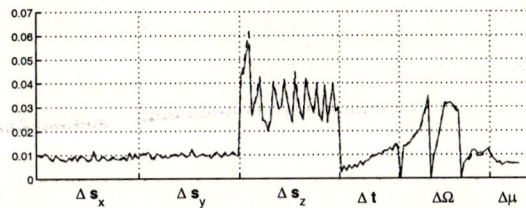

Fig. 6. The square root of the diagonal elements of the covariances in Figure 5 are shown here. This gives the net standard deviation of each parameter in the experimental gauge (8) obtained from the diagonal of the covariance. The solid line is the experimentally measured value and the dashed line is our prediction from the projected normal covariance.

Next we show results for a real image sequence of a chapel in Figure 7 along with the reconstructed shape from SFM. The feature correspondences were determined manually. Not only can we obtain a texture-mapped reconstruction, we can also obtain measurements of similarity invariant properties such as angles with their uncertainties. We found the angle and its uncertainty (in standard deviations) between two walls separated by a buttress: $117° \pm 3.2°$, as well as two other angles on the chapel: $46.2° \pm 2.1°$ and $93.2° \pm 2.6°$ as described in the Figure caption. These quantities are exact and not only up to an unknown transformation. We believe reporting this uncertainty measure is essential for most quantitative analyzes of the shape, and can only be done for gauge invariant properties.

Fig. 7. An image from a 6 image sequence of a chapel is shown on the left with features registered by hand. The reconstruction is on the right. We can obtain quantitative measures and uncertainties from this reconstruction. In this case we estimated the angle between to walls separated by a buttress, and two other angles as illustrated on the far right. The values (anti-clockwise from the top) are: $117° \pm 3.2°$, $46.2° \pm 2.1°$ and $93.2° \pm 2.6°$.

6   Concluding Remarks

We have addressed the question of uncertainty representation when parameter indeterminacies exist in estimation problems. The shape and motion parameters estimated by SFM contain inherent indeterminacies. Hence to apply perturbation analysis, these parameters are first constrained by a gauge and the covariance is estimated in this gauge. Unfortunately the choice of gauge will have significant effects on the uncertainties of the parameters, as illustrated in our results. These effects, however, are "non-physical" and do not correspond to changes in the actual geometric uncertainty which is unaffected by an arbitrary choice of gauge. Thus shape and motion parameter uncertainties contain artifacts of the choice of gauge. The uncertainties of gauge invariant parameters, however, are not affected by these indeterminacies and hence correspond directly to the inherent geometric uncertainty. They thus provide unambiguous measures for the solution uncertainty.

We derived a Geometric Uncertainty Relationship which permits us to compare the geometric uncertainty contained in covariances described under different parametrizations and gauges. Using this relationship we showed that the normal covariance, whose estimation does not need explicit gauge constraints, fully describes the solution uncertainty. We were also able to derive an efficient estimation method for the solution covariance. Using the Geometric Uncertainty Relationship, we showed that this estimate also fully captures the solution uncertainty. Gauge invariant uncertainties can be calculated by transforming this covariance.

References

1. K. B. Atkinson, *Close Range Photogrammetry and Machine Vision*, Whittles Publ., Caithness, Scotland, (1996).
2. R. Hartley, Euclidean reconstruction from uncalibrated views, *Proc. DARPA–ESPRIT Workshop App. Invariants in Comp. Vis.*, Portugal, 1993 187–202.
3. A. Heyden & K. Astrom, Euclidean reconstruction from image sequences with varying and unknown focal length and principal point, *Proc. Comp. Vision Patt. Recog.*, Peurto Rico, 1997 438–443.
4. T. Kanade & D. D. Morris, Factorization methods for structure from motion, *Phil. Trans. R. Soc. Long. A*, 1998 1153–1173.
5. K. Kanatani, *Statistical Optimization for Geometric Computation: Theory and Practice*, Elsevier, Amsterdam, (1996).
6. K. Kanatani, Geometric information criterion for model selection, *Int. J. Comp. Vision* (1998), **26**(3), 171–189.
7. K. Kanatani & D. D. Morris, Gauges and gauge transformations in 3-D reconstruction from a sequence of images, *To appear in ACCV 2000*.
8. L. L. Kontsevich, M. L. Kontsevich & A. K. Shen, Two algorithms for reconstructing shapes, *Avtometriya* (1987), (5), 76–81, (Transl. Optoelec., Instrum. Data Proc., no. 5. 76–81, 1987).
9. D. D. Morris & T. Kanade, A unified factorization algorithm for points, line segments and planes with uncertainty models, *Proc. Sixth Int. Conf. Comp. Vision*, Bombay, India, 1998 696–702.
10. C. Poelman & T. Kanade, A paraperspective factorization method for shape and motion recovery, *IEEE Trans. Patt. Anal. Mach. Intell.* (Mar. 1997), **19**(3), 206–18.
11. L. Quan & T. Kanade, Affine structure from line correspondances with uncalibrated affine cameras, *IEEE Trans. Patt. Anal. Mach. Intell.* (1997), **19**(8), 834–45.
12. P. Sturm & B. Triggs, A factorization based algorithm for multi-image projective structure and motion, *Proc. Euro. Conf. Comp. Vision*, Cambridge, UK, 1996 709–20.
13. R. Szeliski & S. B. Kang, Recovering 3D shape and motion from image streams using non-linear least squares, *J. of Visual Comm. and Image Rep.* (Mar. 1994), **5**(1), 10–28.
14. R. Szeliski & S. B. Kang, Shape ambiguities in structure from motion, *IEEE Trans. Patt. Anal. Mach. Intell.* (May 1997), **19**(5), 506–512.
15. J. I. Thomas, A. Hanson & J. Oliensis, Refining 3D reconstructions: A theoretical and experimental study of the effect of cross-correlations, *CVGIP* (Nov. 1994), **60**(3), 359–370.
16. J. Weng, N. Ahuja & T. Huang, Optimal motion and structure estimation, *IEEE Trans. Patt. Anal. Mach. Intell.* (1993), **15**(9), 864–884.

Discussion

Bill Triggs: When you use your efficient reduction technique, the reduction is triangular not orthogonal, so you should get a different covariance out at the end — it will be gauge-equivalent, but a generalized inverse rather than a Moore-Penrose pseudo-inverse. Can you comment on how large the difference seems to be in practice, and whether looking at one of these covariance matrices would give you a misleading idea of the uncertainties in the other one.

Daniel Morris: That's a good question. There are two issues to consider: the size of the diagonal elements of the covariance matrix and the size of the off-diagonal elements indicating correlation between parameters. The normal covariance will have the smallest trace of all gauge equivalent covariances. For the synthetic example we presented, the trace of our efficient covariance estimation method was 13% larger than that of the normal covariance, and the trace of the covariance of the standard gauge, in which the centroid was fixed, was 30% larger than the normal covariance. However, the normal covariance need not have small off-diagonal elements, and actually in our example it had 50% larger correlation values between shape and motion parameters than our efficient covariance estimate. So numerically our method actually reduced the effect of cross terms. Also, while the magnitudes of the elements in the covariances varied significantly between gauges, the overall structure of the covariances did not seem to significanly change when different gauges were used.

Rick Szeliski: This is a more open-ended, speculative question. When you look, for example, at things like the individual variances of points, you sometimes fail to capture the global things. I guess there are the absolute gauge freedoms that exist in these problems, for example the coordinate or centroid freedom, and then there are other softer ambiguities, depending on the imaging, the bas-relief ambiguity, there are probably others too. I'm just wondering if there is some way we can gain intuition, perhaps through visualization, or some other way to get a handle qualitatively on what the error is in a given reconstruction.

Daniel Morris: The question is, can we gain qualitative information from these covariances?

Rick Szeliski: Is there, for example, some way to pull out that some of these uncertainties are very highly correlated, to be able to just look at the data set and say ...I can tell you very well where it is going to be just like *this*...For example, where you had the angle between two faces, the one that had most to do with how flat the scene was, was the one with the largest error.

Daniel Morris: It is interesting to speculate as to what kind of qualitative information we can obtain from looking at the covariance matrix. In our example we see large correlation effects between the rotation parameters and the Z-component of shape, and I think this corresponds to the bas-relief effect. So you can look at that, and there may be a way of quantifying it, for example, by looking at the eigenvalues. I think that's what you do in your paper on ambiguities to determine how correlated the variables are. It is a bit harder, however, to gain qualitative insight into the uncertainty of invariant properties such as angles from the parameter covariance matrix. To do that it is probably best to directly calculate the covariance matrix of these invariants.

Error Characterization of the Factorization Approach to Shape and Motion Recovery *

Zhaohui Sun[1], Visvanathan Ramesh[2], and A. Murat Tekalp[1]

[1] Dept. of Electrical and Computer Engineering
University of Rochester
Rochester, NY 14627-0126, USA
{zhsun,tekalp}@ece.rochester.edu
[2] Imaging & Visualization Department
Siemens Corporate Research
Princeton, NJ 08540, USA
rameshv@scr.siemens.com

Abstract. This paper is focused on error characterization of the factorization approach to shape and motion recovery from image sequence using results from matrix perturbation theory and covariance propagation for linear models. Given the 2-D projections of a set of points across multiple image frames and small perturbation on image coordinates, first order perturbation and covariance matrices for 3-D affine/Euclidean shape and motion are derived and validated with the ground truth. The propagation of the small perturbation and covariance matrix provides better understanding of the factorization approach and its results, provides error sensitivity information for 3-D affine/Euclidean shape and motion subject to small image error. Experimental results are demonstrated to support the analysis and show how the error analysis and error measures can be used.

1 Introduction

The factorization approach to 3-D shape and motion recovery from image sequence, first proposed in [1], reconstructs 3-D shape and motion in affine and Euclidean spaces given the 2-D projections of a set of points across multiple image frames captured by uncalibrated affine cameras [2]. It employs the facts that the ideal measurement matrix has rank 3 and can be decomposed as 3-D shape and rotation after canceling the translation terms by singular value decomposition, and redundant information is good for robust estimation. The introduction of the factorization approach for orthographic projection [1] was followed by a series of extensions to more general camera models, from weak perspective [3], para-perspective [4], affine [5] to projective projection [6], and methods based on sequential computation [7], line correspondence [8] and occlusion and uncertainty handling [9].

---

* This work is supported by Siemens Corporate Research, Princeton, NJ 08540

B. Triggs, A. Zisserman, R. Szeliski (Eds.): Vision Algorithms'99, LNCS 1883, pp. 218-235, 2000.
© Springer-Verlag Berlin Heidelberg 2000

The factorization approach has attracted significant interest from various researchers who have applied it to a variety of tasks. Therefore it is of great interest to investigate the sensitivity of the estimated 3D shape and motion measurements to perturbations on image measurements. However, to the best knowledge of the authors, no thorough attempt was made for the error sensitivity analysis specific for this method, although there have been quite a few papers addressing error analysis for the structure from motion algorithms [10–13, 9].

One related work is reported in [12] where a general framework of error analysis for structure from motion is proposed and the singular values of the derived Jacobian are used for error interpretation. It is argued in [12] that sensitivity is a property of the problem and not of an implemented technique for the problem. Moreover, they point out that absolute statements about errors in the output are important to understand whether structure from motion is feasible and should be pursued. It is also pointed out that the Jacobian for the problem is singular due to the nature of the inverse problem and hence the eigenvectors of the Jacobian are used to interpret the sensitivity of the results. Our approach falls within the general framework in [12]. However our analysis is specific for the factorization approach. Both methods are only applicable to small perturbation analysis where linearization holds. In addition, if SfM component is one component in a larger vision system, it is important to analyze the sensitivity of the implementation and derive conclusions about the specific technique used in the system. Thus, an analysis of the a sub-class of techniques that perform SfM is necessary. We will show that the perturbation theory on eigensystem, proposed and used for error estimation and analysis for 3-D structure from two perspective views [10, 11], is also applicable to the factorization approach and leads to analytical expressions for the first order shape and motion error measures.

Our analysis uses a step-by-step error propagation through various stages of the factorization approach to characterize the errors at every stage of the process. The various algorithmic stages include: singular value decomposition of the observed measurement matrix to identify the 3 dominant singular values and corresponding eigenvectors. These correspond to the affine shape and motion matrices up to an 3 by 3 affine transform. A subsequent stage applies metric constraints to recover the Euclidean shape and rotation matrices. Ambiguity still exists in this representation as the reference frame is only known up to an arbitrary rotation. To propagate uncertainties through the first stage, we use well known results from matrix perturbation theory to derive the expressions for the perturbations on singular values and eigenvectors [10, 11, 14, 15]. We propagate covariances through each step by assuming that the input perturbations are Gaussian random variables, linearize and do covariance propagation to derive the covariances at each step. The ambiguities in the reconstruction at the different steps make the notion of covariances in these spaces invalid. For example, for an affine shape we can only make relative comparisons of the output deviations to determine what points/frames are more sensitive to input perturbations. We also point out that angle covariances measuring the degree to which relationships such as parallelism and collinearity are preserved in the affine shape (when compared to the Euclidean shape) are useful to characterize the degree to which the intermediate affine shape/motion values are close to the ideal result.

Our paper is organized as follows: Section 2 discusses the theoretical results governing the relationships between input image errors and output errors for affine/Euclidean shape and motion parameter estimates. Section 3 provides a discussion concerning the interpretation of the derived covariance matrices. For instance, we provide insights on how errors can be measured given that the estimated affine shape is known up to an unknown affine transform. Section 4 describes experiments we conducted to address three issues: correctness of theoretical results, example illustration of how errors can be quantified in affine shape/motion, and an illustration of how relative comparisons of reconstruction errors can be made to identify the points/frames which are affected most by input perturbations.

2   Error Characterization

Vectors and matrices will be in bold face. An entity, *e.g.* the shape, may be associated with four variables, the error free shape matrix $\mathbf{S}$, the observed noisy shape matrix $\hat{\mathbf{S}}$, the shape perturbation matrix $\mathbf{\Delta_S}$, and the first order perturbation of the shape matrix $\delta_\mathbf{S}$. According to the definition, we have $\hat{\mathbf{S}} = \mathbf{S} + \mathbf{\Delta_S}$ and $\hat{\mathbf{S}} \simeq \mathbf{S} + \delta_\mathbf{S}$, where $\simeq$ denotes equal in the linear terms. Usually the real shape perturbation matrix $\mathbf{\Delta_S}$ may not be available and we seek for $\delta_\mathbf{S}$ as the first order (linear) approximation of $\mathbf{\Delta_S}$. A matrix $\mathbf{S} = [s_{ij}]_{m \times n}$ with m rows and n columns can also be represented in vector form by column first order (unless stated otherwise) as $\vec{\mathbf{S}}$ with $m \times n$ entities, $\vec{\mathbf{S}} = [s_{11}, s_{21}, \dots, s_{m1}, s_{12}, \dots, s_{m2}, \dots, s_{mn}]^T$.

2.1   Problem Formulation

Recall that the factorization approach recovers 3-D shape (x, y, z coordinates) and motion (affine camera parameters) in affine and Euclidean spaces given the correspondence of P points across F image frames. Our task is to determine the first order approximation of the perturbation and covariance matrices of shape and motion given the observations of 2-D projections of P points across F frames and covariance of the perturbation on image coordinates. The following error analysis of the factorization approach is mainly built upon matrix perturbation theory [10, 14], especially the theorem derived and proved in Appendix A [10], where Weng, Huang and Ahuja used for error analysis of their motion and shape algorithm from two perspective views. The basic ideas are propagating the small perturbation on image coordinates, *i.e.* the perturbation on the registered measurement matrix, to the three dominant singular values and corresponding eigenvectors, therefore to the affine/Euclidean motion and shape matrices, and using the covariance matrices as a vehicle for error measures and applications.

2.2   Affine Shape

Let $m = 2 \times F$ and $n = P$, we first investigate how the perturbation matrix $\mathbf{\Delta_W}$ affects the three largest singular values $\lambda_1, \lambda_2, \lambda_3$ and the corresponding eigenvectors $\mathbf{v_1}, \mathbf{v_2}, \mathbf{v_3}$ of an $m \times n$ measurement matrix $\mathbf{W}$, and thus on the affine shape $\mathbf{S_a} = \mathbf{\Lambda V^T}$, where the singular value decomposition of $\hat{\mathbf{W}}$ is

$$[\hat{\mathbf{W}}]_{m \times n} = \hat{\mathbf{U}} \hat{\mathbf{\Lambda}} \hat{\mathbf{V}}^T \approx [\hat{\mathbf{M}}_\mathbf{a}]_{m \times 3} [\hat{\mathbf{S}}_\mathbf{a}]_{3 \times n}. \tag{1}$$

Before we proceed further, matrices $\mathbf{W}$ and $\mathbf{\Delta_W}$ are scaled down by the maximum absolute value of $\mathbf{W}$, $c = max|w(i,j)|, i = 1, \ldots, m, j = 1, \ldots, n$. This guarantees the maximum absolute value of $\mathbf{\Delta_W}$ is sufficiently small. The scale factor c is later put back to the computed singular values and the perturbation on the singular values.

Let $\mathbf{A}$ be an $n \times n$ symmetric matrix defined as:

$$\mathbf{A} = \mathbf{W^T W} = (\mathbf{U \Lambda V^T})^T (\mathbf{U \Lambda V^T}) = \mathbf{V \Lambda^2 V^T}, \tag{2}$$

we have $\mathbf{V^{-1} A V} = \mathbf{\Lambda}^2 = diag\{\lambda_1^2, \lambda_2^2, \ldots, \lambda_n^2\}$. Matrix $\mathbf{W}$ is usually a rectangular matrix, pre-multiplying with its own transpose yields a symmetric matrix $\mathbf{A}$ so that the Theorem proved in [10] holds.

According to the Theorem [10], the first order perturbations on the three most significant eigenvalues and corresponding eigenvectors of matrix $\mathbf{A}$ are:

$$\delta_{\lambda_i^2} = \mathbf{v_i^T} \mathbf{\Delta_A} \mathbf{v_i},$$
$$\delta_{\mathbf{v_i}} = \mathbf{V} \mathbf{\Delta_i} \mathbf{V^T} \mathbf{\Delta_A} \mathbf{v_i}, \tag{3}$$

where $\mathbf{v_i}$ are the column vectors of $\mathbf{V} = [\mathbf{v_1}, \ldots, \mathbf{v_n}]$, and the diagonal matrix $\mathbf{\Delta_i} = diag\{(\lambda_i^2 - \lambda_1^2)^{-1}, \ldots, 0, \ldots, (\lambda_i^2 - \lambda_n^2)^{-1}\}$ with the i-th diagonal element as 0, and $i = 1, 2, 3$.

The unknowns of $\mathbf{\Delta_A} \mathbf{v_i}$ in (3) can be written as

$$\mathbf{\Delta_A} \mathbf{v_i} = [v_{i1} \mathbf{I_n}, v_{i2} \mathbf{I_n}, \ldots, v_{in} \mathbf{I_n}] \vec{\delta_\mathbf{A}} = \mathbf{H_i} \vec{\delta_\mathbf{A}}, \tag{4}$$

by rewriting the $n \times n$ matrix $\mathbf{\Delta_A}$ as the column-first vector form $\vec{\delta_\mathbf{A}}$ with n^2 elements, where v_{ij} is the j-th element of vector $\mathbf{v_i}$ and $\mathbf{I_n}$ is $n \times n$ identity matrix. $\mathbf{H_i}$ is an $n \times n^2$ matrix with 1 by n submatrices $v_{ik} \mathbf{I_n}$, $k = 1, 2, \ldots, n$, each with $n \times n$ elements.

$\vec{\delta_\mathbf{A}}$ can be further associated with $\vec{\delta_\mathbf{W}}$, so that we have a close form solution for $\delta_{\lambda_i^2}$ and $\delta_{\mathbf{v_i}}$ as a function of $\vec{\delta_\mathbf{W}}$. From the matrix representation of the perturbation on matrix $\mathbf{A}$

$$\mathbf{\Delta_A} = (\mathbf{W} + \mathbf{\Delta_W})^T (\mathbf{W} + \mathbf{\Delta_W}) - \mathbf{W^T W}, \tag{5}$$

the first order approximation

$$[\mathbf{\Delta_A}]_{n \times n} \simeq [\mathbf{W^T}]_{n \times m} [\mathbf{\Delta_W}]_{m \times n} + [\mathbf{\Delta_W^T}]_{n \times m} [\mathbf{W}]_{m \times n} \tag{6}$$

is rewritten as its corresponding vector form

$$\left[\vec{\delta_A}\right]_{n^2 \times 1} = [\mathbf{F_s} + \mathbf{G_s}]_{n^2 \times mn} \left[\vec{\delta w}\right]_{mn \times 1}, \tag{7}$$

where matrix $\mathbf{F_s} = [\mathbf{F_{ij}}]$ has n by n submatrices of $\mathbf{F_{ij}} = \begin{cases} \mathbf{W^T} & if \ \ i = j \\ \mathbf{0} & if \ \ i \neq j \end{cases}$, and matrix $\mathbf{G_s} = [\mathbf{G_{ij}}]$ also has n by n submatrices $\mathbf{G_{ij}}$ with the *j-th* row being the *i-th* column vector of $\mathbf{W}$ and all other rows being zeros. More specifically,

$$\mathbf{F_s} = \begin{bmatrix} \mathbf{W^T} & 0 & \cdots & 0 \\ 0 & \mathbf{W^T} & \cdots & 0 \\ \vdots & \vdots & \ddots & \vdots \\ 0 & 0 & \cdots & \mathbf{W^T} \end{bmatrix} \tag{8}$$

$$\mathbf{G_s} = \begin{bmatrix} w_{11} & \cdots & w_{m1} & \cdots & \cdots & 0 & \cdots & 0 \\ \vdots & \vdots & \vdots & \vdots & \vdots & \vdots & \vdots & \vdots \\ 0 & \cdots & 0 & \cdots & \cdots & w_{11} & \cdots & w_{m1} \\ \vdots & & \vdots & \vdots & & \vdots & & \vdots \\ w_{1n} & \cdots & w_{mn} & \cdots & \cdots & 0 & \cdots & 0 \\ \vdots & \vdots & \vdots & \vdots & \vdots & \vdots & \vdots & \vdots \\ 0 & \cdots & 0 & \cdots & \cdots & w_{1n} & \cdots & w_{mn} \end{bmatrix} \tag{9}$$

Then the perturbations on the eigenvalues and eigenvectors of $\mathbf{A}$ subject to small perturbation on $\mathbf{W}$ are:

$$\delta_{\lambda_i^2} \simeq \mathbf{v_i^T H_i (F_s + G_s)} \vec{\delta w} = \mathbf{D_{\lambda_i}^T} \vec{\delta w},$$
$$\delta_{\mathbf{v_i}} \simeq \mathbf{V \Delta_i V^T H_i (F_s + G_s)} \vec{\delta w} = \mathbf{D_{v_i}} \vec{\delta w}, \tag{10}$$

where $\mathbf{D_{\lambda_i}}$ is a vector with mn elements and $\mathbf{D_{v_i}}$ is a matrix with dimension of $n \times mn$.

Without any constraints on the statistical structure of the small perturbation, we get the covariance matrix of $\mathbf{v_i}$, $i, j = 1, 2, 3$, from (10),

$$\mathbf{\Gamma_{v_i}} = \mathbf{E}\{\delta_{\mathbf{v_i}} \delta_{\mathbf{v_i}}{}^T\} = \mathbf{D_{v_i} \Gamma_{\vec{W}} D_{v_i}}{}^T,$$
$$\mathbf{\Gamma_{v_i v_j}} = \mathbf{E}\{\delta_{\mathbf{v_i}} \delta_{\mathbf{v_j}}{}^T\} = \mathbf{D_{v_i} \Gamma_{\vec{W}} D_{v_j}}{}^T, \tag{11}$$

where $\mathbf{E}$ denotes expectation and $\mathbf{\Gamma_{\vec{W}}}$ is the covariance matrix of the measurement matrix, and the variances of the squares of the singular values λ_i^2 for $i = 1, 2, 3$:

$$\sigma_{\lambda_i^2} = \mathbf{E}\{\delta_{\lambda_i^2} \delta_{\lambda_i^2}^T\} \simeq \mathbf{D_{\lambda_i}^T \Gamma_{\vec{W}} D_{\lambda_i}}$$
$$\sigma_{\lambda_i^2 \lambda_j^2} = \mathbf{E}\{\delta_{\lambda_i^2} \delta_{\lambda_j^2}^T\} \simeq \mathbf{D_{\lambda_i}^T \Gamma_{\vec{W}} D_{\lambda_j}} \tag{12}$$

Under the assumption of identical and independent Gaussian perturbation with zero mean and variance σ^2 for all image points and their components, $\mathbf{\Gamma_{\vec{W}}} =$

$\sigma^2 \mathbf{I}_{mn}$, simpler representations are possible:

$$\mathbf{\Gamma_{v_i}} = \sigma^2 \mathbf{D_{v_i}} \mathbf{D_{v_i}}^T,$$
$$\mathbf{\Gamma_{v_i v_j}} = \sigma^2 \mathbf{D_{v_i}} \mathbf{D_{v_j}}^T. \tag{13}$$

It is well known that the real structure of the errors on 3-D shape and motion is neither independent nor Gaussian distribution. The covariance matrices (11) and (13) are just Gaussian approximation of the real structures for small perturbation. This simplification could lead us to simplified representations and error measures.

At last, we have the first order perturbation on affine shape $\mathbf{S_a} = \mathbf{\Lambda V^T}$ subject to small perturbation on image coordinates, by combining the perturbations on singular values and eigenvectors of $\mathbf{W}$:

$$\mathbf{\Delta_{S_a}} \simeq \delta_{\mathbf{S_a}} = \begin{bmatrix} \delta_{\lambda_1} \mathbf{v_1^T} + \lambda_1 \delta_{\mathbf{v_1}}^{\mathbf{T}} \\ \delta_{\lambda_2} \mathbf{v_2^T} + \lambda_2 \delta_{\mathbf{v_2}}^{\mathbf{T}} \\ \delta_{\lambda_3} \mathbf{v_3^T} + \lambda_3 \delta_{\mathbf{v_3}}^{\mathbf{T}} \end{bmatrix}, \tag{14}$$

where $\delta_{\lambda_i} = \sqrt{\lambda_i^2 + \delta_{\lambda_i}^2} - \lambda_i \simeq \frac{\delta_{\lambda_i}^2}{2\lambda_i}$ (for $|\frac{\delta_{\lambda_i}^2}{\lambda_i^2}| << 1$) are the perturbations on the singular values of $\mathbf{W}$, and their covariances are $\sigma_{\lambda_i} = \frac{1}{4\lambda_i^2}\sigma_{\lambda_i^2}$ and $\sigma_{\lambda_i \lambda_j} = \frac{1}{4\lambda_i \lambda_j}\sigma_{\lambda_i^2 \lambda_j^2}$ (see (12)).

Covariance matrix for affine shape $\mathbf{\Gamma_{S_a}}$

$$\mathbf{\Gamma_{S_a}} = \mathbf{E}\{\vec{\delta}_{\mathbf{S_a}} \vec{\delta}_{\mathbf{S_a}}^T\} = \tag{15}$$

$$\begin{bmatrix} \sigma_{\lambda_1} \mathbf{v_1 v_1}^T + \lambda_1^2 \mathbf{\Gamma_{v_1}} & \sigma_{\lambda_1 \lambda_2} \mathbf{v_1 v_2}^T + \lambda_1 \lambda_2 \mathbf{\Gamma_{v_1 v_2}} & \sigma_{\lambda_1 \lambda_3} \mathbf{v_1 v_3}^T + \lambda_1 \lambda_3 \mathbf{\Gamma_{v_1 v_3}} \\ \sigma_{\lambda_1 \lambda_2} \mathbf{v_2 v_1}^T + \lambda_1 \lambda_2 \mathbf{\Gamma_{v_2 v_1}} & \sigma_{\lambda_2} \mathbf{v_2 v_2}^T + \lambda_2^2 \mathbf{\Gamma_{v_2}} & \sigma_{\lambda_2 \lambda_3} \mathbf{v_2 v_3}^T + \lambda_2 \lambda_3 \mathbf{\Gamma_{v_2 v_3}} \\ \sigma_{\lambda_1 \lambda_3} \mathbf{v_3 v_1}^T + \lambda_1 \lambda_3 \mathbf{\Gamma_{v_3 v_1}} & \sigma_{\lambda_2 \lambda_3} \mathbf{v_3 v_2}^T + \lambda_2 \lambda_3 \mathbf{\Gamma_{v_3 v_2}} & \sigma_{\lambda_3} \mathbf{v_3 v_3}^T + \lambda_3^2 \mathbf{\Gamma_{v_3}} \end{bmatrix}$$

then can be derived from (14) after fitting $\delta_{\mathbf{S_a}}$ into its vector form $\vec{\delta}_{\mathbf{S_a}}$ by row first order, $\vec{\delta}_{\mathbf{S_a}} = [\delta_{\lambda_1} \mathbf{v_1^T} + \lambda_1 \delta_{\mathbf{v_1}}^{\mathbf{T}}, \delta_{\lambda_2} \mathbf{v_2^T} + \lambda_2 \delta_{\mathbf{v_2}}^{\mathbf{T}}, \delta_{\lambda_3} \mathbf{v_3^T} + \lambda_3 \delta_{\mathbf{v_3}}^{\mathbf{T}}]^T$, with the assumption that $\mathbf{E}\{\delta_{\mathbf{v_i}}\} = \mathbf{D_{v_i}} \mathbf{E}\{\vec{\delta}_{\mathbf{W}}\} = 0$.

The representation of $\mathbf{\Gamma_{S_a}}$ in (15) provides us various error measures for affine shapes, from high level error sensitivity summary for affine shape $\|\delta_{\mathbf{S_a}}\| \approx \sqrt{trace\{\mathbf{\Gamma_{S_a}}\}}$ to fine-grained error sensitivity measure for a specific point, say the k-th point, $\|\delta_{\mathbf{S_a^k}}\| \approx \sqrt{trace\{\mathbf{\Gamma_{S_a^k}}\}}$ where covariance matrix $\mathbf{\Gamma_{S_a^k}}$ is an 3×3 matrix extracted from rows and columns of k, $(n+k)$, $(2n+k)$ of covariance matrix $\mathbf{\Gamma_{S_a}}$. $\|\delta_{\mathbf{S_a^k}}\|$ gives us relative error measures for the shape points, e.g. indicating which points are more sensitive to image errors than the others.

It is worth to notice that we are seeking for 3 most significant simple eigenvalues, which are usually distinctive and not close to 0, in the first order perturbation analysis. So the inverse terms, e.g. $(\lambda_i^2 - \lambda_1^2)^{-1}$ in matrix $\mathbf{\Delta_i}$ in (3), are usually quite stable. Recall that the smallest simple eigenvalue (very close to 0) and corresponding eigenvector are sought in [10] where numeric robustness is a big concern. As the ground truth of $\mathbf{W}$ is usually unavailable in real applications, we use the observed $\hat{\mathbf{W}}$, $\hat{\lambda}_i$ and $\hat{\mathbf{V}}$ instead to estimate the first order perturbations.

2.3   Affine Motion

Follow the error analysis for affine shape, and let

$$\mathbf{B} = \mathbf{WW^T} = (\mathbf{U\Lambda V^T})(\mathbf{U\Lambda V^T})^\mathbf{T} = \mathbf{U\Lambda^2 U^T} \tag{16}$$

be an $m \times m$ symmetric matrix. It can be shown that the perturbations on the eigenvalues and eigenvectors of $\mathbf{B}$ subject to small perturbation on $\mathbf{W}$ are:

$$\delta_{\lambda_i^2} \simeq \mathbf{u}_i^T \mathbf{J}_i (\mathbf{F_m} + \mathbf{G_m}) \vec{\delta \mathbf{W}} = \mathbf{D}_{\lambda_i}^T \vec{\delta \mathbf{W}},$$
$$\delta_{\mathbf{u}_i} \simeq \mathbf{U\Delta}_i \mathbf{U^T} \mathbf{J}_i (\mathbf{F_m} + \mathbf{G_m}) \vec{\delta \mathbf{W}} = \mathbf{D}_{\mathbf{u}_i} \vec{\delta \mathbf{W}}, \tag{17}$$

where $\mathbf{D}_{\lambda_i}$ is a vector with mn elements, $\mathbf{D}_{\mathbf{u}_i}$ is a matrix with dimension of $m \times mn$, $\mathbf{u}_i$ are the column vectors of $\mathbf{U} = [\mathbf{u_1}, \dots, \mathbf{u_m}]$, $\mathbf{J}_i = [u_{i1}\mathbf{I_m}, u_{i2}\mathbf{I_m}, \dots, u_{im}\mathbf{I_m}]$ is an $m \times m^2$ matrix with 1 by m submatrices $u_{ik}\mathbf{I_m}$, $k = 1, 2, \dots, m$, each with $m \times m$ elements, $\mathbf{\Delta}_i = diag\{(\lambda_i^2 - \lambda_1^2)^{-1}, \dots, 0, \dots, (\lambda_i^2 - \lambda_n^2)^{-1}\}$ has the i-th diagonal element as 0, $i = 1, 2, 3$, matrix $\mathbf{F_m} = [\mathbf{F_{ij}}]$ has m by n submatrices $\mathbf{F_{ij}}$ with the i-th column being the j-th column vector of $\mathbf{W}$, and matrix $\mathbf{G_m} = [\mathbf{G_{ij}}]$ also has m by n submatrices $\mathbf{G_{ij}}$ with $\mathbf{G_{ij}} = w_{ij}\mathbf{I_m}$, $i.e.$,

$$\mathbf{F_m} = \begin{bmatrix} w_{11} & \cdots & 0 & \cdots & \cdots & w_{1n} & \cdots & 0 \\ \vdots & \vdots & \vdots & \vdots & \vdots & \vdots & \vdots & \vdots \\ w_{m1} & \cdots & 0 & \cdots & \cdots & w_{mn} & \cdots & 0 \\ \vdots & & \vdots & \vdots & \vdots & & \vdots & \\ 0 & \cdots & w_{11} & \cdots & \cdots & 0 & \cdots & w_{1n} \\ \vdots & \vdots & \vdots & \vdots & \vdots & \vdots & \vdots & \vdots \\ 0 & \cdots & w_{m1} & \cdots & \cdots & 0 & \cdots & w_{mn} \end{bmatrix} \tag{18}$$

$$\mathbf{G_m} = \begin{bmatrix} w_{11}\mathbf{I_m} & w_{12}\mathbf{I_m} & \cdots & w_{1n}\mathbf{I_m} \\ w_{21}\mathbf{I_m} & w_{22}\mathbf{I_m} & \cdots & w_{2n}\mathbf{I_m} \\ \vdots & \vdots & \ddots & \vdots \\ w_{m1}\mathbf{I_m} & w_{m2}\mathbf{I_m} & \cdots & w_{mn}\mathbf{I_m} \end{bmatrix} \tag{19}$$

From (17), we get the covariance matrix of $\mathbf{u_i}$,

$$\mathbf{\Gamma_{u_i}} = \mathbf{E}\{\delta_{\mathbf{u}_i}\delta_{\mathbf{u}_i}{}^T\} = \mathbf{D_{u_i}}\mathbf{\Gamma_{\vec{W}}}\mathbf{D_{u_i}}{}^T,$$
$$\mathbf{\Gamma_{u_i u_j}} = \mathbf{E}\{\delta_{\mathbf{u}_i}\delta_{\mathbf{u}_j}{}^T\} = \mathbf{D_{u_i}}\mathbf{\Gamma_{\vec{W}}}\mathbf{D_{u_j}}{}^T. \tag{20}$$

Again under the assumption of identical and independent Gaussian perturbation with zero mean and variance σ^2 for all image points and their components, $\mathbf{\Gamma_{\vec{W}}} = \sigma^2 \mathbf{I_{mn}}$, (20) can be simplified as:

$$\mathbf{\Gamma_{u_i}} = \sigma^2 \mathbf{D_{u_i}}\mathbf{D_{u_i}}{}^T,$$
$$\mathbf{\Gamma_{u_i u_j}} = \sigma^2 \mathbf{D_{u_i}}\mathbf{D_{u_j}}{}^T. \tag{21}$$

The covariance matrices of (20) and (21) are just Gaussian approximation to the error structure on motion matrix.

As affine motion matrix $\mathbf{M_a} = [\mathbf{u_1}, \mathbf{u_2}, \mathbf{u_3}]$ is composed of three eigenvectors corresponding to the three most significant eigenvalues of $\mathbf{B}$, the perturbation on affine motion matrix subject to small perturbations on image coordinates is

$$\delta_{\mathbf{M_a}} = [\delta_{\mathbf{u_1}}, \delta_{\mathbf{u_2}}, \delta_{\mathbf{u_3}}], \tag{22}$$

where $\delta_{\mathbf{u_i}}$ are given by (17). Thus the covariance matrix for affine motion $\mathbf{\Gamma_{M_a}}$ can be derived from (22) after fitting $\delta_{\mathbf{M_a}}$ into its vector form $\vec{\delta}_{\mathbf{M_a}}$ by column first order, $\vec{\delta}_{\mathbf{M_a}} = \left[\delta_{\mathbf{u_1}}{}^T, \quad \delta_{\mathbf{u_2}}{}^T, \quad \delta_{\mathbf{u_3}}{}^T\right]^T$,

$$\mathbf{\Gamma_{M_a}} = \mathbf{E}\{\vec{\delta}_{\mathbf{M_a}} \vec{\delta}_{\mathbf{M_a}}^T\} = \begin{bmatrix} \mathbf{\Gamma_{u_1}} & \mathbf{\Gamma_{u_1 u_2}} & \mathbf{\Gamma_{u_1 u_3}} \\ \mathbf{\Gamma_{u_2 u_1}} & \mathbf{\Gamma_{u_2}} & \mathbf{\Gamma_{u_2 u_3}} \\ \mathbf{\Gamma_{u_3 u_1}} & \mathbf{\Gamma_{u_3 u_2}} & \mathbf{\Gamma_{u_3}} \end{bmatrix}. \tag{23}$$

Similar to $\mathbf{\Gamma_{S_a}}$ in (15), the representation of $\mathbf{\Gamma_{M_a}}$ in (23) also provides various error measures for affine motion, from high level error sensitivity summary for affine motion $\|\delta_{\mathbf{M_a}}\| \approx \sqrt{trace\{\mathbf{\Gamma_{M_a}}\}}$ to the error measure for a specific frame, even a specific axis, such as $\|\delta_{\mathbf{M_a^k}}\| \approx \sqrt{trace\{\mathbf{\Gamma_{M_a^k}}\}}$ for the k-th frame, where covariance matrix $\mathbf{\Gamma_{M_a^k}}$ is an 6×6 matrix extracted from rows and columns of $2k$, $(2k+1)$, $(m+2k)$, $(m+2k+1)$, $(2m+2k)$ and $(2m+2k+1)$ of $\mathbf{\Gamma_{M_a}}$. $\|\delta_{\mathbf{M_a^k}}\|$ tells us which camera frames are more sensitive to image errors than the other frames. The error measures for the x-axis, y-axis and z-axis are just $\|\delta_{\mathbf{u_1}}\|$, $\|\delta_{\mathbf{u_2}}\|$ and $\|\delta_{\mathbf{u_3}}\|$, respectively.

2.4   Euclidean Shape and Motion

Euclidean motion and shape can be recovered by camera auto-calibration [5, 1, 4]. An invertible 3×3 matrix $\hat{\mathbf{Q}}$ is sought, such that $\begin{bmatrix} \hat{\mathbf{m}}_i \\ \hat{\mathbf{n}}_i \end{bmatrix}$ corresponds to the real camera matrix for frame i, where $\hat{\mathbf{m}}_i$ and $\hat{\mathbf{n}}_i$ are the *(2i)-th* and *(2i+1)-th* row vectors of the affine motion matrix $\hat{\mathbf{M}}_a$, and $i = 1, \ldots, F$. The general metric constraints for affine cameras are [5]

$$\begin{bmatrix} \hat{\mathbf{m}}_i^T \hat{\mathbf{Q}} \hat{\mathbf{Q}}^T \hat{\mathbf{m}}_i & \hat{\mathbf{m}}_i^T \hat{\mathbf{Q}} \hat{\mathbf{Q}}^T \hat{\mathbf{n}}_i \\ \hat{\mathbf{m}}_i^T \hat{\mathbf{Q}} \hat{\mathbf{Q}}^T \hat{\mathbf{n}}_i & \hat{\mathbf{n}}_i^T \hat{\mathbf{Q}} \hat{\mathbf{Q}}^T \hat{\mathbf{n}}_i \end{bmatrix} = \mathbf{A}_i \mathbf{A}_i^T, \tag{24}$$

where $\mathbf{A}_i$ is the intrinsic matrix for frame i. Solving matrix $\hat{\mathbf{Q}}$, which can be done by linear method, yields the solutions of motion and shape matrices in Euclidean space, *i.e*

$$\hat{\mathbf{M}}_e = \hat{\mathbf{M}}_a \hat{\mathbf{Q}}, \quad \hat{\mathbf{S}}_e = \hat{\mathbf{Q}}^{-1} \hat{\mathbf{S}}_a. \tag{25}$$

The recovered shape and motion in Euclidean space are still subject to a global scale factor and rotation to be registered with the reference coordinate system where the ground truth resides.

When $\mathbf{Q}$ and $\mathbf{Q}^{-1}$ are given (which is case when evaluation based on ground-truth is done), the first order approximation on the Euclidean shape and motion errors can be simplified as

$$\delta_{\mathbf{M_e}} \approx \delta_{\mathbf{M_a}} \mathbf{Q}, \quad \delta_{\mathbf{S_e}} \approx \mathbf{Q}^{-1} \delta_{\mathbf{S_a}}. \tag{26}$$

By rewriting it as vector form

$$\vec{\delta}_{\mathbf{M_e}} \approx \mathbf{D_Q}\vec{\delta}_{\mathbf{M_a}}, \quad \vec{\delta}_{\mathbf{S_e}} \approx \mathbf{D_{Q^{-1}}}\vec{\delta}_{\mathbf{S_a}}, \qquad (27)$$

we have the close form solution for the covariance matrices of Euclidean motion and shape

$$\boldsymbol{\Gamma}_{\mathbf{M_e}} \approx \mathbf{D_Q}\boldsymbol{\Gamma}_{\mathbf{M_a}}\mathbf{D_Q^T},$$
$$\boldsymbol{\Gamma}_{\mathbf{S_e}} \approx \mathbf{D_{Q^{-1}}}\boldsymbol{\Gamma}_{\mathbf{S_a}}\mathbf{D_{Q^{-1}}^T}. \qquad (28)$$

Under the assumption of $\boldsymbol{\Gamma}_{\vec{\mathbf{W}}} = \sigma^2 \mathbf{I_{mn}}$, it is further simplified as:

$$\boldsymbol{\Gamma}_{\mathbf{M_e}} \approx \sigma^2 \mathbf{D_Q} \mathbf{D_{u_i}} \mathbf{D_{u_i}^T} \mathbf{D_Q^T},$$
$$\boldsymbol{\Gamma}_{\mathbf{S_e}} \approx \sigma^2 \mathbf{D_{Q^{-1}}} \mathbf{D_{v_i}} \mathbf{D_{v_i}^T} \mathbf{D_{Q^{-1}}^T}. \qquad (29)$$

The interpretation of the error measures for Euclidean shape $\|\delta_{\mathbf{S_e}}\| \approx \sqrt{trace\{\boldsymbol{\Gamma}_{\mathbf{S_e}}\}}$, $\|\delta_{\mathbf{S_e^k}}\| \approx \sqrt{trace\{\boldsymbol{\Gamma}_{\mathbf{S_e^k}}\}}$, $k = 1, \ldots, P$ and Euclidean motion $\|\delta_{\mathbf{M_e}}\| \approx \sqrt{trace\{\boldsymbol{\Gamma}_{\mathbf{M_e}}\}}$, $\|\delta_{\mathbf{M_e^k}}\| \approx \sqrt{trace\{\boldsymbol{\Gamma}_{\mathbf{M_e^k}}\}}$, $k = 1, \ldots, F$ are similar to the affine counterparts addressed in Section 2.2 and 2.3. The only difference is that they are more constrained and only a rotation ambiguity is left.

3   Discussion

In this section we discuss key issues addressing: 1) better applicability of the matrix perturbation theory results to factorization analysis over the original application discussed in [10, 11], 2) the use of the error predictions for relative comparisons of sensitivities of output terms to input perturbations, and 3) the interpretation of errors in affine shape, meaning of covariances.

The error characterization approach using the first order approximation is a reasonable approximation to the Jacobian only when the input perturbation is small. And how small should it be really depends on the scene structure, camera configuration, and image noise. One of measures could be

$$\epsilon = \frac{1}{\lambda_1 - \lambda_2} + \frac{1}{\lambda_2 - \lambda_3} + \frac{1}{\lambda_3}, \qquad (30)$$

where $\lambda_1 > \lambda_2 > \lambda_3$ are the three dominant singular values of the measurement matrix. When input perturbation is above certain level, the linear approximation is no longer applicable and the higher order terms will dominate. However, we are only interested in perturbation on the three most dominant singular values and the corresponding eigenvectors, which is more robust than seeking the perturbation on the smallest singular values (usually very close to zero) such as the situation attacked in [10, 11].

It also worths notice that the performance measures derived in (14, 15, 22, 23, 26,28) are subject to a specific eigensystem decided by the scene and camera configuration. When the cameras and shape are fixed, the eigensystem of the registered measurement matrix is also fixed. Due to "small" perturbation on image measurement, not big enough to perturb the eigensystem, we have observations in affine/Euclidean space subject to an unknown but fixed affine/rotation transform. So the local covariance used for relative measures are valid and valuable for relative comparison purposes. For example, by comparing $\|\mathbf{\Gamma}_{\mathbf{S}_{\mathbf{e}}^i}\|$, $i = 1, \ldots, P$ and $\|\mathbf{\Gamma}_{\mathbf{M}_{\mathbf{e}}^j}\|$, $j = 1, \ldots, F$, questions like which 3-D point/frame suffers more error than the others subject to the specific scene structure, camera configuration and image noise can be answered quantitatively. This information is already enough to tell us which point/frame has the worst performance in the group and should be removed first if necessary. Making the same relative comparison also helps us to include further tracking points and frames into the shape and motion reconstruction. An iterative process of the comparisons of the error measures are helpful for picking the right points and frames for performance improvement. We are safe as long as the structure of the eigensystem is preserved.

Since, the estimated affine shape is only defined up to an affine transform, one could ask the question whether the above covariance matrix for the errors $\vec{\delta}_{\mathbf{S}_a}$ is a meaningful quantity to compute. This matrix would only allow relative comparisons since all errors have undergone the same affine transform. Another interesting question that could be asked is on how one could compare various trials wherein the image perturbations are large enough so that the eigensystems are perturbed (e.g. the eigenvectors corresponding to the dominant singular values permute). To answer this question, we use the fact that the same unknown affine transform is applied to every point in the shape matrix. This means that relationships such as parallelism and collinearity for tuples of points in the ideal input Euclidean shape should be preserved after the affine transform. Thus, it makes sense to characterize the error between the difference in the angles of point tuples that satisfy the parallelism/collinearity constraints in the original input shape and estimate the precision parameter for these angle differences. In fact, if two pairs of lines have the same angle between them in Euclidean space, their angles in the affine space would remain the same (since they are undergoing the same unknown affine transform). This fact will be used to characterize errors in the affine motion estimates as well. In this paper, we concentrate mainly on relative comparisons that can be made when the perturbations are small enough.

Another possibility is to remove ambiguity by registration of the estimates for meaningful comparisons. After fixing the affine/rotation ambiguity, the error measures can be even used for comparison of different shape undergoing same motion, or same shape undergoing different motion. Suppose two factorization results are achieved from the same camera configuration and motion, $\mathbf{W}_\alpha = \mathbf{M}_\alpha \mathbf{S}_\alpha$, and $\mathbf{W}_\beta = \mathbf{M}_\beta \mathbf{S}_\beta$. There is a transform $\mathbf{T}$ (an affine transform in affine space and a rotation transform in Euclidean space) between $\mathbf{M}_\alpha$ and $\mathbf{M}_\beta$, and can be solved from linear system $\mathbf{M}_\alpha = \mathbf{M}_\beta \mathbf{T}$. With the transform $\mathbf{T}$ fixed, shapes $\mathbf{S}_\alpha$ and $\mathbf{T}^{-1}\mathbf{S}_\beta$ and the corresponding error measures are comparable. The same approach applies to the situation where shape is fixed. When both scene structure and camera configuration are changing or the image perturbation

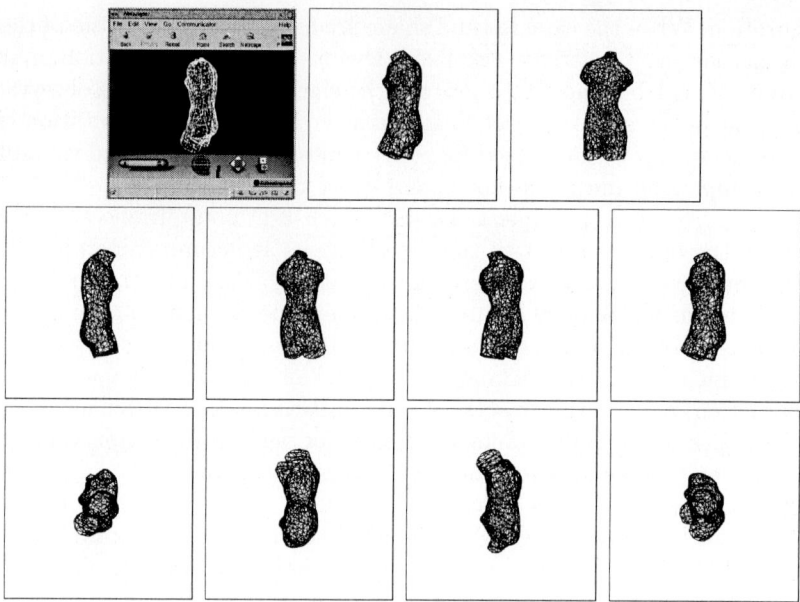

Fig. 1. VRML model VENUS and ten of its projections.

is too large, the error measures with respect to different eigensystems do not provide any meaningful insight for shape and motion distortion.

4   Experiment Results

Experiment results are shown in this section to support the above error analysis and how the results can be used to bring in insights and improve performance.

The first simulation is to prove that the derivations of (14) and (22) based on perturbation theory are correct and valid for small perturbation. A 3-D model VENUS with 711 nodes is projected on 10 image frames, and the point correspondences are perturbed by identical and independent Gaussian noise. The observed 3-D shape and motion errors from the factorization approach are compared against the first order approximations from our error analysis. A close matching of them would be a proof of the derivations. For this purpose, the VENUS model is first normalized in the unit cube $\{x \in (-1,1], y \in (-1,1], z \in (-1,1]\}$. Ten orthographic cameras are simulated, all targeting at the origin. Five of them are distributed uniformly on the unit circle on XZ plane and the other five on the unit circle on YZ plane. The 3-D model and its 10 projections are shown in Fig. 1. Identical and independent Gaussian noises are added to the point coordinates in all frames with size 512×512, $\Delta_u \sim N(0, 4.0)$, $\Delta_v \sim N(0, 1.0)$. The 711 points across 10 frames and the perturbations are fit into the measurement matrix. Affine shape, affine motion, and the first order perturbation on them are calculated based on the factorization approach and the above error analysis. The com-

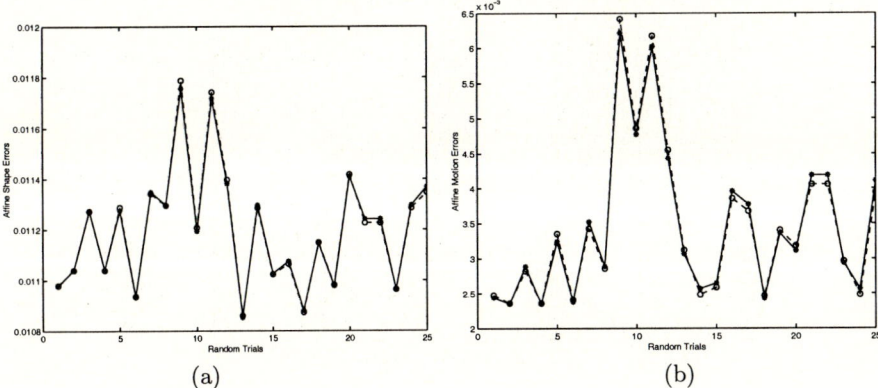

Fig. 2. Norm of computed error (solid line) versus norm of first order perturbation (dotted line) for the VENUS model. (a) $\|\boldsymbol{\Delta}_{\mathbf{S_a}}\| \sim \|\delta_{\mathbf{S_a}}\|$ from (14); (b) $\|\boldsymbol{\Delta}_{\mathbf{M_a}}\| \sim \|\delta_{\mathbf{M_a}}\|$ from (22).

parisons of the observed shape and motion errors, $\|\hat{\mathbf{S}}_a - \mathbf{S}_a\|$ and $\|\hat{\mathbf{M}}_a - \mathbf{M}_a\|$, against the derived first order perturbations on affine shape and motion, $\|\delta_{\mathbf{S_a}}\|$ and $\|\delta_{\mathbf{M_a}}\|$, are shown in Fig. 2 for 25 random trials, where matrix norm is defined as root sum of squares of matrix components, e.g. $\|\mathbf{S}\| = \sqrt{\sum_{i,j} s(i,j)^2}$. It is easy to see the strong correlation between the two curves. Given $\mathbf{Q}$ and $\mathbf{Q}^{-1}$, $\|\delta_{\mathbf{S_e}}\|$ and $\|\delta_{\mathbf{M_e}}\|$ have similar matches.

Next illustration of errors in affine space is demonstrated to check the parallelism relationship. A total of 13 random points are generated in unit cube, where 4 of them specify 2 parallel lines. They are projected on 5 image planes (512×512) by the orthographic cameras in Table 1. Samples from Gaussian distribution with zero mean and standard deviation ranging from 0.1 to 1.5 are simulated as image errors. The errors propagate through the factorization approach and perturb the orientation of the two lines used to be parallel in Euclidean space. The angles in degrees between the two lines are calculated and repeat for 1000 trials to collect the statistics of angle variance. And the result is shown in Fig. 3. The relationship of parallelism is serves as an interpretation of the errors in affine space.

At last, we demonstrate how the shape and motion error measures derived before can be used for relative comparisons. 11 points in unit cube and 5 orthographic cameras are simulated, and details are listed in Table 2 and 1. The 11 points are projected on the 5 image planes (512×512). Small perturbations are added to the image coordinates of the corresponding points. Assuming the noise has identical and independent zero mean Gaussian distribution with standard deviation $\sigma = 0.1, 0.5, 1$, the shape and motion error measures in affine space are shown in Fig. 4 and those in Euclidean space are shown in Fig. 5. By comparing the error measures of $\|\delta_{\mathbf{S_a^i}}\|$, $\|\delta_{\mathbf{M_a^j}}\|$, $\|\delta_{\mathbf{S_e^i}}\|$ and $\|\delta_{\mathbf{M_e^j}}\|$, $i = 1, \ldots, P$, $j = 1, \ldots F$, we can draw conclusions such as point 11 is less sensitive to image

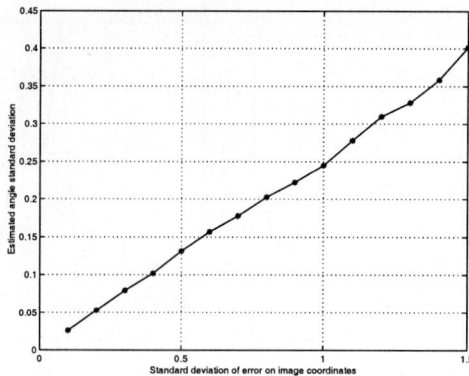

Fig. 3. Estimated standard deviation of the angles between two lines in affine space subject to the errors on image coordinates.

noise than point 4, and frame 3 is more sensitive to image noise than frame 1. This kind of information is already enough to identify which point/frame has the poorest error sensitivity performance, and can be used for integrating further points and frames for performance improvement. Furthermore, not only the 3-D shape and motion but also the relative error sensitivity information can be recovered, and visualized if necessary, given the error perturbation model on the correspondences.

Table 1. Affine and Euclidean motion errors. Five orthographic cameras are simulated on Z-X plane targeting at origin point. The 11 points are captured on the five 512×512 image frames. Identical and independent zero mean Gaussian noises are added to image coordinates of the corresponding points. Given the standard deviation of $\sigma = 0.1, 0.5, 1$ on image coordinates, the estimated corresponding affine motion error and Euclidean motion error are listed in the next 6 columns.

j	Camera Matrix				Affine Error $\|\delta_{\mathbf{M}_a^j}\|$			Euclidean Error $\|\delta_{\mathbf{M}_e^j}\|$		
					$\sigma = 0.1$	$\sigma = 0.5$	$\sigma = 1.0$	$\sigma = 0.1$	$\sigma = 0.5$	$\sigma = 1.0$
1	104.1	0	104.1	255	3.00	6.717	9.499	5.996	13.406	18.959
	0	−147.2	0	255						
2	136	0	56.3	255	3.26	7.29	10.309	6.556	14.66	20.732
	0	−147.2	0	255						
3	147.2	0	0	255	3.424	7.656	10.828	6.928	15.492	21.909
	0	−147.2	0	255						
4	136	0	−56.3	255	3.422	7.651	10.82	6.946	15.532	21.965
	0	−147.2	0	255						
5	104.1	0	−104.1	255	3.257	7.282	10.298	6.607	14.774	20.894
	0	−147.2	0	255						

Table 2. Affine and Euclidean shape errors. Eleven points are distributed asymmetrically in the unit cube, 10 on Z-X plane and 8 on Z axis. Identical and independent zero mean Gaussian noises are added to image coordinates of the corresponding points on 512×512 images. Given the standard deviation of $\sigma = 0.1, 0.5, 1$ on image coordinates, the estimated corresponding affine shape error and Euclidean shape error are listed in the next 6 columns.

Point	(x,y,z)	Affine Error $\|\delta_{S_a^i}\|$			Euclidean Error $\|\delta_{S_e^i}\|$		
i		$\sigma = 0.1$	$\sigma = 0.5$	$\sigma = 1.0$	$\sigma = 0.1$	$\sigma = 0.5$	$\sigma = 1.0$
1	(0,0.28,-1)	1.16314	2.60086	3.67818	0.718179	1.6059	2.27108
2	(-0.28 0 -1)	1.18246	2.64407	3.73928	0.655924	1.46669	2.07421
3	(-0.14 0 -1)	1.04991	2.34766	3.3201	0.605653	1.35428	1.91524
4	(0 0 -0.98)	1.13453	2.53689	3.5877	0.632423	1.41414	1.9999
5	(0 0 -0.84)	1.12433	2.51407	3.55543	0.634903	1.41969	2.00774
6	(0 0 -0.7)	1.11049	2.48312	3.51166	0.632942	1.4153	2.00154
7	(0 0 -0.56)	1.09287	2.44373	3.45596	0.626499	1.4009	1.98117
8	(0 0 -0.42)	1.07129	2.39547	3.38771	0.615433	1.37615	1.94617
9	(0 0 -0.28)	1.0455	2.33781	3.30616	0.599488	1.3405	1.89575
10	(0 0 -0.14)	1.01518	2.27002	3.21029	0.578261	1.29303	1.82862
11	(0 0 0)	0.979918	2.19116	3.09877	0.551142	1.23239	1.74286

5   Conclusion

We have derived the first order perturbation and covariance matrices for affine/ Euclidean shape and motion subject to small perturbation on image coordinates based on matrix perturbation theory, and used them as a vehicle for error measures in applications. Step-by-step error analysis and propagation based on matrix perturbation theory and covariance propagation are derived and validated. Interpretation of the errors in affine space is also addressed. Relative error measures derived from local covariance matrices are used to identify what output points/frames are sensitive to image measurement errors.

Acknowledgment

We would like to thank Professor Terry Boult from Lehigh University for presenting the paper in the Vision Algorithms workshop in spite of his other engagement. We greatly appreciate his efforts. The constructive comments from the anonymous reviewers are also appreciated for improving the paper presentation.

References

1. C. Tomasi and T. Kanade. Shape and motion from image streams under orthography: A factorization method. *International Journal on Computer Vision*, 9(2):137–154, November 1992.
2. Joseph L. Mundy and Andrew Zisserman. *Geometric Invariance in Computer Vision*. The MIT Press, Cambridge, MA, 1992.

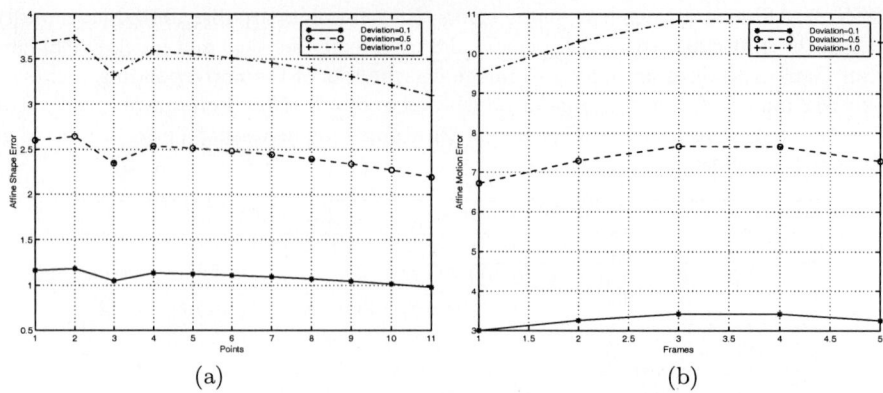

Fig. 4. Error measures for (a) affine shape $\|\delta_{S_a^i}\|$ and (b) affine motion $\|\delta_{M_a^j}\|$. It tells us, for example, point 4 is more sensitive to image error than point 11 and frame 3 is more sensitive to image error than frame 1.

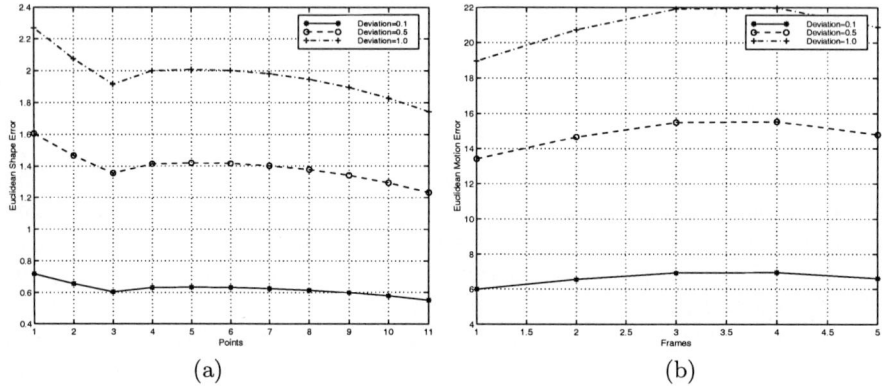

Fig. 5. Error measures for (a) Euclidean shape $\|\delta_{S_e^i}\|$ and (b) Euclidean motion $\|\delta_{S_e^j}\|$. It tells us, for example, point 4 is more sensitive to image error than point 11 and frame 3 is more sensitive to image error than frame 1.

3. D. Weinshall and C. Tomasi. Linear and incremental acquisition of invariant shape models from image sequences. *IEEE Trans. Pattern Analysis Machine Intelligence*, 17(5):512–517, May 1995.

4. C.J. Poelman and T. Kanade. A paraperspective factorization method for shape and motion recovery. *IEEE Trans. Pattern Analysis Machine Intelligence*, 19(3):206–218, March 1997.

5. L. Quan. Self-calibration of an affine camera from multiple views. *International Journal on Computer Vision*, 19(1):93–105, July 1996.

6. P. Sturm and B. Triggs. A factorization based algorithm for multi-image projective structure and motion. In *Computer Vision – ECCV'96*, volume 1065, pages II:709–720. Springer Verlag, Lecture Notes in Computer Science, 1996.

7. T. Morita and T. Kanade. A sequential factorization method for recovering shape and motion from image streams. *IEEE Trans. Pattern Analysis Machine Intelligence*, 19(8):858–867, August 1997.

8. L. Quan and T. Kanade. Affine structure from line correspondences with uncalibrated affine cameras. *IEEE Trans. Pattern Analysis Machine Intelligence*, 19(8):834–845, August 1997.

9. Daniel D. Morris and Takeo Kanade. A unified factorization algorithm for points, line segments and planes with uncertainty. In *International Conference on Computer Vision*, pages 696–702, Bombay, India, 1998.

10. J. Weng, T. S. Huang, and N. Ahuja. Motion and structure from two perspective views: Algorithms, error analysis and error estimation. *IEEE Trans. Pattern Analysis Machine Intelligence*, PAMI-11(5):451–476, May 1989.

11. J. Weng, N. Ahuja, and T.S. Huang. Optimal motion and structure estimation. *IEEE Trans. Pattern Analysis Machine Intelligence*, 15(9):864–884, September 1993.

12. C. Tomasi and J. Zhang. Is structure-from-motion worth pursuing. In *Seventh International Symposium on Robotics Research*, 1995.

13. K. Daniilidis and M. Spetsakis. Understanding noise sensitivity in structure from motion. In Y. Aloimonos, editor, *Visual Navigation*, pages 61–88. Lawrence Erlbaum Associates, Hillsdale, NJ, 1996.

14. J. H. Wilkinson. *The Algebraic Eigenvalue Problem*. Clarendon Press, Oxford, England, 1965.

15. Gene H. Golub and C. F. Van Loan. *Matrix computations*. Johns Hopkins University Press, Baltimore, Maryland, 1996.

Discussion

Last-minute visa problems prevented Zhaohui Sun from attending, so Terry Boult gave the talk. A response from the authors is also included below.

Kenichi Kanatani: Why do you bother with covariance propagation? If you do covariance propagation and you do simulations and your analysis agrees with the experiment, that proves only that your analysis is correct. To me, what is more important is to analyze the theoretical accuracy bound, based in this case on the Fischer information. If you compute the Fischer information and do the simulation and your results agree with the theoretical analysis, then your method is optimal, otherwise it is not. If you once confirm that the method is optimal you can use the Fischer information as the potential, or characteristic, of noise behaviour instead of doing covariance propagation. So to me Fischer information is more essential than covariance propagation.

Terry Boult: This is not my paper, so I'm not going to put on a hat and say I believe this or that is the right approach. But I can answer partially, because we talked about this during visits to Siemens. This paper does covariance propagation using a first-order approximation to the covariance. That's good, but it isn't as useful as propagating the exact covariances would be. But they don't know how to do that yet.

Kenichi Kanatani: The next question is very simple. I think you can do all this covariance propagation analysis using software, using automatic differentiation tools. Why bother with these analytical or Taylor expansions?

Terry Boult: Well, for a particular set of data you could simulate for a long time and say yes, I can do numerical simulation and estimate the covariance by just taking the inputs and outputs. The advantage of doing it analytically is that the approximate output covariance can be directly predicted for any particular set of matrices and cameras.

Kenichi Kanatani: Not numerical simulation. There are software tools available to automatically differentiate given formula expressions.

Terry Boult: Do those tools automatically give the error on the eigenvectors of a matrix? – I'm unaware of such tools. If you can give me a reference I'll pass it back to the authors.

Rick Szeliski: One of your motivations was to identify points that have a lot of uncertainty and throw them out. But when you triangulate a point that is far from you, you typically do have a lot of uncertainty. Yet you don't usually throw it away, you simply declare that it was not very reliably measurable in absolute terms. Could you clarify that?

Terry Boult: Personally, I agree with you. I wouldn't throw points out just because they are noisy. But the SFM problem is completely interspersed, shape and motion come together, so you may be better off temporarily throwing out any especially troublesome points, computing the stabler ones, then recalculating the difficult ones by some other technique. But as I said, the importance of a feature, just because it is distant or possibly unreliable, is different from its noisiness.

Joss Knight: Presumably you could use this in robust correspondence techniques. Incorrectly matched points would have a huge covariance error, and you could just get rid of them and recalculate.

Terry Boult: It's not clear. If you redid this analysis with some points that were very incorrectly matched, the eigenstructure would become very different and the perturbation expansion, at least in theory, would no longer apply. So until someone has implemented and experimented with it, it is not clear how valuable this approach would prove. What happens is that as soon as you get some false correspondences, your fourth eigenvalue increases in value very quickly.

The authors: Note that our paper illustrates how small perturbation analysis can be applied to SVD based estimation schemes. This is of general interest for a whole range of vision problems.

Prof. Kanatani's question is interesting. The Cramér-Rao bound does of course give the optimal minimum variance unbiased estimator. But in the broader context of vision *systems*, accuracy is not the only requirement. The design engineer also has computational constraints to meet, and procedures with suboptimal accuracy may be preferred. Covariance propagation makes perfect sense in this context. To determine how system design choices affect the total system, we need to study the performance as a function of input data, algorithm and tuning parameters. Our philosophy is that each vision algorithm or module should be treated as an estimator (linear or non-linear depending on the sub-task) and characterized in terms of the bias and covariance of its estimates. Suppose SFM is one module of a vision algorithm chain involving point extraction, tracking, SFM (*e.g.* affine shape estimation), and image-based rendering. To predict the final output (image-based rendering) error, we use covariance propagation on a bias-covariance characterization of the error of each module in the chain. The chosen SFM module may satisfy the end-to-end system accuracy and speed requirements without being optimally accurate.

Rick Szeliski and Joss Knight ask the related question of how the covariance estimates should be used in practice. We have not yet explored the practical implications of the theoretical results very thoroughly, but feature selection based on error measures is certainly a possibility. Several issues remain: 1) The error analysis uses small perturbation assumptions. Large deviations (*e.g.* incorrectly matched points) may lead to large changes in the eigensystem, whose effect has not been analyzed. 2) In principle, Rick's observation that one has to keep some points with large variance is correct (as long as there are no matching errors). The point covariances are functions of the geometry (the depths of the 3D point, the camera view points). This makes it difficult to tell whether a large variance was due to insufficient (ill-conditioned) data or outliers (incorrectly matched points). 3) The uncertainty of the image features is a function of the operators used to detect and track them and the underlying geometric and illumination models. Heteroscedasticity is to be expected.

Bootstrapping Errors-in-Variables Models

Bogdan Matei and Peter Meer

Electrical and Computer Engineering Department
Rutgers University, Piscataway, NJ, 08854-8058, USA
matei, meer@caip.rutgers.edu

Abstract. The bootstrap is a numerical technique, with solid theoretical foundations, to obtain statistical measures about the quality of an estimate by using only the available data. Performance assessment through bootstrap provides the same or better accuracy than the traditional error propagation approach, most often without requiring complex analytical derivations. In many computer vision tasks a regression problem in which the measurement errors are point dependent has to be solved. Such regression problems are called *heteroscedastic* and appear in the linearization of quadratic forms in ellipse fitting and epipolar geometry, in camera calibration, or in 3D rigid motion estimation. The performance of these complex vision tasks is difficult to evaluate analytically, therefore we propose in this paper the use of bootstrap. The technique is illustrated for 3D rigid motion and fundamental matrix estimation. Experiments with real and synthetic data show the validity of bootstrap as an evaluation tool and the importance of taking the heteroscedasticity into account.

1 Introduction

No estimation process is complete without reliable information about the accuracy of the solution. Standard error, bias, or confidence interval are among the most often used statistical measures, however, in practice their computation is difficult especially when there is no information available about the distribution of the noise process and the ground truth.

The traditional approach to error analysis in computer vision is *error propagation* [7, pp.125–164][8, 20]. For highly nonlinear transfer functions the validity of error propagation is restricted to a small neighborhood around the estimate. Analytical computation of the required Jacobians is often very difficult.

In this paper we make extensive use of a new paradigm for error analysis with solid theoretical foundations, *the bootstrap*. Being a numerical technique, the bootstrap can substitute the analytical derivations of the error propagation with simulations derived exclusively from the data. More importantly, since the error propagation is only a first order approximation, the bootstrap is more accurate and has a larger applicability [5, pp.313–315]. Though the bootstrap principle looks similar to Monte Carlo simulations, the main difference between them is that the former uses only the corrupted data, while the latter needs ground truth information.

B. Triggs, A. Zisserman, R. Szeliski (Eds.): Vision Algorithms'99, LNCS 1883, pp. 236–252, 2000.
© Springer-Verlag Berlin Heidelberg 2000

The bootstrapping of a regression model, a distinct topic of the bootstrap methodology, was widely investigated in numerous references, yet most of the work was focused on ordinary regression where the explanatory variables are assumed free of measurement errors. The vast majority of regression problems encountered in computer vision applications do however have errors in the explanatory variables. What complicates further the estimation and evaluation of these errors-in-variables (EIV) models is the fact that each measurement might have a different uncertainty about its true value. The linearization of quadratic or bilinear forms encountered in ellipse fitting, respectively epipolar geometry, or the 3D rigid motion with the 3D data extracted from stereo, all yield point dependent measurement errors. The EIV regression having point dependent measurement errors is called *heteroscedastic (HEIV) regression*. By extension the point dependent errors are called next *heteroscedastic noise*.

Since the bootstrap requirement of i.i.d. data is not respected by the HEIV model, the data can not be used directly in the resampling process. In this paper we propose a versatile technique in which the noise affecting the measurements is recovered by an estimator taking into account the heteroscedasticity. The noise process is then transformed to obey the requirements of the bootstrap.

The problem domains chosen to illustrate the bootstrap based error analysis paradigm are the 3D rigid motion and fundamental matrix estimation. The paper is organized as follows. In Section 2 the bootstrap paradigm is introduced. The analysis of rigid motion using bootstrap is presented in Section 3. Bootstrap based performance assessment of the fundamental matrix estimation is described in Section 4.

2   Bootstrap

The bootstrap is a resampling method which extracts valid statistical measures like standard error, bias or confidence intervals in an automatic manner by means of computer intensive simulations using only the available data. Since its introduction in the late 70's by Bradley Efron, the bootstrap has evolved into a very powerful tool supported by numerous theoretical studies. Though the underlying principle is fairly simple, the use of bootstrap in a practical problem should always be preceded by a careful analysis. When the assumptions (to be specified below) upon which the bootstrap is based are violated inconsistent and misleading results may be obtained. A thorough introduction to the bootstrap methodology is the textbook of Efron and Tibshirani [5], while additional material can be found in [4]. A short review is given next.

2.1   Introduction to Bootstrap

A first condition for the validity of the bootstrap procedure is that the available data points $\{z_1, z_2, \cdots, z_n\}$ are i.i.d. Their distribution F is assumed unknown. In the absence of any prior information the empirical distribution $\hat{F}$, obtained by assigning equal probability $1/n$ on each measurement z_i, is used as a representation of the true distribution F. The data is employed to estimate a p-dimensional statistics $\boldsymbol{\theta} = \boldsymbol{\theta}(F)$. Let $\hat{\boldsymbol{\theta}} = g(z_1, z_2, \cdots, z_n)$ be such an estimate. If the probability distribution was known, the computation of the bias or covariance of $\hat{\boldsymbol{\theta}}$ would be immediate and could be achieved by either a theoretical derivation or Monte Carlo simulations as

$$\boldsymbol{\mu}_F(\hat{\boldsymbol{\theta}}) = E_F[\hat{\boldsymbol{\theta}}] - \boldsymbol{\theta}, \quad \mathbf{cov}_F(\hat{\boldsymbol{\theta}}) = E_F\left[\left(\hat{\boldsymbol{\theta}} - E_F[\hat{\boldsymbol{\theta}}]\right)\left(\hat{\boldsymbol{\theta}} - E_F[\hat{\boldsymbol{\theta}}]\right)^{\top}\right], \quad (1)$$

where $E_F[\cdot]$ is the expectation under the probability distribution F. Since F is unknown, the bootstrap approximates (1) by resampling the data from the available $\hat{F}$ distribution. The value z^* is drawn with replacement from $\{z_1, z_2, \cdots, z_n\}$. By repeating this resampling n times a *bootstrap sample* or *bootstrap set*, denoted by $\{z_1^*, z_2^*, \cdots, z_n^*\}$, is generated. Let $\hat{\boldsymbol{\theta}}^* = g(z_1^*, z_2^*, \cdots, z_n^*)$. The bootstrap approximation to (1) is

$$\boldsymbol{\mu}_{\hat{F}}(\hat{\boldsymbol{\theta}}) = E_{\hat{F}}[\hat{\boldsymbol{\theta}}^*] - \hat{\boldsymbol{\theta}}, \quad \mathbf{cov}_{\hat{F}}(\hat{\boldsymbol{\theta}}) = E_{\hat{F}}\left[\left(\hat{\boldsymbol{\theta}}^* - E_{\hat{F}}[\hat{\boldsymbol{\theta}}^*]\right)\left(\hat{\boldsymbol{\theta}}^* - E_{\hat{F}}[\hat{\boldsymbol{\theta}}^*]\right)^{\top}\right]. \quad (2)$$

In practice, the sample moments are used to approximate (2) by generating B bootstrap sets. Thus,

$$\boldsymbol{\mu}_{\hat{F}}(\hat{\boldsymbol{\theta}}) \cong \hat{\boldsymbol{\mu}}_{\hat{\theta}} = \bar{\boldsymbol{\theta}}^* - \hat{\boldsymbol{\theta}} \qquad \bar{\boldsymbol{\theta}}^* = \frac{1}{B}\sum_{b=1}^{B}\hat{\boldsymbol{\theta}}^{*b}, \quad (3)$$

$$\mathbf{cov}_{\hat{F}}(\hat{\boldsymbol{\theta}}) \cong \hat{\boldsymbol{C}}_{\hat{\theta}} = \frac{1}{B-1}\sum_{b=1}^{B}\left[\hat{\boldsymbol{\theta}}^{*b} - \bar{\boldsymbol{\theta}}^*\right]\left[\hat{\boldsymbol{\theta}}^{*b} - \bar{\boldsymbol{\theta}}^*\right]^{\top}. \quad (4)$$

The bias corrected covariance matrix of $\hat{\boldsymbol{\theta}}$ is

$$\hat{\boldsymbol{\Omega}}_{\hat{\theta}} = \hat{\boldsymbol{C}}_{\hat{\theta}} + \boldsymbol{\mu}_{\hat{\theta}}\,\hat{\boldsymbol{\mu}}_{\hat{\theta}}^{\top}. \quad (5)$$

The two approximations, the substitution of $\hat{F}$ for F and the replacement of the sample moments for the true ones, are the main sources of inaccuracy of the bootstrap technique. If the number of measurements is too small (say below 20), the variability of the bootstrap estimates becomes too large for the results to be reliable.

When the assumption of i.i.d. data is not valid the bootstrap may fail. This means that the outliers in the data must be removed before the resampling is performed, i.e. the preprocessing should be robust. Diagnostic methods, like *jackknife after bootstrap* [4, pp.113–123], can be employed to evaluate the bootstrap estimate, however, due to the masking effects these techniques have only limited sensitivity in the presence of significant contamination.

Most of the theoretical results which validate the bootstrap paradigm are obtained by Edgeworth expansions assuming a smooth estimator. For non-smooth estimators there are methods which can be used instead, but they do not enjoy the same accuracy as the bootstrap itself [4, pp.41–44]. The classical example where the bootstrap completely fails is the sample median. One should be therefore extremely circumspect in using the techniques described above for estimators based on the median or other nonlinearities. The bootstrap procedure should be only applied to the data obtained at the *output* of high breakdown point robust estimators like the least median of squares.

The traditional approach based on error propagation approximates $\mathbf{cov}(\hat{\boldsymbol{\theta}})$

$$\hat{\boldsymbol{C}}_{\hat{\theta}} = \sum_{i=1}^{n} \left[\frac{\partial \boldsymbol{g}}{\partial \boldsymbol{z}_i} \right] \boldsymbol{C}_{z_i} \left[\frac{\partial \boldsymbol{g}}{\partial \boldsymbol{z}_i} \right]^{\top} \Bigg|_{z_i = \hat{z}_i} , \tag{6}$$

where $\boldsymbol{C}_{z_i}$ is the covariance of the data $\boldsymbol{z}_i$ and $\left[\frac{\partial \boldsymbol{g}}{\partial \boldsymbol{z}_i} \right]$ is the Jacobian of the transformation from $\boldsymbol{z}_i$ to $\hat{\boldsymbol{\theta}} = \boldsymbol{g}(\boldsymbol{z}_1, \boldsymbol{z}_2, \cdots, \boldsymbol{z}_n)$. Approximating $\mathbf{cov}(\hat{\boldsymbol{\theta}})$ by bootstrap (4) eliminates the need for analytical derivations in the Jacobian calculation, at the expense of an increased amount of computer simulations.

The bootstrap can be also used in constructing elliptical confidence regions for $\hat{\boldsymbol{\theta}}$. They have better coverage compared with the rectangular ones since they exploit the existing correlation between the components of $\hat{\boldsymbol{\theta}}$ and can be obtained even when the normality assumption fails [16].

The exact number of bootstrap samples B required to compute the covariance matrix $\hat{\boldsymbol{C}}_{\hat{\theta}}$ or the confidence regions is difficult to prescribe. In practice, especially when the computation of $\hat{\boldsymbol{\theta}}$ is time consuming, the trade-off is between the accuracy of the bootstrap solution and the time spent on simulations.

We have found that $B = 200$ usually suffices for a good covariance estimation.

2.2   Bootstrap for HEIV Regression

The bootstrap method introduced in Section 2.1 cannot be applied directly to HEIV regression. Assume that the true, unknown measurements $\boldsymbol{z}_{io}$, $i = 1, \cdots, n$ are additively corrupted with heteroscedastic noise $\delta \boldsymbol{z}_i$ having zero mean and point dependent covariance $\boldsymbol{C}_{z_i}$. The covariances are known up to a common multiplicative factor, the noise variance σ^2. The true values $\boldsymbol{z}_{io}$ obey the linear model $\alpha + \boldsymbol{z}_{io}^{\top} \boldsymbol{\theta} = 0$.

The covariance, bias and confidence regions of a given estimator $\{\hat{\boldsymbol{\theta}}, \hat{\alpha}\}$ are obtained by bootstrap using the procedure sketched in Figure 1. An estimator which takes into account the heteroscedasticity of the data (HEIV block) is employed to obtain the corrected data $\hat{\boldsymbol{z}}_i$ by projecting $\boldsymbol{z}_i$ onto hyperplane of the solution $\{\hat{\boldsymbol{\theta}}, \hat{\alpha}\}$. In order to satisfy the i.i.d. condition the residuals $\delta \hat{\boldsymbol{z}}_i = \boldsymbol{z}_i - \hat{\boldsymbol{z}}_i$ are whitened using the corresponding covariances $\boldsymbol{C}_{\delta \hat{z}_i}$. See (A.10) for their expression. The whitened residuals are sampled with replacement and colored with the corresponding covariances $\boldsymbol{C}_{z_i}$. The bootstrapped data is finally obtained by adding the resampled noise to the corrected data $\hat{\boldsymbol{z}}_i$. Any estimator can now be evaluated through bootstrap using (3) and (4).

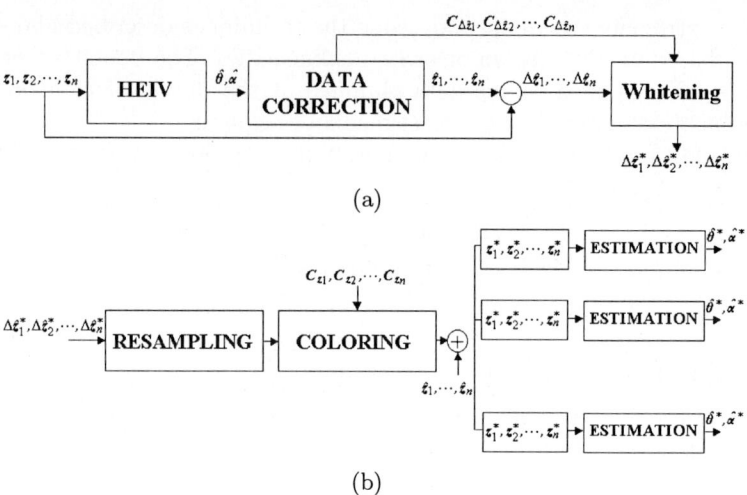

(a)

(b)

Fig. 1. Bootstrapping in a heteroscedastic environment. (a) Recovery of an i.i.d. noise process using the HEIV estimator. (b) Generation of bootstrap samples by coloring the i.i.d. residuals. Any estimator can now be evaluated.

3 Rigid Motion Evaluation

Rigid motion estimation is a basic problem in middle-level computer vision, thoroughly analyzed in numerous papers. Two of the most popular rigid motion estimators are based on the SVD decomposition [1, 24] and on the quaternion representation [11]. Both assume i.i.d. data and give exactly the same results [6]. The 3D rigid motion estimation under heteroscedastic noise was investigated by Pennec and Thirion [20]. They used an extended Kalman filter for finding the motion parameters and obtained closed-form expressions for the covariance of the rotation and translation based on error propagation. However, the data was processed sequentially, and thus not all the available information being taken into account at each processing stage. The computation of the Jacobians entering the expressions of the covariance matrices was quite complex. Recently, Ohta and Kanatani [17] introduced an algorithm for rotation estimation under heteroscedastic noise based on an optimization technique called *renormalization* and provided a lower bound on the covariance of the rotation. However, the analysis was restricted to pure rotation and in the presence of a translation component the estimator was no longer optimal.

The bootstrap methodology introduced in Section 2 is utilized in the sequel in the analysis of 3D rigid motion. Reliable assessment of the accuracy of the solution yielded by an *arbitrary* rigid motion algorithm under heteroscedastic noise is provided using only the available data.

Let the two sets of matched 3D measurements be $U = \{u_1, u_2, \cdots, u_n\}$ and $V = \{v_1, v_2, \cdots, v_n\}$. Each measurement is a corrupted version of the true value, distinguished by the subscript 'o',

$$u_i = u_{io} + \delta u_i \qquad v_i = v_{io} + \delta v_i \ .$$

The heteroscedastic noise has zero-mean and data dependent covariance $E[\delta u_i \delta u_i^\top] = C_{u_i}$, and $E[\delta v_i \delta v_i^\top] = C_{v_i}$ respectively. Rigid motion estimation is a multivariate EIV regression problem, since the true values satisfy the 3D rigid motion constraint

$$v_{io} = R u_{io} + t \ , \tag{7}$$

where R is the 3×3 rotation matrix and t is the translation vector.

The quaternion representation of the rotation matrix transforms (7) into an equivalent multivariate linear regression [16]

$$\alpha + M_o q = 0 \ , \tag{8}$$

where M_o is a 3×4 matrix obtained from the true coordinates, q is the quaternion of the rotation and α is the intercept depending on q and t. A solution of (8) taking into account the heteroscedasticity was presented in [16] and is summarized in Appendix A.

Let $\hat{R}$ and $\hat{t}$ be the rotation and translation given by a consistent rigid motion estimator, i.e. which reaches the true solution asymptotically. We have used the HEIV algorithm which satisfies this consistency requirement.

The residuals $\delta\hat{v}_i = v_i - \hat{v}_i$ and $\delta\hat{u}_i$ (B.1) are obtained by orthogonal projection of the measurements v_i and u_i onto the three dimensional manifold defined by $\hat{R}$ and $\hat{t}$ in $\mathcal{R}^6$. as shown in Appendix B t he corrected points $\hat{v}_i$ and $\hat{u}_i$ can be considered unbiased estimators of the true, unknown measurements $\hat{v}_{io}$ and $\hat{u}_{io}$ when the estimates $\hat{R}$ and $\hat{t}$ are close to the true R and t. The residuals are not i.i.d. having their covariance dependent on the measurement index i. Therefore, to correctly apply the bootstrap procedure a whiten-color cycle is therefore necessary (see Section 2.2).

The bootstrap of residuals method required a consistent estimator. Once the correct noise process is recovered, however, *any* rigid motion estimator (consistent or not) can be analyzed in the same *automatic* manner.

Let $\hat{R}^{*b}$ and $\hat{t}^{*b}$ be the rotation and translation yielded by an *arbitrary* estimator using the bootstrap sample b. The covariance and bias for translation can be estimated using (3) and (4), but for the covariance of rotation the fact that the rotations form a multiplicative group must be taken into account [20]. Let the three-dimensional vector r be the angle-axis representation of the rotation matrix R, defined as $r = f(R)$. The rotation error between the estimate $\hat{R}$ and R is then $\delta\hat{r} = f(\hat{R}R^\top)$, and the bootstrap for the covariance of the rotation $\hat{C}_{\hat{r}}$ uses in (4) the $\delta\hat{r}^{*b} = f(\hat{R}^{*b}\hat{R}^\top)$.

Though confidence regions can be computed separately for $\hat{R}$ and $\hat{t}$, a better joint coverage is obtained by exploiting the existing correlation between the rotation and translation estimates. Define the motion estimation error $\hat{\epsilon}$ as the six-dimensional vector

$$\hat{\epsilon} = \left[(\hat{t} - t)^\top \ \delta\hat{r}^\top \right]^\top \ . \tag{9}$$

The confidence region in $\mathcal{R}^6$ for the rigid motion parameters is constructed using the error terms $\hat{\boldsymbol{\epsilon}}^{*b} = [\,(\hat{\boldsymbol{t}}^{*b} - \hat{\boldsymbol{t}})^\top \; \delta\hat{\boldsymbol{r}}^{*b\top}\,]^\top$, see Section 2.

3.1   Experiments with Synthetic Data

The simulated setting used in our experiments consists of a stereo head moved around a fixed scene. The cameras had zero vergence and focal distance $f = 536$ yielding a field of view of $50°$ on both x and y axes. The baseline of the stereo head was 100 and the image planes were 500×500, all values being in pixel units. The $n = 50$ three-dimensional points were uniformly generated inside a cube with the side length 800 placed at 1300 in front of the cameras. The 3D points are projected onto the image planes, corrupted by adding normal noise with $\sigma = 1$ and then allocated to the nearest lattice site. The 3D information is recovered using Kanatani's triangulation method [14, pp.171–186]. For this type of triangulation there are close form expressions for $\boldsymbol{C}_{v_i}$ and $\boldsymbol{C}_{u_i}$, however we preferred the bootstrap computation described in [16] since is more general, being also applicable to any other triangulation method like those presented in [10, 23].

The bootstrapped covariance matrices $\hat{\boldsymbol{C}}_{u_i}$ inflated to assure an individual coverage of 0.95 are represented in Figure 2 for ten data points. The equivalent error is much higher on the depth and depends on the position of the 3D point in space, thus confirming the theoretical results [2, 21].

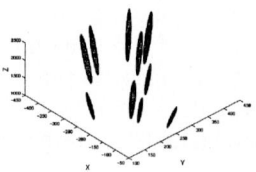

Fig. 2. The covariance matrices $\hat{\boldsymbol{C}}_{u_i}$ extracted by bootstrap for the 3D data points. Note the heteroscedasticity.

The analysis of the rigid motion employed $B = 200$ bootstrap samples generated as discussed in Section 3. The validity of the bootstrap was verified using a Monte Carlo analysis based on the true values and the continuous noise process. Recall that the bootstrap uses *only* the available quantized data.

For both methods the covariance matrices were estimated using $B = 200$ samples. Fifty trials, each having the motion parameters randomly generated (chosen such that the scene remains in the field of view of the cameras) and different 3D point configurations were performed.

In Figure 3 the translation and rotation error $\|\delta t\| = [\mathrm{trace}(\boldsymbol{\Omega}_{\hat{t}})]^{\frac{1}{2}}$, $\|\delta r\| = [\mathrm{trace}(\boldsymbol{\Omega}_{\hat{r}})]^{\frac{1}{2}}$ are plotted for the HEIV and quaternion algorithms using the bootstrap and the Monte Carlo estimates for $\boldsymbol{\Omega}_{\hat{t}}$, $\boldsymbol{\Omega}_{\hat{r}}$ (5).

Note the very good agreement between the bootstrap and Monte Carlo error estimates and the larger translation and rotation error yielded by the quaternion

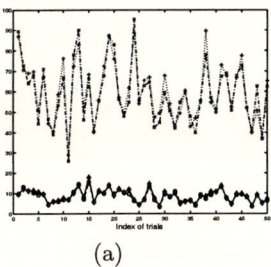 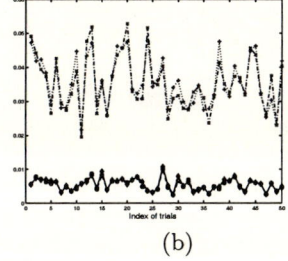

(a)   (b)

Fig. 3. Comparison between the bootstrap (BT) and Monte Carlo (MC) error estimates for HEIV and the quaternion method. (a) Translation, (b) Rotation; 'o' MC estimate for HEIV, 'o' BT estimate for HEIV, '+' MC estimate for quaternion, 'x' BT estimate for quaternion.

method compared with the HEIV algorithm. The same approach can be used to compare the performance of other motion estimators, however, the bootstrap must use the residuals generated by a consistent estimator like HEIV.

3.2 Experiments with Real Data

The CIL-CMU database consists of four data sets: *castle, planar texture, wall & tower* and *copper tea kettle*. Each set consists of 11 frames for which precise ground truth information is available. Lack of space prohibits us to present all the results and we describe only the experiments using the frames 1, 4, 5 and 9 from *the planar texture* set.

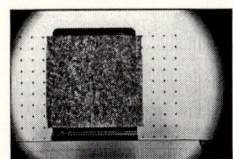 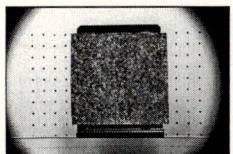

Fig. 4. Frames one and four from the Planar Textures images from CIL-CMU database.

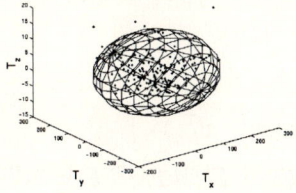 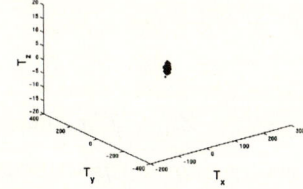

Fig. 5. Uncertainty of the translation estimation for the quaternion (left) and the HEIV (right), evaluated by bootstrap. The ellipsoids assure a 0.95 coverage for the true translation. Both plots are at the same scale.

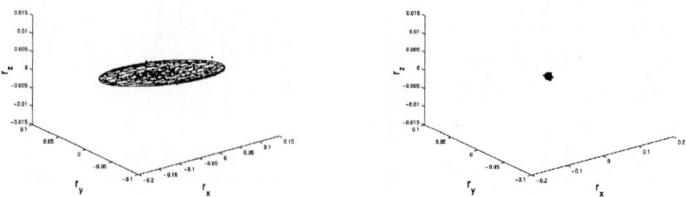

Fig. 6. Uncertainty of the rotation estimation for the quaternion (left) and the HEIV (right) evaluated by bootstrap. The ellipsoids assure a 0.95 coverage for the true rotation. Both plots are at the same scale.

The 3D information was extracted by triangulation from image points obtained by the matching program of Z. Zhang [25]. The estimation used 46 measurements. The true translation was $t = [79.957 \; -0.503 \; -1.220]^\top$ and the rotation in angle-axis representation $r = 0.001 \cdot [0.619 \; 0.193 \; 0.013]$. The quaternion algorithm estimates erroneously the translation and rotation yielding $\hat{t} = [-159.001 \; 69.867 \; 13.050]^\top$, respectively $\hat{r} = [0.035 \; 0.118 \; -0.013]^\top$. On the other hand the HEIV solution is much closer to the true value, being $\hat{t} = [56.094 \; 6.492 \; -1.392]^\top$ and $\hat{r} = [0.004 \; 0.012 \; -0.001]^\top$.

The bootstrapped covariance matrices of the estimates $\hat{R}$, $\hat{t}$ for the quaternion and HEIV methods are plotted in Figures 5 and 6. As expected the quaternion based algorithm has a much larger variability than the HEIV, since it assumes i.i.d. data.

4   Bootstrapping the Fundamental Matrix

The geometry of a stereo head is captured by the epipolar geometry. In the case of uncalibrated cameras the relationship between the two sets of matched points $\{x_{lio}\}$, $\{x_{rio}\}$ in the right, respectively the left image can be expressed using the fundamental matrix F as

$$\varphi(x_{io}, \; F) = \begin{bmatrix} x_{rio}^\top \; 1 \end{bmatrix} F \begin{bmatrix} x_{lio} \\ 1 \end{bmatrix} = 0, \quad x_{io}^\top = [x_{lio}^\top \; x_{rio}^\top], \qquad i = 1, \cdots, n \quad (10)$$

The eight-point algorithm introduced by Longuet-Higgins [19] solves the linearized epipolar constraint

$$\alpha + Z_{io}\theta = 0 \tag{11}$$

$$Z_{io} = Z(x_{io}) = \begin{bmatrix} x_{io}^\top \; \mathrm{vec}\left(x_{rio} \; x_{lio}^\top\right)^\top \end{bmatrix} \tag{12}$$

$$\alpha = F^{(33)} \qquad \theta^\top = [F^{(31)} \; F^{(32)} \; F^{(13)} \; F^{(23)} \; F^{(11)} \; F^{(21)} \; F^{(12)} \; F^{(22)}] \;, \tag{13}$$

where $\mathrm{vec}(A)$ denotes the vectorization of the matrix A. The procedure is equivalent to a Total Least Squares (TLS) solution of a regression model. The sensitivity of the eight-point algorithm to noise affecting the image points is partially remedied by normalizing the image points as shown by Hartley [10]. The normalized eight-point algorithm can be subsequently refined using nonlinear criteria (distance from the noisy image points to the epipolar lines, the Gold Standard, etc.) and the Levenberg-Marquardt optimization technique. A comprehensive review of the nonlinear criteria is [26].

The uncertainty of the fundamental matrix computation can be characterized by the covariance matrix of F and the confidence bands for the epipolar lines [3]. In [3] the covariance of F was computed in two ways: using error propagation and performing Monte Carlo simulations. The former method had the advantage of yielding closed-form covariance estimates, but the computations involved were quite involved. In the latter technique, B realizations of the fundamental matrix were computed by adding normal noise to the *noisy* image points. The sample covariance matrix was finally determined from these fundamental matrix realizations. The ad-hoc choice for the noise standard deviation and the addition of noise on the image points (already noisy) are the major shortcomings of this approach. These deficiencies can be solved by the bootstrap methodology presented below.

The HEIV algorithm can be used to solve (11) and to extract the statistical information required by the bootstrap [15]. Assuming for simplicity that the image points x_{io} are corrupted by zero-mean, i.i.d. noise $\delta x_i \sim GI(0, \sigma^2 I_4)$, the *carriers* Z_{io} are corrupted by *heteroscedastic* noise

$$\delta Z_i \sim GI(0, \sigma^2 C_{Z_i}), \quad C_{Z_i} \approx \left[\frac{\partial Z_i}{\partial x_i}\right] \left[\frac{\partial Z_i}{\partial x_i}\right]^{\mathsf{T}},$$

with $GI(\mu, C)$ standing for general and independent distribution with mean μ and covariance C. The HEIV estimates the noise variance $\hat{\sigma}^2$ in (A.9) and the fundamental matrix $\hat{F}$ from $\hat{\theta}$ and $\hat{\alpha}$. It can be shown (the proof is beyond the scope of the paper) that the HEIV corrected image points $\hat{x}_i$ obeying $\varphi(\hat{x}_i, \hat{F}) = 0$ are obtained by iteratively solving the equation

$$\hat{x}_i = x_i - \left[\frac{\partial Z_i}{\partial \hat{x}_i}\right]^{\mathsf{T}} \hat{\Theta} \hat{\Sigma}_i^{-} \varphi(x_i, \hat{F}) \tag{14}$$

where $\hat{\Theta}$ and $\hat{\Sigma}_i$ are defined in (A.3). The rank-one covariance of the residuals $\delta \hat{x}_i = x_i - \hat{x}_i$ is

$$C_{\delta \hat{x}_i} = \left[\frac{\partial Z_i}{\partial \hat{x}_i}\right]^{\mathsf{T}} \hat{\Theta} \hat{\Sigma}_i^{-} \hat{\Theta}^{\mathsf{T}} \left[\frac{\partial Z_i}{\partial \hat{x}_i}\right]. \tag{15}$$

With the residuals $\delta \hat{x}_i$ and their covariance matrices (15) available, the bootstrap can be applied as shown in Section 2.2.

4.1   Experiments with Synthetic Data

A synthetic camera with the geometry depicted in Figure 7 is used in the following simulations. The image plane is 500×500 and the focal distance is $f = 117$, corresponding to a field of view of 130°, all units being in pixels. The 3D points are generated in a cube with side equal to 2000 and with the center placed in front of the cameras at $Z = 1500$. Normal noise with zero-mean and $\sigma = 3$ was added to $n = 50$ matched image points. To illustrate the potential of the proposed technique we applied it to a well known method for recovering the fundamental matrix, the normalized eight-point algorithm.

Statistical measures for the normalized eight-point estimates are extracted with bootstrap and Monte Carlo simulations for comparison. The HEIV algorithm is used to recover the residuals and their covariance matrices, as described

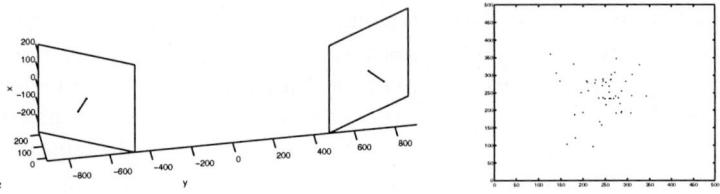

Fig. 7. The stereo head used in the simulations and the points in the left image.

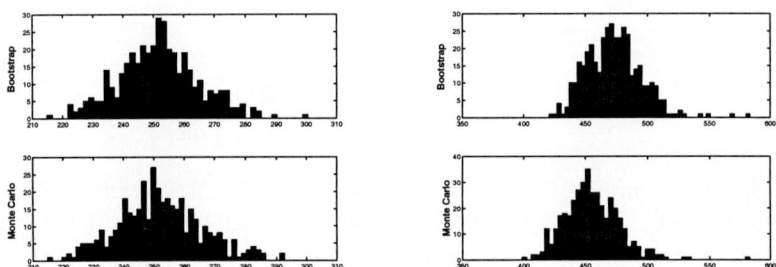

Fig. 8. Histogram of the x (left) and y (right) coordinates of the left epipole estimated with the normalized eight-point algorithm from data obtained through bootstrap and Monte Carlo.

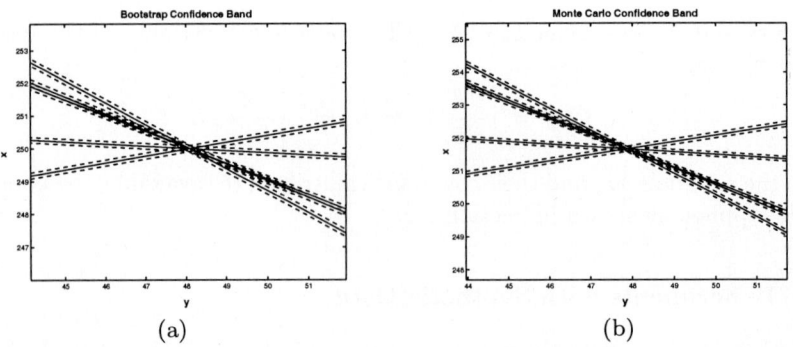

Fig. 9. Confidence bands for the epipolar lines in the right image created with bootstrap (a) and Monte Carlo simulations (b).

above. In Figure 8 the histograms of $B = 400$ bootstrap and Monte Carlo samples of the left epipole estimates are shown. Note the good approximation of the true distribution (Monte Carlo) obtained through bootstrap, which used only *one* set of data points.

Most often the uncertainty in the fundamental matrix estimation is represented through the confidence bands of the epipolar lines [3]. In Figure 9 such confidence bands for four epipolar lines in the right image are plotted using the bootstrap and Monte Carlo estimates for the covariance of $\boldsymbol{F}$. Note the slight difference between the two plots. The bootstrap samples are distributed around $\hat{\boldsymbol{F}}$, the only information available from the image pair. The Monte Carlo simulation, on the other hand, is distributed around the true $\boldsymbol{F}$.

5   Conclusion

We have exploited the bootstrap paradigm for the analysis of heteroscedastic errors-in-variables models. We have shown that through this method valuable information can be recovered solely from the data, which can be integrated into the subsequent processing modules.

Acknowledgments

The support of NSF Grant IRI-9530546 is gratefully acknowledged. The authors thank David Tyler and Yoram Leedan for valuable discussions.

A   HEIV Regression

A short presentation of the HEIV algorithm applied to multivariate regression is given next. Assume that the true values $\boldsymbol{z}_{io}^{(k)} \in \mathcal{R}^p$, $i = 1, \cdots, n$ satisfy the multivariate linear model

$$\boldsymbol{\alpha} + \boldsymbol{Z}_{io}\boldsymbol{\theta} = 0, \qquad \boldsymbol{\theta} \in \mathcal{R}^p, \quad \boldsymbol{\alpha} \in \mathcal{R}^m, \quad \boldsymbol{Z}_{io} = \left[\boldsymbol{z}_{io}^{(1)} \cdots \boldsymbol{z}_{io}^{(m)} \right]^\top .$$

The true values $\boldsymbol{z}_{io}^{(k)}$ are corrupted by heteroscedastic noise $\delta\boldsymbol{z}_i^{(k)}$, $\boldsymbol{z}_i^{(k)} = \boldsymbol{z}_{io}^{(k)} + \delta\boldsymbol{z}_i^{(k)}$ with

$$E\left[\delta\boldsymbol{z}_i^{(k)}\right] = 0, \qquad \mathrm{cov}\left[\delta\boldsymbol{z}_i^{(k)}, \delta\boldsymbol{z}_i^{(l)}\right] = \boldsymbol{C}_i^{(kl)}, \quad k, l = 1, \cdots, m .$$

Define

$$\boldsymbol{w}_{io} = \mathrm{vec}(\boldsymbol{Z}_{io}^\top), \quad \delta\boldsymbol{w}_i = \mathrm{vec}(\delta\boldsymbol{Z}_i^\top), \quad \boldsymbol{C}_i = \left[\boldsymbol{C}_i^{(kl)}\right] .$$

The estimates $\hat{\boldsymbol{\theta}}$, $\hat{\boldsymbol{\alpha}}$ are determined minimizing

$$J = \frac{1}{2} \sum_{i=1}^n (\boldsymbol{w}_i - \boldsymbol{w}_{io})^\top \boldsymbol{C}_i^- (\boldsymbol{w}_i - \boldsymbol{w}_{io}) \tag{A.1}$$

subject to the constraint $\hat{\boldsymbol{\alpha}} + \boldsymbol{Z}_{io}\hat{\boldsymbol{\theta}} = 0$.

In practice $z_{io}^{(k)}$ are unavailable. Let $\hat{z}_i^{(k)}$ be the corrected measurement corresponding to $z_i^{(k)}$. Using the Lagrange multipliers $\eta_i \in \mathcal{R}^m$ (A.1) becomes

$$J = \frac{1}{2} \sum_{i=1}^n (w_i - \hat{w}_i)^\top C_i^- (w_i - \hat{w}_i) + \sum_{i=1}^n \eta_i^\top (\hat{Z}_i \hat{\theta} + \hat{\alpha}) . \tag{A.2}$$

Define the $mp \times m$ matrix $\hat{\Theta}$ and the $m \times m$ matrix $\hat{\Sigma}_i$

$$\hat{\Theta} = I_m \otimes \hat{\theta}, \qquad \hat{\Sigma}_i = \hat{\Theta}^\top C_i \hat{\Theta}, \tag{A.3}$$

where $\otimes$ is the Kroneker product between two matrices. The estimates $\hat{\theta}$, $\hat{\alpha}$ and $\hat{z}_i^{(k)}$ are found by solving the system of equations

$$\nabla_{\hat{\theta}} J = 0, \quad \nabla_{\hat{\alpha}} J = 0, \quad \nabla_{\hat{z}_i^{(k)}} = 0 .$$

After some algebra the estimates $\hat{\theta}$ and $\hat{\alpha}$ are obtained by iteratively solving a generalized eigenvalue problem.

1. Compute an initial solution $\hat{\theta}^{(0)}$, for example the Total Least Squares (TLS) estimate obtained assuming i.i.d. noise. A random initial value, however, sufficed to achieve satisfactory convergence in a large range of problems.
2. Compute the matrices $\hat{\Sigma}_i$, $i = 1, \ldots, n$ using (A.3).
3. Compute the weighted "centroid" matrix $\widetilde{Z}$

$$\widetilde{Z} = \left[\sum_{i=1}^n \hat{\Sigma}_i^{-1} \right]^{-1} \left[\sum_{i=1}^n \hat{\Sigma}_i^{-1} Z_i \right] . \tag{A.4}$$

4. Compute the scatter $S\left[\hat{\theta}^{(j)}\right]$ relative to $\widetilde{Z}$

$$S\left[\hat{\theta}^{(j)}\right] = \sum_{i=1}^n \left[Z_i - \widetilde{Z} \right]^\top \hat{\Sigma}_i^{-1} \left(Z_i - \widetilde{Z} \right) \tag{A.5}$$

and the weighted covariance matrix

$$C\left[\hat{\theta}^{(j)}\right] = \sum_{i=1}^n (\eta_i \otimes I_p)^\top C_i (\eta_i \otimes I_p) \tag{A.6}$$

where the Lagrange multipliers are $\eta_i = \hat{\Sigma}_i^{-1}(Z_i - \widetilde{Z})\hat{\theta}$.
From (A.5), (A.6) $S\left[\hat{\theta}^{(j)}\right]$ and $C\left[\hat{\theta}^{(j)}\right]$ are positive semi-definite.

5. The estimate $\hat{\theta}^{(j+1)}$ is the eigenvector corresponding to the smallest eigenvalue in the generalized eigenproblem

$$S\left[\hat{\theta}^{(j)}\right] \hat{\theta}^{(j+1)} = \lambda C\left[\hat{\theta}^{(j)}\right] \hat{\theta}^{(j+1)} . \tag{A.7}$$

6. Iterate through Steps 2 to 5 until λ becomes one (up to a tolerance). Convergence is achieved after three, four iterations. Let $\hat{\boldsymbol{\theta}}$ be the final estimate.
7. Compute the intercept $\hat{\boldsymbol{\alpha}} = -\tilde{\boldsymbol{Z}}\hat{\boldsymbol{\theta}}$.
8. Compute the corrected measurements $\hat{\boldsymbol{z}}_i^{(k)}$

$$\hat{\boldsymbol{z}}_i^{(k)} = \boldsymbol{z}_i^{(k)} - \left[\sum_{l=1}^{m} \eta_{il} \boldsymbol{C}_i^{(kl)} \right] \hat{\boldsymbol{\theta}} . \tag{A.8}$$

The matrices $\boldsymbol{C}_i$ need to be known only up to a positive multiplicative constant, the equivalent noise variance which can now be estimated as

$$\hat{\sigma}^2 = \frac{\hat{\boldsymbol{\theta}}^{\top} \boldsymbol{S}[\hat{\boldsymbol{\theta}}] \hat{\boldsymbol{\theta}}}{mn - p + 1} . \tag{A.9}$$

The *a posteriori* covariance of $\hat{\boldsymbol{w}}_i = \text{vec}(\hat{\boldsymbol{Z}}_i)$ is

$$\boldsymbol{C}_{\hat{w}_i} = \boldsymbol{C}_i - \boldsymbol{C}_{\delta\hat{w}_i} = \boldsymbol{C}_i - \boldsymbol{C}_i \hat{\boldsymbol{\Theta}} \hat{\boldsymbol{\Sigma}}_i^{-1} \hat{\boldsymbol{\Theta}}^{\top} \boldsymbol{C}_i . \tag{A.10}$$

Note that $\text{rank}(\boldsymbol{C}_{\hat{w}_i}) = \text{rank}(\boldsymbol{C}_i) - m$.

The estimates $\hat{\boldsymbol{\theta}}, \hat{\boldsymbol{\alpha}}, \hat{\boldsymbol{z}}_i^{(k)}$ are consistent, i.e. they converge to the true values as the number of measurements increases. Using Taylor expansions of eigenvectors [18] a first order approximation of the covariance of the estimates $\hat{\boldsymbol{\theta}}, \hat{\boldsymbol{\alpha}}$ is

$$\boldsymbol{C}_{\hat{\theta}} = \hat{\sigma}^2 \left[\boldsymbol{S}(\hat{\boldsymbol{\theta}}) - \boldsymbol{C}(\hat{\boldsymbol{\theta}}) \right]^{-} \qquad \boldsymbol{C}_{\hat{\alpha}} = \tilde{\boldsymbol{Z}} \boldsymbol{C}_{\hat{\theta}} \tilde{\boldsymbol{Z}}^{\top} . \tag{A.11}$$

B   Analysis of the Data Correction for 3D Rigid Motion

Given the estimated motion parameters $\hat{\boldsymbol{R}}$ and $\hat{\boldsymbol{t}}$ we are interested in finding the projections $\hat{\boldsymbol{v}}_i, \hat{\boldsymbol{u}}_i$ of $\boldsymbol{v}_i$ and $\boldsymbol{u}_i$ onto the three dimensional manifold of the solution in $\mathcal{R}^6$ defined by $\hat{\boldsymbol{v}}_i = \hat{\boldsymbol{R}}\hat{\boldsymbol{u}}_i + \hat{\boldsymbol{t}}$. To simplify the notations in the sequel the measurement index i is dropped. Let

$$\boldsymbol{A} = \begin{bmatrix} \boldsymbol{I}_3 & -\hat{\boldsymbol{R}} \end{bmatrix} \quad \boldsymbol{z} = \begin{bmatrix} \boldsymbol{v} \\ \boldsymbol{u} \end{bmatrix} \quad \boldsymbol{w} = \begin{bmatrix} \boldsymbol{v} - \hat{\boldsymbol{t}} \\ \boldsymbol{u} \end{bmatrix} .$$

Thus the solution $\hat{\boldsymbol{w}}$ should satisfy $\boldsymbol{A}\hat{\boldsymbol{w}} = \boldsymbol{0}$, i.e. must be in the three-dimensional null space of $\boldsymbol{A}$. In other words, $\hat{\boldsymbol{w}}$ must be in the range space of a rank 3 matrix $\boldsymbol{B}$, chosen such that $\boldsymbol{A}\boldsymbol{B} = \boldsymbol{0}$. A natural choice is $\boldsymbol{B} = [\hat{\boldsymbol{R}}^{\top} \ \boldsymbol{I}_3]^{\top}$. Then the projection of $\boldsymbol{w}$ onto the space spanned by the columns of $\boldsymbol{B}$ under the metric given by the covariance matrix of $\boldsymbol{w}$, $\boldsymbol{C}_w$ is [22, p.386]

$$\hat{\boldsymbol{w}} = \boldsymbol{B}(\boldsymbol{B}^{\top} \boldsymbol{C}_w^{-1} \boldsymbol{B})^{-1} \boldsymbol{B}^{\top} \boldsymbol{C}_w^{-1} \boldsymbol{w} = \boldsymbol{P}\boldsymbol{w} . \tag{B.1}$$

The measurements in the two sets of 3D points are uncorrelated, therefore

$$\boldsymbol{C}_z = \boldsymbol{C}_w = \begin{bmatrix} \boldsymbol{C}_v & \boldsymbol{0} \\ \boldsymbol{0} & \boldsymbol{C}_u \end{bmatrix} .$$

The projection matrix $\boldsymbol{P}$ can be expressed after some algebra as $\boldsymbol{P} = [\boldsymbol{P}_{ij}]$,

$$\boldsymbol{P}_{11} = \left[\boldsymbol{I}_3 + \boldsymbol{C}_v\hat{\boldsymbol{R}}\boldsymbol{C}_u^{-1}\hat{\boldsymbol{R}}^\top\right]^{-1} \quad \boldsymbol{P}_{22} = \left[\boldsymbol{I}_3 + \boldsymbol{C}_u\hat{\boldsymbol{R}}^\top\boldsymbol{C}_v^{-1}\hat{\boldsymbol{R}}\right]^{-1} \quad (\text{B.2})$$

$$\boldsymbol{P}_{12} = \hat{\boldsymbol{R}}\boldsymbol{P}_{22} \quad \boldsymbol{P}_{21} = \hat{\boldsymbol{R}}^\top\boldsymbol{P}_{11} . \quad (\text{B.3})$$

When the estimates $\hat{\boldsymbol{R}}$ and $\hat{\boldsymbol{t}}$ are close to the true values $\boldsymbol{R}$ and $\boldsymbol{t}$ the weighted least squares projection (B.1) implies that the estimator $\hat{\boldsymbol{z}}$ of $\boldsymbol{z}_o$ can be considered unbiased, and the residuals $\delta\hat{\boldsymbol{z}} = \boldsymbol{z} - \hat{\boldsymbol{z}}$ to have zero mean.

$$E[\hat{\boldsymbol{z}}] = \boldsymbol{z}_o \quad E[\delta\hat{\boldsymbol{z}}] = E[\boldsymbol{z}] - E[\hat{\boldsymbol{z}}] = \boldsymbol{0} . \quad (\text{B.4})$$

Using (B.1) the covariance matrices of $\hat{\boldsymbol{z}}$ and the residuals $\delta\hat{\boldsymbol{z}}$ are

$$\boldsymbol{C}_{\hat{z}} = \boldsymbol{P}\boldsymbol{C}_z\boldsymbol{P}^\top \quad \boldsymbol{C}_{\delta\hat{z}} = [\boldsymbol{I}_6 - \boldsymbol{P}]\boldsymbol{C}_z[\boldsymbol{I}_6 - \boldsymbol{P}]^\top . \quad (\text{B.5})$$

The covariance of the residuals depends only on the rotation and has rank three. From (B.2– B.3) and (B.5) the covariances for $\delta\hat{\boldsymbol{v}}$ and $\delta\hat{\boldsymbol{u}}$ are

$$\boldsymbol{C}_{\delta\hat{v}} = [\boldsymbol{I}_3 - \boldsymbol{P}_{11}]\left[\hat{\boldsymbol{R}}\boldsymbol{C}_u\hat{\boldsymbol{R}}^\top + \boldsymbol{C}_v\right][\boldsymbol{I}_3 - \boldsymbol{P}_{11}]^\top \quad (\text{B.6})$$

$$\boldsymbol{C}_{\delta\hat{u}} = [\boldsymbol{I}_3 - \boldsymbol{P}_{22}]\left[\hat{\boldsymbol{R}}^\top\boldsymbol{C}_v\hat{\boldsymbol{R}} + \boldsymbol{C}_u\right][\boldsymbol{I}_3 - \boldsymbol{P}_{22}]^\top . \quad (\text{B.7})$$

References

1. K.S. Arun, T.S. Huang and S.D. Blostein, "Least-squares fitting of two 3D point sets", *IEEE Transactions on Pattern Analysis and Machine Intelligence*. vol. 9, pp. 698–700, 1987.
2. S.D. Blostein and T.S. Huang, "Error analysis in stereo determination of 3D point positions", *IEEE Transactions on Pattern Analysis and Machine Intelligence*, vol. 9, pp. 752–765, 1987.
3. G. Csurka, C. Zeller, Z. Zhang and O. Faugeras, "Characterizing the Uncertainty of the Fundamental Matrix", *Computer Vision and Image Understanding*, Vol. 68, pp. 18–36, 1997.
4. A.C. Davison and D.V. Hinkley, *Bootstrap Methods and their Application*, Cambridge University Press, 1998.
5. B. Efron and R.J. Tibshirani, *An Introduction to the Bootstrap*, Chapman&Hall, 1993.
6. D.W. Eggert, A. Lorusso and R.B. Fisher, "Estimating 3-D rigid body transformations: A comparison of four major algorithms", *Machine Vision and Applications*, Vol. 9, pp. 272–290, 1997.
7. O. Faugeras, *Three-dimensional Computer Vision. A Geometric Viewpoint*, MIT Press, 1993.
8. S. Yi, R.H. Haralick and L. Shapiro, "Error propagation in machine vision", *Machine Vision and Applications*, vol. 7, pp. 93–114, 1994.
9. R.I. Hartley, "In Defense of the 8-Point Algorithm", *Proceedings of the 5th International Conference on Computer Vision*, Cambridge (MA), pp. 1064-1070, 1995.

10. R. I. Hartley, "Triangulation", *Computer Vision and Image Understanding* , vol. 68, pp. 146-157, 1997.

11. B.K.P. Horn, H.M. Hilden and S. Negahdaripour, "Closed-form solution of absolute orientation using orthonormal matrices," *J. Opt. Soc. Am.* vol. 5, pp. 1127–1135, 1988.

12. K. Kanatani, *Geometric Computation for Machine Vision*, Oxford Science Publications, 1993.

13. K. Kanatani, "Analysis of 3-D rotation fitting," *IEEE Transactions on Pattern Analysis and Machine Intelligence* , vol. 16, No. 5, pp. 543–549, 1994.

14. K. Kanatani, *Statistical Optimization for Geometric Computation: Theory and Practice*, Elsevier, 1996.

15. Y. Leedan and P. Meer, "Estimation with bilinear constraints in computer vision", *Proceedings of the 5th International Conference on Computer Vision*, Bombay, India, pp. 733–738, 1998.

16. B. Matei and P. Meer, "Optimal rigid motion estimation and performance evaluation with bootstrap", *Proceedings of the Computer Vision and Pattern Recognition 99*, Fort Collins Co., vol 1, pp. 339–345, 1999.

17. N. Ohta and K. Kanatani, "Optimal estimation of three-dimensional rotation and reliability evaluation", *Computer Vision - ECCV 98'*, H. Burkhardt, B. Neumann Eds., Lecture Notes in Computer Science, Springer, pp. 175–187, 1998.

18. T. Kato, *A Short Introduction to Perturbation Theory for Linear Operators*, Springer-Verlag, 1982.

19. H.C. Longuet-Higgins, "A Computer Algorithm for Reconstructing a Scene from Two Projections", *Nature*, Vol. 293, pp. 133-135, 1981.

20. X. Pennec and J.P. Thirion, "A framework for uncertainty and validation of 3-D registration methods based on points and frames", *International Journal on Computer Vision*, vol. 25, pp. 203–229, 1997.

21. H. Sahibi and A. Basu, "Analysis of error in depth perception with vergence and spatially varying sensing",*Computer Vision and Image Understanding* vol. 63, pp. 447–461, 1996.

22. L.L. Scharf, *Statistical Signal Processing*, Addison-Wesley, 1990.

23. E. Trucco and A. Verri, *Introductory Techniques for 3-D Computer Vision*, Prentice Hall, 1998.

24. S. Umeyama, "Least-squares estimation of transformation parameters between two point patterns," *IEEE Transactions on Pattern Analysis and Machine Intelligence*, vol. 13, pp. 376–380, 1991.

25. Z. Zhang, R. Deriche, O. Faugeras, Q.-T. Luong, "A robust technique for matching two uncalibrated images through the recovery of unknown epipolar geometry," *Artificial Intelligence*, vol. 78, 87–119, 1995.

26. Z. Zhang, "On the Optimization Criteria Used in Two View Motion Analysis", *IEEE Transactions on Pattern Analysis and Machine Intelligence* , vol. 20, pp. 717–729, 1998.

Discussion

Bill Triggs: Two things. One is just a minor grumble. You say in the earlier part of your talk that optimization, Levenberg-Marquardt, is slow, so you give another method. But your method does a very similar update calculation to Levenberg-Marquardt using a slower algorithm — eigendecomposition rather than linear solution.

Bogdan Matei: The updates are fairly similar. However, the algorithm is designed for errors-in-variables models which are not handled very well by optimization techniques like Levenberg-Marquardt. That's why Levenberg-Marquardt usually needs more iterations to converge.

Bill Triggs: Secondly, with these bootstrap-type methods you're very much a prisoner of the number of samples you have. In statistics, if you try to fit covariances to a high-dimensional model, they're often unstable because you simply don't have enough data to estimate $\mathcal{O}(n^2)$ covariance parameters. So despite its limitations, an analytical approach is in some sense more informative.

Bogdan Matei: Using analytical covariances in performance evaluation would make us the prisoners of elliptical confidence regions and local approximations. With sparse data in a high dimensional space, even a theoretical approach to computing the covariance would experience the same problems in the absence of ground truth information.

Annotation of Video by Alignment to Reference Imagery

Keith J. Hanna, Harpreet S. Sawhney, Rakesh Kumar, Y. Guo, and S. Samarasekara

Sarnoff Corporation, CN5300, Princeton, NJ 08530
khanna@sarnoff.com

Abstract. Video as an entertainment or information source in consumer, military, and broadcast television applications is widespread. Typically however, the video is simply presented to the viewer, with only minimal manipulation. Examples include chroma-keying (often used in news and weather broadcasts) where specific color components are detected and used to control the video source. In the past few years, the advent of digital video and increases in computational power has meant that more complex manipulation can be performed. In this paper we present some highlights of our work in annotating video by aligning features extracted from the video to a reference set of features.

Video insertion and annotation require manipulation of the video stream to composite synthetic imagery and information with real video imagery. The manipulation may involve only the 2D image space or the 3D scene space. The key problems to be solved are : (i) indexing and matching to determine the location of insertion, (ii) stable and jitter-free tracking to compute the time variation of the camera, and (iii) seamlessly blended insertion for an authentic viewing experience. We highlight our approach to these problems by showing three example scenarios: (i) 2D synthetic pattern insertion in live video, (ii) annotation of aerial imagery through geo-registration with stored reference imagery and annotations, and (iii) 3D object insertion in a video for a 3D scene.

1 Introduction

The ability to manipulate video in digital form has opened the potential for numerous applications that may have been difficult to implement with a purely analog representation of video. With the representation of video in terms of its underlying fundamental components of geometry, temporal transformation and appearance of patterns, any or all of these can be manipulated to modify the video stream. Seamless insertion of 2D and 3D objects, and textual and graphical annotations are forms of video manipulation with wide-ranging applications in the commercial, consumer and government worlds. In this paper we present some highlights of our work on annotation and insertion of synthetic objects and information into video and digital imagery.

Video insertion and annotation require manipulation of the video stream to composite synthetic imagery and information with real video imagery. There are a number of dimensions of this problem. First, the insertion may either demand 2D representation of the video and the camera motion, or 3D objects may need to be composited in 3D scenes with arbitrary camera motion. Second, the insertion and manipulation may rely on a small and fixed collection of landmarks in the scene or there may be a large database of stored reference imagery or nothing may be known a priori about the scene.

B. Triggs, A. Zisserman, R. Szeliski (Eds.): Vision Algorithms'99, LNCS 1883, pp. 253–264, 2000.

In the first scenario, we address the problem of inserting 2D patterns into broadcast video with essentially a fixed but pan/tilt/zoom camera. The technology has matured into products that are currently being used on a regular basis for insertion of virtual billboards and game-related synthetic annotations in broadcast sports videos [8], [10]. The second scenario is that of accurately locating current videos of a locale into a stored reference image database and subsequently visualizing the current video stream and the annotations in the database as footprints registered with the database imagery. We are currently building a real-time system for this capability for geo-registration of aerial videos to a reference database [3]. In this scenario, the transformations that relate the video to the database may be 2D or 3D. The final scenario is of a 3D scene imaged with an arbitrarily moving camera and the goal is to be able to insert synthetic 3D objects into the real imagery. No a priori knowledge of the 3D scene is assumed.

The underyling technical problems that need to be solved for the above scenarios are: (i) indexing and matching the video to precisely align locate the video frame, (ii) stable and jitter-free camera pose estimation in 2D and/or 3D, and (iii) seamless insertion of the synthetic pattern and objects for a visually pleasing experience. In this paper we present highlights of our solutions to the technical problems and demonstrate the validity of our approach through visual results.

2   2D Video Insertion

The basic approach for 2D video insertion is in three steps: training, coarse indexing, and fine alignment [4]. The training steps are performed in non real-time in a set-up phase, and the coarse indexing and fine alignment steps are performed in real-time using a hardware system.

In the training step, imagery that will be used as reference for the coarse indexing and fine alignment steps is captured. The target region can be occluded or can enter or leave the field of view when insertion is being performed, and therefore the approach is to record imagery not just of the target region itself, but also of surrounding regions. The images are then aligned to each other so that the location of the target region can be inferred from the recovered locations of surrounding regions.

In the coarse indexing step, regions that have been identified in the reference imagery are located in the current imagery using a hierarchical pattern tree search[2]. The pattern tree comprises a set of templates from the reference imagery and their relative spatial transformation in the coordinate system of the reference imagery. Coarse search begins by correlating the coarsest resolution templates across the current video image. If a potential match is found, then the next template in the pattern tree is correlated with the image using the relative spatial transformation in the pattern tree to compute the location around which correlation should occur. This process is repeated for more templates in the pattern tree, and the model relating the current image to the pattern tree is refined as successive potential matches arc found. A successful search is declared if a sufficient number of templates are matched in the pattern tree.

The fine alignment step recovers the precise transformation between the current image and the reference imagery. The current image is first shifted or warped to the

Fig. 1. Left: Original image from a sequence. Right: The image after manipulation.

reference imagery using the model provided by the coarse search result. The model parameters are then refined using an alignment method described in [1].

Once the precise alignment between the reference and current imagery has been determined, graphics in the coordinate system of the reference imagery can be warped to the coordinates system of the current imagery and inserted.

Figure 1 shows a simple insertion example. The image on the left shows an original frame from a sequence, and the image on the right shows a manipulated frame with a new logo superimposed on top of the left hand box.

3   Geo-registration

Aerial video is rapidly emerging as a low cost, widely used source of imagery for mapping, surveillance and monitoring applications. The mapping between camera co-ordinates in the air and the ground coordinates, called geospatial registration, depends both on the location and orientation of the camera and on the distance and topology of the ground. Rough geospatial registration can be derived from the ESD (Engineering Support Data: obtained from the GPS and inertial navigation units etc.) stream provided by the airborne camera telemetry system and digital terrain map data (from a database). This form of registration is the best available in fielded systems today but does not provide the precision needed for many tasks. Higher precision will be achieved by correlating (and registering) observed video frames to stored references imagery. Application of precise geospatial registration include the overlay of maps, boundaries and other graphical features and annotations onto the video imagery.

We present the details and results of some of the key algorithms we have developed in our laboratory towards implementing the overall system for geo-spatial registration. This work extends the previous body of work based on *still* imagery exploitation using site models [9]. We include more recent work on developing a real-time georegistration system.

3.1   Our Approach

A frame to frame alignment module first computes the spatial transformation between successive images in the video stream. These results are used in both the coarse indexing and fine geo-registration steps as decribed in the following sections.

The engineering support data (ESD: GPS, camera look angle etc.) supplied with the video is decoded to define the initial estimate of the camera model (position and attitude) with respect to the reference database. The camera model is used to apply an image perspective transformation to reference imagery obtained from the database to create a set of synthetic reference images from the perspective of the sensor which are used for coarse search and fine geo-registration.

A coarse indexing module then locates the video imagery more precisely in the reference image. An individual video frame may not contain sufficient information to perform robust matching and therefore results are combined across multiple frames using the results of frame to frame alignment.

A fine geo-registration module then refines this estimate further using the relative information between frames to constrain the solution.

3.2   Frame to Frame Alignment

Video frames are typically acquired at 30 frames a second and contain a lot of frame-to-frame overlap. For typical altitudes and speeds of airborne platforms, the overlaps may range from 4/5 to 49/50th of a single frame. We exploit this overlap by converting a redundant video stream into a compact image stream comprising key frames and parametric models that relate the key frames. For instance, typically 30 frames in a second of standard NTSC resolution (720x480) video containing about 10M pixels may be reduced to a single mosaic image containing only about 200K to 2M pixels depending on the overlap between successive frames. The successive video frames are aligned with low order parametric transformations like translation, affine and projective transformations [6].

3.3   Coarse Indexing/Matching

We present a solution to the coarse matching problem where geometric changes and poor matching of features are handled by combining local appearance matching with global consistency.

In our current real-time implementation, local appearance matching is performed using normalized correlation of multiple image patches in the image. These individual correlation surfaces often have multiple peaks. Disambiguation is obtained by imposing global consistency by combining the frame-to-frame motion information with the correlation surfaces. Specifically, we are looking for a number of potentially poor local matches that exhibit global consistency as the UAV flies along. This is currently implemented by multiplying the correlation surfaces after they have been warped or shifted by the frame-to-frame motion parameters. Figure 2 shows an example of this process. The top row shows three images from UAV video. The middle row shows the results of correlating regions from the reference imagery to the current imagery. Note that there is no single clear peak in the correlation surfaces. The bottom image shows the results of multiplying the correlation surfaces together after warping by a transform computed from the frame to frame parameters. Note that there is now a single peak in the correlation surface.

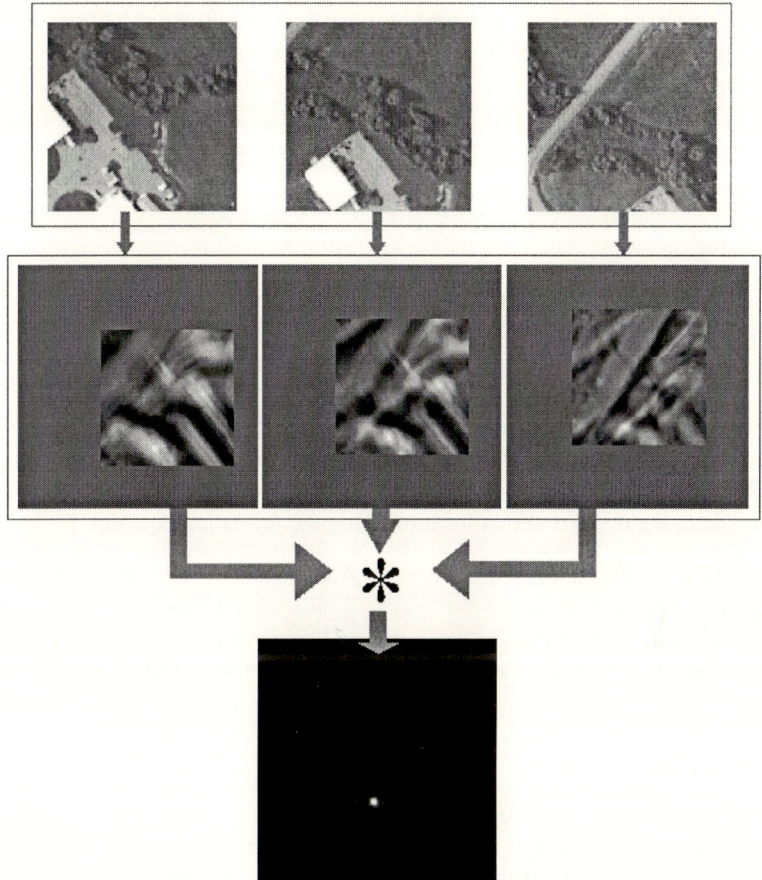

Fig. 2. Top Row: Original key frames. Middle Row: Results of correlating an image portion with the reference imagery. Bottom: Results of multiplying the correlation surfaces after warping using the frame to frame results.

This scheme does not specifically address the occlusion or drastic change of a region, but this is somewhat mitigated by repeating the process on different patches of the image and by selecting the best result as the candidate match.

3.4 Fine Geo-registration

The coarse localization is used to initialize the process of fine alignment. We now present the equations used for fine alignment of video imagery to a co-registered reference mage and depth image. The formulation used is the plane+parallax model developed by [7, 11, 13]. The coordinates of a point in a video image are denoted by (x, y). The coordinates of the corresponding point in the reference image are given by (X_r, Y_r). Each point is the reference image has a parallax value k. The parallax value is computed from a digital elevation map (DEM) which is co-registered with the reference image.

Twelve parameters $a_1...a_{12}$ are used to specify the alignment. The reference image coordinates (X_r, Y_r) are mapped to the ideal video coordinates (X_I, Y_I) by the following equations:

$$X_I = \frac{a_1 * X_r + a_2 * Y_r + a_3 * k(X_r, Y_r) + a_{10}}{a_7 * X_r + a_8 * Y_r + a_9 * k(X_r, Y_r) + a_{12}} \tag{1}$$

$$Y_I = \frac{a_4 * X_r + a_5 * Y_r + a_6 * k(X_r, Y_r) + a_{11}}{a_7 * X_r + a_8 * Y_r + a_9 * k(X_r, Y_r) + a_{12}} \tag{2}$$

Note, since, the right hand side in the above two equations is a ratio of two expressions, the parameters $a_1..a_{12}$ can only be determined up to a scale factor. We typically make parameter $a_{12} = 1$ and solve for the remaining 11 parameters. In the case of the reference image being an orthophoto with a corresponding DEM (digital elevation map), the parallax value k at a location is equal to the DEM value at that location. When the reference image is a real image taken from a frame camera (where the imaging is modeled with perspective projection) the parallax value k at any reference location is calculated from the depth z at that location using the following equation [7, 11, 13]:

$$k = \frac{(z - \bar{z}) * \bar{z}}{z * \sigma_z} \tag{3}$$

where $\bar{z}$ and σ_z are the average and standard deviation of the depth image values.

Parameter Estimation The reference imagery and the current imagery may be significantly different, and also each individual current image may not contain a significant number of image features. Therefore it is not particularly robust to solve for the camera parameters that map the current image to the reference from a single frame. Instead the approach is to use the results from the frame-to-frame processing to constrain the simultaneous solving of several sets of frame to reference parameters. Once a refined set of parameters have been recovered, local image matches between the current and reference imagery are recovered. These matches are then used to refine the sets of parameters as described below.

The output of the coarse search step is an approximate transform between a current image and the reference imagery. The output of the frame-to-frame processing is the transform between successive current images. These are fed into a global minimization algorithm [12] that minimizes the error between virtual points that are created using the frame-to-frame parameters and the coarse search parameters to recover an estimate of the transform between each of the current images and the reference imagery.

The next step is to use image matches between the current and reference imagery at each frame to improve accuracy. This is performed by computing point correspondences using a hierarchical flow algorithm [1]. This algorithm assumes brightness constancy, but the images are pre-filtered with Laplacian filters in order to reduce the impact of illumination changes. The algorithm computes local matches at every image pixel first at a coarse resolution, then refines them at finer resolutions.

These point matches are then sampled and then together with the frame-to-frame parameters are fed into the global minimization algorithm once more [12]. The result is a set of refined parameters for each frame. These parameters are then used to warp or shift the reference imagery to each current image. Point matches between the warped reference imagery and the current imagery can be computed again and used to refine the model parameters even further.

Figure 3 shows a geo-mosaic consisting of current imagery that has been warped and overlaid on top of the reference imagery. Note that the features in the overlaid mosaic line up with features in the reference imagery.

Fig. 3. A geo-mosaic warped and overlaid on the refence imagery.

Figure 4 shows a frame from the output of a real-time geo-registration system that is being built at Sarnoff that uses a VFE-200 processor for frame to frame alignment and for coarse search, and an SGI computer for fine alignment. The current imagery is shown in the center of the figure, and annotations and the reference imagery in the background have been aligned to it. Remaining misalignments are due to the use of a distortion-free camera model in the current development phase of the real-time system.

4   3D Match Move

In geo-registration we assumed that reference models and reference imagery existed. Annotating the video in that case, involved solving for the pose of the video frames with respect to the reference image. In many applications such as in film production, reference imagery and models are often not available. The problem here therefore is that given a video sequence of N frames, we wish to compute the camera poses (the rotations and translations) without the knowledge of the 3D model and with some rough knowledge

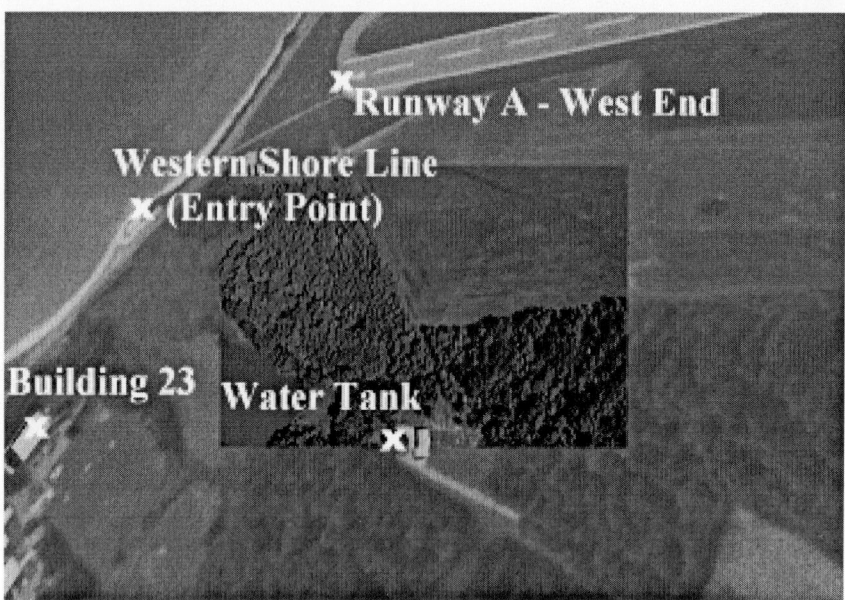

Fig. 4. A frame from UAV video overlayed on the warped reference imagery with annotations being displayed

of the internal parameters of the camera. The approach should work with a variety of different 3D camera motions, especially those in which novel parts of the scene appear and disappear relatively rapidly. Of course, imaging scenarios in which features remain fairly persistent, as in fixated motions, are also naturally handled. A sparse collection of 3D features are also computed in the process of pose computation. In general, the problems of correspondence over the sequence, camera pose and 3D structure estimation, and camera calibration estimation are tied together. Solving all the problems in a single optimization problem is complex and will in general not lead to stable and correct solutions. Therefore, we adopt a strategy of progressive complexity with feedback in which earlier stages work on smaller subsequences of the data and generate inputs for the latter stages which estimate consistent poses over the entire sequence. The advantage of dividing the problem into subsequence estimates and then combining these is threefold: (i) better computational efficiency since global bundle block adjustment for all frames is expensive, (ii) progressively better generation of estimates leading to a global maximum likelihood estimation, and (iii) limited build up of error due to small scale concatenation of local pose estimates (akin to [12, 14]).

4.1   Pose Estimation for Unmodeled Scenes

We divide the pose estimation problem for unmodeled scenes into the following different steps:

1. Feature Tracking: Our method allows for frame-to-frame patch tracking while allowing for new features to emerge and older features to disappear. The first step is to choose new features in every new frame. Features are chosen on the basis of their contrast strength and distinctiveness with respect to their local neighborhoods. In any given frame both new points and points projected from a previous frame are checked for flow consistency at their locations. Points that are flow consistent are kept for further tracking. The process of instantiation of new points, projection of previous points into a new frame and flow consistency checks is repeated over the whole sequence to obtain multi-frame point tracks.

2. Pairwise estimation of camera poses: Initial estimates for the camera poses are computed using the fundamental matrix constraint. The fundamental matrix can be computed by a number of known techniques. We employ Zhang's [15] algorithm that combines a linear method for initialization, and then refines it with a method that employs image based error minimization. Furthermore, outliers are rejected using a least median squares minimization. The final fundamental matrix is computed using the image based error measure after outlier rejection. With the knowledge of the approximately known calibration, the fundamental matrix can be decomposed into the camera pose matrices using the technique of Hartley [5].

3. Computation of camera poses for sub-sequences: In order to exploit the static rigid scene constraint, the pairwise camera estimates are used to create consistent camera pose estimates and the corresponding 3D point locations over short subsequences. Point tracks that persist for the time period of each subsequence are used to create the consistent estimates. In order to compute the maximum likelihood estimates for the camera poses and 3D points for the subsequence, a bundle block adjustment is applied.

4. Aligning sub-sequences: Subsequence computation is performed with a few frames overlap between consecutive sub-sequences. The points that are visible in two overlapping sub-sequences are used to solve for absolute orientation that relate the coordinate systems of the two sub-sequences. This is used to represent both the subsequences in a common coordinate system, so that they may be stitched together.

5. Refinement of poses over sequence: The stitching of subsequences allows the representation of poses and the 3D points in a single coordinate system. However, point tracks that are common across more than one sub-sequence provide constraints for further global adjustment of the 3D parameters. In the final step, bundle block adjustment is applied to the complete set of frames and 3D points. For computational efficiency, this adjustment can be applied in small sets of arbitrary frames or can be applied to the complete set. The interesting aspect of the representation here is that any combination of internal parameters, pose parameters or 3D points can be adjusted while maintaining a global representation.

4.2   3D Insertion Using Computed Poses

Accurate and stable pose estimation important for the application of 3D match move in which synthetic objects are inserted into real images and their viewpoints are mimicked according to the real camera's pose and internal parameters. Now we show examples of

Fig. 5. Three frames of the *Garden* sequence with synthetic 3D flamingoes inserted. The 3D placement was done only in one frame, and all others were generated through rendering using the automatically computed poses.

3D match move using the pose estimation technique presented in the earlier part of the paper.

Fig. 5 shows three frames from a garden sequence with synthetic 3D flamingos inserted. The 3D placement was performed manually only in one frame, and all others were generated through rendering using the automatically computed poses. It is to be emphasized that the placement of the synthetics has been done with respect to one frame only. Therefore, there is minimal interaction demanded of the user. It is also to be emphasized that both in the still image displays as well as in the videos, no drift or jitter in the objects in any of the frames is noticeable. This is a qualitative visual validation of the stability of pose and 3D structure computation of the algorithm developed.

References

1. J. R. Bergen, P. Anandan, K. J. Hanna, and R. Hingorani. Hierarchical model-based motion estimation. In *European Conference on Computer Vision*, Santa-Margherita Ligure, Italy, 1992.
2. Burt et. al. Object tracking with a moving camera. In *IEEE Workshop on Visual Motion, Irvine CA*, 1989.
3. R. Kumar et al. Registration of video to geo-referenced imagery. In *Proc. International Conference on Pattern Recognition*, 1998.
4. K. Hanna and P. Burt. US Patent 5,566,251 - October 15, 1996.
5. R. I. Hartley. Estimation of relative camera positions for uncalibrated cameras. In *Proc. 2nd European Conference on Computer Vision*, pages 579–587, 1992.
6. Michal Irani. Applications of image mosaics. In *International Conference on Computer Vision*, Cambridge, MA, November 1995.
7. R. Kumar, P. Anandan, and K. Hanna. Direct recovery of shape from multiple views: a parallax based approach. In *Proc 12th ICPR*, 1994.
8. Princeton Video Image. http://www.pvimage.com.
9. RADIUS PI Reports and Technical papers. Proc. darpa image understanding workshop, 1996. pp. 255–525.
10. R. Rosser and M. Leach. US Patent 5,264,933 - November 23, 1993.
11. Harpreet Sawhney. 3D geometry from planar parallax. In *Proc. CVPR 94*, June 1994.
12. Harpreet S. Sawhney, Steve Hsu, and R. Kumar. Robust video mosaicing through topology inference and local to global alignment. In *ECCV*, pages 103–119, 1998.
13. A. Shashua and N. Navab. Relative affine structure, theory and application to 3d reconstruction from 2d views. In *IEEE Conference on Computer Vision and Pattern Recognition*, June 1994.
14. R. Szeliski and H. Shum. Creating full view panoramic image mosaics and environment maps. In *Proc. of SIGGRAPH*, pages 251–258, 1997.
15. Z. Zhang et al. A robust technique for matching two uncalibrated images through the recovery of the unknown epipolar geometry. *Artificial Intelligence*, 78:87–119, 1995.

Discussion

Rick Szeliski: You showed the sequence with the flamingo inserted. How much effort would it be today, to insert a flamingo behind the fence — with occlusions, and not the situation you planned for?

Keith Hanna: That's a good question. Obviously one way to do it would be to recover or build a 3D model of the scene. But you need to compare how long it takes to make the 3D model with someone going in and delineating the occlusion by hand. In Hollywood, they do a lot by hand, so if we want to get more into Hollywood, we need to understand what they do. Here they'd probably do a pose estimation then delineate by hand, maybe with the help of tracking tools. As computer vision people we'd like to build a 3D model and then do everything ourselves, but in practice in many applications we'd be wasting our time actually trying to do that.

Yongduek Seo: The graphics object inserted in the video scene is very stable. Do you have any special method?

Keith Hanna: Basically all the approaches use iterative refinement. You recover a first estimate of your poses, and depths, then use those to refine iteratively, to get closer to registration. The reason for the accuracy is just continual iterative refinement of the parameters to improve the alignment. Five or six iterations is usually enough.

Yongduek Seo: How large are the images?

Keith Hanna: Just regular sizes, 720×480 here I think. All the video stuff is standard 768×480. The movie ones are bigger, about 1k.

Luc Robert: First I'd like to add to your answer to Rick's question. Hollywood people are very skilled, but sometimes they simply can't do it by hand, or it's too painful like painting individual pixels. So, 3D maps are something they use a lot. They often build 3D models just to predict binary image maps for compositing. That would be a good solution for the fence.

I have a question about the example with the baseball player moving in front of the billboard. You clearly handle the occlusion, but the background is green. Can you also do it against an arbitrary, non-color-key-able background?

Keith Hanna: When there is a lot of background texture, detecting the difference is much harder, and any slight misalignment shows up very clearly. Even a tenth of a pixel is visible if you have a high-contrast edge. There are other constraints you can use, like motion or spatial continuity, but typically it's much easier when the background is flat.

Another interesting thing you may have seen is video insertion on the ground in soccer. There we do a video mixing of about 75% logo and 25% grass background. There are a couple of reasons for that. One is that the texture of the grass comes through, so it really looks like the logo is painted on the grass. In soccer it looks great actually, we were all blown away when we saw that! But the second reason is that it makes the occlusion analysis a little easier — errors are less noticeable if you do a little mixing.

Computer-Vision for the Post-production World: Facts and Challenges through the REALViZ Experience

Luc Robert

REALViZ S.A., BP037, 06901 Sophia Antipolis, France
Luc.Robert@realviz.com

Luc Robert described the products being developed at REALViZ and their application to special effects and post production in the film industry. In particular the MatchMover product which is a "3-D Camera Tracker" computing a camera for each frame of the film by tracking 2-D features through an image sequence. We include below the discussion following his presentation.

Harpreet Sawhney: In the case of 2D tracking it's easy to figure out when things start going wrong. But when you go to MatchMoving with camera estimation and so forth, how do you tell a non-expert user what to do when the computation has gone wrong?

Luc Robert: Well, you write lots of pages of documentation, hoping that the user won't have to read them... Yes, this is one of the most difficult parts of MatchMoving, making things clear to the user when they're sometimes not even clear to us. You can provide survey tools that inspect image residuals, time averages, anything that might be useful. But beyond that it's not clear.

Yongduek Seo: I did some similar work, and in that case, although the results were very good in parameter space, we still found some trembling and things like that in the real video. Does this happen with your system? Also, you are using Euclidean parameters, I wonder if you have considered a calibration-free approach.

Luc Robert: As far as the first question is concerned, yes, even with our software, the thing sometimes wiggles and the trajectories are a little shaky. So you have to provide the user with tools for smoothing out parameters, or trying to fix things by hand if necessary. One case where it often happens is when you compute a trajectory with variable zoom. There is a near-ambiguity between zooming and moving forward, so the estimated camera trajectory can be very jagged in the z-direction. But you can usually fix that by applying a smoothing filter to the zoom parameter and recomputing the other parameters. If the objects you insert in the scene are exactly between the points you track, it's usually OK even without smoothing. But when you add 'noise amplifiers' — objects which go much further than the points you've tracked — you start seeing vibrations and for this filtering is pretty efficient. I don't like it because it means that the algorithm has in some sense failed, but it's the best solution we've found up till now.

B. Triggs, A. Zisserman, R. Szeliski (Eds.): Vision Algorithms'99, LNCS 1883, pp. 265–266, 2000.
© Springer-Verlag Berlin Heidelberg 2000

Fig. 1. A synthetic car inserted in a real scene using the REALViZ software.

As for the second question, unfortunately we have to fit into the standard production pipeline. So we get images here and we produce camera files there. The camera files have to be read by animation packages, which do not handle projective cameras. So we have to do Euclidean stuff. Otherwise no one would be able to use the results.

Joe Mundy: Given that a person in the loop is essential in most circumstances, how do you think the computer vision community should be thinking about algorithms to best take advantage of human interaction?

Luc Robert: I don't really know. I think that when things are not very clear to you, you can't explain them to someone else, and usually the reverse is true. In MatchMoving, the MatchMovers are usually cameramen, because they understand best how a synthetic camera is looking at the world.

Joe Mundy: What this suggests to me is that the user-interface needs to be much more tightly coupled to the computer vision algorithms. Rather than just pointing, there has to be a deeper interaction with the imagery. It seems to me that perhaps we should start to look more carefully at what people have done in human factors research. There's been a tremendous amount of research for fields like piloting aircraft, and maybe an invited talk at a computer vision conference on that material would be useful.

About Direct Methods

M. Irani[1] and P. Anandan[2]

[1] Dept. of Computer Science and Applied Mathematics,
The Weizmann Inst. of Science, Rehovot, Israel.
irani@wisdom.weizmann.ac.il
[2] Microsoft Research, One Microsoft Way,
Redmond, WA 98052, USA.
anandan@microsoft.com

1 Introduction

This report provides a brief summary of the review of "Direct Methods", which was presented by Michal Irani and P. Anandan.

In the present context, we define "Direct Methods" as methods for motion and/or shape estimation, which recover the unknown parameters directly from *measurable image quantities* at *each pixel* in the image. This is contrast to the "feature-based methods", which first extract a sparse set of distinct features from each image separately, and then recover and analyze their correspondences in order to determine the motion and shape. Feature-based methods minimize an error measure that is based on *distances* between a few corresponding features, while direct methods minimize an error measure that is based on direct image information collected from *all pixels* in the image (such as image brightness, or brightness-based cross-correlation, etc).

2 The Brightness Constraint

The starting point for most direct methods is the "brightness constancy constraint", namely, given two images $J(x, y)$ and $I(x, y)$,

$$J(x, y) = I(x + u(x, y), y + v(x, y)),$$

where (x, y) are pixel coordinates, and (u, v) denotes the displacement of pixel (x, y) between the two images. Assuming small (u, v), and linearizing I around (x, y), we can obtain the following well-established constraint [7]:

$$I_x u + I_y v + I_t = 0, \tag{1}$$

where (I_x, I_y) are the spatial derivatives of the image brightness, and $I_t = I - J$. All the quantities in these equations are functions of image position (x, y), hence every pixel provides one such equation that constrains the displacement of that pixel. However, since the displacement of each pixel is defined by two quantities, u and v, the brightness constraint alone is insufficient to determine

B. Triggs, A. Zisserman, R. Szeliski (Eds.): Vision Algorithms'99, LNCS 1883, pp. 267–277, 2000.
© Springer-Verlag Berlin Heidelberg 2000

the displacement of a pixel. A second constraint is provided by a "global motion model", namely a model that describes the variation of the image motion across the entire image. These models can be broadly divided into two classes: Two-dimensional (2D) motion models and three-dimensional (3D) motion models. Below we describe how direct methods have been used in connection with these two classes of models. A more complete description of a hierarchy of different motion models can be found in [1].

3   2D Global Motion Models

The 2D motion models use a single global 2D parametric transformation to define the displacement of every pixel contained in their region of support. A frequently used model is the *affine* motion model[1], which is described by the equations:

$$u(x, y) = a_1 + a_2 x + a_3 y$$
$$v(x, y) = a_4 + a_5 x + a_6 y \tag{2}$$

The affine motion model is a very good approximation for the induced image motion when the camera is imaging *distant* scenes, such as in airborne video or in remote surveillance applications. Other 2D models which have been used by direct methods include the *Quadratic* motion model [1, 14], which describes the motion of a planar surface under small camera rotation, and the 2D *projective* transformation (a homography) [19], which describes the exact image motion of an arbitrary planar surface between two discrete *uncalibrated* perspective views.

The method of employing the global motion constraint is similar, regardless of the selected 2D global motion model. As an example, we briefly describe here how this is done for the affine transformation.

We can substitute the affine motion of Equation 2 into the brightness constraint in Equation 1 to obtain,

$$I_x(a_1 + a_2 x + a_3 y) + I_y(a_4 + a_5 x + a_6 y) + I_t = 0. \tag{3}$$

Thus each pixel provides one constraint on the six unknown global parameters $(a_1, \ldots, a_6)$. Since these parameters are *global* (i.e., the same parameters are shared by all the pixels), therefore, theoretically, six independent constraints from six different pixels are adequate to recover these parameters. In practice, however, the constraints from *all* the pixels within the region of analysis (could be the entire image) are combined to minimize the error:

$$E(a_1, \ldots, a_6) = \sum (I_x(a_1 + a_2 x + a_3 y) + I_y(a_4 + a_5 x + a_6 y) + I_t)^2 \tag{4}$$

Note that different pixels contribute differently to this error measure. For example, a pixel along a horizontal edge in the image will have significant I_y, but zero

---

[1] The affine transformation accurately describes the motion of a an arbitrary planar surface for a fully rectified pair of cameras - i.e., when the optical axes are parallel and the baseline is strictly sideways.

I_x, and hence will only constrain the estimation of the parameters (a_4, a_5, a_6) and not the others. Likewise a pixel along a vertical edge will only constrain the estimation of the parameters (a_1, a_2, a_3). On the other hand, at a corner-like pixel and within a highly textured region, both the components of the gradient will be large, and hence the pixel will constrain all the parameters of the global affine transformation. Finally, a pixel in a homogeneous area will contribute little to the error since the gradient will be very small.

In other words, the direct methods use information from all the pixels, weighting the contribution of each pixel according to the underlying image structure around that pixel. This eliminates the need for explicitly recovering distinct features. In fact, even images which contains no distinct feature points can be analyzed, as long as there is sufficient image gradient along different directions in different parts of the image.

4   Coarse-to-Fine Iterative Estimation

The basic process described above relies on *linearizing* the image brightness function (Equation 1). This linearization is a good approximation when (u, v) are small (e.g., less than one pixel). However, this is rarely satisfied in real video sequences. The scope of the direct methods has therefore been extended to handle a significantly larger range of motions via *coarse-to-fine* processing, using *iterative refinement* within a multi-resolution pyramid.

The basic observation behind coarse-to-fine estimation is that given proper filtering and subsampling, the induced image motion decreases as we go from full resolution images (fine pyramid levels) to small resolution images (coarse pyramid levels). The analysis starts at the coarsest resolution level, where the image motion is very small. The estimated global motion parameters are used to warp one image toward the other, bringing the two images closer to each other. The estimation process is then repeated between the *warped* images. Several iterations (typically 4 or 5) of warping and refinement are used to further increase the search range. After a few iterations, the parameters are propagated to the next (finer) pyramid level, and the process is repeated there. This iterative-refine estimation process is repeated and propagated all the way up to the finest resolution level, to yield the final motion parameters. A more complete description of the coarse-to-fine approach can be found in [1].

With the use of coarse-to-fine refinement, direct methods have been extended to handle image motions typically upto 10-15 percent of the image size. This range is more than adequate for handling the type of motions found in real video sequences. Direct methods are also used for aligning images taken by different cameras, whose degree of misalignment does not exceed the abovementioned range. For larger misalignments, an initial estimate is required.

5   Properties of Direct Methods

In addition to the use of constraints from all the pixels, weighted according to the information available at each pixel, direct methods have a number of properties that have made them attractive in practice. Here we note three of these: (i) high sub-pixel accuracy, and (ii) the "locking property", and (iii) dense recovery of shape in the case of 3D estimation. Properties (i) and (ii) are briefly explained in this section, while property (iii) is referred to in Section 6.

5.1   Sub-pixel Accuracy

Since direct methods use "confidence-weighted" local constraints from every pixel in the image to estimate a few global motion parameters (typically 6 or 8), these parameters are usually estimated to very high precision. As a result, the displacement vector induced at each pixel by the global motion model is precise upto a fraction of a pixel (misalignment error is usually less than 0.1 pixel). This has led to its use in a number of practical situations including mosaicing [11, 9, 18, 17], video enhancement [11, 9], and super resolution [12], all of which require sub pixel alignment of images. Figure 1 shows an example of a mosaic constructed by aligning a long sequence of video frames using a direct method with a frame-to-frame affine motion model. Note that the alignment is seamless. Figure 2 shows an example of video enhancement. Note the improvement in the fine details in the image, such as the windows of the building. For examples of Super-Resolution using direct image alignment see [12].

5.2   Locking Property and Outlier Rejection

Direct methods can successfully estimate global motion even in the presence of multiple motions and/or outliers. Burt, et. al. [3] used a frequency-domain analysis to show that the coarse-to-fine refinement process allows direct methods to "lock-on" to a single dominant motion even when multiple motions are present. While their analysis focuses on the case of global translation, in practice, direct methods have been successful of handling outliers even for affine and other parametric motions. Irani et. al. [14] achieved further robustness by using an iterative reweighting approach with an outlier measure that is easy to compute from image measurements. Black and Anandan [2] used M-estimators to recover the dominant global motion in the presence of outliers. Figure 3 (from [13]) shows an example of dominant motion selection, in which the second motion (a person walking across the room) occupies a significant area of the image. Other examples of dominant motion selection can be found in a number of papers in the literature (e.g., see [2, 14, 13]).

6   3D Motion Models

So far, we have focused on using direct methods for estimating global 2D parametric motions. In these cases, a small number (typically 6 or 8) parameters

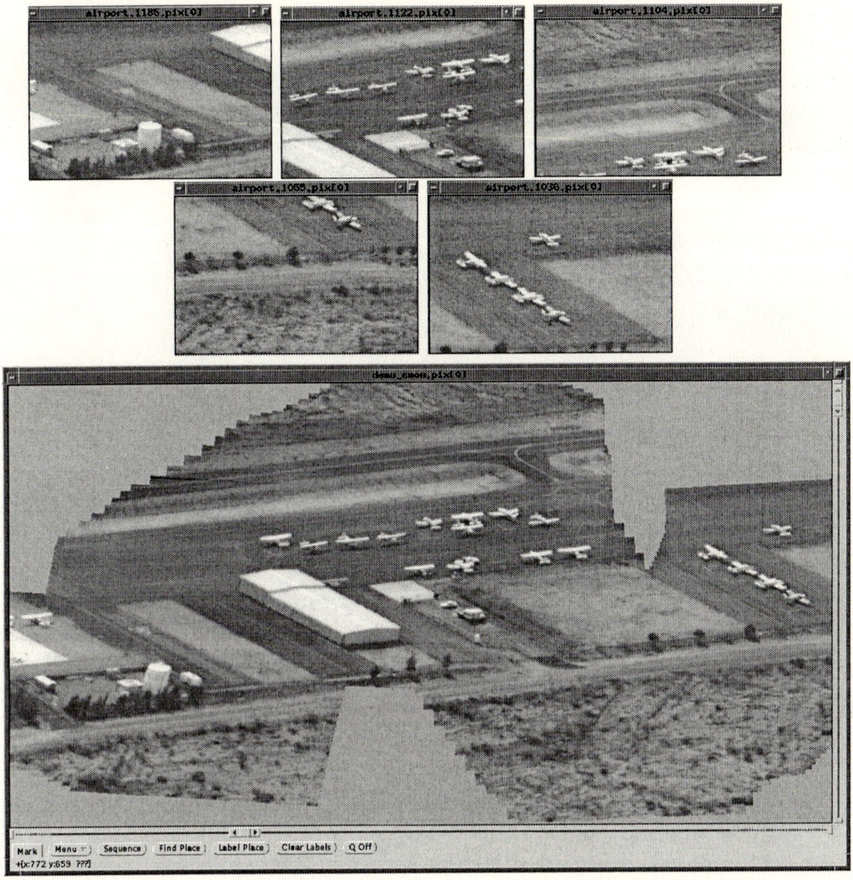

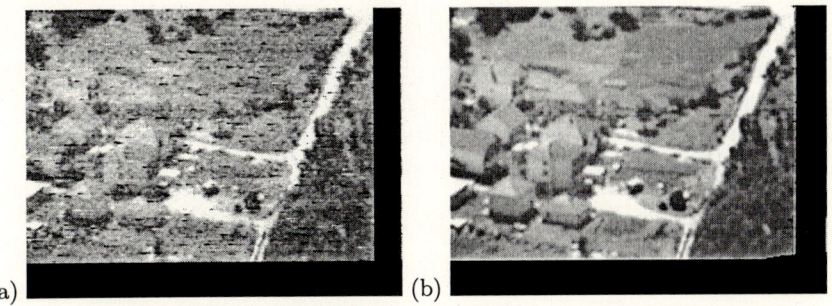

(a)

(b)

Fig. 1. **Panoramic mosaic of an airport video clip.**   (a) A few representative frames from a one-minute-long video clip. The video shows an airport being imaged from the air with a moving camera. (b) The mosaic image built from all frames of the input video clip. Note that the alignment is seamless.

(a)   (b)

Fig. 2. **Video enhancement.**   (a) One out of 20 noisy frames (all frames are of similar quality). (b) The corresponding enhanced frame in the enhanced video sequence (all the frames in the enhanced video are of the same quality).

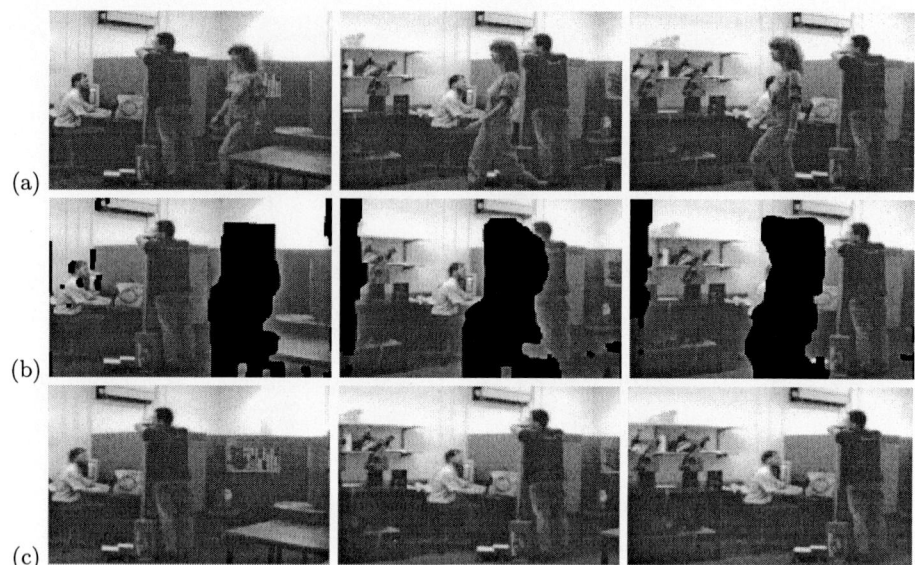

Fig. 3. Dominant motion selection and outlier rejection. (a) 3 representative frames from the sequence. There are two motions present – that induced by the panning camera, and that induced by the walking woman. (b) Outlier pixels detected in those frame are marked in blacks. Those are pixels found to be moving inconsistently with the detected dominant motion. Those pixels correspond to the walking woman, to her reflection in the desk, to the boundaries of the image frames, and to some noisy pixels. (c) Full reconstructions of the dominant layer (the background) in all frames. The girl, her reflection, and the noise are removed from the video sequence by filling in the black regions with gray-level information from other frames according to the computed dominant background motion.

can describe the motion of every pixel in the region consistent with the global motion. However, these 2D motion models cannot model frame-to-frame motion when significant camera translation and non-planar depth variations are present. These scenarios require 3D motion models. The 3D motion models consist of two sets of parameters: a set of global parameters, which represent the effects of camera motion, and a set of local parameters (one per pixel), which represents the 3D structure or the "shape"[2]. Examples of 3D motion models include:
(i) The instantaneous velocity field model:

$$u = -xy\Omega_X + (1 + x^2)\Omega_Y - y\Omega_Z + (T_X - T_Z x)/Z$$
$$v = -(1 + y^2)\Omega_X + xy\Omega_Y + x\Omega_Z + (T_Y - T_Z y)/Z,$$

where $(\Omega_X, \Omega_Y, \Omega_Z)$ and (T_X, T_Y, T_Z) denote the camera rotation and translation parameters, and Z the depth value represents the local shape.

---

[2] These types of 3D models are referred to as "quasi-parametric" models in [1].

(ii) The discrete 3D motion model, parameterized in terms of a homography and the epipole:

$$u = \frac{h_1 x + h_2 y + h_3 + \gamma t_1}{h_7 x + h_8 y + h_9 + \gamma t_3} - x$$

$$v = \frac{h_4 x + h_5 y + h_6 + \gamma t_2}{h_7 x + h_8 y + h_9 + \gamma t_3} - y$$

where $(h_1, \ldots, h_9)$ denote the parameters of the homography, (t_1, t_2, t_3) represents the epipole in homogeneous coordinates, and γ represents the local shape.
(iii) The plane+parallax model:

$$u = x^w - x = \frac{\gamma}{1 + \gamma t_3}(t_3 x - t_1)$$

$$v = y^w - y = \frac{\gamma}{1 + \gamma t_3}(t_3 y - t_2)$$

where (x^w, y^w) correspond the image locations obtained after *warping* the image according to the induced homography (2D projective transformation) of a dominant planar surface (See [15, 10] for more details). Direct methods have been applied in conjunction with 3D motion models to simultaneously recover the global camera motion parameters and the local shape parameters from image measurements. For example, [4, 5] have used the instantaneous velocity equations to recover the camera motion and shape from two and multiple images. Szeliski and Kang [20] directly recovered the homography, the epipole, and the local shape from image intensity variations, and Kumar et. al. [15] and Irani et. al. [10] have applied direct methods using the plane+parallax model with two and multiple frames, respectively.

All of these examples of using direct methods with 3D motion models use multi-resolution coarse-to-fine estimation to handle large search ranges. The computational methods are roughly similar to each other and are based on the approach described in [1] for quasi-parametric model.

Figure 4 shows an example of applying the plane+parallax model to the "block sequence" [15]. These results were obtained using the multiframe technique described in [10]. A natural outcome of using the direct approach with a 3D motion model is the recovery of a *dense* shape map of the scene, as is illustrated in Figure 4. Dense recovery is made possible because at *every* pixel the Brightness Constancy Equation 1 provides *one line constraint*, while the epipolar-constraint provides *another line constraint*. The intersection of these two line constraints uniquely defines the displacement of the pixel. Other examples of using direct methods for dense 3D shape and motion recovery can be found in the various papers cited above.

7   Handling Changes in Brightness

Since the brightness constancy constraint is central to the direct methods, a natural question arises concerning the applicability of these techniques when the

 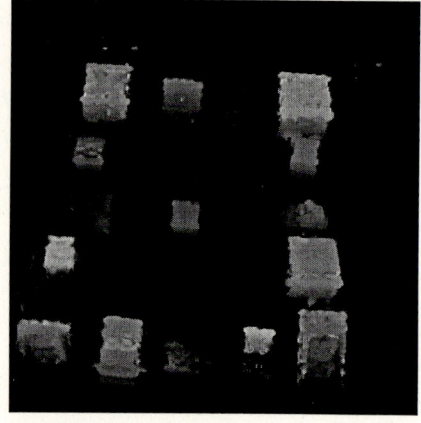

(a) (b)

Fig. 4. Shape recovery using the Plane+Parallax model. (a) One frame from the sequence. (b) The recovered shape (relative to the carpet plane). Brighter values correspond to taller points.

brightness of a pixel is *not* constant over multiple images. There are two ways of handling such changes. The first approach is to renormalize the image intensities to reduce the effects of such changes in brightness over time. For example, normalizing the images to remove global changes in mean and contrast often handles effects of overall lighting changes. More local variations can be handled by using Laplacian pyramid representations and by applying local contrast normalizations to the Laplacian filtered images (see [6] for a *real-time* direct affine estimation algorithm which uses Laplacian pyramid images together with some local contrast normalization).

A second (and more recent) approach to handling brightness variation is to generalize the entire approach to use other local match measures besides the brightness error. This approach is discussed in more detail in Section 8.

8   Other Local Match Measures

Irani and Anandan [8] describe a general approach for extending direct methods to handle any user defined local match measure. In particular, instead of applying the linearization and the iterative refinement to *brightness surfaces*, the regression in [8] is applied directly to *normalized-correlation surfaces*, which are measured at *every pixel* in the image. A *global* affine transformation is sought, which *simultaneously* maximizes as many *local* correlation values as possible. This is done without prior commitment to particular local matches. The choice of local displacements is constrained on one hand by the global motion model (could be a 2D affine transformation or a 3D epipolar constraint), and on the other hand by the local correlation variations.

Irani and Anandan show that with some image pre-filtering, the *direct* correlation based approach can be applied to even extreme cases of image matching, such as *multi-sensor* image alignment. Figure 5 shows the results of applying their approach to recovering a global 2D affine transformation needed to align an infra-red (IR) image with an electro-optic (video) image. More recently, Mandelbaum, et. al. [16] have extended this approach to simultaneously recover the 3D global camera motion and the dense local shape.

9   Summary

In this paper we have briefly described the class of methods for motion estimation called direct methods. Direct methods use measurable image information, such as brightness variations or image cross-correlation measures, which is integrated from all the pixels to recover 2D or 3D information. This is in contrast to feature-based methods that rely on the correspondence of a sparse set of highly reliable image features.

Direct methods have been used to recover 2D global parametric motion models (e.g., affine transforms, quadratic transforms, or homographies), as well as 3D motion models. In the 3D case, the direct methods recover the *dense* 3D structure of the scene simultaneously with the camera motion parameters (or epipolar geometry). Direct methods have been shown to recover pixel motion upto high subpixel precision. They have also been applied to real-image sequences containing multiple motions and outliers, especially in the case of 2D motion models. The recent use of cross-correlation measures within direct methods have extended their applicability to image sequences containing significant brightness variations over time, as well as to alignment of images obtained by sensors of different sensing modalities (such as IR and video). Direct methods are capable of recovering misalignments of up to 10-15 % of the image size. For larger misalignments, an initial estimate is required.

References

1. J.R. Bergen, P. Anandan, K.J. Hanna, and R. Hingorani. Hierarchical model-based motion estimation. In *European Conference on Computer Vision*, pages 237–252, Santa Margarita Ligure, May 1992.
2. M.J. Black and P. Anandan. The robust estimation of multiple motions: Parametric and piecewise-smooth flow fields. *Computer Vision and Image Understanding*, 63:75–104, 1996.
3. P.J. Burt, R. Hingorani, and R.J. Kolczynski. Mechanisms for isolating component patterns in the sequential analysis of multiple motion. In *IEEE Workshop on Visual Motion*, pages 187–193, Princeton, New Jersey, October 1991.
4. K. Hanna. Direct multi-resolution estimation of ego-motion and structure from motion. In *IEEE Workshop on Visual Motion*, pages 156–162, Princeton, NJ, October 1991.
5. K. J. Hanna and N. E. Okamoto. Combining stereo and motion for direct estimation of scene structure. In *International Conference on Computer Vision*, pages 357–365, Berlin, May 1993.

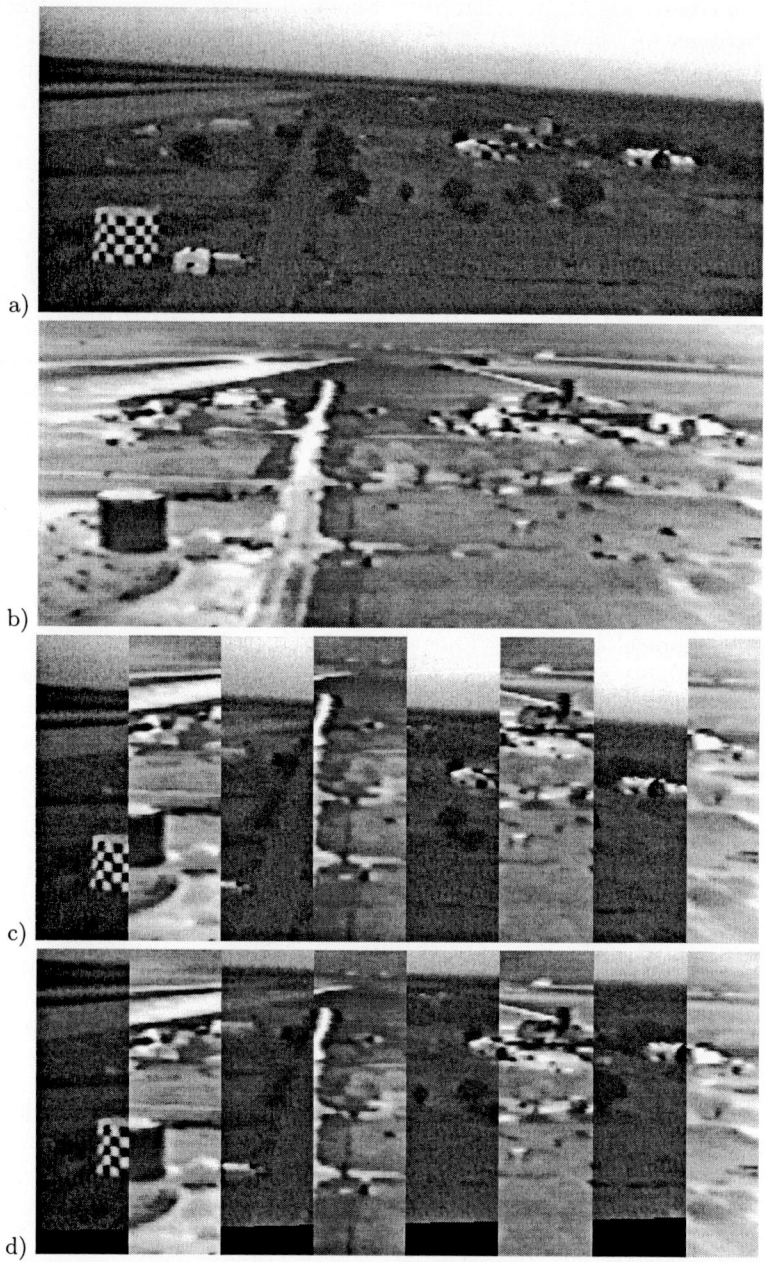

Fig. 5. Multi-sensor Alignment. (a) EO (video) image. (b) IR (Infra-Red) image. (c) Composite (spliced) display *before* alignment. (d) Composite (spliced) display *after* alignment. Note in particular the perfect alignment of the water-tank at the bottom left of the images, the building with the arched-doorway at the right, and the roads at the top left of the images.

6. M. Hansen, P. Anandan, K. Dana, G. van der Wal, and P. Burt. Real-time scene stabilization and mosaic construction. In *Proc. of the Workshop on Applications of Computer Vision II*, Sarasota, Fl., 1994.

7. B.K.P. Horn and B.G. Schunck. Determining optical flow. *Artificial Intelligence*, 17:185–203, 1981.

8. M. Irani and P. Anandan. Robust multi-sensor image alignment. In *International Conference on Computer Vision*, Bombay, January 1998.

9. M. Irani, P. Anandan, J. Bergen, R. Kumar, and S. Hsu. Efficient representations of video sequences and their application. *Signal Processing: Image Communication*, 8(4), 1996.

10. M. Irani, P. Anandan, and M. Cohen. Direct recovery of planar-parallax from multiple frames. In *Vision Algorithms 99*, Corfu, September 1999.

11. M. Irani, P. Anandan, and S. Hsu. Mosaic based representations of video sequences and their applications. In *International Conference on Computer Vision*, pages 605–611, Cambridge, MA, November 1995.

12. M. Irani and S. Peleg. Improving resolution by image registration. *CVGIP: Graphical Models and Image Processing*, 53:231–239, May 1991.

13. M. Irani and S. Peleg. Using motion analysis for image enhancement. *Journal of Visual Communication and Image Representation*, 4(4):324–335, December 1993.

14. M. Irani, B. Rousso, and S. Peleg. Computing occluding and transparent motions. *International Journal of Computer Vision*, 12:5–16, February 1994.

15. R. Kumar, P. Anandan, and K. Hanna. Direct recovery of shape from multiple views: a parallax based approach. In *Proc 12th ICPR*, pages 685–688, 1994.

16. R.Mandelbaum, G. Salgian, and H. Sawhney. Correlation-based estimation of ego-motion and structure from motion and stereo. In *International Conference on Computer Vision*, pages 544–550, Corfu, September 1999.

17. H.S. Sawhney and S. Ayer. Compact representations of videos through dominant and multiple motion estimation. *IEEE Trans. on Pattern Analysis and Machine Intelligence*, 18:814–830, 1996.

18. R. Szeliski. Image mosaicing for tele-reality applications. Technical Report CRL 94/2, DEC Cambridge Research Lab, May 1994.

19. R. Szeliski and J. Coughlan. Hierarchical spline-based image registration. In *IEEE Conference on Computer Vision and Pattern Recognition*, pages 194–201, June 1994.

20. R. Szeliski and S.B. Kang. Direct methods for visual scene reconstruction. In *Workshop on Representations of Visual Scenes*, 1995.

Feature Based Methods
for Structure and Motion Estimation

P. H. S. Torr[1] and A. Zisserman[2]

[1] Microsoft Research Ltd, 1 Guildhall St
Cambridge CB2 3NH, UK
philtorr@microsoft.com
[2] Department of Engineering Science, University of Oxford
Oxford, OX1 3PJ, UK
az@robots.ox.ac.uk

1   Introduction

This report is a brief overview of the use of "feature based" methods in structure and motion computation. A companion paper by Irani and Anandan [16] reviews "direct" methods.

Direct methods solve two problems simultaneously: the motion of the camera and the correspondence of every pixel. They effect a global minimization using all the pixels in the image, the starting point of which is (generally) the image brightness constraint (as explained in the companion paper).

By contrast we advocate a feature based approach. This involves a strategy of concentrating computation on areas of the image where it is possible to get good correspondence, and from these an initial estimate of camera geometry is made. This geometry is then used to guide correspondence in regions of the image where there is less information. Our thesis is as follows:

Structure and motion recovery should proceed by first extracting features, and then using these features to compute the image matching relations. It should not proceed by simultaneously estimating motion and dense pixel correspondences.

The "image matching relations" referred to here arise from the camera motion alone, not from the scene structure. These relations are the part of the motion that can be computed directly from image correspondences. For example, if the camera translates between two views then the image matching relation is the epipolar geometry of the view-pair.

The rest of this paper demonstrates that there are cogent theoretical and practical reasons for advocating this thesis when attempting to recover structure *and* motion from images. We illustrate the use of feature based methods on two examples. First, in section 2, we describe in detail a feature based algorithm for registering multiple frames to compute a mosaic. The frames are obtained by a camera rotating about its centre, and the algorithm estimates the point-to-point homography map relating the views. Second, section 3 discusses the more general case of structure and motion computation from images obtained by a camera rotating *and* translating. Here it is shown how feature matching methods form the basis for a dense 3D reconstruction of the scene (where depth is obtained for

B. Triggs, A. Zisserman, R. Szeliski (Eds.): Vision Algorithms'99, LNCS 1883, pp. 278–294, 2000.

every pixel). Section 4 explores the strengths and weaknesses of feature based and direct methods, and summarises the reasons why feature based methods perform so well.

2   Mosaic Computation

Within this section the feature based approach to mosaicing is described. Given a sequence of images acquired by a camera rotating about its centre, the objective is to fuse together the set of images to produce a single panoramic mosaic image of the scene. For this particular camera motion, corresponding image points (i.e. projections of the same scene point) are related by a point-to-point planar homography map which depends only on the camera rotation and internal calibration, and does not depend on the scene structure (depth of the scene points). This map also applies if the camera "pans and zooms" (changes focal length whilst rotating).

A planar homography (also known as a plane projective transformation, or collineation) is specified by eight independent parameters. The homography is represented as a 3×3 matrix that transforms homogeneous image coordinates as:

$$\mathbf{x}' = \mathbf{H}\mathbf{x}.$$

We first describe the computation of a homography between an image pair, and then show how this computation is extended to a set of three or more images.

2.1   Image Pairs

The automatic feature based algorithm for computing a homography between two images is summarized in table 1, with an example given in figure 1.

The point features used (developed by Harris [12]) are known as interest points or "corners". However, as can be seen from figure 1 (c) & (d), the term corner is misleading as these point features do not just occur at classical corners (intersection of lines). Thus we prefer the term interest point. Typically there can be hundreds or thousands of interest points detected in an image.

It is worth noting two things about the algorithm. First, interest points are not matched purely using geometry – i.e. only using a point's position. Instead, the intensity neighbourhood of the interest point is also used to rank possible matches by computing a normalized cross correlation between the point's neighbourhood and the neighbourhood of a possible match. Second, robust estimation methods are an essential part of the algorithm: more than 40% of the putative matches between the interest points (obtained by the best cross correlation score and proximity) are incorrect. It is the RANSAC algorithm that identifies the correct correspondences.

Given the inlying interest point correspondences: $\{\mathbf{x}_i \leftrightarrow \mathbf{x}_i'\}, i = 1 \ldots n$, the final estimate of the homography is obtained by minimizing the following cost function,

$$\sum_i d(\mathbf{x}_i, \hat{\mathbf{x}}_i)^2 + d(\mathbf{x}_i', \hat{\mathbf{x}}_i')^2 \tag{1}$$

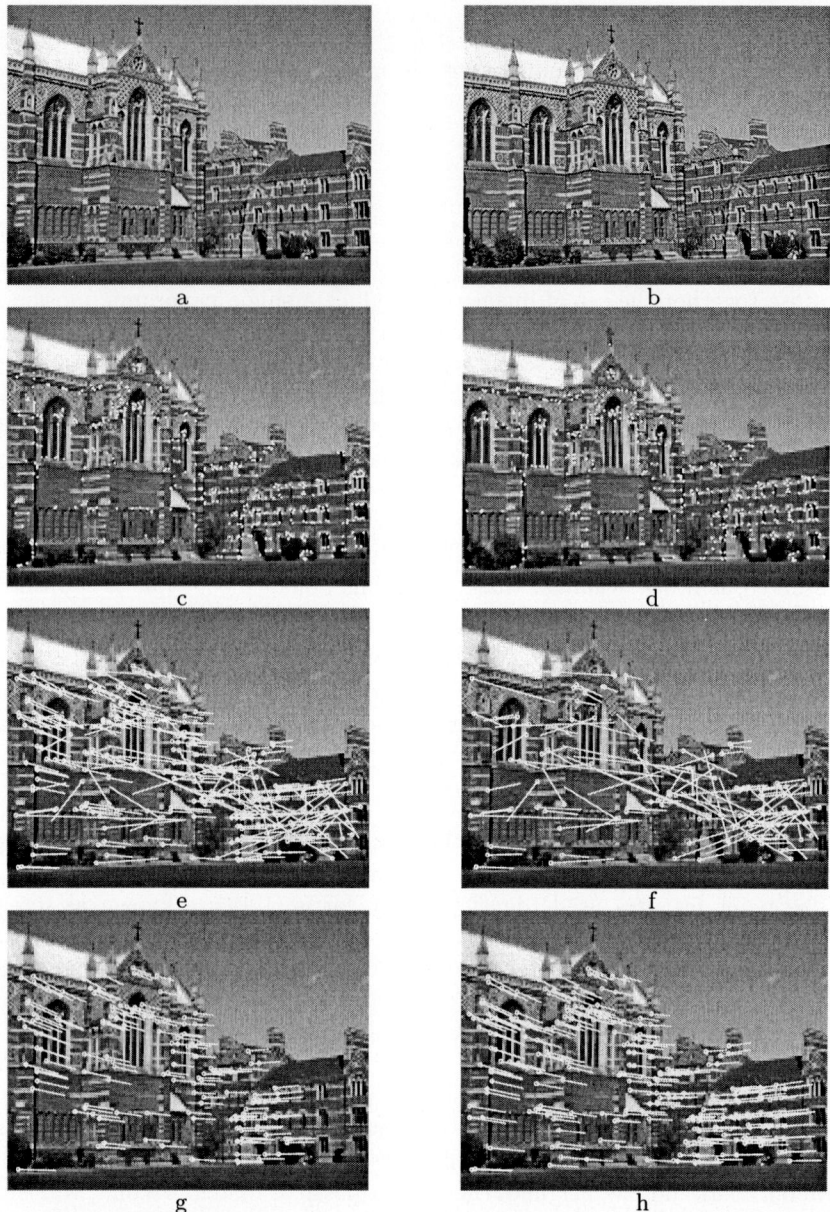

Fig. 1. Automatic computation of a homography between two images using the algorithm of table 1. *(a) (b) Images of Keble College, Oxford. The motion between views is a rotation about the camera centre so the images are exactly related by a homography. The images are 640 × 480 pixels. (c) (d) Detected point features superimposed on the images. There are approximately 500 features on each image. The following results are superimposed on the left image: (e) 268 putative matches shown by the line linking matched points, note the clear mismatches; (f) RANSAC outliers — 117 of the putative matches; (g) RANSAC inliers — 151 correspondences consistent with the estimated* **H**; *(h) final set of 262 correspondences after guided matching and MLE. The estimated* **H** *is accurate to subpixel resolution.*

Table 1. *The main steps in the algorithm to automatically estimate a homography between two images using RANSAC and features. Further details are given in [14].*

<u>Objective</u> Compute the 2D homography between two images.

<u>Algorithm</u>

1. **Features:** Compute interest point features in each image to sub pixel accuracy (e.g. Harris corners [12]).
2. **Putative correspondences:** Compute a set of interest point matches based on proximity and similarity of their intensity neighbourhood.
3. **RANSAC robust estimation:** Repeat for N samples
   (a) Select a random sample of 4 correspondences and compute the homography **H**.
   (b) Calculate a geometric image distance error for each putative correspondence.
   (c) Compute the number of inliers consistent with **H** by the number of correspondences for which the distance error is less than a threshold.
   Choose the **H** with the largest number of inliers.
4. **Optimal estimation:** re-estimate **H** from all correspondences classified as inliers, by minimizing the maximum likelihood cost function (1) using a suitable numerical minimizer (e.g. the Levenberg-Marquardt algorithm [24]).
5. **Guided matching:** Further interest point correspondences are now determined using the estimated **H** to define a search region about the transferred point position.

The last two steps can be iterated until the number of correspondences is stable.

---

where $d(\mathbf{x}, \mathbf{y})$ is the geometric distance between the image points $\mathbf{x}$ and $\mathbf{y}$. The cost is minimized over the homography $\widehat{\mathbf{H}}$ and corrected points $\{\hat{\mathbf{x}}_i\}$ such that $\hat{\mathbf{x}}_i' = \widehat{\mathbf{H}}\hat{\mathbf{x}}_i$. This gives the maximum likelihood estimate of the homography under the assumption of Gaussian measurement noise in the position of the image points. A fuller discussion of the estimation algorithm is given in [14] with variations and improvements (the use of MLESAC rather than RANSAC) given in [34].

2.2   From Image Ppairs to a Mosaic

The two frame homography estimation algorithm can readily be extended to constructing a mosaic for a sequence as follows:

1. Compute interest point features in each frame.
2. Compute homographies and correspondences between frames using these point features.
3. Compute a maximum likelihood estimate of the homographies and points over all frames.
4. Use the estimated homographies to map all frames onto one of the input frames to form the mosaic.

In computing the maximum likelihood estimate the homographies are parametrized to be consistent across frames. So, for example, the homography between the first and third frame is obtained exactly from the composition of homographies between the first and second, and second and third as $\mathbf{H}_{13} = \mathbf{H}_{23}\,\mathbf{H}_{12}$. This is achieved by computing all homographies with respect to a single set of corrected points $\hat{\mathbf{x}}_i$. Details are given in [7].

The application of this algorithm to a 100 frame image sequence is illustrated in figures 2 and 3. The result is a seamless mosaic obtained to subpixel accuracy.

a

b

Fig. 2. Automatic panoramic mosaic construction. (a) Every 10th frame of a 100 frame sequence acquired by a hand held cam-corder approximately rotating about its lens centre. Note, each frame has a quite limited field of view, and there is no common overlap between all frames. (b) The computed mosaic which is seamless, with frames aligned to subpixel accuracy. The computation method is described in [7].

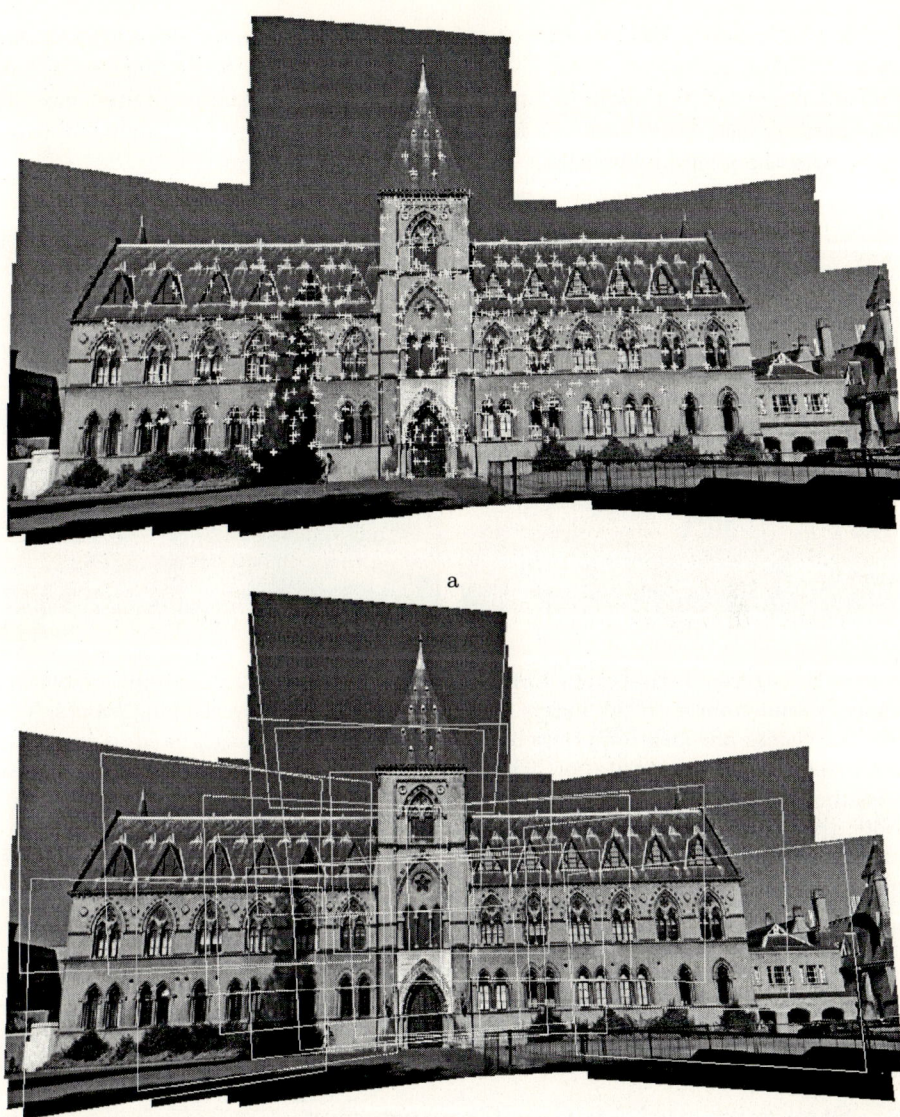

Fig. 3. Details of the mosaic construction of figure 2. (a) 1000 of the 2500 points used in the maximum likelihood estimation, note the density of points across the mosaic. (b) Every 5th frame (indicated by its outline), note again the lack of frame overlap. A super-resolution detail of this mosaic is shown in figure 4.

The mosaic can then form the basis for a number of applications such as video summary [17], motion removal [19], auto-calibration [13], and super-resolution. For example, figure 4 shows a super-resolution detail of the computed mosaic. The method used [8] is based on MAP estimation, which gives a slight improvement over the generally excellent Irani and Peleg algorithm [18].

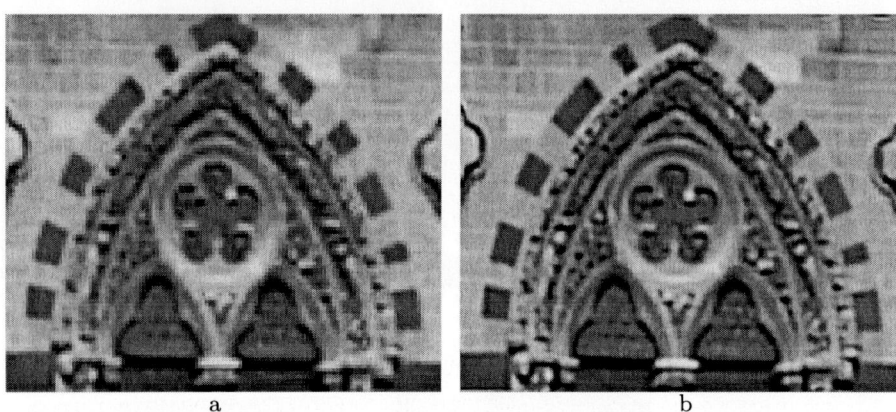

a   b

Fig. 4. Super-resolution detail of the mosaic of figure 2. The super-resolution image is built from a set 20 images obtained from partially overlapping frames. The original frames are jpeg compressed. (a) One of the set of images used as input for the super-resolution computation. The image is 130×110 pixels, and has the highest resolution of the 20 used. (b) The computed double resolution image (260×220 pixels). Note, the reduction in aliasing (e.g. on the dark bricks surrounding the Gothic arch) and the improvement in sharpness of the edges of the brick drapery. Details of the method are given in [8].

To summarize: in this case the "image matching relation" is a homography which is computed from point feature correspondences. Once the homography is estimated the correspondence of every pixel is determined.

3   Structure and Motion Computation

This section gives an example of (metric) reconstruction of the scene and cameras directly from an image sequence. This involves computing the cameras up to a scaled Euclidean transformation of 3-space (auto-calibration) and a dense model of the scene. The method proceeds in two overall steps:

1. Compute cameras for all frames of the sequence.
2. Compute a dense scene reconstruction with correspondence aided by the multiple view geometry.

Unlike in the mosaicing example, in this case the camera centre is moving and consequently the map between corresponding pixels depends on the depth of the scene points, i.e. for general scene structure there is not a simple map (such as a homography) global to the image.

3.1   Computing Cameras for an Image Sequence

The method follows a similar path to that of computing a mosaic.

1. **Features:** Compute interest point features in each image.
2. **Multiple view point correspondences:** Compute two-view interest point correspondences and simultaneously the fundamental matrix $\mathbf{F}$ between pairs of frames, e.g. using robust estimation on minimal sets of 7 points, as described in [32]; Compute three-view interest point correspondences and simultaneously the trifocal tensor between image triplets, e.g. using robust estimation on minimal sets of 6 points, as described in [33]; Weave together these 2-view and 3-view reconstructions to get an initial estimation of 3D points and cameras for all frames [10]. This initial reconstruction provides the basis for bundle adjustment.
3. **Optimal estimation:** Compute the maximum likelihood estimate of the 3D points and cameras by minimizing reprojection error over all points. This is bundle adjustment and determines a projective reconstruction. The cost function is the sum of squared distances between the measured image points $\mathbf{x}_j^i$ and the projections of the estimated 3D points using the estimated cameras:

$$\min_{\hat{\mathbf{P}}^i, \hat{\mathbf{X}}_j} \sum_{ij} d(\hat{\mathbf{P}}^i \hat{\mathbf{X}}_j, \mathbf{x}_j^i)^2 \tag{2}$$

where $\hat{\mathbf{P}}^i$ is the estimated camera matrix for the ith view, $\hat{\mathbf{X}}_j$ is the jth estimated 3D point, and $d(\mathbf{x}, \mathbf{y})$ is the geometric image distance between the homogeneous points $\mathbf{x}$ and $\mathbf{y}$.
4. **Auto-calibration:** Remove the projective ambiguity in the reconstruction using constraints on the cameras such as constant aspect ratio, see e.g. [23].

Further details of automatic computation of cameras for a sequence are given in [1, 3, 4, 10, 14, 22, 30, 31].

3.2   Computing a Dense Reconstruction

Given the cameras, the multi-view geometry is used to help solve for dense correspondences. There is a large body of literature concerning methods for obtaining surface depths given the camera geometry: a classical stereo algorithm may be used, for example an area based algorithm such as [9, 20]; or space carving, e.g.[21, 28]; or surface primitives may be fitted directly, e.g. piecewise planar models [2] or piecewise generalized cylinders [15]; or optical flow may be used, constrained by epipolar geometry [36].

Figure 5 shows an example of automatic camera recovery from five images, followed by automatic dense stereo reconstruction using an area based algorithm. The method is described in [23].

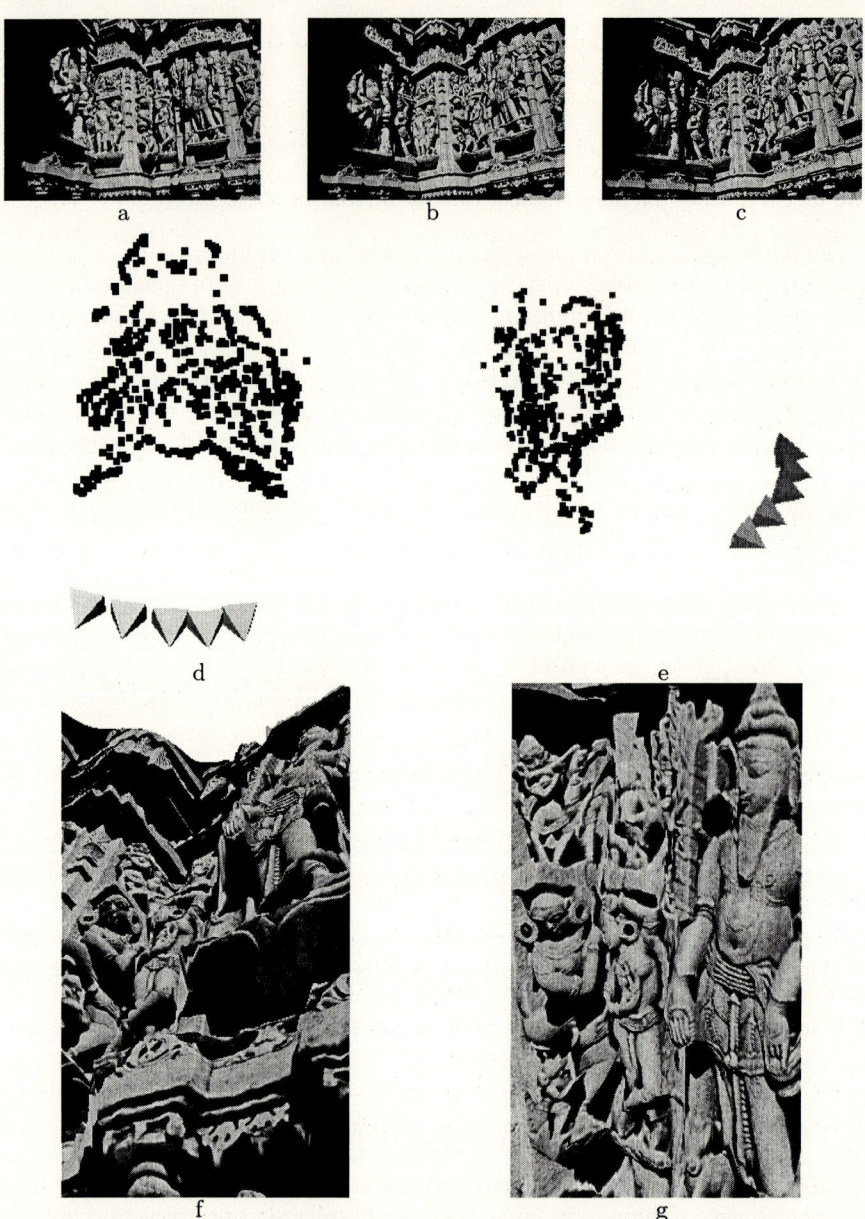

Fig. 5. Automatic generation of a texture mapped 3D model from an image sequence. The input is a sequence of images acquired by a hand held camera. The output is a 3D VRML model of the cameras and scene geometry. (a)–(c) three of the five input images. (d) and (e) two views of a metric reconstruction computed from interest points matched over the five images. The cameras are represented by pyramids with apex at the computed camera centre. (f) and (g) two views of the texture mapped 3D model computed from the original images and reconstructed cameras using an area based stereo algorithm. Figures courtesy of Marc Pollefeys, Reinhard Koch, and Luc Van Gool [23].

To summarize: the key point is that features are a convenient intermediate step from input images to dense 3D reconstruction. In this case the "image matching relations" are epipolar geometry, trifocal geometry, etc that may be computed from image interest point correspondences. This is equivalent to recovering the cameras up to a common projective transformation of 3-space. After computing the cameras, the features need not be used at all in the subsequent dense scene reconstruction.

4   Comparison of the Feature Based and Direct Methods

Within this section the two methods are contrasted. We highlight three aspects of the structure and motion recovery problem: invariance, optimal estimation, and the computational efficiency of the methods. Then list the current state of the art.

4.1   The Importance of Invariance

Features have a wide range of *photometric* invariance. For example, although thus far we have only discussed interest points, lines may be detected in an image as an intensity discontinuity (an "edge"). The invariance arises because a discontinuity is still detectable even under large changes in illumination conditions between two images. Features also have a wide range of *geometric* invariance – lines are invariant to projective transformations (a line is mapped to a line), and consequently line features may be detected under any projective transformation of the image.

In the case of Harris interest points, the feature is detected at the local minima of an autocorrelation function. This minima is also invariant to a wide range of photometric and geometric image transformations, as has been demonstrated by Schmid *et al* [27]. Consequently, the detected interest point across a set of images corresponds to the same 3D point.

This photometric and geometric invariance is perhaps the primary motivation for adopting a feature based approach.

In direct approaches it is necessary to provide a photometric map between corresponding pixels, for example the map might be that the image intensities are constant (image brightness constraint), or that corresponding pixels are related by a monotonic function. If this map is incorrect, then erroneous correspondences between pixels will result. In contrast in feature based methods a photometric map is used only to *guide* interest point correspondence.

As an example, consider normalized cross correlation on neighbourhoods. This measure is used in the algorithms included in this paper to *rank* matches. Normalized cross-correlation is invariant to a local affine transformation of intensities (scaling plus offset). If, in a particular imaging situation, the cross-correlation measure is not invariant to the actual photometric map between the images, then the ranking of the matches may be erroneous. However, the position of the interest points is (largely) invariant to this photometric map. Thus with the immunity to mismatches provided by robust estimation, the transformation estimated from the interest points will still be correct. It is for this reason that the estimated camera geometry is largely unaffected by errors in the model of (or invariance to) the photometric map.

If normalized cross-correlation is used in a direct method, and is invariant to the actual photometric map, then in principle the correct pixel correspondence will be obtained. However, if it is not invariant to the actual photometric map, then direct methods may systematically degrade but feature based methods will not.

As a consequence, feature based methods are able to cope with severe viewing and photometric distortion, and this has enabled wide base line matching algorithms to be developed. An example is given in figure 6.

Fig. 6. Wide baseline matching. *Three images acquired from very different viewpoints with a hand-held camera. The trifocal tensor is estimated automatically from interest point matches and a global homography affinity score. Five of the matched points are shown together with their corresponding epipolar lines in the second and third images. The epipolar geometry is determined from the estimated trifocal tensor. Original images courtesy of RobotVis INRIA Sophia Antipolis. The wide baseline method is described in [25].*

4.2   Optimal Estimation

A significant advantage of the feature based approach is that it readily lends itself to a bundle adjustment method over a long sequence, and this provides a maximum likelihood estimate of the estimated quantities (homographies in the mosaic example, cameras in the structure and motion example). This reveals a key difference between the feature based and direct methods: in feature based approaches the errors are uncorrelated between features so that statistical independence is a valid assumption in estimation.

Consider the "least squares" cost functions that are typically used (e.g. (2)). For this to be a valid maximum likelihood estimation two criteria must be satisfied: first, each of the squares to be summed must be the log likelihood of that error, and second each must be conditionally independent of any of the other errors. In the case of feature based methods the sum of squared error that is minimized is the distance between the backprojected reconstructed 3D point and its measured correspondence in each image. There is evidence that these errors are independent and distributed with zero mean in a Gaussian manner [35]. The same cannot be said when using the brightness constraint equation to estimate global motion models [5, 11]. Because the quantities involved are image derivatives obtained by smoothing the image there is a large amount of conditional dependence between the errors. It is not clear what effect this violation of the conditions for maximum likelihood estimation might be but it is possible that the results produced may be biased.

To summarize: for direct methods it is not straightforward to write down a practical likelihood function for all pixels. Modelling of noise and statistics is much more complicated, and simple assumptions of independence invalid. Thus attempting a global minimization treating all the errors as if they were uncorrelated will lead to a biased result.

4.3   Computational Efficiency and Convergence

Consider computing the fundamental matrix from two views. Interest point correspondences yield highly accurate camera locations at little computational cost. If instead every pixel in the image is used to calculate the epipolar geometry the computational cost rises dramatically. Furthermore the result could not have been improved on as only pixels where the correspondence is well established are used (the point features). Use of every pixels means introducing much noisy data, as correspondence simply cannot be determined in homogeneous regions of the image either from the brightness constraint or from cross correlation. Thus the introduction of such pixels could potentially introduce more outliers, which in turn may cause incorrect convergence of the minimization. To determine correspondence in these regions requires additional constraints such as local smoothness.

To summarize: features can be thought of as a computational device to leap frog us to a solution using just the good (less noisy) data first, and then incorporating the bad (more noisy) data once we are near a global minima.

4.4   Scope and Applications

Finally we list some of the current achievements of feature based structure from motion schemes and ask how direct methods compare with this. A list of this sort will of course date, but it is indicative of the implementation ease and computational success of the two approaches.

Automatic estimation of the fundamental matrix and trifocal tensor. Point features facilitate automatic estimation of the fundamental matrix and trifocal tensor. There is a wide choice of algorithms available for interest points. These algorithms are based on robust statistics – this means that they are robust to effects such as occlusion and small independent motions in an otherwise rigid scene.

The fundamental matrix cannot be estimated from normal flow alone. The trifocal tensor can [29], but results comparable to the feature based algorithms have yet to be demonstrated. Direct methods can include robustness to minor occlusion and small independent motions. Although pyramid methods can be deployed to cope with larger disparities direct methods have met with only limited success with wide base line cases.

Application to image sequences. Features have enabled automatic computation of cameras for extended video sequences over a very wide range of camera motions and scenes. This includes auto-calibration of the camera. An example is shown in figure 7 of camera computation with auto-calibration for hundreds of frames.

In contrast direct methods have generally been restricted to scenes amenable to a "plane plus parallax" approach, i.e. where the scene is dominated by a plane so that homographies may be computed between images.

Features other than points. Although this paper has concentrated on interest point features, other features such as lines and curves may also be used to compute multi-view relations. For example, figure 8 shows an example of a homography computed automatically from an imaged planar outline between two views.

5   Conclusions

It is often said (by the unlearned) that feature based methods only furnish a sparse representation of the scene. **This is missing the point**, feature based methods are a way of initializing camera geometry/image matching relations so that a dense reconstruction method can follow.

The extraction of features – *the seeds of perception* [6] – is an intermediate step, a computational artifice that culls the useless data and affords the use of powerful statistical techniques such as RANSAC and bundle adjustment.

The purpose of this paper has not been to argue against the use of direct methods where appropriate (for instance in the mosaicing problem under small image deformations). Rather it has been to suggest that for more general structure and motion problems, the currently most successful way to proceed is via the extraction of photometrically invariant features. The benefit being that just a few high information features can be used to find the correct ball park of the solution. Once this is found more information may be introduced, and a "direct" method can be used to improve the result.

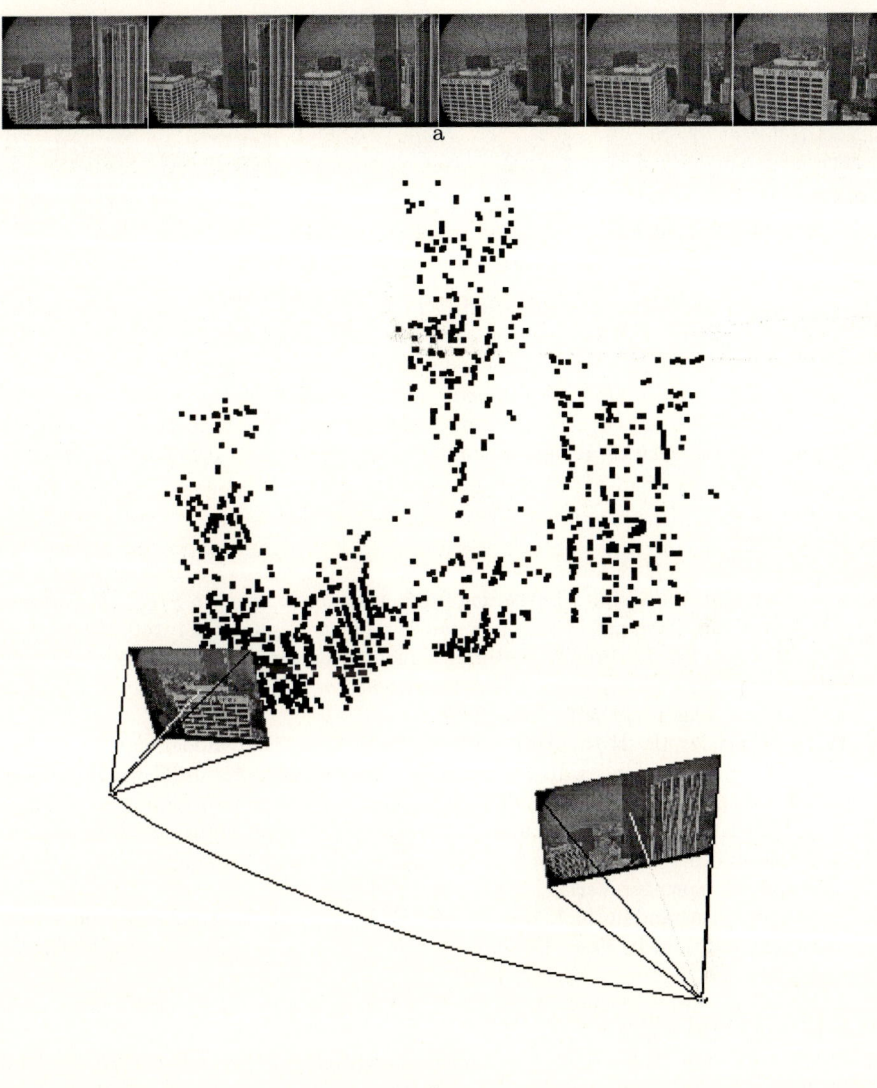

Fig. 7. Reconstruction from extended image sequences. (a) Six frames from 120 frames of a helicopter shot. (b) Automatically computed cameras and 3D points. The cameras are shown for just the start and end frames for clarity, with the path between them indicated by the black curve. The computation method is described in [10].

Acknowledgements

The mosaicing and super-resolution results given here were produced by David Capel, and the fundamental matrix and cameras for an image sequence by Andrew Fitzgibbon. We are very grateful to both of them.

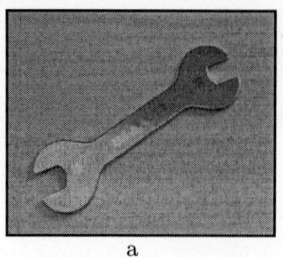
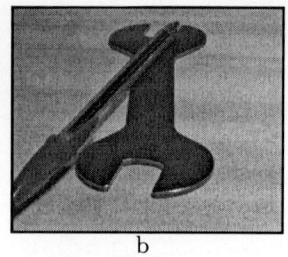
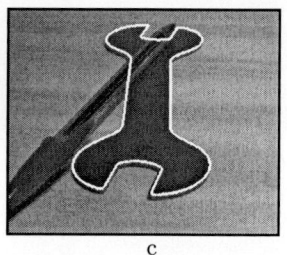

a   b   c

Fig. 8. Computing homographies using curve features. *The homography between the plane of the spanner in (a) and (b) is computed automatically from segments of the outline curve. This curve is obtained using a Canny-like edge detector. Note the severe perspective distortion in (b). The mapped outline is shown in (c). The computation method is robust to partial occlusion and involves identifying projectively covariant points on the curve such as bi-tangents and inflections. Details are given in [26].*

References

1. S. Avidan and A. Shashua. Threading fundamental matrices. In *Proc. 5th European Conference on Computer Vision, Freiburg, Germany*, pages 124–140, 1998.
2. C. Baillard and A. Zisserman. Automatic reconstruction of piecewise planar models from multiple views. In *Proc. IEEE Conference on Computer Vision and Pattern Recognition*, pages 559–565, June 1999.
3. P. A. Beardsley, P. H. S. Torr, and A. Zisserman. 3D model aquisition from extended image sequences. In *Proc. 4th European Conference on Computer Vision, LNCS 1065, Cambridge*, pages 683–695, 1996.
4. P. A. Beardsley, A. Zisserman, and D. W. Murray. Navigation using affine structure and motion. In *Proc. European Conference on Computer Vision*, LNCS 800/801, pages 85–96. Springer-Verlag, 1994.
5. J. Bergen, P. Anandan, K.J. Hanna, and R. Hingorani. Hierarchical model-based motion estimation. In *Proc. European Conference on Computer Vision*, LNCS 588, pages 237–252. Springer-Verlag, 1992.
6. J. M. Brady. Seeds of perception. In *Proceedings of the 3rd Alvey Vision Conference*, pages 259–265, 1987.
7. D. Capel and A. Zisserman. Automated mosaicing with super-resolution zoom. In *Proc. IEEE Conference on Computer Vision and Pattern Recognition, Santa Barbara*, pages 885–891, June 1998.
8. D. Capel and A. Zisserman. Super-resolution enhancement of text image sequences. In *Proc. International Conference on Pattern Recognition*, 2000.
9. I.J. Cox, S.L. Hingorani, and S.B. Rao. A maximum likelihood stereo algorithm. *Computer vision and image understanding*, 63(3):542–567, 1996.
10. A. W. Fitzgibbon and A. Zisserman. Automatic camera recovery for closed or open image sequences. In *Proc. European Conference on Computer Vision*, pages 311–326. Springer-Verlag, June 1998.
11. K.J. Hanna and E. Okamoto. Combining stereo and motion analysis for direct estimation of scene structure. In *Proc. IEEE Conference on Computer Vision and Pattern Recognition*, pages 357–365, 1993.
12. C. J. Harris and M. Stephens. A combined corner and edge detector. In *Proc. 4th Alvey Vision Conference, Manchester*, pages 147–151, 1988.

13. R. I. Hartley. Self-calibration from multiple views with a rotating camera. In *Proc. European Conference on Computer Vision*, LNCS 800/801, pages 471–478. Springer-Verlag, 1994.

14. R. I. Hartley and A. Zisserman. *Multiple View Geometry in Computer Vision*. Cambridge University Press, ISBN: 0521623049, 2000.

15. P. Havaldar and G. Medioni. Segmented shape descriptions from 3-view stereo. In *Proc. International Conference on Computer Vision*, pages 102–108, 1995.

16. M. Irani and P. Anandan. About direct methods. In *Vision Algorithms: Theory and Practice*. Springer-Verlag, 2000.

17. M. Irani, P. Anandan, and S. Hsu. Mosaic based representations of video sequences and their applications. In *Proc. 5th International Conference on Computer Vision, Boston*, pages 605–611, 1995.

18. M. Irani and S. Peleg. Motion analysis for image enhancement: Resolution, occlusion, and transparency. *Journal of Visual Communication and Image Representation*, 4:324–335, 1993.

19. M. Irani, B. Rousso, and S. Peleg. Computing occluding and transparent motions. *International Journal of Computer Vision*, 12(1):5–16, 1994.

20. R. Koch. 3D surface reconstruction from stereoscopic image sequences. In *Proc. 5th International Conference on Computer Vision, Boston*, pages 109–114, 1995.

21. K. Kutulakos and S. Seitz. A theory of shape by space carving. In *Proc. 7th International Conference on Computer Vision, Kerkyra, Greece*, pages 307–314, 1999.

22. S. Laveau. *Géométrie d'un système de N caméras. Théorie, estimation et applications*. PhD thesis, INRIA, 1996.

23. M. Pollefeys, R. Koch, and L. Van Gool. Self calibration and metric reconstruction in spite of varying and unknown internal camera parameters. In *Proc. 6th International Conference on Computer Vision, Bombay, India*, pages 90–96, 1998.

24. W. Press, B. Flannery, S. Teukolsky, and W. Vetterling. *Numerical Recipes in C*. Cambridge University Press, 1988.

25. P. Pritchett and A. Zisserman. Matching and reconstruction from widely separated views. In R. Koch and L. Van Gool, editors, *3D Structure from Multiple Images of Large-Scale Environments, LNCS 1506*, pages 78–92. Springer-Verlag, June 1998.

26. C. Rothwell, A. Zisserman, D. Forsyth, and J. Mundy. Planar object recognition using projective shape representation. *International Journal of Computer Vision*, 16(2), 1995.

27. C. Schmid, R. Mohr, and C. Bauckhage. Comparing and evaluating interest points. In *Proc. International Conference on Computer Vision*, pages 230–235, 1998.

28. S.M. Seitz and C.R. Dyer. Photorealistic scene reconstruction by voxel coloring. In *Proc. IEEE Conference on Computer Vision and Pattern Recognition, Puerto Rico*, pages 1067–1073, 1997.

29. G. Stein and A. Shashua. Model-based brightness constraints: on direct estimation of structure and motion. In *Proc. IEEE Conference on Computer Vision and Pattern Recognition*, pages 400–406, 1997.

30. P. Sturm. *Vision 3D non calibrée: Contributions à la reconstruction projective et étude des mouvements critiques pour l'auto calibrage*. PhD thesis, INRIA Rhône-Alpes, 1997.

31. P. H. S. Torr, A. W. Fitzgibbon, and A. Zisserman. The problem of degeneracy in structure and motion recovery from uncalibrated image sequences. *International Journal of Computer Vision*, 32(1):27–44, August 1999.

32. P. H. S. Torr and D. W. Murray. The development and comparison of robust methods for estimating the fundamental matrix. *International Journal of Computer Vision*, 24(3):271–300, 1997.

33. P. H. S. Torr and A. Zisserman. Robust parameterization and computation of the trifocal tensor. *Image and Vision Computing*, 15:591–605, 1997.

34. P. H. S. Torr and A. Zisserman. Robust computation and parameterization of multiple view relations. In *Proc. 6th International Conference on Computer Vision, Bombay, India*, pages 727–732, January 1998.

35. P. H. S. Torr, A. Zisserman, and S. Maybank. Robust detection of degenerate configurations for the fundamental matrix. *Computer Vision and Image Understanding*, 71(3):312–333, September 1998.

36. J. Weber and J. Malik. Rigid body segmentation and shape description from dense optical flow under weak perspective. In *Proc. International Conference on Computer Vision*, pages 251–256, 1995.

Discussion for Direct versus Features Session

This section contains the discussion following the special panel session comparing direct and feature-based methods for motion analysis. The positions of the panelists are given in the previous two papers, by Irani & Anandan [1], and by Torr & Zisserman [2].

Discussion

Harpreet Sawhney: I don't think the issue is really feature based or direct methods. There are many intermediate situations between these two extremes. An example is Sarnoff's VideoBrush. It can align multiple, distorted images with only 10–20% overlap between them. The initial step uses a direct method to determine translations which roughly align the images. This is based on a search over a correlation surface. Then, as in feature based methods, it bundle adjusts homographies to align all the images, but it does not suffer from the problem of feature based methods where the cost rises with the number of features.

Andrew Zisserman: There's certainly room for combining the methods and VideoBrush is a good example. In general though a direct method is suitable for estimating a global transformation by a restricted search over a small number of unknown parameters, such as the translation and rotation in the VideoBrush application. But if, for example, there is a a very severe projective transformation where it is necessary to estimate eight parameters, then a feature based method is really needed.

Shmuel Peleg: As Harpreet Sawhney mentioned, feature based and direct methods are just two extremes. Take the example that Michal Irani showed, where a correlation surface is computed for every pixel. This means that each pixel can be thought of as a feature point. If you throw away the 90% of these pixels that don't have a clear correlation maximum, then you have sparse feature based matching. Or you can keep the entire correlation which is the direct method.

Rick Szeliski: Regarding Andrew Zisserman's point that you can't easily do something like the fundamental matrix with direct measurements, I've always thought that the fundamental matrix is kind of a strange beast. It's really only a way to get the camera matrices. If you formulate the problem as plane plus parallax then what Michal Irani showed, and what we and the people at Sarnoff did back in 1994, is that the direct method will pop out the camera matrix fairly easily. Maybe you have to try a couple of hypotheses for the epipole but after that gradient descent is enough. I don't see our inability to solve a two-frame algebraic problem as a severe impediment to finding all of the cameras and the structure.

B. Triggs, A. Zisserman, R. Szeliski (Eds.): Vision Algorithms'99, LNCS 1883, pp. 295–297, 2000.
© Springer-Verlag Berlin Heidelberg 2000

Andrew Zisserman: I agree that we compute the fundamental matrix in order to get the cameras and then the scene reconstruction. We would claim that, at the moment, feature-based methods can deal with much more severe distortions between the two views than direct methods. The reason is that direct methods really have to model to some extent the photometric and geometric distortions (such as the global homography in the plane plus parallax approach). While feature based methods do not require such an accurate model.

Michal Irani: Why do you say that? I showed the multisensor fusion example, which doesn't assume photometric invariance. The claim that direct methods require the constant brightness assumption is just a red herring.

Philip Torr: To reply to Rick Szeliski's point, there's no guarantee that the direct method will converge, especially when the camera movement is large. On the other hand a feature based method can be used to get a good initial approximation to a solution, and then additional image information can be used after that. The main thesis is just that: initialize with a feature based method, and refine the results later with a direct one if necessary. Also, features are not only points: we could use lines or curves as well.

Joss Knight: In both cases, if there are large differences it seems that you need to have some pre-knowledge to decide what image pre-processing technique is needed to get alignable images or patches.

Michal Irani: The multi-sensor correlation method that I showed at the end is actually quite general. You can apply it to any kind of images. Assumptions like brightness constancy are less expensive, but they are not necessary.

Philip Torr: Just to add to the controversy, I note that Jitendra Malik has always argued strongly against features, but when he was doing the car monitoring project he ended up resorting to feature based methods. I'm interested in his experience.

Jitendra Malik: From a scientific or aesthetic point of view, I don't think there's any comparison. The world consists of surfaces, and the visual world consists of the perception of surfaces, with occlusion, non-rigid motion, *etc.*

For engineering purposes, if it so happens that there's just a single moving camera and you can reduce your world to a collection of 20 or 30 points, that's fine. But it's engineering, not fundamental vision. Even then, when I look at Andrew Zisserman's or Luc van Gool's demos I always find a very large number of windows, doors and such like. That's fine too, but there's an empirical question: Suppose I picked lots of video tapes at random, how often would features give me a better initialization, and how often would direct be better? – It's an empirical question and one should ask it.

P. Anandan: That reminds me that so far, we have been talking as if structure from motion was the only thing worth doing. But there are a lot of other things like tracking walking people and motion segmentaion. Michael Black and others have had a fair bit of success extending models like the rigid affine one to deal with these situations, applying direct brightness-based methods to compute the parameters. Video is not like multisensor imagery – simple motion models are enough, and even if the brightness varies, simple preprocessing actually does the trick most of the time.

One of the things which initiated this debate in my mind is that back in 91–93 Keith Hanna published a couple of good papers on direct methods for doing structure from motion, which I suspect that most of the features people in the audience have not read.

Philip Torr: On the other hand, Andrew Blake's person tracking work is feature based.

P. Anandan: Yes. All I'm saying is that the applicability of direct methods goes farther than you think.

Harpreet Sawhney: Phil Torr suggested that feature-based methods should be used to initialize direct ones. Actually, I don't think that I've ever done that. If you need to compute dense displacement fields between nearby frames, you have the choice of a purely 2D method, or one that applies 3D rigidity constraints like Keith Hanna's. In my experience the 3D methods give you much more accurate flow fields.

References

1. M. Irani and P. Anandan. About direct methods. In B. Triggs, A. Zisserman, and R. Szeliski, editors, *Vision Algorithms: Theory and Practice*, number 1883 in LNCS, pages 267–278, Corfu, Greece, September 2000. Springer-Verlag.
2. P. H. S. Torr and A. Zisserman. Feature based methods for structure and motion estimation. In B. Triggs, A. Zisserman, and R. Szeliski, editors, *Vision Algorithms: Theory and Practice*, number 1883 in LNCS, pages 279–295, Corfu, Greece, September 2000. Springer-Verlag.

Bundle Adjustment — A Modern Synthesis

Bill Triggs[1], Philip F. McLauchlan[2], Richard I. Hartley[3], and Andrew W. Fitzgibbon[4]

[1] INRIA Rhône-Alpes, 655 avenue de l'Europe, 38330 Montbonnot, France
Bill.Triggs@inrialpes.fr
http://www.inrialpes.fr/movi/people/Triggs
[2] School of Electrical Engineering, Information Technology & Mathematics
University of Surrey, Guildford, GU2 5XH, U.K.
P.McLauchlan@ee.surrey.ac.uk
[3] General Electric CRD, Schenectady, NY, 12301
hartley@crd.ge.com
[4] Dept of Engineering Science, University of Oxford, 19 Parks Road, OX1 3PJ, U.K.
awf@robots.ox.ac.uk

Abstract. This paper is a survey of the theory and methods of photogrammetric bundle adjustment, aimed at potential implementors in the computer vision community. Bundle adjustment is the problem of refining a visual reconstruction to produce jointly optimal structure and viewing parameter estimates. Topics covered include: the choice of cost function and robustness; numerical optimization including sparse Newton methods, linearly convergent approximations, updating and recursive methods; gauge (datum) invariance; and quality control. The theory is developed for general robust cost functions rather than restricting attention to traditional nonlinear least squares.

Keywords: Bundle Adjustment, Scene Reconstruction, Gauge Freedom, Sparse Matrices, Optimization.

1 Introduction

This paper is a survey of the theory and methods of bundle adjustment aimed at the computer vision community, and more especially at potential implementors who already know a little about bundle methods. Most of the results appeared long ago in the photogrammetry and geodesy literatures, but many seem to be little known in vision, where they are gradually being reinvented. By providing an accessible modern synthesis, we hope to forestall some of this duplication of effort, correct some common misconceptions, and speed progress in visual reconstruction by promoting interaction between the vision and photogrammetry communities.

Bundle adjustment is the problem of refining a visual reconstruction to produce *jointly optimal* 3D structure and viewing parameter (camera pose and/or calibration) estimates. *Optimal* means that the parameter estimates are found by minimizing some cost function that quantifies the model fitting error, and *jointly* that the solution is simultaneously optimal with respect to both structure and camera variations. The name refers to the 'bundles'

This work was supported in part by the European Commission Esprit LTR project CU-MULI (B. Triggs), the UK EPSRC project GR/L34099 (P. McLauchlan), and the Royal Society (A. Fitzgibbon). We would like to thank A. Zisserman, A. Grün and W. Förstner for valuable comments and references.

B. Triggs, A. Zisserman, R. Szeliski (Eds.): Vision Algorithms'99, LNCS 1883, pp. 298–372, 2000.
© Springer-Verlag Berlin Heidelberg 2000

of light rays leaving each 3D feature and converging on each camera centre, which are 'adjusted' optimally with respect to both feature and camera positions. Equivalently — unlike *independent model methods*, which merge partial reconstructions without updating their internal structure — all of the structure and camera parameters are adjusted together 'in one bundle'.

Bundle adjustment is really just a large sparse geometric parameter estimation problem, the parameters being the combined 3D feature coordinates, camera poses and calibrations. Almost everything that we will say can be applied to many similar estimation problems in vision, photogrammetry, industrial metrology, surveying and geodesy. Adjustment computations are a major common theme throughout the measurement sciences, and once the basic theory and methods are understood, they are easy to adapt to a wide variety of problems. Adaptation is largely a matter of choosing a numerical optimization scheme that exploits the problem structure and sparsity. We will consider several such schemes below for bundle adjustment.

Classically, bundle adjustment and similar adjustment computations are formulated as nonlinear least squares problems [19, 46, 100, 21, 22, 69, 5, 73, 109]. The cost function is assumed to be quadratic in the feature reprojection errors, and robustness is provided by explicit outlier screening. Although it is already very flexible, this model is not really general enough. Modern systems often use non-quadratic M-estimator-like distributional models to handle outliers more integrally, and many include additional penalties related to overfitting, model selection and system performance (priors, MDL). For this reason, we will *not* assume a least squares / quadratic cost model. Instead, the cost will be modelled as a sum of opaque contributions from the independent information sources (individual observations, prior distributions, overfitting penalties ...). The functional forms of these contributions and their dependence on fixed quantities such as observations will usually be left implicit. This allows many different types of robust and non-robust cost contributions to be incorporated, without unduly cluttering the notation or hiding essential model structure. It fits well with modern sparse optimization methods (cost contributions are usually sparse functions of the parameters) and object-centred software organization, and it avoids many tedious displays of chain-rule results. Implementors are assumed to be capable of choosing appropriate functions and calculating derivatives themselves.

One aim of this paper is to correct a number of misconceptions that seem to be common in the vision literature:

- **"Optimization / bundle adjustment is slow":** Such statements often appear in papers introducing yet another heuristic Structure from Motion (SFM) iteration. The claimed slowness is almost always due to the unthinking use of a general-purpose optimization routine that completely ignores the problem structure and sparseness. Real bundle routines are *much* more efficient than this, and usually considerably more efficient and flexible than the newly suggested method (§6, 7). That is why bundle adjustment remains the dominant structure refinement technique for real applications, after 40 years of research.

- **"Only linear algebra is required":** This is a recent variant of the above, presumably meant to imply that the new technique is especially simple. Virtually all iterative refinement techniques use only linear algebra, and bundle adjustment is simpler than many in that it only solves linear systems: it makes no use of eigen-decomposition or SVD, which are themselves complex iterative methods.

- **"Any sequence can be used":** Many vision workers seem to be very resistant to the idea that reconstruction problems should be planned in advance (§11), and results checked afterwards to verify their reliability (§10). System builders should at least be aware of the basic techniques for this, even if application constraints make it difficult to use them. The extraordinary extent to which weak geometry and lack of redundancy can mask gross errors is too seldom appreciated, *c.f.* [34, 50, 30, 33].

- **"Point P is reconstructed accurately":** In reconstruction, just as there are no absolute references for position, there are none for uncertainty. The 3D coordinate frame is itself uncertain, as it can only be located relative to uncertain reconstructed features or cameras. All other feature and camera uncertainties are expressed relative to the frame and inherit its uncertainty, so statements about them are meaningless until the frame and its uncertainty are specified. Covariances can look completely different in different frames, particularly in object-centred versus camera-centred ones. See §9.

There is a tendency in vision to develop a profusion of *ad hoc* adjustment iterations. Why should you use bundle adjustment rather than one of these methods? :

- **Flexibility:** Bundle adjustment gracefully handles a very wide variety of different 3D feature and camera types (points, lines, curves, surfaces, exotic cameras), scene types (including dynamic and articulated models, scene constraints), information sources (2D features, intensities, 3D information, priors) and error models (including robust ones). It has no problems with missing data.

- **Accuracy:** Bundle adjustment gives precise and easily interpreted results because it uses accurate statistical error models and supports a sound, well-developed quality control methodology.

- **Efficiency:** Mature bundle algorithms are comparatively efficient even on very large problems. They use economical and rapidly convergent numerical methods and make near-optimal use of problem sparseness.

In general, as computer vision reconstruction technology matures, we expect that bundle adjustment will predominate over alternative adjustment methods in much the same way as it has in photogrammetry. We see this as an inevitable consequence of a greater appreciation of optimization (notably, more effective use of problem structure and sparseness), and of systems issues such as quality control and network design.

Coverage: We will touch on a good many aspects of bundle methods. We start by considering the camera projection model and the parametrization of the bundle problem §2, and the choice of error metric or cost function §3. §4 gives a rapid sketch of the optimization theory we will use. §5 discusses the network structure (parameter interactions and characteristic sparseness) of the bundle problem. The following three sections consider three types of implementation strategies for adjustment computations: §6 covers second order Newton-like methods, which are still the most often used adjustment algorithms; §7 covers methods with only first order convergence (most of the *ad hoc* methods are in this class); and §8 discusses solution updating strategies and recursive filtering bundle methods. §9 returns to the theoretical issue of gauge freedom (datum deficiency), including the theory of inner constraints. §10 goes into some detail on quality control methods for monitoring the accuracy and reliability of the parameter estimates. §11 gives some brief hints on network design, *i.e.* how to place your shots to ensure accurate, reliable reconstruction. §12 completes the body of the paper by summarizing the main conclusions and giving some provisional recommendations for methods. There are also several appendices. §A gives a brief historical overview of the development of bundle methods, with literature references.

§B gives some technical details of matrix factorization, updating and covariance calculation methods. §C gives some hints on designing bundle software, and pointers to useful resources on the Internet. The paper ends with a glossary and references.

General references: Cultural differences sometimes make it difficult for vision workers to read the photogrammetry literature. The collection edited by Atkinson [5] and the manual by Karara [69] are both relatively accessible introductions to close-range (rather than aerial) photogrammetry. Other accessible tutorial papers include [46, 21, 22]. Kraus [73] is probably the most widely used photogrammetry textbook. Brown's early survey of bundle methods [19] is well worth reading. The often-cited manual edited by Slama [100] is now quite dated, although its presentation of bundle adjustment is still relevant. Wolf & Ghiliani [109] is a text devoted to adjustment computations, with an emphasis on surveying. Hartley & Zisserman [62] is an excellent recent textbook covering vision geometry from a computer vision viewpoint. For nonlinear optimization, Fletcher [29] and Gill *et al* [42] are the traditional texts, and Nocedal & Wright [93] is a good modern introduction. For linear least squares, Björck [11] is superlative, and Lawson & Hanson is a good older text. For more general numerical linear algebra, Golub & Van Loan [44] is the standard. Duff *et al* [26] and George & Liu [40] are the standard texts on sparse matrix techniques. We will not discuss initialization methods for bundle adjustment in detail, but appropriate reconstruction methods are plentiful and well-known in the vision community. See, *e.g.*, [62] for references.

Notation: The structure, cameras, *etc.*, being estimated will be parametrized by a single large **state vector** $\mathbf{x}$. In general the state belongs to a nonlinear manifold, but we linearize this locally and work with small linear state displacements denoted $\delta\mathbf{x}$. Observations (*e.g.* measured image features) are denoted $\underline{\mathbf{z}}$. The corresponding predicted values at parameter value $\mathbf{x}$ are denoted $\mathbf{z} = \mathbf{z}(\mathbf{x})$, with **residual prediction error** $\triangle\mathbf{z}(\mathbf{x}) \equiv \underline{\mathbf{z}} - \mathbf{z}(\mathbf{x})$. However, observations and prediction errors usually only appear implicitly, through their influence on the **cost function** $\mathbf{f}(\mathbf{x}) = \mathbf{f}(predz(\mathbf{x}))$. The cost function's **gradient** is $\mathbf{g} \equiv \frac{d\mathbf{f}}{d\mathbf{x}}$, and its **Hessian** is $\mathbf{H} \equiv \frac{d^2\mathbf{f}}{d\mathbf{x}^2}$. The **observation-state Jacobian** is $\mathbf{J} \equiv \frac{d\mathbf{z}}{d\mathbf{x}}$. The dimensions of $\delta\mathbf{x}, \delta\mathbf{z}$ are $n_\mathbf{x}, n_\mathbf{z}$.

2   Projection Model and Problem Parametrization

2.1   The Projection Model

We begin the development of bundle adjustment by considering the basic image projection model and the issue of problem parametrization. Visual reconstruction attempts to recover a model of a 3D scene from multiple images. As part of this, it usually also recovers the poses (positions and orientations) of the cameras that took the images, and information about their internal parameters. A simple scene model might be a collection of isolated 3D features, *e.g.*, points, lines, planes, curves, or surface patches. However, far more complicated scene models are possible, involving, *e.g.*, complex objects linked by constraints or articulations, photometry as well as geometry, dynamics, *etc*. One of the great strengths of adjustment computations — and one reason for thinking that they have a considerable future in vision — is their ability to take such complex and heterogeneous models in their stride. Almost any *predictive parametric* model can be handled, *i.e.* any model that *predicts* the values of some known measurements or descriptors on the basis of some continuous *parametric* representation of the world, which is to be estimated from the measurements.

Similarly, many possible camera models exist. Perspective projection is the standard, but the affine and orthographic projections are sometimes useful for distant cameras, and more exotic models such as push-broom and rational polynomial cameras are needed for certain applications [56, 63]. In addition to pose (position and orientation), and simple internal parameters such as focal length and principal point, real cameras also require various types of **additional parameters** to model internal aberrations such as radial distortion [17–19, 100, 69, 5].

For simplicity, suppose that the scene is modelled by individual static 3D features $\mathbf{X}_p$, $p = 1 \ldots n$, imaged in m shots with camera pose and internal calibration parameters $\mathbf{P}_i$, $i = 1 \ldots m$. There may also be further calibration parameters $\mathbf{C}_c$, $c = 1 \ldots k$, constant across several images (*e.g.*, depending on which of several cameras was used). We are given uncertain measurements $\underline{x}_{ip}$ of some subset of the possible image features x_{ip} (the true image of feature $\mathbf{X}_p$ in image i). For each observation $\underline{x}_{ip}$, we assume that we have a **predictive model** $x_{ip} = x(\mathbf{C}_c, \mathbf{P}_i, \mathbf{X}_p)$ based on the parameters, that can be used to derive a **feature prediction error**:

$$\triangle x_{ip}(\mathbf{C}_c, \mathbf{P}_i, \mathbf{X}_p) \;\equiv\; \underline{x}_{ip} - x(\mathbf{C}_c, \mathbf{P}_i, \mathbf{X}_p) \tag{1}$$

In the case of image observations the predictive model is image projection, but other observation types such as 3D measurements can also be included.

To estimate the unknown 3D feature and camera parameters from the observations, and hence reconstruct the scene, we minimize some measure (discussed in §3) of their total prediction error. Bundle adjustment is the model refinement part of this, starting from given initial parameter estimates (*e.g.*, from some approximate reconstruction method). Hence, it is essentially a matter of optimizing a complicated nonlinear cost function (the total prediction error) over a large nonlinear parameter space (the scene and camera parameters).

We will not go into the analytical forms of the various possible feature and image projection models, as these do not affect the general structure of the adjustment network, and only tend to obscure its central simplicity. We simply stress that the bundle framework is flexible enough to handle almost any desired model. Indeed, there are so many different combinations of features, image projections and measurements, that it is best to regard them as black boxes, capable of giving measurement predictions based on their current parameters. (For optimization, first, and possibly second, derivatives with respect to the parameters are also needed).

For much of the paper we will take quite an abstract view of this situation, collecting the scene and camera parameters to be estimated into a large **state vector** $\mathbf{x}$, and representing the cost (total fitting error) as an abstract function $f(\mathbf{x})$. The cost is really a function of the feature prediction errors $\triangle x_{ip} = \underline{x}_{ip} - x(\mathbf{C}_c, \mathbf{P}_i, \mathbf{X}_p)$. But as the observations $\underline{x}_{ip}$ are constants during an adjustment calculation, we leave the cost's dependence on them and on the projection model $x(\cdot)$ implicit, and display only its dependence on the parameters $\mathbf{x}$ actually being adjusted.

2.2   Bundle Parametrization

The bundle adjustment parameter space is generally a high-dimensional nonlinear manifold — a large Cartesian product of projective 3D feature, 3D rotation, and camera calibration manifolds, perhaps with nonlinear constraints, *etc*. The state $\mathbf{x}$ is not strictly speaking a vector, but rather a point in this space. Depending on how the entities that it contains are

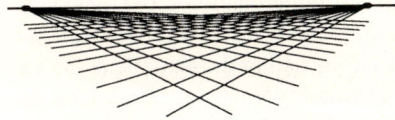

Fig. 1. Vision geometry and its error model are essentially projective. Affine parametrization introduces an artificial singularity at projective infinity, which may cause numerical problems for distant features.

represented, x can be subject to various types of complications including singularities, internal constraints, and unwanted internal degrees of freedom. These arise because geometric entities like rotations, 3D lines and even projective points and planes, do not have simple global parametrizations. Their local parametrizations are nonlinear, with singularities that prevent them from covering the whole parameter space uniformly (*e.g.* the many variants on Euler angles for rotations, the singularity of affine point coordinates at infinity). And their global parametrizations either have constraints (*e.g.* quaternions with $\|q\|^2 = 1$), or unwanted internal degrees of freedom (*e.g.* homogeneous projective quantities have a scale factor freedom, two points defining a line can slide along the line). For more complicated compound entities such as matching tensors and assemblies of 3D features linked by coincidence, parallelism or orthogonality constraints, parametrization becomes even more delicate.

Although they are in principle equivalent, different parametrizations often have profoundly different numerical behaviours which greatly affect the speed and reliability of the adjustment iteration. The most suitable parametrizations for optimization are as uniform, finite and well-behaved as possible *near the current state estimate*. Ideally, they should be locally close to linear in terms of their effect on the chosen error model, so that the cost function is locally nearly quadratic. Nonlinearity hinders convergence by reducing the accuracy of the second order cost model used to predict state updates (§6). Excessive correlations and parametrization singularities cause ill-conditioning and erratic numerical behaviour. Large or infinite parameter values can only be reached after excessively many finite adjustment steps.

Any given parametrization will usually only be well-behaved in this sense over a relatively small section of state space. So to guarantee uniformly good performance, however the state itself may be represented, *state updates should be evaluated using a stable* **local** *parametrization based on increments from the current estimate*. As examples we consider 3D points and rotations.

3D points: Even for calibrated cameras, vision geometry and visual reconstructions are intrinsically projective. If a 3D $(X\ Y\ Z)^{\top}$ parametrization (or equivalently a homogeneous affine $(X\ Y\ Z\ 1)^{\top}$ one) is used for very distant 3D points, large X, Y, Z displacements are needed to change the image significantly. *I.e.*, in $(X\ Y\ Z)$ space the cost function becomes very flat and steps needed for cost adjustment become very large for distant points. In comparison, with a homogeneous projective parametrization $(X\ Y\ Z\ W)^{\top}$, the behaviour near infinity is natural, finite and well-conditioned so long as the normalization keeps the homogeneous 4-vector finite at infinity (by sending $W \to 0$ there). In fact, there is no immediate visual distinction between the images of real points near infinity and virtual ones 'beyond' it (all camera geometries admit such virtual points as *bona fide* projective constructs). The optimal reconstruction of a real 3D point may even be virtual in this sense, if image noise happens to push it 'across infinity'. Also, there is nothing to stop a reconstructed point wandering beyond infinity and back during the optimization. This sounds bizarre at first, but it is an inescapable consequence of the fact that the natural geometry and error model for visual reconstruction is projective rather than affine.

Projectively, *infinity is just like any other place*. Affine parametrization $(X \, Y \, Z \, 1)^\top$ is acceptable for points near the origin with close-range convergent camera geometries, but it is disastrous for distant ones because it artificially cuts away half of the natural parameter space, and hides the fact by sending the resulting edge to infinite parameter values. Instead, you should use a homogeneous parametrization $(X \, Y \, Z \, W)^\top$ for distant points, *e.g.* with spherical normalization $\sum X_i^2 = 1$.

Rotations: Similarly, experience suggests that quasi-global 3 parameter rotation parametrizations such as Euler angles cause numerical problems unless one can be certain to avoid their singularities and regions of uneven coverage. Rotations should be parametrized using either quaternions subject to $\|q\|^2 = 1$, or local perturbations $R \, \delta R$ or $\delta R \, R$ of an existing rotation R, where δR can be any well-behaved 3 parameter small rotation approximation, *e.g.* $\delta R = (I + [\delta r]_\times)$, the Rodriguez formula, local Euler angles, *etc.*

State updates: Just as state vectors x represent points in some nonlinear space, state updates $x \rightarrow x + \delta x$ represent displacements in this nonlinear space that often can not be represented exactly by vector addition. Nevertheless, we assume that we can locally linearize the state manifold, locally resolving any internal constraints and freedoms that it may be subject to, to produce an unconstrained vector δx parametrizing the possible local state displacements. We can then, *e.g.*, use Taylor expansion in δx to form a local cost model $f(x + \delta x) \approx f(x) + \frac{df}{dx} \delta x + \frac{1}{2} \delta x^\top \frac{d^2 f}{dx^2} \delta x$, from which we can estimate the state update δx that optimizes this model (§4). The displacement δx need not have the same structure or representation as x — indeed, if a well-behaved local parametrization is used to represent δx, it generally will not have — but we must at least be able to update the state with the displacement to produce a new state estimate. We write this operation as $x \rightarrow x + \delta x$, even though it may involve considerably more than vector addition. For example, apart from the change of representation, an updated quaternion $q \rightarrow q + dq$ will need to have its normalization $\|q\|^2 = 1$ corrected, and a small rotation update of the form $R \rightarrow R(1 + [r]_\times)$ will not in general give an exact rotation matrix.

3   Error Modelling

We now turn to the choice of the cost function $f(x)$, which quantifies the total prediction (image reprojection) error of the model parametrized by the combined scene and camera parameters x. Our main conclusion will be that robust statistically-based error metrics based on total (inlier + outlier) log likelihoods should be used, to correctly allow for the presence of outliers. We will argue this at some length as it seems to be poorly understood. The traditional treatments of adjustment methods consider only least squares (albeit with data trimming for robustness), and most discussions of robust statistics give the impression that the choice of robustifier or M-estimator is wholly a matter of personal whim rather than data statistics.

Bundle adjustment is essentially a parameter estimation problem. Any parameter estimation paradigm could be used, but we will consider only **optimal point estimators**, whose output is by definition the single parameter vector that minimizes a predefined **cost function** designed to measure how well the model fits the observations and background knowledge. This framework covers many practical estimators including maximum likelihood (ML) and maximum a posteriori (MAP), but not explicit Bayesian model averaging. Robustification, regularization and model selection terms are easily incorporated in the cost.

A typical ML cost function would be the summed negative log likelihoods of the prediction errors of all the observed image features. For Gaussian error distributions, this reduces to the sum of squared covariance-weighted prediction errors (§3.2). A MAP estimator would typically add cost terms giving certain structure or camera calibration parameters a bias towards their expected values.

The cost function is also a tool for statistical interpretation. To the extent that lower costs are uniformly 'better', it provides a natural model preference ordering, so that cost iso-surfaces above the minimum define natural confidence regions. Locally, these regions are nested ellipsoids centred on the cost minimum, with size and shape characterized by the **dispersion matrix** (the inverse of the cost function Hessian $H = \frac{d^2f}{dx^2}$ at the minimum). Also, the residual cost at the minimum can be used as a test statistic for model validity (§10). _E.g._, for a negative log likelihood cost model with Gaussian error distributions, twice the residual is a χ^2 variable.

3.1 Desiderata for the Cost Function

In adjustment computations we go to considerable lengths to optimize a large nonlinear cost model, so it seems reasonable to require that the refinement should actually improve the estimates in some objective (albeit statistical) sense. Heuristically motivated cost functions can not usually guarantee this. They almost always lead to biased parameter estimates, and often severely biased ones. A large body of statistical theory points to maximum likelihood (ML) and its Bayesian cousin maximum a posteriori (MAP) as the estimators of choice. ML simply selects the model for which the total probability of the observed data is highest, or saying the same thing in different words, for which the _total posterior probability_ of the model given the observations is highest. MAP adds a prior term representing background information. ML could just as easily have included the prior as an additional 'observation': so far as estimation is concerned, the distinction between ML / MAP and prior / observation is purely terminological.

Information usually comes from many independent sources. In bundle adjustment these include: covariance-weighted reprojection errors of individual image features; other measurements such as 3D positions of control points, GPS or inertial sensor readings; predictions from uncertain dynamical models (for 'Kalman filtering' of dynamic cameras or scenes); prior knowledge expressed as soft constraints (_e.g._ on camera calibration or pose values); and supplementary sources such as overfitting, regularization or description length penalties. Note the variety. One of the great strengths of adjustment computations is their ability to combine information from disparate sources. Assuming that the sources are statistically independent of one another given the model, the total probability for the model given the combined data is the product of the probabilities from the individual sources. To get an additive cost function we take logs, so the total log likelihood for the model given the combined data is the sum of the individual source log likelihoods.

Properties of ML estimators: Apart from their obvious simplicity and intuitive appeal, ML and MAP estimators have strong statistical properties. Many of the most notable ones are **asymptotic**, _i.e._ they apply in the limit of a large number of independent measurements, or more precisely in the **central limit** where the posterior distribution becomes effectively Gaussian[1]. In particular:

---

[1] Cost is additive, so as measurements of the same type are added the entire cost surface grows in direct proportion to the amount of data n_z. This means that the _relative_ sizes of the cost and all of

- Under mild regularity conditions on the observation distributions, the posterior distribution of the ML estimate converges asymptotically in probability to a Gaussian with covariance equal to the dispersion matrix.
- The ML estimate asymptotically has zero bias and the lowest variance that any unbiased estimator can have. So in this sense, ML estimation is at least as good as any other method[2].

Non-asymptotically, the dispersion is not necessarily a good approximation for the covariance of the ML estimator. The asymptotic limit is usually assumed to be a valid for well-designed highly-redundant photogrammetric measurement networks, but recent sampling-based empirical studies of posterior likelihood surfaces [35, 80, 68] suggest that the case is much less clear for small vision geometry problems and weaker networks. More work is needed on this.

The effect of incorrect error models: It is clear that incorrect modelling of the observation distributions is likely to disturb the ML estimate. Such mismodelling is to some extent inevitable because error distributions stand for influences that we can not fully predict or control. To understand the distortions that unrealistic error models can cause, first realize that geometric fitting is really a special case of parametric probability density estimation. For each set of parameter values, the geometric image projection model and the assumed observation error models combine to predict a probability density for the observations. Maximizing the likelihood corresponds to fitting this *predicted observation density* to the observed data. The geometry and camera model only enter indirectly, via their influence on the predicted distributions.

Accurate noise modelling is just as critical to successful estimation as accurate geometric modelling. The most important mismodelling is failure to take account of the possibility of **outliers** (aberrant data values, caused *e.g.*, by blunders such as incorrect feature correspondences). We stress that so long as the assumed error distributions model the behaviour of *all* of the data used in the fit (including *both* inliers *and* outliers), the above properties of ML estimation including asymptotic minimum variance remain valid in the presence of outliers. In other words, *ML estimation is naturally robust*: there is no

---

its derivatives — and hence the size r of the region around the minimum over which the second order Taylor terms dominate all higher order ones — remain roughly constant as n_z increases. Within this region, the total cost is roughly quadratic, so if the cost function was taken to be the posterior log likelihood, the posterior distribution is roughly Gaussian. However the curvature of the quadratic (*i.e.* the inverse dispersion matrix) increases as data is added, so the posterior standard deviation shrinks as $\mathcal{O}\big(\sigma/\sqrt{n_z - n_x}\big)$, where $\mathcal{O}(\sigma)$ characterizes the average standard deviation from a single observation. For $n_z - n_x \gg (\sigma/r)^2$, essentially the entire posterior probability mass lies inside the quadratic region, so the posterior distribution converges asymptotically in probability to a Gaussian. This happens at *any* proper isolated cost minimum at which second order Taylor expansion is locally valid. The approximation gets better with more data (stronger curvature) and smaller higher order Taylor terms.

[2] This result follows from the **Cramér-Rao bound** (*e.g.* [23]), which says that the covariance of any unbiased estimator is bounded below by the **Fisher information** or mean curvature of the posterior log likelihood surface $\langle (\widehat{x} - \overline{x})(\widehat{x} - \overline{x})^\top \rangle \succeq -\langle \frac{d^2 \log p}{dx^2} \rangle$ where p is the posterior probability, x the parameters being estimated, $\widehat{x}$ the estimate given by any unbiased estimator, $\overline{x}$ the true underlying x value, and $A \succeq B$ denotes positive semidefiniteness of $A - B$. Asymptotically, the posterior distribution becomes Gaussian and the Fisher information converges to the inverse dispersion (the curvature of the posterior log likelihood surface at the cost minimum), so the ML estimate attains the Cramér-Rao bound.

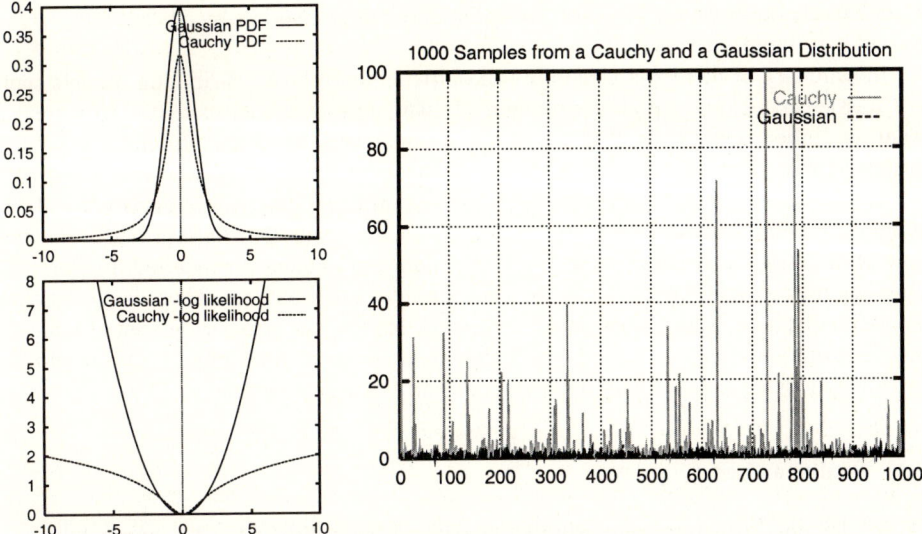

Fig. 2. Beware of treating any bell-shaped observation distribution as a Gaussian. Despite being narrower in the peak and broader in the tails, the probability density function of a Cauchy distribution, $p(x) = \left(\pi(1 + x^2)\right)^{-1}$, does not look so very different from that of a Gaussian (*top left*). But their negative log likelihoods are very different (*bottom left*), and large deviations ("outliers") are *much* more probable for Cauchy variates than for Gaussian ones (*right*). In fact, the Cauchy distribution has infinite covariance.

need to robustify it so long as realistic error distributions were used in the first place. A distribution that models both inliers and outliers is called a **total distribution**. There is no need to separate the two classes, as ML estimation does not care about the distinction. If the total distribution happens to be an explicit mixture of an inlier and an outlier distribution (*e.g.*, a Gaussian with a locally uniform background of outliers), outliers can be labeled after fitting using likelihood ratio tests, but this is in no way essential to the estimation process.

It is also important to realize the extent to which superficially similar distributions can differ from a Gaussian, or equivalently, how extraordinarily rapidly the tails of a Gaussian distribution fall away compared to more realistic models of real observation errors. See figure 2. In fact, unmodelled outliers typically have very severe effects on the fit. To see this, suppose that the real observations are drawn from a fixed (but perhaps unknown) underlying distribution $p_0(\underline{z})$. The *law of large numbers* says that their empirical distributions (the observed distribution of each set of samples) converge asymptotically in probability to $p_0(\underline{z})$. So for each model, the negative log likelihood cost sum $- \sum_i \log p_{\text{model}}(\underline{z}_i | \underline{x})$ converges to $-n_{\underline{z}} \int p_0(\underline{z}) \log(p_{\text{model}}(\underline{z}|\underline{x}))\, d\underline{z}$. Up to a model-independent constant, this is $n_{\underline{z}}$ times the **relative entropy** or **Kullback-Leibler divergence** $\int p_0(\underline{z}) \log(p_0(\underline{z})/p_{\text{model}}(\underline{z}|\underline{x}))\, d\underline{z}$ of the model distribution w.r.t. the true one $p_0(\underline{z})$. Hence, even if the model family does not include p_0, *the ML estimate converges asymptotically to the model whose predicted observation distribution has* minimum relative entropy *w.r.t.* p_0. (See, *e.g.* [96, proposition 2.2]). It follows that ML estimates are typically very sensitive to unmodelled outliers, as regions which are relatively probable under p_0 but highly *im*probable under the model make large contributions to the relative entropy. In contrast, allowing for outliers where none actually occur causes relatively little distortion, as no region which is probable under p_0 will have large $-\log p_{\text{model}}$.

In summary, if there is a possibility of outliers, non-robust distribution models such as Gaussians should be replaced with more realistic long-tailed ones such as: mixtures of a narrow 'inlier' and a wide 'outlier' density, Cauchy or α-densities, or densities defined piecewise with a central peaked 'inlier' region surrounded by a constant 'outlier' region[3]. We emphasize again that poor robustness is due entirely to unrealistic distributional assumptions: the maximum likelihood framework itself is naturally robust provided that the total observation distribution including both inliers and outliers is modelled. In fact, real observations can seldom be cleanly divided into inliers and outliers. There is a hard core of outliers such as feature correspondence errors, but there is also a grey area of features that for some reason (a specularity, a shadow, poor focus, motion blur ...) were not as accurately located as other features, without clearly being outliers.

3.2   Nonlinear Least Squares

One of the most basic parameter estimation methods is **nonlinear least squares**. Suppose that we have vectors of observations $\underline{z}_i$ predicted by a model $z_i = z_i(x)$, where x is a vector of model parameters. Then nonlinear least squares takes as estimates the parameter values that minimize the **weighted Sum of Squared Error (SSE)** cost function:

$$f(x) \equiv \tfrac{1}{2} \sum_i \triangle z_i(x)^\top W_i \triangle z_i(x), \qquad \triangle z_i(x) \equiv \underline{z}_i - z_i(x) \qquad (2)$$

Here, $\triangle z_i(x)$ is the feature prediction error and W_i is an arbitrary symmetric positive definite (SPD) **weight matrix**. Modulo normalization terms independent of x, the weighted SSE cost function coincides with the negative log likelihood for observations $\underline{z}_i$ perturbed by Gaussian noise of mean zero and covariance W_i^{-1}. So for least squares to have a useful statistical interpretation, the W_i should be chosen to approximate the inverse measurement covariance of $\underline{z}_i$. Even for non-Gaussian noise with this mean and covariance, the **Gauss-Markov theorem** [37, 11] states that if the models $z_i(x)$ are linear, least squares gives the Best Linear Unbiased Estimator (BLUE), where 'best' means minimum variance[4].

Any weighted least squares model can be converted to an unweighted one ($W_i = 1$) by pre-multiplying $\underline{z}_i, z_i, \triangle z_i$ by any $L_i^\top$ satisfying $W_i = L_i L_i^\top$. Such an L_i can be calculated efficiently from W_i or W_i^{-1} using Cholesky decomposition (§B.1). $\overline{\triangle z}_i = L_i^\top \triangle z_i$ is called a **standardized residual**, and the resulting unweighted least squares problem $\min_x \tfrac{1}{2} \sum_i \|\overline{\triangle z}_i(x)\|^2$ is said to be in **standard form**. One advantage of this is that optimization methods based on linear least squares solvers can be used in place of ones based on linear (normal) equation solvers, which allows ill-conditioned problems to be handled more stably (§B.2).

Another peculiarity of the SSE cost function is its indifference to the natural boundaries between the observations. If observations $\underline{z}_i$ from any sources are assembled into a

---

[3] The latter case corresponds to a hard inlier / outlier decision rule: for any observation in the 'outlier' region, the density is constant so the observation has no influence at all on the fit. Similarly, the mixture case corresponds to a softer inlier / outlier decision rule.

[4] It may be possible (and even useful) to do better with either biased (towards the correct solution), or nonlinear estimators.

compound observation vector $\underline{z} \equiv (\underline{z}_1^{\top}, \dots, \underline{z}_k^{\top})^{\top}$, and their weight matrices W_i are assembled into compound block diagonal weight matrix $W \equiv \mathrm{diag}(W_1, \dots, W_k)$, the weighted squared error $f(x) \equiv \frac{1}{2} \triangle z(x)^{\top} W \triangle z(x)$ is the same as the original SSE cost function, $\frac{1}{2} \sum_i \triangle z_i(x)^{\top} W_i \triangle z_i(x)$. The general quadratic form of the SSE cost is preserved under such compounding, and also under arbitrary linear transformations of $\underline{z}$ that mix components from different observations. The only place that the underlying structure is visible is in the block structure of W. Such invariances do not hold for essentially any other cost function, but they simplify the formulation of least squares considerably.

3.3   Robustified Least Squares

The main problem with least squares is its high sensitivity to outliers. This happens because the Gaussian has extremely small tails compared to most real measurement error distributions. For robust estimates, we must choose a more realistic likelihood model (§3.1). The exact functional form is less important than the general way in which the expected types of outliers enter. A single blunder such as a correspondence error may affect one or a few of the observations, but it will usually leave all of the others unchanged. This locality is the whole basis of robustification. If we can decide which observations were affected, we can down-weight or eliminate them and use the remaining observations for the parameter estimates as usual. If all of the observations had been affected about equally (*e.g.* as by an incorrect projection model), we might still know that something was wrong, but not be able to fix it by simple data cleaning.

We will adopt a 'single layer' robustness model, in which the observations are partitioned into independent groups $\underline{z}_i$, each group being irreducible in the sense that it is accepted, down-weighted or rejected as a whole, independently of all the other groups. The partitions should reflect the types of blunders that occur. For example, if feature correspondence errors are the most common blunders, the two coordinates of a single image point would naturally form a group as both would usually be invalidated by such a blunder, while no other image point would be affected. Even if one of the coordinates appeared to be correct, if the other were incorrect we would usually want to discard both for safety. On the other hand, in stereo problems, the four coordinates of each pair of corresponding image points might be a more natural grouping, as a point in one image is useless without its correspondent in the other one.

Henceforth, when we say *observation* we mean *irreducible group of observations treated as a unit by the robustifying model. I.e.*, our observations need not be scalars, but they must be units, probabilistically independent of one another irrespective of whether they are inliers or outliers.

As usual, each independent observation $\underline{z}_i$ contributes an independent term $f_i(x \mid \underline{z}_i)$ to the total cost function. This could have more or less any form, depending on the expected total distribution of inliers and outliers for the observation. One very natural family are the **radial distributions**, which have negative log likelihoods of the form:

$$f_i(x) \equiv \tfrac{1}{2} \rho_i(\triangle z_i(x)^{\top} W_i \triangle z_i(x)) \tag{3}$$

Here, $\rho_i(s)$ can be any increasing function with $\rho_i(0) = 0$ and $\frac{d}{ds}\rho_i(0) = 1$. (These guarantee that at $\triangle z_i = 0$, f vanishes and $\frac{d^2 f_i}{dz_i^2} = W_i$). Weighted SSE has $\rho_i(s) = s$, while more robust variants have sublinear ρ_i, often tending to a constant at ∞ so that distant outliers are entirely ignored. The dispersion matrix W_i^{-1} determines the spatial spread of $\underline{z}_i$, and up to scale its covariance (if this is finite). The radial form is preserved under arbitrary affine transformations of $\underline{z}_i$, so within a group, all of the observations are on an equal footing in the same sense as in least squares. However, non-Gaussian radial distributions are almost never *separable*: the observations in $\underline{z}_i$ can neither be split into independent subgroups, nor combined into larger groups, without destroying the radial form. Radial cost models do not have the remarkable isotropy of non-robust SSE, but this is exactly what we wanted, as it ensures that all observations in a group will be either left alone, or down-weighted together.

As an example of this, for image features polluted with occasional large outliers caused by correspondence errors, we might model the error distribution as a Gaussian central peak plus a uniform background of outliers. This would give negative log likelihood contributions of the form $f(x) = -\log\left(\exp(-\frac{1}{2}\chi_{ip}^2) + \epsilon\right)$ instead of the non-robust weighted SSE model $f(x) = \frac{1}{2}\chi_{ip}^2$, where $\chi_{ip}^2 = \triangle x_{ip}^\top W_{ip} \triangle x_{ip}$ is the squared weighted residual error (which is a χ^2 variable for a correct model and Gaussian error distribution), and ϵ parametrizes the frequency of outliers.

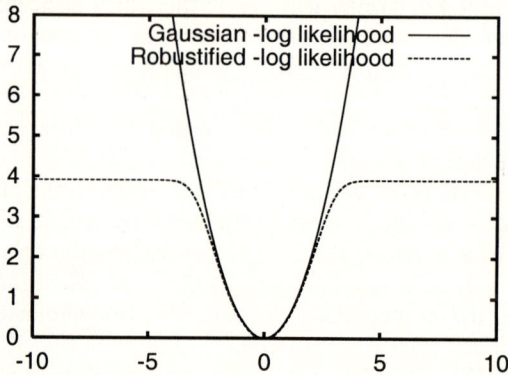

3.4   Intensity-Based Methods

The above models apply not only to geometric image features, but also to intensity-based matching of image patches. In this case, the observables are image gray-scales or colors I rather than feature coordinates u, and the error model is based on intensity residuals. To get from a point projection model $u = u(x)$ to an intensity based one, we simply compose with the assumed local intensity model $I = I(u)$ (*e.g.* obtained from an image template or another image that we are matching against), premultiply point Jacobians by point-to-intensity Jacobians $\frac{dI}{du}$, *etc.* The full range of intensity models can be implemented within this framework: pure translation, affine, quadratic or homographic patch deformation models, 3D model based intensity predictions, coupled affine or spline patches for surface coverage, *etc.*, [1, 52, 55, 9, 110, 94, 53, 97, 76, 104, 102]. The structure of intensity based bundle problems is very similar to that of feature based ones, so all of the techniques studied below can be applied.

We will not go into more detail on intensity matching, except to note that it is the real basis of feature based methods. Feature detectors are optimized for detection not localization. To localize a detected feature accurately we need to match (some function of) the image intensities in its region against either an idealized template or another image of the feature, using an appropriate geometric deformation model, *etc*. For example, suppose that the intensity matching model is $f(u) = \frac{1}{2} \iint \rho(\|\delta \mathbf{I}(u)\|^2)$ where the integration is over some image patch, $\delta \mathbf{I}$ is the current intensity prediction error, u parametrizes the local geometry (patch translation & warping), and $\rho(\cdot)$ is some intensity error robustifier. Then the cost gradient in terms of u is $g_u^\top = \frac{df}{du} = \iint \rho'\, \delta \mathbf{I}^\top \frac{d\mathbf{I}}{du}$. Similarly, the cost Hessian in u in a Gauss-Newton approximation is $H_u = \frac{d^2 f}{du^2} \approx \iint \rho'' \, (\frac{d\mathbf{I}}{du})^\top \frac{d\mathbf{I}}{du}$. In a feature based model, we express $u = u(x)$ as a function of the bundle parameters, so if $J_u = \frac{du}{dx}$ we have a corresponding cost gradient and Hessian contribution $g_x^\top = g_u^\top J_u$ and $H_x = J_u^\top H_u J_u$. In other words, the intensity matching model is locally equivalent to a quadratic feature matching one on the 'features' $u(x)$, with effective weight (inverse covariance) matrix $W_u = H_u$. All image feature error models in vision are ultimately based on such an underlying intensity matching model. As feature covariances are a function of intensity gradients $\iint \rho'' \, (\frac{d\mathbf{I}}{du})^\top \frac{d\mathbf{I}}{du}$, they can be both highly variable between features (depending on how much local gradient there is), and highly anisotropic (depending on how directional the gradients are). *E.g.*, for points along a 1D intensity edge, the uncertainty is large in the along edge direction and small in the across edge one.

3.5 Implicit Models

Sometimes observations are most naturally expressed in terms of an implicit observation-constraining model $h(x, z) = 0$, rather than an explicit observation-predicting one $z = z(x)$. (The associated image error still has the form $f(\underline{z} - z)$). For example, if the model is a 3D curve and we observe points on it (the noisy images of 3D points that may lie anywhere along the 3D curve), we can predict the whole image curve, but not the exact position of each observation along it. We only have the constraint that the noiseless image of the observed point would lie on the noiseless image of the curve, if we knew these. There are basically two ways to handle implicit models: nuisance parameters and reduction.

Nuisance parameters: In this approach, the model is made explicit by adding additional 'nuisance' parameters representing something equivalent to model-consistent estimates of the unknown noise free observations, *i.e.* to z with $h(x, z) = 0$. The most direct way to do this is to include the entire parameter vector z as nuisance parameters, so that we have to solve a constrained optimization problem on the extended parameter space (x, z), minimizing $f(\underline{z} - z)$ over (x, z) subject to $h(x, z) = 0$. This is a sparse constrained problem, which can be solved efficiently using sparse matrix techniques (§6.3). In fact, for image observations, the subproblems in z (optimizing $f(\underline{z} - z)$ over z for fixed $\underline{z}$ and x) are small and for typical f rather simple. So in spite of the extra parameters z, optimizing this model is not significantly more expensive than optimizing an explicit one $z = z(x)$ [14, 13, 105, 106]. For example, when estimating matching constraints between image pairs or triplets [60, 62], instead of using an explicit 3D representation, pairs or triplets of corresponding image points can be used as features z_i, subject to the epipolar or trifocal geometry contained in x [105, 106].

However, if a smaller nuisance parameter vector than z can be found, it is wise to use it. In the case of a curve, it suffices to include just one nuisance parameter per observation, saying where along the curve the corresponding noise free observation is predicted to lie. This model exactly satisfies the constraints, so it converts the implicit model to an unconstrained explicit one $z = z(x, \lambda)$, where λ are the along-curve nuisance parameters.

The advantage of the nuisance parameter approach is that it gives the exact optimal parameter estimate for x, and jointly, optimal x-consistent estimates for the noise free observations z.

Reduction: Alternatively, we can regard $h(x, \underline{z})$ rather than $\underline{z}$ as the observation vector, and hence fit the parameters to the explicit log likelihood model for $h(x, \underline{z})$. To do this, we must transfer the underlying error model / distribution $f(\triangle z)$ on $\underline{z}$ to one $f(h)$ on $h(x, \underline{z})$. In principle, this should be done by marginalization: the density for h is given by integrating that for $\triangle z$ over all $\triangle z$ giving the same h. Within the point estimation framework, it can be approximated by replacing the integration with maximization. Neither calculation is easy in general, but in the asymptotic limit where first order Taylor expansion $h(x, \underline{z}) = h(x, z + \triangle z) \approx 0 + \frac{dh}{dz} \triangle z$ is valid, the distribution of h is a marginalization or maximization of that of $\triangle z$ over affine subspaces. This can be evaluated in closed form for some robust distributions. Also, standard covariance propagation gives (more precisely, this applies to the h and $\triangle z$ dispersions):

$$\langle h(x, \underline{z}) \rangle \approx 0, \qquad \langle h(x, \underline{z}) \, h(x, \underline{z})^\top \rangle \approx \frac{dh}{dz} \langle \triangle z \, \triangle z^\top \rangle \frac{dh}{dz}^\top = \frac{dh}{dz} \, W^{-1} \, \frac{dh}{dz}^\top \quad (4)$$

where W^{-1} is the covariance of $\triangle z$. So at least for an outlier-free Gaussian model, the reduced distribution remains Gaussian (albeit with x-dependent covariance).

4 Basic Numerical Optimization

Having chosen a suitable model quality metric, we must optimize it. This section gives a very rapid sketch of the basic local optimization methods for differentiable functions. See [29, 93, 42] for more details. We need to minimize a cost function $f(x)$ over parameters x, starting from some given initial estimate x of the minimum, presumably supplied by some approximate visual reconstruction method or prior knowledge of the approximate situation. As in §2.2, the parameter space may be nonlinear, but we assume that local displacements can be parametrized by a local coordinate system / vector of free parameters δx. We try to find a displacement $x \rightarrow x + \delta x$ that locally minimizes or at least reduces the cost function. Real cost functions are too complicated to minimize in closed form, so instead we minimize an approximate **local model** for the function, *e.g.* based on Taylor expansion or some other approximation at the current point x. Although this does not usually give the exact minimum, with luck it will improve on the initial parameter estimate and allow us to iterate to convergence. The art of reliable optimization is largely in the details that make this happen even without luck: which local model, how to minimize it, how to ensure that the estimate is improved, and how to decide when convergence has occurred. If you not are interested in such subjects, use a professionally designed package (§C.2): details *are* important here.

4.1 Second Order Methods

The reference for all local models is the quadratic Taylor series one:

$$f(x + \delta x) \approx f(x) + g^\top \delta x + \tfrac{1}{2} \delta x^\top H \, \delta x \qquad g \equiv \frac{df}{dx}(x) \qquad H \equiv \frac{d^2 f}{dx^2}(x) \quad (5)$$

quadratic local model $\qquad\qquad$ gradient vector $\qquad$ Hessian matrix

For now, assume that the Hessian H is positive definite (but see below and §9). The local model is then a simple quadratic with a unique global minimum, which can be found explicitly using linear algebra. Setting $\frac{df}{dx}(x + \delta x) \approx H\,\delta x + g$ to zero for the stationary point gives the **Newton step**:

$$\delta x = -H^{-1}g \tag{6}$$

The estimated new function value is $f(x + \delta x) \approx f(x) - \frac{1}{2}\delta x^\top H\,\delta x = f(x) - \frac{1}{2}g^\top H^{-1}g$. Iterating the Newton step gives **Newton's method**. This is the canonical optimization method for smooth cost functions, owing to its exceptionally rapid theoretical and practical convergence near the minimum. For quadratic functions it converges in one iteration, and for more general analytic ones its **asymptotic convergence** is **quadratic**: as soon as the estimate gets close enough to the solution for the second order Taylor expansion to be reasonably accurate, the residual state error is approximately *squared* at each iteration. This means that the number of significant digits in the estimate approximately doubles at each iteration, so starting from any reasonable estimate, at most about $\log_2(16) + 1 \approx 5$–6 iterations are needed for full double precision (16 digit) accuracy. Methods that potentially achieve such rapid asymptotic convergence are called **second order methods**. This is a high accolade for a local optimization method, but it can only be achieved if the Newton step is asymptotically well approximated. Despite their conceptual simplicity and asymptotic performance, Newton-like methods have some disadvantages:

- To guarantee convergence, a suitable step control policy must be added (§4.2).
- Solving the $n \times n$ Newton step equations takes time $\mathcal{O}(n^3)$ for a dense system (§B.1), which can be prohibitive for large n. Although the cost can often be reduced (very substantially for bundle adjustment) by exploiting sparseness in H, it remains true that Newton-like methods tend to have a high cost per iteration, which increases relative to that of other methods as the problem size increases. For this reason, it is sometimes worthwhile to consider more approximate **first order methods** (§7), which are occasionally more efficient, and generally simpler to implement, than sparse Newton-like methods.
- Calculating second derivatives H is by no means trivial for a complicated cost function, both computationally, and in terms of implementation effort. The **Gauss-Newton** method (§4.3) offers a simple analytic approximation to H for nonlinear least squares problems. Some other methods build up approximations to H from the way the gradient g changes during the iteration are in use (see §7.1, Krylov methods).
- The asymptotic convergence of Newton-like methods is sometimes felt to be an expensive luxury when far from the minimum, especially when damping (see below) is active. However, it must be said that Newton-like methods generally do require significantly fewer iterations than first order ones, even far from the minimum.

4.2 Step Control

Unfortunately, Newton's method can fail in several ways. It may converge to a saddle point rather than a minimum, and for large steps the second order cost prediction may be inaccurate, so there is no guarantee that the true cost will actually decrease. To guarantee convergence to a minimum, the step must follow a local **descent direction** (a direction with a non-negligible component down the local cost gradient, or if the gradient is zero near a saddle point, down a negative curvature direction of the Hessian), and it must make reasonable progress in this direction (neither so little that the optimization runs slowly or stalls, nor so much that it greatly overshoots the cost minimum along this direction). It is also necessary to decide when the iteration has converged, and perhaps to limit any over-large steps that are requested. Together, these topics form the delicate subject of **step control**.

To choose a descent direction, one can take the Newton step direction if this descends (it may not near a saddle point), or more generally some combination of the Newton and gradient directions. **Damped Newton methods** solve a regularized system to find the step:

$$(H + \lambda W)\,\delta x = -g \tag{7}$$

Here, λ is some weighting factor and W is some positive definite weight matrix (often the identity, so $\lambda \to \infty$ becomes gradient descent $\delta x \propto -g$). λ can be chosen to limit the step to a dynamically chosen maximum size (**trust region methods**), or manipulated more heuristically, to shorten the step if the prediction is poor (**Levenberg-Marquardt methods**).

Given a descent direction, progress along it is usually assured by a **line search** method, of which there are many based on quadratic and cubic 1D cost models. If the suggested (*e.g.* Newton) step is δx, line search finds the α that actually minimizes f along the line $x + \alpha\,\delta x$, rather than simply taking the estimate $\alpha = 1$.

There is no space for further details on step control here (again, see [29, 93, 42]). However note that poor step control can make a huge difference in reliability and convergence rates, especially for ill-conditioned problems. Unless you are familiar with these issues, it is advisable to use professionally designed methods.

4.3   Gauss-Newton and Least Squares

Consider the nonlinear weighted SSE cost model $f(x) \equiv \frac{1}{2}\,\triangle z(x)^\top W \triangle z(x)$ (§3.2) with prediction error $\triangle z(x) = \underline{z} - z(x)$ and weight matrix W. Differentiation gives the gradient and Hessian in terms of the **Jacobian** or **design matrix** of the predictive model, $J \equiv \frac{dz}{dx}$:

$$g \equiv \frac{df}{dx} = \triangle z^\top W J \qquad\qquad H \equiv \frac{d^2 f}{dx^2} = J^\top W J + \sum_i (\triangle z^\top W)_i \frac{d^2 z_i}{dx^2} \tag{8}$$

These formulae could be used directly in a damped Newton method, but the $\frac{d^2 z_i}{dx^2}$ term in H is likely to be small in comparison to the corresponding components of $J^\top W J$ if either: (*i*) the prediction error $\triangle z(x)$ is small; or (*ii*) the model is nearly linear, $\frac{d^2 z_i}{dx^2} \approx 0$. Dropping the second term gives the **Gauss-Newton approximation** to the least squares Hessian, $H \approx J^\top W J$. With this approximation, the Newton step prediction equations become the **Gauss-Newton** or **normal** equations:

$$(J^\top W J)\,\delta x = -J^\top W \triangle z \tag{9}$$

The Gauss-Newton approximation is extremely common in nonlinear least squares, and practically all current bundle implementations use it. Its main advantage is simplicity: the second derivatives of the projection model $z(x)$ are complex and troublesome to implement.

In fact, the normal equations are just one of many methods of solving the weighted linear least squares problem[5] $\min_{\delta x} \frac{1}{2}(J\,\delta x - \triangle z)^{\top} W\,(J\,\delta x - \triangle z)$. Another notable method is that based on QR decomposition (§B.2, [11, 44]), which is up to a factor of two slower than the normal equations, but much less sensitive to ill-conditioning in J [6].

Whichever solution method is used, the main disadvantage of the Gauss-Newton approximation is that when the discarded terms are not negligible, the convergence rate is greatly reduced (§7.2). In our experience, such reductions are indeed common in highly nonlinear problems with (at the current step) large residuals. For example, near a saddle point the Gauss-Newton approximation is *never* accurate, as its predicted Hessian is always at least positive semidefinite. However, for well-parametrized (*i.e.* locally near linear, §2.2) bundle problems under an outlier-free least squares cost model evaluated near the cost minimum, the Gauss-Newton approximation is usually very accurate. Feature extraction errors and hence $\triangle z$ and W^{-1} have characteristic scales of at most a few pixels. In contrast, the nonlinearities of $z(x)$ are caused by nonlinear 3D feature-camera geometry (perspective effects) and nonlinear image projection (lens distortion). For typical geometries and lenses, neither effect varies significantly on a scale of a few pixels. So the nonlinear corrections are usually small compared to the leading order linear terms, and bundle adjustment behaves as a near-linear small residual problem.

However note that this does *not* extend to robust cost models. Robustification works by introducing strong nonlinearity into the cost function at the scale of typical feature reprojection errors. For accurate step prediction, the optimization routine must take account of this. For radial cost functions (§3.3), a reasonable compromise is to take account of the exact second order derivatives of the robustifiers $\rho_i(\cdot)$, while retaining only the first order Gauss-Newton approximation for the predicted observations $z_i(x)$. If ρ'_i and ρ'' are respectively the first and second derivatives of ρ_i at the current evaluation point, we have a **robustified Gauss-Newton approximation**:

$$g_i = \rho'_i\, J_i^{\top} W_i\, \triangle z_i \qquad H_i \approx J_i^{\top}\left(\rho'_i\, W_i + 2\,\rho''_i\,(W_i\,\triangle z_i)\,(W_i\,\triangle z_i)^{\top}\right) J_i \qquad (10)$$

So robustification has two effects: (*i*) it down-weights the entire observation (both g_i and H_i) by ρ'_i; and (*ii*) it makes a rank-one reduction[7] of the curvature H_i in the radial ($\triangle z_i$) direction, to account for the way in which the weight changes with the residual. There are reweighting-based optimization methods that include only the first effect. They still find the true cost minimum $g = 0$ as the g_i are evaluated exactly[8], but convergence may

---

[5] Here, the dependence of J on x is ignored, which amounts to the same thing as ignoring the $\frac{d^2 z_i}{dx^2}$ term in H.

[6] The QR method gives the solution to a relative error of about $\mathcal{O}(C\epsilon)$, as compared to $\mathcal{O}(C^2\epsilon)$ for the normal equations, where C is the condition number (the ratio of the largest to the smallest singular value) of J, and ϵ is the machine precision (10^{-16} for double precision floating point).

[7] The useful robustifiers ρ_i are sublinear, with $\rho'_i < 1$ and $\rho''_i < 0$ in the outlier region.

[8] Reweighting is also sometimes used in vision to handle projective homogeneous scale factors rather than error weighting. *E.g.*, suppose that image points $(u/w, v/w)^{\top}$ are generated by a homogeneous projection equation $(u, v, w)^{\top} = P(X, Y, Z, 1)^{\top}$, where P is the 3×4 homogeneous image projection matrix. A scale factor reweighting scheme might take derivatives w.r.t. u, v while treating the inverse weight w as a constant within each iteration. Minimizing the resulting globally bilinear linear least squares error model over P and $(X, Y, Z)^{\top}$ does *not* give the true cost minimum: it zeros the gradient-ignoring-w-variations, not the true cost gradient. Such schemes should not be used for precise work as the bias can be substantial, especially for wide-angle lenses and close geometries.

be slowed owing to inaccuracy of H, especially for the mainly radial deviations produced by non-robust initializers containing outliers. H_i has a direction of negative curvature if $\rho_i'' \, \Delta z_i^\top W_i \, \Delta z_i < -\frac{1}{2}\rho_i'$, but if not we can even reduce the robustified Gauss-Newton model to a local unweighted SSE one for which linear least squares methods can be used. For simplicity suppose that W_i has already reduced to 1 by premultiplying z_i and J_i by $L_i^\top$ where $L_i L_i^\top = W_i$. Then minimizing the **effective squared error** $\frac{1}{2}\|\overline{\delta z}_i - \overline{J}_i \, \delta x\|^2$ gives the correct second order robust state update, where $\alpha \equiv \mathrm{RootOf}(\frac{1}{2}\alpha^2 - \alpha - \rho_i''/\rho_i' \|\Delta z_i\|^2)$ and:

$$\overline{\delta z}_i \equiv \frac{\sqrt{\rho_i'}}{1-\alpha} \, \Delta z_i(x) \qquad \overline{J}_i \equiv \sqrt{\rho_i'} \left(1 - \alpha \frac{\Delta z_i \, \Delta z_i^\top}{\|\Delta z_i\|^2} \right) J_i \qquad (11)$$

In practice, if $\rho_i'' \|\Delta z_i\|^2 \lesssim -\frac{1}{2}\rho_i'$, we can use the same formulae but limit $\alpha \le 1 - \epsilon$ for some small ϵ. However, the full curvature correction is not applied in this case.

4.4   Constrained Problems

More generally, we may want to minimize a function $f(x)$ subject to a set of constraints $c(x) = 0$ on x. These might be scene constraints, internal consistency constraints on the parametrization (§2.2), or constraints arising from an implicit observation model (§3.5). Given an initial estimate x of the solution, we try to improve this by optimizing the quadratic local model for f subject to a linear local model of the constraints c. This linearly constrained quadratic problem has an exact solution in linear algebra. Let g, H be the gradient and Hessian of f as before, and let the first order expansion of the constraints be $c(x+\delta x) \approx c(x) + C \, \delta x$ where $C \equiv \frac{dc}{dx}$. Introduce a vector of Lagrange multipliers λ for c. We seek the $x+\delta x$ that optimizes $f + c^\top \lambda$ subject to $c = 0$, $i.e.$ $0 = \frac{d}{dx}(f + c^\top \lambda)(x+\delta x) \approx g + H \, \delta x + C^\top \lambda$ and $0 = c(x+\delta x) \approx c(x) + C \, \delta x$. Combining these gives the **Sequential Quadratic Programming (SQP)** step:

$$\begin{pmatrix} H & C^\top \\ C & 0 \end{pmatrix} \begin{pmatrix} \delta x \\ \lambda \end{pmatrix} = - \begin{pmatrix} g \\ c \end{pmatrix}, \quad f(x + \delta x) \approx f(x) - \frac{1}{2} \begin{pmatrix} g^\top & c^\top \end{pmatrix} \begin{pmatrix} H & C^\top \\ C & 0 \end{pmatrix}^{-1} \begin{pmatrix} g \\ c \end{pmatrix} \quad (12)$$

$$\begin{pmatrix} H & C^\top \\ C & 0 \end{pmatrix}^{-1} = \begin{pmatrix} H^{-1} - H^{-1}C^\top D^{-1}C H^{-1} & H^{-1}C^\top D^{-1} \\ D^{-1}C H^{-1} & -D^{-1} \end{pmatrix}, \qquad D \equiv C H^{-1} C^\top \quad (13)$$

At the optimum δx and c vanish, but $C^\top \lambda = -g$, which is generally non-zero.

An alternative constrained approach uses the linearized constraints to eliminate some of the variables, then optimizes over the rest. Suppose that we can order the variables to give partitions $x = (x_1 \ x_2)^\top$ and $C = (C_1 \ C_2)$, where C_1 is square and invertible. Then using $C_1 x_1 + C_2 x_2 = Cx = -c$, we can solve for x_1 in terms of x_2 and c: $x_1 = -C_1^{-1}(C_2 x_2 + c)$. Substituting this into the quadratic cost model has the effect of eliminating x_1, leaving a smaller unconstrained **reduced problem** $\overline{H}_{22} x_2 = -\overline{g}_2$, where:

$$\overline{H}_{22} \equiv H_{22} - H_{21} C_1^{-1} C_2 - C_2^\top C_1^{-\top} H_{12} + C_2^\top C_1^{-\top} H_{11} C_1^{-1} C_2 \quad (14)$$

$$\overline{g}_2 \equiv g_2 - C_2^\top C_1^{-\top} g_1 - (H_{21} - C_2^\top C_1^{-\top} H_{11}) C_1^{-1} c \quad (15)$$

(These matrices can be evaluated efficiently using simple matrix factorization schemes [11]). This method is stable provided that the chosen C_1 is well-conditioned. It works well for dense problems, but is not always suitable for sparse ones because if C is dense, the reduced Hessian $\overline{H}_{22}$ becomes dense too.

For least squares cost models, constraints can also be handled within the linear least squares framework, *e.g.* see [11].

4.5   General Implementation Issues

Before going into details, we mention a few points of good numerical practice for large-scale optimization problems such as bundle adjustment:

Exploit the problem structure: Large-scale problems are almost always highly structured and bundle adjustment is no exception. In professional cartography and photogrammetric site-modelling, bundle problems with thousands of images and many tens of thousands of features are regularly solved. Such problems would simply be infeasible without a thorough exploitation of the natural structure and sparsity of the bundle problem. We will have much to say about sparsity below.

Use factorization effectively: Many of above formulae contain matrix inverses. This is a convenient short-hand for theoretical calculations, but *numerically, matrix inversion is almost never used*. Instead, the matrix is decomposed into its Cholesky, LU, QR, *etc.*, factors and these are used directly, *e.g.* linear systems are solved using forwards and backwards substitution. This is much faster and numerically more accurate than explicit use of the inverse, particularly for sparse matrices such as the bundle Hessian, whose factors are still quite sparse, but whose inverse is always dense. Explicit inversion is required only occasionally, *e.g.* for covariance estimates, and even then only a few of the entries may be needed (*e.g.* diagonal blocks of the covariance). Factorization is the heart of the optimization iteration, where most of the time is spent and where most can be done to improve efficiency (by exploiting sparsity, symmetry and other problem structure) and numerical stability (by pivoting and scaling). Similarly, certain matrices (subspace projectors, Householder matrices) have (diagonal)+(low rank) forms which should not be explicitly evaluated as they can be applied more efficiently in pieces.

Use stable local parametrizations: As discussed in §2.2, the parametrization used for step prediction need not coincide with the global one used to store the state estimate. It is more important that it should be finite, uniform and locally as nearly linear as possible. If the global parametrization is in some way complex, highly nonlinear, or potentially ill-conditioned, it is usually preferable to use a stable local parametrization based on perturbations of the current state for step prediction.

Scaling and preconditioning: Another parametrization issue that has a profound and too-rarely recognized influence on numerical performance is **variable scaling** (the choice of 'units' or reference scale to use for each parameter), and more generally **preconditioning** (the choice of which linear combinations of parameters to use). These represent the linear part of the general parametrization problem. The performance of gradient descent and most other linearly convergent optimization methods is critically dependent on preconditioning, to the extent that for large problems, they are seldom practically useful without it.

One of the great advantages of the Newton-like methods is their theoretical independence of such scaling issues[9]. But even for these, scaling makes itself felt indirectly in

---

[9] Under a linear change of coordinates $x \to Tx$ we have $g \to T^{-\top} g$ and $H \to T^{-\top} H T^{-1}$, so the Newton step $\delta x = -H^{-1} g$ varies correctly as $\delta x \to T \delta x$, whereas the gradient one $\delta x \sim g$

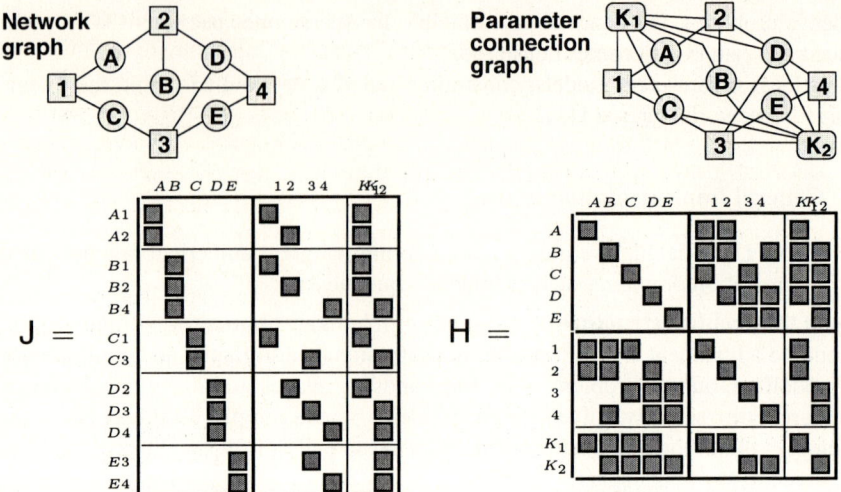

Fig. 3. The network graph, parameter connection graph, Jacobian structure and Hessian structure for a toy bundle problem with five 3D features A–E, four images 1–4 and two camera calibrations K_1 (shared by images 1,2) and K_2 (shared by images 3,4). Feature A is seen in images 1,2; B in 1,2,4; C in 1,3; D in 2–4; and E in 3,4.

several ways: (*i*) Step control strategies including convergence tests, maximum step size limitations, and damping strategies (trust region, Levenberg-Marquardt) are usually all based on some implicit norm $\|\delta\mathsf{x}\|^2$, and hence change under linear transformations of x (*e.g.*, damping makes the step more like the non-invariant gradient descent one). (*ii*) Pivoting strategies for factoring H are highly dependent on variable scaling, as they choose 'large' elements on which to pivot. Here, 'large' *should* mean 'in which little numerical cancellation has occurred' but with uneven scaling it becomes 'with the largest scale'. (*iii*) The choice of gauge (datum, §9) may depend on variable scaling, and this can significantly influence convergence [82, 81].

For all of these reasons, it is important to choose variable scalings that relate meaningfully to the problem structure. This involves a judicious comparison of the relative influence of, *e.g.*, a unit of error on a nearby point, a unit of error on a very distant one, a camera rotation error, a radial distortion error, *etc.* For this, it is advisable to use an 'ideal' Hessian or weight matrix rather than the observed one, otherwise the scaling might break down if the Hessian happens to become ill-conditioned or non-positive during a few iterations before settling down.

5   Network Structure

Adjustment networks have a rich structure, illustrated in figure 3 for a toy bundle problem. The free parameters subdivide naturally into blocks corresponding to: 3D feature coordinates A, ... , E; camera poses and unshared (single image) calibration parameters 1, ... , 4; and calibration parameters shared across several images K_1, K_2. Parameter blocks

varies incorrectly as $\delta\mathsf{x} \rightarrow \mathsf{T}^{-\top}\delta\mathsf{x}$. The Newton and gradient descent steps agree only when $\mathsf{T}^\top\mathsf{T} = \mathsf{H}$.

interact only via their joint influence on image features and other observations, *i.e.* via their joint appearance in cost function contributions. The abstract structure of the measurement network can be characterized graphically by the **network graph** (top left), which shows which features are seen in which images, and the **parameter connection graph** (top right) which details the sparse structure by showing which parameter blocks have direct interactions. Blocks are linked if and only if they jointly influence at least one observation. The cost function Jacobian (bottom left) and Hessian (bottom right) reflect this sparse structure. The shaded boxes correspond to non-zero blocks of matrix entries. Each block of rows in the Jacobian corresponds to an observed image feature and contains contributions from each of the parameter blocks that influenced this observation. The Hessian contains an off-diagonal block for each edge of the parameter connection graph, *i.e.* for each pair of parameters that couple to at least one common feature / appear in at least one common cost contribution[10].

Two layers of structure are visible in the Hessian. The **primary structure** consists of the subdivision into structure (A–E) and camera (1–4, K_1–K_2) submatrices. Note that the structure submatrix is block diagonal: 3D features couple only to cameras, not to other features. (This would no longer hold if inter-feature measurements such as distances or angles between points were present). The camera submatrix is often also block diagonal, but in this example the sharing of unknown calibration parameters produces off-diagonal blocks. The **secondary structure** is the internal sparsity pattern of the structure-camera Hessian submatrix. This is dense for small problems where all features are seen in all images, but in larger problems it often becomes quite sparse because each image only sees a fraction of the features.

All worthwhile bundle methods exploit at least the primary structure of the Hessian, and advanced methods exploit the secondary structure as well. The secondary structure is particularly sparse and regular in surface coverage problems such grids of photographs in aerial cartography. Such problems can be handled using a fixed 'nested dissection' variable reordering (§6.3). But for the more irregular connectivities of close range problems, general sparse factorization methods may be required to handle secondary structure.

Bundle problems are by no means limited to the above structures. For example, for more complex scene models with moving or articulated objects, there will be additional connections to object pose or joint angle nodes, with linkages reflecting the kinematic chain structure of the scene. It is often also necessary to add constraints to the adjustment, *e.g.* coplanarity of certain points. One of the greatest advantages of the bundle technique is its ability to adapt to almost arbitrarily complex scene, observation and constraint models.

---

[10] The Jacobian structure can be described more directly by a bipartite graph whose nodes correspond on one side to the observations, and on the other to the parameter blocks that influence them. The parameter connection graph is then obtained by deleting each observation node and linking each pair of parameter nodes that it connects to. This is an example of elimination graph processing (see below).

6 Implementation Strategy 1: Second Order Adjustment Methods

The next three sections cover implementation strategies for optimizing the bundle adjustment cost function $f(x)$ over the complete set of unknown structure and camera parameters x. This section is devoted to second-order Newton-style approaches, which are the basis of the great majority of current implementations. Their most notable characteristics are rapid (second order) asymptotic convergence but relatively high cost per iteration, with an emphasis on exploiting the network structure (the sparsity of the Hessian $H = \frac{d^2 f}{dx^2}$) for efficiency. In fact, the optimization aspects are more or less standard (§4, [29, 93, 42]), so we will concentrate entirely on efficient methods for solving the linearized Newton step prediction equations $\delta x = -H^{-1} g$, (6). For now, we will assume that the Hessian H is non-singular. This will be amended in §9 on gauge freedom, without changing the conclusions reached here.

6.1 The Schur Complement and the Reduced Bundle System

Schur complement: Consider the following block triangular matrix factorization:

$$M = \begin{pmatrix} A & B \\ C & D \end{pmatrix} = \begin{pmatrix} 1 & 0 \\ C A^{-1} & 1 \end{pmatrix} \begin{pmatrix} A & 0 \\ 0 & \overline{D} \end{pmatrix} \begin{pmatrix} 1 & A^{-1} B \\ 0 & 1 \end{pmatrix}, \qquad \overline{D} \equiv D - C A^{-1} B \quad (16)$$

$$\begin{pmatrix} A & B \\ C & D \end{pmatrix}^{-1} = \begin{pmatrix} 1 & -A^{-1} B \\ 0 & 1 \end{pmatrix} \begin{pmatrix} A^{-1} & 0 \\ 0 & \overline{D}^{-1} \end{pmatrix} \begin{pmatrix} 1 & 0 \\ -C A^{-1} & 1 \end{pmatrix} = \begin{pmatrix} A^{-1} + A^{-1} B \overline{D}^{-1} C A^{-1} & -A^{-1} B \overline{D}^{-1} \\ -\overline{D}^{-1} C A^{-1} & \overline{D}^{-1} \end{pmatrix}$$
$$(17)$$

Here A must be square and invertible, and for (17), the whole matrix must also be square and invertible. $\overline{D}$ is called the **Schur complement** of A in M. If both A and D are invertible, complementing on D rather than A gives

$$\begin{pmatrix} A & B \\ C & D \end{pmatrix}^{-1} = \begin{pmatrix} \overline{A}^{-1} & -\overline{A}^{-1} B D^{-1} \\ -D C \overline{A}^{-1} & D^{-1} + D^{-1} C \overline{A}^{-1} B D^{-1} \end{pmatrix}, \qquad \overline{A} = A - B D^{-1} C$$

Equating upper left blocks gives the **Woodbury formula**:

$$(A \pm B D^{-1} C)^{-1} = A^{-1} \mp A^{-1} B (D \pm C A^{-1} B)^{-1} C A^{-1} \quad (18)$$

This is the usual method of updating the inverse of a nonsingular matrix A after an update (especially a low rank one) $A \to A \pm B D^{-1} C$. (See §8.1).

Reduction: Now consider the linear system $\begin{pmatrix} A & B \\ C & D \end{pmatrix} \begin{pmatrix} x_1 \\ x_2 \end{pmatrix} = \begin{pmatrix} b_1 \\ b_2 \end{pmatrix}$. Pre-multiplying by $\begin{pmatrix} 1 & 0 \\ -C A^{-1} & 1 \end{pmatrix}$ gives $\begin{pmatrix} A & B \\ 0 & \overline{D} \end{pmatrix} \begin{pmatrix} x_1 \\ x_2 \end{pmatrix} = \begin{pmatrix} b_1 \\ \overline{b}_2 \end{pmatrix}$ where $\overline{b}_2 \equiv b_2 - C A^{-1} b_1$. Hence we can use Schur complement and forward substitution to find a **reduced system** $\overline{D} x_2 = \overline{b}_2$, solve this for x_2, then back-substitute and solve to find x_1:

$$\begin{array}{ccc} \overline{D} \equiv D - C A^{-1} B & & \\ \overline{b}_2 \equiv b_2 - C A^{-1} b_1 & \overline{D} x_2 = \overline{b}_2 & A x_1 = b_1 - B x_2 \\ \text{Schur complement} + & \text{reduced system} & \text{back-substitution} \\ \text{forward substitution} & & \end{array} \quad (19)$$

Note that the reduced system entirely subsumes the contribution of the x_1 rows and columns to the network. Once we have reduced, we can pretend that the problem does not involve x_1 at all — it can be found later by back-substitution if needed, or ignored if not. This is the basis of all recursive filtering methods. In bundle adjustment, if we use the primary subdivision into feature and camera variables and subsume the structure ones, we get the **reduced camera system** $\overline{H}_{CC} x_C = \overline{g}_C$, where:

$$\overline{H}_{CC} \equiv H_{CC} - H_{CS} H_{SS}^{-1} H_{SC} = H_{CC} - \sum_p H_{Cp} H_{pp}^{-1} H_{pC}$$
$$\overline{g}_C \equiv g_C - H_{CS} H_{SS}^{-1} g_S = g_C - \sum_p H_{Cp} H_{pp}^{-1} g_p \tag{20}$$

Here, 'S' selects the structure block and 'C' the camera one. H_{SS} is block diagonal, so the reduction can be calculated rapidly by a sum of contributions from the individual 3D features 'p' in S. Brown's original 1958 method for bundle adjustment [16, 19, 100] was based on finding the reduced camera system as above, and solving it using Gaussian elimination. Profile Cholesky decomposition (§B.3) offers a more streamlined method of achieving this.

Occasionally, long image sequences have more camera parameters than structure ones. In this case it is more efficient to reduce the camera parameters, leaving a **reduced structure system**.

6.2 Triangular Decompositions

If D in (16) is further subdivided into blocks, the factorization process can be continued recursively. In fact, there is a family of block (lower triangular)*(diagonal)*(upper triangular) factorizations $A = LDU$:

$$
\begin{pmatrix} A_{11} & A_{12} & \cdots & A_{1n} \\ A_{21} & A_{22} & \cdots & A_{2n} \\ \vdots & \vdots & \ddots & \vdots \\ A_{m1} & A_{m2} & \cdots & A_{mn} \end{pmatrix} = \begin{pmatrix} L_{11} & & & \\ L_{21} & L_{22} & & \\ \vdots & \vdots & \ddots & \\ L_{m1} & L_{m2} & \cdots & L_{mr} \end{pmatrix} \begin{pmatrix} D_1 & & & \\ & D_2 & & \\ & & \ddots & \\ & & & D_r \end{pmatrix} \begin{pmatrix} U_{11} & U_{12} & \cdots & \cdots & U_{1n} \\ & U_{22} & \cdots & \cdots & U_{2n} \\ & & \ddots & & \vdots \\ & & & \cdots & U_{rn} \end{pmatrix}
$$
$$\tag{21}$$

See §B.1 for computational details. The main advantage of triangular factorizations is that they make linear algebra computations with the matrix much easier. In particular, if the input matrix A is square and nonsingular, linear equations $Ax = b$ can be solved by a sequence of three recursions that implicitly implement multiplication by $A^{-1} = U^{-1} D^{-1} L^{-1}$:

$$Lc = b \qquad c_i \leftarrow L_{ii}^{-1}\left(b_i - \sum_{j<i} L_{ij} c_j\right) \qquad \text{forward substitution} \tag{22}$$

$$Dd = c \qquad d_i \leftarrow D_i^{-1} c_i \qquad\qquad\qquad\qquad \text{diagonal solution} \tag{23}$$

$$Ux = d \qquad x_i \leftarrow U_{ii}^{-1}\left(d_i - \sum_{j>i} U_{ij} x_j\right) \qquad \text{back-substitution} \tag{24}$$

Forward substitution corrects for the influence of earlier variables on later ones, diagonal solution solves the transformed system, and back-substitution propagates corrections due to later variables back to earlier ones. In practice, this is usual method of solving linear equations such as the Newton step prediction equations. It is stabler and much faster than explicitly inverting A and multiplying by A^{-1}.

The diagonal blocks L_{ii}, D_i, U_{ii} can be set arbitrarily provided that the product $L_{ii} D_i U_{ii}$ remains constant. This gives a number of well-known factorizations, each optimized for a different class of matrices. **Pivoting** (row and/or column exchanges designed to improve the conditioning of L and/or U, §B.1) is also necessary in most cases, to ensure stability. Choosing $L_{ii} = D_{ii} = 1$ gives the (block) **LU decomposition** $A = L U$, the matrix representation of (block) Gaussian elimination. Pivoted by rows, this is the standard method for non-symmetric matrices. For symmetric A, roughly half of the work of factorization can be saved by using a symmetry-preserving $LDL^\top$ factorization, for which D is symmetric and $U = L^\top$. The pivoting strategy must also preserve symmetry in this case, so it has to permute columns in the same way as the corresponding rows. If A is symmetric positive definite we can further set $D = 1$ to get the **Cholesky decomposition** $A = L L^\top$. This is stable even without pivoting, and hence extremely simple to implement. It is the standard decomposition method for almost all unconstrained optimization problems including bundle adjustment, as the Hessian is positive definite near a non-degenerate cost minimum (and in the Gauss-Newton approximation, almost everywhere else, too). If A is symmetric but only positive *semi*definite, **diagonally pivoted Cholesky decomposition** can be used. This is the case, *e.g.* in subset selection methods of gauge fixing (§9.5). Finally, if A is symmetric but indefinite, it is not possible to reduce D stably to 1. Instead, the **Bunch-Kaufman method** is used. This is a diagonally pivoted $LDL^\top$ method, where D has a mixture of 1×1 and 2×2 diagonal blocks. The augmented Hessian $\begin{pmatrix} H & C \\ C^\top & 0 \end{pmatrix}$ of the Lagrange multiplier method for constrained optimization problems (12) is always symmetric indefinite, so Bunch-Kaufman is the recommended method for solving constrained bundle problems. (It is something like 40% faster than Gaussian elimination, and about equally stable).

Another use of factorization is matrix inversion. Inverses can be calculated by factoring, inverting each triangular factor by forwards or backwards substitution (52), and multiplying out: $A^{-1} = U^{-1} D^{-1} L^{-1}$. However, explicit inverses are rarely used in numerical analysis, it being both stabler and much faster in almost all cases to leave them implicit and work by forward/backward substitution w.r.t. a factorization, rather than multiplication by the inverse. One place where inversion *is* needed in its own right, is to calculate the dispersion matrix (inverse Hessian, which asymptotically gives the posterior covariance) as a measure of the likely variability of parameter estimates. The dispersion can be calculated by explicit inversion of the factored Hessian, but often only a few of its entries are needed, *e.g.* the diagonal blocks and a few key off-diagonal parameter covariances. In this case (53) can be used, which efficiently calculates the covariance entries corresponding to just the nonzero elements of L, D, U.

6.3   Sparse Factorization

To apply the above decompositions to sparse matrices, we must obviously avoid storing and manipulating the zero blocks. But there is more to the subject than this. As a sparse matrix is decomposed, zero positions tend to rapidly **fill in** (become non-zero), essentially because decomposition is based on repeated linear combination of matrix rows, which is generically non-zero wherever any one of its inputs is. Fill-in depends strongly on the order in which variables are eliminated, so efficient sparse factorization routines attempt to minimize either operation counts or fill-in by re-ordering the variables. (The Schur process is fixed in advance, so this is the only available freedom). Globally minimizing either operations or fill-in is NP complete, but reasonably good heuristics exist (see below).

Variable order affects stability (pivoting) as well as speed, and these two goals conflict to some extent. Finding heuristics that work well on both counts is still a research problem.

Algorithmically, fill-in is characterized by an **elimination graph** derived from the parameter coupling / Hessian graph [40, 26, 11]. To create this, nodes (blocks of parameters) are visited in the given elimination ordering, at each step linking together all unvisited nodes that are currently linked to the current node. The coupling of block i to block j via visited block k corresponds to a non-zero Schur contribution $\mathsf{L}_{ik} \mathsf{D}_k^{-1} \mathsf{U}_{kj}$, and at each stage the subgraph on the currently unvisited nodes is the coupling graph of the current reduced Hessian. The amount of fill-in is the number of new graph edges created in this process.

Pattern Matrices   We seek variable orderings that approximately minimize the total operation count or fill-in over the whole elimination chain. For many problems a suitable ordering can be fixed in advance, typically giving one of a few standard pattern matrices such as band or arrowhead matrices, perhaps with such structure at several levels.

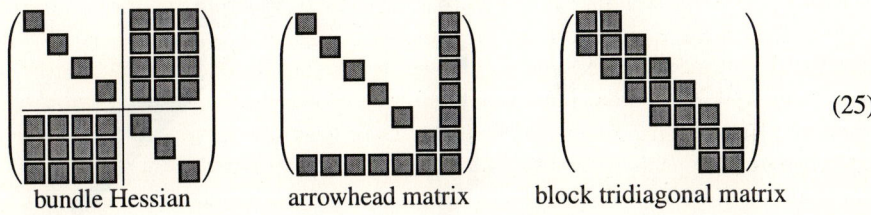

$$(25)$$

bundle Hessian arrowhead matrix block tridiagonal matrix

The most prominent pattern structure in bundle adjustment is the primary subdivision of the Hessian into structure and camera blocks. To get the reduced camera system (19), we treat the Hessian as an arrowhead matrix with a broad final column containing all of the camera parameters. Arrowhead matrices are trivial to factor or reduce by block 2×2 Schur complementation, *c.f.* (16, 19). For bundle problems with many independent images and only a few features, one can also complement on the image parameter block to get a reduced *structure* system.

Another very common pattern structure is the block tridiagonal one which characterizes all singly coupled chains (sequences of images with only pairwise overlap, Kalman filtering and other time recursions, simple kinematic chains). Tridiagonal matrices are factored or reduced by recursive block 2×2 Schur complementation starting from one end. The L and U factors are also block tridiagonal, but the inverse is generally dense.

Pattern orderings are often very natural but it is unwise to think of them as immutable: structure often occurs at several levels and deeper structure or simply changes in the relative sizes of the various parameter classes may make alternative orderings preferable. For more difficult problems there are two basic classes of on-line ordering strategies. *Bottom-up* methods try to minimize fill-in locally and greedily at each step, at the risk of global short-sightedness. *Top-down* methods take a divide-and-conquer approach, recursively splitting the problem into smaller sub-problems which are solved quasi-independently and later merged.

Top-Down Ordering Methods   The most common top-down method is called **nested dissection** or **recursive partitioning** [64, 57, 19, 38, 40, 11]. The basic idea is to recursively split the factorization problem into smaller sub-problems, solve these independently, and

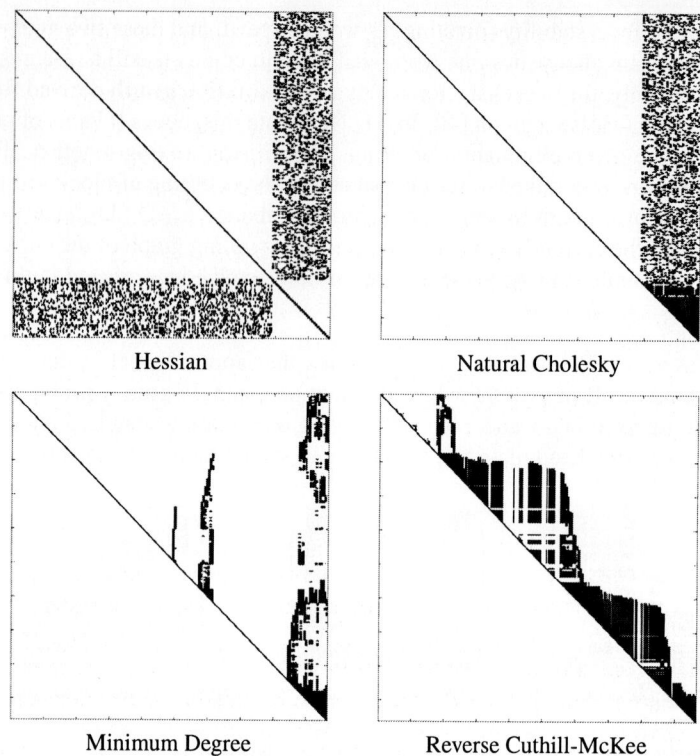

Hessian	Natural Cholesky
Minimum Degree	Reverse Cuthill-McKee

Fig. 4. A bundle Hessian for an irregular coverage problem with only local connections, and its Cholesky factor in natural (structure-then-camera), minimum degree, and reverse Cuthill-McKee ordering.

then glue the solutions together along their common boundaries. Splitting involves choosing a **separating set** of variables, whose deletion will separate the remaining variables into two or more independent subsets. This corresponds to finding a **(vertex) graph cut** of the elimination graph, *i.e.* a set of vertices whose deletion will split it into two or more disconnected components. Given such a partitioning, the variables are reordered into connected components, with the separating set ones last. This produces an 'arrowhead' matrix, *e.g.* :

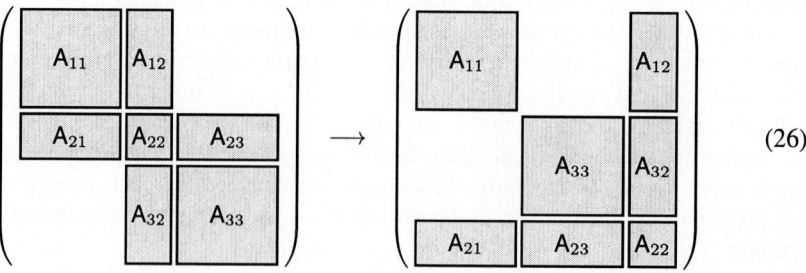

$$\begin{pmatrix} A_{11} & A_{12} & \\ A_{21} & A_{22} & A_{23} \\ & A_{32} & A_{33} \end{pmatrix} \longrightarrow \begin{pmatrix} A_{11} & & A_{12} \\ & A_{33} & A_{32} \\ A_{21} & A_{23} & A_{22} \end{pmatrix} \tag{26}$$

The arrowhead matrix is factored by blocks, as in reduction or profile Cholesky, taking account of any internal sparsity in the diagonal blocks and the borders. Any suitable factorization method can be used for the diagonal blocks, including further recursive partitionings.

Nested dissection is most useful when comparatively small separating sets can be found. A trivial example is the primary structure of the bundle problem: the camera variables separate the 3D structure into independent features, giving the standard arrowhead form of the bundle Hessian. More interestingly, networks with good geometric or temporal locality (surface- and site-covering networks, video sequences) tend to have small separating sets based on spatial or temporal subdivision. The classic examples are geodesic and aerial cartography networks with their local 2D connections — spatial bisection gives simple and very efficient recursive decompositions for these [64, 57, 19].

For sparse problems with less regular structure, one can use graph partitioning algorithms to find small separating sets. Finding a globally minimal partition sequence is NP complete but several effective heuristics exist. This is currently an active research field. One promising family are multilevel schemes [70, 71, 65, 4] which decimate (subsample) the graph, partition using *e.g.* a spectral method, then refine the result to the original graph. (These algorithms should also be very well-suited to graph based visual segmentation and matching).

Bottom-Up Ordering Methods Many bottom-up variable ordering heuristics exist. Probably the most widespread and effective is **minimum degree ordering**. At each step, this eliminates the variable coupled to the fewest remaining ones (*i.e.* the elimination graph node with the fewest unvisited neighbours), so it minimizes the number $\mathcal{O}(n_{\text{neighbours}}^2)$ of changed matrix elements and hence FLOPs for the step. The minimum degree ordering can also be computed quite rapidly without explicit graph chasing. A related ordering, **minimum deficiency**, minimizes the fill-in (newly created edges) at each step, but this is considerably slower to calculate and not usually so effective.

Fill-in or operation minimizing strategies tend to produce somewhat fragmentary matrices that require pointer- or index-based sparse matrix implementations (see fig. 4). This increases complexity and tends to reduce cache locality and pipeline-ability. An alternative is to use **profile matrices** which (for lower triangles) store all elements in each row between the first non-zero one and the diagonal in a contiguous block. This is easy to implement (see §B.3), and practically efficient so long as about 30% or more of the stored elements are actually non-zero. Orderings for this case aim to minimize the sum of the profile lengths rather than the number of non-zero elements. Profiling enforces a multiply-linked chain structure on the variables, so it is especially successful for linear / chain-like / one dimensional problems, *e.g.* space or time sequences. The simplest profiling strategy is **reverse Cuthill-McKee** which chooses some initial variable (very preferably one from one 'end' of the chain), adds all variables coupled to that, then all variables coupled to those, *etc.*, then reverses the ordering (otherwise, any highly-coupled variables get eliminated early on, which causes disastrous fill-in). More sophisticated are the so-called **banker's strategies**, which maintain an active set of all the variables coupled to the already-eliminated ones, and choose the next variable — from the active set (King [72]), it and its neighbours (Snay [101]) or all uneliminated variables (Levy [75]) — to minimize the new size of the active set at each step. In particular, **Snay's banker's algorithm** is reported to perform well on geodesy and aerial cartography problems [101, 24].

For all of these automatic ordering methods, it often pays to do some of the initial work by hand, *e.g.* it might be appropriate to enforce the structure / camera division beforehand and only order the reduced camera system. If there are nodes of particularly high degree such as inner gauge constraints, the ordering calculation will usually run faster and the quality may also be improved by removing these from the graph and placing them last by hand.

The above ordering methods apply to both Cholesky / LDL^T decomposition of the Hessian and QR decomposition of the least squares Jacobian. Sparse QR methods can be implemented either with Givens rotations or (more efficiently) with sparse Householder transformations. Row ordering is important for the Givens methods [39]. For Householder ones (and some Givens ones too) the **multifrontal** organization is now usual [41, 11], as it captures the natural parallelism of the problem.

7   Implementation Strategy 2: First Order Adjustment Methods

We have seen that for large problems, factoring the Hessian H to compute the Newton step can be both expensive and (if done efficiently) rather complex. In this section we consider alternative methods that avoid the cost of exact factorization. As the Newton step can not be calculated, such methods generally only achieve first order (linear) asymptotic convergence: when close to the final state estimate, the error is asymptotically reduced by a constant (and in practice often depressingly small) factor at each step, whereas quadratically convergent Newton methods roughly double the number of significant digits at each step. So first order methods require more iterations than second order ones, but each iteration is usually much cheaper. The relative efficiency depends on the relative sizes of these two effects, both of which can be substantial. For large problems, the reduction in work per iteration is usually at least $\mathcal{O}(n)$, where n is the problem size. But whereas Newton methods converge from $\mathcal{O}(1)$ to $\mathcal{O}(10^{-16})$ in about $1 + \log_2 16 = 5$ iterations, linearly convergent ones take respectively $\log 10^{-16} / \log(1 - \gamma) = 16, 350, 3700$ iterations for reduction $\gamma = 0.9, 0.1, 0.01$ per iteration. Unfortunately, reductions of only 1% or less are by no means unusual in practice (§7.2), and the reduction tends to decrease as n increases.

7.1   First Order Iterations

We first consider a number of common first order methods, before returning to the question of why they are often slow.

Gradient descent: The simplest first order method is **gradient descent**, which "slides down the gradient" by taking $\delta x \sim g$ or $H_a = 1$. Line search is needed, to find an appropriate scale for the step. For most problems, gradient descent is spectacularly inefficient unless the Hessian actually happens to be very close to a multiple of 1. This can be arranged by preconditioning with a linear transform L, $x \rightarrow L x$, $g \rightarrow L^{-T} g$ and $H \rightarrow L^{-T} H L^{-1}$, where $L L^T \sim H$ is an approximate Cholesky factor (or other left square root) of H, so that $H \rightarrow L^{-T} H L^{-1} \sim 1$. In this very special case, preconditioned gradient descent approximates the Newton method. Strictly speaking, gradient descent is a cheat: the gradient is a covector (linear form on vectors) not a vector, so it does not actually define a direction in the search space. Gradient descent's sensitivity to the coordinate system is one symptom of this.

Alternation: Another simple approach is **alternation**: partition the variables into groups and cycle through the groups optimizing over each in turn, with the other groups held fixed. This is most appropriate when the subproblems are significantly easier to optimize than the full one. A natural and often-rediscovered alternation for the bundle problem is

resection-intersection, which interleaves steps of *resection* (finding the camera poses and if necessary calibrations from fixed 3D features) and *intersection* (finding the 3D features from fixed camera poses and calibrations). The subproblems for individual features and cameras are independent, so only the diagonal blocks of H are required.

Alternation can be used in several ways. One extreme is to optimize (or perhaps only perform one step of optimization) over each group in turn, with a state update and re-evaluation of (the relevant components of) g, H after each group. Alternatively, some of the re-evaluations can be simulated by evaluating the linearized effects of the parameter group update on the other groups. *E.g.*, for resection-intersection with structure update $\delta x_S = -H_{SS}^{-1} g_S(x_S, x_C)$ (where 'S' selects the structure variables and 'C' the camera ones), the updated camera gradient is exactly the gradient of the reduced camera system, $g_C(x_S + \delta x_S, x_C) \approx g_C(x_S, x_C) + H_{CS}\delta x_S = g_C - H_{CS} H_{SS}^{-1} g_C$. So the total update for the cycle is $\begin{pmatrix} \delta x_S \\ \delta x_C \end{pmatrix} = -\begin{pmatrix} H_{SS}^{-1} & 0 \\ -H_{CC}^{-1} H_{CS} H_{SS}^{-1} & H_{CC}^{-1} \end{pmatrix} \begin{pmatrix} g_S \\ g_C \end{pmatrix} = \begin{pmatrix} H_{SS} & 0 \\ H_{CS} & H_{CC} \end{pmatrix}^{-1} \begin{pmatrix} g_S \\ g_C \end{pmatrix}$. In general, this correction propagation amounts to solving the system as if the above-diagonal triangle of H were zero. Once we have cycled through the variables, we can update the full state and relinearize. This is the **nonlinear Gauss-Seidel method**. Alternatively, we can split the above-diagonal triangle of H off as a correction (back-propagation) term and continue iterating $\begin{pmatrix} H_{SS} & 0 \\ H_{CS} & H_{CC} \end{pmatrix} \begin{pmatrix} \delta x_S \\ \delta x_C \end{pmatrix}_{(k)} = -\begin{pmatrix} g_S \\ g_C \end{pmatrix} - \begin{pmatrix} 0 & H_{SC} \\ 0 & 0 \end{pmatrix} \begin{pmatrix} \delta x_S \\ \delta x_C \end{pmatrix}_{(k-1)}$ until (hopefully) $\begin{pmatrix} \delta x_S \\ \delta x_C \end{pmatrix}$ converges to the full Newton step $\delta x = -H^{-1}g$. This is the **linear Gauss-Seidel method** applied to solving the Newton step prediction equations. Finally, alternation methods always tend to underestimate the size of the Newton step because they fail to account for the cost-reducing effects of including the back-substitution terms. **Successive Over-Relaxation (SOR)** methods improve the convergence rate by artificially lengthening the update steps by a heuristic factor $1 < \gamma < 2$.

Most if not all of the above alternations have been applied to both the bundle problem and the independent model one many times, *e.g.* [19, 95, 2, 108, 91, 20]. Brown considered the relatively sophisticated SOR method for aerial cartography problems as early as 1964, before developing his recursive decomposition method [19]. None of these alternations are very effective for traditional large-scale problems, although §7.4 below shows that they can sometimes compete for smaller highly connected ones.

Krylov subspace methods: Another large family of iterative techniques are the **Krylov subspace methods**, based on the remarkable properties of the power subspaces $\text{Span}(\{A^k b | k = 0 \ldots n\})$ for fixed A, b as n increases. Krylov iterations predominate in many large-scale linear algebra applications, including linear equation solving.

The earliest and greatest Krylov method is the **conjugate gradient** iteration for solving a positive definite linear system or optimizing a quadratic cost function. By augmenting the gradient descent step with a carefully chosen multiple of the previous step, this manages to minimize the quadratic model function over the entire k^{th} Krylov subspace at the kth iteration, and hence (in exact arithmetic) over the whole space at the n_x^{th} one. This no longer holds when there is round-off error, but $\mathcal{O}(n_x)$ iterations usually still suffice to find the Newton step. Each iteration is $\mathcal{O}(n_x^2)$ so this is not in itself a large gain over explicit factorization. However convergence is significantly faster if the eigenvalues of H are tightly clustered away from zero: if the eigenvalues are covered by intervals $[a_i, b_i]_{i=1\ldots k}$, convergence occurs in $\mathcal{O}\left(\sum_{i=1}^{k} \sqrt{b_i/a_i}\right)$ iterations [99, 47, 48][11]. Preconditioning (see below)

---

[11] For other eigenvalue based based analyses of the bundle adjustment covariance, see [103, 92].

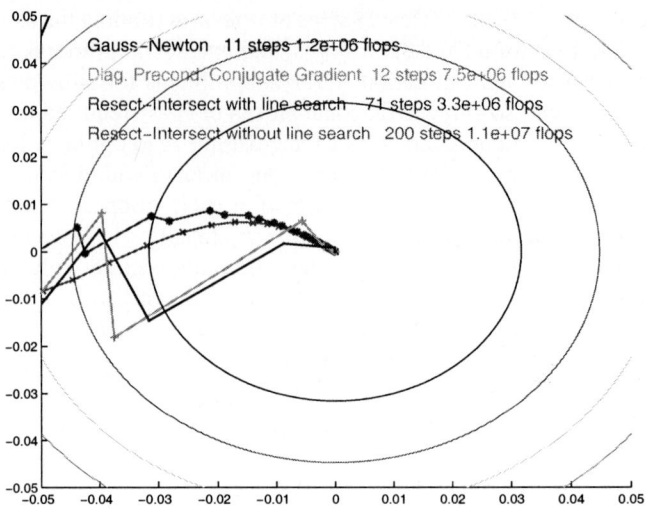

Fig. 5. An example of the typical behaviour of first and second order convergent methods near the minimum. This is a 2D projection of a small but ill-conditioned bundle problem along the two most variable directions. The second order methods converge quite rapidly, whether they use exact (Gauss-Newton) or iterative (diagonally preconditioned conjugate gradient) linear solver for the Newton equations. In contrast, first order methods such as resection-intersection converge slowly near the minimum owing to their inaccurate model of the Hessian. The effects of mismodelling can be reduced to some extent by adding a line search.

aims at achieving such clustering. As with alternation methods, there is a range of possible update / re-linearization choices, ranging from a fully nonlinear method that relinearizes after each step, to solving the Newton equations exactly using many linear iterations. One major advantage of conjugate gradient is its simplicity: there is no factorization, all that is needed is multiplication by H. For the full nonlinear method, H is not even needed — one simply makes a line search to find the cost minimum along the direction defined by g and the previous step.

One disadvantage of nonlinear conjugate gradient is its high sensitivity to the accuracy of the line search. Achieving the required accuracy may waste several function evaluations at each step. One way to avoid this is to make the information obtained by the conjugation process more explicit by building up an explicit approximation to H or H^{-1}. **Quasi-Newton** methods such as the BFGS method do this, and hence need less accurate line searches. The quasi-Newton approximation to H or H^{-1} is dense and hence expensive to store and manipulate, but **Limited Memory Quasi-Newton (LMQN)** methods often get much of the desired effect by maintaining only a low-rank approximation.

There are variants of all of these methods for least squares (Jacobian rather than Hessian based) and for constrained problems (non-positive definite matrices).

7.2 Why Are First Order Methods Slow?

To understand why first order methods often have slow convergence, consider the effect of approximating the Hessian in Newton's method. Suppose that in some local parametrization x centred at a cost minimum x = 0, the cost function is well approximated by a quadratic near 0: $f(x) \approx \frac{1}{2}x^\top H x$ and hence $g(x) \equiv H x$, where H is the true Hessian. For most first order methods, the predicted step is linear in the gradient g. If we adopt a Newton-like state update $\delta x = -H_a^{-1} g(x)$ based on some approximation H_a to H, we get an iteration:

$$x_{k+1} = x_k - H_a^{-1} g(x_k) \approx (1 - H_a^{-1} H) x_k \approx (1 - H_a^{-1} H)^{k+1} x_0 \qquad (27)$$

The numerical behaviour is determined by projecting x_0 along the eigenvectors of $1 - H_a^{-1} H$. The components corresponding to large-modulus eigenvalues decay slowly and hence asymptotically dominate the residual error. For generic x_0, the method converges 'linearly' (*i.e.* exponentially) at rate $\|1 - H_a^{-1} H\|_2$, or diverges if this is greater than one. (Of course, the exact Newton step $\delta x = -H^{-1} g$ converges in a single iteration, as $H_a = H$). Along eigen-directions corresponding to positive eigenvalues (for which H_a overestimates H), the iteration is over-damped and convergence is slow but monotonic. Conversely, along directions corresponding to negative eigenvalues (for which H_a underestimates H), the iteration is under-damped and zigzags towards the solution. If H is underestimated by a factor greater than two along any direction, there is divergence. Figure 5 shows an example of the typical asymptotic behaviour of first and second order methods in a small bundle problem.

Ignoring the camera-feature coupling: As an example, many approximate bundle methods ignore or approximate the off-diagonal feature-camera blocks of the Hessian. This amounts to ignoring the fact that the cost of a feature displacement can be partially offset by a compensatory camera displacement and vice versa. It therefore significantly overestimates the total 'stiffness' of the network, particularly for large, loosely connected networks. The fact that off-diagonal blocks are *not* negligible compared to the diagonal ones can be seen in several ways:

- Looking forward to §9, before the gauge is fixed, the full Hessian is singular owing to gauge freedom. The diagonal blocks by themselves are well-conditioned, but including the off-diagonal ones entirely cancels this along the gauge orbit directions. Although gauge fixing removes the resulting singularity, it can not change the fact that the off-diagonal blocks have enough weight to counteract the diagonal ones.

- In bundle adjustment, certain well-known ambiguities (poorly-controlled parameter combinations) often dominate the uncertainty. Camera distance and focal length estimates, and structure depth and camera baseline ones (bas-relief), are both strongly correlated whenever the perspective is weak and become strict ambiguities in the affine limit. The well-conditioned diagonal blocks of the Hessian give no hint of these ambiguities: when both features and cameras are free, the overall network is *much* less rigid than it appears to be when each treats the other as fixed.

- During bundle adjustment, local structure refinements cause 'ripples' that must be propagated throughout the network. The camera-feature coupling information carried in the off-diagonal blocks is essential to this. In the diagonal-only model, ripples can propagate at most one feature-camera-feature step per iteration, so it takes many iterations for them to cross and re-cross a sparsely coupled network.

These arguments suggest that any approximation H_a to the bundle Hessian H that suppresses or significantly alters the off-diagonal terms is likely to have large $\|1 - H_a^{-1} H\|$ and hence slow convergence. This is exactly what we have observed in practice for all such methods that we have tested: near the minimum, convergence is linear and for large problems often extremely slow, with $\|1 - H_a^{-1} H\|_2$ very close to 1. The iteration may either zigzag or converge slowly and monotonically, depending on the exact method and parameter values.

Line search: The above behaviour can often be improved significantly by adding a line search to the method. In principle, the resulting method converges for *any* positive definite H_a. However, accurate modelling of H is still highly desirable. Even with no rounding errors, an exactly quadratic (but otherwise unknown) cost function and exact line searches (*i.e.* the minimum along the line is found exactly), the most efficient generic line search based methods such as conjugate gradient or quasi-Newton require at least $\mathcal{O}(n_x)$ iterations to converge. For large bundle problems with thousands of parameters, this can already be prohibitive. However, if knowledge about H is incorporated via a suitable *preconditioner*, the number of iterations can often be reduced substantially.

7.3 Preconditioning

Gradient descent and Krylov methods are sensitive to the coordinate system and their practical success depends critically on good preconditioning. The aim is to find a linear transformation $x \rightarrow T x$ and hence $g \rightarrow T^{-\top} g$ and $H \rightarrow T^{-\top} H T$ for which the transformed H is near 1, or at least has only a few clusters of eigenvalues well separated from the origin. Ideally, T should be an accurate, low-cost approximation to the left Cholesky factor of H. (Exactly evaluating this would give the expensive Newton method again). In the experiments below, we tried conjugate gradient with preconditioners based on the diagonal blocks of H, and on **partial Cholesky decomposition**, dropping either all filled-in elements, or all that are smaller than a preset size when performing Cholesky decomposition. These methods were not competitive with the exact Gauss-Newton ones in the 'strip' experiments below, but for large enough problems it is likely that a preconditioned Krylov method would predominate, especially if more effective preconditioners could be found.

An exact Cholesky factor of H from a previous iteration is often a quite effective preconditioner. This gives hybrid methods in which H is only evaluated and factored every few iterations, with the Newton step at these iterations and well-preconditioned gradient descent or conjugate gradient at the others.

7.4 Experiments

Figure 6 shows the relative performance of several methods on two synthetic projective bundle adjustment problems. In both cases, the number of 3D points increases in proportion to the number of images, so the dense factorization time is $\mathcal{O}(n^3)$ where n is the number of points or images. The following methods are shown: 'Sparse Gauss-Newton' — sparse Cholesky decomposition with variables ordered naturally (features then cameras); 'Dense Gauss-Newton' — the same, but (inefficiently) ignoring all sparsity of the Hessian; 'Diag. Conj. Gradient' — the Newton step is found by an iterative conjugate gradient linear system solver, preconditioned using the Cholesky factors of the diagonal blocks of the Hessian; 'Resect-Intersect' — the state is optimized by alternate steps of resection and intersection, with relinearization after each. In the 'spherical cloud' problem, the points are uniformly distributed within a spherical cloud, all points are visible in all images, and the camera geometry is strongly convergent. These are ideal conditions, giving a low diameter network graph and a well-conditioned, nearly diagonal-dominant Hessian. All of the methods converge quite rapidly. Resection-intersection is a competitive method for

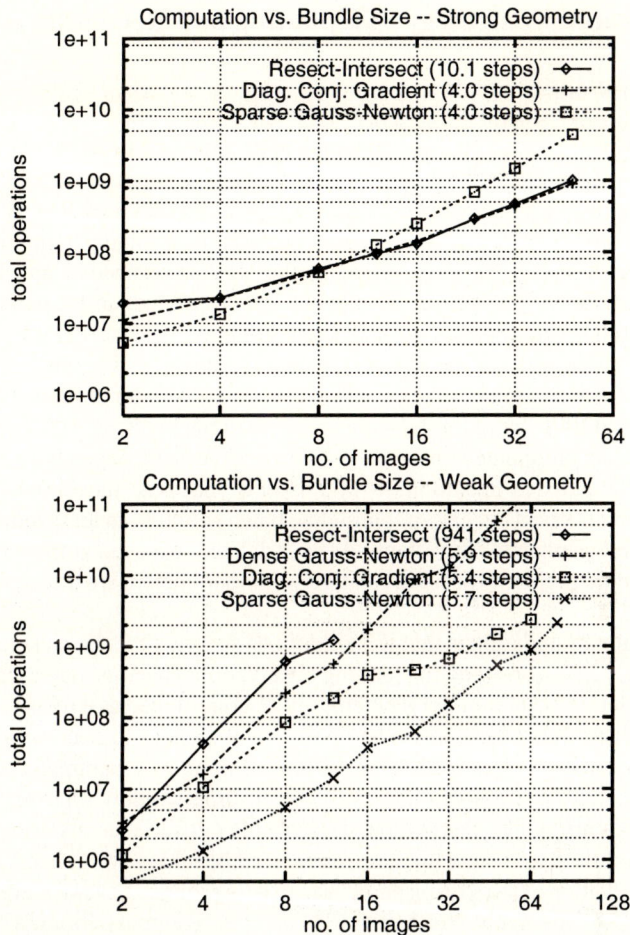

Fig. 6. Relative speeds of various bundle optimization methods for strong 'spherical cloud' and weak 'strip' geometries.

larger problems owing to its low cost per iteration. Unfortunately, although this geometry is often used for testing computer vision algorithms, it is atypical for large-scale bundle problems. The 'strip' experiment has a more representative geometry. The images are arranged in a long strip, with each feature seen in about 3 overlapping images. The strip's long thin weakly-connected network structure gives it large scale low stiffness 'flexing' modes, with correspondingly poor Hessian conditioning. The off-diagonal terms are critical here, so the approximate methods perform very poorly. Resection-intersection is slower even than dense Cholesky decomposition ignoring all sparsity. For 16 or more images it fails to converge even after 3000 iterations. The sparse Cholesky methods continue to perform reasonably well, with the natural, minimum degree and reverse Cuthill-McKee orderings all giving very similar run times in this case. For all of the methods that we tested, including resection-intersection with its linear per-iteration cost, the total run time for long chain-like geometries scaled roughly as $\mathcal{O}(n^3)$.

8   Implementation Strategy 3: Updating and Recursion

8.1   Updating Rules

It is often convenient to be able to **update** a state estimate to reflect various types of changes, *e.g.* to incorporate new observations or to delete erroneous ones ('**downdating**'). Parameters may have to be added or deleted too. Updating rules are often used recursively, to incorporate a series of observations one-by-one rather than solving a single batch system. This is useful in on-line applications where a rapid response is needed, and also to provide preliminary predictions, *e.g.* for correspondence searches. Much of the early development of updating methods was aimed at on-line data editing in aerial cartography workstations.

The main challenge in adding or deleting observations is efficiently updating either a factorization of the Hessian H, or the covariance H^{-1}. Given either of these, the state update δx is easily found by solving the Newton step equations $H \, \delta x = -g$, where (assuming that we started at an un-updated optimum $g = 0$) the gradient g depends only on the newly added terms. The Hessian update $H \rightarrow H \pm B W B^{\top}$ needs to have relatively low rank, otherwise nothing is saved over recomputing the batch solution. In least squares the rank is the number of independent observations added or deleted, but even without this the rank is often low in bundle problems because relatively few parameters are affected by any given observation.

One limitation of updating is that it is seldom as accurate as a batch solution owing to build-up of round-off error. Updating (adding observations) itself is numerically stable, but downdating (deleting observations) is potentially ill-conditioned as it reduces the positivity of the Hessian, and may cause previously good pivot choices to become arbitrarily bad. This is particularly a problem if all observations relating to a parameter are deleted, or if there are repeated insertion-deletion cycles as in time window filtering. Factorization updating methods are stabler than Woodbury formula / covariance updating ones.

Consider first the case where no parameters need be added nor deleted, *e.g.* adding or deleting an observation of an existing point in an existing image. Several methods have been suggested [54, 66]. Mikhail & Helmering [88] use the Woodbury formula (18) to update the covariance H^{-1}. This simple approach becomes inefficient for problems with many features because the sparse structure is not exploited: the full covariance matrix is dense and we would normally avoid calculating it in its entirety. Grün [51, 54] avoids this problem by maintaining a running copy of the reduced camera system (20), using an incremental Schur complement / forward substitution (16) to fold each new observation into this, and then re-factorizing and solving as usual after each update. This is effective when there are many features in a few images, but for larger numbers of images it becomes inefficient owing to the re-factorization step. Factorization updating methods such as (55, 56) are currently the recommended update methods for most applications: they allow the existing factorization to be exploited, they handle any number of images and features and arbitrary problem structure efficiently, and they are numerically more accurate than Woodbury formula methods. The Givens rotation method [12, 54], which is equivalent to the rank 1 Cholesky update (56), is probably the most common such method. The other updating methods are confusingly named in the literature. Mikhail & Helmering's method [88] is sometimes called 'Kalman filtering', even though no dynamics and hence no actual filtering is involved. Grün's reduced camera system method [51] is called 'triangular factor update (TFU)', even though it actually updates the (square) reduced Hessian rather than its triangular factors.

For updates involving a previously unseen 3D feature or image, new variables must also be added to the system. This is easy. We simply choose where to put the variables in the elimination sequence, and extend H and its L,D,U factors with the corresponding rows and columns, setting all of the newly created positions to zero (except for the unit diagonals of LDL$^\top$'s and LU's L factor). The factorization can then be updated as usual, presumably adding enough cost terms to make the extended Hessian nonsingular and couple the new parameters into the old network. If a direct covariance update is needed, the Woodbury formula (18) can be used on the old part of the matrix, then (17) to fill in the new blocks (equivalently, invert (54), with $D_1 \leftarrow A$ representing the old blocks and $D_2 \leftarrow 0$ the new ones).

Conversely, it may be necessary to delete parameters, *e.g.* if an image or 3D feature has lost most or all of its support. The corresponding rows and columns of the Hessian H (and rows of g, columns of J) must be deleted, and all cost contributions involving the deleted parameters must also be removed using the usual factorization downdates (55, 56). To delete the rows and columns of block b in a matrix A, we first delete the b rows and columns of L, D, U. This maintains triangularity and gives the correct trimmed A, except that the blocks in the lower right corner $A_{ij} = \sum_{k \leq \min(i,j)} L_{ik} D_k U_{kj}$, $i, j > b$ are missing a term $L_{ib} D_b U_{bj}$ from the deleted column b of L / row b of U. This is added using an update $+L_{*b} D_b U_{b*}$, $* > b$. To update A^{-1} when rows and columns of A are deleted, permute the deleted rows and columns to the end and use (17) backwards: $(A_{11})^{-1} = (A^{-1})_{11} - (A^{-1})_{12} (A^{-1})_{22}^{-1} (A^{-1})_{21}$.

It is also possible to freeze some live parameters at fixed (current or default) values, or to add extra parameters / unfreeze some previously frozen ones, *c.f.* (48, 49) below. In this case, rows and columns corresponding to the frozen parameters must be deleted or added, but no other change to the cost function is required. Deletion is as above. To insert rows and columns A_{b*}, A_{*b} at block b of matrix A, we open space in row and column b of L, D, U and fill these positions with the usual recursively defined values (51). For $i, j > b$, the sum (51) will now have a contribution $L_{ib} D_b U_{bj}$ that it should not have, so to correct this we downdate the lower right submatrix $* > b$ with a cost cancelling contribution $-L_{*b} D_b U_{b*}$.

8.2   Recursive Methods and Reduction

Each update computation is roughly quadratic in the size of the state vector, so if new features and images are continually added the situation will eventually become unmanageable. We must limit what we compute. In principle parameter refinement never stops: each observation update affects all components of the state estimate and its covariance. However, the refinements are in a sense trivial for parameters that are not directly coupled to the observation. If these parameters are eliminated using reduction (19), the observation update can be applied directly to the reduced Hessian and gradient[12]. The eliminated parameters can then be updated by simple back-substitution (19) and their covariances by (17). In particular, if we cease to receive new information relating to a block of parameters (an image that has been fully treated, a 3D feature that has become invisible), they and all the observations relating to them can be subsumed once-and-for-all in a reduced Hessian and gradient on the remaining parameters. If required, we can later re-estimate the

---

[12] In (19), only D and b_2 are affected by the observation as it is independent of the subsumed components A, B, C, b_1. So applying the update to $\overline{D}, b_2$ has the same effect as applying it to D, b_2.

eliminated parameters by back-substitution. Otherwise, we do not need to consider them further.

This elimination process has some limitations. Only 'dead' parameters can be eliminated: to merge a new observation into the problem, we need the current Hessian or factorization entries for all parameter blocks relating to it. Reduction also commits us to a linearized / quadratic cost approximation for the eliminated variables at their current estimates, although to the extent that this model is correct, the remaining variables can still be treated nonlinearly. It is perhaps best to view reduction as the first half-iteration of a full nonlinear optimization: by (19), the Newton method for the full model can be implemented by repeated cycles of reduction, solving the reduced system, and back-substitution, with relinearization after each cycle, whereas for eliminated variables we stop after solving the first reduced system. Equivalently, reduction evaluates just the reduced components of the full Newton step and the full covariance, leaving us the option of computing the remaining eliminated ones later if we wish.

Reduction can be used to refine estimates of relative camera poses (or fundamental matrices, *etc.*) for a fixed set of images, by reducing a sequence of feature correspondences to their camera coordinates. Or conversely, to refine 3D structure estimates for a fixed set of features in many images, by reducing onto the feature coordinates.

Reduction is also the basis of recursive (Kalman) filtering. In this case, one has a (*e.g.* time) series of system state vectors linked by some probabilistic transition rule ('dynamical model'), for which we also have some observations ('observation model'). The parameter space consists of the combined state vectors for all times, *i.e.* it represents a path through the states. Both the dynamical and the observation models provide "observations" in the sense of probabilistic constraints on the full state parameters, and we seek a maximum likelihood (or similar) parameter estimate / path through the states. The full Hessian is block tridiagonal: the observations couple only to the current state and give the diagonal blocks, and dynamics couples only to the previous and next ones and gives the off-diagonal blocks (differential observations can also be included in the dynamics likelihood). So the model is large (if there are many time steps) but very sparse. As always with a tridiagonal matrix, the Hessian can be decomposed by recursive steps of reduction, at each step Schur complementing to get the current reduced block $\overline{\mathsf{H}}_t$ from the previous one $\overline{\mathsf{H}}_{t-1}$, the off-diagonal (dynamical) coupling $\mathsf{H}_{t\,t-1}$ and the current unreduced block (observation Hessian) H_t: $\overline{\mathsf{H}}_t = \mathsf{H}_t - \mathsf{H}_{t\,t-1}\,\overline{\mathsf{H}}_{t-1}^{-1}\,\mathsf{H}_{t\,t-1}^{\top}$. Similarly, for the gradient $\overline{\mathsf{g}}_t = \mathsf{g}_t - \mathsf{H}_{t\,t-1}\,\overline{\mathsf{H}}_{t-1}^{-1}\,\overline{\mathsf{g}}_{t-1}$, and as usual the reduced state update is $\delta\mathsf{x}_t = -\overline{\mathsf{H}}_t^{-1}\,\overline{\mathsf{g}}_t$.

This forwards reduction process is called **filtering**. At each time step it finds the optimal (linearized) current state estimate given all of the previous observations and dynamics. The corresponding unwinding of the recursion by back-substitution, **smoothing**, finds the optimal state estimate at each time given both past and future observations and dynamics. The usual equations of Kalman filtering and smoothing are easily derived from this recursion, but we will not do this here. We emphasize that filtering is merely the first half-iteration of a nonlinear optimization procedure: even for nonlinear dynamics and observation models, we can find the exact maximum likelihood state path by cyclic passes of filtering and smoothing, with relinearization after each.

For long or unbounded sequences it may not be feasible to run the full iteration, but it can still be very helpful to run short sections of it, *e.g.* smoothing back over the last 3–4 state estimates then filtering forwards again, to verify previous correspondences and anneal the effects of nonlinearities. (The traditional **extended Kalman filter** optimizes

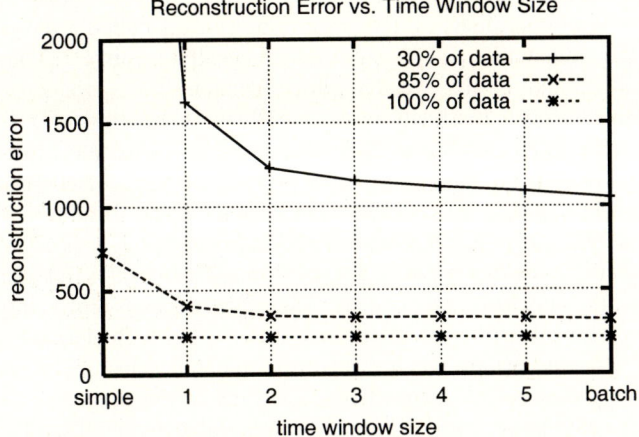

Fig. 7. The residual state estimation error of the VSDF sequential bundle algorithm for progressively increasing sizes of rolling time window. The residual error at image $t = 16$ is shown for rolling windows of 1–5 previous images, and also for a 'batch' method (all previous images) and a 'simple' one (reconstruction / intersection is performed independently of camera location / resection). To simulate the effects of decreasing amounts of image data, 0%, 15% and 70% of the image measurements are randomly deleted to make runs with 100%, 85% and only 30% of the supplied image data. The main conclusion is that window size has little effect for strong data, but becomes increasingly important as the data becomes weaker.

nonlinearly over just the current state, assuming all previous ones to be linearized). The effects of variable window size on the Variable State Dimension Filter (VSDF) sequential bundle algorithm [85, 86, 83, 84] are shown in figure 7.

9   Gauge Freedom

Coordinates are a very convenient device for reducing geometry to algebra, but they come at the price of some arbitrariness. The coordinate system can be changed at any time, without affecting the underlying geometry. This is very familiar, but it leaves us with two problems: (*i*) algorithmically, we need some concrete way of deciding which particular coordinate system to use at each moment, and hence *breaking* the arbitrariness; (*ii*) we need to allow for the fact that the results may look quite different under different choices, even though they represent the same underlying geometry.

Consider the choice of 3D coordinates in visual reconstruction. The only objects in the 3D space are the reconstructed cameras and features, so we have to decide where to place the coordinate system relative to these ... Or in coordinate-centred language, where to place the reconstruction relative to the coordinate system. Moreover, bundle adjustment updates and uncertainties can perturb the reconstructed structure almost arbitrarily, so we must specify coordinate systems not just for the current structure, but also for *every possible nearby one*. Ultimately, this comes down to constraining the coordinate values of certain aspects of the reconstructed structure — features, cameras or combinations of these — whatever the rest of the structure might be. Saying this more intrinsically, the coordinate frame is specified and held fixed with respect to the chosen reference elements, and the rest of the geometry is then expressed in this frame as usual. In measurement science such a set of coordinate system specifying rules is called a **datum**, but we will follow the wider mathematics and physics usage and call it a **gauge**[13]. The freedom in the choice of coordinate fixing rules is called **gauge freedom**.

As a gauge anchors the coordinate system rigidly to its chosen reference elements, perturbing the reference elements has no effect on their own coordinates. Instead, it changes the coordinate system itself and hence systematically changes the coordinates of all the *other* features, while leaving the reference coordinates fixed. Similarly, uncertainties in the reference elements do not affect their own coordinates, but appear as highly correlated uncertainties in all of the *other* reconstructed features. The moral is that *structural perturbations and uncertainties are highly relative*. Their form depends profoundly on the gauge, and especially on how this changes as the state varies (*i.e.* which elements it holds fixed). The effects of disturbances are *not* restricted to the coordinates of the features actually disturbed, but may appear almost anywhere depending on the gauge.

In visual reconstruction, the differences between object-centred and camera-centred gauges are often particularly marked. In object-centred gauges, object points appear to be relatively certain while cameras appear to have large and highly correlated uncertainties. In camera-centred gauges, it is the camera that appears to be precise and the object points that appear to have large correlated uncertainties. One often sees statements like "the reconstructed depths are very uncertain". This may be true in the camera frame, yet the object may be very well reconstructed in its own frame — it all depends on what fraction of the total depth fluctuations are simply due to global uncertainty in the camera location, and hence identical for all object points.

Besides 3D coordinates, many other types of geometric parametrization in vision involve arbitrary choices, and hence are subject to gauge freedoms [106]. These include the choice of: homogeneous scale factors in homogeneous-projective representations; supporting points in supporting-point based representations of lines and planes; reference plane in plane + parallax representations; and homographies in homography-epipole representations of matching tensors. In each case the symptoms and the remedies are the same.

9.1   General Formulation

The general set up is as follows: We take as our state vector x the set of all of the 3D feature coordinates, camera poses and calibrations, *etc.*, that enter the problem. This state space has internal symmetries related to the arbitrary choices of 3D coordinates, homogeneous scale factors, *etc.*, that are embedded in x. Any two state vectors that differ only by such choices represent the same underlying 3D geometry, and hence have exactly the same image projections and other intrinsic properties. So under change-of-coordinates equivalence, the state space is partitioned into classes of intrinsically equivalent state vectors, each class representing exactly one underlying 3D geometry. These classes are called **gauge orbits**. Formally, they are the group orbits of the state space action of the relevant **gauge group** (coordinate transformation group), but we will not need the group structure below. A state space function represents an intrinsic function of the underlying geometry if and only if it is constant along each gauge orbit (*i.e.* coordinate system independent). Such quantities

---

[13] Here, *gauge* just means reference frame. The sense is that of a reference against which something is *judged* (O.Fr. jauger, gauger). Pronounce $g\bar{e}^i dj$.

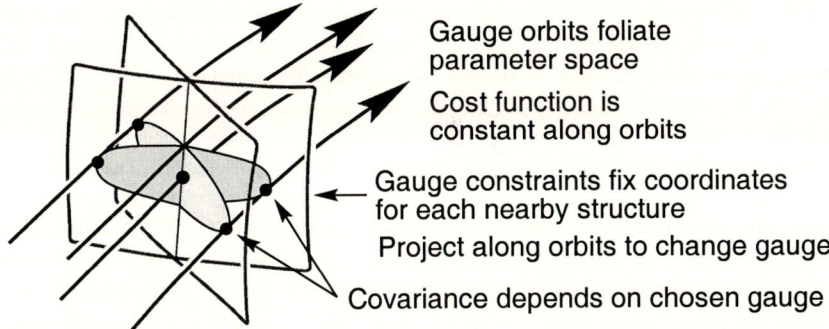

Fig. 8. Gauge orbits in state space, two gauge cross-sections and their covariances.

are called **gauge invariants**. We want the bundle adjustment cost function to quantify 'intrinsic merit', so it must be chosen to be gauge invariant.

In visual reconstruction, the principal gauge groups are the $3 + 3 + 1 = 7$ dimensional group of 3D similarity (scaled Euclidean) transformations for Euclidean reconstruction, and the 15 dimensional group of projective 3D coordinate transformations for projective reconstruction. But other gauge freedoms are also present. Examples include: (*i*) The arbitrary scale factors of homogeneous projective feature representations, with their 1D rescaling gauge groups. (*ii*) The arbitrary positions of the points in 'two point' line parametrizations, with their two 1D motion-along-line groups. (*iii*) The underspecified 3×3 homographies used for 'homography + epipole' parametrizations of matching tensors [77, 62, 106]. For example, the fundamental matrix can be parametrized as $F = [e]_\times H$ where e is its left epipole and H is the inter-image homography induced by any 3D plane. The choice of plane gives a freedom $H \to H + e\,a^\top$ where a is an arbitrary 3-vector, and hence a 3D linear gauge group.

Now consider how to specify a gauge, *i.e.* a rule saying how each possible underlying geometry near the current one should be expressed in coordinates. Coordinatizations are represented by state space points, so this is a matter of choosing exactly one point (structure coordinatization) from each gauge orbit (underlying geometry). Mathematically, the gauge orbits foliate (fill without crossing) the state space, and a gauge is a local transversal 'cross-section' $\mathcal{G}$ through this foliation. See fig. 8. Different gauges represent different but geometrically equivalent coordinatization rules. Results can be mapped between gauges by pushing them along gauge orbits, *i.e.* by applying local coordinate transformations that vary depending on the particular structure involved. Such transformations are called **S-transforms** ('similarity' transforms) [6, 107, 22, 25]. Different gauges through the same central state represent coordinatization rules that agree for the central geometry but differ for perturbed ones — the S-transform is the identity at the centre but not elsewhere.

Given a gauge, only state perturbations that lie within the gauge cross-section are authorized. This is what we want, as such state perturbations are in one-to-one correspondence with perturbations of the underlying geometry. Indeed, any state perturbation is equivalent to some on-gauge one under the gauge group (*i.e.* under a small coordinate transformation that pushes the perturbed state along its gauge orbit until it meets the gauge cross-section). State perturbations along the gauge orbits are uninteresting, because they do not change the underlying geometry at all.

Covariances are averages of squared perturbations and must also be based on on-gauge perturbations (they would be infinite if we permitted perturbations along the gauge orbits, as there is no limit to these — they do not change the cost at all). So covariance matrices are gauge-dependent and in fact represent ellipsoids tangent to the gauge cross-section at the cost minimum. They can look very different for different gauges. But, as with states, S-transforms map them between gauges by projecting along gauge orbits / state equivalence classes.

Note that there is no intrinsic notion of orthogonality on state space, so it is meaningless to ask which state-space directions are 'orthogonal' to the gauge orbits. This would involve deciding when two different structures have been "expressed in the same coordinate system", so every gauge believes its own cross section to be orthogonal and all others to be skewed.

9.2   Gauge Constraints

We will work near some point x of state space, perhaps a cost minimum or a running state estimate. Let n_x be the dimension of x and n_g the dimension of the gauge orbits. Let f, g, H be the cost function and its gradient and Hessian, and G be any $n_x \times n_g$ matrix whose columns span the local gauge orbit directions at x [14]. By the exact gauge invariance of f, its gradient and Hessian vanish along orbit directions: $g^\top G = 0$ and $H G = 0$. Note that the gauged Hessian H is singular with (at least) rank deficiency n_g and null space G. This is called **gauge deficiency**. Many numerical optimization routines assume nonsingular H, and must be modified to work in gauge invariant problems. The singularity is an expression of indifference: when we come to calculate state updates, any two updates ending on the same gauge orbit are equivalent, both in terms of cost and in terms of the change in the underlying geometry. All that we need is a method of telling the routine which particular update to choose.

Gauge constraints are the most direct means of doing this. A gauge cross-section $\mathcal{G}$ can be specified in two ways: (*i*) *constrained form:* specify n_g local constraints $d(x)$ with $d(x) = 0$ for points on $\mathcal{G}$; (*ii*) *parametric form:* specify a function $x(y)$ of $n_x - n_g$ independent local parameters y, with $x = x(y)$ being the points of $\mathcal{G}$. For example, a **trivial gauge** is one that simply freezes the values of n_g of the parameters in x (usually feature or camera coordinates). In this case we can take $d(x)$ to be the parameter freezing constraints and y to be the remaining unfrozen parameters. Note that once the gauge is fixed the problem is no longer gauge invariant — the whole purpose of $d(x), x(y)$ is to *break* the underlying gauge invariance.

Examples of trivial gauges include: (*i*) using several visible 3D points as a 'projective basis' for reconstruction (*i.e.* fixing their projective 3D coordinates to simple values, as in [27]); and (*ii*) fixing the components of one projective 3×4 camera matrix as $(I \; 0)$, as in [61] (this only partially fixes the 3D projective gauge — 3 projective 3D degrees of freedom remain unfixed).

---

[14] A suitable G is easily calculated from the infinitesimal action of the gauge group on x. For example, for spatial similarities the columns of G would be the $n_g = 3 + 3 + 1 = 7$ state velocity vectors describing the effects of infinitesimal translations, rotations and changes of spatial scale on x.

Linearized gauge: Let the local linearizations of the gauge functions be:

$$d(x + \delta x) \approx d(x) + D\,\delta x \qquad\qquad D \equiv \frac{dd}{dx} \qquad (28)$$

$$x(y + \delta y) \approx x(y) + Y\,\delta y \qquad\qquad Y \equiv \frac{dx}{dy} \qquad (29)$$

Compatibility between the two gauge specification methods requires $d(x(y)) = 0$ for all y, and hence $D\,Y = 0$. Also, since $\mathcal{G}$ must be transversal to the gauge orbits, $D\,G$ must have full rank n_g and $(Y\;G)$ must have full rank n_x. Assuming that x itself is on $\mathcal{G}$, a perturbation $x + \delta x_{\mathcal{G}}$ is on $\mathcal{G}$ to first order iff $D\,\delta x_{\mathcal{G}} = 0$ or $\delta x_{\mathcal{G}} = Y\,\delta y$ for some δy.

Two $n_x \times n_x$ rank $n_x - n_g$ matrices characterize $\mathcal{G}$. The **gauge projection matrix** $P_{\mathcal{G}}$ implements linearized projection of state displacement vectors δx along their gauge orbits onto the local gauge cross-section: $\delta x \to \delta x_{\mathcal{G}} = P_{\mathcal{G}}\,\delta x$. (The projection is usually non-orthogonal: $P_{\mathcal{G}}^{\mathsf{T}} \neq P_{\mathcal{G}}$). The **gauged covariance matrix** $V_{\mathcal{G}}$ plays the role of the inverse Hessian. It gives the cost-minimizing Newton step within $\mathcal{G}$, $\delta x_{\mathcal{G}} = -V_{\mathcal{G}}\,g$, and also the asymptotic covariance of $\delta x_{\mathcal{G}}$. $P_{\mathcal{G}}$ and $V_{\mathcal{G}}$ have many special properties and equivalent forms. For convenience, we display some of these now[15] — let $V \equiv (H + D^{\mathsf{T}} B\,D)^{-1}$ where B is any nonsingular symmetric $n_g \times n_g$ matrix, and let $\mathcal{G}'$ be any other gauge:

$$V_{\mathcal{G}} \equiv Y\,(Y^{\mathsf{T}} H\,Y)^{-1}\,Y^{\mathsf{T}} = V\,H\,V = V - G\,(D\,G)^{-1}\,B^{-1}\,(D\,G)^{-\mathsf{T}}\,G^{\mathsf{T}} \qquad (30)$$

$$= P_{\mathcal{G}}\,V = P_{\mathcal{G}}\,V_{\mathcal{G}} = P_{\mathcal{G}}\,V_{\mathcal{G}'}\,P_{\mathcal{G}}^{\mathsf{T}} \qquad (31)$$

$$P_{\mathcal{G}} \equiv 1 - G\,(D\,G)^{-1}\,D = Y\,(Y^{\mathsf{T}} H\,Y)^{-1}\,Y^{\mathsf{T}} H = V\,H = V_{\mathcal{G}}\,H = P_{\mathcal{G}}\,P_{\mathcal{G}'} \qquad (32)$$

$$P_{\mathcal{G}}\,G = 0, \qquad P_{\mathcal{G}}\,Y = Y, \qquad D\,P_{\mathcal{G}} = D\,V_{\mathcal{G}} = 0 \qquad (33)$$

$$g^{\mathsf{T}}\,P_{\mathcal{G}} = g^{\mathsf{T}}, \qquad H\,P_{\mathcal{G}} = H, \qquad V_{\mathcal{G}}\,g = V\,g \qquad (34)$$

These relations can be summarized by saying that $V_{\mathcal{G}}$ is the $\mathcal{G}$-supported generalized inverse of H and that $P_{\mathcal{G}}$: (*i*) projects along gauge orbits ($P_{\mathcal{G}}\,G = 0$); (*ii*) projects onto the gauge cross-section $\mathcal{G}$ ($D\,P_{\mathcal{G}} = 0$, $P_{\mathcal{G}}\,Y = Y$, $P_{\mathcal{G}}\delta x = \delta x_{\mathcal{G}}$ and $V_{\mathcal{G}} = P_{\mathcal{G}}\,V_{\mathcal{G}'}\,P_{\mathcal{G}}^{\mathsf{T}}$); and (*iii*) preserves gauge invariants (*e.g.* $f(x + P_{\mathcal{G}}\,\delta x) = f(x + \delta x)$, $g^{\mathsf{T}}\,P_{\mathcal{G}} = g^{\mathsf{T}}$ and $H\,P_{\mathcal{G}} = H$). Both $V_{\mathcal{G}}$ and H have rank $n_x - n_g$. Their null spaces D^{T} and G are transversal but otherwise unrelated. $P_{\mathcal{G}}$ has left null space D and right null space G.

State updates: It is straightforward to add gauge fixing to the bundle update equations. First consider the constrained form. Enforcing the gauge constraints $d(x + \delta x_{\mathcal{G}}) = 0$ with Lagrange multipliers λ gives an SQP step:

$$\begin{pmatrix} H & D^{\mathsf{T}} \\ D & 0 \end{pmatrix} \begin{pmatrix} \delta x_{\mathcal{G}} \\ \lambda \end{pmatrix} = - \begin{pmatrix} g \\ d \end{pmatrix}, \qquad \begin{pmatrix} H & D^{\mathsf{T}} \\ D & 0 \end{pmatrix}^{-1} = \begin{pmatrix} V_{\mathcal{G}} & G\,(D\,G)^{-1} \\ (D\,G)^{-\mathsf{T}}\,G^{\mathsf{T}} & 0 \end{pmatrix} \qquad (35)$$

so $\quad \delta x_{\mathcal{G}} = -(V_{\mathcal{G}}\,g + G\,(D\,G)^{-1}\,d), \qquad \lambda = 0 \qquad (36)$

This is a rather atypical constrained problem. For typical cost functions the gradient has a component pointing away from the constraint surface, so $g \neq 0$ at the constrained minimum

---

[15] These results are most easily proved by inserting strategic factors of $(Y\;G)(Y\;G)^{-1}$ and using $H\,G = 0$, $D\,Y = 0$ and $(Y\;G)^{-1} = \begin{pmatrix} (Y^{\mathsf{T}} H\,Y)^{-1}\,Y^{\mathsf{T}} H \\ (D\,G)^{-1}\,D \end{pmatrix}$. For any $n_g \times n_g$ B in-

cluding 0, $\begin{pmatrix} Y^{\mathsf{T}} \\ G^{\mathsf{T}} \end{pmatrix} (H + D^{\mathsf{T}} B\,D) (Y\;G) = \begin{pmatrix} Y^{\mathsf{T}} H\,Y & 0 \\ 0 & (D\,G)^{\mathsf{T}} B\,(D\,G) \end{pmatrix}$. If B is nonsingular,

$V = (H + D^{\mathsf{T}} B\,D)^{-1} = Y\,(Y^{\mathsf{T}} H\,Y)^{-1}\,Y^{\mathsf{T}} + G\,(D\,G)^{-1}\,B^{-1}\,(D\,G)^{-\mathsf{T}}\,G^{\mathsf{T}}$.

and a non-vanishing force $\lambda \neq 0$ is required to hold the solution on the constraints. Here, the cost function and its derivatives are entirely indifferent to motions along the orbits. Nothing actively forces the state to move off the gauge, so the constraint force λ vanishes everywhere, g vanishes at the optimum, and the constrained minimum value of f is identical to the unconstrained minimum. The only effect of the constraints is to correct any gradual drift away from $\mathcal{G}$ that happens to occur, via the d term in $\delta x_{\mathcal{G}}$.

A simpler way to get the same effect is to add a gauge-invariance breaking term such as $\frac{1}{2}d(x)^\top B\,d(x)$ to the cost function, where B is some positive $n_g \times n_g$ weight matrix. Note that $\frac{1}{2}d(x)^\top B\,d(x)$ has a unique minimum of 0 on each orbit at the point $d(x) = 0$, *i.e.* for x on $\mathcal{G}$. As f is constant along gauge orbits, optimization of $f(x) + \frac{1}{2}d(x)^\top B\,d(x)$ along each orbit enforces $\mathcal{G}$ and hence returns the orbit's f value, so global optimization will find the global constrained minimum of f. The cost function $f(x) + \frac{1}{2}d(x)^\top B\,d(x)$ is nonsingular with Newton step $\delta x_{\mathcal{G}} = V(g + D^\top B\,d)$ where $V = (H + D^\top B\,D)^{-1}$ is the new inverse Hessian. By (34, 30), this is identical to the SQP step (36), so the SQP and cost-modifying methods are equivalent. This strategy works only because no force is required to keep the state on-gauge — if this were not the case, the weight B would have to be infinite. Also, for dense D this form is not practically useful because $H + D^\top B\,D$ is dense and hence slow to factorize, although updating formulae can be used.

Finally, consider the parametric form $x = x(y)$ of $\mathcal{G}$. Suppose that we already have a current reduced state estimate y. We can approximate $f(x(y + \delta y))$ to get a reduced system for δy, solve this, and find $\delta x_{\mathcal{G}}$ afterwards if necessary:

$$(Y^\top H\,Y)\,\delta y = -Y^\top g, \qquad \delta x_{\mathcal{G}} = Y\,\delta y = -V_{\mathcal{G}}\,g \qquad (37)$$

The $(n_x - n_g) \times (n_x - n_g)$ matrix $Y^\top H\,Y$ is generically nonsingular despite the singularity of H. In the case of a trivial gauge, Y simply selects the submatrices of g, H corresponding to the unfrozen parameters, and solves for these. For less trivial gauges, both Y and D are often dense and there is a risk that substantial fill-in will occur in all of the above methods.

Gauged covariance: By (30) and standard covariance propagation in (37), the covariance of the on-gauge fluctuations $\delta x_{\mathcal{G}}$ is $E\left[\delta x_{\mathcal{G}}\,\delta x_{\mathcal{G}}^\top\right] = Y\,(Y^\top H\,Y)^{-1}\,Y^\top = V_{\mathcal{G}}$. $\delta x_{\mathcal{G}}$ never moves off $\mathcal{G}$, so $V_{\mathcal{G}}$ represents a rank $n_x - n_g$ covariance ellipsoid 'flattened onto $\mathcal{G}$'. In a trivial gauge, $V_{\mathcal{G}}$ is the covariance $(Y^\top H\,Y)^{-1}$ of the free variables, padded with zeros for the fixed ones.

Given $V_{\mathcal{G}}$, the linearized gauged covariance of a function $h(x)$ is $\frac{dh}{dx} V_{\mathcal{G}} \frac{dh}{dx}^\top$ as usual. If $h(x)$ is gauge invariant (constant along gauge orbits) this is just its ordinary covariance. Intuitively, $V_{\mathcal{G}}$ and $\frac{dh}{dx} V_{\mathcal{G}} \frac{dh}{dx}^\top$ depend on the gauge because they measure not absolute uncertainty, but uncertainty relative to the reference features on which the gauge is based. Just as there are no absolute reference frames, there are no absolute uncertainties. The best we can do is relative ones.

Gauge transforms: We can change the gauge at will during a computation, *e.g.* to improve sparseness or numerical conditioning or re-express results in some standard gauge. This is simply a matter of an **S-transform** [6], *i.e.* pushing all gauged quantities along their gauge orbits onto the new gauge cross-section $\mathcal{G}$. We will assume that the base point x is unchanged. If not, a fixed (structure independent) change of coordinates achieves this. Locally, an S-transform then linearizes into a linear projection along the orbits spanned by G onto the new gauge constraints given by D or Y. This is implemented by the $n_x \times n_x$ rank $n_x - n_g$ non-orthogonal projection matrix $P_{\mathcal{G}}$ defined in (32). The projection preserves all gauge invariants — *e.g.* $f(x + P_G \, \delta x) = f(x + \delta x)$ — and it cancels the effects of projection onto any other gauge: $P_G \, P_{G'} = P_G$.

9.3   Inner Constraints

Given the wide range of gauges and the significant impact that they have on the appearance of the state updates and covariance matrix, it is useful to ask which gauges give the "smallest" or "best behaved" updates and covariances. This is useful for interpreting and comparing results, and it also gives beneficial numerical properties. Basically it is a matter of deciding which features or cameras we care most about and tying the gauge to some stable average of them, so that gauge-induced correlations in them are as small as possible. For object reconstruction the resulting gauge will usually be object-centred, for vehicle navigation camera-centred. We stress that such choices are only a matter of superficial appearance: in principle, all gauges are equivalent and give identical values and covariances for all gauge invariants.

Another way to say this is that it is only for gauge invariants that we can find meaningful (coordinate system independent) values and covariances. But one of the most fruitful ways to create invariants is to locate features w.r.t. a basis of reference features, *i.e.* w.r.t. the gauge based on them. The choice of inner constraints is thus a choice of a stable basis of compound features w.r.t. which invariants can be measured. By including an average of many features in the compound, we reduce the invariants' dependence on the basis features.

As a performance criterion we can minimize some sort of weighted average size, either of the state update or of the covariance. Let W be an $n_x \times n_x$ information-like weight matrix encoding the relative importance of the various error components, and L be any left square root for it, $L L^\top = W$. *The local gauge at x that minimizes the weighted size of the state update $\delta x_G^\top \, W \, \delta x_G$, the weighted covariance sum* $\mathrm{Trace}(W \, V_G) = \mathrm{Trace}(L^\top V_G \, L)$, *and the L_2 or Frobenius norm of* $L^\top V_G \, L$, *is given by the* **inner constraints** *[87, 89, 6, 22, 25]*[16]:

$$D \, \delta x = 0 \qquad \text{where} \qquad D \equiv G^\top W \qquad\qquad (38)$$

The corresponding covariance V_G is given by (30) with $D = G^\top W$, and the state update is $\delta x_G = -V_G \, g$ as usual. Also, if W is nonsingular, V_G is given by the weighted rank $n_x - n_g$ pseudo-inverse $L^{-\top} \left(L^{-1} H L^{-\top} \right)^\dagger L^{-1}$, where $W = L L^\top$ is the Cholesky decomposition of W and $(\cdot)^\dagger$ is the Moore-Penrose pseudo-inverse.

---

[16] *Sketch proof*: For $W = 1$ (whence $L = 1$) and diagonal $H = \left(\begin{smallmatrix} \Lambda & 0 \\ 0 & 0 \end{smallmatrix} \right)$, we have $G = \left(\begin{smallmatrix} 0 \\ 1 \end{smallmatrix} \right)$ and $g = \left(\begin{smallmatrix} g' \\ 0 \end{smallmatrix} \right)$ as $g^\top G = 0$. Any gauge G transversal to G has the form $\overline{D} = (-\overline{B} \ \ \overline{C})$ with nonsingular $\overline{C}$. Premultiplying by $\overline{C}^{-1}$ reduces $\overline{D}$ to the form $D = (-B \ \ 1)$ for some $n_g \times (n_x - n_g)$ matrix B. It follows that $P_G = \left(\begin{smallmatrix} 1 & 0 \\ B & 0 \end{smallmatrix} \right)$ and $V_G = \left(\begin{smallmatrix} 1 \\ B \end{smallmatrix} \right) \Lambda^{-1} (1 \ \ B^\top)$, whence $\delta x_G^\top W \, \delta x_G = g^\top V_G \, W \, V_G \, g = g'^\top \Lambda^{-1} \left(1 + B^\top B \right) \Lambda^{-1} g'$ and $\mathrm{Trace}(V_G) = \mathrm{Trace}(\Lambda^{-1}) + \mathrm{Trace}(B \, \Lambda^{-1} B^\top)$. Both criteria are clearly minimized by taking $B = 0$, so $D = (0 \ \ 1) = G^\top W$ as claimed. For nonsingular $W = L L^\top$, scaling the coordinates by $x \to L x$ reduces us to $W \to 1$, $g^\top \to g^\top L^{-1}$ and $H \to L^{-1} H L^{-\top}$. Eigen-decomposition then reduces us to diagonal H. Neither transformation affects $\delta x_G^\top W \, \delta x_G$ or $\mathrm{Trace}(W \, V_G)$, and back substituting gives the general result. For singular W, use a limiting argument on $D = G^\top W$. Similarly, using V_G as above, $B \to 0$, and hence the inner constraint, minimizes the L_2 and Frobenius norms of $L^\top V_G \, L$. Indeed, by the interlacing property of eigenvalues [44, §8.1], $B \to 0$ minimizes *any* strictly non-decreasing rotationally invariant function of $L^\top V_G \, L$ (*i.e.* any strictly non-decreasing function of its eigenvalues).   □

The inner constraints are covariant under global transformations $x \rightarrow t(x)$ provided that W is transformed in the usual information matrix / Hessian way $W \rightarrow T^{-\top} W T^{-1}$ where $T = \frac{dt}{dx}$ [17]. However, such transformations seldom preserve the form of W (diagonality, $W = 1$, *etc.*). If W represents an isotropic weighted sum over 3D points[18], its form is preserved under global 3D Euclidean transformations, and rescaled under scalings. But this extends neither to points under projective transformations, nor to camera poses, 3D planes and other non-point-like features even under Euclidean ones. (The choice of origin has a significant influence For poses, planes, *etc.* : changes of origin propagate rotational uncertainties into translational ones).

Inner constraints were originally introduced in geodesy in the case $W = 1$ [87]. The meaning of this is entirely dependent on the chosen 3D coordinates and variable scaling. In bundle adjustment there is little to recommend $W = 1$ unless the coordinate origin has been carefully chosen and the variables carefully pre-scaled as above, *i.e.* $x \rightarrow L^\top x$ and hence $H \rightarrow L^{-1} H L^{-\top}$, where $W \sim LL^\top$ is a fixed weight matrix that takes account of the fact that the covariances of features, camera translations and rotations, focal lengths, aspect ratios and lens distortions, all have entirely different units, scales and relative importances. For $W = 1$, the gauge projection P_G becomes orthogonal and symmetric.

9.4 Free Networks

Gauges can be divided roughly into **outer gauges**, which are locked to predefined external reference features giving a **fixed network** adjustment, and **inner gauges**, which are locked only to the recovered structure giving a **free network** adjustment. (If their weight W is concentrated on the external reference, the inner constraints give an outer gauge). As above, well-chosen inner gauges do not distort the intrinsic covariance structure so much as most outer ones, so they tend to have better numerical conditioning and give a more representative idea of the true accuracy of the network. It is also useful to make another, slightly different fixed / free distinction. In order to control the gauge deficiency, any gauge fixing method must at least specify which motions are *locally* possible at each iteration. However, it is not indispensable for these local decisions to cohere to enforce a global gauge. A method is **globally fixed** if it does enforce a global gauge (whether inner or outer), and **globally free** if not. For example, the standard photogrammetric inner constraints [87, 89, 22, 25] give a globally free inner gauge. They require that the cloud of reconstructed points should not be translated, rotated or rescaled under perturbations (*i.e.* the centroid and average directions and distances from the centroid remain unchanged). However, they do not specify where the cloud actually is and how it is oriented and scaled, and they do not attempt to correct for any gradual drift in the position that may occur during the optimization iterations, *e.g.* owing to accumulation of truncation errors. In contrast, McLauchlan globally fixes the inner gauge by locking it to the reconstructed centroid and scatter matrix [82, 81]. This seems to give good numerical properties (although more testing is required to determine whether there is much improvement over a globally free

---

[17] $G \rightarrow TG$ implies that $D \rightarrow DT^{-1}$, whence $V_G \rightarrow TV_G T^\top$, $P_G \rightarrow TP_G T^{-1}$, and $\delta x_G \rightarrow T \delta x_G$. So $\delta x_G^\top W \delta x_G$ and $\mathrm{Trace}(W V_G)$ are preserved.

[18] This means that it vanishes identically for all non-point features, camera parameters, *etc.*, and is a weighted identity matrix $W_i = w_i I_{3 \times 3}$ for each 3D point, or more generally it has the form $\overline{W} \otimes I_{3 \times 3}$ on the block of 3D point coordinates, where $\overline{W}$ is some $n_{\mathrm{points}} \times n_{\mathrm{points}}$ inter-point weighting matrix.

inner gauge), and it has the advantage of actually fixing the coordinate system so that direct comparisons of solutions, covariances, *etc.*, are possible. Numerically, a globally fixed gauge can be implemented either by including the 'd' term in (36), or simply by applying a rectifying gauge transformation to the estimate, at each step or when it drifts too far from the chosen gauge.

9.5   Implementation of Gauge Constraints

Given that all gauges are in principle equivalent, it does not seem worthwhile to pay a high computational cost for gauge fixing during step prediction, so methods requiring large dense factorizations or (pseudo-)inverses should not be used directly. Instead, the main computation can be done in any convenient, low cost gauge, and the results later transformed into the desired gauge using the gauge projector[19] $P_G = 1 - G(DG)^{-1}D$. It is probably easiest to use a trivial gauge for the computation. This is simply a matter of deleting the rows and columns of g, H corresponding to n_g preselected parameters, which should be chosen to give a reasonably well-conditioned gauge. The choice can be made automatically by a **subset selection** method (*c.f.*, *e.g.* [11]). H is left intact and factored as usual, except that the final dense (owing to fill-in) submatrix is factored using a stable pivoted method, and the factorization is stopped n_g columns before completion. The remaining $n_g \times n_g$ block (and the corresponding block of the forward-substituted gradient g) should be zero owing to gauge deficiency. The corresponding rows of the state update are set to zero (or anything else that is wanted) and back-substitution gives the remaining update components as usual. This method effectively finds the n_g parameters that are least well constrained by the data, and chooses the gauge constraints that freeze these by setting the corresponding δx_G components to zero.

10   Quality Control

This section discusses quality control methods for bundle adjustment, giving diagnostic tests that can be used to detect outliers and characterize the overall accuracy and reliability of the parameter estimates. These techniques are not well known in vision so we will go into some detail. Skip the technical details if you are not interested in them.

Quality control is a serious issue in measurement science, and it is perhaps here that the philosophical differences between photogrammetrists and vision workers are greatest: the photogrammetrist insists on good equipment, careful project planning, exploitation of prior knowledge and thorough error analyses; while the vision researcher advocates a more casual, flexible 'point-and-shoot' approach with minimal prior assumptions. Many applications demand a judicious compromise between these virtues.

A basic maxim is "quality = accuracy + reliability"[20]. The absolute *accuracy* of the system depends on the imaging geometry, number of measurements, *etc.* But theoretical

---

[19] The projector P_G itself is never calculated. Instead, it is applied in pieces, multiplying by D, *etc.* The gauged Newton step δx_G is easily found like this, and selected blocks of the covariance $V_G = P_G V_{G'} P_G^T$ can also be found in this way, expanding P_G and using (53) for the leading term, and for the remaining ones finding $L^{-1}D^T$, *etc.*, by forwards substitution.

[20] 'Accuracy' is sometimes called 'precision' in photogrammetry, but we have preferred to retain the familiar meanings from numerical analysis: 'precision' means numerical error / number of working digits and 'accuracy' means statistical error / number of significant digits.

precision by itself is not enough: the system must also be *reliable* in the face of out-liers, small modelling errors, and so forth. The key to reliability is the intelligent use of *redundancy*: the results should represent an internally self-consistent consensus among many independent observations, no aspect of them should rely excessively on just a few observations.

The photogrammetric literature on quality control deserves to be better known in vision, especially among researchers working on statistical issues. Förstner [33, 34] and Grün [49, 50] give introductions with some sobering examples of the effects of poor design. See also [7, 8, 21, 22]. All of these papers use least squares cost functions and scalar measurements. Our treatment generalizes this to allow robust cost functions and vector measurements, and is also slightly more self-consistent than the traditional approach. The techniques considered are useful for data analysis and reporting, and also to check whether design requirements are realistically attainable during project planning. Several properties should be verified. **Internal reliability** is the ability to detect and remove large aberrant observations using internal self-consistency checks. This is provided by traditional outlier detection and/or robust estimation procedures. **External reliability** is the extent to which any remaining *un*detected outliers can affect the estimates. **Sensitivity analysis** gives useful criteria for the quality of a design. Finally, **model selection tests** attempt to decide which of several possible models is most appropriate and whether certain parameters can be eliminated.

10.1   Cost Perturbations

We start by analyzing the approximate effects of adding or deleting an observation, which changes the cost function and hence the solution. We will use second order Taylor expansion to characterize the effects of this. Let $f_-(x)$ and $f_+(x) \equiv f_-(x) + \delta f(x)$ be respectively the total cost functions without and with the observation included, where $\delta f(x)$ is the cost contribution of the observation itself. Let $g_\pm, \delta g$ be the gradients and $H_\pm, \delta H$ the Hessians of $f_\pm, \delta f$. Let x_0 be the unknown true underlying state and $x_\pm$ be the minima of $f_\pm(x)$ (*i.e.* the optimal state estimates with and without the observation included). Residuals at x_0 are the most meaningful quantities for outlier decisions, but x_0 is unknown so we will be forced to use residuals at $x_\pm$ instead. Unfortunately, as we will see below, these are biased. The bias is small for strong geometries but it can become large for weaker ones, so to produce uniformly reliable statistical tests we will have to correct for it. The fundamental result is: *For any sufficiently well behaved cost function, the* **difference in fitted residuals** $f_+(x_+) - f_-(x_-)$ *is asymptotically an unbiased and accurate estimate of* $\delta f(x_0)$ [21]:

$$\delta f(x_0) \approx f_+(x_+) - f_-(x_-) + \nu, \quad \nu \sim \mathcal{O}\left(\|\delta g\|/\sqrt{n_z - n_x}\right), \quad \langle \nu \rangle \sim 0 \quad (39)$$

---

[21] *Sketch proof*: From the Newton steps $\delta x_\pm \equiv x_\pm - x_0 \approx -H_\pm^{-1} g_\pm(x_0)$ at x_0, we find that $f_\pm(x_\pm) - f_\pm(x_0) \approx -\frac{1}{2}\delta x_\pm^\top H_\pm \delta x_\pm$ and hence $\nu \equiv f_+(x_+) - f_-(x_-) - \delta f(x_0) \approx \frac{1}{2}\left(\delta x_-^\top H_- \delta x_- - \delta x_+^\top H_+ \delta x_+\right)$. ν is unbiased to relatively high order: by the central limit property of ML estimators, the asymptotic distributions of $\delta x_\pm$ are Gaussian $\mathcal{N}(0, H_\pm^{-1})$, so the expectation of both $\delta x_\pm^\top H_\pm \delta x_\pm$ is asymptotically the number of free model parameters n_x. Expanding $\delta x_\pm$ and using $g_+ = g_- + \delta g$, the leading term is $\nu \approx -\delta g(x_0)^\top x_-$, which asymptotically has normal distribution $\nu \sim \mathcal{N}(0, \delta g(x_0)^\top H_-^{-1} \delta g(x_0))$ with standard deviation of order $\mathcal{O}\left(\|\delta g\|/\sqrt{n_z - n_x}\right)$, as $x_- \sim \mathcal{N}(0, H_-^{-1})$ and $\|H_-\| \sim \mathcal{O}(n_z - n_x)$.   □

Note that by combining values at two known evaluation points $x_\pm$, we simulate a value at a third unknown one x_0. The estimate is not perfect, but it is the best that we can do in the circumstances.

There are usually many observations to test, so to avoid having to refit the model many times we approximate the effects of adding or removing observations. Working at $x_\pm$ and using the fact that $g_\pm(x_\pm) = 0$, the Newton step $\delta x \equiv x_+ - x_- \approx -H_\mp^{-1} \delta g(x_\pm)$ implies a change in fitted residual of:

$$f_+(x_+) - f_-(x_-) \approx \delta f(x_\pm) \pm \tfrac{1}{2} \delta x^\top H_\mp \, \delta x$$
$$= \delta f(x_\pm) \pm \tfrac{1}{2} \delta g(x_\pm)^\top H_\mp^{-1} \delta g(x_\pm) \tag{40}$$

So $\delta f(x_+)$ systematically underestimates $f_+(x_+) - f_-(x_-)$ and hence $\delta f(x_0)$ by about $\tfrac{1}{2} \delta x^\top H_- \, \delta x$, and $\delta f(x_-)$ overestimates it by about $\tfrac{1}{2} \delta x^\top H_+ \, \delta x$. These biases are of order $\mathcal{O}(1/(n_z - n_x))$ and hence negligible when there is plenty of data, but they become large at low redundancies. Intuitively, including δf improves the estimate on average, bringing about a 'good' reduction of δf, but it also overfits δf slightly, bringing about a further 'bad' reduction. Alternatively, the reduction in δf on moving from x_- to x_+ is bought at the cost of a slight increase in f_- (since x_- was already the minimum of f_-), which should morally also be 'charged' to δf.

When deleting observations, we will usually have already evaluated H_+^{-1} (or a corresponding factorization of H_+) to find the Newton step near x_+, whereas (40) requires H_-^{-1}. And vice versa for addition. Provided that $\delta H \ll H$, it is usually sufficient to use $H_\pm^{-1}$ in place of $H_\mp^{-1}$ in the simple tests below. However if the observation couples to relatively few state variables, it is possible to calculate the relevant components of $H_\mp^{-1}$ fairly economically. If '$*$' means 'select the k variables on which δH, δg are non-zero', then $\delta g^\top H^{-1} \delta g = (\delta g^*)^\top (H^{-1})^* \delta g^*$ and[22] $(H_\mp^{-1})^* = \left(((H_\pm^{-1})^*)^{-1} \mp \delta H^* \right)^{-1} \approx (H_\pm^{-1})^* \pm (H_\pm^{-1})^* \, \delta H^* \, (H_\pm^{-1})^*$. Even without the approximation, this involves at most a $k \times k$ factorization or inverse. Indeed, for least squares δH is usually of even lower rank (= the number of independent observations in δf), so the Woodbury formula (18) can be used to calculate the inverse even more efficiently.

10.2   Inner Reliability and Outlier Detection

In robust cost models nothing special needs to be done with outliers — they are just normal measurements that happen be downweighted owing to their large deviations. But in non-robust models such as least squares, explicit outlier detection and removal are essential for inner reliability. An effective diagnostic is to estimate $\delta f(x_0)$ using (39, 40), and significance-test it against its distribution under the null hypothesis that the observation is an inlier. For the least squares cost model, the null distribution of $2 \, \delta f(x_0)$ is χ_k^2 where k is the number of independent observations contributing to δf. So if α is a suitable χ_k^2 significance threshold, the typical one-sided significance test is:

$$\alpha \overset{?}{\leq} 2 \, (f(x_+) - f(x_-)) \approx 2 \, \delta f(x_\pm) \pm \delta g(x_\pm)^\top H_\mp^{-1} \delta g(x_\pm) \tag{41}$$
$$\approx \triangle z_i(x_\pm)^\top \left(W_i \pm W_i \, J_i^\top H_\mp^{-1} J_i \, W_i \right) \triangle z_i(x_\pm) \tag{42}$$

---

[22] *C.f.* the lower right corner of (17), where the '$*$' components correspond to block 2, so that $((H_\pm^{-1})^*)^{-1}$ is 'D_2', the Schur complement of the remaining variables in $H_\pm$. Adding δH^* changes the 'D' term but not the Schur complement correction.

As usual we approximate $H_{\mp}^{-1} \approx H_{\pm}^{-1}$ and use x_- results for additions and x_+ ones for deletions. These tests require the fitted covariance matrix $H_{\pm}^{-1}$ (or, if relatively few tests will be run, an equivalent factorization of $H_{\pm}$), but given this they are usually fairly economical owing to the sparseness of the observation gradients $\delta g(x_\pm)$. Equation (42) is for the nonlinear least squares model with residual error $\triangle z_i(x) \equiv \underline{z}_i - z_i(x)$, cost $\frac{1}{2} \triangle z_i(x)^\top W_i \triangle z_i(x)$ and Jacobian $J_i = \frac{dz_i}{dx}$. Note that even though $\underline{z}_i$ induces a change in *all* components of the observation residual $\triangle z$ via its influence on δx, only the immediately involved components $\triangle z_i$ are required in (42). The bias-correction-induced change of weight matrix $W_i \rightarrow W_i \pm W_i J_i^\top H_{\mp}^{-1} J_i W_i$ accounts for the others. For non-quadratic cost functions, the above framework still applies but the cost function's native distribution of negative log likelihood values must be used instead of the Gaussian's $\frac{1}{2} \chi^2$.

In principle, the above analysis is only valid when at most one outlier causes a relatively small perturbation δx. In practice, the observations are repeatedly scanned for outliers, at each stage removing any discovered outliers (and perhaps reinstating previously discarded observations that have become inliers) and refitting. The net result is a form of M-estimator routine with an abruptly vanishing weight function: *outlier deletion is just a roundabout way of simulating a robust cost function*. (Hard inlier/outlier rules correspond to total likelihood functions that become strictly constant in the outlier region).

The tests (41, 42) give what is needed for outlier decisions based on *fitted* state estimates $x_\pm$, but for planning purposes it is also useful to know how large a gross error must typically be w.r.t. the *true* state x_0 before it is detected. Outlier detection is based on the uncertain fitted state estimates, so we can only give an average case result. No adjustment for $x_\pm$ is needed in this case, so the average **minimum detectable gross error** is simply:

$$\alpha \overset{?}{\leq} 2\,\delta f(x_0) \approx \triangle z(x_0)^\top W \triangle z(x_0) \tag{43}$$

10.3 Outer Reliability

Ideally, the state estimate should be as insensitive as possible to any remaining errors in the observations. To estimate how much a particular observation influences the final state estimate, we can directly monitor the displacement $\delta x \equiv x_+ - x_- \approx H_{\mp}^{-1} \delta g_\pm(x_\pm)$. For example, we might define an importance weighting on the state parameters with a criterion matrix U and monitor absolute displacements $\|U \, \delta x\| \approx \|U H_{\mp}^{-1} \delta g(x_\pm)\|$, or compare the displacement δx to the covariance $H_{\pm}^{-1}$ of $x_\pm$ by monitoring $\delta x^\top H_{\mp} \delta x \approx \delta g_\pm(x_\pm)^\top H_{\mp}^{-1} \delta g_\pm(x_\pm)$. A bound on $\delta g(x_\pm)$ of the form[23] $\delta g \, \delta g^\top \preceq V$ for some positive semidefinite V implies a bound $\delta x \, \delta x^\top \preceq H_{\mp}^{-1} V H_{\mp}^{-1}$ on δx and hence a bound $\|U \, \delta x\|^2 \leq \mathcal{N}(U H_{\mp}^{-1} V H_{\mp}^{-1} U^\top)$ where $\mathcal{N}(\cdot)$ can be L_2 norm, trace or Frobenius norm. For a robust

---

[23] This is a convenient intermediate form for deriving bounds. For positive semidefinite matrices A, B, we say that B **dominates** A, $B \succeq A$, if $B - A$ is positive semidefinite. It follows that $\mathcal{N}(U A U^\top) \leq \mathcal{N}(U B U^\top)$ for any matrix U and any matrix function $\mathcal{N}(\cdot)$ that is non-decreasing under positive additions. Rotationally invariant non-decreasing functions $\mathcal{N}(\cdot)$ include all non-decreasing functions of the eigenvalues, *e.g.* L_2 norm $\max \lambda_i$, trace $\sum \lambda_i$, Frobenius norm $\sqrt{\sum \lambda_i^2}$. For a vector a and positive B, $a^\top B a \leq k$ if and only if $a a^\top \preceq k B^{-1}$. (*Proof:* Conjugate by $B^{1/2}$ and then by a $(B^{1/2} a)$-reducing Householder rotation to reduce the question to the equivalence of $0 \preceq \mathrm{Diag}\left(k - u^2, k, \ldots, k\right)$ and $u^2 \leq k$, where $u^2 = \|B^{1/2} a\|^2$). Bounds of the form $\|U a\|^2 \leq k \mathcal{N}(U B^{-1} U^\top)$ follow for any U and any $\mathcal{N}(\cdot)$ for which $\mathcal{N}(v v^\top) = \|v\|^2$, *e.g.* L_2 norm, trace, Frobenius norm.

cost model in which δg is globally bounded, this already gives asymptotic bounds of order $\mathcal{O}(\|H^{-1}\|\|\delta g\|) \sim \mathcal{O}(\|\delta g\|/\sqrt{n_z - n_x})$ for the state perturbation, regardless of whether an outlier occurred. For non-robust cost models we have to use an inlier criterion to limit δg. For the least squares observation model with rejection test (42), $\triangle z \triangle z^\top \preceq \alpha \left(W_i \pm W_i J_i^\top H_\mp^{-1} J_i W_i\right)^{-1}$ and hence the maximum state perturbation due to a declared-inlying observation $\underline{z}_i$ is:

$$\delta x \, \delta x^\top \preceq \alpha H_\mp^{-1} J_i W_i \left(W_i \pm W_i J_i^\top H_\mp^{-1} J_i W_i\right)^{-1} W_i J_i^\top H_\mp^{-1}$$

$$= \alpha \left(H_-^{-1} - H_+^{-1}\right) \tag{44}$$

$$\approx \alpha H_\pm^{-1} J_i W_i^{-1} J_i^\top H_\pm^{-1} \tag{45}$$

so, e.g., $\delta x^\top H_\pm \, \delta x \leq \alpha \operatorname{Trace}\left(J_i H_\pm^{-1} J_i^\top W_i^{-1}\right)$ and $\|U \, \delta x\|^2 \leq \alpha \operatorname{Trace} J_i H_\pm^{-1} U^\top U H_\pm^{-1} J_i^\top W_i^{-1}$, where W_i^{-1} is the nominal covariance of $\underline{z}_i$. Note that these bounds are based on changes in the *estimated* state x_+. They do not directly control perturbations w.r.t. the *true* one x_0. The combined influence of several ($k \ll n_z - n_x$) observations is given by summing their δg's.

10.4 Sensitivity Analysis

This section gives some simple figures of merit that can be used to quantify network redundancy and hence reliability. First, in $\delta f(x_0) \approx \delta f(x_+) + \frac{1}{2} \delta g(x_+)^\top H_-^{-1} \delta g(x_+)$, each cost contribution $\delta f(x_0)$ is split into two parts: the *visible residual* $\delta f(x_+)$ at the fitted state x_+; and $\frac{1}{2} \delta x^\top H_- \, \delta x$, the *change in the base cost* $f_-(x)$ due to the state perturbation $\delta x = H_-^{-1} \delta g(x_+)$ induced by the observation. Ideally, we would like the state perturbation to be small (for stability) and the residual to be large (for outlier detectability). In other words, we would like the following **masking factor** to be small ($m_i \ll 1$) for each observation:

$$m_i \equiv \frac{\delta g(x_+)^\top H_-^{-1} \delta g(x_+)}{2 \, \delta f(x_+) + \delta g(x_+)^\top H_-^{-1} \delta g(x_+)} \tag{46}$$

$$= \frac{\triangle z_i(x_+)^\top W_i J_i H_-^{-1} J_i^\top W_i \triangle z_i(x_+)}{\triangle z_i(x_+)^\top \left(W_i + W_i J_i H_-^{-1} J_i^\top W_i\right) \triangle z_i(x_+)} \tag{47}$$

(Here, δf should be normalized to have minimum value 0 for an exact fit). If m_i is known, the outlier test becomes $\delta f(x_+)/(1 - m_i) \geq \alpha$. The masking m_i depends on the relative size of δg and δf, which in general depends on the functional form of δf and the specific deviation involved. For robust cost models, a bound on δg may be enough to bound m_i for outliers. However, for least squares case ($\triangle z$ form), and more generally for quadratic cost models (such as robust models near the origin), m_i depends only on the direction of $\triangle z_i$, not on its size, and we have a global L_2 matrix norm based bound $m_i \leq \frac{\nu}{1+\nu}$ where $\nu = \|L^\top J_i H_-^{-1} J_i^\top L\|_2 \leq \operatorname{Trace}\left(J_i H_-^{-1} J_i^\top W\right)$ and $L L^\top = W_i$ is a Cholesky decomposition of W_i. (These bounds become equalities for scalar observations).

The stability of the state estimate is determined by the total cost Hessian (information matrix) H. A large H implies a small state estimate covariance H^{-1} and also small responses $\delta x \approx -H^{-1} \delta g$ to cost perturbations δg. The **sensitivity numbers** $s_i \equiv \operatorname{Trace}(H_+^{-1} \delta H_i)$ are a useful measure of the relative amount of information contributed to H_+ by each observation. They sum to the model dimension — $\sum_i s_i = n_x$ because $\sum_i \delta H_i = H_+$

— so they count "how many parameters worth" of the total information the observation contributes. Some authors prefer to quote **redundancy numbers** $r_i \equiv n_i - s_i$, where n_i is the effective number of independent observations contained in $\underline{z}_i$. The redundancy numbers sum to $n_z - n_x$, the total redundancy of the system. In the least squares case, $s_i = \text{Trace}(J_i H_+^{-1} J_i^\top W)$ and $m_i = s_i$ for scalar observations, so the scalar outlier test becomes $\delta f(x_+)/r_i \geq \alpha$. Sensitivity numbers can also be defined for subgroups of the parameters in the form $\text{Trace}(U H^{-1} \delta H)$, where U is an orthogonal projection matrix that selects the parameters of interest. Ideally, the sensitivities of each subgroup should be spread evenly across the observations: a large s_i indicates a heavily weighted observation, whose incorrectness might significantly compromise the estimate.

10.5   Model Selection

It is often necessary to chose between several alternative models of the cameras or scene, *e.g.* additional parameters for lens distortion, camera calibrations that may or may not have changed between images, coplanarity or non-coplanarity of certain features. Over-special models give biased results, while over-general ones tend to be noisy and unstable. We will consider only **nested models**, for which a more general model is specialized to a more specific one by freezing some of its parameters at default values (*e.g.* zero skew or lens distortion, equal calibrations, zero deviation from a plane). Let: x be the parameter vector of the more general model; $f(x)$ be its cost function; $c(x) = 0$ be the parameter freezing constraints enforcing the specialization; k be the number of parameters frozen; x_0 be the true underlying state; x_g be the optimal state estimate for the general model (*i.e.* the unconstrained minimum of $f(x)$); and x_s be the optimal state estimate for the specialized one (*i.e.* the minimum of $f(x)$ subject to the constraints $c(x) = 0$). Then, under the null hypothesis that the specialized model is correct, $c(x_0) = 0$, and in the asymptotic limit in which $x_g - x_0$ and $x_s - x_0$ become Gaussian and the constraints become locally approximately linear across the width of this Gaussian, the difference in fitted residuals $2 (f(x_s) - f(x_g))$ has a χ_k^2 distribution[24]. So if $2 (f(x_s) - f(x_g))$ is less than some suitable χ_k^2 decision threshold α, we can accept the hypothesis that the additional parameters take their default values, and use the specialized model rather than the more general one[25].

As before, we can avoid fitting one of the models by using a linearized analysis. First suppose that we start with a fit of the more general model x_g. Let the linearized constraints at x_g be $c(x_g + \delta x) \approx c(x_g) + C \delta x$, where $C \equiv \frac{dc}{dx}$. A straightforward Lagrange multiplier calculation gives:

$$2 (f(x_s) - f(x_g)) \approx c(x_g)^\top (C H^{-1} C^\top)^{-1} c(x_g)$$
$$x_s \approx x_g - H^{-1} C^\top (C H^{-1} C^\top)^{-1} c(x_g)$$

(48)

Conversely, starting from a fit of the more specialized model, the unconstrained minimum is given by the Newton step: $x_g \approx x_s - H^{-1} g(x_s)$, and $2 (f(x_s) - f(x_g)) \approx g(x_s)^\top H^{-1} g(x_s)$, where $g(x_s)$ is the residual cost gradient at x_s. This requires the general-model covariance

---

[24] This happens irrespective of the observation distributions because — unlike the case of adding an observation — the same observations and cost function are used for both fits.

[25] In practice, small models are preferable as they have greater stability and predictive power and less computational cost. So the threshold α is usually chosen to be comparatively large, to ensure that the more general model will not be chosen unless there is strong evidence for it.

H^{-1} (or an equivalent factorization of H), which may not have been worked out. Suppose that the additional parameters were simply appended to the model, $x \rightarrow (x, y)$ where x is now the reduced parameter vector of the specialized model and y contains the additional parameters. Let the general-model cost gradient at (x_s, y_s) be $\left(\begin{smallmatrix} 0 \\ h \end{smallmatrix} \right)$ where $h = \frac{df}{dy}$, and its Hessian be $\left(\begin{smallmatrix} H & A^{\top} \\ A & B \end{smallmatrix} \right)$. A straightforward calculation shows that:

$$2\left(f(x_s, y_s) - f(x_g, y_g)\right) \approx h^{\top} \left(B - A H^{-1} A^{\top}\right)^{-1} h$$

$$\left(\begin{smallmatrix} x_g \\ y_g \end{smallmatrix} \right) \approx \left(\begin{smallmatrix} x_s \\ y_s \end{smallmatrix} \right) + \left(\begin{smallmatrix} H^{-1} A^{\top} \\ -1 \end{smallmatrix} \right) \left(B - A H^{-1} A^{\top}\right)^{-1} h \tag{49}$$

Given H^{-1} or an equivalent factorization of H, these tests are relatively inexpensive for small k. They amount respectively to one step of Sequential Quadratic Programming and one Newton step, so the results will only be accurate when these methods converge rapidly.

Another, softer, way to handle nested models is to apply a prior $\delta f_{prior}(x)$ peaked at the zero of the specialization constraints $c(x)$. If this is weak the data will override it when necessary, but the constraints may not be very accurately enforced. If it is stronger, we can either apply an 'outlier' test (39, 41) to remove it if it appears to be incorrect, or use a **sticky prior** — a prior similar to a robust distribution, with a concentrated central peak and wide flat tails, that will hold the estimate near the constraint surface for weak data, but allow it to 'unstick' if the data becomes stronger.

Finally, more heuristic rules are often used for model selection in photogrammetry, for example deleting any additional parameters that are excessively correlated (correlation coefficient greater than ~ 0.9) with other parameters, or whose introduction appears to cause an excessive increase in the covariance of other parameters [49, 50].

11   Network Design

Network design is the problem of planning camera placements and numbers of images before a measurement project, to ensure that sufficiently accurate and reliable estimates of everything that needs to be measured are found. We will not say much about design, merely outlining the basic considerations and giving a few useful rules of thumb. See [5, chapter 6], [79, 78], [73, Vol.2 §4] for more information.

Factors to be considered in network design include: scene coverage, occlusion / visibility and feature viewing angle; field of view, depth of field, resolution and workspace constraints; and geometric strength, accuracy and redundancy. The basic quantitative aids to design are covariance estimation in a suitably chosen gauge (see §9) and the quality control tests from §10. Expert systems have been developed [79], but in practice most designs are still based on personal experience and rules of thumb.

In general, geometric stability is best for 'convergent' (close-in, wide baseline, high perspective) geometries, using wide angle lenses to cover as much of the object as possible, and large film or CCD formats to maximize measurement precision. The wide coverage maximizes the overlap between different sub-networks and hence overall network rigidity, while the wide baselines maximize the sub-network stabilities. The practical limitations on closeness are workspace, field of view, depth of field, resolution and feature viewing angle constraints.

Maximizing the overlap between sub-networks is very important. For objects with several faces such as buildings, images should be taken from corner positions to tie the face sub-networks together. For large projects, large scale overview images can be used to tie together close-in densifying ones. When covering individual faces or surfaces, overlap and hence stability are improved by taking images with a range of viewing angles rather than strictly fronto-parallel ones (*e.g.*, for the same number of images, pan-move-pan-move or interleaved left-looking and right-looking images are stabler than a simple fronto-parallel track). Similarly, for buildings or turntable sequences, using a mixture of low and high viewpoints helps stability.

For reliability, one usually plans to see each feature point in at least four images. Although two images in principle suffice for reconstruction, they offer little redundancy and no resistance against feature extraction failures. Even with three images, the internal reliability is still poor: isolated outliers can usually be detected, but it may be difficult to say which of the three images they occurred in. Moreover, 3–4 image geometries with widely spaced (*i.e.* non-aligned) centres usually give much more isotropic feature error distributions than two image ones.

If the bundle adjustment will include self-calibration, it is important to include a range of viewing angles. For example for a flat, compact object, views might be taken at regularly spaced points along a 30–45° half-angle cone centred on the object, with 90° optical axis rotations between views.

12   Summary and Recommendations

This survey was written in the hope of making photogrammetric know-how about bundle adjustment — the simultaneous optimization of structure and camera parameters in visual reconstruction — more accessible to potential implementors in the computer vision community. Perhaps the main lessons are the extraordinary versatility of adjustment methods, the critical importance of exploiting the problem structure, and the continued dominance of second order (Newton) algorithms, in spite of all efforts to make the simpler first order methods converge more rapidly.

We will finish by giving a series of recommendations for methods. At present, these must be regarded as very provisional, and subject to revision after further testing.

Parametrization: (§2.2, 4.5) During step prediction, avoid parameter singularities, infinities, strong nonlinearities and ill-conditioning. Use well-conditioned local (current value + offset) parametrizations of nonlinear elements when necessary to achieve this: the local step prediction parametrization can be different from the global state representation one. The ideal is to make the parameter space error function as isotropic and as near-quadratic as possible. Residual rotation or quaternion parametrizations are advisable for rotations, and projective homogeneous parametrizations for distant points, lines and planes (*i.e.* 3D features near the singularity of their affine parametrizations, affine infinity).

Cost function: (§3) The cost should be a realistic approximation to the negative log likelihood of the total (inlier + outlier) error distribution. The exact functional form of the distribution is not too critical, however: (*i*) Undue weight should not be given to outliers by making the tails of the distribution (the predicted probability of outliers) unrealistically small. (NB: Compared to most real-world measurement distributions, the tails of a Gaussian *are* unrealistically small). (*ii*) The dispersion matrix or inlier covariance should be a realistic estimate of the actual inlier measurement dispersion, so that the transition between inliers and outliers is in about the right place, and the inlier errors are correctly weighted during fitting.

Optimization method: (§4, 6, 7) For **batch problems** use a second order Gauss-Newton method with sparse factorization (see below) of the Hessian, unless:

- The problem is so large that exact sparse factorization is impractical. In this case consider either iterative linear system solvers such as Conjugate Gradient for the Newton step, or related nonlinear iterations such as Conjugate Gradient, or preferably Limited Memory Quasi-Newton or (if memory permits) full Quasi-Newton (§7, [29, 93, 42]). (None of these methods require the Hessian). If you are in this case, it would pay to investigate professional large-scale optimization codes such as MINPACK-2, LANCELOT, or commercial methods from NAG or IMSL (see §C.2).

- If the problem is medium or large but dense (which is unusual), and if it has strong geometry, alternation of resection and intersection may be preferable to a second order method. However, in this case Successive Over-Relaxation (SOR) would be even better, and Conjugate Gradient is likely to be better yet.

- In all of the above cases, good preconditioning is critical (§7.3).

For **on-line problems** (rather than batch ones), use factorization updating rather than matrix inverse updating or re-factorization (§B.5). In time-series problems, investigate the effect of changing the time window (§8.2, [83, 84]), and remember that Kalman filtering is only the first half-iteration of a full nonlinear method.

Factorization method: (§6.2, B.1) For speed, preserve the symmetry of the Hessian during factorization by using: Cholesky decomposition for positive definite Hessians (*e.g.* unconstrained problems in a trivial gauge); pivoted Cholesky decomposition for positive semi-definite Hessians (*e.g.* unconstrained problems with gauge fixing by subset selection §9.5); and Bunch-Kauffman decomposition (§B.1) for indefinite Hessians (*e.g.* the augmented Hessians of constrained problems, §4.4). Gaussian elimination is stable but a factor of two slower than these.

Variable ordering: (§6.3) The variables can usually be ordered by hand for regular networks, but for more irregular ones (*e.g.* close range site-modelling) some experimentation may be needed to find the most efficient overall ordering method. If reasonably compact profiles can be found, profile representations (§6.3, B.3) are simpler to implement and faster than general sparse ones (§6.3).

- For dense networks use a profile representation and a "natural" variable ordering: either features then cameras, or cameras then features, with whichever has the fewest parameters last. An explicit reduced system based implementation such as Brown's method [19] can also be used in this case (§6.1, A).

- If the problem has some sort of 1D temporal or spatial structure (*e.g.* image streams, turntable problems), try a profile representation with natural (simple connectivity) or Snay's banker's (more complex connectivity) orderings (§6.3, [101, 24]). A recursive on-line updating method might also be useful in this case.

- If the problem has 2D structure (*e.g.* cartography and other surface coverage problems) try nested dissection, with hand ordering for regular problems (cartographic blocks), and a multilevel scheme for more complex ones (§6.3). A profile representation may or may not be suitable.

- For less regular sparse networks, the choice is not clear. Try minimum degree ordering with a general sparse representation, Snay's Banker's with a profile representation, or multilevel nested dissection.

For all of the automatic variable ordering methods, try to order any especially highly connected variables last by hand, before invoking the method.

Gauge fixing: (§9) For efficiency, use either a trivial gauge or a subset selection method as a working gauge for calculations, and project the results into whatever gauge you want later by applying a suitable gauge projector P_G (32). Unless you have a strong reason to use an external reference system, the output gauge should probably be an inner gauge centred on the network elements you care most about, *i.e.* the observed features for a reconstruction problem, and the cameras for a navigation one.

Quality control and network design: (§10) A robust cost function helps, but for overall system reliability you still need to plan your measurements in advance (until you have developed a good intuition for this), and check the results afterwards for outlier sensitivity and over-modelling, using a suitable quality control procedure. Do not underestimate the extent to which either low redundancy, or weak geometry, or over-general models can make gross errors undetectable.

A   Historical Overview

This appendix gives a brief history of the main developments in bundle adjustment, including literature references.

Least squares: The theory of combining measurements by minimizing the sum of their squared residuals was developed independently by Gauss and Legendre around 1795–1820 [37, 74], [36, Vol.IV, 1–93], about 40 years *after* robust L_1 estimation [15]. Least squares was motivated by estimation problems in astronomy and geodesy and extensively applied to both fields by Gauss, whose remarkable 1823 monograph [37, 36] already contains almost the complete modern theory of least squares including elements of the theory of probability distributions, the definition and properties of the Gaussian distribution, and a discussion of bias and the "Gauss-Markov" theorem, which states that least squares gives the Best Linear Unbiased Estimator (BLUE) [37, 11]. It also introduces the $LDL^\top$ form of symmetric Gaussian elimination and the Gauss-Newton iteration for nonlinear problems, essentially in their modern forms although without explicitly using matrices. The 1828 supplement on geodesy introduced the Gauss-Seidel iteration for solving large nonlinear systems. The economic and military importance of surveying lead to extensive use of least squares and several further developments: Helmert's nested dissection [64] — probably the first systematic sparse matrix method — in the 1880's, Cholesky decomposition around 1915, Baarda's theory of reliability of measurement networks in the 1960's [7, 8], and Meissl [87, 89] and Baarda's [6] theories of uncertain coordinate frames and free networks [22, 25]. We will return to these topics below.

Second order bundle algorithms: Electronic computers capable of solving reasonably large least squares problems first became available in the late 1950's. The basic photogrammetric bundle method was developed for the U.S. Air Force by Duane C. Brown and his co-workers in 1957–9 [16, 19]. The initial focus was aerial cartography, but by the late 1960's bundle methods were also being used for close-range measurements[26]. The links with geodesic least squares and the possibility of combining geodesic and other types of measurements with the photogrammetric ones were clear right from the start. Initially

---

[26] **Close range** means essentially that the object has significant depth relative to the camera distance, *i.e.* that there is significant perspective distortion. For aerial images the scene is usually shallow compared to the viewing height, so focal length variations are very difficult to disentangle from depth variations.

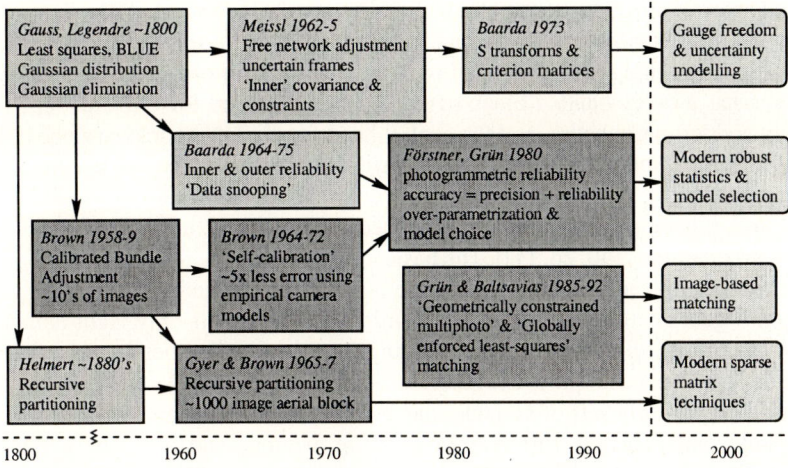

Fig. 9. A schematic history of bundle adjustment.

the cameras were assumed to be calibrated[27], so the optimization was over object points and camera poses only. **Self calibration** (the estimation of internal camera parameters during bundle adjustment) was first discussed around 1964 and implemented by 1968 [19]. Camera models were greatly refined in the early 1970's, with the investigation of many alternative sets of **additional (distortion) parameters** [17–19]. Even with stable and carefully calibrated aerial photogrammetry cameras, self calibration significantly improved accuracies (by factors of around 2–10). This lead to rapid improvements in camera design as previously unmeasurable defects like film platten non-flatness were found and corrected. Much of this development was lead by Brown and his collaborators. See [19] for more of the history and references.

Brown's initial 1958 bundle method [16, 19] uses block matrix techniques to eliminate the structure parameters from the normal equations, leaving only the camera pose parameters. The resulting **reduced camera subsystem** is then solved by dense Gaussian elimination, and back-substitution gives the structure. For self-calibration, a second reduction from pose to calibration parameters can be added in the same way. Brown's method is probably what most vision researchers think of as 'bundle adjustment', following descriptions by Slama [100] and Hartley [58, 59]. It is still a reasonable choice for small dense networks[28], but it rapidly becomes inefficient for the large sparse ones that arise in aerial cartography and large-scale site modelling.

For larger problems, more of the natural sparsity has to be exploited. In aerial cartography, the regular structure makes this relatively straightforward. The images are arranged in **blocks** — rectangular or irregular grids designed for uniform ground coverage, formed from parallel 1D **strips** of images with about 50–70% forward overlap giving adjacent stereo pairs or triplets, about 10–20% side overlap, and a few known ground control points

---

[27] **Calibration** always denotes *internal* camera parameters ("interior orientation") in photogrammetric terminology. External calibration is called **pose** or **(exterior) orientation**.

[28] A photogrammetric network is **dense** if most of the 3D features are visible in most of the images, and **sparse** if most features appear in only a few images. This corresponds directly to the density or sparsity of the off-diagonal block (feature-camera coupling matrix) of the bundle Hessian.

sprinkled sparsely throughout the block. Features are shared only between neighbouring images, and images couple in the reduced camera subsystem only if they share common features. So if the images are arranged in strip or cross-strip ordering, the reduced camera system has a triply-banded block structure (the upper and lower bands representing, *e.g.*, right and left neighbours, and the central band forward and backward ones). Several efficient numerical schemes exist for such matrices. The first was Gyer & Brown's 1967 **recursive partitioning** method [57, 19], which is closely related to Helmert's 1880 geodesic method [64]. (Generalizations of these have become one of the major families of modern sparse matrix methods [40, 26, 11]). The basic idea is to split the rectangle into two halves, recursively solving each half and gluing the two solutions together along their common boundary. Algebraically, the variables are reordered into left-half-only, right-half-only and boundary variables, with the latter (representing the only coupling between the two halves) eliminated last. The technique is extremely effective for aerial blocks and similar problems where small *separating sets* of variables can be found. Brown mentions adjusting a block of 162 photos on a machine with only 8k words of memory, and 1000 photo blocks were already feasible by mid-1967 [19]. For less regular networks such as site modelling ones it may not be feasible to choose an appropriate variable ordering beforehand, but efficient on-line ordering methods exist [40, 26, 11] (see §6.3).

Independent model methods: These approximate bundle adjustment by calculating a number of partial reconstructions independently and merging them by pairwise 3D alignment. Even when the individual models and alignments are separately optimal, the result is suboptimal because the the stresses produced by alignment are not propagated back into the individual models. (Doing so would amount to completing one full iteration of an optimal recursive decomposition style bundle method — see §8.2). Independent model methods were at one time the standard in aerial photogrammetry [95, 2, 100, 73], where they were used to merge individual stereo pair reconstructions within aerial strips into a global reconstruction of the whole block. They are always less accurate than bundle methods, although in some cases the accuracy can be comparable.

First order & approximate bundle algorithms: Another recurrent theme is the use of approximations or iterative methods to avoid solving the full Newton update equations. Most of the plausible approximations have been rediscovered several times, especially variants of alternate steps of resection (finding the camera poses from known 3D points) and intersection (finding the 3D points from known camera poses), and the linearized version of this, the block Gauss-Seidel iteration. Brown's group had already experimented with Block Successive Over-Relaxation (BSOR — an accelerated variant of Gauss-Seidel) by 1964 [19], before they developed their recursive decomposition method. Both Gauss-Seidel and BSOR were also applied to the independent model problem around this time [95, 2]. These methods are mainly of historical interest. For large sparse problems such as aerial blocks, they can not compete with efficiently organized second order methods. Because some of the inter-variable couplings are ignored, corrections propagate very slowly across the network (typically one step per iteration), and many iterations are required for convergence (see §7).

Quality control: In parallel with this algorithmic development, two important theoretical developments took place. Firstly, the Dutch geodesist W. Baarda led a long-running working group that formulated a theory of statistical reliability for least squares estimation [7, 8]. This greatly clarified the conditions (essentially **redundancy**) needed to ensure that outliers could be detected from their residuals (**inner reliability**), and that any remaining undetected outliers had only a limited effect on the final results (**outer reliability**). A. Grün [49, 50] and W. Förstner [30, 33, 34] adapted this theory to photogrammetry around 1980, and also gave some early correlation and covariance based model selection heuristics designed to control over-fitting problems caused by over-elaborate camera models in self calibration.

Datum / gauge freedom: Secondly, as problem size and sophistication increased, it became increasingly difficult to establish sufficiently accurate control points for large geodesic and photogrammetric networks. Traditionally, the network had been viewed as a means of 'densifying' a fixed control coordinate system — propagating control-system coordinates from a few known control points to many unknown ones. But this viewpoint is suboptimal when the network is intrinsically more accurate than the control, because most of the apparent uncertainty is simply due to the uncertain definition of the control coordinate system itself. In the early 1960's, Meissl studied this problem and developed the first **free network** approach, in which the reference coordinate system floated freely rather than being locked to any given control points [87, 89]. More precisely, the coordinates are pinned to a sort of average structure defined by so-called **inner constraints**. Owing to the removal of control-related uncertainties, the nominal structure covariances become smaller and easier to interpret, and the numerical bundle iteration also converges more rapidly. Later, Baarda introduced another approach to this theory based on **S-transforms** — coordinate transforms between uncertain frames [6, 21, 22, 25].

Least squares matching: All of the above developments originally used manually extracted image points. Automated image processing was clearly desirable, but it only gradually became feasible owing to the sheer size and detail of photogrammetric images. Both feature based, *e.g.* [31, 32], and direct (region based) [1, 52, 55, 110] methods were studied, the latter especially for matching low-contrast natural terrain in cartographic applications. Both rely on some form of **least squares matching** (as image correlation is called in photogrammetry). Correlation based matching techniques remain the most accurate methods of extracting precise translations from images, both for high contrast photogrammetric targets and for low contrast natural terrain. Starting from around 1985, Grün and his co-workers combined region based least squares matching with various geometric constraints. **Multi-photo geometrically constrained matching** optimizes the match over multiple images simultaneously, subject to the inter-image matching geometry [52, 55, 9]. For each surface patch there is a single search over patch depth and possibly slant, which *simultaneously* moves it along epipolar lines in the other images. Initial versions assumed known camera matrices, but a full patch-based bundle method was later investigated [9]. Related methods in computer vision include [94, 98, 67]. **Globally enforced least squares matching** [53, 97, 76] further stabilizes the solution in low-signal regions by enforcing continuity constraints between adjacent patches. Patches are arranged in a grid and matched using local affine or projective deformations, with additional terms to penalize mismatching at patch boundaries. Related work in vision includes [104, 102]. The inter-patch constraints give a sparsely-coupled structure to the least squares matching equations, which can again be handled efficiently by recursive decomposition.

B   Matrix Factorization

This appendix covers some standard material on matrix factorization, including the technical details of factorization, factorization updating, and covariance calculation methods. See [44, 11] for more details.

Terminology: Depending on the factorization, 'L' stands for lower triangular, 'U' or 'R' for upper triangular, 'D' or 'S' for diagonal, 'Q' or 'U', 'V' for orthogonal factors.

B.1   Triangular Decompositions

Any matrix A has a family of block (lower triangular)*(diagonal)*(upper triangular) factorizations $A = LDU$:

$$
\begin{matrix} A \end{matrix} \quad = \quad \begin{matrix} L \end{matrix} \qquad \begin{matrix} D \end{matrix} \qquad \begin{matrix} U \end{matrix}
$$

$$
\begin{pmatrix} A_{11} & A_{12} & \cdots & A_{1n} \\ A_{21} & A_{22} & \cdots & A_{2n} \\ \vdots & \vdots & \ddots & \vdots \\ A_{m1} & A_{m2} & \cdots & A_{mn} \end{pmatrix} = \begin{pmatrix} L_{11} & & & \\ L_{21} & L_{22} & & \\ \vdots & \vdots & \ddots & \\ L_{m1} & L_{m2} & \cdots & L_{mr} \end{pmatrix} \begin{pmatrix} D_1 & & & \\ & D_2 & & \\ & & \ddots & \\ & & & D_r \end{pmatrix} \begin{pmatrix} U_{11} & U_{12} & \cdots & \cdots & U_{1n} \\ & U_{22} & \cdots & \cdots & U_{2n} \\ & & \ddots & & \vdots \\ & & & \cdots & U_{rn} \end{pmatrix}
$$

$$(50)$$

$$
\left. \begin{aligned} L_{ii} \, D_i \, U_{ii} &= \overline{A}_{ii}, & i = j \\ L_{ij} &\equiv \overline{A}_{ij} \, U_{jj}^{-1} \, D_j^{-1}, & i > j \\ U_{ij} &\equiv D_i^{-1} L_{ii}^{-1} \overline{A}_{ij}, & i < j \end{aligned} \right\} \qquad \begin{aligned} \overline{A}_{ij} &\equiv A_{ij} - \sum_{k < \min(i,j)} L_{ik} \, D_k \, U_{kj} \\ &= A_{ij} - \sum_{k < \min(i,j)} \overline{A}_{ik} \, \overline{A}_{kk}^{-1} \overline{A}_{kj} \end{aligned} \qquad (51)
$$

Here, the diagonal blocks $D_1 \ldots D_{r-1}$ must be chosen to be square and invertible, and r is determined by the rank of A. The recursion (51) follows immediately from the product $A_{ij} = (LDU)_{ij} = \sum_{k \le \min(i,j)} L_{ik} \, D_k \, U_{kj}$. Given such a factorization, linear equations can be solved by forwards and backwards substitution as in (22–24).

The diagonal blocks of L, D, U can be chosen freely subject to $L_{ii} \, D_{ii} \, U_{ii} = \overline{A}_{ii}$, but once this is done the factorization is uniquely defined. Choosing $L_{ii} = D_{ii} = 1$ so that $U_{ii} = \overline{A}_{ii}$ gives the (block) **LU decomposition** $A = LU$, the matrix representation of (block) Gaussian elimination. Choosing $L_{ii} = U_{ii} = 1$ so that $D_i = \overline{A}_{ii}$ gives the **LDU decomposition**. If A is symmetric, the LDU decomposition preserves the symmetry and becomes the **LDL$^\top$ decomposition** $A = LDL^\top$ where $U = L^\top$ and $D = D^\top$. If A is symmetric positive definite we can set $D = 1$ to get the **Cholesky decomposition** $A = LL^\top$, where $L_{ii} \, L_{ii}^\top = \overline{A}_{ii}$ (recursively) defines the Cholesky factor L_{ii} of the positive definite matrix $\overline{A}_{ii}$. (For a scalar, $\mathrm{Chol}(a) = \sqrt{a}$.) If all of the blocks are chosen to be 1×1, we get the conventional scalar forms of these decompositions. These decompositions are obviously equivalent, but for speed and simplicity it is usual to use the most specific one that applies: LU for general matrices, LDL$^\top$ for symmetric ones, and Cholesky for symmetric positive definite ones. For symmetric matrices such as the bundle Hessian, LDL$^\top$ / Cholesky are 1.5–2 times faster than LDU / LU. We will use the general form (50) below as it is trivial to specialize to any of the others.

Loop ordering: From (51), the ij block of the decomposition depends only on the the upper left $(m-1) \times (m-1)$ submatrix and the first m elements of row i and column j of A, where $m = \min(i,j)$. This allows considerable freedom in the ordering of operations during decomposition, which can be exploited to enhance parallelism and improve memory cache locality.

Fill in: If A is sparse, its L and U factors tend to become ever denser as the decomposition progresses. Recursively expanding $\overline{A}_{ik}$ and $\overline{A}_{kj}$ in (51) gives contributions of the form $\pm A_{ik}\, \overline{A}_{kk}^{-1} A_{kl} \cdots A_{pq}\, \overline{A}_{qq}^{-1} A_{qj}$ for $k, l \ldots p, q < \min(i,j)$. So even if A_{ij} is zero, if there is any path of the form $i \to k \to l \to \ldots \to p \to q \to j$ via non-zero A_{kl} with $k, l \ldots p, q < \min(i,j)$, the ij block of the decomposition will generically **fill-in** (become non-zero). The amount of fill-in is strongly dependent on the ordering of the variables (*i.e.* of the rows and columns of A). Sparse factorization methods (§6.3) manipulate this ordering to minimize either fill-in or total operation counts.

Pivoting: For positive definite matrices, the above factorizations are very stable because the **pivots** $\overline{A}_{ii}$ must themselves remain positive definite. More generally, the pivots may become ill-conditioned causing the decomposition to break down. To deal with this, it is usual to search the undecomposed part of the matrix for a large pivot at each step, and permute this into the leading position before proceeding. The stablest policy is **full pivoting** which searches the whole submatrix, but usually a less costly **partial pivoting** search over just the current column (**column pivoting**) or row (**row pivoting**) suffices. Pivoting ensures that L and/or U are relatively well-conditioned and postpones ill-conditioning in D for as long as possible, but it can not ultimately make D any better conditioned than A is. Column pivoting is usual for the LU decomposition, but if applied to a symmetric matrix it destroys the symmetry and hence doubles the workload. **Diagonal pivoting** preserves symmetry by searching for the largest remaining diagonal element and permuting both its row and its column to the front. This suffices for positive semidefinite matrices (*e.g.* gauge deficient Hessians). For general symmetric indefinite matrices (*e.g.* the augmented Hessians $\left(\begin{smallmatrix} H & C \\ C^\top & 0 \end{smallmatrix}\right)$ of constrained problems (12)), off-diagonal pivots can not be avoided[29], but there are fast, stable, symmetry-preserving pivoted $LDL^\top$ decompositions with block diagonal D having 1×1 and 2×2 blocks. Full pivoting is possible (**Bunch-Parlett decomposition**), but **Bunch-Kaufman decomposition** which searches the diagonal and only one or at most two columns usually suffices. This method is nearly as fast as pivoted Cholesky decomposition (to which it reduces for positive matrices), and as stable LU decomposition with partial pivoting. **Åsen's method** has similar speed and stability but produces a tridiagonal D. The constrained Hessian $\left(\begin{smallmatrix} H & C \\ C^\top & 0 \end{smallmatrix}\right)$ has further special properties owing to its zero block, but we will not consider these here — see [44, §4.4.6 Equilibrium Systems].

B.2   Orthogonal Decompositions

For least squares problems, there is an alternative family of decompositions based on orthogonal reduction of the Jacobian $J = \frac{dz}{dx}$. Given any rectangular matrix A, it can be decomposed as $A = Q R$ where R is upper triangular and Q is orthogonal (*i.e.*, its columns are orthonormal unit vectors). This is called the **QR decomposition** of A. R is identical to the right Cholesky factor of $A^\top A = (R^\top Q^\top)(Q R) = R^\top R$. The solution of the linear

---

[29] The archetypical failure is the unstable $LDL^\top$ decomposition of the well-conditioned symmetric indefinite matrix $\left(\begin{smallmatrix} \epsilon & 1 \\ 1 & 0 \end{smallmatrix}\right) = \left(\begin{smallmatrix} 1 & 0 \\ 1/\epsilon & 1 \end{smallmatrix}\right) \left(\begin{smallmatrix} \epsilon & 0 \\ 0 & -1/\epsilon \end{smallmatrix}\right) \left(\begin{smallmatrix} 1 & 1/\epsilon \\ 0 & 1 \end{smallmatrix}\right)$, for $\epsilon \to 0$. Fortunately, for small diagonal elements, permuting the dominant off-diagonal element next to the diagonal and leaving the resulting 2×2 block undecomposed in D suffices for stability.

least squares problem $\min_x \|A x - b\|^2$ is $x = R^{-1} Q^T b$, and $R^{-1} Q^T$ is the Moore-Penrose pseudo-inverse of A. The QR decomposition is calculated by finding a series of simple rotations that successively zero below diagonal elements of A to form R, and accumulating the rotations in Q, $Q^T A = R$. Various types of rotations can be used. **Givens rotations** are the fine-grained extreme: one-parameter 2×2 rotations that zero a single element of A and affect only two of its rows. **Householder reflections** are coarser-grained reflections in hyperplanes $1 - 2\frac{v v^T}{\|v\|^2}$, designed to zero an entire below-diagonal column of A and affecting all elements of A in or below the diagonal row of that column. Intermediate sizes of Householder reflections can also be used, the 2×2 case being computationally equivalent, and equal up to a sign, to the corresponding Givens rotation. This is useful for sparse QR decompositions, *e.g.* multifrontal methods (see §6.3 and [11]). The Householder method is the most common one for general use, owing to its speed and simplicity. Both the Givens and Householder methods calculate R explicitly, but Q is not calculated directly unless it is explicitly needed. Instead, it is stored in factorized form (as a series of 2×2 rotations or Householder vectors), and applied piecewise when needed. In particular, $Q^T b$ is needed to solve the least squares system, but it can be calculated progressively as part of the decomposition process. As for Cholesky decomposition, QR decomposition is stable without pivoting so long as A has full column rank and is not too ill-conditioned. For degenerate A, Householder QR decomposition with column exchange pivoting can be used. See [11] for more information about QR decomposition.

Both QR decomposition of A and Cholesky decomposition of the normal matrix $A^T A$ can be used to calculate the Cholesky / QR factor R and to solve least squares problems with design matrix / Jacobian A. The QR method runs about as fast as the normal / Cholesky one for square A, but becomes twice as slow for long thin A (*i.e.* many observations in relatively few parameters). However, the QR is numerically much stabler than the normal / Cholesky one in the following sense: if A has condition number (ratio of largest to smallest singular value) c and the machine precision is ϵ, the QR solution has relative error $\mathcal{O}(c\epsilon)$, whereas the normal matrix $A^T A$ has condition number c^2 and its solution has relative error $\mathcal{O}(c^2\epsilon)$. This matters only if $c^2\epsilon$ approaches the relative accuracy to which the solution is required. For example, even in accurate bundle adjustments, we do not need relative accuracies greater than about $1 : 10^6$. As $\epsilon \sim 10^{-16}$ for double precision floating point, we can safely use the normal equation method for $c(J) \lesssim 10^5$, whereas the QR method is safe up to $c(J) \lesssim 10^{10}$, where J is the bundle Jacobian. In practice, the Gauss-Newton / normal equation approach is used in most bundle implementations.

Individual Householder reflections are also useful for projecting parametrizations of geometric entities orthogonal to some constraint vector. For example, for quaternions or homogeneous projective vectors X, we often want to enforce spherical normalization $\|X\|^2 = 1$. To first order, only displacements δX orthogonal to X are allowed, $X^T \delta X = 0$. To parametrize the directions we can move in, we need a basis for the vectors orthogonal to X. A Householder reflection Q based on X converts X to $(1\ 0 \ldots 0)^T$ and hence the orthogonal directions to vectors of the form $(0\ * \ldots *)^T$. So if U contains rows $2-n$ of Q, we can reduce Jacobians $\frac{d}{dX}$ to the $n - 1$ independent parameters δu of the orthogonal subspace by post-multiplying by U^T, and once we have solved for δu, we can recover the orthogonal $\delta X \approx U \delta u$ by premultiplying by U. Multiple constraints can be enforced by successive **Householder reductions** of this form. This corresponds exactly to the **LQ method** for solving constrained least squares problems [11].

$$L = \text{profile\_cholesky\_decomp}(A)$$
$$\textbf{for } i = 1 \textbf{ to } n \textbf{ do}$$
$$\quad \textbf{for } j = \text{first}(i) \textbf{ to } i \textbf{ do}$$
$$\quad\quad a = A_{ij} - \sum_{k=\max(\text{first}(i),\text{first}(j))}^{j-1} L_{ik}\, L_{jk}$$
$$\quad\quad L_{ij} = (j < i) \; ? \; a / L_{jj} \; : \; \sqrt{a}$$

$$x = \text{profile\_cholesky\_forward\_subs}(A, b)$$
$$\textbf{for } i = \text{first}(b) \textbf{ to } n \textbf{ do}$$
$$\quad x_i = \left(b_i - \sum_{k=\max(\text{first}(i),\text{first}(b))}^{i-1} L_{ik}\, x_k \right) / L_{ii}$$

$$y = \text{profile\_cholesky\_back\_subs}(A, x)$$
$$y = x$$
$$\textbf{for } i = \text{last}(b) \textbf{ to } 1 \textbf{ step } -1 \textbf{ do}$$
$$\quad \textbf{for } k = \max(\text{first}(i), \text{first}(y)) \textbf{ to } i \textbf{ do}$$
$$\quad\quad y_k = y_k - y_i\, L_{ik}$$
$$\quad y_i = y_i / L_{ii}$$

Fig. 10. A complete implementation of profile Cholesky decomposition.

B.3 Profile Cholesky Decomposition

One of the simplest sparse methods suitable for bundle problems is **profile Cholesky decomposition**. With natural (features then cameras) variable ordering, it is as efficient as any method for dense networks (*i.e.* most features visible in most images, giving dense camera-feature coupling blocks in the Hessian). With suitable variable ordering[30], it is also efficient for some types of sparse problems, particularly ones with chain-like connectivity.

Figure 10 shows the complete implementation of profile Cholesky, including decomposition $L\,L^{\top} = A$, forward substitution $x = L^{-1}b$, and back substitution $y = L^{-\top}x$. $\text{first}(b), \text{last}(b)$ are the indices of the first and last nonzero entries of b, and $\text{first}(i)$ is the index of the first nonzero entry in row i of A and hence L. If desired, L, x, y can overwrite A, b, x during decomposition to save storage. As always with factorizations, the loops can be reordered in several ways. These have the same operation counts but different access patterns and hence memory cache localities, which on modern machines can lead to significant performance differences for large problems. Here we store and access A and L consistently by rows.

B.4 Matrix Inversion and Covariances

When solving linear equations, forward-backward substitutions (22, 24) are much faster than explicitly calculating and multiplying by A^{-1}, and numerically stabler too. Explicit inverses are only rarely needed, *e.g.* to evaluate the dispersion ("covariance") matrix H^{-1}. Covariance calculation is expensive for bundle adjustment: no matter how sparse H may be, H^{-1} is always dense. Given a triangular decomposition $A = L\,D\,U$, the most obvious way to calculate A^{-1} is via the product $A^{-1} = U^{-1}\,D^{-1}\,L^{-1}$, where L^{-1} (which is lower triangular) is found using a recurrence based on either $L^{-1}L = 1$ or $L\,L^{-1} = 1$ as follows (and similarly but transposed for U):

$$(L^{-1})_{ii} = (L_{ii})^{-1}, \quad (L^{-1})_{ji} = -L_{jj}^{-1}\left(\sum_{k=i}^{j-1} L_{jk}\,(L^{-1})_{ki}\right) = -\left(\sum_{k=i+1}^{j}(L^{-1})_{jk}\,L_{ki}\right)L_{ii}^{-1}$$
$$i=1...n\,,\;\; j=i+1...n \qquad\qquad i=n...1\,,\;\; j=n...i+1$$

$$(52)$$

---

[30] Snay's Banker's strategy (§6.3, [101, 24]) seems to be one of the most effective ordering strategies.

Alternatively [45, 11], the diagonal and the (zero) upper triangle of the linear system $\mathsf{U}\,\mathsf{A}^{-1} = \mathsf{D}^{-1}\mathsf{L}^{-1}$ can be combined with the (zero) lower triangle of $\mathsf{A}^{-1}\mathsf{L} = \mathsf{U}^{-1}\mathsf{D}^{-1}$ to give the direct recursion ($i = n \ldots 1$ and $j = n \ldots i+1$):

$$(\mathsf{A}^{-1})_{ji} \;=\; -\left(\sum_{k=i+1}^{n} (\mathsf{A}^{-1})_{jk}\,\mathsf{L}_{ki} \right) \mathsf{L}_{ii}^{-1}, \qquad (\mathsf{A}^{-1})_{ij} \;=\; -\mathsf{U}_{ii}^{-1}\left(\sum_{k=i+1}^{n} \mathsf{U}_{ik}\,(\mathsf{A}^{-1})_{kj} \right)$$

$$(\mathsf{A}^{-1})_{ii} \;=\; \mathsf{U}_{ii}^{-1}\left(\mathsf{D}_i^{-1}\mathsf{L}_{ii}^{-1} - \sum_{k=i+1}^{n} \mathsf{U}_{ik}\,(\mathsf{A}^{-1})_{ki} \right) \;=\; \left(\mathsf{U}_{ii}^{-1}\mathsf{D}_i^{-1} - \sum_{k=i+1}^{n} (\mathsf{A}^{-1})_{ik}\,\mathsf{L}_{ki} \right) \mathsf{L}_{ii}^{-1}$$

$$(53)$$

In the symmetric case $(\mathsf{A}^{-1})_{ji} = (\mathsf{A}^{-1})_{ij}$ so we can avoid roughly half of the work. If only a few blocks of A^{-1} are required (*e.g.* the diagonal ones), this recursion has the property that the blocks of A^{-1} associated with the filled positions of L and U can be calculated without calculating any blocks associated with unfilled positions. More precisely, to calculate $(\mathsf{A}^{-1})_{ij}$ for which L_{ji} ($j > i$) or U_{ji} ($j < i$) is non-zero, we do not need any block $(\mathsf{A}^{-1})_{kl}$ for which $\mathsf{L}_{lk} = \mathsf{0}$ ($l > k$) or $\mathsf{U}_{lk} = \mathsf{0}$ ($l < k$) [31]. This is a significant saving if L, U are sparse, as in bundle problems. In particular, given the covariance of the reduced camera system, the 3D feature variances and feature-camera covariances can be calculated efficiently using (53) (or equivalently (17), where $\mathsf{A} \leftarrow \mathsf{H}_{ss}$ is the block diagonal feature Hessian and D_2 is the reduced camera one).

B.5   Factorization Updating

For on-line applications (§8.2), it is useful to be able to **update** the decomposition $\mathsf{A} = \mathsf{L}\,\mathsf{D}\,\mathsf{U}$ to account for a (usually low-rank) change $\mathsf{A} \to \overline{\mathsf{A}} \equiv \mathsf{A} \pm \mathsf{B}\,\mathsf{W}\,\mathsf{C}$. Let $\overline{\mathsf{B}} \equiv \mathsf{L}^{-1}\mathsf{B}$ and $\overline{\mathsf{C}} \equiv \mathsf{C}\,\mathsf{U}^{-1}$ so that $\mathsf{L}^{-1}\overline{\mathsf{A}}\,\mathsf{U}^{-1} = \mathsf{D} \pm \overline{\mathsf{B}}\,\mathsf{W}\,\overline{\mathsf{C}}$. This low-rank update of D can be LDU decomposed efficiently. Separating the first block of D from the others we have:

$$\begin{pmatrix} \mathsf{D}_1 & \\ & \mathsf{D}_2 \end{pmatrix} \pm \begin{pmatrix} \overline{\mathsf{B}}_1 \\ \overline{\mathsf{B}}_2 \end{pmatrix} \mathsf{W} \begin{pmatrix} \overline{\mathsf{C}}_1 & \overline{\mathsf{C}}_2 \end{pmatrix} \;=\; \begin{pmatrix} 1 & \\ \pm \overline{\mathsf{B}}_2\,\mathsf{W}\,\overline{\mathsf{C}}_1\,\overline{\mathsf{D}}_1^{-1} & 1 \end{pmatrix} \begin{pmatrix} \overline{\mathsf{D}}_1 & \\ & \overline{\mathsf{D}}_2 \end{pmatrix} \begin{pmatrix} 1 & \pm \overline{\mathsf{D}}_1^{-1}\overline{\mathsf{B}}_1\,\mathsf{W}\,\overline{\mathsf{C}}_2 \\ & 1 \end{pmatrix}$$

$$\overline{\mathsf{D}}_1 \;\equiv\; \mathsf{D}_1 \pm \overline{\mathsf{B}}_1\,\mathsf{W}\,\overline{\mathsf{C}}_1 \qquad\qquad \overline{\mathsf{D}}_2 \;\equiv\; \mathsf{D}_2 \pm \overline{\mathsf{B}}_2 \left(\mathsf{W} \mp \mathsf{W}\,\overline{\mathsf{C}}_1\,\overline{\mathsf{D}}_1^{-1}\overline{\mathsf{B}}_1\,\mathsf{W} \right) \overline{\mathsf{C}}_2$$

$$(54)$$

$\overline{\mathsf{D}}_2$ is a low-rank update of D_2 with the same $\overline{\mathsf{C}}_2$ and $\overline{\mathsf{B}}_2$ but a different W. Evaluating this recursively and merging the resulting L and U factors into L and U gives the updated

---

[31] This holds because of the way fill-in occurs in the LDU decomposition. Suppose that we want to find $(\mathsf{A}^{-1})_{ij}$, where $j > i$ and $\mathsf{L}_{ji} \neq \mathsf{0}$. For this we need $(\mathsf{A}^{-1})_{kj}$ for all non-zero U_{ik}, $k > i$. But for these $\overline{\mathsf{A}}_{jk} = \mathsf{L}_{ji}\,\mathsf{D}_i\,\mathsf{U}_{ik} + \ldots + \mathsf{A}_{jk} \neq \mathsf{0}$, so $(\mathsf{A}^{-1})_{kj}$ is associated with a filled position and will already have been evaluated.

decomposition[32] $\overline{A} = \overline{L}\,\overline{D}\,\overline{U}$:

$$W^{(1)} \leftarrow \pm W; \quad B^{(1)} \leftarrow B; \quad C^{(1)} \leftarrow C;$$

for $i = 1$ **to** n **do**

$$\overline{B}_i \leftarrow B_i^{(i)}; \quad \overline{C}_i \leftarrow C_i^{(i)}; \quad \overline{D}_i \leftarrow D_i + \overline{B}_i W^{(i)} \overline{C}_i;$$

$$W^{(i+1)} \leftarrow W^{(i)} - W^{(i)} \overline{C}_i \overline{D}_i^{-1} \overline{B}_i W^{(i)} = \left((W^{(i)})^{-1} + \overline{C}_i D_i^{-1} \overline{B}_i \right)^{-1}; \qquad (55)$$

for $j = i + 1$ **to** n **do**

$$B_j^{(i+1)} \leftarrow B_j^{(i)} - L_{ji} \overline{B}_i; \quad \overline{L}_{ji} \leftarrow L_{ji} + B_j^{(i+1)} W^{(i+1)} \overline{C}_i D_i^{-1};$$

$$C_j^{(i+1)} \leftarrow C_j^{(i)} - \overline{C}_i U_{ij}; \quad \overline{U}_{ij} \leftarrow U_{ij} + D_i^{-1} \overline{B}_i W^{(i+1)} C_j^{(i+1)};$$

The W^{-1} form of the W update is numerically stabler for additions ('+' sign in $A \pm B W C$ with positive W), but is not usable unless $W^{(i)}$ is invertible. In either case, the update takes time $\mathcal{O}\left((k^2 + b^2)N^2\right)$ where A is $N \times N$, W is $k \times k$ and the D_i are $b \times b$. So other things being equal, k should be kept as small as possible (*e.g.* by splitting the update into independent rows using an initial factorization of W, and updating for each row in turn). The scalar Cholesky form of this method for a rank one update $A \rightarrow A + w\,b\,b^\top$ is:

$$w^{(1)} \leftarrow w; \quad b^{(1)} \leftarrow b;$$

for $i = 1$ **to** n **do**

$$\overline{b}_i \leftarrow b_i^{(i)}/L_{ii}; \quad \overline{d}_i \leftarrow 1 + w^{(i)} \overline{b}_i^2; \quad \overline{L}_{ii} \leftarrow L_{ii} \sqrt{\overline{d}_i};$$

$$w^{(i+1)} \leftarrow w^{(i)}/\overline{d}_i;$$

for $j = i + 1$ **to** n **do**

$$b_j^{(i+1)} \leftarrow b_j^{(i)} - L_{ji} \overline{b}_i; \quad \overline{L}_{ji} \leftarrow \left(L_{ji} + b_j^{(i+1)} w^{(i+1)} \overline{b}_i \right) \sqrt{\overline{d}_i};$$

$$\qquad (56)$$

This takes $\mathcal{O}(n^2)$ operations. The same recursion rule (and several equivalent forms) can be derived by reducing $(L\ b)^\top$ to an upper triangular matrix using Givens rotations or Householder transformations [43, 11].

C   Software

C.1   Software Organization

For a general purpose bundle adjustment code, an extensible object-based organization is natural. The measurement network can be modelled as a network of objects, representing *measurements and their error models* and the different types of *3D features* and *camera models* that they depend on. It is obviously useful to allow the measurement, feature and camera types to be open-ended. Measurements may be 2D or 3D, implicit or explicit, and many different robust error models are possible. Features may range from points through curves and homographies to entire 3D object models. Many types of camera and lens

---

[32] Here, $B_j^{(i)} = B_j - \sum_{k=1}^{i-1} L_{jk} \overline{B}_k = \sum_{k=i}^{j} L_{jk} \overline{B}_k$ and $C_j^{(i)} = C_j - \sum_{k=1}^{i-1} \overline{C}_k L_{kj} = \sum_{k=i}^{j} \overline{C}_k U_{kj}$ accumulate $L^{-1}B$ and $C\,U^{-1}$. For the L, U updates one can also use $W^{(i+1)} \overline{C}_i D_i^{-1} = W^{(i)} \overline{C}_i \overline{D}_i^{-1}$ and $D_i^{-1} \overline{B}_i W^{(i+1)} = \overline{D}_i^{-1} \overline{B}_i W^{(i)}$.

distortion models exist. If the scene is dynamic or articulated, additional nodes representing 3D transformations (kinematic chains or relative motions) may also be needed.

The main purpose of the network structure is to predict observations and their Jacobians w.r.t. the free parameters, and then to integrate the resulting first order parameter updates back into the internal 3D feature and camera state representations. Prediction is essentially a matter of systematically propagating values through the network, with heavy use of the chain rule for derivative propagation. The network representation must interface with a numerical linear algebra one that supports appropriate methods for forming and solving the sparse, damped Gauss-Newton (or other) step prediction equations. A fixed-order sparse factorization may suffice for simple networks, while automatic variable ordering is needed for more complicated networks and iterative solution methods for large ones.

Several extensible bundle codes exist, but as far as we are aware, none of them are currently available as freeware. Our own implementations include:

- CARMEN [59] is a program for camera modelling and scene reconstruction using iterative nonlinear least squares. It has a modular design that allows many different feature, measurement and camera types to be incorporated (including some quite exotic ones [56, 63]). It uses sparse matrix techniques similar to Brown's reduced camera system method [19] to make the bundle adjustment iteration efficient.

- HORATIO (http://www.ee.surrey.ac.uk/Personal/P.McLauchlan/horatio/html, [85], [86], [83], [84]) is a C library supporting the development of efficient computer vision applications. It contains support for image processing, linear algebra and visualization, and will soon be made publicly available. The bundle adjustment methods in Horatio, which are based on the Variable State Dimension Filter (VSDF) [83, 84], are being commercialized. These algorithms support sparse block matrix operations, arbitrary gauge constraints, global and local parametrizations, multiple feature types and camera models, as well as batch and sequential operation.

- VXL: This modular C++ vision environment is a new, lightweight version of the TargetJr/IUE environment, which is being developed mainly by the Universities of Oxford and Leuven, and General Electric CRD. The initial public release on http://www.robots.ox.ac.uk/~vxl will include an OpenGL user interface and classes for multiple view geometry and numerics (the latter being mainly C++ wrappers to well established routines from Netlib — see below). A bundle adjustment code exists for it but is not currently planned for release [28, 62].

C.2 Software Resources

A great deal of useful numerical linear algebra and optimization software is available on the Internet, although more commonly in FORTRAN than in C/C++. The main repository is NETLIB at http://www.netlib.org/. Other useful sites include: the 'Guide to Available Mathematical Software' GAMS at http://gams.nist.gov; the NEOS guide http://www-fp.mcs.anl.gov/otc/Guide/, which is based in part on Moré & Wright's guide book [90]; and the Object Oriented Numerics page http://oonumerics.org. For large-scale dense linear algebra, LAPACK (http://www.netlib.org/lapack, [3]) is the best package available. However it is optimized for relatively large problems (matrices of size 100 or more), so if you are solving many small ones (size less than 20 or so) it may be faster to use the older LINPACK and EISPACK routines. These libraries all use the BLAS (Basic Linear Algebra Subroutines) interface for low level matrix manipulations, optimized versions of which are available from most processor vendors. They are all FORTRAN based, but C/C++ versions and interfaces exist (CLAPACK, http://www.netlib.org/clapack; LAPACK++, http://math.nist.gov/lapack++). For sparse matrices there is a bewildering array of packages. One good one is Boeing's SPOOLES (http://www.netlib.org/linalg/spooles/spooles.2.2.html) which implements sparse Bunch-Kaufman decomposition in C with several ordering methods. For iterative linear system solvers implementation is seldom difficult, but there are again many methods and implementations. The 'Templates' book [10] contains potted code. For nonlinear optimization there are various older codes such as MINPACK, and more recent codes designed mainly for very large problems such as MINPACK-2 (ftp://info.mcs.anl.gov/pub/MINPACK-2) and LANCELOT (http://www.cse.clrc.ac.uk/Activity/LANCELOT). (Both of these latter codes have good reputations for other large scale problems, but as far as we are aware they have not yet been tested on bundle adjustment). All of the above packages are freely available. Commercial vendors such as NAG (ttp://www.nag.co.uk) and IMSL (www.imsl.com) have their own optimization codes.

Glossary

This glossary includes a few common terms from vision, photogrammetry, numerical optimization and statistics, with their translations.

Additional parameters: Parameters added to the basic perspective model to represent lens distortion and similar small image deformations.

α-distribution: A family of wide tailed probability distributions, including the **Cauchy distribution** ($\alpha = 1$) and the Gaussian ($\alpha = 2$).

Alternation: A family of simplistic and largely outdated strategies for nonlinear optimization (and also iterative solution of linear equations). Cycles through variables or groups of variables, optimizing over each in turn while holding all the others fixed. Nonlinear alternation methods usually relinearize the equations after each group, while **Gauss-Seidel** methods propagate first order corrections forwards and relinearize only at the end of the cycle (the results are the same to first order). **Successive over-relaxation** adds momentum terms to speed convergence. See **separable problem**. Alternation of **resection** and **intersection** is a naïve and often-rediscovered bundle method.

Asymptotic limit: In statistics, the limit as the number of independent measurements is increased to infinity, or as the second order moments dominate all higher order ones so that the posterior distribution becomes approximately Gaussian.

Asymptotic convergence: In optimization, the limit of small deviations from the solution, *i.e.* as the solution is reached. **Second order** or **quadratically convergent** methods such as **Newton's method** *square* the norm of the residual at each step, while **first order** or **linearly convergent** methods such as **gradient descent** and **alternation** only reduce the error by a constant factor at each step.

Banker's strategy: See **fill in**, §6.3.

Block: A (possibly irregular) grid of overlapping photos in aerial cartography.

Bunch-Kauffman: A numerically efficient factorization method for symmetric indefinite matrices, $A = L D L^T$ where L is lower triangular and D is block diagonal with 1×1 and 2×2 blocks (§6.2, B.1).

Bundle adjustment: Any refinement method for visual reconstructions that aims to produce jointly optimal structure and camera estimates.

Calibration: In photogrammetry, this always means *internal* calibration of the cameras. See **inner orientation**.

Central limit theorem: States that maximum likelihood and similar estimators asymptotically have Gaussian distributions. The basis of most of our perturbation expansions.

Cholesky decomposition: A numerically efficient factorization method for symmetric positive definite matrices, $A = L L^\top$ where L is lower triangular.

Close Range: Any photogrammetric problem where the scene is relatively close to the camera, so that it has significant depth compared to the camera distance. Terrestrial photogrammetry as opposed to **aerial cartography**.

Conjugate gradient: A cleverly accelerated first order iteration for solving positive definite linear systems or minimizing a nonlinear cost function. See **Krylov subspace**.

Cost function: The function quantifying the total residual error that is minimized in an adjustment computation.

Cramér-Rao bound: See **Fisher information**.

Criterion matrix: In network design, an ideal or desired form for a covariance matrix.

Damped Newton method: Newton's method with a stabilizing step control policy added. See **Levenberg-Marquardt**.

Data snooping: Elimination of outliers based on examination of their residual errors.

Datum: A reference coordinate system, against which other coordinates and uncertainties are measured. Our principle example of a **gauge**.

Dense: A matrix or system of equations with so few known-zero elements that it may as well be treated as having none. The opposite of **sparse**. For photogrammetric networks, **dense** means that the off-diagonal structure-camera block of the Hessian is dense, *i.e.* most features are seen in most images.

Descent direction: In optimization, any search direction with a downhill component, *i.e.* that locally reduces the cost.

Design: The process of defining a measurement network (placement of cameras, number of images, *etc.*) to satisfy given accuracy and quality criteria.

Design matrix: The observation-state Jacobian $J = \frac{dz}{dx}$.

Direct method: Dense correspondence or reconstruction methods based directly on cross-correlating photometric intensities or related descriptor images, without extracting geometric features. See **least squares matching, feature based method**.

Dispersion matrix: The inverse of the cost function **Hessian**, a measure of distribution spread. In the **asymptotic limit**, the covariance is given by the dispersion.

Downdating: On-the-fly removal of observations, without recalculating everything from scratch. The inverse of **updating**.

Elimination graph: A graph derived from the **network graph**, describing the progress of **fill in** during sparse matrix factorization.

Empirical distribution: A set of samples from some probability distribution, viewed as an sum-of-delta-function approximation to the distribution itself. The **law of large numbers** asserts that the approximation asymptotically converges to the true distribution in probability.

Fill-in: The tendency of zero positions to become nonzero as sparse matrix factorization progresses. **Variable ordering strategies** seek to minimize fill-in by permuting the variables before factorization. Methods include **minimum degree, reverse Cuthill-McKee, Banker's strategies**, and **nested dissection**. See §6.3.

Fisher information: In parameter estimation, the mean curvature of the posterior log likelihood function, regarded as a measure of the certainty of an estimate. The **Cramér-Rao bound** says that any unbiased estimator has covariance $\geq$ the inverse of the Fisher information.

Free gauge / free network: A **gauge** or **datum** that is defined internally to the measurement network, rather than being based on predefined reference features like a **fixed gauge**.

Feature based: Sparse correspondence / reconstruction methods based on geometric image features (points, lines, homographies . . .) rather than direct photometry. See **direct method**.

Filtering: In sequential problems such as time series, the estimation of a current value using all of the previous measurements. **Smoothing** can correct this afterwards, by integrating also the information from future measurements.

First order method / convergence: See **asymptotic convergence**.

Gauge: An internal or external reference coordinate system defined for the current state and (at least) small variations of it, against which other quantities *and their uncertainties* can be measured. The 3D coordinate gauge is also called the **datum**. A **gauge constraint** is any constraint fixing a specific gauge, *e.g.* for the current state and arbitrary (small) displacements of it. The fact that the gauge can be chosen arbitrarily without changing the underlying structure is called **gauge freedom** or **gauge invariance**. The rank-deficiency that this transformation-invariance of the cost function induces on the Hessian is called **gauge deficiency**. Displacements that violate the gauge constraints can be corrected by applying an **S-transform**, whose linear form is a **gauge projection matrix** P_G.

Gauss-Markov theorem: This says that for a linear system, least squares weighted by the true measurement covariances gives the Best (minimum variance) Linear Unbiased Estimator or BLUE.

Gauss-Newton method: A Newton-like method for nonlinear least squares problems, in which the Hessian is approximated by the Gauss-Newton one $H \approx J^T W J$ where J is the **design matrix** and W is a weight matrix. The **normal equations** are the resulting Gauss-Newton step prediction equations $(J^T W J)\, \delta x = -(J W \triangle z)$.

Gauss-Seidel method: See **alternation**.

Givens rotation: A 2×2 rotation used to as part of orthogonal reduction of a matrix, *e.g.* QR, SVD. See **Householder reflection**.

Gradient: The derivative of the cost function w.r.t. the parameters $g = \dfrac{df}{dx}$.

Gradient descent: Naïve optimization method which consists of steepest descent (in some given coordinate system) down the gradient of the cost function.

Hessian: The second derivative matrix of the cost function $H = \dfrac{d^2 f}{dx^2}$. Symmetric and positive (semi-)definite at a cost minimum. Measures how 'stiff' the state estimate is against perturbations. Its inverse is the **dispersion matrix**.

Householder reflection: A matrix representing reflection in a hyperplane, used as a tool for orthogonal reduction of a matrix, *e.g.* QR, SVD. See **Givens rotation**.

Independent model method: A suboptimal approximation to bundle adjustment developed for aerial cartography. Small local 3D models are reconstructed, each from a few images, and then glued together via **tie features** at their common boundaries, without a subsequent adjustment to relax the internal stresses so caused.

Inner: Internal or intrinsic.

Inner constraints: **Gauge constraints** linking the gauge to some weighted average of the reconstructed features and cameras (rather than to an externally supplied reference system).

Inner orientation: Internal camera calibration, including lens distortion, *etc*.

Inner reliability: The ability to either resist outliers, or detect and reject them based on their residual errors.

Intersection: (of optical rays). Solving for 3D feature positions given the corresponding image features and known 3D camera poses and calibrations. See **resection, alternation**.

Jacobian: See **design matrix**.

Krylov subspace: The linear subspace spanned by the iterated products $\{A^k b | k = 0 \ldots n\}$ of some square matrix A with some vector b, used as a tool for generating linear algebra and nonlinear optimization iterations. **Conjugate gradient** is the most famous Krylov method.

Kullback-Leibler divergence: See **relative entropy**.

Least squares matching: Image matching based on photometric intensities. See **direct method**.

Levenberg-Marquardt: A common damping (step control) method for nonlinear least squares problems, consisting of adding a multiple λD of some positive definite weight matrix D to the Gauss-Newton Hessian before solving for the step. Levenberg-Marquardt uses a simple rescaling based heuristic for setting λ, while **trust region** methods use a more sophisticated step-length based one. Such methods are called **damped Newton** methods in general optimization.

Local model: In optimization, a local approximation to the function being optimized, which is easy enough to optimize that an iterative optimizer for the original function can be based on it. The second order Taylor series model gives **Newton's method**.

Local parametrization: A parametrization of a nonlinear space based on offsets from some current point. Used during an optimization step to give better local numerical conditioning than a more global parametrization would.

LU decomposition: The usual matrix factorization form of Gaussian elimination.

Minimum degree ordering: One of the most widely used automatic variable ordering methods for sparse matrix factorization.

Minimum detectable gross error: The smallest outlier that can be detected on average by an outlier detection method.

Nested dissection: A top-down divide-and-conquer **variable ordering method** for sparse matrix factorization. Recursively splits the problem into disconnected halves, dealing with the **separating set** of connecting variables last. Particularly suitable for surface coverage problems. Also called **recursive partitioning**.

Nested models: Pairs of models, of which one is a specialization of the other obtained by freezing certain parameters(s) at prespecified values.

Network: The interconnection structure of the 3D features, the cameras, and the measurements that are made of them (image points, *etc.*). Usually encoded as a graph structure.

Newton method: The basic iterative second order optimization method. The **Newton step** state update $\delta x = -H^{-1} g$ minimizes a local quadratic Taylor approximation to the cost function at each iteration.

Normal equations: See **Gauss-Newton method**.

Nuisance parameter: Any parameter that had to be estimated as part of a nonlinear parameter estimation problem, but whose value was not really wanted.

Outer: External. See **inner**.

Outer orientation: Camera pose (position and angular orientation).

Outer reliability: The influence of unremoved outliers on the final parameter estimates, *i.e.* the extent to which they are reliable even though some (presumably small or lowly-weighted) outliers may remain undetected.

Outlier: An observation that deviates significantly from its predicted position. More generally, any observation that does not fit some preconceived notion of how the observations should be distributed, and which must therefore be removed to avoid disturbing the parameter estimates. See **total distribution**.

Pivoting: Row and/or column exchanges designed to promote stability during matrix factorization.

Point estimator: Any estimator that returns a single "best" parameter estimate, *e.g.* maximum likelihood, maximum a posteriori.

Pose: 3D position and orientation (angle), *e.g.* of a camera.

Preconditioner: A linear change of variables designed to improve the accuracy or convergence rate of a numerical method, *e.g.* a first order optimization iteration. **Variable scaling** is the diagonal part of preconditioning.

Primary structure: The main decomposition of the bundle adjustment variables into structure and camera ones.

Profile matrix: A storage scheme for sparse matrices in which all elements between the first and the last nonzero one in each row are stored, even if they are zero. Its simplicity makes it efficient even if there are quite a few zeros.

Quality control: The monitoring of an estimation process to ensure that accuracy requirements were met, that outliers were removed or down-weighted, and that appropriate models were used, *e.g.* for **additional parameters**.

Radial distribution: An observation error distribution which retains the Gaussian dependence on a squared residual error $r = \mathsf{x}^{\mathsf{T}} \mathsf{W} \mathsf{x}$, but which replaces the exponential $e^{-r/2}$ form with a more robust long-tailed one.

Recursive: Used of filtering-based reconstruction methods that handle sequences of images or measurements by successive updating steps.

Recursive partitioning: See **nested dissection**.

Reduced problem: Any problem where some of the variables have already been eliminated by partial factorization, leaving only the others. The **reduced camera system** (20) is the result of reducing the bundle problem to only the camera variables. (§6.1, 8.2, 4.4).

Redundancy: The extent to which any one observation has only a small influence on the results, so that it could be incorrect or missing without causing problems. Redundant consenses are the basis of reliability. **Redundancy numbers** r are a heuristic measure of the amount of redundancy in an estimate.

Relative entropy: An information-theoretic measure of how badly a model probability density p_1 fits an actual one p_0: the mean (w.r.t. p_0) log likelihood contrast of p_0 to p_1, $\langle \log(p_0/p_1) \rangle_{p_0}$.

Resection: (of optical rays). Solving for 3D camera poses and possibly calibrations, given image features and the corresponding 3D feature positions. See **intersection**.

Resection-intersection: See **alternation**.

Residual: The error $\triangle \mathsf{z}$ in a predicted observation, or its cost function value.

S-transformation: A transformation between two **gauges**, implemented locally by a **gauge projection matrix** $\mathsf{P}_\mathcal{G}$.

Scaling: See **preconditioner**.

Schur complement: Of A in $\left(\begin{smallmatrix} \mathsf{A} & \mathsf{B} \\ \mathsf{C} & \mathsf{D} \end{smallmatrix} \right)$ is $\mathsf{D} - \mathsf{C}\,\mathsf{A}^{-1}\mathsf{B}$. See §6.1.

Second order method / convergence: See **asymptotic convergence**.

Secondary structure: Internal structure or sparsity of the off-diagonal feature-camera coupling block of the bundle Hessian. See **primary structure**.

Self calibration: Recovery of camera (internal) calibration during bundle adjustment.

Sensitivity number: A heuristic number s measuring the sensitivity of an estimate to a given observation.

Separable problem: Any optimization problem in which the variables can be separated into two or more subsets, for which optimization over each subset given all of the others is significantly easier than simultaneous optimization over all variables. Bundle adjustment is separable into 3D structure and cameras. **Alternation** (successive optimization over each subset) is a naïve approach to separable problems.

Separating set: See **nested dissection**.

Sequential Quadratic Programming (SQP): An iteration for constrained optimization problems, the constrained analogue of **Newton's method**. At each step optimizes a **local model** based on a quadratic model function with linearized constraints.

Sparse: "Any matrix with enough zeros that it pays to take advantage of them" (Wilkinson).

State: The bundle adjustment parameter vector, including all scene and camera parameters to be estimated.

Sticky prior: A robust prior with a central peak but wide tails, designed to let the estimate 'unstick' from the peak if there is strong evidence against it.

Subset selection: The selection of a stable subset of 'live' variables on-line during pivoted factorization. *E.g.*, used as a method for selecting variables to constrain with trivial gauge constraints (§9.5).

Successive Over-Relaxation (SOR): See **alternation**.

Sum of Squared Errors (SSE): The nonlinear least squares cost function. The (possibly weighted) sum of squares of all of the residual feature projection errors.

Total distribution: The error distribution expected for *all* observations of a given type, including both inliers and outliers. *I.e.* the distribution that should be used in maximum likelihood estimation.

Trivial gauge: A **gauge** that fixes a small set of predefined reference features or cameras at given coordinates, irrespective of the values of the other features.

Trust region: See **Levenberg-Marquardt**.

Updating: Incorporation of additional observations without recalculating everything from scratch.

Variable ordering strategy: See **fill-in**.

Weight matrix: An information (inverse covariance) like matrix matrix W, designed to put the correct relative statistical weights on a set of measurements.

Woodbury formula: The matrix inverse updating formula (18).

References

[1] F. Ackermann. Digital image correlation: Performance and potential applications in photogrammetry. *Photogrammetric Record*, 11(64):429–439, 1984.

[2] F. Amer. Digital block adjustment. *Photogrammetric Record*, 4:34–47, 1962.

[3] E. Anderson, Z. Bai, C. Bischof, S. Blackford, J. Demmel, J. Dongarra, J. Du Croz, A. Greenbaum, S. Hammarling, A. McKenney, and D. Sorensen. *LAPACK Users' Guide, Third Edition*. SIAM Press, Philadelphia, 1999. LAPACK home page: http://www.netlib.org/lapack.

[4] C. Ashcraft and J. W.-H. Liu. Robust ordering of sparse matrices using multisection. *SIAM J. Matrix Anal. Appl.*, 19:816–832, 1998.

[5] K. B. Atkinson, editor. *Close Range Photogrammetry and Machine Vision*. Whittles Publishing, Roseleigh House, Latheronwheel, Caithness, Scotland, 1996.

[6] W. Baarda. S-transformations and criterion matrices. *Netherlands Geodetic Commission, Publications on Geodesy*, New Series, Vol.5, No.1 (168 pages), 1967.

[7] W. Baarda. Statistical concepts in geodesy. *Netherlands Geodetic Commission Publications on Geodesy*, New Series, Vol.2, No.4 (74 pages), 1967.

[8] W. Baarda. A testing procedure for use in geodetic networks. *Netherlands Geodetic Commission Publications on Geodesy*, New Series, Vol.2, No.5 (97 pages), 1968.

[9] E. P. Baltsavias. *Multiphoto Geometrically Constrained Matching*. PhD thesis, ETH-Zurich, 1992.

[10] R. Barrett, M. W. Berry, T. F. Chan, J. Demmel, J. Donato, J. Dongarra, V. Eijkhout, R. Pozo, C. Romine, and H. van der Vorst. *Templates for the Solution of Linear Systems: Building Blocks for Iterative Methods*. SIAM Press, Philadelphia, 1993.

[11] Åke Björck. *Numerical Methods for Least Squares Problems*. SIAM Press, Philadelphia, PA, 1996.

[12] J. A. R. Blais. Linear least squares computations using Givens transformations. *Canadian Surveyor*, 37(4):225–233, 1983.

[13] P. T. Boggs, R. H. Byrd, J. E. Rodgers, and R. B. Schnabel. Users reference guide for ODR-PACK 2.01: Software for weighted orthogonal distance regression. Technical Report NISTIR 92-4834, NIST, Gaithersburg, MD, June 1992.

[14] P. T. Boggs, R. H. Byrd, and R. B. Schnabel. A stable and efficient algorithm for nonlinear orthogonal regression. *SIAM J. Sci. Statist. Comput*, 8:1052–1078, 1987.

[15] R. J. Boscovich. De litteraria expeditione per pontificiam ditionem, et synopsis amplioris operis, ac habentur plura ejus ex exemplaria etiam sensorum impressa. *Bononiensi Scientarum et Artum Instituto Atque Academia Commentarii*, IV:353–396, 1757.

[16] D. C. Brown. A solution to the general problem of multiple station analytical stereotriangulation. Technical Report RCA-MTP Data Reduction Technical Report No. 43 (or AFMTC TR 58-8), Patrick Airforce Base, Florida, 1958.

[17] D. C. Brown. Close range camera calibration. *Photogrammetric Engineering*, XXXVII(8), August 1971.

[18] D. C. Brown. Calibration of close range cameras. *Int. Archives Photogrammetry*, 19(5), 1972. Unbound paper (26 pages).

[19] D. C. Brown. The bundle adjustment — progress and prospects. *Int. Archives Photogrammetry*, 21(3), 1976. Paper number 3–03 (33 pages).

[20] Q. Chen and G. Medioni. Efficient iterative solutions to m-view projective reconstruction problem. In *Int. Conf. Computer Vision & Pattern Recognition*, pages II:55–61. IEEE Press, 1999.

[21] M. A. R. Cooper and P. A. Cross. Statistical concepts and their application in photogrammetry and surveying. *Photogrammetric Record*, 12(71):637–663, 1988.

[22] M. A. R. Cooper and P. A. Cross. Statistical concepts and their application in photogrammetry and surveying (continued). *Photogrammetric Record*, 13(77):645–678, 1991.

[23] D. R. Cox and D. V. Hinkley. *Theoretical Statistics*. Chapman & Hall, 1974.

[24] P. J. de Jonge. A comparative study of algorithms for reducing the fill-in during Cholesky factorization. *Bulletin Géodésique*, 66:296–305, 1992.

[25] A. Dermanis. The photogrammetric inner constraints. *J. Photogrammetry & Remote Sensing*, 49(1):25–39, 1994.

[26] I. Duff, A. M. Erisman, and J. K. Reid. *Direct Methods for Sparse Matrices*. Oxford University Press, 1986.

[27] O. Faugeras. What can be seen in three dimensions with an uncalibrated stereo rig? In G. Sandini, editor, *European Conf. Computer Vision*, Santa Margherita Ligure, Italy, May 1992. Springer-Verlag.

[28] A. W. Fitzgibbon and A. Zisserman. Automatic camera recovery for closed or open image sequences. In *European Conf. Computer Vision*, pages 311–326, Freiburg, 1998.

[29] R. Fletcher. *Practical Methods of Optimization*. John Wiley, 1987.

[30] W. Förstner. Evaluation of block adjustment results. *Int. Arch. Photogrammetry*, 23-III, 1980.

[31] W. Förstner. On the geometric precision of digital correlation. *Int. Arch. Photogrammetry & Remote Sensing*, 24(3):176–189, 1982.

[32] W. Förstner. A feature-based correspondence algorithm for image matching. *Int. Arch. Photogrammetry & Remote Sensing*, 26 (3/3):150–166, 1984.

[33] W. Förstner. The reliability of block triangulation. *Photogrammetric Engineering & Remote Sensing*, 51(8):1137–1149, 1985.

[34] W. Förstner. Reliability analysis of parameter estimation in linear models with applications to mensuration problems in computer vision. *Computer Vision, Graphics & Image Processing*, 40:273–310, 1987.

[35] D. A. Forsyth, S. Ioffe, and J. Haddon. Bayesian structure from motion. In *Int. Conf. Computer Vision*, pages 660–665, Corfu, 1999.

[36] C. F. Gauss. *Werke*. Königlichen Gesellschaft der Wissenschaften zu Göttingen, 1870–1928.

[37] C. F. Gauss. *Theoria Combinationis Observationum Erroribus Minimis Obnoxiae (Theory of the Combination of Observations Least Subject to Errors)*. SIAM Press, Philadelphia, PA, 1995. Originally published in *Commentatines Societas Regiae Scientarium Gottingensis Recentiores* 5, 1823 (*Pars prior, Pars posterior*), 6, 1828 (*Supplementum*). Translation and commentary by G. W. Stewart.

[38] J. A. George. Nested dissection of a regular finite element mesh. *SIAM J. Numer. Anal.*, 10:345–363, 1973.

[39] J. A. George, M. T. Heath, and E. G. Ng. A comparison of some methods for solving sparse linear least squares problems. *SIAM J. Sci. Statist. Comput.*, 4:177–187, 1983.

[40] J. A. George and J. W.-H. Liu. *Computer Solution of Large Sparse Positive Definite Systems*. Prentice-Hall, 1981.

[41] J. A. George and J. W.-H. Liu. Householder reflections versus Givens rotations in sparse orthogonal decomposition. *Lin. Alg. Appl.*, 88/89:223–238, 1987.

[42] P. Gill, W. Murray, and M. Wright. *Practical Optimization*. Academic Press, 1981.

[43] P. E. Gill, G. H. Golub, W. Murray, and M. Saunders. Methods for modifying matrix factorizations. *Math. Comp.*, 28:505–535, 1974.

[44] G. Golub and C. F. Van Loan. *Matrix Computations*. Johns Hopkins University Press, 3rd edition, 1996.

[45] G. Golub and R. Plemmons. Large-scale geodetic least squares adjustment by dissection and orthogonal decomposition. *Linear Algebra Appl.*, 34:3–28, 1980.

[46] S. Granshaw. Bundle adjustment methods in engineering photogrammetry. *Photogrammetric Record*, 10(56):181–207, 1980.

[47] A. Greenbaum. Behaviour of slightly perturbed Lanczos and conjugate-gradient recurrences. *Linear Algebra Appl.*, 113:7–63, 1989.

[48] A. Greenbaum. *Iterative Methods for Solving Linear Systems*. SIAM Press, Philadelphia, 1997.

[49] A. Grün. Accuracy, reliability and statistics in close range photogrammetry. In *Inter-Congress Symposium of ISP Commission V*, page Presented paper. Unbound paper No.9 (24 pages), Stockholm, 1978.

[50] A. Grün.   Precision   and   reliability   aspects   in   close   range   photogrammetry. *Int. Arch. Photogrammetry*, 11(23B):378–391, 1980.

[51] A. Grün. An optimum algorithm for on-line triangulation. In *Symposium of Commission III of the ISPRS*, Helsinki, 1982.

[52] A. Grün. Adaptive least squares correlation — concept and first results. Intermediate Research Report to Helava Associates, Ohio State University. 13 pages, March 1984.

[53] A. Grün. Adaptive kleinste Quadrate Korrelation and geometrische Zusatzinformationen. *Vermessung, Photogrammetrie, Kulturtechnik*, 9(83):309–312, 1985.

[54] A. Grün. Algorithmic aspects of on-line triangulation. *Photogrammetric Engineering & Remote Sensing*, 4(51):419–436, 1985.

[55] A. Grün and E. P. Baltsavias. Adaptive least squares correlation with geometrical constraints. In *SPIE Computer Vision for Robots*, volume 595, pages 72–82, Cannes, 1985.

[56] R. Gupta and R. I. Hartley. Linear pushbroom cameras. *IEEE Trans. Pattern Analysis & Machine Intelligence*, September 1997.

[57] M. S. Gyer. The inversion of the normal equations of analytical aerotriangulation by the method of recursive partitioning. Technical report, Rome Air Development Center, Rome, New York, 1967.

[58] R. Hartley. Euclidean reconstruction from multiple views. In 2nd *Europe-U.S. Workshop on Invariance*, pages 237–56, Ponta Delgada, Azores, October 1993.

[59] R. Hartley. An object-oriented approach to scene reconstruction. In *IEEE Conf. Systems, Man & Cybernetics*, pages 2475–2480, Beijing, October 1996.

[60] R. Hartley. Lines and points in three views and the trifocal tensor. *Int. J. Computer Vision*, 22(2):125–140, 1997.

[61] R. Hartley, R. Gupta, and T. Chang. Stereo from uncalibrated cameras. In *Int. Conf. Computer Vision & Pattern Recognition*, pages 761–4, Urbana-Champaign, Illinois, 1992.

[62] R. Hartley and A. Zisserman. *Multiple View Geometry in Computer Vision*. Cambridge University Press, 2000.

[63] R. I. Hartley and T. Saxena. The cubic rational polynomial camera model. In *Image Understanding Workshop*, pages 649–653, 1997.

[64] F. Helmert. *Die Mathematischen und Physikalischen Theorien der höheren Geodäsie*, volume 1 Teil. Teubner, Leipzig, 1880.

[65] B. Hendrickson and E. Rothberg. Improving the run time and quality of nested dissection ordering. *SIAM J. Sci. Comput.*, 20:468–489, 1998.

[66] K. R. Holm. Test of algorithms for sequential adjustment in on-line triangulation. *Photogrammetria*, 43:143–156, 1989.

[67] M. Irani, P. Anadan, and M. Cohen. Direct recovery of planar-parallax from multiple frames. In *Vision Algorithms: Theory and Practice*. Springer-Verlag, 2000.

[68] K. Kanatani and N. Ohta. Optimal robot self-localization and reliability evaluation. In *European Conf. Computer Vision*, pages 796–808, Freiburg, 1998.

[69] H. M. Karara. *Non-Topographic Photogrammetry*. Americal Society for Photogrammetry and Remote Sensing, 1989.

[70] G. Karypis and V. Kumar. Multilevel k-way partitioning scheme for irregular graphs. *J. Parallel & Distributed Computing*, 48:96–129, 1998.

[71] G. Karypis and V. Kumar. A fast and highly quality multilevel scheme for partitioning irregular graphs. *SIAM J. Scientific Computing*, 20(1):359–392, 1999. For METIS code see http://www-users.cs.umn.edu/ karypis/.

[72] I. P. King. An automatic reordering scheme for simultaneous equations derived from network systems. *Int. J. Numer. Meth. Eng.*, 2:479–509, 1970.

[73] K. Kraus. *Photogrammetry*. Dümmler, Bonn, 1997. Vol.1: Fundamentals and Standard Processes. Vol.2: Advanced Methods and Applications. Available in German, English & several other languages.

[74] A. M. Legendre. *Nouvelles méthodes pour la détermination des orbites des comètes*. Courcier, Paris, 1805. Appendix on least squares.

[75] R. Levy. Restructuring the structural stiffness matrix to improve computational efficiency. *Jet Propulsion Lab. Technical Review*, 1:61–70, 1971.

[76] M. X. Li. *Hierarchical Multi-point Matching with Simultaneous Detection and Location of Breaklines*. PhD thesis, KTH Stockholm, 1989.

[77] Q.-T. Luong, R. Deriche, O. Faugeras, and T. Papadopoulo. On determining the fundamental matrix: Analysis of different methods and experimental results. Technical Report RR-1894, INRIA, Sophia Antipolis, France, 1993.

[78] S. Mason. Expert system based design of close-range photogrammetric networks. *J. Photogrammetry & Remote Sensing*, 50(5):13–24, 1995.

[79] S. O. Mason. *Expert System Based Design of Photogrammetric Networks*. Ph.D. Thesis, Institut für Geodäsie und Photogrammetrie, ETH Zürich, May 1994.

[80] B. Matei and P. Meer. Bootstrapping a heteroscedastic regression model with application to 3D rigid motion evaluation. In *Vision Algorithms: Theory and Practice*. Springer-Verlag, 2000.

[81] P. F. McLauchlan. Gauge independence in optimization algorithms for 3D vision. In *Vision Algorithms: Theory and Practice*, Lecture Notes in Computer Science, Corfu, September 1999. Springer-Verlag.

[82] P. F. McLauchlan. Gauge invariance in projective 3D reconstruction. In *Multi-View Modeling and Analysis of Visual Scenes*, Fort Collins, CO, June 1999. IEEE Press.

[83] P. F. McLauchlan. The variable state dimension filter. Technical Report VSSP 5/99, University of Surrey, Dept of Electrical Engineering, December 1999.

[84] P. F. McLauchlan. A batch/recursive algorithm for 3D scene reconstruction. In *Int. Conf. Computer Vision & Pattern Recognition*, Hilton Head, South Carolina, 2000.

[85] P. F. McLauchlan and D. W. Murray. A unifying framework for structure and motion recovery from image sequences. In E. Grimson, editor, *Int. Conf. Computer Vision*, pages 314–20, Cambridge, MA, June 1995.

[86] P. F. McLauchlan and D. W. Murray. Active camera calibration for a Head-Eye platform using the Variable State-Dimension filter. *IEEE Trans. Pattern Analysis & Machine Intelligence*, 18(1):15–22, 1996.

[87] P. Meissl. Die innere Genauigkeit eines Punkthaufens. *Österreichische Zeitschrift für Vermessungswesen*, 50(5): 159–165 and 50(6): 186–194, 1962.

[88] E. Mikhail and R. Helmering. Recursive methods in photogrammetric data reduction. *Photogrammetric Engineering*, 39(9):983–989, 1973.

[89] E. Mittermayer. Zur Ausgleichung freier Netze. *Zeitschrift für Vermessungswesen*, 97(11):481–489, 1962.

[90] J. J. Moré and S. J. Wright. *Optimization Software Guide*. SIAM Press, Philadelphia, 1993.

[91] D. D. Morris and T. Kanade. A unified factorization algorithm for points, line segments and planes with uncertainty. In *Int. Conf. Computer Vision*, pages 696–702, Bombay, 1998.

[92] D. D. Morris, K. Kanatani, and T. Kanade. Uncertainty modelling for optimal structure and motion. In *Vision Algorithms: Theory and Practice*. Springer-Verlag, 2000.

[93] J. Nocedal and S. J. Wright. *Numerical Optimization*. Springer-Verlag, 1999.

[94] M. Okutomi and T. Kanade. A multiple-baseline stereo. *IEEE Trans. Pattern Analysis & Machine Intelligence*, 15(4):353–363, 1993.

[95] D. W. Proctor. The adjustment of aerial triangulation by electronic digital computers. *Photogrammetric Record*, 4:24–33, 1962.

[96] B. D. Ripley. *Pattern Recognition and Neural Networks*. Cambridge University Press, 1996.

[97] D. Rosenholm. Accuracy improvement of digital matching for elevation of digital terrain models. *Int. Arch. Photogrammetry & Remote Sensing*, 26(3/2):573–587, 1986.

[98] S. Roy and I. Cox. A maximum-flow formulation of the n-camera stereo correspondence problem. In *Int. Conf. Computer Vision*, Bombay, 1998.

[99] Y. Saad. On the rates of convergence of Lanczos and block-Lanczos methods. *SIAM J. Numer. Anal.*, 17:687–706, 1980.

[100] C. C. Slama, editor. *Manual of Photogrammetry*. American Society of Photogrammetry and Remote Sensing, Falls Church, Virginia, USA, 1980.

[101] R. A. Snay. Reducing the profile of sparse symmetric matrices. *Bulletin Géodésique*, 50:341–352, 1976. Also NOAA Technical Memorandum NOS NGS-4, National Geodetic Survey, Rockville, MD.

[102] R. Szeliski, S. B. Kang, and H. Y. Shum. A parallel feature tracker for extended image sequences. Technical Report CRL 95/2, DEC Cambridge Research Labs, May 1995.

[103] R. Szeliski and S. B. Kang. Shape ambiguities in structure from motion. In *European Conf. Computer Vision*, pages 709–721, Cambridge, 1996.

[104] R. Szeliski and H. Y. Shum. Motion estimation with quadtree splines. In *Int. Conf. Computer Vision*, pages 757–763, Boston, 1995.

[105] B. Triggs. A new approach to geometric fitting. Available from http://www.inrialpes.fr/movi/people/Triggs, 1997.

[106] B. Triggs. Optimal estimation of matching constraints. In R. Koch and L. Van Gool, editors, *3D Structure from Multiple Images of Large-scale Environments SMILE'98*, Lecture Notes in Computer Science. Springer-Verlag, 1998.

[107] G. L. Strang van Hees. Variance-covariance transformations of geodetic networks. *Manuscripta Geodaetica*, 7:1–20, 1982.

[108] X. Wang and T. A. Clarke. Separate adjustment of close range photogrammetric measurements. *Int. Symp. Photogrammetry & Remote Sensing*, XXXII, part 5:177–184, 1998.

[109] P. R. Wolf and C. D. Ghilani. *Adjustment Computations: Statistics and Least Squares in Surveying and GIS*. John Wiley & Sons, 1997.

[110] B. P. Wrobel. Facets stereo vision (FAST vision) — a new approach to computer stereo vision and to digital photogrammetry. In *ISPRS Intercommission Conf. Fast Processing of Photogrammetric Data*, pages 231–258, Interlaken, Switzerland, June 1987.

Discussion for Session on Bundle Adjustment

This section contains the discussion that followed the special panel session on bundle adjustment.

Discussion

Kenichi Kanatani: This is a question related to Richard's talk. You have observations and a camera model, you derive some error function and you minimize over all possible parameter values. But shouldn't you also be optimizing over different camera models?

Richard Hartley: That sounds a bit like a loaded question. You're getting into the area of model selection for the cameras, which I know you've done some work on yourself. My point of view here is that usually you know what sort of camera you have, a perspective or push-broom camera or whatever. You may want to choose between an affine approximation and a full projective camera, or how many radial distortion parameters to include, but that's beyond the scope of what I would normally call bundle adjustment. You often need to initialize and bundle adjust several times with different models, so that you can compare them and choose the best. I do that in my program, for example to decide whether points are coplanar or not. You can use scientific methods like AIC for it if you want.

Bill Triggs: The place in photogrammetry where this really comes up is "additional parameters" modelling things like lens distortion, non-flatness of film, *etc*, where there is no single best model. Such parameters improve the fit significantly, but if you add too many, yes, you overfit, and the results get worse. The usual decision criteria in photogrammetry are based on predicted covariance matrices. If you add a parameter and the estimated covariance of the something that you want to measure (3D points or whatever) jumps, or if there is more than say 95% correlation between some pairs of parameters, you declare overfitting and back off.

The other point is that in many cases, a little regularization — adding a small prior covariance — is enough to stabilize parameter combinations that are sometimes poorly controlled, without biasing the results too much in cases when they are better controlled by the measurements. So within limits, you can often just take a general model with lots of parameters and fit that, letting the prior smooth things out if necessary.

P. Anandan: My question is also about model selection. With bundle-adjustment, if you have impoverished data — planar scene, narrow field of view, noisy points and maybe some outliers, things like that — the question is how stable is bundle-adjustment under these conditions. Assuming that you've got a decent initial estimate, is it likely that you'll actually get the correct solution, or will this kind of error cause you to fail. Is there any wisdom on this?

B. Triggs, A. Zisserman, R. Szeliski (Eds.): Vision Algorithms'99, LNCS 1883, pp. 373–375, 2000.
© Springer-Verlag Berlin Heidelberg 2000

Richard Hartley: My practical experience is that when these situations occur, data that's too planar say, it's best if you can find some sort of additional constraint to include. Maybe you don't know the focal length, but you think it's surely 1000 ± 500; or the points may not be coplanar, but they're probably coplanar with some large deviation of ten-thousand feet say. That stabilizes your solution by putting soft constraints on it.

Andrew Fitzgibbon: I agree, and this is also what Bill was talking about. If you're viewing a planar scene you're going to see large correlations in your focal lengths and motion parameters. If you damp some of the camera parameters when you discover these correlations, you'll get a more reliable motion estimate from your planar scene.

Richard Hartley: You can estimate the camera from a planar scene provided you start with constraints on the cameras, like known principal point.

Bill Triggs: I think our responses so far have missed an important point. What is bundle adjustment? – It's just minimization of your best guess at the true statistical error for the problem, over all the parameters that you think are important for the problem. If bundle adjustment is unstable, that's really another way of saying that you just don't have enough information to stably estimate things in the situation you think you're in. If some other method — say a linearized one — appears to give you stabler results, its lying. Either it's biased, or it's estimating a different error model or parameters.

P. Anandan: Maybe I'm misunderstanding. Isn't there also the approach of minimizing taking a local descent type of approach, so it's not just the optimization function that could be wrong?

Bill Triggs: Bundle adjustment *is* a local descent approach. Of course, you might have convergence to the wrong local minimum.

P. Anandan: Yes, that's what I'm talking about. . .

Bill Triggs: If bundle adjustment gives you a wrong local minimum, that minimum is a feature of the true statistical error surface. So it's likely that other methods which attempt to approximate this surface will have similar behaviour from a similar initialization.

Harry Shum: First a comment: who cares about bundle adjustment if you have a wrong model? Secondly, I want to ask Richard about camera models. You mentioned quite a few, and there were at least two that I wasn't aware of — the 2D camera and the polynomial cameras.

Richard Hartley: The 2D camera is just my name for the cases where you have a homography between the world and the images (no translation or planar scene), or where the camera is a mapping from a plane in 3D onto a line. That includes the linear push-broom sensors used in sensing satellites, and some X-ray sensors that image a point source of X-rays on a linear sensor.

The rational polynomial camera is a general model used in the US intelligence community. It approximately fits a large number of different sensors: ordinary cameras, SAR, push-broom and push-sweep cameras, and lots of others that I'm unaware of. Basically, whereas an ordinary perspective camera maps a point in space to the quotient of two linear polynomials in the 3D point coordinates, the rational polynomial camera uses a quotient of two higher degree polynomials. I have a paper on it in a DARPA IU workshop proceedings if you want the details.

Summary of the Panel Session

P. Anandan[1], O. Faugeras[2], R. Hartley[3], J. Malik[4], and J. Mundy[3]

[1] Microsoft Research, One Microsoft Way, Redmond, WA 98052, USA
anandan@microsoft.com
[2] INRIA, 2004 route des Lucioles, B.P. 93, 06902 Sophia-Antipolis, France
Olivier.Faugeras@sophia.inria.fr
[3] General Electric CRD, Schenectady, NY, 12301
hartley@crd.ge.com
[4] Dept. of EECS, University of California, Berkeley, CA 94720, USA
malik@cs.berkeley.edu

1 Introduction

The workshop ended with a 75 minute panel session, with Richard Hartley, P. Anandan, Jitendra Malik, Joe Mundy and Olivier Faugeras as panelists. Each panelist selected a topic related to the workshop theme that he felt was important and gave a short position statement on it, followed by questions and discussion.

2 Richard Hartley

Richard Hartley discussed error modelling and self-calibration, arguing that we should be willing to accept practical compromises rather than leaning too heavily towards theoretical ideals.

As far as error modelling is concerned, he argued that the precise details of the assumed error model do not usually seem to be very important in practice. So given that we seldom know what the true underlying error model is, it does not seem worthwhile to go to great lengths to get the last few percent of precision. On the other hand, when combining grossly different error models it *is* important to compensate at least approximately, for example by applying normalizing transformations to the data. Rather than relying too much on theoretical optima, you should choose a realistic performance metric (for example epipolar line distances in fundamental matrix estimation) and monitor how well you have done.

On calibration *vs.* self-calibration, he argued that it was usually unwise to pretend that you know nothing at all about the cameras, as self-calibration from minimal data (such as only vanishing skew) is often very unstable. It is often more accurate in practice, *e.g.* to assume a known principal point at the centre of the image, rather than hoping that a completely unknown one will be estimated accurately enough. This sort of information can be included as a prior under maximum *a posteriori* (MAP) estimation.

B. Triggs, A. Zisserman, R. Szeliski (Eds.): Vision Algorithms'99, LNCS 1883, pp. 376–382, 2000.

3   P. Anandan

P. Anandan focused on the limited domain of applicability of current 3D reconstruction algorithms, and of our reconstruction paradigm in general. He observed that for limited classes of scenes we can already do many things:

1. Our geometric reconstruction algorithms are nearly optimal. Given a suitable set of initial correspondences (even with some outliers), we can recover multi-camera geometry and do 'point-cloud' 3D reconstruction nearly as well as the data will support. And for at least some classes of scene, suitable initial correspondences can also be recovered.
2. Our techniques for 3D surface representation are also very advanced. We can do multi-base line stereo to get good quality dense 2.5-D maps, put the results into surface fitting techniques to get recover 3D shapes, *etc.*

However, the domain of applicability of all this is limited. Today's algorithms work fine for sparse 3D scenes with only a few objects, simple photometry and few or no inter-object occlusions. But they cannot handle:

- Scenes with significant 3D clutter — your desk, shutters, tree branches through which the background is seen, *etc.*
- Scenes with complex photometry, reflections from one surface onto another, translucency. Almost any scene with glass windows or shiny objects that reflect others cannot currently be processed.
- Scenes with almost any nontrivial dynamics — moving people, *etc.*

The point is that if you casually shoot a video in an ordinary everyday environment, it will almost certainly not be processable by current reconstruction algorithms.

To make progress, grouping and segmentation need to be more tightly integrated with reconstruction. One good way to do this is layered representations built using mixture models and Bayesian estimation. Layers have relatively simple geometry, are capable of handling occlusions and transparency, and provide a natural model for both local continuity and global occlusion coherence.

4   Jitendra Malik

Jitendra Malik argued that "the vision community should return to vision from photogrammetry":

1. We should declare victory on the reconstruction of 3D geometry. The mathematics of SFM, shape-from-texture, reconstruction from monocular views of constrained classes such as symmetric objects and SOR's, *etc*, is now worked out, or is at the 95% point. Even though we do not yet have reliable fully automatic reconstruction software, the hurdles lie elsewhere.
2. The correspondence problem, particularly dense correspondence as needed for surfaces, is far from being solved. This problem cannot be solved robustly

and accurately by treating it as a pure, modularized matching problem in isolation from other visual processing. Variations on themes of maximizing image cross-correlation can only go so far. Regions without texture and discontinuities will be the bane of all such algorithms. Coupling correspondence with structure recovery helps but that too is only part of the solution.

3. The era where SFM (and other geometrically posed problems) could be profitably studied in isolation is over. Problems like correspondence are intimately linked to grouping and perceptual organization, perhaps even to recognition. Many apparent difficulties in correspondence simply vanish in such an integrated view. *E.g.* we can match untextured regions on a group to group basis, aligning sharply at discontinuities using the monocular information.

Several of these issues have the tinge of the bad old days of AI-inspired vision, with lots of talk but no real, solid results. But there is an ongoing revival, based on powerful new techniques from probabilistic modeling, graph theory, learning theory *etc.* Some (biased) samples: his own group's work on image segmentation; Andrew Blake's group's work on tracking; Forsyth's and Zhu's use of MCMC techniques for recognition. He ended by encouraging more people to "join the good fight"...

Discussion

The reaction from the audience in the discussion that followed Jitendra Malik's presentation was generally supportive:

Jean Ponce: I completely agree with Jitendra, but I think that the problem is not with geometry alone. People have also looked at photometry, illumination *etc*, and all of these fail because of poor segmentation. Looking at inference systems like probabilities is a good idea, but it's still going to be very scary. So long as we don't know how to solve segmentation, vision is going to remain a very dirty problem. I find this a little discouraging, but I think that it's the good fight, and that we should all be working on it.

Rick Szeliski: I want to thank Jitendra for a very stimulating position. I think that a positive example of the potential of learning techniques is the tremendous advances made in face recognition and matching. For example Thomas Vetter's and Chris Taylor's groups have both been able to build 3D models from single images. If we're willing to consider constrained sub-problems, and if we have enough training data to learn from, then working systems can be built that do not necessarily have any sort of geometric interpretation, but that are able to learn to do the right thing by example.

5   Joe Mundy

Joe Mundy discussed systems issues. It now takes man years of effort to develop a competent 3-D vision system. These difficulties cut across various subject areas and levels of representation, and they present a formidable barrier to the next generation of applications.

Code is currently developed essentially one thesis at a time. There is little representational unity. Cross-fertilization between (or even within) labs is limited, so a great deal of time is wasted reinventing things that have already been done. For example it cost GE 1-2 man years of effort to start working on video. Also, graduate students are not usually experienced software designers, and relatively little of their code is stable and well-organized enough to be reused.

He then gave a brief history of the TargetJr C++ vision environment, and suggested that it was a reasonable success: it has been used in a number of projects, it supplies a unified environment for student training, and code sharing across labs has actually occurred. However the current version is not perfect: it is a big system (100k lines of code) requiring a heavy infra-structure, and C++ is not easy (tests showed that only 1 in 10 C++ programmers really know the language). It is likely that TargetJr will evolve to a more open, modular, client-server architecture with a lightweight Java GUI, a Corba or DCOM backplane, and specialist modules for the various vision and graphics tasks.

He finished by advocating the Linux/Open Source software model as the most suitable way to sustain such large, collaborative software efforts. Any restrictions on distribution or commercial use prevent potential collaborators from contributing. (An example is the 'pay for commercial use' licence of the Esprit CGAL computational geometry library, http://www.cs.uu.nl/CGAL, which excluded it from consideration for TargetJr).

In the discussion, Richard Szeliski suggested that standardization was difficult when there was disagreement over representations, which algorithms to use, and details like border effects. Joe Mundy replied that in some areas such as spatial indexing and Hough voting, there was enough agreement to standardize many representations and algorithms, and in more difficult ones such as edge detection at least the input and output representation could be standardized, as in TargetJr which supports a number of different edge detectors.

6   Olivier Faugeras

Olivier Faugeras made a number of points in support of the geometric approach to vision:

1. If we believe Popper's definition of scientific knowledge based on the falsifiability of theories, we have to accept that like physics, chemistry, biology and computer science, vision geometry — structure from motion and so forth — is a science. The objects of study are well defined. Quantitative theories exist and can be tested and criticized by independent observers. But the softer areas of computer vision (correspondence, perceptual organization ...) are *not* currently sciences. What phenomena are they trying to study and make quantitative theories of? What experimental procedures can be used to invalidate these theories?

2. Far from being irrelevant to 'real' vision, the geometric theories developed over the last 10 years to model structure from motion, self-calibration, stratified vision, *etc*, are highly pertinent. They both deepen our understanding of what is going on when we point cameras at the world, and help to make practical applications easier to solve. Also, representations of knowledge are and should be application dependent. Geometry often turns out to be the most appropriate representation.

3. On the future of vision geometry, he suggested that geometric theorem proving may prove to be an effective tool for many problems, then argued that the old AI vision problems need to be seriously reexamined from the standpoint of both biological vision and mathematics, *e.g.* by asking what it really means to segment a set of images.

Discussion

Michal Irani: I must say I'm a little puzzled by your definition of science. According to you, something becomes science only after it has been solved and you have the theory for it. So when Galileo had the hypothesis that the earth is round, he was dealing with religion not science, and he was probably being naive. That's my interpretation of your definition.

Olivier Faugeras: I guess my statement was unclear. What I'm saying is that theories live and die. Science is the way you build and refute them, so the problem has not been solved just because you have a theory. The Copernican theory of gravitational attraction was shown to be wrong by Newton, for example. The important thing is that theories must be criticized, and this doesn't happen enough in our field. People come up with theories for structure from motion, but they're not being criticized enough.

P. Anandan: I think that it's unnecessary to worry about whether vision is a science or not. It's a field of study that has scientific components, but also other components. Also, I wanted say that Olivier made an important point in identifying vision and AI as having the same sort of difficulties. Ultimately, AI and vision are about trying to develop a theory of reasoning. I think that reasoning is the only phenomenon that we could actually identify as being studied at a theoretical level. All the other things with geometry and optics are important, but the problem that I think eludes us, and will continue to elude us is a theory of reasoning.

Jitendra Malik: I think that we should be very clear about what vision is. Vision is not a science, and structure from motion is not a science. Vision is a sort of a hybrid field with several components: mathematics, science, and engineering.

First, the mathematical component. This has a precise formulation such as "given k points in n views can I recover X". Most of the basic results in structure from motion are mathematical theorems, and for a theorem you have a simple test: is it valid or not? Mathematics is a good thing, but it's not a science.

Secondly there's science, which is fundamentally about empirical phenomena. Biological vision is a science, but I'm not sure whether computer vision is. If you have phenomena, you can construct models for them, compare with empirical results, and see how they fit. I think that the view of science being primarily driven by Popper's falsifiability is a bit naive. We have to think of it more in terms of Kuhn's paradigm shifts. It is an evolutionary process. It's true that in the end, scientific papers get written in a falsifiable sense, with some experiment, control, and so forth. But the way things actually happen is that there is some collection of facts, vaguely understood, then some model of them, then somebody else comes along with some inconvenient facts. Models stick around, or get replaced finally by new ones. That's the way it works, it doesn't get falsified with a single fact.

Finally, there is the engineering aspect of computer vision. For this we have very clear criteria. Ultimately, in engineering there are specific tasks with specific performance criteria. You want to recover depth? – Well, measure the depth, say what your computer vision algorithm does, compute a percentage error. It's very simple.

But since we are in a field that has all of these things mixed together, what we have to do is just keep trying to do good stuff. It's more important to do good stuff than to worry about whether it is maths, science, or engineering.

7   General Discussion

The discussion and questions after the presentations was rather diverse and can only be summarized briefly here. The point that came out most clearly was that people had never forgotten about segmentation, perceptual organization and so forth. But for a time there was a feeling that new ideas were needed before we could start making progress on these problems, whereas vision geometry was developing very rapidly. However the tide appears to be turning: there seemed to be a remarkably strong consensus (at least among the vocal minority!) that we will make significant advances on these difficult mid- and high-level vision problems in the near future, notably:

1. By exploiting domain constraints, using purpose built parametric models and optimization/learning over a suitable training set (*e.g.* for face representation, medical applications, as in work by Thomas Vetter, Chris Taylor, Andrew Blake).
2. By applying 'new wave Bayesian' methods — probabilistic networks, HMM's and MRF's for knowledge representation, sampling (MCMC, Condensation) for calculations, parameter and structure learning algorithms.

Nobody (vocally) disagreed either that significant advances would be made, or that these rather mathematical tools were the appropriate ones. Even the suggestion that Bayesian networks might prove to be an effective model of some aspects of human cognition went unchallenged. This consensus was perhaps surprising given the geometric orientation of the workshop. Certainly, we would not have expected to find it a few years ago. But large-scale statistics and optimization seem now to have become main stream tools.

Comfortingly, there was also a consensus that whether computer vision counts as mathematics, science, or engineering, it is a domain worth studying.

Author Index

Lecture Notes in Computer Science

For information about Vols. 1–1804
please contact your bookseller or Springer-Verlag

Vol. 1846: H. Lu, A. Zhou (Eds.), Web-Age Information Management. Proceedings, 2000. XIII, 462 pages. 2000

Vol. 1847: R. Dyckhoff (Ed.), Automated Reasoning with Analytic Tableaux and Related Methods. Proceedings, 2000. X, 441 pages. 2000. (Subseries LNAI).

Vol. 1848: R. Giancarlo, D. Sankoff (Eds.), Combinatorial Pattern Matching. Proceedings, 2000. XI, 423 pages. 2000.

Vol. 1849: C. Freksa, W. Brauer, C. Habel, K.F. Wender (Eds.), Spatial Cognition II. XI, 420 pages. 2000. (Subseries LNAI).

Vol. 1850: E. Bertino (Ed.), ECOOP 2000 – Object-Oriented Programming. Proceedings, 2000. XIII, 493 pages. 2000.

Vol. 1851: M.M. Halldórsson (Ed.), Algorithm Theory – SWAT 2000. Proceedings, 2000. XI, 564 pages. 2000.

Vol. 1852: T. Thierauf, The Computational Complexity of Equivalence and Isomorphism Problems. VIII, 135 pages. 2000.

Vol. 1853: U. Montanari, J.D.P. Rolim, E. Welzl (Eds.), Automata, Languages and Programming. Proceedings, 2000. XVI, 941 pages. 2000.

Vol. 1854: G. Lacoste, B. Pfitzmann, M. Steiner, M. Waidner (Eds.), SEMPER — Secure Electronic Marketplace for Europe. XVIII, 350 pages. 2000.

Vol. 1855: E.A. Emerson, A.P. Sistla (Eds.), Computer Aided Verification. Proceedings, 2000. X, 582 pages. 2000.

Vol. 1857: J. Kittler, F. Roli (Eds.), Multiple Classifier Systems. Proceedings, 2000. XII, 404 pages. 2000.

Vol. 1858: D.-Z. Du, P. Eades, V. Estivill-Castro, X. Lin, A. Sharma (Eds.), Computing and Combinatorics. Proceedings, 2000. XII, 478 pages. 2000.

Vol. 1860: M. Klusch, L. Kerschberg (Eds.), Cooperative Information Agents IV. Proceedings, 2000. XI, 285 pages. 2000. (Subseries LNAI).

Vol. 1861: J. Lloyd, V. Dahl, U. Furbach, M. Kerber, K.-K. Lau, C. Palamidessi, L. Moniz Pereira, Y. Sagiv, P.J. Stuckey (Eds.), Computational Logic – CL 2000. Proceedings, 2000. XIX, 1379 pages. 2000. (Subseries LNAI).

Vol. 1862: P.G. Clote, H. Schwichtenberg (Eds.), Computer Science Logic. Proceedings, 2000. XIII, 543 pages. 2000.

Vol. 1863: L. Carter, J. Ferrante (Eds.), Languages and Compilers for Parallel Computing. Proceedings, 1999. XII, 500 pages. 2000.

Vol. 1864: B. Y. Choueiry, T. Walsh (Eds.), Abstraction, Reformulation, and Approximation. Proceedings, 2000. XI, 333 pages. 2000. (Subseries LNAI).

Vol. 1865: K.R. Apt, A.C. Kakas, E. Monfroy, F. Rossi (Eds.), New Trends Constraints. Proceedings, 1999. X, 339 pages. 2000. (Subseries LNAI).

Vol. 1866: J. Cussens, A. Frisch (Eds.), Inductive Logic Programming. Proceedings, 2000. X, 265 pages. 2000. (Subseries LNAI).

Vol. 1867: B. Ganter, G.W. Mineau (Eds.), Conceptual Structures: Logical, Linguistic, and Computational Issues. Proceedings, 2000. XI, 569 pages. 2000. (Subseries LNAI).

Vol. 1868: P. Koopman, C. Clack (Eds.), Implementation of Functional Languages. Proceedings, 1999. IX, 199 pages. 2000.

Vol. 1869: M. Aagaard, J. Harrison (Eds.), Theorem Proving in Higher Order Logics. Proceedings, 2000. IX, 535 pages. 2000.

Vol. 1872: J. van Leeuwen, O. Watanabe, M. Hagiya, P.D. Mosses, T. Ito (Eds.), Theoretical Computer Science. Proceedings, 2000. XV, 630 pages. 2000.

Vol. 1876: F. J. Ferri, J.M. Iñesta, A. Amin, P. Pudil (Eds.), Advances in Pattern Recognition. Proceedings, 2000. XVIII, 901 pages. 2000.

Vol. 1877: C. Palamidessi (Ed.), CONCUR 2000 – Concurrency Theory. Proceedings, 2000. XI, 612 pages. 2000.

Vol. 1878: J.P. Bowen, S. Dunne, A. Galloway, S. King (Eds.), ZB 2000: Formal Specification and Development in Z and B. Proceedings, 2000. XIV, 511 pages. 2000.

Vol. 1879: M. Paterson (Ed.), Algorithms – ESA 2000. Proceedings, 2000. IX, 450 pages. 2000.

Vol. 1880: M. Bellare (Ed.), Advances in Cryptology – CRYPTO 2000. Proceedings, 2000. XI, 545 pages. 2000.

Vol. 1881: C. Zhang, V.-W. Soo (Eds.), Design and Applications of Intelligent Agents. Proceedings, 2000. X, 183 pages. 2000. (Subseries LNAI).

Vol. 1883: B. Triggs, A. Zisserman, R. Szeliski (Eds.), Vision Algorithms: Theory and Practice. Proceedings, 1999. X, 383 pages. 2000.

Vol. 1886: R. Mizoguchi, J. Slaney /Eds.), PRICAI 2000: Topics in Artificial Intelligence. Proceedings, 2000. XX, 835 pages. 2000. (Subseries LNAI).

Vol. 1889: M. Anderson, P. Cheng, V. Haarslev (Eds.), Theory and Application of Diagrams. Proceedings, 2000. XII, 504 pages. 2000. (Subseries LNAI).

Vol. 1892: P. Brusilovsky, O. Stock, C. Strapparava (Eds.), Adaptive Hypermedia and Adaptive Web-Based Systems. Proceedings, 2000. XIII, 422 pages. 2000.

Vol. 1893: M. Nielsen, B. Rovan (Eds.), Mathematical Foundations of Computer Science 2000. Proceedings, 2000. XIII, 710 pages. 2000.

Vol. 1896: R. W. Hartenstein, H. Grünbacher (Eds.), Field-Programmable Logic and Applications. Proceedings, 2000. XVII, 856 pages. 2000.

Vol. 1897: J. Gutknecht, W. Weck (Eds.), Modular Programming Languages. Proceedings, 2000. XII, 299 pages. 2000.

Vol. 1899: H.-H. Nagel, F.J. Perales López (Eds.), Articulated Motion and Deformable Objects. Proceedings, 2000. X, 183 pages. 2000.

Vol. 1900: A. Bode, T. Ludwig, W. Karl, R. Wismüller (Eds.), Euro-Par 2000 Parallel Processing. Proceedings, 2000. XXXV, 1368 pages. 2000.

Vol. 1912: Y. Gurevich, P.W. Kutter, M. Odersky, L. Thiele (Eds.), Abstract State Machines. Proceedings, 2000. X, 381 pages. 2000.

Vol. 1913: K. Jansen, S. Khuller (Eds.), Approximation Algorithms for Combinatorial Optimization. Proceedings, 2000. IX, 275 pages. 2000.